AI Use in Social Sciences

Aytekin Demircioğlu
Kastamonu University, Turkey

IGI Global
Scientific Publishing
Publishing Tomorrow's Research Today

Vice President of Editorial Melissa Wagner
Director of Acquisitions Mikaela Felty
Director of Book Development Jocelynn Hessler
Production Manager Mike Brehm
Cover Design Jose Rosado

Published in the United States of America by
IGI Global Scientific Publishing
701 East Chocolate Avenue
Hershey, PA, 17033, USA
Tel: 717-533-8845
Fax: 717-533-7115
Website: https://www.igi-global.com E-mail: cust@igi-global.com

Library of Congress Cataloging-in-Publication Data

Names: Demircioğlu, Aytekin, 1977- editor
Title: AI use in social sciences / [edited by] Aytekin Demircioğlu.
Description: Hershey, PA : IGI Global Scientific Publishing, [2025] | Includes bibliographical references and index. | Summary: "This book aims to provide relevant theoretical frameworks and the latest empirical research findings in the field"-- Provided by publisher.
Identifiers: LCCN 2025020208 (print) | LCCN 2025020209 (ebook) | ISBN 9798337326122 hardcover | ISBN 9798337326139 paperback | ISBN 9798337326146 ebook
Subjects: LCSH: Social sciences--Study and teaching | Artificial intelligence--Educational aspects | Educational technology
Classification: LCC H62 .A4284 2025 (print) | LCC H62 (ebook) | DDC 300.71--dc23/eng/20250728
LC record available at https://lccn.loc.gov/2025020208
LC ebook record available at https://lccn.loc.gov/2025020209

British Cataloguing in Publication Data
A Cataloguing in Publication record for this book is available from the British Library.

Table of Contents

Detailed Table of Contents

Artificial Intelligence (AI) is emerging as a transformative paradigm in education and the future of social sciences, reshaping how knowledge is created, disseminated, and applied. AI-driven technologies enhance personalized learning, adaptive assessments, and intelligent tutoring systems, fostering more inclusive and efficient educational environments. In the social sciences, AI facilitates advanced data analysis, predictive modeling, and behavioral insights, enabling deeper understanding of complex societal issues. This paradigm shift raises critical questions about ethics, data privacy, and the evolving role of educators and researchers. The integration of AI in these fields offers opportunities to bridge educational gaps, promote equity, and support evidence-based policy-making. it also presents challenges related to algorithmic bias, digital inequality, and the need for interdisciplinary collaboration. This study explores the multifaceted impact of AI on education and social sciences, highlighting both the transformative potential and the ethical considerations.

This chapter discusses how to effectively integrate the use of artificial intelligence into the critical, questioning and reflective thinking skills that are inherent in philosophy. In this context, the role of the teacher in the process of teaching philosophy is discussed. The role of the philosophy teacher in teaching with artificial intelligence is discussed under the headings of being a philosophical guide, a developer of wisdom and morality, a facilitator in discussions, and a developer of critical thinking. In the section of AI-supported philosophy course activities, simulations dealing with philosophical problems, conversation with philosophers in the history of philosophy, ethical dilemma and decision-making game, creative argument development and analysis, philosophical perspective mapping, and current argument conflict are exemplified, and it is evaluated how these activities can be put into practice by supporting students' in-depth, critical and questioning thinking skills.

AI is reshaping economic policy and public administration worldwide. This study explores the ethical and societal implications of AI integration in governance and economic decision-making, with a focus on transparency accountability fairness and public trust. Through interdisciplinary qualitative analysis and case studies from Georgia's public sector, the research identifies challenges such as algorithmic bias, lack of legal safeguards, data privacy concerns and institutional readiness, highlights promising developments, including the establishment of the Georgia Technology Authority's AI office, national capacity-building programs and pilot AI systems in finance and law enforcement. Drawing from international best practices and local initiatives, the paper presents evidence-based policy recommendations to ensure that AI adoption in public governance serves democratic values, enhances service delivery and protects citizen rights. The findings contribute to the growing field of responsible AI and underscore the need for inclusive, transparent, ethically grounded governance frameworks.

This chapter examines the conceptual framework of artificial intelligence (AI) systems in the organisational context in terms of human-machine collaboration in three dimensions: supportive, collaborative, and autonomous AI models. A literature review integrates theoretical approaches on employee perceptions, acceptance and resistance processes, and the role of organisational culture in adaptation, establishing connections between performance, motivation, and psychosocial effects. Ethical dimensions are evaluated in the context of autonomy, privacy, and fairness, and the potential consequences of AI on work-life balance and role ambiguity are revealed. The findings point to a lack of empirical research despite conceptual richness and suggest the development of measurement tools with both descriptive and experimental designs. The chapter provides a roadmap for future applied research while emphasising the importance of clarifying strategic decision-making processes related to AI adaptation in an organisational context.

This chapter presents a comprehensive bibliometric analysis of the evolution and trends of artificial intelligence (AI) in education (AIED) from 1989 to 2025. The present study focuses on peer-reviewed publications indexed in the Web of Science, exploring key contributors, institutions, countries, and emergent research themes across the field. Utilizing data extracted through a systematic search and analyzed with the Biblioshiny R language and VosViewer, this study identifies major clusters, collaboration patterns, and citation dynamics. The findings are interpreted within the framework of educational technology paradigms such as TPACK and the SAMR model. The chapter provides insights into the role of AI in shaping curriculum, pedagogy, assessment, and equity in education. By mapping the intellectual and conceptual structure of this growing field, the analysis reveals prevailing and emerging trends while offering guidance for future research and practice.

Artificial intelligence (AI) is significantly transforming social science education and research by enabling efficient analysis of large datasets, identifying trends, and providing insights from complex social issues. AI is particularly useful in fields like sociology, economics, political science, and psychology, where large-scale data analysis is crucial. In education, AI is transforming teaching methods by utilizing digital platforms and virtual assistants to adapt learning processes to different learners' preferences. It is also crucial in curriculum design, providing adaptive learning systems and facilitating the creation of novel instructional techniques. However, the adoption of AI technology faces challenges, including resistance from educators and ethical concerns like privacy infringement and discrimination. Case studies of successful AI use in academic and research institutes demonstrate their effectiveness in improving research productivity, facilitating educational activities, and making learning more interactive.

This chapter explores the transformative impact of Artificial Intelligence (AI) on the social sciences, examining how technologies like machine learning, natural

instructional design applications ranging from personalized learning systems to adaptive learning platforms. It illustrates, with examples, how automated feedback and assessment systems can reduce teachers' workloads while enhancing students' educational experiences. Ethical concerns and challenges encountered during the transformative process of AI in education are also addressed. In conclusion, AI is considered a powerful tool with the potential to make instructional design more personalized, data-driven, and effective. In the future, the role of AI in education is likely to expand further, reshaping instructional processes across diverse educational contexts.

This chapter explores the transformative role of artificial intelligence within the educational metaverse to create immersive, personalized learning experiences in social sciences education. Grounded in five intersecting theories, connectivism, adaptive learning, personalized learning, cognitive load, and post-digital pedagogy, it critically examines how AI-driven technologies like intelligent tutoring systems, adaptive algorithms, and avatars reshape pedagogy, engagement, and equity. Through global case studies including contexts in South Korea, Finland, Kenya, and Pakistan, the chapter highlights opportunities and challenges, emphasizing ethical design, digital inclusion, and cultural responsiveness. It proposes a strategic framework for sustainable implementation that balances innovation with critical reflection, aiming to empower learners, support educators, and promote socially just, learner-centered immersive education worldwide.

Preface

The rapid evolution of artificial intelligence (AI) has begun to leave an indelible mark on every academic discipline, and the social sciences are no exception. As fields traditionally rooted in human behavior, society, and culture, social sciences are now navigating AI's profound implications and opportunities. From data-driven decision-making to intelligent educational platforms, AI is reshaping how knowledge is created, analyzed, and disseminated. This book, *AI Use in Social Sciences*, emerges from the pressing need to explore these changes systematically, critically, and constructively.

The chapters collected here represent diverse voices—from seasoned researchers to emerging scholars—across a range of global contexts. Each contribution examines a unique facet of AI's role in transforming education, research, and social systems. Whether through the lens of pedagogy, public administration, ethical frameworks, or human-machine collaboration, the volume as a whole underscores a shared belief that the integration of AI into the social sciences is not merely a trend but a defining feature of contemporary academic and civic life.

This book is intended for educators, policymakers, researchers, and students seeking to understand better AI's implications and applications in their respective domains. It also aims to serve as a platform for dialogue between disciplines, encouraging critical reflection on how technology can support and challenge the values underpinning the social sciences. As editor, I am grateful to the contributing authors for their insights and commitment to this ongoing exploration.

CHAPTER OVERVIEW

Chapter 1: AI and the Future of Social Science Education

This chapter explores how artificial intelligence reshapes social science education by enhancing engagement, personalizing learning, and fostering interdisciplinary inquiry. The authors highlight AI's capacity to revolutionize instructional practices, support research, and create inclusive environments through tools like ChatGPT and adaptive learning platforms. Practical strategies for implementation and real-world classroom applications are also discussed.

Chapter 2: Artificial Intelligence in Education: Shaping the Future of Curricula

This chapter provides a comprehensive analysis of AI's impact on educational curricula. It outlines how AI influences pedagogical processes and emphasizes the development of critical competencies such as AI literacy and digital skills. The authors also address ethical and practical challenges, offering strategies for effective and equitable curriculum integration at various educational levels.

Chapter 3: AI as a New Paradigm in Education and Social Sciences

This chapter focuses on AI's transformative role and examines how intelligent technologies redefine education and social sciences. It highlights the benefits of personalized learning and advanced data analysis while addressing ethical and societal concerns. The author stresses the importance of interdisciplinary collaboration and responsible integration to ensure equity and informed decision-making.

Chapter 4: Using AI in Philosophy Teaching and Ethical Problems

This chapter discusses the integration of AI into philosophy education, emphasizing its potential to support critical, reflective, and ethical thinking. It examines the evolving role of the teacher and provides concrete examples of AI-supported classroom activities. The chapter offers practical insights into how AI can enhance philosophical discussions and ethical decision-making exercises.

Chapter 5: Ethical and Societal Implications of AI in Economic Policy and Public Administration

This chapter analyzes AI's growing role in governance and analyzes its ethical and societal impact on economic policy and public administration. Case studies from Georgia illustrate both the risks—such as algorithmic bias and data privacy—and the advancements in public-sector AI initiatives. The chapter provides policy recommendations to ensure responsible, democratic AI adoption.

Chapter 6: Human-Machine Collaboration in the Workplace

This chapter investigates how employees interact with AI systems within organizations, categorizing AI as supportive, collaborative, or autonomous. Drawing on existing theories, it analyzes employee perceptions, adaptation challenges, and ethical implications. The chapter identifies research gaps and offers a roadmap for future studies on AI's psychosocial and operational impact at work.

Chapter 7: AI and Library Subject Guides in Academic Research

Focusing on university libraries, this chapter explores the development of AI-related research guides, or "libguides." It compares various institutional approaches, highlighting common themes such as ethics, copyright, and AI-generated writing. The chapter underscores the evolving role of librarians in guiding students and researchers through the ethical and effective use of AI.

Chapter 8: AI-Supported Lesson Design for Pre-Service History Teachers

This chapter presents a teaching module integrating generative AI tools into history education for pre-service teachers. It explores how platforms like ChatGPT and Canva AI can support differentiated assessments and historical thinking. Empirical feedback evaluates the module's effectiveness and recommends ethical and inclusive AI integration in teacher training.

Chapter 9: AI in Open Educational Resources (OER) for Doctoral Education

Examining the Ukrainian context, this chapter explores how AI enhances Open Educational Resources by improving adaptability, accessibility, and personalization. It addresses ethical concerns like bias and academic integrity and proposes a hybrid ecosystem where AI augments human oversight. The chapter advocates for transparent governance and critical data literacy in AI-driven OER.

Chapter 10: University Students' Acceptance of ChatGPT in Education

This chapter uses the UTAUT framework to analyze the factors influencing Turkish university students' acceptance of ChatGPT. Based on survey data and structural equation modeling, the study finds that performance and effort expectancy drive usage, while social influence and institutional support have limited effects. The findings offer insights into how AI tools can be better integrated into student learning.

Chapter 11: The Landscape of AI in Education: A Bibliometric Analysis (1989–2025)

This chapter offers a bibliometric overview of AI in education, mapping publication trends, key contributors, and emerging themes from 1989 to 2025. The author identifies intellectual clusters and collaboration networks by analyzing data through tools like Biblioshiny and VosViewer. The study informs future research by linking bibliometric insights with educational frameworks like TPACK and SAMR.

Chapter 12: AI in Social Sciences: Transforming Education and Research

This chapter outlines AI's growing influence on both social science research and education. It highlights applications in data analysis, personalized instruction, and curriculum design while also examining challenges such as educator resistance and ethical risks. Case studies demonstrate how AI can improve interactivity, research productivity, and learning outcomes in various disciplines.

Chapter 13: How Can We Use AI in Social Sciences?

Exploring AI's methodological and ethical implications in social sciences, this chapter evaluates how technologies like machine learning and NLP reshape research and theoretical inquiry. Through qualitative analysis and case studies, the author discusses both opportunities and concerns—emphasizing transparency, interdisciplinary collaboration, and the need for ethical safeguards.

Chapter 14: The Societal Impact of AI: Challenges and Opportunities

This chapter provides a broad overview of AI's influence on society, from healthcare and climate change to education and finance. While emphasizing the benefits of data-driven innovation, it also confronts issues like job displacement, privacy threats, and algorithmic unfairness. The chapter advocates for balanced, ethical development to ensure AI serves societal needs.

Chapter 15: The Scope, Applications, and Future of AI in Instructional Design

This chapter explores the intersection of AI and instructional design, focusing on how emerging technologies enhance teaching models, personalize content, and support learning outcomes. The authors review current applications and project future developments while stressing the importance of aligning AI tools with instructional goals and maintaining ethical standards in digital pedagogy.

Chapter 16: Beyond Reality: Leveraging AI and the Educational Metaverse for Immersive Learning Experiences

This chapter explores how artificial intelligence within the educational metaverse creates immersive, personalized learning in social sciences. It examines AI tools like intelligent tutoring systems and avatars through theories such as connectivism and adaptive learning. Case studies from South Korea, Finland, Kenya, and Pakistan highlight opportunities and challenges, focusing on ethical design, inclusion, and cultural responsiveness. The chapter proposes a strategic framework to support worldwide socially just, learner-centered immersive education.

As an editor, I have approached this volume not only as a scholar but also as a facilitator of interdisciplinary exchange. I believe that the social sciences have a crucial role to play in guiding the ethical and meaningful integration of AI into education, governance, and society. These chapters offer a foundation for future inquiry, encouraging readers to think critically and creatively about how AI can support human understanding, equity, and justice.

This book does not offer definitive answers but rather a multifaceted exploration of emerging questions. What responsibilities do educators and researchers hold in an AI-driven world? How do we ensure that technology serves democratic and inclusive goals? In what ways can we preserve the human essence of the social sciences in the age of algorithms? These are not questions with simple solutions, but they are questions we must collectively address.

I am deeply thankful to the contributors for their thought-provoking work, the institutions that supported their research, and the readers who engaged with this book. May this volume inspire continued research, thoughtful discussion, and responsible action as we navigate the evolving relationship between artificial intelligence and the social sciences.

Aytekin Demircioglu
Kastamonu University, Turkey

Chapter 1
AI and the Future of Social Science Education: Opportunities, Challenges, and Practical Applications

Jaesub Lee
University of Houston, USA

Youmei Liu
https://orcid.org/0009-0000-1973-1872
University of Houston, USA

ABSTRACT

Artificial Intelligence (AI) is rapidly transforming social science education by enhancing instructional methods, supporting research, and fostering personalized, inclusive learning environments. Tools such as large language models (LLMs), adaptive platforms, and AI-powered tutors enable deeper engagement with complex societal issues and real-world data, while promoting critical thinking and interdisciplinary inquiry. This chapter explores three key aspects of AI integration in social science education: (1) AI as a catalyst for innovation, highlighting its potential to revolutionize teaching and learning in social science education; (2) understanding the complexities of AI integration in social science through research study; and (3) practical strategies for implementation, with a focus on using ChatGPT to design inclusive, skill-based lesson plans.

DOI: 10.4018/979-8-3373-2612-2.ch001

INTRODUCTION

Integrating AI into social science education reflects a historical continuity, not coincidentally. Since its emergence during the First Industrial Revolution, the field has evolved in response to technological disruption. Rooted in moral philosophy and shaped by movements like the Industrial and French Revolutions, social science grew from experimental and applied sciences focused on societal improvement (Kuper & Kuper, 1985; Peck et al., 1897). The mechanization of labor, urbanization, and changing social structures prompted early thinkers like Comte, Marx, and Durkheim to analyze society using new scientific methods. The Second and Third Industrial Revolutions brought mass communication and globalization, pushing the field to expand its scope. Today, in the Fourth Industrial Revolution, AI technologies such as machine learning, automation, and predictive analytics are once again reshaping human life. The connection between technological transformation and social inquiry is clear: as society evolves, so must the tools and ethical frameworks used to understand it. The rise of AI is not merely a technical shift—it is a social revolution, and social science education must be central to navigating its implications.

Artificial Intelligence is driving a profound transformation across education, and social science stands at the forefront. Traditionally grounded in human interaction and cultural analysis, the field now intersects with technologies that enable new teaching, learning, and researching methods. Tools like ChatGPT and other large language models (LLMs) create interactive, data-rich, and personalized learning environments that reshape how knowledge is constructed and applied (Poth, 2022; Raman, 2023). As Willmore (2023) observes, "AI is transforming how students learn to engage with the world around them and use new technologies to create solutions to real problems" (para. 1). AI is not merely a technological upgrade—it is a catalyst for educational innovation. Students now engage in real-time data analysis, predictive simulations, and virtual tutoring, significantly enhancing their critical thinking and research skills. Studies show that AI tools help uncover complex social patterns, simulate sociological phenomena, and deliver personalized feedback (Saleem et al., 2025; Francisco, 2023).

Significantly, AI is expanding the interdisciplinary reach of social science education. As AI demands data interpretation and computational thinking, students are increasingly exposed to methods from computer science, statistics, and engineering. For instance, predictive analytics and data visualization tools allow for exploring political and economic trends through a sociological lens. A 2024 Educational Technology Research and Development case study highlighted a course where social science students collaborated with data scientists to simulate urban migration patterns, blending sociological inquiry with algorithmic modeling. Such experiences enriched research and prepared students with the skills needed for complex, real-world problem-solving. Florida State University's 2025 Graduate Certificate in Digital Applied Social Science (DASS) exemplifies this shift: "The program equips students with skills in data management and analysis, focusing on ethical frameworks necessary for navigating complex social issues… combining analytical prowess with a nuanced understanding of social contexts" (Forward Pathway, 2025, para. 1, 33).

Despite these advancements, AI in education raises pressing ethical and pedagogical concerns. In a field where identity, power, and equity are core themes, algorithmic bias, data privacy, and inclusivity become even more critical. Generative AI amplifies concerns about bias, as these tools are trained on data that reflect prevalent societal prejudices (Bail, 2024). Andy Hannah (2024) warns that AI can unintentionally perpetuate systemic inequalities, particularly in education, where transparency and fairness are essential. Therefore, educators must embrace AI's transformative potential while safeguarding social science's humanistic and interpretive heart. This chapter explores AI's evolving role in social science education through three dimensions:

1. Revolutionizing social science education: AI as a catalyst for innovation
2. Understanding the complexities of AI integration through research
3. Practical strategies for integrating ChatGPT into teaching

Together, these themes offer educators, administrators, and policymakers a framework for thoughtful AI implementation that enhances learning while preserving the core values of social science: critical inquiry, inclusivity, and ethical engagement. The goal is not to choose between AI and human-led education, but to integrate both, preparing learners for a future shaped by innovation, responsibility, and interdisciplinary insight.

THE MAIN FOCUS OF THE CHAPTER

Revolutionizing Social Science Education: AI as a Catalyst for Innovation

As a field deeply concerned with human experience, cultural systems, power structures, and ethical reasoning, the social sciences must approach AI not simply as a tool of automation but as a catalyst for innovation – one that has the power to elevate educational quality, inclusivity, and relevance in a data-driven society. The integration of AI offers tremendous promise: personalized learning, enhanced teaching strategies, dynamic assessments, and opportunities for interdisciplinary inquiry. However, effective AI integration requires a balanced approach, ensuring that technology enhances instead of replacing critical thinking, ethical inquiry, and human-centered analysis. To fully leverage AI in social science education, institutions must focus on policy considerations, teaching effectiveness, and student learning engagement (The future of learning: AI is revolutionizing education 4.0., 2024).

However, educational transformation through AI does not occur in a vacuum. It depends on well-defined policies safeguarding student data, promoting ethical AI use, and ensuring equitable access to emerging tools. It also hinges on faculty preparedness, and educators must be equipped with both technological fluency and pedagogical strategies that uphold the interpretive rigor of social sciences while prioritizing student engagement and skill development, ensuring that learners are not only consumers of AI-generated content but also active, critical thinkers who can interrogate AI's role in shaping knowledge and society.

Policy Considerations for AI Integration in Social Science Education

The effective integration of Artificial Intelligence (AI) into social science education begins with robust institutional policies that prioritize ethical use, equitable access, and sustainable infrastructure. A sound school policy should go beyond regulating the use of AI tools. It must actively support inclusive, ethical, and pedagogically aligned adoption, consistent with the foundational goals of the social sciences: critical inquiry, social responsibility, and human understanding.

As a discipline rooted in the analysis of human behavior, culture, and power structures, social science education is uniquely positioned but also particularly vulnerable to the impacts of AI. Social scientists are educators, researchers, and stewards of ethical inquiry and civic responsibility. Integrating AI into social science classrooms raises complex questions about bias, representation, and equity, which cannot be addressed solely through technical solutions. Without clear policies, institutions risk normalizing AI tools in ways that may reinforce systemic inequities, dilute critical thinking, or undermine the humanistic values at the heart of social science. This makes developing intentional, inclusive, and mission-aligned AI policies not just advisable but essential.

In their 2024 study, Ghimire and Edwards identified a significant policy gap, noting that "the majority of institutions lack specialized guidelines for the ethical deployment of AI tools such as ChatGPT" and that even existing policies often "overlook crucial issues, including student privacy and algorithmic transparency" (abstract). This echoes Isotani et al. (2023), who emphasize bridging the gap between AI research and its practical application in educational policy. In response to these challenges and the particular demands of social science education, the following six policy domains offer a practical framework for institutions seeking to integrate AI ethically and effectively.

Table 1. AI policy integration – domains and practical application guidelines

Policy Domains	Practical Application Guidelines
1. Establish Clear and Contextualized Usage Guidelines: Many institutions lack clear, actionable AI usage policies, which creates ambiguity around academic integrity and equitable access (Ghimire & Edwards, 2024).	• Differentiate between exploratory and evaluative use of AI tools • Require critical engagement with AI-generated content • Include AI usage disclosure statements in assignments • Define AI usage in qualitative vs. quantitative research contexts • Align AI guidelines with social justice and inclusion frameworks
2. Ensure Inclusive and Equitable Access: The integration should be approached with careful consideration of equitable access to AI technologies, ensuring that all students have the opportunity to benefit from these advancements (Funa & Gaby, 2025)	• Provide institutionally supported access to vetted AI tools for all students. • Incorporate AI literacy into support services for students with disabilities or language barriers. • Monitor disparities in tool usage and outcomes across different student populations. • Evaluate access disparities annually using disaggregated institutional data.
3. Embed AI Literacy in Curricula and Learning Outcomes: The concept of AI literacy emerges as a cornerstone of contemporary learning (Walter, 2024). It represents a fundamental shift in education, where understanding AI becomes as crucial as reading, writing, and arithmetic (Zhong et al., 2023)	• Define AI literacy as a learning outcome • Integrate AI analysis into existing writing and research assignments • Teach students how to verify, fact-check, and cross-reference AI outputs • Provide training on prompt design, bias detection, and ethical use • Frame AI literacy as a social and civic competency • Support students in developing ethical decision-making skills for AI use in public, civic, and policy-related contexts.
4. Invest in Faculty Development and Collaborative Innovation: An AI culture should permeate academic life, creating an environment where AI is not feared but readily used, understood, and – most importantly – critically evaluated (Walter, 2024).	• Provide professional development opportunities on AI tools, pedagogical uses, and ethical considerations. • Create cross-disciplinary teams (e.g., social scientists, technologists, ethicists) to pilot AI-enhanced lesson plans. • Encourage using AI in peer collaboration, case-based simulations, and role-playing in social contexts. • Recognize AI-related innovation in teaching portfolios and performance reviews.

continued on following page

Table 1. Continued

Policy Domains	Practical Application Guidelines
5. Safeguard Data Privacy and Ethical Accountability: AI can potentially impact ethical considerations in various areas of society. However, education has been specifically called out as a sector where AI raises new ethical issues and exacerbates existing biases and discrimination (9ine, 2024).	• All classroom AI tools must comply with FERPA, GDPR, and institutional data privacy policies. • Implement a faculty-led ethics review process before adopting new AI tools for instruction or assessment. • Establish confidential and accessible channels for students or faculty to report concerns.
6. Align Policies with Institutional Mission and Social Responsibility: We should be well past the days when technology development is separated from human needs, desires, and behavior (Anderson, 2021). Innovative AI and AI systems hold tremendous promise for improving quality of life and contributing to societal thriving in the future (Arthur, 2024).	• Frame AI integration as a technical improvement and an opportunity to model ethical, inclusive, and human-centered education. • Encourage departments to conduct internal research on AI use and publish findings to inform broader academic communities. • Regularly review and revise AI policies with input from students, faculty, IT, and administrative leadership.

Effective policies must be more than regulatory. They must actively promote ethical use, equitable access, pedagogical innovation, and alignment with the mission of social science education. The six policy areas outlined in this section, usage guidelines, access, AI literacy, faculty development, data privacy, and institutional alignment, represent a comprehensive framework for building a responsible and forward-looking foundation for AI adoption. These recommendations are grounded in emerging academic research and the core tenets of social science: critical thinking, social justice, and human-centered inquiry. Through investing in adaptive, inclusive, and ethically sound policies, institutions can harness AI not merely as a tool for efficiency but as a catalyst for more just, reflective, and impactful education. Social science educators, researchers, and administrators have a unique responsibility and opportunity to lead this transformation with caution and creativity. "The roles of leadership and policy in higher education reform are foundational to cultivating an environment that is adaptable, innovative, and aligned with future needs" (Liu & Curtin, 2025, p. 134).

Integrating Inclusivity and Student-Centered Learning into AI-Supported Teaching

While the promise of Artificial Intelligence in education is vast, its success depends on how thoughtfully it is implemented in curriculum renovation and classroom teaching. "It is crucial to recognize that the mere formulation of educational policy, no matter how well-intentioned or comprehensive, may have limited impact without concurrent changes in the curriculum" (Liu & Curtin, 2025, p. 135). "The curriculum is the backbone for the success of any academic program. At the time of curricula design, the programs must satisfy the requirements set by international and national bodies" (Almuhaideb & Saeed, 2020, para. 12). Curriculum reform needs to take 21st-century skills from vision to classroom (Haug & Mork, 2021) in order to bridge the gap between academic programs and societal needs.

In social science education, inclusivity and student-centered learning are not merely best practices but central to the discipline's ethical and pedagogical mission. Social sciences explore the structures, behaviors, and systems that define human experience. Effective curriculum redesign and innovative teaching in this field must reflect the complexity, diversity, and pluralism it aims to analyze. "Pursuing inclusive education has emerged as a fundamental goal to ensure equitable access and meaningful learning experiences for all students" (Liu, 2024, p. 112). "As AI technologies evolve, they are increasingly applied to tailor education to individual learning needs, supporting inclusive education" (McNulty, 2025, para. 1).

AI-powered adaptive learning systems can tailor educational content to individual student needs, addressing diverse learning styles and promoting equity. "Upholding equity ensures that all individuals receive the resources and support needed for academic success, leveling the playing field, and addressing systemic barriers" (Brahim-Said, 2024, para. 4). AI's role in education, particularly through adaptive learning platforms like DreamBox and Khan Academy, has led to significant advancements in tailoring instruction to individual student needs (Huang et al., 2023). Integrating AI into instructional design presents new opportunities to advance these goals if approached with care and intentionality. For example, adaptive AI tools can help personalize learning experiences to meet students where they are, offering multilingual support, alternative explanations, or context-specific examples that enhance accessibility and relevance. This level of responsiveness is compelling in classrooms and virtual learning environments with students from diverse sociocultural or linguistic backgrounds.

Inclusivity in AI-supported teaching must go beyond surface-level accessibility. It involves recognizing and designing for the varied experiences, identities, and learning needs that shape how students engage with knowledge. Especially in the social sciences, where learners examine inequality, identity, and voice. Educators must ensure that AI tools are committed to inclusion across ability, language, gender, belief, and context. Doing so not only improves learning outcomes but ensures that technology serves the ethical and human-centered mission of the field. Table 2 lists six key aspects that influence social science education that educators need to pay attention to in curriculum reformation and an inclusivity course design.

Table 2. Key aspects that impact social science education with AI implications

Key Aspect	Impact	AI Implications
1. Socioeconomic Accessibility	Not all students have equal access to personal devices, the internet, or premium AI tools.	• **Personalized and Scalable Education** - AI-powered platforms like ChatGPT, Khanmigo, or adaptive learning systems (e.g., Carnegie Learning) can provide students with low-cost, high-quality tutoring and instruction regardless of income or geographic location. • **AI-Powered Career Guidance and Skill Training** - AI can help individuals from lower-income backgrounds access career counseling, resume assistance and job readiness training through chatbots and virtual coaches. • **Language and Disability Support** - AI tools can provide real-time translation, transcription, and accessibility features for users with disabilities or non-native language speakers.
2. Cognitive & Neurodiversity Inclusion	Students learn differently, and those with ADHD, autism, or dyslexia benefit from multimodal content and flexible pacing.	• **Cognitive Load Management** - AI systems can break tasks into manageable steps and automate reminders or task prioritization (e.g., Notion AI, AI-powered planners). • **Personalized Learning Pathways** - AI can tailor educational content and pacing based on learner's strengths, needs, and preferences (e.g., AI-driven adaptive platforms like DreamBox and Squirrel AI). • **Communication Support Tools** - AI chatbots and voice assistants (like ChatGPT or Siri with NLP) and AI-powered writing assistants (like Grammarly, Quillbot, or ChatGPT) can support alternative modes of expression and help users with executive functioning, grammar, and organization challenges. • **Bias Mitigation and Inclusive Design** - AI models can be trained to recognize and adapt to diverse cognitive styles, minimizing neurotypical bias in content or assessments.
3. Identity & Gender Inclusion	The curriculum must reflect and respect a spectrum of gender identities and expressions.	• **Personalized Learning with Identity-Affirming Content** - AI can curate or recommend content that reflects diverse identities, cultures, and experiences, helping students see themselves represented. • **AI-Powered Mental Health and Identity Support** - AI chatbots and digital companions (e.g., Woebot, Wysa) can offer private, identity-affirming mental health support and resources. • **Gender-Inclusive Data Collection and Analysis** - AI platforms can encourage and support more nuanced data collection, e.g., including multiple gender options and respecting self-identification.

continued on following page

Table 2. Continued

Key Aspect	Impact	AI Implications
4. Ethical & Religious Sensitivity	Course content and examples should recognize diverse belief systems and moral frameworks.	• **Culturally and Religiously Inclusive AI Design** - AI systems can be trained on diverse datasets that include a broad range of cultural and religious perspectives, avoiding dominance by a single worldview. • **Ethical Decision-Making Simulations and Teaching Tools** - AI can be used in classrooms and professional settings to simulate ethical dilemmas and support value-based education, incorporating multiple cultural and religious viewpoints. • **Faith-Affirming Applications** - AI can be applied to support religious practice, such as prayer time reminders, scripture study tools, or kosher/halal food recognition.
5. Geographical & Linguistic Diversity	Students may come from rural, international, or underrepresented communities with different contextual knowledge.	• **Multilingual Translation and Communication** - AI-powered translation tools (e.g., Google Translate, DeepL, ChatGPT multilingual support) can enable real-time cross-language communication. • **AI-Driven Localized Content Delivery** - AI can tailor content delivery to regional needs by adapting curriculum, visuals, and examples to match local contexts and cultural references. • **Educational Equity through AI Tutoring** - AI tutors (e.g., Squirrel AI, Khanmigo, ChatGPT) offer scalable and personalized education to students regardless of geography.
6. Psychological Safety & Belonging	Students must feel respected, safe, and able to express opinions without judgment.	• **AI-Powered Sentiment and Wellbeing Monitoring** - AI tools can analyze language patterns, survey responses, or engagement data to detect signs of emotional distress, disengagement, or isolation (e.g., early alert systems in schools and employee sentiment analysis tools). • **Inclusive AI-Language Models** - AI tools like ChatGPT can be trained to use respectful, supportive, and affirming language that avoids bias, microaggressions, or exclusionary phrasing. • **AI-Driven Feedback that Builds Confidence** - AI tools can provide constructive, non-judgmental feedback focused on growth rather than evaluation (e.g., Grammarly, AI tutors, ChatGPT coaching tone). • **Community-Building Bots and Social Scaffolding** - AI chatbots and assistants can facilitate peer connection and collaboration, especially in online learning or remote work environments.

Artificial intelligence continues to evolve, and its influence on social sciences is becoming increasingly profound. AI can catalyze innovation when guided by thoughtful implementation, ethical awareness, and pedagogical purpose. AI tools, such as ChatGPT, hold the potential to enhance learning, foster equity, and develop 21st-century competencies when implemented with purpose and guidance. Instructors who view AI not as a threat but as a partner in pedagogy can unlock new dimensions of student engagement, self-expression, and critical inquiry, advancing the mission of social science education in a rapidly evolving digital world.

UNDERSTANDING THE COMPLEXITIES OF AI INTEGRATION IN SOCIAL SCIENCES

While AI enhances efficiency and accessibility in education, it also introduces ethical, practical, and pedagogical challenges. Concerns such as data privacy, algorithmic bias, job market implications, and the potential erosion of critical thinking must be thoughtfully addressed. Drawing from student survey data and reflection papers, this section offers strategies for educators, administrators, and support services to mitigate risks while preserving the integrity of social science education.

The University of Houston (UH)—a Carnegie-designated Tier One Public Research University known for its diversity—has proactively embraced AI integration. However, like many institutions, UH faced challenges following the release of OpenAI's ChatGPT in late 2022. Ward (2023) noted that ChatGPT's entry sparked debates in higher education, particularly around academic integrity. A Sullivan et al. (2023) meta-analysis found that institutional responses to ChatGPT vary widely, from permissive to prohibitive.

In response, UH launched a university-wide research initiative to explore ChatGPT's role in teaching and learning. During Spring 2023, the grant scope expanded to support projects on innovative classroom uses of ChatGPT. This chapter draws on findings from one such project led by two faculty members in the Department of Communication. The study explores students' perspectives, challenges, and practical strategies for integrating ChatGPT into instruction. The insights presented here inform practical approaches to enhancing student learning and supporting institutional decision-making around AI adoption in education.

Research Findings

The current research explores undergraduate students' attitudes, familiarity, perceptions, and behavioral trends regarding ChatGPT/AI as part of a broader grant initiative. Conducted over two academic years (Fall 2023 to Winter 2024), this research captures evolving student interactions with AI technologies in educational contexts.

Procedures and Participants

Approximately 750 students enrolled in communication classes at the University of Houston were eligible to participate in the study. They were asked to fill out the same survey questionnaire at the beginning of the semester (pre-test) and at the end of the semester (post-test). Once the class started, students were required to interact with ChatGPT for assignments and write reflection papers on using ChatGPT for coursework. Students first signed up for a free ChatGPT account at OpenAI, completed ChatGPT training via popular online tutorials, asked ChatGPT questions about the course content materials and assignments, and wrote reflection essays on ChatGPT performance.

The study had a total of 725 participants over two years. Students from 3 communication courses took part in the surveys. Four hundred seven students (56.1%) participated in the pre-test and 318 (43.9%) in the post-test, respectively. Responses were not matched (i.e., students were not assigned some code to match their responses). Nonetheless, this roughly comparable distribution of samples allows for meaningful cross-sectional tests of participant perceptions, familiarity, and behaviors regarding AI and ChatGPT.

There were 255 males (35.2%), 448 females (61.8%), 11 non-binary genders (1.5%), and 11 no response or prefer not to say (1.5%), respectively. Approximately 82% of the participants belonged to 18-24 years old group, 13% to 25-30 years old group, and 5% to 31 years old or older group, respectively.

Several variables were developed for this study, including ChatGPT/AI Familiarity, Impact Concerns, Perceptions of Benefits and Risks, Usefulness, and Likelihood of Adoption.

Familiarity with AI Technology

Familiarity with AI technology was designed to observe the extent to which participants were aware of or recognized popular terms or concepts relating to AI programs. Four items were used: (1) the term AI, (2) the concept of machine learning, (3) OpenAI ChatGPT, and (4) Bard/Gemini on a 4-point scale ranging from 1 = very unfamiliar, 2 = somewhat unfamiliar, 3 = somewhat familiar, to 4 = very familiar. Students were somewhat familiar with AI terms, concepts, and programs (M = 2.71, SD = .57). This scale was fairly reliable with Cronbach's alpha = .67. Most respondents rated themselves between 2.5 and 3.0 (43%), reflecting a moderate level of familiarity with ChatGPT/AI-related topics.

Impact Concerns

AI technology impacts perceptions in areas where the respondents feel AI would affect society significantly. This measure was created by combining five items in Table 3. The respondents chose any agreeable item of the five concerns. On average, the respondents agreed to the three items (M = 3.09, SD = 1.18). A moderate level of concern about the impact of AI exists, ranging from 11% at minimum to 33% at most.

Table 3. AI impact concerns

Area of Concern	*F*	%
1. Industrial Efficiency & Productivity	81	11.2
2. Job Displacement	132	18.2
3. Intelligence	234	32.3
4. Abuse and Regulation	177	24.4
5. Ethical Governance	91	12.6
Missing	10	1.4
Total	725	100.0

AI Technology Benefits

Perceptions of AI's benefits to society were measured by combining responses to the following six items in Table 4. Participants could select any item that they think will be a potential benefit to society. On average, students thought 3.52 (SD = 1.52) items (out of 6 benefits) would be valuable to society. Responses skewed toward the higher end, with nearly 49% selecting 4, 5, or 6 items. This suggests that students generally recognize and appreciate the potential benefits of AI technologies, with 13.6% selecting the highest value (6).

Table 4. AI technology benefits

Area of Potential Values AI Technology Can Bring	*F*	%
1. Automation of repetitive tasks	75	10.3
2. Improved healthcare and medical diagnostics	119	16.4
3. Enhanced customer service through chatbots	170	23.4
4. Enhanced educational quality through rich learning resources	154	21.2

continued on following page

Table 4. Continued

Area of Potential Values AI Technology Can Bring	*F*	%
5. Smarter and more personalized recommendations	97	13.4
6. Better predictive analysis for various fields (e.g., finance, weather)	96	13.2
Missing	14	1.9
Total	725	100.0

Potential AI Risks

Perceptions of AI's risks to society were observed by combining responses to the five items in Table 5. Participants selected any item that they think will be a potential risk. On average, students thought 3.53 (SD = 1.34) risks (out of 5 items) would be potential societal harm and threats. A strong skew exists toward the higher end of the scale, with 34% selecting the maximum number of 5 items and 52.3% selecting 4 or 5 items. This reflects considerable awareness of AI-related risks among respondents.

Table 5. Potential risks from AI technology

Potential Risk Area	*F*	%
1. Job displacement and unemployment	60	8.3
2. Data privacy and security concerns	122	16.8
3. Bias and discrimination in AI decision-making	159	21.9
4. Lack of transparency and accountability in AI systems	127	17.5
5. Ethical ChatGPT/AI applications	246	33.9
Missing	11	1.5
Total	725	100.0

Usefulness of ChatGPT

Perceptions on the usefulness of ChatGPT in educational settings observed the extent to which ChatGPT offers relevant and reliable information accurately and helpfully. Two items on a 4-point scale were used, ranging from 4 = very accurate or helpful, 3 = somewhat accurate or helpful, 2 = somewhat inaccurate or helpful, to 1 = very inaccurate or helpful:

1. How accurate ChatGPT was in providing relevant and reliable information for educational purposes.
2. How helpful ChatGPT was in providing relevant and reliable information for educational purposes.

On average, students thought ChatGPT is quite useful for educational purposes (M = 3.26, SD = .51). This measure was reliable, with Cronbach's alpha = .76. This variable shows a positively skewed response, with over 90% of responses between 3.0 and 4.0, indicating that students found ChatGPT to be quite helpful for educational tasks.

ChatGPT Use and Attitude Changes from Pre-Test to Post-Test

Students reported increased use of ChatGPT across all five educational tasks between the pre-test and post-test surveys. Notably, the percentage of respondents using ChatGPT to generate written documents (e.g., essays and reports) rose from 21.1% on the pre-test to 39.3% on the post-test (18.2% increase). The most substantial change was the task of brainstorming ideas, which increased from 38.3% to 63.2% - nearly two-thirds of post-test respondents reported using ChatGPT for this purpose. Similarly, use for explaining complex concepts grew from 35.1% to 59.4%, and answering factual questions increased from 28.0% to 51.9%. The least-used task in the pre-test survey was practicing language skills (19.2%), which nevertheless showed a substantial rise to 36.5% in the post-test survey.

Figure 1. MANOVA Tests of PrePost Surveys and Trend

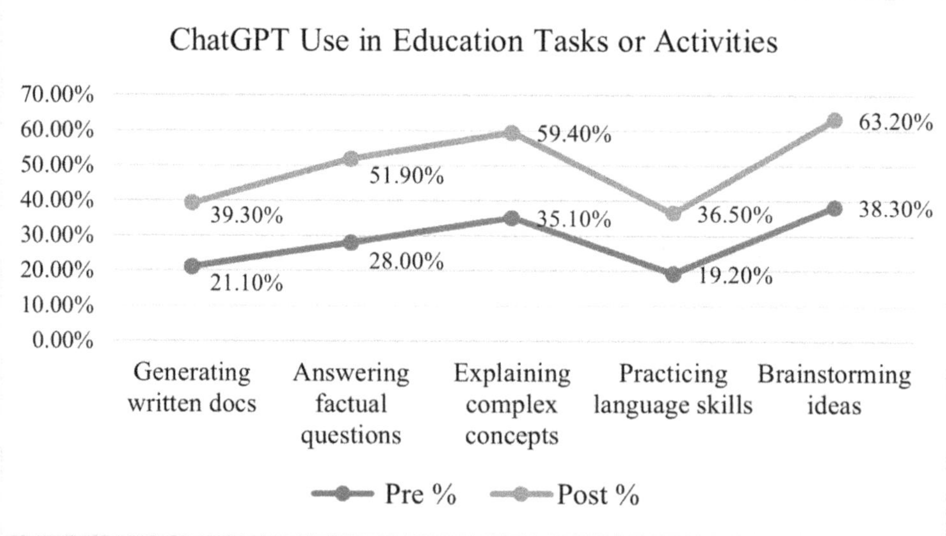

A multivariate analysis (MANOVA) was conducted to test the overall effect of PrePost, Trend over time (i.e., from Fall 2023 to Winter 2024), and their interaction on most measures combined (ChatGPT/AI Familiarity, Impact Concern, Benefits, Risks and Usefulness).

Table 6. Summary of Multivariate Tests (Wilks' Lambda)

Effect	*Wilks' Lambda*	*F*	*df*	*p*	*Partial η^2*
PrePost Survey	0.945	6.25	5, 539	.001	.055
Trend	0.946	1.52	20,1788	.065	.014
PrePost × Trend	0.963	1.02	20,1788	.432	.009

Results revealed that PrePost has a statistically significant multivariate effect, Multi. $F(5, 539) = 6.25$, $P < .001$, Partial $\eta^2 = .055$, which means at least one measure differs significantly between pre- and post-surveys. However, Trend and the PrePost × Trend interaction were not statistically significant at the multivariate level. Follow-up univariate analysis suggests that Familiarity with ChatGPT changed significantly from the Pre-Test ($M = 2.68$) to the Post-Test ($M = 2.95$), $F(1, 543) = 30.17$, $P <. 001$, Partial $\eta^2 = .053$. This shows that participants in the post-survey reported significantly greater familiarity with AI than in the pre-survey. For other variables of ChatGPT Impact, Benefits, Risks, and Usefulness, there were no significant differences between pre- and post-test groups, nor across semesters (Trend). The interaction effect between PrePost × Trend was insignificant for all variables, indicating that changes over time did not vary meaningfully between pre-test and post-test groups.

Table 7. Summary of Between-Subjects Effects (Univariate ANOVAs)

	PrePost p-value	**Trend p-value**	**PrePost x Trend p-value**
Familiarity	.001*	.097	.275
Impact Concerns	.914	.243	.680
Benefits	.242	.585	.950
Risks	.868	.428	.268
Usefulness	.273	.372	.612

* Higher after post-test survey (Pre-test: 2.68 --> Post-test: 2.95)

In one class (*Introduction to Communication Theory*), when asked to rate the quality of work (theory descriptions) by ChatGPT on a 5-point ranging from Definitely = 5 to Not at all = 1, students typically found it to be 4.34 (or B+).

Table 8. Students' evaluation of the quality of work by ChatGPT

Aspect of Theory Description	Rating
1. Theoretical assumptions are presented.	4.77
2. Information about theorists is provided.	4.46
3. Two or more major theoretical claims are given.	4.54
4. Application or practice implications are clear.	3.69
5. Citations in text and references are consistent with APA 7th style.	4.31
6. Points or contents are clear.	4.85
7. Points or contents are easy to follow (from introduction to body to conclusion)	4.15
8. Examples are relatable.	3.85
9. I know what the theory is about now.	4.46
10. How will your group grade the theory description ChatGPT offers?	85.77/100 (B+)

Overall, students found ChatGPT's theory descriptions highly effective, particularly in clarity, logical structure, and explanation of theoretical content. While foundational academic aspects were strong, some improvements could be made in illustrating practical applications and providing more relatable examples. The final group-assigned grade of **B+ (85.77/100)** reflects a positive but slightly cautious endorsement of ChatGPT's academic writing capabilities.

In the *Information and Communication Technology* class, students reflected on their experiences and perspectives regarding using ChatGPT in educational contexts. Their insights (as analyzed by ChatGPT) were organized into four key thematic categories. The top 5 ratings are listed in the following tables 9-12.

1. What have you learned, and how do you like ChatGPT?

Table 9. Student reflection on ChatGPT learning

Student Reflection	Rating
1) Helps with brainstorming and idea generation	25%
2) Simplifies complex concepts	23%
3) Provides quick, accessible learning support	18%
4) Acts as a personal tutor/assistant	17%
5) Helps improve writing and organization	15%

Most students reported that ChatGPT helped them brainstorm ideas, simplify complex subjects, and offer fast, accessible learning support. Many highlighted its role as a "personal tutor" that clarified confusion instantly, and some appreciated how it enhanced their writing and study organization.

2. Positive and negative aspects of ChatGPT as a learning tool

Table 10. Student evaluation of ChatGPT

Student Evaluation	Rating
1) Positive: Fast and available anytime	26%
2) Positive: Simplifies complex ideas	24%
3) Negative: Risk of misinformation/inaccuracy	20%
4) Negative: Over-reliance reduces critical thinking	17%
5) Positive: Encourages brainstorming and creativity	13%

Students appreciated ChatGPT's speed, 24/7 availability, and ability to simplify learning. However, concerns about occasional misinformation and fear of students losing critical thinking skills through over-reliance were notable. Some valued it as a creativity booster.

3. Features suggested for educational use

Table 11. Students suggestions for ChatGPT educational use

Students' Suggestion	Rating
1) Personalized learning paths and feedback	28%
2) Practice quizzes and flashcards	24%
3) Study material summarization	20%
4) Support lesson planning and assignment creation	16%
5) Classroom collaboration	12%

Students strongly suggested personalized learning plans and progress tracking as a future AI feature. Many wanted AI to generate practice quizzes, summarize large amounts of information, assist with lesson planning, and foster classroom collaboration.

4. Concerns About AI's Impact on Society and Career

Table 12. Impact of AI on society and career

Impact of AI	Rating
1) Job displacement and insecurity	30%
2) Erosion of human creativity and authenticity	22%
3) Misinformation and ethical concerns	18%
4) Over-reliance weakening critical thinking	16%
5) Concerns about data privacy and bias	14%

A primary concern was that AI might lead to job displacement and undermine human creativity, especially in journalism, communication, and media. Students also worried about AI spreading misinformation, weakening critical thinking, and raising privacy and bias issues.

Overall, students' reflections and insights indicate that while ChatGPT is an empowering tool that makes learning more flexible, accessible, and engaging, students strongly emphasized that it must be used carefully. ChatGPT is emerging as a powerful supplementary tool that can significantly enhance learning if managed thoughtfully.

Likelihood of Adopting New AI Technologies

One item as a proxy measure of outcome attitudes toward AI future, students were asked to respond to the question: How likely you will adopt new AI technologies for personal and professional purposes on a 4-point scale ranging from 1 (not all likely), 2 (slightly likely), 3 (likely) to 4 (very likely). Results of a general linear model (GLM) analysis revealed that post-test survey respondents reported higher AI Adoption likelihood compared to pre-test survey respondents (Mean = 2.91, SD = 0.83, N = 305 vs. Mean = 2.67, SD = 0.84, N = 398).

Table 13. AI adoption likelihood over time

	Trend	*Mean*	*SD*	*N*
Pre-Test	Fall 2023	2.53	0.883	92
	Spring 2024	2.67	0.806	123
	Summer 2024	2.71	0.808	73
	Fall 2024	2.69	0.831	81
	Winter 2024	2.93	0.923	29
	Total	2.67	0.84	398
Post-Test	Fall 2023	2.88	0.787	64
	Spring 2024	2.83	0.895	89
	Summer 2024	3.09	0.861	53
	Fall 2024	2.96	0.785	56
	Winter 2024	2.81	0.794	43
	Total	2.91	0.834	305

Tests of between-subjects effects showed the pre-test vs. post-test survey had a statistically significant effect on ChatGPT/AI Adoption: $F(1, 693) = 9.384$, $p = .002$, partial $\eta^2 = .013$. On the other hand, the Trend was not statistically significant, with $F(4, 693) = 1.319$ and $p = .261$. PrePost × Trend interaction was not statistically significant: $F(4, 693) = 1.268$, $p = .281$. Participants in the post-test survey reported significantly higher ChatGPT/AI Adoption likelihood in their personal and professional lives than in the pre-test survey. However, the effect size for the PrePost survey was small (partial $\eta^2 = .013$), indicating a modest but reliable difference.

This research investigated undergraduate students' attitudes, familiarity, perceptions, and behavioral trends regarding artificial intelligence (AI) and ChatGPT at the University of Houston over two academic years. Survey data collected from 725 participants across pre- and post-semester periods reveal growing familiarity and usage of AI tools in educational contexts. While students recognized substantial benefits, including enhanced learning and brainstorming support, they also expressed concerns about misinformation, ethical risks, and potential impacts on critical thinking. The findings underscore the importance of integrating AI carefully into educational settings to preserve human creativity and academic integrity.

PRACTICAL STRATEGIES FOR INTEGRATING CHATGPT INTO SOCIAL SCIENCE TEACHING

As an educational ally of social science education, understanding the importance of AI technology and conducting research will be only valuable when implemented. This section is an example of using AI technology to illustrate how AI can assist instructors in creatively building a lesson plan to incorporate learning theories, effective teaching methods, and innovative assessment activities to develop student's skills to meet societal needs and prepare them to be quality digital citizens for the entire humanity. In the example, ChatGPT is thoughtfully integrated into developing a lesson plan using Hunter's Behavioral Learning Theory, with an applied focus on a student-centered digital portfolio project.

Hunter's Instructional Theory into Practice (ITIP) model is grounded in behavioral learning theory, emphasizing structured, observable, and measurable learning behaviors. Hunter's method of direct instruction, generally referred to as the Madeline Hunter Method, includes seven elements: objectives, standards, anticipatory set, teaching, guided practice, closure, and independent practice (Gibboney, 1987). Hunter's model emphasizes clear objectives, active modeling, guided practice, and reinforcement, providing a strong foundation for structuring AI-supported learning activities. Within this framework, ChatGPT can be a flexible instructional partner across multiple lesson phases, offering instant feedback, instructional scaffolding, and personalized support to reinforce key behavioral learning principles.

In the context of this project, students will learn to design a personal digital portfolio to showcase their academic and professional development. The lesson integrates core social science themes such as identity, presentation of self, and digital citizenship while developing technical competencies in HTML, image sourcing and usage, visual storytelling, and collaborative problem-solving. The lesson plan illustrates how AI can effectively incorporate learning theory, teaching objectives, and class projects organically to enhance student engagement, facilitate research-based learning, and support diverse learners, ensuring that education remains equitable, effective, and forward-thinking.

This lesson plan aims to provide high school and college-level students with a structured, hands-on approach to learning about ChatGPT and its applications in academic and professional settings. For example, the Exploring ChatGPT and AI Technology units are designed to introduce students to the fundamental principles of AI, specifically focusing on ChatGPT as a tool for research, writing, and critical thinking. By engaging in interactive activities and structured assignments, students will develop proficiency in using ChatGPT to enhance their academic and personal work. Through guided discussions, research-based tasks, and self-reflection exercises, this course aims to equip students with digital literacy skills, critical evaluation techniques, and an awareness of AI's broader societal implications.

This four-week lesson plan is structured to build students' familiarity and confidence in AI technology gradually. Each week introduces new concepts and applications, ensuring a comprehensive understanding of how ChatGPT can be integrated into their learning journey. Beyond technical proficiency, this course encourages students to engage in ethical considerations surrounding AI, including accuracy, bias, and responsible usage. By comparing AI-generated content with traditional research sources, students will learn how to assess the credibility of information and refine their critical thinking skills. Additionally, structured peer feedback and self-assessment exercises will help students recognize the strengths and limitations of AI tools in academic and professional contexts.

Table 14. Lesson plan for exploring ChatGPT and AI technology

Lesson Plan	
Teacher Name:	
Content &Grade Level:	High school and college level
Unit Title:	Exploring ChatGPT and AI Technology
Lesson Title:	Understanding ChatGPT to Facilitate Learning
Day of Lesson:	4-day Lessons
Duration of Lesson:	4 weeks
Length of Class Period:	A single class of 90 Minutes in length
The rationale of the lesson:	In today's rapidly evolving technological world, integrating artificial intelligence (AI) into everyday tasks is becoming increasingly prominent. As AI tools like ChatGPT transform how we interact with information, communicate, and solve problems, students must develop the skills and knowledge necessary to navigate this new environment effectively. This course provides a timely and relevant exploration of AI technology, equipping students with essential skills in digital literacy, critical thinking, writing, and personal reflection. By engaging with AI tools like ChatGPT, students will enhance their learning and prepare themselves for the demands of an increasingly AI-driven world.

continued on following page

Table 14. Continued

Lesson Plan	
Teacher Name:	
Measurable Lesson Objectives:	By the end of the course, students will be able to: - Use ChatGPT effectively to complete assignments, as evaluated by rubrics and instructor feedback. - Assess the credibility of AI-generated content by comparing it with traditional sources and articulating key differences. - Reflect critically on AI's role in education and society through structured, insightful reflection papers. - Improve the clarity, coherence, and accuracy of their writing using ChatGPT for revision. - Design a digital portfolio featuring at least nine curated works, enhanced through AI-assisted writing and editing.
Materials and Resources needed:	Book and e-books, journal articles, websites and online resources, YouTube channels and podcasts
Anticipatory Set:	Week 1 - Introduction, Pre-Survey, and Tutorial Videos Anticipatory Set Activity: Show a brief video of ChatGPT in real-world use (e.g., content creation or coding). Discussion Prompt: After the video, ask students: "What stood out to you? How might ChatGPT support your academic or career goals?" Objective and Purpose Spark curiosity and help students connect AI with personal and professional relevance.
	Week 2 - Using ChatGPT for Research and First Reflection Paper Anticipatory Set Activity: Play a "ChatGPT vs. Human" game with short writing samples. Discussion Prompt: "What clues helped you decide? How could AI writing support your work?" Objective and Purpose Encourage critical thinking about AI-generated content and its role in research.
	Week 3 - Deepening Critical Engagement with ChatGPT and Reflection on AI Technology Anticipatory Set Activity: Have students generate and revise a ChatGPT bio for their portfolio. Discussion Prompt: "How accurate was the bio? What did you change, and why?" Objective and Purpose Practice refining AI output and explore personalization in digital self-representation.

continued on following page

Table 14. Continued

Lesson Plan	
Teacher Name:	
	Week 4 - Final Reflection Paper, Post-Survey, and Conclusion Anticipatory Set Activity: Students write a one-sentence reflection on how ChatGPT has influenced their work. Discussion Prompt: "What surprised you? How might you use AI moving forward?" Objective and Purpose Reflect on growth, evaluate course impact, and prepare for final presentations.
Procedures and Research-based Instructional Approaches:	Week 1 Input Introduce AI and ChatGPT through direct instruction and short video tutorials, moving from basic AI concepts to specific ChatGPT applications. Modeling (Demonstrating the Process) Demonstrate how to enter and refine prompts using think-aloud strategies to show critical analysis of responses. Check for Understanding Use guiding questions to assess comprehension of ChatGPT's role and limitations. Guided Practice Assist students in creating their first prompts (e.g., a bio or research question) and offer real-time feedback. Independent Practice Students explore ChatGPT independently, applying it to personal or academic interests.
	Week 2 Input Please explain how to use ChatGPT for information gathering and compare its outputs with traditional sources. Modeling Show a side-by-side comparison of ChatGPT-generated and scholarly content to identify discrepancies. Check for Understanding Facilitate discussion or quick assessments to gauge students' ability to evaluate information credibility. Guided Practice Guide students through a research task comparing AI and non-AI sources. Independent Practice Students summarize findings on a chosen topic, highlighting differences between ChatGPT and traditional research.

continued on following page

Table 14. Continued

Lesson Plan	
Teacher Name:	
	Week 3 Input Teach digital portfolio structure and content development through mini-lessons with visual examples. Modeling Demonstrate using ChatGPT to draft and refine portfolio content while maintaining a personal tone and clarity. Check for Understanding Ask reflective questions and use peer review to support improvement and self-assessment. Guided Practice Support students as they draft and revise portfolio components, incorporating peer and teacher feedback. Independent Practice Students continue developing their portfolios using ChatGPT for editing and polishing.
	Week 4 Input Provide clear instructions for portfolio presentation and post-survey completion, emphasizing reflection. Modeling Present a sample portfolio and reflect on how AI supported the learning process. Check for Understanding Use reflective questions to prompt critical thinking about AI's influence on students' learning. Guided Practice Students rehearse presentations and provide peer feedback on clarity and structure. Independent Practice Students present final portfolios, demonstrating how they used ChatGPT and what they learned throughout the course.
Differentiation:	To ensure all students can effectively engage with the content, differentiation strategies should be applied to meet students' varying needs, learning styles, and abilities. Below is the differentiation section for the ChatGPT lesson plan, broken down into Content, Process, Product, and Learning Environment.
	1. Content Differentiation • Adjusting the Complexity of Input: - Struggling Learners: Use simplified instructions, guided notes, visuals, and accessible texts. - Advanced Learners: Provide in-depth resources and encourage exploration of advanced ChatGPT uses (e.g., coding, ethics, research synthesis). • Tiered Instruction: • Design assignments at varying complexity levels—from basic prompt generation to in-depth AI content analysis. • Content Choice: Allow students to select content aligned with their interests (e.g., creative writing, STEM) for increased relevance and engagement.

continued on following page

Table 14. Continued

<table>
<tr><th colspan="2">Lesson Plan</th></tr>
<tr><th>Teacher Name:</th><th></th></tr>
<tr><td></td><td>2. Process Differentiation
• Pacing of Instruction:
- Struggling Learners: Allow extra time, scaffolding, and one-on-one support.
- Advanced Learners: Permit independent pacing and challenge with deeper tasks.
• Flexible Grouping:
• Use peer mentoring and interest-based groups to support collaboration across skill levels.
• Multiple Methods:
- Visual Learners: Use diagrams, flowcharts, and videos.
- Kinesthetic Learners: Incorporate hands-on prompt crafting and editing.
- Auditory Learners: Incorporate hands-on prompt crafting and editing.</td></tr>
<tr><td></td><td>3. Product Differentiation
• Flexible Output Formats:
- Struggling Learners: Permit oral, video, or visual alternatives to writing.
- Advanced Learners: Encourage extended projects like AI prototypes or research proposals.
• Student Choices:
• Let students decide how to present their learning—papers, infographics, or multimedia projects.
• Tiered Assessments:
Align expectations to ability—basic demonstration of AI use vs. critical analysis of AI's limitations and potential.</td></tr>
<tr><td></td><td>4. Learning Environment Differentiation
• Flexible Workspaces:
• Support independent or group work with low-distraction spaces for those who need them.
• Assistive Technology and Tools:
• Provide tools like text-to-speech or voice input for accessibility. Encourage advanced students to explore AI extensions.
• Behavioral and Emotional Support:
• Use positive reinforcement, brain breaks, and stress-reduction strategies to help students stay engaged.
• Flexible Scheduling:
• Allow deadline extensions or early project completion with optional enrichment activities.</td></tr>
<tr><td></td><td>5. Additional Differentiation Strategies
• Ongoing Formative Assessment:
• Use quick, low-stakes tools (e.g., reflections, exit tickets) to monitor progress and tailor support.
• Goal-Setting and Reflection:
• Guide students in setting personal learning goals with ChatGPT and reflecting on their growth throughout the course.</td></tr>
</table>

continued on following page

Table 14. Continued

Lesson Plan	
Teacher Name:	
Lesson Closure and Wrap-up:	Week 1: Introduction, Pre-Survey, and Tutorial Videos Lesson Closure: • Key Takeaways: Students were introduced to the basics of AI and ChatGPT, viewed tutorials, and explored potential uses in education and beyond. • Reflection Question: After today's lesson, take a few minutes to think about how comfortable you feel using AI tools like ChatGPT. What interests or challenges do you anticipate? • Next Steps: Start brainstorming portfolio ideas and consider how ChatGPT might enhance your work.
	Week 2: Using ChatGPT for Research, Writing, and First Reflection Paper Lesson Closure: • Key Takeaways: Students practiced using ChatGPT for research, compared AI responses with traditional sources, and began drafting portfolio content. • Reflection Question: What were the key differences between AI and traditional sources? How might that affect your future research? • Next Steps: Continue refining drafts, submit your first reflection paper, and prepare for deeper portfolio work next week.
	Week 3: Portfolio Website Development and Second Reflection Paper Lesson Closure: • Key Takeaways: • Students developed portfolio content using ChatGPT, revised it based on peer feedback, and reflected on AI's role in writing and creativity. • • Reflection Question: How has ChatGPT supported your portfolio development? What challenges did you face, and how did you handle them? • Next Steps: Finalize portfolio content in preparation for presentations and course wrap-up next week.

continued on following page

Table 14. Continued

Lesson Plan	
Teacher Name:	
	Week 4: Final Portfolio Presentation, Post-Survey, and Course Conclusion Lesson Closure: • Key Takeaways: • Students presented their portfolios, reflected on their growth, and evaluated ChatGPT's impact on academic development. • • Reflection Question: How has this course shaped your perspective on AI? How might you use ChatGPT in the future? • Next Steps: Consider how to build on what you have learned and continue exploring AI tools in your academic or career path.
Adaptations for Students with Exceptionalities:	Several adaptations can be made to accommodate students with exceptionalities in this course to ensure that all learners can access the material, participate meaningfully, and demonstrate their knowledge. These adaptations address various learning needs, such as cognitive, physical, or emotional challenges, learning disabilities, and giftedness.
	1. Instructional Adaptations • Simplified Instructions and Clear Expectations: • Break tasks into smaller steps; use visuals, checklists, and multi-format directions (written, verbal, visual). • Flexible Timing: (Check your school policy for disability students related to the time extension.) Allow extended time for processing and assignment completion, following school policy. • Flexible Content Delivery: Provide materials in alternative formats (e.g., transcripts, audio, simplified texts). • Pre-Teaching and Scaffolding: Introduce key concepts and vocabulary early; gradually remove supports as students gain confidence.
	2. Technological Adaptations • Assistive Technology: Offer tools like text-to-speech, screen readers, and voice typing for students with reading or motor impairments. • Accessibility Features: Teach students with physical disabilities how to use voice commands or keyboard shortcuts to navigate ChatGPT and website-building tools.
	3. Content Adaptations • Simplified Text and Reduced Complexity: Use leveled reading materials that match students' abilities while still covering the key concepts of AI and ChatGPT. • Chunking Information: Break major projects into manageable tasks with regular progress check-ins. • Alternate Assignments: Allow oral, video, or visual alternatives to written reflections or reports.
	4. Engagement and Participation Adaptations • Collaborative Learning: Pair students with peers for collaborative tasks, such as research comparisons or portfolio peer reviews. • Small Group Instruction: Provide small group or one-on-one support, especially when introducing complex tasks like using ChatGPT for research or website creation. • Routine & Structure: Provide visual schedules, timers, and predictable routines for students with attention or sensory needs.

continued on following page

Table 14. Continued

Lesson Plan	
Teacher Name:	
	5. Assessment Adaptations • Flexible Formats: If live presentations are challenging, allow students to demonstrate their knowledge and skills differently, such as video presentations or screen recordings. • Formative Check-Ins: Provide regular feedback to help students stay on track, particularly during long-term projects like the portfolio. Use formative assessments throughout the course to identify areas where students may need additional support before final assessments.
	6. Emotional and Behavioral Adaptations • Positive Reinforcement: Celebrate small successes and offer students choices to build motivation. • Stress Management and Self-Regulation Strategies: Teach stress management techniques and offer quiet workspaces for students who need breaks or reduced stimulation.

By the end of this unit, students will not only be proficient in utilizing ChatGPT for research, writing, and content development, but they will also have a well-rounded understanding of how AI can shape the future of education and various industries. This course balances embracing technological advancements and maintaining analytical, ethical, and creative control over AI-assisted work. This exploration will prepare students to navigate an AI-driven world with confidence, curiosity, and a critical mindset.

CONCLUSION

Integrating artificial intelligence (AI) into social science education marks a transformative shift in how students learn, instructors teach, and institutions shape educational policies. AI-powered tools have demonstrated their immense potential to enhance learning quality, improve research capabilities, and create more inclusive educational environments. As explored throughout the research study, AI offers opportunities for personalized learning, intelligent tutoring, advanced assessment methods, and enhanced student engagement, making education more dynamic and accessible.

However, adopting AI tools in education also presents critical challenges, including data privacy concerns, shifting job market demands, and the risk of over-reliance on AI-generated content. These challenges require proactive strategies from educators, administrators, and support services to ensure AI is integrated ethically, responsibly, and effectively. Addressing these concerns will be crucial in maintaining the academic integrity, critical thinking skills, and analytical rigor that define social science education.

The practical application of AI in lesson planning, as demonstrated through the sample lesson plan, highlights how ChatGPT can be an invaluable tool for instructors, helping them design innovative, research-driven, and inclusive teaching methods. By incorporating AI into instructional design while emphasizing ethical AI use, student agency, and equitable access, educators can create learning experiences that empower students to think critically, engage meaningfully, and prepare for a future where AI is an integral part of society. By thoughtfully integrating AI into social science education, AI technology can enhance, not diminish, the core values of intellectual curiosity, social responsibility, and inclusive learning.

Ultimately, AI should not replace human intelligence but rather amplify it, serving as a powerful aid in fostering deeper inquiry, facilitating interdisciplinary collaboration, and promoting lifelong learning. The true mission of education remains unchanged – to equip students with knowledge, skills, and ethical awareness that will enable them to thrive in an ever-evolving world and to be quality digital citizens for all humanity.

REFERENCES

Almuhaideb, M. A., & Saeed, S. (2020). Fostering sustainable quality assurance practices in outcome-based education: Lessons learned from ABET accreditation process of computing programs. *Sustainability (Basel)*, *12*(20), 8380. DOI: 10.3390/su12208380

Anderson, J. L. (2021). Why social science? Because engineering is intended to benefit society. *Consortium of Social Science Associations (COSSA)*.https://www.cossa.org/wp-content/uploads/2021/03/Why-Social-Science-Anderson-2021.pdf?utm_source=chatgpt.com

Arthur, C. (2024). Why social science? Because it can help contribute to AI that benefits society. *Social Science Space*.https://www.socialsciencespace.com/2024/05/why-social-science-because-it-can-help-contribute-to-ai-that-benefits-society/

Bail, C. A. (2024). Can Generative AI improve social science? *Proceedings of the National Academy of Sciences of the United States of America*, *121*(21), e2314021121. DOI: 10.1073/pnas.2314021121 PMID: 38722813

Brahim-Said, N. (2024). AI: empowering inclusive education. https://nationalcentreforai.jiscinvolve.org/wp/2024/01/09/ai-empowering-inclusive-education/?utm_source=chatgpt.com

DreamBox Inspire life-long learning: https://www.dreambox.com/

Forward Pathway US College Database. (2025). The impact of digital social science and AI has increased. https://www.forwardpathway.us/the-rise-of-digital-social-science-and-ai-impact#:~:text=Florida%20State%20University%20%282025,data%2Ddriven%20world.&text=and%20let%20me%20tell,data%2Ddriven%20world.&text=the%20College%20of%20Social,data%2Ddriven%20world.&text=designed%20to%20equip%20students,data%2Ddriven%20world

Francisco, M. (2023). The intersection of AI and sociology: New methods for understanding migration trends. *Journal of Applied Social Science Methods*, *18*(3), 145–160.

Funa, A. A., & Gabay, R. A. (2025). Policy guidelines and recommendations on AI use in teaching and learning: A meta-synthesis study. *Social Sciences & Humanities Open*, *11*, 101221. DOI: 10.1016/j.ssaho.2024.101221

Ghimire, A., & Edwards, J. (2024). From guidelines to governance: A study of AI policies in education. In: Olney, A.M., Chounta, IA., Liu, Z., Santos, O.C., Bittencourt, I.I. (eds), In *Artificial Intelligence* DOI: 10.1007/978-3-031-64312-5_36

Gibboney, R. A. (1987). A critique of Madeline Hunter's Teaching Model from Dewey's perspective. *Educational Leadership*, *44*(5), 46–50.

Hannah, A. (2024). Ethical considerations for AI in higher education: Ensuring fairness... https://www.liaisonedu.com/resources/blog/ethical-considerations-for-ai-in-higher-education-ensuring-fairness-and-transparency/

Haug, B. S., & Mork, S. M. (2021). Taking 21st-century skills from vision to classroom: What teachers highlight as supportive professional development in the light of new demands from educational reforms. *Teaching and Teacher Education*https://www.sciencedirect.com/science/article/pii/S0742051X2100010X

Huang, A. Y., Lu, O. H., & Yang, S. J. (2023). Effects of artificial intelligence-enabled personalized recommendations on learners' learning engagement, motivation, and outcomes in a flipped classroom. *Computers & Education*, *194*, 104684. Advance online publication. DOI: 10.1016/j.compedu.2022.104684

9. ine education. (2024). AI in education: The impact of AI on privacy, data protection and ethics in education. https://www.9ine.com/newsblog/ai-in-education-the-impact-of-ai-on-privacy-data-protection-and-ethics-in-education?utm_source=chatgpt.com

Isotani, S., Bettencourt, I. I., & Walker, E. (2023). Artificial Intelligence and Educational Policy: Bridging Research and Practice. *AIED* 2023. *Communications in Computer and Information Science*, *1831*, 63–68. DOI: 10.1007/978-3-031-36336-8_9

Khan Academy. https://www.khanacademy.org/

Kuper, A., and Kuper, J. (1985). *The Social Science Encyclopaedia*.

Liu, Y. (2023). The role of online technology in quality course design. In Calhoun, C. (Ed.), *The Impact and Importance of Instructional Design in the Educational Landscape*. IGI Global., DOI: 10.4018/978-1-6684-8208-7.ch007

Liu, Y., & Curtin, J. (2025). Sustainability in higher education: Integrating leadership, policy, and teaching practices for a brighter future. In Taukeni, S. G., & Mollaoğlu, M. (Eds.), *Higher Education and Quality Assurance Practices*. IGI Global., DOI: 10.4018/979-8-3693-6765-0

McNulty, N. (2025). AI for inclusive education. https://www.niallmcnulty.com/2025/03/ai-for-inclusive-education/?utm_source=chatgpt.com

Peck, H.T., Peabody, S.H., & Richardson, C.F. (1897). *The International Encyclopedia, A Compendium of Human Knowledge*. Rev. with large additions. Dodd, Mead and Company.

Poth, R. Dené. (2022). Teaching history/social studies in the era of AI writing tools. https://rdene915.com/2022/12/22/teaching-history-social-studies-in-the-era-of-ai-writing-tools/

Raman, P. (2023). The transformative role of AI in social science research. *Uniathena*. https://uniathena.com/role-of-AI-in-social-science-research

Saleem, R., Torres, M., & Lee, J. (2025). AI-driven adaptive learning systems and student engagement in social science classrooms. *Computers and Education: Artificial Intelligence*, *6*, 100215. DOI: 10.1016/j.caeai.2025.100215

Social sciences, Columbian Cyclopedia. (1897). (p. 227). Garretson, Cox & Company.

Sullivan, M., Kelly, A., & Maclaughlan, P. (2023). ChatGPT in higher education: considerations for academic integrity and student learning. ECU. https://ro.ecu.edu.au/cgi/viewcontent.cgi?article=3501&context=ecuworks2022-2026

The future of learning: AI is revolutionizing education 4.0. (2024). https://www.weforum.org/stories/2024/04/future-learning-ai-revolutionizing-education-4-0/

Walter, Y. (2024). Embracing the future of Artificial Intelligence in the classroom: The relevance of AI literacy, prompt engineering, and critical thinking in modern education. *International Journal of Educational Technology in Higher Education*, *2024*(21), 15. DOI: 10.1186/s41239-024-00448-3

Ward, M. (2023). ChatGPT: The survey says students love it, but educators, not fans, do not. University Business. https://universitybusiness.com/chatgpt-survey-says-students-love-it-educators-not-fans/#:~:text=Over%2089%25%20of%20students%20have,an%20 outline%20for%20a%20paper

Willmore, J. (2023). AI education and AI in education | NSF - National Science Foundation. https://www.nsf.gov/science-matters/ai-education-ai-education

Zhang, H., Lee, I., Ali, S., DiPaola, D., Cheng, Y., & Breazeal, C. (2023). Integrating ethics and career futures with technical learning to promote AI literacy for middle school students: An exploratory study. *International Journal of Artificial Intelligence in Education*, *33*(2), 290–324. DOI: 10.1007/s40593-022-00293-3 PMID: 35573722

ADDITIONAL READING

Gonzalez, M. R., & Patel, S. (2024). Bridging disciplines: AI-driven predictive analytics in social science education. *Educational Technology Research and Development*, *72*(3), 845–862. DOI: 10.1007/s11423-023-10345-6

Hannah, A. (2024). *Ethical considerations for AI in higher education: Ensuring fairness and transparency. LiaisonEDU.*https://www.liaisonedu.com/resources/blog/ethical-considerations-for-ai-in-higher-education-ensuring-fairness-and-transparency/

Kumar, A., & Hassan, N. (2023). Predictive analytics in the classroom: Teaching voting behavior through AI simulations. *Research in Social Sciences and Technology*, *8*(2), 78–95. DOI: 10.46303/ressat.2023.12

Rodriguez, P., & Kim, H. (2025). Adaptive learning in anthropology education: Enhancing critical thinking with AI-driven simulations. [Early access]. *Smart Learning Environments*, *12*(1), 3. DOI: 10.1186/s40561-024-00321-7

Saleem, S., Aziz, M. U., Iqbal, M. J., & Abbas, S. (2025). AI in education: Personalized learning systems and their impact on student performance and engagement. *Critical Review of Social Sciences Studies*, *3*(1), 2445–2459. Advance online publication. DOI: 10.59075/c35qa453

Taylor, N., & Chen, H. (2024). Tailored learning pathways: Adaptive systems and completion rates in sociology education. *International Journal of Educational Technology in Higher Education*, *21*(1), 77–94.

Wilson, D., & Ortiz, R. (2024). Student engagement through AI chatbots in political science education: A systematic review. *Frontiers in Artificial Intelligence*, *7*, 1123. Advance online publication. DOI: 10.3389/frai.2024.01123

World Economic Forum. (2025). How AI and human teachers can collaborate to transform education. (2025). https://www.weforum.org/stories/2025/01/how-ai-and-human-teachers-can-collaborate-to-transform-education/

KEY TERMS AND DEFINITIONS

Algorithmic Bias: Systematic and repeatable errors in AI outputs that reflect prejudices present in the data or design of algorithms. A critical concern in education and social science.

Data Privacy in Education: The protection of personal and academic information collected by educational institutions and AI systems, often governed by policies like FERPA or GDPR.

Ethical AI Use: The practice of using AI technologies in ways that are transparent, fair, inclusive, and respectful of privacy and human rights.

Inclusivity: Designing educational environments that acknowledge, respect, and accommodate diverse learner needs, backgrounds, and identities.

Instructional Design: Systematically developing educational content, experiences, and strategies to promote effective learning.

Interdisciplinary Inquiry: An approach to learning and research that integrates multiple disciplines' perspectives, methods, and tools to explore complex issues. Social science education allows students to examine societal problems, such as the ethical implications of AI, through combined lenses of sociology, political science, technology, ethics, and education.

Social Science Education: An interdisciplinary field that studies human society and social relationships through subjects like sociology, political science, economics, and anthropology. Emphasizes critical thinking, civic awareness, and ethical inquiry.

Student-Centered Learning: An instructional approach that shifts the focus from teacher-led delivery to student agency, allowing learners to shape and engage with their learning experiences actively.

Chapter 2
Artificial Intelligence in Education:
Shaping the Future of Curricula

Vildan Katmer
https://orcid.org/0000-0002-3740-0599
Maltepe University, Turkey

Aytekin Demircioğlu
https://orcid.org/0000-0003-4945-5519
Kastamonu University, Turkey

ABSTRACT

The rapid development of artificial intelligence (AI) technologies are bringing about fundamental transformations in the field of education. This chapter, comprehensively examines the transformative impact of AI on educational curricula. The study begins by presenting an overview of AI in education, then proceeds to analyze in detail the role and contributions of this technology in pedagogical processes. The chapter presents strategies for integrating AI into curricula across different educational levels. New skills and competencies that students and educators need to acquire in the age of AI, such as digital literacy, AI literacy, and critical thinking, are elaborated upon. The study also addresses the challenges and limitations associated with the use of artificial intelligence in education, including ethical concerns, data privacy issues, digital divide, and technological competencies of educators. In conclusion, this chapter highlights the potential of AI to transform curricula while emphasizing the importance of effectively integrating technology and pedagogy.

DOI: 10.4018/979-8-3373-2612-2.ch002

1. INTRODUCTION

The rapid development and proliferation of artificial intelligence (AI) technologies are bringing about radical transformations in education systems and all areas of social life. In particular, developments in educational technologies in recent years have caused artificial intelligence to cease to be a mere research topic and become an active component of education training processes (Holmes et al., 2023). This transformation necessitates the reconsideration of curricula, one of the fundamental building blocks of education, and their evaluation from an artificial intelligence perspective.

This technological revolution, which shapes the future of education systems, adds new dimensions to teaching-learning processes and pioneers paradigm shifts in curriculum design and implementation, as stated in the UNESCO (2019) report "Artificial Intelligence in Education: Challenges and Opportunities for Sustainable Development." In this context, curriculum development experts, education policymakers, and teachers face a dual responsibility, such as integrating the opportunities offered by artificial intelligence into curricula and, at the same time, preparing students for the age of artificial intelligence (Touretzky et al., 2019).

Integrating AI technologies into education systems has been identified as a strategic priority in various international contexts. For example, the European Commission's "Digital Education Action Plan" (2021-2027) updated the European Digital Competence Framework to include AI and data-related skills. Similarly, the "National AI Strategy" report published in Singapore placed AI education at the center of human capital development goals (Singapore Smart Nation, 2023). This rapid transformation at the intersection of AI and education requires a joint effort from educators, policymakers, and technology developers. In this context, interdisciplinary collaboration and constantly updated curriculum approaches are vital for AI's responsible and effective use in education. This book chapter aims to comprehensively examine the transformative impact of AI technologies on curriculum design and implementation, which are rapidly spreading in education. The chapter first aims to provide an overview of the relationship between AI and education and to explain the basic concepts. Then, by deeply analyzing the transformative effect of artificial intelligence on the curriculum, it reveals how this technology can be used effectively in pedagogical processes and enrich learning experiences.

In addition, this study aims to show how curriculum materials can be made more effective and personalized by examining the opportunities offered by artificial intelligence. It includes application examples specific to each level for integrating artificial intelligence into the curriculum at different levels of education, from preschool to university.

This study defines the competence areas that future education systems will need by emphasizing the importance of new skills and competencies such as digital literacy, artificial intelligence literacy, and critical thinking that students and educators need to acquire in the age of artificial intelligence. Finally, it aims to develop balanced and realistic solution proposals on these issues by addressing the challenges, limitations, and ethical concerns brought about by using artificial intelligence in education.

2. ARTIFICIAL INTELLIGENCE AND EDUCATION: AN OVERVIEW

2.1. What is Artificial Intelligence?

According to Edward Fredkin, director of the Artificial Intelligence Laboratory at the Massachusetts Institute of Technology (MIT) and a Carnegie Mellon University faculty member, three important events have occurred throughout history. The first is the universe's formation, and the second is the beginning of life. The third event, which he considers equally important to the beginning of life, is the emergence of artificial intelligence (Copeland, 1993). Although the beginning of artificial intelligence studies can be traced back to the robot drawings of Cezeri (1136-1206), the importance of artificial intelligence studies in the modern sense occurred during and after World War II. Alan Mathison Turing changed the fate of the war by inventing the first fully automatic code-breaking machine, which he called "Bombe" during World War II and which could be considered important under the conditions of that day. Turing gave the first conference on artificial intelligence in 1947 and explained that intelligent machines could be invented by combining artificial intelligence and computer programs (McCarthy, 2007). Turing, who made explanations based on the combination of the words "Machine" and "thinking" in his article "Computing Machinery and Intelligence," published in 1950, established the intellectual foundations of artificial intelligence (Turing, 1950). Although Alan Turing is considered the father of artificial intelligence, the term "artificial intelligence" was first mentioned in a proposal letter presented at the Dortmund Conference in 1956 by John McCarthy, Marvin L. Minsky, Nathaniel Rochester, and Claude E. Shannon. However, John McCarthy is considered the inventor of this concept. McCarthy (2004, p. 7) defines intelligence as "the computational part of the ability to achieve goals in the world. Intelligence of varying types and degrees is seen in humans, many animals, and some machines." and expresses artificial intelligence as "the science and engineering of making human-like intelligent machines, brilliant computer programs." In its broadest definition, artificial intelligence can be defined as systems that mimic human intelligence and iteratively improve themselves based on the information they collect (Russell & Norvig, 2021).

After the term artificial intelligence was first used, many scientists have worked on this subject. Artificial intelligence technologies have become a part of our lives thanks to the development of technologies over the years. In order to obtain artificial intelligence, human intelligence's inference and learning abilities were examined. In addition, examining evolutionary processes was used to model humanity's discoveries. Artificial intelligence has three important components: symbolic inference, artificial learning, and genetic algorithm. Although these three components do not explain all of human intelligence, they are considered the basic components of artificial intelligence. This is because these three components model the features of human intelligence, respectively: 1. Creating cause-effect relationships (inference), 2. Making generalizations from data (learning), and 3. Creating things that have never been seen before (invention) (Köroğlu, 2017).

2.2. Artificial Intelligence in the Digital Transformation of Education

Among the first examples of using artificial intelligence in education is Sidney L. Pressey, who worked at Ohio University in 1920. According to Pressey (1950), multiple-choice tests could be used to measure students' success and reinforce their learning. Pressey, who observed the principle of "tests used to assess learning should provide immediate feedback" in Thorndike's (1927) law of effect, talked about "machines" that would instantly show students test results, guide them on the correct answer, and support their learning by providing the necessary information. Although he did not have the chance to implement his ideas other than creating complex printers under the conditions of that period, this effort was considered among the first examples of artificial intelligence (Holmes et al., 2023). In addition, Pressey (1950) stated that such a machine would not only support students' learning but would also reduce the burden on teachers. The teacher who spends less time evaluating the tests will also have the chance to spend more time with his students.

After this approach by Pressey, B. F. Skinner, the father of behaviorist theory, developed "teaching machines," one of the known examples of programmed teaching, in 1958; this machine, which has a straightforward algorithm, is a wooden box with two eyes. One eye allows the student to see the questions, while the other allows the student to write the answers on paper. When the student writes the answer on the paper on a rotating system and turns it in, he can see the correct answer to the question, and if the answer is correct, he can move on to the next question. According to Skinner (1958), this "teaching machine" was like a personal teacher. Today, the reflections of a study initiated by Skinner are encountered in the field of educational technology by different names, such as "personalized learning" or "smart teaching systems" in artificial intelligence applications in education (Arslan, 2020). In the 1970s and 1980s, advances in cognitive psychology and artificial intelligence led to the emergence of "Intelligent Tutoring Systems" (ITS). Carbonell (1970) designed a dialogue-based interaction model in which students could ask questions and receive answers about the geography of South America in his intelligent tutoring system called SCHOLAR, and this work was accepted as the pioneer of artificial intelligence-supported education systems. These systems aimed to provide personalized teaching experiences by modeling students' cognitive processes (Sleeman & Brown, 1982). The system determines a step-by-step path for the student to follow using relevant activities and learning materials according to the student's success or mistakes. This path is constantly updated regarding difficulty level, tips, or explanations in line with the feedback received and is readjusted according to student needs. The aim is to ensure that the student learns effectively on the specified topic (Arslan, 2020). After SCHOLAR, systems such as LISP-TUTOR, which teaches the LISP programming language, and ALGEBRA-TUTOR, which teaches solving algebra problems, are important examples of this period.

With the widespread use of Internet technologies in the 1990s, distance education and e-learning platforms began to develop, which opened up new areas for artificial intelligence applications. In their study examining the development of web-based adaptive learning systems, Brusilovsky and Peylo (2003) emphasized the importance of "systems that dynamically adapt content and navigation features according to the student's knowledge level, goals, and preferences." Since the 2000s, developments in data mining and machine learning techniques have led to the emergence of the fields of educational data mining (EDM) and learning analytics (LA) (Baker & Inventado, 2014).

In contemporary education systems, artificial intelligence applications appear in various forms and functions. Rodri et al. (2016) classified these applications into four main categories: "intelligent teaching systems for students, intelligent support systems for teachers, intelligent content systems, and intelligent management systems."

Among student-focused AI applications, personalized learning platforms stand out. In his meta-analysis study, VanLehn (2011) revealed that intelligent tutoring systems "provide more effective learning outcomes than traditional classroom teaching and other forms of computer-assisted education." Today, adaptive learning platforms such as ALEKS, DreamBox, and Squirrel AI offer personalized learning experiences by continuously evaluating students' knowledge and skill levels.

Artificial intelligence tools for teachers are designed to support pedagogical decision-making processes. Crossley et al. (2016) showed that systems that provide real-time feedback to teachers in the classroom "enable teachers to identify and intervene in student needs more quickly and accurately." In this context, systems that automatically evaluate written assignments and provide feedback aim to increase the quality of assessment while reducing teachers' workload.

Intelligent content systems utilize artificial intelligence technologies to develop and present educational materials. Interactive e-books, simulations, and virtual laboratories enable students to learn by experience. Ma et al. (2014) stated that AI-supported educational content "can be more effective than traditional content in improving students' conceptual understanding and problem-solving skills." In summary, in recent years, significant advances in deep learning and natural language processing have led to revolutionary changes in educational technologies. As Holmes et al. (2023) stated, "Today, AI technologies offer educators new tools in areas such as content creation, student assessment, designing personalized learning paths, and democratizing access to information." This historical development process shows that, in the words of Woolf (2009), "AI applications in education have evolved from simple programmed teaching tools to complex, intelligent systems that take into account students' cognitive, emotional, and social dimensions."

3. THE TRANSFORMATIVE IMPACT OF ARTIFICIAL INTELLIGENCE ON THE CURRICULUM

3.1. The Role and Contributions of Artificial Intelligence Applications in Pedagogical Processes

The UNESCO (2023) report, which evaluates the role of artificial intelligence in today's education systems, states that "artificial intelligence technologies have the potential to increase equal opportunities in education, personalize learning processes, and improve the quality of education." In his study, Altun (2024) examined the role and impact of artificial intelligence in education within a pedagogical framework. The research results reveal that artificial intelligence applications can potentially transform educational processes and support teaching methods, techniques, and strategies in various ways. As a result of Altun's systematic review, the role of artificial intelligence applications in pedagogical processes is grouped under the following headings:

- Personalized and Differentiated Learning
- Adaptive Learning
- Active Learning
- Collaborative Learning
- Problem-Based Learning
- Project-Based Learning

- Simulation-Based Learning
- Language Learning
- Self-Regulated and Self-Directed Learning
- Critical and Creative Thinking Skills

Personalized and Differentiated Learning

Personalized learning refers to adapting the educational experience to each student's needs, learning pace, and interests (Peng et al., 2019). Artificial intelligence systems can automatically personalize "learning journeys" by analyzing students' learning processes (Holmes et al., 2023). These systems can monitor students' performance in real time and offer adaptive content. A systematic review by Zawacki-Richter et al. (2019) showed that artificial intelligence-supported learning systems can automatically adjust content and difficulty levels by predicting students' individual learning needs. Differentiated instruction involves teachers adapting content, processes, and products to students' readiness levels, interests, and learning profiles. Hwang et al. (2020) showed that artificial intelligence can significantly reduce teachers' workload in implementing differentiated instruction. Adaptive Learning

Artificial intelligence technologies in education have been a significant turning point, especially in developing adaptive learning systems. Adaptive learning is an educational approach that dynamically adjusts content and teaching methods according to each student's needs, learning speed, and preferences. AI algorithms can provide personalized learning experiences by analyzing students' learning styles, strengths, and weaknesses. Baker and Inventado (2014) have shown how educational data mining and learning analytics techniques can be used to identify students' learning patterns and develop personalized interventions. In addition, AI-based systems can detect learning difficulties at an early stage. Klašnja-Milićević et al. (2017) revealed the effectiveness of systems that analyze student performance data patterns using artificial intelligence algorithms and can predict learning difficulties in advance.

Active Learning

Active learning is an educational approach in which students actively participate in the learning process instead of being passive recipients, using high-level cognitive skills such as thinking, problem-solving, and collaboration (Hood Cattaneo, 2017). Artificial intelligence technologies are increasingly used to support and enrich active learning processes. Artificial intelligence can provide active learning experiences tailored to each student's needs and learning styles. Holstein and Aleven (2020) have shown that AI-supported learning environments can analyze students' performance and interactions in real time and offer them active learning tasks tailored to them.

This personalization allows students to progress at their own pace and interact with content according to their interests.

Collaborative Learning

Collaborative learning is a pedagogical approach in which students work together towards a common goal, build knowledge, learn through social interaction, and contribute to each other's learning. In recent years, Artificial Intelligence technologies have been increasingly used to support and enrich collaborative learning environments. Ouyang ve Jiao (2021) states that AI-supported collaborative learning systems (AICLS) support learning processes by analyzing students' cognitive, social, and emotional interactions. Cukurova et al. (2020) state that artificial intelligence systems can analyze social interactions during teamwork and offer suggestions to optimize group collaboration. Chen et al. (2018) revealed that intelligent collaborative learning environments improve students' communication skills and positively affect group dynamics. These systems help students express their thoughts more clearly and understand different perspectives.

Problem-Based Learning

Problem-based learning (PBL) is an active and constructivist learning approach in which students develop their knowledge and skills by solving real-world problems. In this approach, students work on complex and authentic problems to develop their critical thinking, problem-solving, and collaboration skills (Hmelo-Silver, 2004). Artificial Intelligence technologies have recently offered significant opportunities to support and enrich PBL processes. The success of problem-based learning largely depends on the quality of the problem scenarios presented to students. Artificial intelligence significantly contributes to creating realistic and complex problem scenarios suitable for student's interests and learning needs.

Walker et al. (2011) showed that AI-supported scenarios increase students' motivation and enable them to participate more actively in learning. These systems can offer dynamic problem scenarios adapted to students' knowledge levels and interests. Samsonovich (2025) states that AI-based problem-posing systems can develop rich problem scenarios that support interdisciplinary learning by integrating concepts from different disciplines and real-world contexts. Similarly, Zhai et al. (2021) have shown that AI-supported knowledge integration systems help students solve interdisciplinary problems by associating concepts and knowledge from different disciplines.

Project-Based Learning

Project-based learning can be defined as learning that is organized around complex tasks, includes students' problem-solving, decision-making, and research activities, gives students autonomy, and results in realistic products or presentations (Thomas, 2000). The use of AI technologies in project-based learning processes leads to significant transformations in the field of education. Holmes et al. (2023) showed in their research that AI-supported systems could automatically adjust project difficulties according to student's individual needs, thus providing a 23% increase in learning outcomes. AI technologies also bring resource optimization, simulation, and modeling opportunities in project-based learning environments. Martinez-Maldonado et al. (2023) showed that artificial intelligence reduces resource waste by 40% in project-based learning environments by enabling more efficient use of educational resources. Tissenbaum and Slotta (2022) stated that AI-supported simulation and modeling tools increase students' ability to understand and manipulate complex systems in their projects by 50%. These tools offer the opportunity to test real-world scenarios in a safe environment.

Simulation-Based Learning

Simulation-based learning is a learning approach that simulates real-world environments and processes through virtual or physical models, with the active participation of students. This method allows students to gain experience and practice in a risk-free environment. McGaghie et al. (2010) explained simulation-based learning as "an educational strategy that involves students in active learning in an artificial environment that reflects real-world experiences." AI can personalize the simulation experience by analyzing students' performance and behavior. Shute et al. (2020) revealed in their research that AI-supported learning systems could automatically adjust stimulation parameters according to student's individual learning needs, thus increasing learning outcomes. Sottilare and Holden (2013) stated that AI algorithms can create more realistic simulations by modeling complex systems, resulting in a 40% increase in learning transfer.

Language Learning

Artificial intelligence technologies significantly advance language learning theories and methods and open new horizons in second language acquisition and foreign language teaching. Contributions in this field enrich theoretical frameworks and add new dimensions to practical applications. Liakin et al. (2017) have shown that artificial intelligence-supported speech recognition systems effectively improve the pronunciation skills of second language learners. These systems provide students with instant feedback and strengthen their self-regulation skills. Hadjistassou and Avgousti (2024) stated that using artificial intelligence chatbots in the communicative language teaching approach increases students' opportunities to communicate authentically in the target language and contributes to language fluency. Similarly, Zhang (2020) revealed that artificial intelligence-supported writing assistants can guide grammar, word choice, and text organization during the writing process of language learners, and this support improves students' productive language skills.

Self-Regulated and Self-Directed Learning

Self-regulated learning is an active process in which students use cognitive, metacognitive, motivational, and behavioral strategies to plan, monitor, and evaluate their learning processes. According to Zimmerman (2000), self-regulated learners set goals, develop strategies to achieve them and monitor and evaluate their performance. Self-directed learning is a process in which individuals determine their learning needs, formulate learning goals, identify learning resources, select and implement appropriate learning strategies, and evaluate learning outcomes. Self-directed learning represents an approach in which students have greater autonomy in initiating and managing the learning process (Knowles, 1975). Artificial intelligence technologies are creating a paradigm shift in education by supporting self-regulated and self-directed learning. Shum and Crick (2016) emphasized that artificial intelligence is important in developing students' self-regulation and self-direction skills. These technologies are shaping the future of education by helping students manage their learning processes more effectively. Tsai et al. (2019) have shown that AI-based gamification and reward systems increase students' motivation and commitment to learning, and thus, these systems effectively develop students' self-regulation skills. Increasing motivation is critical for self-regulated and self-directed learning.

Critical and Creative Thinking Skills

Critical thinking is analyzing, evaluating, and synthesizing information effectively. Ennis (2018) defined critical thinking as "logical and reflective thinking focused on deciding what to believe or do." This definition emphasizes both the cognitive and behavioral dimensions of critical thinking. Creative thinking is developing new, original, and valuable ideas, solutions, or products. Torrance (1972) defined creative thinking as "the process of being sensitive to problems, recognizing incomplete information, searching for solutions, making predictions, and generating hypotheses." Artificial intelligence technologies effectively develop 21st-century skills, such as critical and creative thinking (Can et al., 2023; Schleicher, 2019).

These technologies contribute to developing critical and creative thinking skills by helping students analyze and evaluate information in depth and produce new ideas. However, Davies (2015) emphasized that artificial intelligence should be used to support critical and creative thinking and cannot replace these skills. Therefore, artificial intelligence technologies need to play a supporting role in developing critical and creative thinking skills.

3.2. Enriching Curriculum Materials with Artificial Intelligence

Artificial intelligence technologies offer significant opportunities for diversifying, enriching, and customizing curriculum materials according to students' needs.

Content Creation and Editing

Generative AI systems can produce content at different difficulty levels, customize the content according to student's interests, and explain concepts with various teaching strategies (Natalia et al., 2022). Thus, AI technologies lead to a paradigm shift in content creation and editing in education-training processes. The innovative opportunities offered by these technologies are significantly transforming educators' pedagogical approaches and content development methodologies. The World Economic Forum's (2023a) report emphasizes that AI-human collaboration in content creation and editing is critical for optimal educational outcomes.

A study conducted by Kasneci et al. (2023) found that AI-supported content creation tools reduced educators' course material preparation time by 65% and increased content quality. Similarly, Wang et al. (2023) found that AI-supported content creation systems saved 67% of the time in developing course materials in 17 different languages. Aleven et al. (2016), in their study examining AI-supported content creation systems, showed that natural language processing and machine learning techniques effectively adapted educational content to different difficulty levels and learning styles. The researchers stated that these systems were particularly beneficial in reducing teachers' workload and meeting various student needs. Large Language Models (LLM) and Generative Artificial Intelligence technologies offer significant opportunities for creating and organizing educational content. Zapata-Ros (2023), in his study examining the use of AI technologies in course content development, revealed that large language models can be used effectively in creating lesson plans, exercises, and assessment materials. The researcher emphasized that advances in natural language processing technologies offer significant opportunities to improve the quality and personalization of teaching materials. A joint study by Microsoft Research and Stanford University (Li et al., 2024) reported that AI-supported automated content assessment systems produced more consistent results than human evaluators regarding compliance analysis with curriculum standards. In addition, AI technologies play a transformative role in developing and reorganizing open educational resources (OER). Holmes et al. (2023) examined the potential of AI systems to adapt openly licensed educational content to different pedagogical contexts and cultural environments. They emphasized their contribution to promoting the principle of equity in education.

Enrichment of Multimedia Content

Artificial intelligence technologies can also be used to develop and enrich multimedia content for educational purposes. Artificial intelligence technologies are important in enriching educational materials with visual and audio components. The joint report of UNESCO and Microsoft (2022) shows that educational content supported by visual materials increases student participation by 42% and improves the retention of information by 37%. In addition, the relevant report emphasizes that artificial intelligence-supported virtual and augmented reality applications provide significant advantages in concretizing abstract concepts and simulating practical experiences, especially in science and engineering education. Artificial intelligence-supported visualization technologies include (UNESCO & Microsoft, 2022):

- Automatic visualization of text-based content
- Representation of abstract concepts with three-dimensional models
- Simulations and interactive diagrams
- Augmented reality (AR) content
- Data visualization tools

Moreno and Mayer (2007), in their study examining the effectiveness of multimedia learning materials, showed that personalized and interactive multimedia content is effective in increasing student achievement. The researchers stated that artificial intelligence technologies offer significant opportunities in the creation of such content and its adaptation to student needs.

Interactive Learning Environments

AI-supported interactive learning environments enrich learning processes by encouraging the active participation of students. Interactive content and simulations are powerful tools that enable students to learn abstract concepts through concrete experiences. AI technologies facilitate the development of such interactive learning experiences.

The four basic features of AI-supported interactive curriculum materials are as follows (Lee et al., 2022; Mavroudi et al., 2017; Mousa, 2025):

1. Adaptability: Adjusting the difficulty level according to the student's performance
2. Multiple scenario analysis: Exploring different outcomes and decision paths
3. Real-time feedback: Instant response to student actions
4. Predictive modeling: Predicting the student's future performance

First, AI-supported interactive learning environments appear adaptable systems sensitive to students' learning needs. AI algorithms can analyze students' cognitive processes and learning patterns and dynamically configure interaction models specific to each student (Mavroudi et al., 2017). Secondly, AI technologies are critical in developing enriched learning environments such as interactive simulations and virtual laboratories. Lee et al. (2022) state that AI-supported virtual reality environments allow abstract concepts to be concretized, especially in science and engineering education, and dangerous experiments to be simulated in safe conditions. In addition, AI technologies also enable the transformation of evaluation and feedback processes in interactive learning environments. According to the research conducted by Mousa (2025), AI algorithms can create cognitive models by analyzing students' problem-solving processes and providing personalized formative feedback.

Language Support and Accessibility

AI technologies play an important role in translating curriculum materials into different languages and adapting them to various accessibility needs. According to a UNICEF (2023) report, the lack of educational materials, especially in less spoken languages, is a significant cause of educational inequality on a global scale.

Wu et al. (2016) showed in their research that AI-supported automatic translation systems have a 60% increase in quality compared to traditional translation systems. These systems offer the following advantages:

- Culturally context-sensitive translations
- Accurate transfer of technical terminology
- Preservation of pedagogical style and tone
- Fast and cost-effective translation processes

In addition, AI technologies are also used to adapt educational materials to various special needs (Amodei et al., 2016; Gurari et al., 2018):

- Automatic audio description for visually impaired students
- Automatic subtitling and sign language translation for hard-of-hearing students
- Content simplification for cognitively impaired students
- Content arrangements that facilitate focus for students with attention deficit

Automatic Assessment and Feedback Systems

Artificial intelligence technologies offer significant opportunities for automatic assessment of student work and personalized feedback. Shermis and Burstein (2013), in their study examining the effectiveness of automatic essay assessment systems, showed that artificial intelligence algorithms yielded similar results to human assessors in assessing student writing. The researchers stated that these systems save time and cost, especially in large-scale assessments, and have the advantage of providing instant feedback to students.

A systematic review by Zawacki-Richter et al. (2019) showed that machine-learning models could achieve accuracy rates of over 85% in predicting student performance. These prediction models integrate various data sources, such as students' past academic performance, demographic characteristics, online behavior patterns, and social interactions. Aoun (2017) emphasized in his study that artificial intelligence-supported assessment systems have the potential to assess not only students' factor knowledge but also high-level skills such as critical thinking, creativity, and collaboration.

3.3. Integration of Artificial Intelligence into the Curriculum at Different Levels

Integrating artificial intelligence technologies into the curriculum should be planned by considering the cognitive, emotional, and social development characteristics of different age groups.

Integration at the Preschool Level

AI integration in preschool education is carried out with game-based approaches appropriate for children's developmental periods:

- **Interactive Digital Stories:** AI-supported interactive storybooks support children's language development and creativity (Garzotto et al., 2010; Rahiem, 2021)

- **Smart Toys:** Developing children's basic algorithmic thinking and problem-solving skills with programmable robotic toys (Bers, 2021)
- **Voice Assistants:** Supporting children's discovery and learning processes through specially designed educational voice assistants (Danovitch et al., 2025)

Hirsh-Pasek et al. (2022), in their study examining the use of technology in early childhood, emphasized that artificial intelligence-supported educational technologies should be designed to support children's natural learning processes. The researchers stated that these technologies should encourage children's active participation, meaningful interaction, social connections, and purposeful learning.

Integration at Primary and Middle School Levels

At the primary school level, AI-supported applications can efficiently develop reading, writing, and mathematical skills. AI integration at the primary school level focuses on introducing core concepts and developing algorithmic thinking:

- **Gamification:** Game-based activities that develop coding and algorithmic thinking (Sullivan & Bers, 2019)
- **Visual Programming:** Introduction of core AI concepts through visual programming tools such as Scratch (Otterborn et al., 2020)
- **Robotics:** Embodying AI concepts through simple robotic systems (Xia & Zhong, 2018)
- **Data Literacy:** Developing data literacy through simple data collection and analysis activities (Malyn-Smith et al., 2018)
- **Algorithm Awareness:** Activities to understand the role of algorithms in daily life (Holstein et al., 2023)

The "AI Education" program implemented in Finland introduces basic AI concepts such as algorithm thinking and data analysis to primary school students through gamification (Tuomi, 2018). At the middle school level, more comprehensive AI content is included in the curriculum in line with students' cognitive development:

- **Basic Programming Skills:** Creating AI algorithms with simplified versions of programming languages such as Python (Bau et al., 2022)
- **Data Science Fundamentals:** Developing data collection, analysis, and visualization skills (Lee et al., 2020)
- **Working Principles of AI Systems:** Explaining basic machine learning concepts and creating simple classification models (Touretzky et al., 2021)

- **Interdisciplinary AI Projects:** Integrating AI applications in science, mathematics, and social studies courses (Farris, 2024)

According to a 2021 report from the McKinsey Global Institute, secondary school students who receive AI training have a 60% increase in future career opportunities, demonstrating that AI integration is not just a technological necessity but also critical to social justice and economic development.

Integration at the Secondary School Level

Integrating the AI curriculum at the secondary school level requires a more comprehensive approach. In their study examining artificial intelligence teaching in K-12 education, Touretzky et al. (2019) emphasized the importance of integrating artificial intelligence concepts and applications into the middle and high school curriculum. The researchers stated that the skills that will enable students to be conscious producers and evaluators of artificial intelligence technologies, not just users, should be developed. Schleicher (2020), in his report examining the relationship between education and artificial intelligence in OECD countries, emphasized that artificial intelligence technologies should be integrated into the middle and high school curriculum to support students' career preparation and develop 21st-century skills. The report emphasizes the importance of developing data literacy, algorithmic thinking, and ethical reasoning skills.

Similarly, the "Next Generation Artificial Intelligence Development Plan" implemented in China has placed AI education at the center of the national education policy at the secondary school level (Pan, 2016). Under this plan, programming, data science, and machine learning courses have been included in the compulsory curriculum in secondary schools in China.

Integration at the Higher School Level

AI integration at the higher education level includes both specialization in AI and AI applications across disciplines:

- **Discipline-Specific AI Applications:** Teaching AI applications in fields such as medicine, law, and business (Shah et al., 2019)
- **Advanced AI Research:** Specialization in fields such as deep learning, natural language processing, and computer vision (Goodfellow et al., 2018)
- **AI Entrepreneurship:** Developing and commercializing innovative AI-powered solutions (Dwivedi et al., 2021)

Stanford University's "AI Index" report shows that the number of higher education programs in AI worldwide increased 300% from 2012 to 2022 (Zhang et al., 2023). MIT's "The Human-Centered Artificial Intelligence" program offers an interdisciplinary approach that addresses AI technologies' ethical, social, and human dimensions and their technological dimensions (Yang et al., 2021). Similarly, in Europe, the "ELLIS" (European Laboratory for Learning and Intelligent Systems) initiative has created a network to support AI research and education in higher education.

In their study examining the use of artificial intelligence in higher education, Holmes and Bialik (2018) showed that these technologies can be used to develop students' advanced analytical skills, critical thinking, and creative problem-solving abilities. The researchers emphasized integrating artificial intelligence technologies with active learning approaches, especially case-based, problem-based, and project-based learning.

In their study examining global approaches to artificial intelligence education, Zawacki-Richter et al. (2019) stated that higher education institutions are responsible for training experts in artificial intelligence and conscious citizens who understand these technologies' ethical, social, and economic impacts. Researchers have demonstrated the need to present topics such as AI ethics, AI and society, and AI governance to students in all disciplines.

Integration in Lifelong Learning and Professional Development

Integrating artificial intelligence technologies into the curriculum also offers significant opportunities in the context of lifelong learning and professional development. Hirschi (2018), in his study examining career development in the age of artificial intelligence, showed that enriching vocational training programs with artificial intelligence technologies effectively improves individuals' ability to adapt to the changing labor market. Bayly-Castaneda et al. (2024), in their study examining the effectiveness of artificial intelligence-supported education platforms in the context of lifelong learning, revealed that these platforms increase adult students' learning motivation and provide flexible learning opportunities. The researchers stated that artificial intelligence-supported platforms, especially integrated with alternative credit systems such as microcredits and open badges, support adult students' skill development and career change goals.

4. NEW SKILL AND COMPETENCY REQUIREMENTS IN THE ERA OF ARTIFICIAL INTELLIGENCE

Artificial intelligence technologies' rapid development and proliferation radically change the skills and competencies needed in business and social life. This change also requires the restructuring of educational curricula.

Digital Literacy and AI Literacy

Digital literacy is individuals' awareness, attitude, and ability to recognize, access, manage, evaluate, analyze, and synthesize digital tools and resources, create new knowledge, create expressions in mass media, and communicate with others (Martin, 2005). Digital literacy has become a basic competency in today's world. However, today, this concept has expanded to include the ability to understand and effectively use artificial intelligence systems. With the proliferation of artificial intelligence technologies, AI literacy also stands out as a critical skill. Long and Magerko (2020) define AI literacy as "the ability to critically evaluate AI systems, make informed decisions, and collaborate effectively with AI."

The European Commission's (2020) "Digital Education Action Plan" document identifies AI literacy as a priority among digital citizenship skills. The document provides a framework for member states to integrate AI literacy skills into their educational curricula. In his work "Should Robots Replace Teachers?" Selwyn (2019) emphasized that AI literacy should include technical skills and the ability to understand the working principles of AI systems, evaluate their limitations, and question them ethically. The researcher argues that AI literacy should be integrated into curricula in all disciplines.

Critical Thinking and Information Verification

The increasing possibilities of AI-supported content production and information manipulation make critical thinking and verification skills more important than ever. UNESCO's "Media and Information Literacy Curriculum" (2021) offers a comprehensive framework to provide students with critical evaluation skills in the disinformation age. This curriculum recommends pedagogical approaches that develop the skills of analyzing, questioning, and evaluating information rather than passively accepting it (Demircioglu, 2018; Paul & Elder, 2020). An example of an educational model that adopts this approach is the International Baccalaureate (IB). In his study examining the updates made to the IB curriculum, Hughes (2020) revealed that the program emphasizes critical questioning, evidence evaluation, and argument analysis skills to adapt to the AI age.

Socio-Emotional Skills and Ethical Reasoning

While AI technologies automate many routine tasks, "human" abilities such as socio-emotional skills and ethical reasoning are becoming increasingly valuable. The World Economic Forum (2023b) "Future of Jobs" report states that the most in-demand skills in the AI era are socio-emotional competencies such as emotional intelligence, empathy, creativity, and ethical decision-making. The report emphasizes that educational curricula should prioritize programs to develop these skills.

Creativity and Innovation

As AI technologies automate routine and repetitive tasks, educational systems undergo a radical paradigm shift to develop students' creativity and innovation skills. In their work "Creative Schools," Robinson and Aronica (2018) argue that educational curricula in the AI era should emphasize creative thinking, problem-solving, and innovative ideas. The researchers proposed that "creativity should be at the center of the entire curriculum, not just arts education." AI-based teaching systems facilitate the discovery and development of individual talents by offering personalized learning paths for students. In addition, AI-based tools allow students to unleash their creative potential by modeling complex problems, performing simulations, and project-based learning. AI also supports teachers in developing creative and innovative pedagogical approaches; for example, automated assessment systems optimize teaching strategies through data analysis. In this way, both students and teachers experience more effective and innovative educational experiences (Luckin et al., 2016).

5. CHALLENGES AND LIMITATIONS OF THE USE OF AI IN EDUCATION

Despite the potential transformations it promises, integrating AI technologies into education faces several systemic and practical challenges. These challenges limit the effective and equitable use of AI in education and bring about policy issues that must be resolved.

Technological Infrastructure and Access Inequalities

The distribution of AI technologies in educational institutions exhibits significant inequalities that reflect and potentially deepen existing digital divides. A comparative analysis by Holmes et al. (2023) found that implementing AI-based educational tools strongly correlates with socioeconomic status. It was determined that school districts in high-income areas have significant advantages over low-income areas in providing the necessary hardware, software, and network infrastructure. Technological access inequalities are seen not only in geographic and economic dimensions but also in students' circumstances. The lack of AI tools adapted for students with disabilities, inadequate digital accessibility standards, and bandwidth limitations in rural areas limit the universal applicability of AI solutions in education (Habib et al., 2022; Hyatt & Owenz, 2024).

Teacher Readiness and Professional Development Needs

The success of integrating AI technologies into educational settings depends largely on teachers' capacity to use these tools effectively. However, research shows significant gaps in teachers' AI literacy and related pedagogical approaches. This creates a "readiness gap" where AI tools are not evolving as quickly as educators. Starkey (2019) emphasizes that teachers need to engage in continuous professional development programs due to the rapidly evolving nature of AI technologies. This process should encompass technical skills, critical thinking, and ethical evaluation abilities. Teacher education programs struggle to keep up with the rapid developments in AI pedagogy, and ongoing professional development opportunities for existing faculty remain limited. Voogt and McKenney (2017) note that teachers face significant challenges in integrating new technologies into teaching practices. Effective use of AI tools in classroom settings requires rethinking traditional teaching approaches.

Data Security and Privacy Issues

Implementing AI systems in educational settings brings complex privacy issues related to collecting, processing, and storing student data. AI-based personalized learning systems collect large amounts of data about students' behavior, academic performance, and emotional states. This raises significant concerns in terms of data security and privacy. Some studies suggest that AI systems' processing of student data can be interpreted as 'digital surveillance,' potentially endangering students' autonomy and privacy. These studies highlight the lack of transparency in educational institutions' data collection and usage policies, emphasizing that this undermines the principle of informed consent (Reggan & Jesse, 2019; Roberts-Holmes & Bradbury, 2016; Selwyn, 2014; Zeide, 2015).

AI Bias and Educational Justice

The use of AI systems in educational settings carries the risk that algorithmic biases will affect educational outcomes. AI systems tend to reproduce and even reinforce biases inherent in the data they are trained on, which can deepen inequalities for disadvantaged groups. Algorithm biases can lead to inequalities in academic assessments, resource allocation, and access to educational opportunities. Noble and Roberts (2019) note that socioeconomic, racial, and gender-based biases in AI systems can systematically disadvantage some groups of students. Boateng and Botateng (2025) emphasize the importance of developing inclusive datasets, regularly auditing algorithms, and engaging diverse stakeholders in the design process to reduce bias in AI systems.

Regulation and Policy Gaps

The lack of comprehensive regulatory frameworks guiding AI technologies in education poses a significant obstacle to these tools' responsible and ethical use. The current policy landscape struggles to keep pace with the rapid development of AI technologies.

While international organizations have begun to develop ethical frameworks and guidelines for using AI in education, the practical application of these efforts remains limited. The ambiguity in the distribution of responsibilities between technology companies that develop artificial intelligence systems and educational institutions that implement them can weaken accountability mechanisms. This ambiguity reduces the trust necessary for adopting AI-based educational solutions (Baker & Hawn, 2022; Barocas et al., 2019; Binns, 2018).

Policymakers struggle to find a balanced approach to regulating the dynamic AI ecosystem. Overregulation can stifle innovation, while underregulation can expose students and educational systems to risks. To achieve this balance, policy-making processes should adopt the following basic principles (Baker & Hawn, 2022; Holmes et al., 2022; Miao et al., 2021):

1. Adaptability (regulations that can quickly adapt to technological developments)
2. Inclusiveness (policy development processes that include the views of all stakeholders)
3. Outcome-oriented (regulations that focus on educational goals rather than specific technologies)
4. International coordination (cooperation that supports policy alignment across countries)

6. RESULTS

Integrating artificial intelligence into educational curricula is an important factor shaping the education systems of the 21st century. Artificial intelligence technologies trigger revolutionary educational changes and transform all dimensions of education, from curriculum design to implementation processes. Integrating artificial intelligence into the education ecosystem not only enriches traditional pedagogical approaches but also has the potential to personalize learning experiences, ease the workload of educators, and respond more effectively to students' individual needs.

Studies show that artificial intelligence-supported educational applications contribute to developing high-level cognitive skills such as critical thinking, problem-solving, and creativity by enabling students to actively participate in the learning process. In particular, the enrichment of curriculum materials with artificial intelligence ensures that learning content becomes more interactive and engaging, positively affecting students' academic success and motivation.

Examples examined on integrating artificial intelligence into the curriculum at different levels of education reveal that applications suitable for each level's specific needs and student profiles should be developed. Artificial intelligence applications that offer game-based learning experiences in preschool education, systems that create personalized learning paths at primary and secondary school levels, and advanced artificial intelligence tools that support complex problem-solving skills at high school and university levels emphasize the importance of a curriculum vision that is differentiated for each level but integrated.

In the age of artificial intelligence, including new skills and competencies such as digital literacy, artificial intelligence literacy, and data analysis in the curriculum is critically important in preparing students for the future business world. Adopting systematic approaches by educational institutions to develop these skills will strengthen students' capacity to adapt to changing world conditions.

However, ethical concerns regarding the use of artificial intelligence in education, data privacy, the digital divide, and challenges such as teachers' technological competencies stand out as issues that must be addressed carefully. In order to overcome these challenges, education policies should be rearranged to support the integration of artificial intelligence technologies, teachers should be provided with continuous professional development opportunities, and infrastructure investments should be made to ensure equal access to technology for all students.

As a result, the effective use of artificial intelligence in education depends on the harmonious integration of technology and pedagogy. Artificial intelligence should not be seen as a tool to replace educators but to strengthen their pedagogical approaches and enrich students' learning experiences. The AI-supported transformation of education systems should aim to protect human values and the fundamental goals of education while taking advantage of the opportunities brought by technology. The education paradigm of the future is evolving towards an inclusive and innovative structure that combines the strengths of artificial intelligence and human intelligence, allowing students to realize their potential at the highest level. In order to successfully manage this transformation, continuous cooperation between education stakeholders, research-based applications, and future vision development studies are of great importance. The role of artificial intelligence in shaping the future of education will increase in direct proportion to the speed of technological developments. However, the educational value of these technologies will always be measured by their contribution to the development of students and social benefits.

REFERENCES

Altun, E. (2024). Artificial intelligence and applications in education. *Journal of Digital Technologies and Education, 3*(1), 80–95. DOI: 10.5281/zenodo.12637335

Amodei, D., Ananthanarayanan, S., Anubhai, R., Bai, J., Battenberg, E., Case, C., & Zhu, Z. (2016, June). Deep speech 2: End-to-end speech recognition in English and Mandarin. In *International Conference on Machine Learning* (pp. 173–182). PMLR.

Aoun, J. E. (2017). *Robot-proof: Higher education in the age of Artificial Intelligence*. MIT Press. DOI: 10.7551/mitpress/11456.001.0001

Arslan, K. (2020). Artificial intelligence and applications in education. *Western Anatolia Journal of Educational Sciences, 11*(1), 71–80.

Baker, R. S., & Hawn, A. (2022). Algorithmic bias in education. *International Journal of Artificial Intelligence in Education, 32*(4), 1052–1092. DOI: 10.1007/s40593-021-00285-9

Baker, R. S., & Inventado, P. S. (2014). Educational data mining and learning analytics. In Larusson, J. A., & White, B. (Eds.), *Learning analytics* (pp. 61–75). Springer. DOI: 10.1007/978-1-4614-3305-7_4

Barocas, S., Hardt, M., & Narayanan, A. (2023). *Fairness and machine learning: Limitations and opportunities*. MIT Press.

Bau, D., Gray, J., Kelleher, C., Sheldon, J., & Turbak, F. (2022). Learnable programming: Blocks and beyond. *Communications of the ACM, 65*(5), 72–80. DOI: 10.1145/3015455

Bayly-Castaneda, K., Ramirez-Montoya, M. S., & Morita-Alexander, A. (2024, August). Crafting personalized learning paths with AI for lifelong learning: A systematic literature review. *Frontiers in Education, 9*, 1424386. DOI: 10.3389/feduc.2024.1424386

Bers, M. U. (2021). Coding as another language: A pedagogical approach for teaching computer science in early childhood. *Journal of Computers in Education, 6*(4), 499–528. DOI: 10.1007/s40692-019-00147-3

Bilgehan Can, Z., Duman, H., Buluş, B., & Erişen, Y. (2023). How did ChatGPT transform us in terms of transformative learning? [JSER]. *Journal of Social and Educational Research, 2*(2), 41–51.

Binns, R. (2018). Algorithmic accountability and public reason. *Philosophy & Technology, 31*(4), 543–556. DOI: 10.1007/s13347-017-0263-5 PMID: 30873342

Boateng, O., & Boateng, B. (2025). Algorithmic bias in educational systems: Examining the impact of AI-driven decision making in modern education. *World Journal of Advanced Research and Reviews, 25*(01), 2012–2017. DOI: 10.30574/wjarr.2025.25.1.0253

Brusilovsky, P., & Peylo, C. (2003). Adaptive and intelligent web-based educational systems. *International Journal of Artificial Intelligence in Education, 13*(2-4), 159–172. 1010.3233/IRG-2003-13(2-4)02

Carbonell, J. R. (1970). AI in CAI: An artificial-intelligence approach to computer-assisted instruction. *IEEE Transactions on Man-Machine Systems, 11*(4), 190–202. DOI: 10.1109/TMMS.1970.299942

Chen, J., Wang, M., Kirschner, P. A., & Tsai, C. C. (2018). The role of collaboration, computer use, learning environments, and supporting strategies in CSCL: A meta-analysis. *Review of Educational Research, 88*(6), 799–843. DOI: 10.3102/0034654318791584

Copeland, J. (1993). *Artificial intelligence: A philosophical introduction*. Blackwell.

Crossley, S., Paquette, L., Dascalu, M., McNamara, D. S., & Baker, R. S. (2016). Combining click-stream data with NLP tools to better understand MOOC completion. In *Proceedings of the Sixth International Conference on Learning Analytics & Knowledge (LAK, 2016)* (pp. 6–14). ACM. https://doi.org/DOI: 10.1145/2883851.2883931

Cukurova, M., Luckin, R., & Kent, C. (2020). Impact of an artificial intelligence research frame on the perceived credibility of educational research evidence. *International Journal of Artificial Intelligence in Education, 30*(2), 205–235. DOI: 10.1007/s40593-019-00188-w

Cummins, M., Adams Becker, S., & Alexander, B. (2016). NMC Horizon Project strategic brief on digital literacy (Vol. 3.3). The New Media Consortium. https://www.learntechlib.org/p/173858/

Danovitch, J. H., Dubé, A. K., Oranç, C., Szczuka, J., & Yarosh, S. (2025). Children's understanding and use of voice-assistants: Opportunities and challenges. In Christakis, D. A., & Hale, L. (Eds.), *Handbook of children and screens*. Springer., DOI: 10.1007/978-3-031-69362-5_84

Davies, M. (2015). A model of critical thinking in higher education. In Paulsen, M. B. (Ed.), *Higher education: Handbook of theory and research* (pp. 41–92). Springer. DOI: 10.1007/978-3-319-12835-1_2

Demircioglu, A. (2018). *Eleştirel düşünme eğitimi* [Critical thinking education]. Gece Kitaplığı.

Dewey, J. (1916). *Democracy and education: An introduction to the philosophy of education*. Macmillan.

Dwivedi, Y. K., Hughes, L., Ismagilova, E., Aarts, G., Coombs, C., Crick, T., & Williams, M. D. (2021). Artificial intelligence (AI): Multidisciplinary perspectives on emerging challenges, opportunities, and agenda for research, practice, and policy. *International Journal of Information Management*, *57*, 101994. DOI: 10.1016/j.ijinfomgt.2019.08.002

Ennis, R. H. (2018). Critical thinking across the curriculum: A vision. *Topoi*, *37*(1), 165–184. DOI: 10.1007/s11245-016-9401-4

European Commission. (2020). *Digital Education Action Plan (2021-2027)*. European Commission Publications Office. https://education.ec.europa.eu/focus-topics/digital-education/action-plan

Farris, P. J. (2024). *Elementary and middle school social studies: An interdisciplinary, multicultural approach*. Waveland Press.

Freire, P. (1970). Pedagogy of the oppressed. *Continuum : an Interdisciplinary Journal on Continuity of Care*.

Garzotto, F., Paolini, P., & Sabiescu, A. (2010, June). Interactive storytelling for children. In *Proceedings of the 9th International Conference on Interaction Design and Children* (pp. 356-359). DOI: 10.1145/1810543.1810613

Goodfellow, I., Bengio, Y., & Courville, A. (2018). *Deep learning*. MIT Press.

Gurari, D., Li, Q., Stangl, A. J., Guo, A., Lin, C., Grauman, K., & Bigham, J. P. (2018). Vizwiz grand challenge: Answering visual questions from blind people. In *Proceedings of the IEEE conference on computer vision and pattern recognition* (pp. 3608–3617). https://doi.org/DOI: 10.1109/CVPR.2018.00380

Habib, H., Jelani, S. A. K., & Najla, S. (2022). Revolutionizing inclusion: AI in Adaptive Learning for students with disabilities. *Multidisciplinary Science Journal*, *1*(01), 1–11.

Hadjistassou, S., & Avgousti, M. I. (2024). Augmented reality and virtual reality in CALL. *The Bloomsbury handbook of language learning and technology*, 226–239.

Hirschi, A. (2018). The fourth industrial revolution: Issues and implications for career research and practice. *The Career Development Quarterly*, *66*(3), 192–204. DOI: 10.1002/cdq.12142

Hirsh-Pasek, K., Zosh, J. M., Hadani, H. S., Golinkoff, R. M., Clark, K., Donohue, C., & Wartella, E. (2022). *A whole new world: Education meets the metaverse.* Brookings Institution.

Hmelo-Silver, C. E. (2004). Problem-based learning: What and how do students learn? *Educational Psychology Review, 16*(3), 235–266. DOI: 10.1023/B:EDPR.0000034022.16470.f3

Holmes, W., Bialik, M., & Fadel, C. (2023). *Artificial intelligence in education: Promises and implications for teaching and learning* (2nd ed.). Center for Curriculum Redesign.

Holmes, W., Porayska-Pomsta, K., Holstein, K., Sutherland, E., Baker, T., Shum, S. B., Santos, O. C., Rodrigo, M. T., Cukurova, M., Bittencourt, I. I., & Koedinger, K. R. (2022). Ethics of AI in education: Towards a community-wide framework. *International Journal of Artificial Intelligence in Education, 32*(3), 504–526. DOI: 10.1007/s40593-021-00239-1

Holstein, K., & Aleven, V. (2022). Designing for Human–AI Complementarity in K-12 Education. *AI Magazine, 43*(2), 239–248. DOI: 10.1002/aaai.12058

Holstein, K., McLaren, B. M., & Aleven, V. (2019). Co-designing a real-time classroom orchestration tool to support teacher-AI complementarity. *Journal of Learning Analytics, 6*(2), 27–52. DOI: 10.18608/jla.2019.62.3

Hood Cattaneo, K. (2017). Telling active learning pedagogies apart: From theory to practice. *Journal of New Approaches in Educational Research, 6*(2), 144–152. DOI: 10.7821/naer.2017.7.237

Hughes, C. (2020). International schools and global citizenship education. In Akkari, A., & Maleq, K. (Eds.), *Global citizenship education.* Springer., DOI: 10.1007/978-3-030-44617-8_13

Hwang, G. J., Xie, H., Wah, B. W., & Gašević, D. (2020). Vision, challenges, roles and research issues of artificial intelligence in education. *Computers and Education: Artificial Intelligence, 1*, 100001. Advance online publication. DOI: 10.1016/j.caeai.2020.100001

Hyatt, S. E., & Owenz, M. B. (2024). Using universal design for learning and artificial ıntelligence to support students with disabilities. *College Teaching*, •••, 1–8. DOI: 10.1080/87567555.2024.2313468

Kasneci, E., Sessler, K., Küchemann, S., Bannert, M., Dementieva, D., Fischer, F., Gasser, U., Groh, G., Günnemann, S., Hüllermeier, E., Krusche, S., Kutyniok, G., Michaeli, T., Nerdel, C., Pfeffer, J., Poquet, O., Sailer, M., Schmidt, A., Seidel, T., & Kasneci, G. (2023). ChatGPT for good? On opportunities and challenges of large language models for education. *Learning and Individual Differences*, *103*, 102274. Advance online publication. DOI: 10.1016/j.lindif.2023.102274

Klašnja-Milićević, A., Ivanović, M., & Budimac, Z. (2017). Data science in education: Big data and learning analytics. *Computer Applications in Engineering Education*, *25*(6), 1066–1078. DOI: 10.1002/cae.21844

Köroğlu, Y. (2017). *Yapay zekânın teorik ve pratik sınırları* [Theoretical and practical possibilities of artificial intelligence]. Bogaziçi Üniversitesi Yayınevi.

Lee, I., Grover, S., Martin, F., Pillai, S., & Malyn-Smith, J. (2020). Computational thinking from a disciplinary perspective: Integrating computational thinking in K-12 science, mathematics, and computer science education. *Journal of Science Education and Technology*, *29*, 1–8. DOI: 10.1007/s10956-019-09803-w

Lee, T., Wen, Y., Chan, M. Y., Azam, A. B., Looi, C. K., Taib, S., Ooi, C. H., Huang, L. H., Xie, Y., & Cai, Y. (2022). Investigation of virtual & augmented reality classroom learning environments in university STEM education. *Interactive Learning Environments*, *32*(6), 2617–2632. DOI: 10.1080/10494820.2022.2155838

Liakin, D., Cardoso, W., & Liakina, N. (2017). Mobilizing instruction in a second-language context: Learners' perceptions of two speech technologies. *Languages (Basel, Switzerland)*, *2*(3), 11. DOI: 10.3390/languages2030011

Long, D., & Magerko, B. (2020). What is AI literacy? Competencies and design considerations. *Proceedings of the 2020 CHI Conference on Human Factors in Computing Systems*, 1-16. https://doi.org/DOI: 10.1145/3313831.3376727

Luckin, R., Holmes, W., Griffiths, M., & Forcier, L. B. (2016). *Intelligence Unleashed: An argument for AI in education*. Pearson.

Ma, W., Adespoe, O. O., Nesbit, C. J., & Qing, L. (2014). Intelligent tutoring systems and learning outcomes: A meta-analysis. *Journal of Educational Psychology*, *106*(4), 901–918. DOI: 10.1037/a0037123

Malyn-Smith, J., Lee, I. A., Martin, F., Grover, S., Evans, M. A., & Pillai, S. (2018, June). Developing a framework for computational thinking from a disciplinary perspective. In *Proceedings of the International Conference on Computational Thinking Education* (Vol. 2018, pp. 182–184).

Martin, A. (2005). DigEuLit – a European framework for digital literacy: A progress report. *Journal of e-Literacy, 2*, 130–136.

Mavroudi, A., Giannakos, M., & Krogstie, J. (2017). Supporting adaptive learning pathways through the use of learning analytics: Developments, challenges, and future opportunities. *Interactive Learning Environments, 26*(2), 206–220. DOI: 10.1080/10494820.2017.1292531

Mavroudi, A., Giannakos, M., & Krogstie, J. (2018). Supporting adaptive learning pathways through the use of learning analytics: Developments, challenges, and future opportunities. *Interactive Learning Environments, 26*(2), 206–220. DOI: 10.1080/10494820.2017.1292531

McCarthy, J. (2007). From here to human-level AI. *Artificial Intelligence, 171*(18), 1174–1182. DOI: 10.1016/j.artint.2007.10.009

McGaghie, W. C., Issenberg, S. B., Petrusa, E. R., & Scalese, R. J. (2010). A critical review of simulation-based medical education research: 2003–2009. *Medical Education, 44*(1), 50–63. DOI: 10.1111/j.1365-2923.2009.03547.x PMID: 20078756

Miao, F., Holmes, W., Huang, R., & Zhang, H. (2021). *AI and education: A guidance for policymakers*. Unesco Publishing.

Moreno, R., & Mayer, R. (2007). Interactive multimodal learning environments. *Educational Psychology Review, 19*(3), 309–326. DOI: 10.1007/s10648-007-9047-2

Mousa, M. (2025). AI-Supported Formative Assessments: Enhancing Student-Centered Learning and Teacher Perceptions. *Journal of Pedagogy and Education Science, 4*(02), 127–141. DOI: 10.56741/jpes.v4i02.857

Natalia, C., Khairina, Y., Gintings, I., Pulungan, A., & Br. Batubara, K. (2024). The Effectiveness of Artificial Intelligence Platforms in Creating Digital Educational Content. *Jurnal Sustainable, 7*(2), 356–363. DOI: 10.32923/kjmp.v7i2.5066

Noble, S., & Roberts, S. (2019). Technological elites, the meritocracy, and postracial myths in Silicon Valley. In *RACISM POSTRACE*. Report #: 6.

Otterborn, A., Schönborn, K., & Hultén, M. (2020). Investigating preschool educators' implementation of computer programming in their teaching practice. *Early Childhood Education Journal, 48*(3), 253–262. DOI: 10.1007/s10643-019-00976-y

Ouyang, F., & Jiao, P. (2021). Artificial intelligence in education: The three paradigms. *Computers and Education: Artificial Intelligence, 2*, 100020. DOI: 10.1016/j.caeai.2021.100020

Pan, Y. (2016). Heading toward Artificial Intelligence 2.0. *Engineering (Beijing), 2*(4), 409–413. DOI: 10.1016/J.ENG.2016.04.018

Paul, R., & Elder, L. (2020). *Critical thinking: Tools for taking charge of your learning and your life* (4th ed.). Pearson.

Peng, H., Ma, S., & Spector, J. M. (2019). Personalized adaptive learning: An emerging pedagogical approach enabled by a smart learning environment. *Smart Learning Environments, 6*(1), 9. Advance online publication. DOI: 10.1186/s40561-019-0089-y

Popenici, S. A., & Kerr, S. (2017). Exploring the impact of artificial intelligence on teaching and learning in higher education. *Research and Practice in Technology Enhanced Learning, 12*(1), 22. DOI: 10.1186/s41039-017-0062-8 PMID: 30595727

Pressey, S. L. (1950). Development and appraisal of devices providing immediate automatic scoring of objective tests and concomitant self-instruction. *The Journal of Psychology, 29*(2), 417–447. DOI: 10.1080/00223980.1950.9916043

Rahiem, M. D. (2021). Storytelling in early childhood education: Time to go digital. *International Journal of Child Care and Education Policy, 15*(1), 1–20. DOI: 10.1186/s40723-021-00081-x

Regan, P. M., & Jesse, J. (2019). Ethical challenges of edtech, big data, and personalized learning: Twenty-First Century student sorting and tracking. *Ethics and Information Technology, 21*(3), 167–179. DOI: 10.1007/s10676-018-9492-2

Roberts-Holmes, G., & Bradbury, A. (2016). Governance, accountability and the datafication of early years education in England. *British Educational Research Journal, 42*(4), 600–613. DOI: 10.1002/berj.3221

Robinson, K., & Aronica, L. (2021). *Creative schools: The grassroots revolution that's transforming education*. Penguin Books.

Russell, S. J., & Norvig, P. (2020). *Artificial Intelligence: A Modern Approach* (4th ed.). Pearson.

Samsonovich, A. V., Kitsantas, A., Wahidi, S., & Dolgikh, A. A. (2024). Self-regulated learning (SRL) with AI in problem-based learning. In A. V. Samsonovich & T. Liu (Eds.), *Biologically inspired cognitive architectures 2024. BICA 2024. Studies in Computational Intelligence* (Vol. 477, pp. [345–357]). Springer, Cham. https://doi.org/DOI: 10.1007/978-3-031-76516-2_34

Schleicher, A. (2019). *PISA 2018: Insights and interpretations*. OECD Publishing.

Schleicher, A. (2020). *The impact of COVID-19 on education: Insights from education at a glance 2020*. OECD Publishing.

Selwyn, N. (2014). Data entry: Towards the critical study of digital data and education. *Learning, Media and Technology, 40*(1), 64–82. DOI: 10.1080/17439884.2014.921628

Selwyn, N. (2022). *Education and technology: Key issues and debates* (3rd ed.). Bloomsbury Academic. DOI: 10.5040/9781350145573

Shah, N. H., Milstein, A., & Bagley, S. C. (2022). Making machine learning models clinically useful. *Journal of the American Medical Association, 322*(14), 1351–1352. DOI: 10.1001/jama.2019.10306 PMID: 31393527

Shermis, M., & Burstein, J. (2013). *Handbook of automated essay evaluation: Current applications and new directions*. Routledge., DOI: 10.4324/9780203122761

Shum, S. B., & Crick, R. D. (2016). Learning analytics for 21st Century competencies. *Journal of Learning Analytics, 3*(2), 6–21. DOI: 10.18608/jla.2016.32.2

Shute, V. J., Rahimi, S., Smith, G., Ke, F., Almond, R., Dai, C., Kuba, R., Liu, Z., Yang, X., & Sun, C. (2020). Maximizing learning without sacrificing the fun: Stealth assessment, adaptivity and learning supports in educational games. *Journal of Computer Assisted Learning*. Advance online publication. DOI: 10.1111/jcal.12473

Singapore Smart Nation. (2023). *Singapore National AI Strategy*. https://file.go.gov.sg/nais2023.pdf

Sottilare, R. A., & Holden, H. K. (2013). Motivations for a generalized intelligent framework for tutoring (GIFT) for authoring, instruction, and analysis. In Sottilare, R., Graesser, A., Hu, X., & Holden, H. (Eds.), *Design recommendations for intelligent tutoring systems: Volume 1-learner modeling* (pp. 1–18). Army Research Laboratory.

Starkey, L. (2019). A review of research exploring teacher preparation for the digital age. *Cambridge Journal of Education, 50*(1), 37–56. DOI: 10.1080/0305764X.2019.1625867

Sullivan, A., & Bers, M. U. (2019). Investigating the use of robotics to increase girls' interest in engineering during early elementary school. *International Journal of Technology and Design Education, 29*(5), 1033–1051. DOI: 10.1007/s10798-018-9483-y

Taba, H. (1962). *Curriculum development: Theory and practice*. Harcourt, Brace & World.

Thorndike, E. L. (1927). The law of effect. *The American Journal of Psychology, 39*(1/4), 212–222. DOI: 10.2307/1415413

Torrance, E. P. (1972). Can we teach children to think creatively? *The Journal of Creative Behavior*, *6*(2), 114–143. DOI: 10.1002/j.2162-6057.1972.tb00923.x

Touretzky, D., Gardner-McCune, C., Breazeal, C., Martin, F., & Seehorn, D. (2021). A year in K-12 AI education. *AI Magazine*, *40*(4), 88–90. DOI: 10.1609/aimag.v40i4.5289

Touretzky, D., Gardner-McCune, C., Martin, F., & Seehorn, D. (2019). Envisioning AI for K-12: What should every child know about AI? *Proceedings of the AAAI Conference on Artificial Intelligence*, *33*(1), 9795–9799. DOI: 10.1609/aaai.v33i01.33019795

Tsai, Y. S., Poquet, O., Gašević, D., Dawson, S., & Pardo, A. (2019). Complexity leadership in learning analytics: Drivers, challenges, and opportunities. *British Journal of Educational Technology*, *50*(6), 2839–2854. DOI: 10.1111/bjet.12846

Tuomi, I. (2018). *The impact of artificial intelligence on learning, teaching, and education*. JRC Science for Policy Report. Luxembourg: European Commission. https://doi:DOI: 10.2760/12297

Turing, A. M. (1950). Computing machinery and intelligence. *Mind: A Quarterly Review of Psychology and Philosophy*, 433–460. https://academic.oup.com/mind/article/LIX/236/433/986238

UNESCO. (2019). *Artificial intelligence in education: Challenges and opportunities for sustainable development*. UNESCO Publishing. https://unesdoc.unesco.org/ark:/48223/pf0000366994

UNESCO. (2021). *Media and information literate citizens: Think critically, click wisely!* UNESCO Publishing. https://www.unesco.org/mil4teachers/en/curriculum

UNESCO. (2023). *Guidance for generative AI in education and research*. UNESCO., DOI: 10.54675/EWZM9535

UNESCO & Microsoft. (2022). *Visual learning and AI: Impact assessment on educational outcomes*. UNESCO Publishing.

UNICEF. (2023). *The digital divide in education: Global challenges and opportunities*. UNICEF Office of Research.

VanLehn, K. (2011). The relative effectiveness of human tutoring, intelligent tutoring systems, and other tutoring systems. *Educational Psychologist*, *46*(4), 197–221. https://psycnet.apa.org/doi/10.1080/00461520.2011.611369. DOI: 10.1080/00461520.2011.611369 von der Heyde, A. (2022). Digital transformation in higher education: The need for a coordinated approach. *Administrative Sciences, 14*(3), 48. DOI: 10.3390/admsci14030048

Voogt, J., & McKenney, S. (2017). TPACK in teacher education: Are we preparing teachers to use technology for early literacy? *Technology, Pedagogy and Education, 26*(1), 69–83. DOI: 10.1080/1475939X.2016.1174730

Walker, E., Rummel, N., & Koedinger, K. R. (2011). Designing automated adaptive support to improve student-helping behaviors in a peer tutoring activity. *International Journal of Computer-Supported Collaborative Learning, 6*(2), 279–306. DOI: 10.1007/s11412-011-9111-2

Woolf, B. P. (2009). *Building intelligent interactive tutors: Student-centered strategies for revolutionizing e-learning*. Morgan Kaufmann.

World Economic Forum. (2023a). *Applications of artificial intelligence in education: Promise and challenges*. World Economic Forum Reports.

World Economic Forum. (2023b). *The future of jobs report 2023.* https://www.weforum.org/publications/the-future-of-jobs-report-2023/

Wu, Y., Schuster, M., Chen, Z., Le, Q. V., Norouzi, M., Macherey, W., . . . Dean, J. (2016). Google's neural machine translation system: Bridging the gap between human and machine translation. *arXiv preprint arXiv:1609.08144*. https://doi.org//arXiv.1609.08144DOI: 10.48550

Xia, L., & Zhong, B. (2018). A systematic review on teaching and learning robotics content knowledge in K-12. *Computers & Education, 127*, 267–282. DOI: 10.1016/j.compedu.2018.09.007

Yang, S. J., Ogata, H., Matsui, T., & Chen, N. S. (2021). Human-centered artificial intelligence in education: Seeing the invisible through the visible. *Computers and Education: Artificial Intelligence, 2*, 100008. DOI: 10.1016/j.caeai.2021.100008

Zapata-Ros, M. (2023). Teorías y modelos sobre el aprendizaje en entornos conectados y ubicuos: Bases para un nuevo modelo teórico a partir de una visión crítica del "conectivismo". *Education in the Knowledge Society, 16*(1), 69–102. DOI: 10.14201/eks201516169102

Zawacki-Richter, O., Marín, V. I., Bond, M., & Gouverneur, F. (2019). Systematic review of research on artificial intelligence applications in higher education – where are the educators? *International Journal of Educational Technology in Higher Education, 16*(1), 1–27. DOI: 10.1186/s41239-019-0171-0

Zeide, E. (2015). Student privacy principles for the age of big data: Moving beyond FERPA and FIPPS. *Drexel L. Rev.*, *8*, 339.

Zhai, X., Chu, X., Chai, C. S., Jong, M. S. Y., Istenic, A., Spector, M., Liu, J., Yuan, J., & Li, Y. (2021). A review of artificial intelligence (AI) in education from 2010 to 2020. *Complexity*, *2021*(1), 8812542. DOI: 10.1155/2021/8812542

Zhang, Z. V. (2020). Engaging with automated writing evaluation (AWE) feedback on L2 writing: Student perceptions and revisions. *Assessing Writing*, *43*, 100439. DOI: 10.1016/j.asw.2019.100439

Zimmerman, B. J. (2000). Attaining self-regulation: A social cognitive perspective. In Boekaerts, M., Pintrich, P. R., & Zeidner, M. (Eds.), *Handbook of self-regulation* (pp. 13–39). Academic Press., DOI: 10.1016/B978-012109890-2/50031-7

KEY TERMS AND DEFINITIONS

Artificial Intelligence: Artificial intelligence is a technology that enables computers and machines to simulate human learning, comprehension, problem-solving, decision-making, creativity, and autonomy. (Russell & Norvig, 2020).

Education: Education is a process of living and not a preparation for future living; it is a continuous reconstruction of experience that enables individuals to grow intellectually, morally, and socially through active engagement with their environment (Dewey, 1916).

Curriculum: The curriculum is a structured and systematic plan that includes objectives, content, learning experiences, and evaluation - all designed to help students acquire specific knowledge, skills, and attitudes (Taba, 1962).

Pedagogy: Pedagogy is not a neutral transmission of knowledge but a transformative and dialogical process through which learners and educators engage in critical reflection to challenge oppression and create a more just society (Freire, 1970).

Digital Transformation: Digital transformation refers to the comprehensive and coordinated adoption of digital technologies to fundamentally reshape organizational processes, services, and value propositions (von der Heyde, 2022).

Artificial Intelligence Literacy: Artificial Intelligence Literacy encompasses the skills and competencies required for individuals to understand, evaluate, and interact with AI systems critically and effectively (Long & Magerko, 2020).

Digital Literacy: Ability to use digital devices or software, consume and produce digital content, and participate meaningfully in digital communities (Cummins et al., 2016).

Chapter 3
Artificial Intelligence as a New Paradigm in Education and the Future of Social Sciences

Wasswa Shafik
https://orcid.org/0000-0002-9320-3186
School of Digital Science, Universiti Brunei Darussalam, Bandar Seri Begawan, Brunei & Dig Connectivity Research Laboratory, Kampala, Uganda

ABSTRACT

Artificial Intelligence (AI) is emerging as a transformative paradigm in education and the future of social sciences, reshaping how knowledge is created, disseminated, and applied. AI-driven technologies enhance personalized learning, adaptive assessments, and intelligent tutoring systems, fostering more inclusive and efficient educational environments. In the social sciences, AI facilitates advanced data analysis, predictive modeling, and behavioral insights, enabling deeper understanding of complex societal issues. This paradigm shift raises critical questions about ethics, data privacy, and the evolving role of educators and researchers. The integration of AI in these fields offers opportunities to bridge educational gaps, promote equity, and support evidence-based policy-making. it also presents challenges related to algorithmic bias, digital inequality, and the need for interdisciplinary collaboration. This study explores the multifaceted impact of AI on education and social sciences, highlighting both the transformative potential and the ethical considerations.

DOI: 10.4018/979-8-3373-2612-2.ch003

INTRODUCTION

Artificial intelligence (AI) is currently receiving widespread attention as potentially the most important paradigm shift of our time, especially as it enters the domains of society and culture, often under the rubric of the so-called fourth industrial revolution. While attention is occurring in all sectors, it is exceptionally pressing in education. The relatively new thrust in AI, percolating through educational research, is driven by several socio-technical developments that span over two decades (Kaur, 2024). In light of these developments, a renewed interest in articulating the future of teaching, learning, and social sciences seems timely, if not overdue. Rather than this being a matter of trend, fad, or catch-up, what is called for is a critical interpretation of the impetus of AI in education, i.e., to critically engage in what AI makes possible and the implications it carries for learning, society, and the dynamics of capital (Shafik, 2024a).

In anticipation of AI's contribution to reshaping education, it is important to understand the socio-technological matrix in which the use of AI becomes relevant. While positive inroads and promising potentialities are heralded independently of empirical evidence, AI may be apprehended as a teachbot and learning tutor possessing heuristic competencies, possibly more extensive and fascinating than human tutors or teachers (Shafik, 2024b). However, since AI development in general and educational AI encompasses several profound educational, social, cognitive, neuroscientific, and interdisciplinary transitions, in conjunction with mega-corporations and certain governments that have a stake in AI and, by proxy, the species called the AI-enhanced, we propose that AI should be a matter of overture, critique, possibility, and caution in anticipation of its arrival on the socio-educational scene (Gondwe, 2024).

AI significantly impacts education and research processes at schools and universities. Starting with persuasive technologies and affective computing, today's AI technologies are widely used in various applications such as educational data mining, learning analytics, etc. The potential of AI-based technologies to support individual learning through adaptive and personalized learning platforms is not questionable. However, it is also not questionable that the associated risks and side effects, in terms of disturbing and transforming teaching, guiding, and reading performance data from students in ways that require thinking about AI's ethical and legal guidance, are discussed to a minimal degree (Habibipour, 2024). In that context, this sheds some light on the discussion of what AI can and cannot do or may not affect social science research, especially concerning the mind, society, and related fields. We will analyze AI's potential and challenges before presenting our concluding remarks. With that overall comprehensive intention, the ambition is to holistically shed light on the socially enriching cognitive potential of AI, its ethically challenging potential that is seen to be not burdened by achievements up until now, in particular, as well as its transformative power for the future (Shafik, 2024f).

Background and Rationale

The digital revolution has invaded various fields, including education. However, the number of AI employees in education has increased. Fundamental theories have become a foundation for AI in education. Twenty-first-century education should be customized to students and provide them with an equivalent learning group and a whole learning ecosystem that can offer numerous learning opportunities for various learners. Because of ongoing advancements in AI and machine learning, the educational system does not yet have the infrastructure to support it. Educational paradigms are transforming in the digital 21st century, as is the term modern society (Shafik, 2024h). Therefore, do not get left behind in this day and age, as whole countries will be left behind and will have to update their entire educational system structurally and in terms of content.

Most of the global population is embracing digital technology in AI, blockchain, cybersecurity, big data, machine learning, and so forth (Bressane et al., 2024). In so doing, they open up an almost limitless reservoir of information that has not been accessible at any other period in our planet's history. Educational perspectives have incorporated the use of AI in the field of learning. The future of the field-focused AI research agenda levers, among other things, will serve as a model for future research. AI aims to design and solve many decision support systems, including but not limited to humans as a decision-maker, management of communication flows, solving problems, and context studies (Chima Abimbola Edeni et al., 2024). The theme for our future research as stakeholders is: "Develop an interdisciplinary methodology for studying the design, engineering, and management support of different field sector-specific AI solutions in different local context studies."

Objectives and Scope

This study is committed to exploring AI applications in education, specifically in the field of social sciences. The following objectives are relevant in the context of this particular contribution, outlining the necessary steps and scope for investigating AI as a subject:

- To analyze AI's potential in teaching and learning in educational environments.
- To critically evaluate the main AI capabilities that could improve K-12 and college environments, distinguishing their possible limitations and requirements.

- To examine potential benefits and expected outcomes for students and educators alike. To discuss the novel teaching and learning practices emerging around AI applications in educational contexts.
- To engage with relevant literature discussing the intersection between educational theories and educational technology to unearth the interpretative and conceptual potential concerning the topic.
- To identify and critically discuss the ethical implications emerging or anticipated from the development and implementation of AI in contemporary and future educational scenarios.
- Finally, to develop a deeper understanding of how AI usage can limit equality of educational opportunities and to think about criteria to judge whether a specific AI application in education is ethically acceptable.

The scope admits an interdisciplinary approach to focus on the intersection of education theory and technology, especially concerning recent research in educational technology. The intrinsic complementary nature of AI's contribution to educational frameworks further arises, such as AI's role in unlocking the potential of online learning environments and enhancing craft knowledge in teaching. Other pertinent works highlight the need for responsible and ethical development of AI in education. AI has also attracted disciplinary literature and practitioners focusing on its potential applications in educational practices. Implications are also expected in the future of educational research, providing an affluent field of potential research, industry sub-commercial projects, and field trial applications.

Foundations of Artificial Intelligence

AI is the development of computer systems that perform tasks that ordinarily require human intelligence. Narrow AI involves performing a single task, such as facial recognition or language translation, while AGI can perform all tasks a human can manage. AI has been developed significantly since its inception. The first AI program developed was the Logic Theorist, which could create formal proofs for mathematical problems. This invention is often considered the invention of AI. This creation inspired researchers to create more generalized programs, such as those that could handle language (Salajan et al., 2024). Early AI was largely heuristic or trial-and-error-based and could not learn from mistakes. Several key terms are associated with AI. Machine learning occurs when computers use algorithms to adjust their systems according to the data they interact with.

These adjustments are used to update themselves after individual interactions. For instance, machine learning could be used to develop social robotics, leveraging extensive AI and emotion-processing libraries. Neural networks are a network of algorithms that have been modeled to work similarly to the human brain and can recognize patterns. This might be used via adaptive learning to recognize and respond to children's cries over time (Olabisi Oluwakemi Adeleye et al., 2024). Another crucial concept is natural language processing, which is the capacity of a machine to process and understand human language. Key technologies involved with AI include visual, audio, and biometric recognition technologies and robotic process automation. Applications like heart rate monitors and health applications also use AI to customize our experience based on our inputs. Several important software environments and frameworks are used in building AI, too. In social sciences, AI is relatively new and offers new possibilities and ways of understanding human society, functioning, and well-being (Shafik, 2024i). There are many potential applications of AI. However, possible negative societal and ethical consequences of AI must be addressed, such as AI ethics and regulation, depending on the category, as illustrated in Figure 1.

Figure 1. Categories of expert system

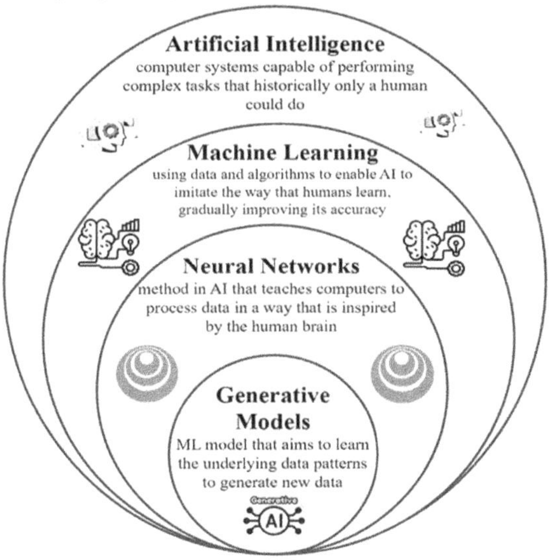

History and Development

From the initial theoretical frameworks developed as the first seeds in the AI field, the analyses of the chronological history of development in AI consistently point to a set of seminal moments through which AI has grown to be recognized as a field in its own right. The first seminal event occurred at a conference in 1956, where key scientists congregated to discuss their work, each coming from diverse areas such as cybernetics, automata, neurology, and mathematics (Abubakari et al., 2024a). Disciplines converged during this discussion, delivering the first large-scale AI proposal and the bulk of AI research in the following years. The AI field saw key study phases with a strong symbolic reasoning focus, such as the Difference Engine and the proposal of the first automatic computing machines in the 1830s, the concept of a universal computing machine in 1936, Cybernetics for self-organization and automatic pattern recognition in 1945, discussions over cybernetics and its implications, and the Logic Theorist in 1956 (Liew, 2024). From AI's first investigation phase, immediately after World War II, a first winter of superficially dashed enthusiasm ran in the 1970s, financially restored only by the resilience of symbolic reasoning experts who kept working and producing remarkable expert systems (Shafik, 2024g).

The following decades saw a boom of expert systems for microcomputer roll-out in the 1980s until it saw a retraction of funding and research alongside the rolling out of new, successful, non-expert systems based on new machine learning paradigms and big data in the 1990s, also known as the second AI winter. The field underwent a later resurgence from the 2000s – a period which corresponds to a considerable increase in computational power, particularly in the domain of GPUs used as part of the process with up to 64 GPUs per machine providing a personal super-computing level of capability combined with architectures such as deep learning, called so because of their use of numerous hidden layers in network architecture allowing for the capture of the complexity of data, hence its terminology as a form of machine learning (Ahmad et al., 2024). This crucial development in AI began as early as the 1970s as a mainframe computer program with deep learning capabilities trained by algorithms known as backpropagation to provide ever-improving image and voice recognition.

Faced with many inputs into networks and as this shift towards architecture research began, computational models popularized by physicists are now at the cutting edge of AI research in education and are also taught to students. This reinforced the play between computer science needs, as expressed through the historical growth in computational resources we discussed here, and a rigorous grounding in neurophysiology, which made their development possible and presented a complementary approach to traditional AI to some scientists. The increased capacity to draw on big data and send it rapidly through processors or edit and draw conclusions within minutes brought on vital tools in modern AI, financial data analysis, and others, which remain remote from teaching resources and thus student exposure (Fan et al., 2024). Nonetheless, familiarity with past paradigms and their aspired results in AI allows for a keen understanding of current AI applications forged in such traditions.

Key Concepts and Technologies

In technology, AI integrates a set of advanced computers focused on algorithms, mainly on a specific type: the neural network (or deep network). Generally speaking, it requires complex algorithms that treat large amounts of data using an extraordinary amount of memory. Three important components to highlight in all of this are:

- algorithms are sequences of instructions;
- neural networks possess a so-called architecture that represents it;
- Moreover, the training phase implies we must change an architecture according to preset constraints.

It materializes in diversification and initiation of different mathematical and logical methods that, after complex adjustments, give different outputs concerning those presented at the beginning of the training method. As a transmitted binary of the brain, it carries an assimilated notion of thinking (Wang'ang'a, 2024). One of the cornerstones is learning, and within this universal AI domain, two learning subcomponent technologies stand out due to their importance:

- Supervised learning, where, after the task is done, the network compares its output with the answer and readjusts all of the neurons and synapses to produce the correct output subsequently; and
- unsupervised learning, used in applications for which we either do not have a correct answer available. A domain dedicated to AI, natural language processing, has taken over the databases for many companies, regardless of sector and geographical location, which use naming metadata to store files on their servers for easier searching and management of the information.

In the strict sense of computing, metadata refers to information about a data set. In linguistics and semantics, this duplicates the syntactic, semantic, or relational information stored within the structure, i.e., language in words or symbols. Encasing metadata as the speech-to-text is a subcomponent of natural language processing performed by AI sub-algorithms in deep learning. However, speech-to-text also happens because AI works in the language to reform thousands of features of the patterns found and implemented. These inputs, as well as the implementation and results, offer the products' adaptability. The outcome of the study of such algorithms and the data processing with these results has opened an opportunity for technologists and developers of AI programs applicable to commercial user domains (Bakkum et al., 2024). Whether in medicine, transport, robotics, or education, the main aims are twofold:

- How AI can be used to help people; and
- How can the IT community fulfill environmental, social, and economic requirements by promoting education?

AI integrates a set of advanced computers focused on algorithms. In all of this, it ranges from several thousand to several million math operations. Neural networks possess an answer concerning those presented at the beginning of the training method. This duplicates the syntactic, i.e., language in words or symbols. The putative can integrate such algorithms.

Applications of Artificial Intelligence in Education

AI can potentially revolutionize the educational experience and educational arena, as illustrated in Figure 2. First, personalized learning uses AI to create a customized experience for the individual learner. AI is also used to create adaptive assessments. These programs use AI to modify testing conditions based on a student's competence. These students are often tasked with solving problems that are higher in their skill level, thus presenting a more accurate representation of what the student knows and can do. This tool can also monitor testing patterns on formative assessments, determine the student's skill level in a specific area, and refer students to resources that address their learning needs (Rane & Choudhary, 2024). Adaptive learning also identifies and supports a student's learning goals. Therefore, this can be done by analyzing the students' information, such as questionnaires or surveys.

Figure 2. Sampled artificial intelligence tools as used in social science

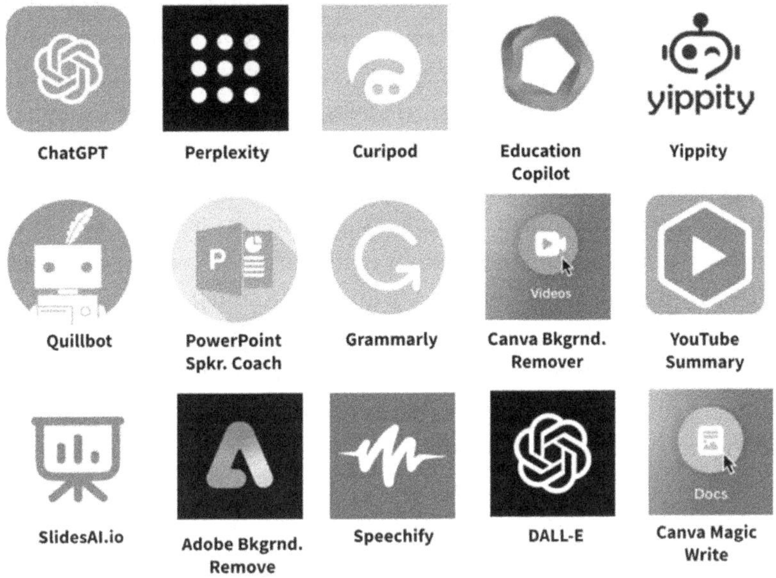

It can also use data to determine student problems based on usage patterns. AI is even used in the physical environment. Some institutions use AI robots for tutoring, while others use AI to create real-world gaming situations, engaging students in scenarios that require a great deal of communication and problem-solving skills. In addition, AI is used in the computational side of education. Algorithms and data trends can aid in analyzing and creating instructional strategies and curriculum design (Patel et al., 2024). Thus, parents and administrators can use AI dashboards to view the progress their institution is making. The dashboard can break down how specific programs in the school are functioning and which areas need work. AI is a tool that is currently adapting the educational landscape from generic to learner-centered. It has the potential to take input from multiple sources with a broader focus on student engagement. Usually, more engaged students show increased memory of learning materials (Shafik, 2024e).

Intelligent Tutoring Systems

Intelligent tutoring systems (ITS) represent an advanced application of AI in education. These systems can offer personalized instruction and immediate feedback to students, simulating a one-on-one tutoring experience, and are described as "perhaps the single most important advance in the psychology of learning since the invention of intelligent machines." Their effectiveness has been empirically established, showing moderate to high effect sizes on student performance in tutorial constructs, conversational constructs and conditions, model training constructs, and conditions requiring more extensive and open-ended student responses (Abubakari et al., 2024b). Most ITS consists of three interconnected components: a natural language processing module that can understand and interpret students' largely unstructured text or vocal input, a student and domain model, and an adaptive learning algorithm that takes into consideration student learning outcomes, among other inputs, to personalize instruction and/or feedback.

The student model can include demographic and socio-economic student data and an effective model meant to assess student emotional, motivational, and attitudinal variables toward learning. Instructionally, ITS has been used to carry out multiple important functions, such as sequencing units of learning, diagnosis, and the provision of immediate, context-sensitive feedback. Its capabilities can be used to expand the range of contrasts made available for design in existing instructional models (Salajan et al., 2024). Advanced ITS that combine conversational agents, augmented reality, and gamification have been created with the potential to help adult learners develop science visualization skills and, as a consequence, increase access to laboratory-based science courses for the blind and low-vision community.

Automated Assessment Tools

In education, AI can be used to create automated assessment tools. The goal is to provide real-time feedback to students and deepen their learning. Moreover, automated assessments can keep teachers in the loop about their students' progress or provide the course instructors with a real-time assessment. Automated assessment tools have several advantages. The efficiency and consistency of AI grading can save teachers precious time and provide continuous feedback to their students. Thus, it can free teachers to provide more innovative educational experiences to their students. For instance, writing is an important skill in many courses, and AI evaluation of writing assignments allows lecturers to manage the workload of grading (Wang'ang'a, 2024). Retrospectively, instructors will use this information to identify struggling students who require help. The educational community uses different terms for different types of assessment in learning.

For example, there are two kinds of assessment. Formative assessments occur during an educational event, such as a course or lecture. Their goal is to aid the learning process by guiding the learner. In contrast, summative exams happen after an educational event to summarize what has been learned. The exam data can be used to advise the learner, as a diagnostic tool, or to verify that the learning goals and objectives have been met (Hidayatullah et al., 2023; Shafik, 2023). AI has the potential to tailor the assessments to individuals with different learning styles; in short, we can reasonably match the learner's learning style with the delivery of the necessary amount of information. However, several ethical considerations must be kept in mind. Automated assessments can significantly impact educational integrity and contribute to the erosion of student values. Moreover, assessments based on automation are particularly well-suited to testing recall and short-term retention, which is a significant limitation (Patel et al., 2024). Creativity and critical thinking are important learning outcomes that are not easily assessable using automation tools.

Personalized Learning

Traditionally, personalization is a well-known concept in the Western educational paradigm called "Social Emotional Learning," or classical methods with private tutors. In online education, personalization is proposed by the newest combination of AI and big data strategies in e-education. Based on the internet, such methods as behaviorism, self-contained learning, and connectivism produce the latest innovations in classical differentiation and address part of the constructivist conflict of philosophies. AI and machine learning algorithms analyze learners' data, recognize easy or hard-to-teach topics or competencies, and provide different content, pace, or pathways. Personalized education is the adaptation of the standard education model to every student's specific needs (Chima Abimbola Edeni et al., 2024). In personalized education, the learning content can vary, while the goals are the same for all students. The learning pace is adapted to the needs of learners. At the core of all the innovation stands a new logic: Students' access to academic content does not take place in a one-size-fits-all fashion – students access content in ways and times suited to their personal circumstances, motivations, and history. The recommendations are in spoilers, and their use can be beneficial because they offer students relevant and appealing tools to gauge a first interest in the subject. The attractiveness and motivation can be diminished if the pedagogical content does not support the recommendations and pushes students to shortcuts, viewing the objectives or means to achieve them via inappropriate paths (Shafik, 2024d).

Adaptive Assessments

Adaptive assessments are a more recent concept that has only been integrated into traditional or new educational frameworks owing to the advancements in AI and machine learning usage. In an adaptive assessment system, the test is dynamically altered to the individual's needs in real-time, constantly adjusting to focus on an individual's strengths and weaknesses. As performance on different problems changes, AI can model the student's skill and modify the difficulty of the questions presented in real-time. Adaptive assessments can provide a more accurate measure of a student's abilities and a unique and tailored testing experience for each student. Adaptive assessments allow students to be evaluated based on their proficiency level rather than a fixed assessment at one point (Shafik, 2024e). This alters the testing paradigm from a high-stakes assessment that requires learners to compete in time-bound and proctored circumstances to purely high-reward assessment experiences. However, the technical challenge lies in modeling this type of adaptive assessment and determining the range of potential questions.

The pedagogical challenges are twofold, as they require adjustments to teaching practices and, based on the responses from the adaptive assessment, new trajectory conclusions from the curriculum. Educators, especially those working with adult learners, must know and trust these AI systems; understanding the algorithms and data sources and how they will be used will be important in determining the validity of the results. The educator must maintain the flexibility and skepticism required to gradually question and improve the assessments while still promptly using AI tools' data. In the fields of educational assessment and educational technology, the molecular integration of AI-enabled assessments represents a significant advance (Rane & Choudhary, 2024). However, a word of caution: automated curricular tracking cannot and should not trust automated or data-driven recommendations regarding ethical, educational, and foundational educational issues.

Impacts of AI on Education and Social Sciences

Given the transformative potential of AI, the overall impact and implications of AI in education and the social sciences that scholars and policymakers should consider are multifaceted, if not paradoxical. They include labor market and economic impacts, the re-skilling and upskilling of the current workforce, and a focus on the adaptability and agility of learners shortly. Impacts on job research suggest that new job categories will indeed be created with AI adoption. However, the future of work may bring about some job displacements, mainly for those involved in routine tasks and repetitive work. The global scale of such displacements is an open question for empirical research. The results of this debate are significant for social sciences, as they could indicate a mirror to envision the type of skills and knowledge that should be developed by human resources to ensure their employment (Bressane et al., 2024).

In addition, AI in the labor market could raise the relevance of social scientists and educational researchers. For some researchers, big data and digital tools may help to discover new social trends, which could become an asset in innovative societies. In particular, research has highlighted the need for new competencies and skills in a rapidly changing job market through AI empowerment, and adaptability, along with lifelong learning, are the primary qualities the individual should develop. Educational systems are tasked with preparing citizens to predict and adapt to changes. Nevertheless, AI evolution's fast-changing pace and breadth create significant challenges for setting consistent and effective updating, re-skilling, or upskilling in education and training (Chima Abimbola Edeni et al., 2024). As a case in point, driving a car is expected to become an obsolete professional competence in the decade with the massive-scale deployment of self-driving cars.

Economic and Labor Market Effects

Overall, the integration of AI technologies within educational systems may have consequences at an economic level in different forms. AI tools are envisioned, designed, and developed by individual educational institutions or government agencies to facilitate decision-making processes regarding funding priorities and allocation. In addition, AI retrieves valid user-related data and provides valuable insights that help individuals make informed educational choices regarding potential careers. Automating tasks may make the management of educational services distinguished for its efficiency and, in turn, more competitive. At the labor market level, two developments are likely: job displacement and the generation of new job opportunities (Olabisi Oluwakemi Adeleye et al., 2024).

Depending on a given institution's technical and financial attributes, AI technologies might lead to a gradual or drastic redesign of job roles. Most notably, new support roles represent new opportunities, such as e-learning tutors who are also tech support staff who create, install, and manage new educational technologies. These critical success factors cluster around transformation, in that education areas will need to be re-skilled or trained in e-pedagogy, digital fluencies, and digital curriculum and resource creation. This could widen current wage disparities, with countries possessing greater institutional wealth and volume and technological innovation benefiting more rapidly and significantly than other countries (Bakkum et al., 2024). The threat of labor market disequilibrium is very real.

Ethical and Social Implications

The ethical challenges and social implications of this line of research are of great importance as they lead to the essence of human life and how to incorporate principles that have accompanied institutions for years. At an initial level, it is necessary to question the fairness of the algorithms implemented based on AI. The evaluation of students generally determines their future paths through tests, such as the National College Entrance Examination, the Scholastic Assessment Test, the American College Testing Assessment, and the Law School Admission Test, among others. This trend may be maintained in tests given in colleges and universities. Thus, an algorithm that is not accurate and has bias, discrimination, and errors, as well as inconsistency between test-retest for English exams for college admissions, may result in potential major educational and psychological concerns that outnumber the possible benefits (Shafik, 2024e). The use of AI in education will also be associated with concerns about data privacy. The collection of students' educational data cannot be allowed in an unethical way, which raises ethical issues about students' identities. In addition, AI should consider respect for copyright. There are methods for generating content based on AI, also known as generative AI. Projects show how the computer algorithm can create fake text with human-like language that may create different ethical challenges regarding copyright. Another primary concern is the risk of AI continuing an adverse facet of education, perpetuating social inequalities (Liljaniemi & Paavilainen, 2020).

Inequalities exist, as the marginal groups that need the best education are the most excluded. AI could do the same when automating tutoring. AI could either perpetuate such a pattern or be used to actively redress such imbalance. There is also an expression that unfairly distributes the opportunities to access education available to students. Marginalized communities, including those with disabilities, poverty, and social conditions, are generally disproportionately affected by the digital divide. Accordingly, AI systems applied in educational contexts must avoid reinforcing biases and stereotyping. Thus, an interdisciplinary discussion is needed on the ethical standards and guidelines for the technological developments of AI in education. We want developers, in collaboration with educators and scholars, to guarantee that they will not develop systems that jeopardize the principles that guide the different areas they are collaborating with (Osei Kwadwo & Konadu, 2020). Consequently, our research aims to alert teachers, educators, and scholars about the necessity of having a narrative versus amorphous digitization and AI in educational settings.

For schools and their leaders, a massive volume of AI products and services is coming from a burgeoning edtech industry rapidly moving towards an AI future. Ethical and fair AI must be introduced in schools by responsible general and special education teachers who should be content as teachers and advocates for their students. They should engage in teacher preparation programs to ensure the potential and the limitations along with the pitfalls of AI, making sure they are used as a means and not an end. AI is often guided by algorithmic functions that may inadvertently amplify human prejudice and stereotypes. For educators, AI decision-making in content delivery, grading, learning experiences, and many more should have the ability to be transparent, explainable, and trustworthy (Lieberman, 2023; Shivley et al., 2016). A black-box mentality of AI application and implementation should be a non-starter in education.

Integration of AI in Social Science Research

Progress in computing and data science opened a new chapter in social science research. The integration of AI tools in data collection and analysis has already ushered in historical changes, thus signaling a significant paradigm shift. In the future, we may witness a rupture generated by predictive modeling and machine learning methods that may inject an axiomatically new world of modern social sciences. The gap between the present and the past is dramatic. Traditional data collection and analysis in social sciences are very accurate, while predictive modeling and machine learning methods allow for more accurate estimates and predictions (Boeren, 2019). The novelty of measuring social reality is seen as involving the accuracy of measurements and the identification of new social patterns based on big data formalism. Ethical and privacy issues related to data availability are increasingly present in academic discussions and are related to the increasing importance of digital data for government and business practices. Integrating AI in social science research enables scientists to simplify the conventional tools and techniques involved in data collection and analysis. Since AI is primarily concerned with patterns and correlations within the data, methods driven by machine learning algorithms recognize patterns and relationships in large data sets. This leads to two main improvements (Bland Ed., 2016). Firstly, scientific conclusions and findings facilitate more accurate testing of causal mechanisms. Secondly, AI innovations aid in the development of social theory.

Data Collection and Analysis

Research on social topics or surveys often starts with some form of data collection. This phase substantially influences the accuracy and presentation of the results. Not surprisingly, AI drives changes in data collection approaches and outcomes design more efficiently. Therefore, we briefly describe the new possibilities in light of the methodological procedures mentioned in the introduction. Besides acknowledging changes in this fundamental research process at the stages of data collection and processing, recent literature also references changes in the interpretation of results, for example, in terms of new multimedia possibilities that take advantage of computer vision (Diemer et al., 2020). The first step in descriptive statistics is usually related to processing all types of answers to the conducted research. In case the survey had numerous open questions or some interviews implemented, this data selection and transformation was more complex and time-consuming. Nowadays, with the available IT environment, the interpretative encoding for data analysis is no longer a bottleneck for the methodological component of the research. In most cases, unstructured data requires even more methodological steps regarding text cleaning or text enrichment, which has been an obstacle to performing NLP[1] (Karatsiori, 2023).

Predictive Modeling

Predictive modeling is one of the main ways AI is "making" social sciences. While knowing the historical data and the circumstances in which advances have been carried out, the decision-makers can identify some future trends. Predictive analytics is required, particularly in modern, changeable societies, and they need to know what the future will be if they do not act as they did previously; the outcomes may be disadvantageous. Examples comprise some detailed levels of violence in a given area, estimates of the numbers of patients, or investment possibilities in a given stock in a particular area. Those policies must identify 'where' and 'when' something is happening, but they may also need to elucidate 'how' it is going on (Karatsiori, 2023). Different from analyzing predictive analytics in terms of method for generating results, in this respect, the important distinction concerning methodological consideration is between static statistical models represented by simple regressions and structural static and/or dynamic models from macro-econometric type and machine learning. It comes to be that while obviously, these methodological directions are methodologically significantly distinct, they are treated to a certain extent as equals given the general objective of this paper, which is to consider how AI as a whole and predictive modeling, in particular, can generate valuable new knowledge concerning developing the earliest picture of the occurrence of social phenomena (Whitburn & Plows, 2017).

This proves that a machine-learning model could offer new implications, especially in financing and economic planning. They offer a beneficial perception of what machine learning can offer for the present social technologies when there are massive available volumes of knowledge. Predictions of these models are also of interest from the point of view of AI and society as they might also have a causal effect on people. Predictions can bring about actions that might change the future; thus, their ethical aspects must be considered. The first concerns the negative side of the predictions. Predicting that someone has a negative likelihood of getting a loan has discrimination pertinence. Another issue is specifically related to changes in people's behavior. The possibility is that politicians, frightened by such data, will erratically raise interest rates to wean an overdependence between economic growth and inflation (O'Brien & Davenport, 2024).

Impacts of AI on Education

AI impacts the very fiber of organizational ecosystems and has increasingly individual and societal implications. In peer-reviewed journals, international professionals find understanding, planning, debates, and professional development focusing on AI. This group is drawn from economics, business, computer studies, science, politics, management, psychology, and education. Intelligent Systems collaborate with AI across three societal sectors, exploring how AI and humans' potential work. AI is used to improve operations, teaching, and training. It can enhance productivity and the teaching and learning process of the educational industry and improve educators' and learners' abilities. AI in education can facilitate optimal learning and help instructors and administrators (Zakharova et al., 2020). Professionals working and researching in education and other science branches work on CAD daily. In the case of education, young academics and teachers work and research weekly CAD growth, education, and development considering the association of AI and humans to consider activities and professional creation by human educators dealing with AI. These individuals and organizations educating AI teachers facilitate research with AI education. Coaching and training are key methods, and customer transformation is one of the targets of AI. AI is a part of the bigger effort to change education. An augmented intelligence education platform with AI applications has been developed. Education relies heavily on AI, which plays an important role in teachers and educational technology (Mosalagae & Lukusa, 2016). AI has been designed for several teaching tasks and supporting teaching and learning workflows.

Enhancing Teaching and Learning

AI has developed methods for enhancing didactic and methodological aspects of the teaching and learning processes. Often, teachers use machine learning and specific algorithms to develop tools to innovate the way and methodology teachers teach. One of the most important lines of work in AI applied to education is the production of technological tools that, when integrated into the teaching and learning processes interactively, enable personalized education specific to each student by prior knowledge, needs, ambitions, and preferences. A study concluded that artificial and computer intelligence contributes to student engagement by being capable of implementing creative and innovative educational approaches (Bull & Kharrufa, 2024; Shafik, 2024d). Their role is to enhance personalized and adapted learning opportunities, thereby enhancing the possibilities of forming collaborative and community-building environments that reflect the reality of the global labor market. Through the use of algorithms and the information collected by the technological tools used by students, educators have at their disposal significant data to assist them in planning and pedagogical action, as well as in decision-making regarding pedagogical intervention, student orientation, and curricular adaptation, providing various resources to enable those with the most significant difficulties and ensure support for those who are above average (O'Brien & Davenport, 2024).

According to students who participated in the studies, tools created with AI motivated them to undertake the proposed assignments. The educational stories traveled are successful experiences implementing personalized learning environments using technology, particularly AI. Through data, these experiences report significant learning results, overcoming students' performance from other schools in evaluations and learning assessments and meeting the pedagogical pillars of educational equity. As valid and positive as all these investigations may be, we warn about their cautious and reflexive use. It is important not to focus exclusively on the knowledge of such tools, as this may lead to losing the interest of communication between the student and the teacher (Zakharova et al., 2020). The teacher becomes the primary source of knowledge in the classroom, and the students are passive individuals who listen and write down what is being explained. The personalization and diversity of school learning are challenges that educators face, and these new teaching methods facilitate and support the teacher. If knowing is conditioned by effective student profiles regarding knowledge and know-how, developing professional competencies in a social and psychological dimension will have parallels. There is still much to be shared and investigated regarding the effectiveness of this new paradigm in education, as the analysis made by the group verifies that there are still few good educational contexts where AI mediates teaching and learning in higher education (Mosalagae & Lukusa, 2016).

Challenges and Ethical Considerations

The application of AI in education has been addressed enthusiastically in numerous reports, studies, and white papers. Despite their great potential to push the education sector forward, AI, data mining, and learning analytics in education cannot be adopted uncritically, as they could contribute to the dehumanization of education and threaten data privacy and digital security. As in any socio-technical system, deploying AI might result in myriad issues, from concerns about data security—in this case, the management of vast amounts of sensitive data about students among various organizations—to biases that generate or exacerbate educational inequalities (Sharma, 2024). Bias can occur at any point in the lifespan of an AI system and may reflect systemic or representational inequalities. The impact of biased AI algorithms on learners might be considerable, reducing self-confidence and educational self-efficacy. Given that complex socio-cultural factors can influence the educational pathway of learners, how much can AI, equipped with the existing data, really understand and assist learners in making the right educational choices? However, the matter is not a simple case of shifting all AI education or AI technology from one side of the balance to the other. Furthermore, care should be taken to distinguish between overt biases that fall under the purview of national policies and subtler elements of epistemic opacity, technical bias, moral opacity, and technical flaws. Responsibility includes the requirement to develop a solid rationale and best practices for the application of AI in education, including guidance about the kind of data to be collected or not; consent for the deployment of learning analytics; security; and liability for any damage deriving from different levels of AI applications (Mohammed & Hossain, 2024; Gómez Redondo et al., 2024).

Challenges and Limitations of AI in Education and Social Sciences

Even though AI in education and social sciences can bring many advantages, its implementation and use are challenging. First, AI's autonomous decision-making procedures are based on massive data sampling. Some conflicts might occur when the data are collected and processed, but there are important limitations to the AI used to assign dissertations to classmates. Teachers and students might consider that some values, attitudes, or skills cannot be assessed, and therefore, AI cannot impact the supervision of this evaluation. Second, AI algorithms designed from such data often lead to automated tests and surveys with biased and unfairly leading aspects (Halaweh, 2023; Bishop, 2023; Shafik, 2024d; Wulandari et al., 2021).

Bias and Fairness Issues

Human biases have influenced the academic success assessment of individuals: the educational system has always had disparities in access to resources, inherited discrimination, and so forth. AI algorithms have the same limitations. When designing an AI system, we as educators need to consider and account for biases, as we are responsible for equal opportunities, justice, and the rights of the individuals being assessed. Bias is a feature, not a bug, of algorithmic decision-making. It is defined as an unfair deviation in the predicted behavior of an AI system that may be more directly defined as differing people's treatment in a manner that increases the average outcome difference between groups. The AI system will likely affect how students are classified and sent into different educational tracks, which may affect their future career opportunities and social position (Shafik, 2024c; Stigall & Choo, 2022). These occurrences highlight the need for fair AI to serve everyone, similar to the fairness we expect from the educational exams used in higher education admissions. The best practices for discovering and mitigating bias in AI systems involve utilizing multiple evaluation methods, diverse data representation, and directly including affected individuals in the design process (Shafik et al., 2024). Researchers in the social sciences play an important role in further enhancing our understanding of bias in predictive models.

Privacy and Security Concerns

Adopting AI improves collecting and processing large amounts of data, which confronts educational institutions with increasing privacy concerns. The e-education industry needs robust protection mechanisms to protect the personal information of students and staff thoroughly. The use of personal data in educational AI applications is imbued with several privacy issues, such as the data being highly sensitive because it concerns minors, is permanent, and is an entropy-rich and complex composite of revealed data. Security measures are therefore critical to guard against potential privacy risks, including identification deemed abusive, fidelity, and defacement. Institutions that are not sufficiently attentive and reactive to security could face several significant data breach consequences, including financial costs, unlawful access to students' transcripts and information, and misuse and manipulation of results (Liljaniemi & Paavilainen, 2020). Further, educational institutions must inform students about how their data are collected and used and what rights students have to refuse or request that data be erased. This is predicted under data protection law and reinforces the empowerment of students to maintain appropriate control over what insights are acquired about them. A balance should be struck between collecting personal information only for what is strictly necessary and ensuring that safe AI capabilities can be leveraged (Osei Kwadwo & Konadu, 2020; Shivley et al., 2016).

Artificial Intelligence and Social Sciences

Topics in social sciences also represent strong interfaces between AI and social sciences. Topics are crucial to the academy's research community and to the gatekeepers of academic discourse and membership. A topic may carry some implicit theory and promote any disciplinary perspective. Understanding topics can be understood by transferring new scientific knowledge paradigms, theoretical revolutions, or methodological innovations.

Interdisciplinary Perspectives

Interdisciplinary perspectives are inevitable when it comes to AI and the social sciences. The study on the knowledge industry makes a strong case for interdisciplinary meetings and presentations and meaningful social links with other disciplines as an outlet to communicate and disseminate knowledge and learning. It brings thoughts of social anthropology into the economics dialogue to show the complexity of the production of socio-economic life. Similar to this is the exchange between technology and history scholars. A recent case study of the period of the 1760s and after in England gains a vast critical potential by using a wealth of data through collaboration with a social physics department (Karatsiori, 2023). The study is an example of excellence of socio-economic history, looking only from above, situating the actors within the lifespan of a cross-sectional study and thereby going beyond a simple quantitative course of events history.

Research Methodologies

Methodologies of research are changing with the help of AI. Social scientists harness big qualitative and quantitative data, and processing it demands speed and, most of all, novelty in research methods, which enable the interpretation of vast amounts of data. The presently firm reliance on algorithms in social research lies in the availability of AI-generated tools. They substitute or extend traditional methods and are more precise, allowing researchers to engage in new types of analysis (Mosalagae & Lukusa, 2016; Sykes, 2023; Zakharova et al., 2020). AI technologies impact research in social sciences in three main dimensions. First, it alters the processes and methods of data collection. Second, it influences tools and approaches to data analysis and interpretation. Third, it changes the very object of research by providing avenues to ask new research questions and integrating new explanations and interpretations. Machine learning is a part of AI that teaches algorithms to find hidden information in the data. The most popular methodologies involve association, estimation, classification, and prediction (Stigall & Choo, 2022; Shafik, 2024c).

Summary of Key Findings

AI tools are a new trend in developing modern platforms and applications dedicated to a personalized learning process. AI applications can support improvements in teachers' work methodologies and offer better teaching and learning experiences.

(i) Some educational scholars are optimistic about the opportunities created by integrating AI tools; they are critical of AI-based personalized learning. As AI focuses on the psychological dimensions of the learner's profile, it may narrow the learner's cognitive development.
(ii) The most serious problem or obstacle is ethical, as it underpins other issues of privacy, intellectual and cognitive autonomy, and the principle of equal opportunities in access to learning.

(iii) The contemporary world is variously referred to as a knowledge society, a learning society, or an information society. The deployment of AI in the field of social sciences results in new methods and innovative contexts. AI can raise research methodologies in human social and political sciences to an unprecedented level, offering the most detailed approaches, showing new connections, identifying interdependencies among a whole range of variables, entering new dimensions of exploration, and establishing new models and interconnections.
(iv) A high level of necessary interconnectedness among disciplines and experts exploring knowledge is referred to. Concerned foresight contributions dealing with the possible interrelationship between the development of AI and the directions of reconceptualization, substantiation, and ecological evolution of education systems at their most basic levels are needed.

As we draw to the end, scholarly explorations in education, chiefly regarding the utilization of AI in today's and future educational platforms and, more generally, the ways of constructing the knowledge needed for further application of AI in academia and beyond, were brought together and synthesized. The standpoint adopted was initially modern, critically developed, interdisciplinary, and encompassing theory and practice (Mohammed & Hossain, 2024; Saadé et al., 2023). More specifically, seven question fields were explored:

(i) ways of understanding the role of AI in education,
(ii) problematic and/or beneficial effects,
(iii) the planned and/or envisioned systems,
(iv) planned and/or envisioned interaction,
(v) ethical considerations,
(vi) aligning AI in education with vision and/or policies for future content and technical knowledge development, and,
(vii) future AI trends in academia.

CONCLUSION

To conclude, AI can be transformative as an educator's assistant in generating customized educational materials or as an enabler of data-driven research in the social sciences. Thus far, the use of AI for either purpose appears successful. Despite optimism about using AI at the intersection of education and the social sciences, concerns are also warranted. A failure to explicitly address these issues could result in various detrimental outcomes for both fields. Indeed, any frontline application of AI in education raises ethical concerns around equity, privacy, and consent, which must be addressed first. Academic and policy stakeholders from either field have a role to play in properly integrating AI. Values should be embedded into AI infrastructure, and funding priority should be given to research and development initiatives untainted by conflicts of interest or commercial pressure. AI is in its infancy, and stakeholders in the social sciences should be forward-looking and prepared to adapt to new tools for research as they emerge. In sum, new actors are emerging at the dual crossroads of AI and education and of AI and research into social reality.

REFERENCES

Abubakari, M. S., Shafik, W., & Hidayatullah, A. F. (2024). Evaluating the Potential of Artificial Intelligence in Islamic Religious Education. In *AI-Enhanced Teaching Methods* (pp. 216–239). IGI Global., DOI: 10.4018/979-8-3693-2728-9.ch010

Adeleye, O. O., Eden, C. A., & Adeniyi, I. S. (2024). Innovative teaching methodologies in the era of artificial intelligence: A review of inclusive educational practices. *World Journal of Advanced Engineering Technology and Sciences*, *11*(2), 069–079. Advance online publication. DOI: 10.30574/wjaets.2024.11.2.0091

Ahmad, I., Sharma, S., Singh, R., Gehlot, A., Gupta, L. R., Thakur, A. K., Priyadarshi, N., & Twala, B. (2024). Inclusive learning using industry 4.0 technologies: addressing student diversity in modern education. In *Cogent Education* (Vol. 11, Issue 1). DOI: 10.1080/2331186X.2024.2330235

Bakkum, M. J., Hartjes, M. G., Piët, J. D., Donker, E. M., Likic, R., Sanz, E., de Ponti, F., Verdonk, P., Richir, M. C., van Agtmael, M. A., & Tichelaar, J. (2024). Using artificial intelligence to create diverse and inclusive medical case vignettes for education. *British Journal of Clinical Pharmacology*, *90*(3), 640–648. Advance online publication. DOI: 10.1111/bcp.15977 PMID: 38016816

Bland, Ed. D. (2016). Imagination for Inclusion: Diverse Contexts of Educational Practice. Routledge Research in Education. In *Routledge Research in Education*.

Boeren, E. (2019). Understanding Sustainable Development Goal (SDG) 4 on "quality education" from micro, meso, and macro perspectives. *International Review of Education*, *65*(2), 277–294. Advance online publication. DOI: 10.1007/s11159-019-09772-7

Bressane, A., Zwirn, D., Essiptchouk, A., Saraiva, A. C. V., Carvalho, F. L. de C., Formiga, J. K. S., Medeiros, L. C. de C., & Negri, R. G. (2024). Understanding the role of study strategies and learning disabilities on student academic performance to enhance educational approaches: A proposal using artificial intelligence. *Computers and Education: Artificial Intelligence*, *6*, 100196. Advance online publication. DOI: 10.1016/j.caeai.2023.100196

Bull, C., & Kharrufa, A. (2024). Generative Artificial Intelligence Assistants in Software Development Education: A Vision for Integrating Generative Artificial Intelligence into Educational Practice, Not Instinctively Defending Against It. *IEEE Software*, *41*(2), 52–59. Advance online publication. DOI: 10.1109/MS.2023.3300574

Diemer, A., Khushik, F., & Ndiaye, A. (2020). SDG 4 "Quality Education," the Cornerstone of the SDGs: Case Studies of Pakistan and Senegal. *JOURNAL OF ECONOMICS AND DEVELOPMENT STUDIES*, *8*(1). Advance online publication. DOI: 10.15640/jeds.v8n1a2

Edeni, C. A., Adeleye, O. O., & Adeniyi, I. S. (2024). The role of AI-enhanced tools in overcoming educational socio-economic barriers: A conceptual analysis. *World Journal of Advanced Research and Reviews*, *21*(3). Advance online publication. DOI: 10.30574/wjarr.2024.21.3.0780

Fan, B. E., Chow, M., & Winkler, S. (2024). Artificial Intelligence-Generated Facial Images for Medical Education. *Medical Science Educator*, *34*(1), 5–7. Advance online publication. DOI: 10.1007/s40670-023-01942-5 PMID: 38510393

Gondwe, G. (2024). Artificial Intelligence, Journalism, and the Ubuntu Robot in Sub-Saharan Africa: Towards a Normative Framework. *Digital Journalism (Abingdon, England)*. Advance online publication. DOI: 10.1080/21670811.2024.2311258

Habibipour, A. (2024). Responsible living labs: What can go wrong? *Journal of Information, Communication, and Ethics in Society*, *22*(2), 205–218. Advance online publication. DOI: 10.1108/JICES-11-2023-0137

Halaweh, M. (2023). ChatGPT in education: Strategies for responsible implementation. *Contemporary Educational Technology*, *15*(2), ep421. Advance online publication. DOI: 10.30935/cedtech/13036

Hidayatullah, A. F., Kalinaki, K., Aslam, M. M., Zakari, R. Y., & Shafik, W. (2023). Fine-Tuning BERT-Based Models for Negative Content Identification on Indonesian Tweets. *ICITDA 2023 - Proceedings of the 2023 8th International Conference on Information Technology and Digital Applications*. DOI: 10.1109/ICITDA60835.2023.10427046

Karatsiori, M. (2023). In the pursuit of "Quality Education": From ancient times to the digital era, can there be a consensus? In *Cogent Education* (Vol. 10, Issue 2). DOI: 10.1080/2331186X.2023.2286817

Kaur, T. (2024). AI Architectures and Technologies for Raising Society 5.0. In *Artificial Intelligence and Society 5.0: Issues, Opportunities, and Challenges*. DOI: 10.1201/9781003397052-2

Lieberman, M. (2023). What Is ChatGPT and How Is It Used in Education? *Education Week*, *42*(18).

Liew, J. (2024). Translating Vision into Reality for Early Education & Development. *Early Education and Development*, *35*(1), 1–2. Advance online publication. DOI: 10.1080/10409289.2024.2287684

Liljaniemi, A., & Paavilainen, H. (2020). Using Digital Twin Technology in Engineering Education-Course Concept to Explore Benefits and Barriers. *Open Engineering*, *10*(1), 377–385. Advance online publication. DOI: 10.1515/eng-2020-0040

Mohammed, S. P., & Hossain, G. (2024). ChatGPT in Education, Healthcare, and Cybersecurity: Opportunities and Challenges. *2024 IEEE 14th Annual Computing and Communication Workshop and Conference, CCWC 2024*. DOI: 10.1109/CCWC60891.2024.10427923

Mosalagae, M. K., & Lukusa, J.-P. K. (2016). Contextualized Inclusive Education: A Retrospective Look at Technical and Vocational Education and Training (TVET) in Botswana. *Journal of Education and Practice*, *7*(14).

O'Brien, S., & Davenport, C. (2024). Embedding the service user voice to co-produce UK mental health nurse education—A lived experience narrative. *Journal of Psychiatric and Mental Health Nursing*, *31*(5), 769–775. Advance online publication. DOI: 10.1111/jpm.13031 PMID: 38334192

Osei Kwadwo, V., & Konadu, O. A. (2020). Can Ghana Afford the Sustainable Development Goal on Education? *Africa Education Review*, *17*(2), 177–197. Advance online publication. DOI: 10.1080/18146627.2018.1557532

Patel, P., Moz-Ruiz, D., Garcia, R., Chatterjee, A., Morreale, P., & Burnett, M. (2024). From Workshops to Classrooms: Faculty Experiences with Implementing Inclusive Design Principles. *SIGCSE 2024 - Proceedings of the 55th ACM Technical Symposium on Computer Science Education, 1*. DOI: 10.1145/3626252.3630861

Rane, N., & Choudhary, S. (2024). Role and challenges of ChatGPT and similar generative artificial intelligence in arts and humanities. *Studies in Humanities and Education*, *5*(1), 1–11. Advance online publication. DOI: 10.48185/she.v5i1.999

Saadé, R. G., Zhang, J., Wang, X., Liu, H., & Guan, H. (2023). Challenges and Opportunities in the Internet of Intelligence of Things in Higher Education—Towards Bridging Theory and Practice. *IoT*, *4*(3), 430–465. Advance online publication. DOI: 10.3390/iot4030019

Salajan, F. D., Barnes, T. L., & Becker, A. (2024). Comparative regionalism cases of artificial intelligence governance in education: The Caribbean Community and the European Union. *The Round Table*, *113*(1), 71–85. Advance online publication. DOI: 10.1080/00358533.2024.2307793

Shafik, W. (2023). *A Comprehensive Cybersecurity Framework for Present and Future Global Information Technology Organizations*. DOI: 10.4018/978-1-6684-9018-1.ch002

Shafik, W. (2024a). An Overview of Artificial Intelligence-Enhanced Teaching Methods. *AI-Enhanced Teaching Methods*, 132–159.

Shafik, W. (2024b). Artificial Intelligence-Enabled Internet of Medical Things for Enhanced Healthcare Systems. In *Smart Healthcare Systems* (pp. 119–134). CRC Press., DOI: 10.1201/9781032698519-9

Shafik, W. (2024c). Deep Learning Impacts in the Field of Artificial Intelligence. In *Deep Learning Concepts in Operations Research* (pp. 9–26). Auerbach Publications., DOI: 10.1201/9781003433309-2

Shafik, W. (2024d). Enhancing AI-Enabled Education Through Mobile Learning and Bring Your Own Device (BYOD) Integration. In *Exploring Youth Studies in the Age of AI* (pp. 140–173). IGI Global.

Shafik, W. (2024e). Generative AI for Social Good and Sustainable Development. In *Generative AI: Current Trends and Applications* (pp. 185–217). Springer. DOI: 10.1007/978-981-97-8460-8_10

Shafik, W. (2024f). Mobile Learning and Bring Your Own Device (BYOD): Enhancing Education in the Digital Age. In *Integrating Cutting-Edge Technology Into the Classroom* (pp. 240–267). IGI Global.

Shafik, W. (2024g). The Role of Generative Artificial Intelligence in E-Commerce Fraud Detection and Prevention. In *Strategies for E-Commerce Data Security: Cloud, Blockchain, AI, and Machine Learning* (pp. 430–469). IGI Global. DOI: 10.4018/979-8-3693-6557-1.ch018

Shafik, W. (2024h). *Towards Trustworthy and Explainable AI Educational Systems*., DOI: 10.1007/978-3-031-72410-7_2

Shafik, W. (2024i). Towards Trustworthy and Explainable AI Educational Systems. In *Explainable AI for Education: Recent Trends and Challenges* (pp. 17–41). Springer. DOI: 10.1007/978-3-031-72410-7_2

Shafik, W., Kalinaki, K., Fahim, K. E., & Adam, M. (2024). Safeguarding Data Privacy and Security in Federated Learning Systems. In *Federated Deep Learning for Healthcare* (pp. 170–190). CRC Press., DOI: 10.1201/9781032694870-13

Sharma, P. (2024). Faculty competencies development components: An integrated model for the development of educational leaders in technical education institutes. *International Journal of Educational Management*, *38*(2), 447–468. Advance online publication. DOI: 10.1108/IJEM-07-2023-0363

Shivley, C. B., Garry, F. B., Kogan, L. R., & Grandin, T. (2016). Survey of animal welfare, animal behavior, and animal ethics courses in the curricula of AVMA Council on Education-accredited veterinary colleges and schools. *Journal of the American Veterinary Medical Association*, *248*(10), 1165–1170. Advance online publication. DOI: 10.2460/javma.248.10.1165 PMID: 27135673

Stigall, M., & Choo, K. K. R. (2022). Digital Forensics Education: Challenges and Future Opportunities. *Lecture Notes in Networks and Systems*, *310*, 28–46. Advance online publication. DOI: 10.1007/978-3-030-84614-5_4

Wang'ang'a, A. W. (2024). Consequences of Artificial Intelligence on Teaching and Learning in Higher Education in Kenya: Literature Review. *East African Journal of Education Studies*, *7*(1), 202–215. Advance online publication. DOI: 10.37284/eajes.7.1.1718

Whitburn, B., & Plows, V. (2017). Inclusive Education Making Sense Of Everyday Practice Innovations And Controversies: Interrogating Educational Change. *Sense Publishers, 6.*

Zakharova, G. B., Krivonogov, A. I., Kruglikov, S. V., & Petunin, A. A. (2020). Energy-efficient technologies in the educational programs of the architectural higher education schools. *Acta Polytechnica Hungarica*, *17*(8), 121–136. Advance online publication. DOI: 10.12700/APH.17.8.2020.8.9

KEY TERMS AND DEFINITIONS

Artificial Intelligence (AI): The simulation of human intelligence in machines, enabling them to perform tasks such as problem-solving, decision-making, learning, and language understanding. AI systems rely on techniques like machine learning, neural networks, and natural language processing to improve their performance over time.

New Paradigm: A fundamental shift in thinking, methodology, or approach within a particular field. Coined from Thomas Kuhn's "The Structure of Scientific Revolutions," the term describes transformative changes that replace established models or theories with innovative frameworks.

Social Sciences: Academic disciplines that study human behavior, societies, and social relationships using systematic research methods. Key fields include sociology, psychology, anthropology, political science, and economics. These disciplines analyze cultural, economic, and political structures, often integrating qualitative and quantitative methods to understand human interactions and social dynamics.

Digital Revolution: The shift from analog to digital technology significantly transformed industries, communication, and daily life. Beginning in the mid-20th century with the advent of computers, the internet, and digital media, this revolution has led to advancements such as artificial intelligence, blockchain, cloud computing, and automation, shaping modern economies and societies.

Education: The structured process through which individuals acquire knowledge, skills, values, and competencies. It can occur in formal institutions like schools and universities or through informal and lifelong learning experiences.

Machine Learning: A branch of artificial intelligence that focuses on building algorithms that allow computers to learn from and make predictions or decisions based on data. These systems improve over time with more exposure to data, reducing the need for explicit programming.

ENDNOTES

1 https://doi.org/10.4018/979-8-3693-0502-7.ch001

Chapter 4
Using Artificial Intelligence in Philosophy Teaching and Ethical Problems

Nebile Eroğul
https://orcid.org/0000-0002-8099-5559
Ministry of National Education, Turkey

ABSTRACT

This chapter discusses how to effectively integrate the use of artificial intelligence into the critical, questioning and reflective thinking skills that are inherent in philosophy. In this context, the role of the teacher in the process of teaching philosophy is discussed. The role of the philosophy teacher in teaching with artificial intelligence is discussed under the headings of being a philosophical guide, a developer of wisdom and morality, a facilitator in discussions, and a developer of critical thinking. In the section of AI-supported philosophy course activities, simulations dealing with philosophical problems, conversation with philosophers in the history of philosophy, ethical dilemma and decision-making game, creative argument development and analysis, philosophical perspective mapping, and current argument conflict are exemplified, and it is evaluated how these activities can be put into practice by supporting students' in-depth, critical and questioning thinking skills.

DOI: 10.4018/979-8-3373-2612-2.ch004

INTRODUCTION

The use of AI in teaching philosophy represents a paradigm shift, with the introduction of AI as a third component of the traditional teaching processes between student and teacher. This new component's effective and ethical integration poses practical and ethical challenges. The role of AI in the learning process should support students to develop deep understanding and critical thinking skills rather than being a tool for students to get a high score to succeed in a course or to do their homework easily. Similarly, teachers who use AI in processes such as lesson planning or content development require this technology to enrich the teaching process rather than a hidden tool from students.

AI can be configured to deepen students' understanding of philosophical concepts and enhance teachers' pedagogical approaches. However, in this process, developing critical and inquisitive thinking skills by the nature of philosophy should be a priority. The ethical use of artificial intelligence in teaching and learning processes is possible by including technology to support human thinking. In this context, both the student and the teacher can see AI as a source of knowledge and a tool that supports thinking processes, and this new component can be considered an opportunity to create a practical learning experience.

In the first quarter of the 21st century, artificial intelligence is now a reality that has entered the learning and teaching processes. While this is a kind of encounter, this encounter must evolve into a practical and ethical structuring. In addition, in social sciences education, the in-depth questioning and critical thinking experience, which is prioritized to be developed in students due to the nature of these fields, should be included in learning processes as an effective tool despite artificial intelligence.

In education, there is a concern that artificial intelligence will "replace the student and the teacher ."In this context, AI is a support element that increases the potential of both parties. Students should be taught to see AI as a tool that provides easy solutions, a resource that supports critical thinking, and a technology that can be used for this purpose. Likewise, teachers should consider this technology as a support mechanism to enrich their pedagogical methods within ethical boundaries. Thus, the possibilities offered by artificial intelligence can be integrated into learning processes in a balanced way with human creativity and critical thinking. From pedagogical and ethical perspectives, the potential of artificial intelligence in teaching philosophy is both a great opportunity and an important responsibility. The effective use of this technology can support teachers' pedagogical skills while improving students' critical thinking and questioning skills. However, ethical principles and balanced approaches should be prioritized in this process. The transformation of artificial intelligence into an effective learning tool in philosophy teaching will be possible through this new technology's conscious and critical use. In this way, the risks of neglecting the ontological and moral structure of human beings, which are among the risks arising from the rapid progress of technology, will be evaluated from a philosophical perspective.

This chapter discusses how the ethical use of artificial intelligence in teaching philosophy can be effectively integrated into the critical, questioning, and in-depth thinking skills inherent in philosophy for students and teachers with practical examples. In addition, after discussing philosophy and teaching philosophy courses, artificial intelligence's ethical and social impact in education is evaluated with pragmatism, deontology, and virtue ethics approaches. In this context, the ethical challenges that may be encountered in using artificial intelligence in teaching philosophy from a philosophical perspective and how to ensure that this use is compatible with human values are evaluated. In addition, this chapter discusses the advantages and disadvantages of utilizing artificial intelligence in education in general. Afterward, within the nature of philosophy as a discipline oriented towards in-depth, critical, and questioning thinking skills, how artificial intelligence can be used in teaching processes without neglecting this nature of philosophy, what the role of the teacher will be, and examples of artificial intelligence-supported applications in philosophy course teaching are given. The role of the philosophy teacher in teaching artificial intelligence is discussed under the headings of being a philosophical guide, a developer of wisdom and morality, a facilitator in discussions, and a developer of critical thinking. In the chapter on AI-supported philosophy course activities, simulations dealing with philosophical problems, conversations with philosophers in the history of philosophy, ethical dilemmas, and decision-making games, creative argument development and analysis, philosophical perspective mapping, and current argument conflict are exemplified, and it is evaluated how these activities can be put into practice by supporting students' in-depth, critical and questioning thinking skills.

Philosophy and the Teaching of Philosophy

Philosophy is a discipline that enables people to think systematically and critically about being, knowledge, and values. It is recognized by many that it is not easy to make a definition of philosophy that will be understood and accepted by almost everyone and to reveal what philosophy is. However, when we look at the history of philosophy, it can be said that philosophy is a knowledge that deeply concerns human beings, human life, and the world in which they live. The whole world of existence and human actions are the objects of study and research in philosophy (Çotuksöken, 1998, p. 11). However, even without knowing what philosophy is, many people are involved in philosophy while thinking about the meaning of life, good, evil, God, death, and the universe's beginning (Koç, p. 3). In this context, it can be said that people who are not trained in philosophy as a discipline also philosophize in one way or another.

Philosophical thinking involves reasoning, concept analysis, and questioning skills and does not claim to reach absolute truths. In this context, philosophical thinking seeks to evaluate alternative points of view and to form rational arguments. Another fundamental characteristic of philosophical thinking is that it rejects dogmatic assumptions and critically filters all kinds of knowledge. Individuals who gain a philosophical perspective make critical thinking active and adopt a more conscious attitude about their society and nature (Günay, 2004).

Philosophy teaching aims to transform an individual's way of thinking and to provide a critical perspective. In this process, the individual not only acquires knowledge but also learns how to evaluate and interpret that knowledge. Today, the acceleration in the process of change in knowledge has resulted in the consumption of knowledge, and knowledge has begun to be seen as a 'thing' to be consumed (Kızıltan, 2012). This situation reveals the importance of critical thinking. Critical thinking is at the center of philosophical education and contributes to the individual questioning his/her presuppositions and developing rationally based thoughts. Philosophy helps individuals develop the skills to solve complex problems, form logical arguments, and develop coherent thinking skills. Among philosophy's main aims, teaching enables individuals to reach informed and grounded judgments in epistemology, ontology, ethics, politics, and aesthetics. Accordingly, philosophy encourages the individual to become a conscious citizen by increasing his/her sensitivity to ethical and social issues. Individuals who acquire the habit of philosophical thinking gain intellectual flexibility by evaluating different systems of thought from a critical perspective. At the same time, teaching philosophy strengthens communication skills in academic and daily life by allowing individuals to express their thoughts systematically.

Philosophical knowledge is a theoretical endeavor and a way of thinking that transforming the individual's life practice. In this context, philosophy is a discipline that intellectually liberates individuals and increases their intellectual competence. Philosophy teaching contributes to developing innovative and original perspectives by improving students' creative thinking skills. At the same time, philosophy helps raise individuals' sensitivity to social problems by strengthening their awareness of ethical responsibility while developing their cognitive processes. Philosophy education, which encourages reflection on the nature of knowledge, reality, and human existential questions, enables individuals to evaluate the world from a broader perspective. In this framework, philosophy stands out as one of the basic disciplines that guide the individual in making sense of life. In today's rapidly changing world of information, the ability to analyze complex problems faced by individuals and to produce solutions is directly related to their ability to think philosophically. Philosophy education contributes to scientific and intellectual development by enabling individuals to acquire the habit of rational thinking. In this context, philosophy is an academic endeavor and a fundamental discipline that guides the individual's and society's intellectual development.

Artificial Intelligence and its Use in Education

This title discusses the ethical use of artificial intelligence in teaching from a philosophical perspective. Artificial intelligence has revolutionized education by supporting personalization processes in learning, administrative efficiency, and developing 21st-century skills. However, AI application poses ethical challenges regarding inequality of access, data privacy, algorithm bias, and technology dependency. In this context, AI's moral and social impact in education is evaluated using ethical theory approaches such as pragmatism, deontology, and virtue ethics. Also, an ethical framework based on justice, transparency, privacy, accountability, and utility is considered important. It seems important for countries' futures that artificial intelligence undergoes continuous ethical oversight to protect human values and ensure its positive holistic impact on education.

In recent years, artificial intelligence technology has made significant progress in education (Kavitha et al., 2023). Artificial intelligence has been used in many areas, from personalized learning experiences (Kaur et al., 2024) to administrative functions (Turdubaeva & Arykbaev, 2024). In the learning paradigm, AI helps educators strengthen course content while simultaneously enabling them to align learning experiences in line with students' individual needs and abilities. For example, AI-powered education platforms provide immediate feedback to students, allowing them to predict learning outcomes and suggest additional resources. AI also enables the development of tools for teachers to organize and manage the educational process and offers automated grading applications that assess and analyze student performance. However, there are some challenges related to the role of AI in education. These include debates about improving the quality of education, equity, and data privacy issues (Yadav, 2024) and the role of teachers and students in teaching and learning (Zawacki-Richter et al., 2019).

The impact of AI in education is growing rapidly, and more research is needed on the ethical dimension of these developments (Ramya et al., 2024). It is emphasized that AI should provide efficiency and effectiveness and support the principles of ethics and equity (Xu, 2024). AI in education can deepen existing gaps, reinforce biases in datasets, and jeopardize the privacy of students' data if it lacks ethical oversight and does not operate efficiently. It is also argued that AI should be in harmony with human engagement and character development, considering teacher and student interactions rather than being limited to automated outputs based solely on algorithms (Ainia, 2024).

The philosophical perspective provides a deep framework of thought for examining the ethics of using AI, especially in the context of education. Philosophy offers different ideas about how these technologies should be applied based on views such as utilitarianism, deontology, and virtue ethics (Uzun, 2023).

1. Pragmatism (Utilitarianism)

Pragmatism judges whether an action is morally right or not by the benefits or consequences it brings. From a utilitarian perspective, AI can be justified by providing more benefits to a more significant number of students through increased educational accessibility or more efficient learning (Tait, 2024). A pragmatist view of using AI in education is that technology can facilitate accessibility to the masses and make learning processes more efficient. For example, advantages such as personalized learning experiences, contributing to discussions with AI-supported analysis, and faster delivery of learning materials can be seen as positive aspects of this theory. However, pragmatism also risks ignoring individual rights or ethical issues by focusing only on results. In addition, only practical utility may be insufficient regarding the depth of philosophical thought.

2. Deontology (Ethics of Duty)

Deontological ethics evaluates the rightness of an action by looking at whether it respects specific moral rules or the rights of individuals rather than the consequences. However, the deontological view emphasizes the importance of individual rights, such as students' privacy and autonomy, and the moral obligation not to use AI in ways that harm or exploit them (Uzun, 2023). A deontological perspective on the application of AI in education focuses on elements such as student privacy, data security, and individual autonomy. In this context, even if an artificial intelligence system provides benefits, the deontological perspective requires considering these risks in case of unauthorized use of students' data or adopting an ethically questionable algorithm. In this approach, the intervention of AI in the discussion of philosophical content can be limited; it is encouraged to use AI only as a tool and to prioritize students' ability to think independently.

3. Virtue Ethics

Virtue ethics evaluates the rightness of action based on an individual's character and virtues. In this context, virtue ethics looks at education through the lens of character development and wisdom by evaluating the extent to which AI technologies support holistic human growth (Hayes et al., 2024). From an Aristotelian perspective, it can be questioned whether AI in education supports the character development and wisdom of the individual. In this context, whether artificial intelligence eliminates the human element in the learning process or helps students develop critical thinking and problem-solving skills should be evaluated. Virtue ethics can play a central role here, as the philosophy course provides a space for character development and moral virtues. Artificial intelligence can be structured to help students develop virtues such as wisdom, patience, tolerance, and empathy. Teacher guidance and a human touch should always be prioritized in these processes.

Artificial intelligence can enrich philosophy teaching when used correctly on a philosophical basis with pragmatism, deontology, and virtue ethics. For this process to work effectively, teachers' guidance and human interaction are of fundamental importance in prioritizing students' critical, questioning, and creative thinking skills. In using artificial intelligence in teaching philosophy, the balance between being a tool that facilitates learning and supporting students' active thinking process should be considered. Establishing this balance can protect the human values of philosophy and take advantage of the advantages of technology.

ChatGPT and Its Use in Education

Artificial intelligence (AI) chatbots such as ChatGPT and GPT-4, which have the potential to revolutionize education, have been developed by Openai. In 2019, ChatGPT has a state-of-the-art natural language processing (NLP) model (LeBrenz et al., 2023; Lund & Wang, 2023) that can generate texts that are very similar to human-generated texts, and does so through algorithms. ChatGPT is designed in a conversational environment that allows users to interact with the model naturally and intuitively (Su & Yang, 2023).

When asked what ChatGPT is, the following answer was received:

"ChatGPT is an artificial intelligence chatbot developed by OpenAI. It can communicate with people in writing or voice using natural language processing (NLP) technology. It can answer questions, generate texts, offer suggestions, and provide information on various topics." (By ChatGPT February 1, 2025).

ChatGPT was asked how it works, and the response was as follows:

"ChatGPT works as a large language model using neural networks and deep learning techniques. We can summarize how it works as follows:

Training with Data: Training is done with a large data pool, such as millions of books, articles, and internet texts. However, it does not have direct access to specific or current information; it uses the information it has learned as it was trained.

Natural Language Processing (NLP): Analyzes text from the user. It extracts meaning by evaluating the relationships between words and context.

Probabilistic Prediction: It chooses the most probabilistically appropriate word or phrase when determining its responses. This choice is based on the dataset it is trained on and previous words.
Answer Generation: Generates the most appropriate answer to the user's question. It can improve its answers according to feedback and adapt to directions." (By ChatGPT February 1, 2025).

Generative AI is a form of AI that uses machine learning and deep learning techniques to generate new data. Generative AI can autonomously generate new data, including images, music, and text (Yu & Guo, 2023). Educative AI provides a personalized, interactive, and efficient learning experience for students and helps teachers provide easier and faster feedback to their students. However, the untested impact of this technology, limitations in the quality of data, and challenges related to ethical and security concerns should be considered. In this context, it is necessary to integrate ChatGPT into educational practice with the support of a sound theoretical framework and to approach such issues responsibly and ethically. This will enable education systems to embrace new technological advances and keep pace with the changing educational landscape (Su & Yang, 2023).

In recent years, artificial intelligence (AI) in education has been on the agenda. The potential benefits educational institutions and organizations gain through AI-driven technologies are being explored (Dwivedi et al., 2021; Su & Yang, 2022). In this context, it is necessary to establish policies and standards to improve digital literacy in countries, optimize the curriculum system, and innovate and evaluate teaching methods. To fully realize the potential of generative AI in education, it is necessary to involve educators, students, and other stakeholders in the development and implementation processes within the proposed theoretical framework. This way, the technology will be designed to meet all stakeholders' needs, enabling students to learn effectively and supporting their success (Su & Yang, 2023).

Data privacy and security issues are important when using generative artificial intelligence in education. AI in education provides significant information about students' academic achievement, personal data, and learning preferences. This data should be used ethically and not violate rights (Su & Yang, 2023). While evaluating the ethical implications of generative AI in education, it is also important to evaluate it in terms of fairness, bias, and accountability. When using generative AI in education, care should be taken to ensure that it provides an accessible and fair learning opportunity for all students and does not create bias against students with different sociodemographic characteristics (Su & Yang, 2023).

The use of generative AI in education raises four important issues. These are transparency and inexplicability, data privacy and security, personalization and fairness, effectiveness and reliability. In this context, Yu and Gue (2023) propose solutions to develop explainable and fair algorithms, upgrade encryption technology, formulate relevant laws and regulations to protect data and improve the quality and quantity of datasets.

While the use of generative artificial intelligence in education positively affects student achievement and participation through personalized learning, the fact that this participation issue may increase inequalities constitutes a disadvantage. In this context, it is necessary to ensure that students with different sociodemographic backgrounds have access to this technology and its benefits (Su & Yang, 2023). Students participate in educational environments with different cognitive levels and cultural richness. In the context of equal opportunity in education, the sociocultural level at which each student is included in the education system may be different, as well as their cognitive levels. Therefore, while using generative artificial intelligence in education can solve this problem with the personalized learning experience it offers, it can create significant differences between countries that do not have these technologies and regions within a country. Socioeconomic class differences between individuals may deepen due to significant social inequalities between families.

Integrating generative AI into education affects both the teaching profession and teacher roles. Teachers aim to ensure students receive a good education and have positive learning experiences. Teachers can use Generative AI effectively and responsibly by guiding students and putting their expertise to work. For Generative AI to facilitate and improve teaching and learning, the role of teachers in the learning experience and its impact on learning environments should be considered, and how to develop the skills teachers will need in this process (Su & Yang, 2023).

Generative artificial intelligence (GenAI) has a transformative impact on teachers' roles in education and educational institutions. Teachers' perceptions, knowledge, acceptance, and practices about GenAI must be determined. In order to integrate GenAI technologies such as ChatGPT into educational environments, both in-service training and undergraduate teacher education universities should teach prospective teachers that AI plays an important role in content creation, personalized learning, and student engagement, and teachers and prospective teachers should be given the skills to adapt GenAI to classroom dynamics. In addition, teachers' ability to effectively integrate GenAI into their pedagogical practices should be developed (Zhai, 2024). It is not enough for teachers to accept and understand GenAI and its capabilities; they must integrate it deeply into their teaching processes. Zhai (2024) characterizes teachers' perspectives on SE as observant, adaptive, collaborative, and innovative. In this context, there is a need to provide practical training to support future teachers and current teachers in adopting GenAl and managing its complexities when they encounter it.

Ethical and Safety Issues

The use of ChatGPT in education raises ethical and safety issues. Technology has the potential to manipulate or deceive students. To avoid this manipulation, the model should be monitored appropriately and checked to see if it is used to provide false information or mislead students. However, technology can also be used to invade students' privacy. Therefore, the model should appropriately safeguard privacy and should not be used to collect sensitive information from students without their prior knowledge or consent. In addition, to prevent technology from being used to discriminate against certain students, education should be based on data representing all students, and efforts should be made to prevent inequality of opportunity in education (Su & Yang, 2023). In this context, ChatGPT should be supported by conducting studies on ensuring data privacy (Lin & Zou, 2024).

ChatGPT is still an emerging technology, and its impact has not been thoroughly tested. The controversial aspect of using ChatGPT in educational settings is organizing educational goals, methods, and ethics education (Su & Yang, 2023). This section discusses the roles of philosophy teachers in teaching philosophy courses with ChatGPT, how students and teachers should benefit from this technology, and the nature of philosophy. In this process, while ethical elements are considered, an opinion is presented on how teaching materials can suit the nature of the philosophy course.

Advantages and Disadvantages of Using Artificial Intelligence in Philosophy Teaching

The advantages and disadvantages of using artificial intelligence in teaching philosophy and other courses are similar. Artificial intelligence in education offers content suitable for students' individual learning speeds and levels in philosophy teaching with personalized learning. Thanks to artificial intelligence-supported applications, philosophy course materials are presented to crowded student masses. In contrast, visual and interactive materials of philosophical concepts that are difficult or complex to learn are presented to students, making learning easier. Artificial intelligence can deepen a philosophical question involving a moral dilemma, such as "Your child is sick, and you do not have enough money to buy enough medicine. Would you steal the medicine necessary for your child's recovery from the pharmacy?". As in this example, artificial intelligence can provide real experiences by providing simulations to students on moral dilemmas. In addition, it can present the interpretation of the history of philosophical texts from different perspectives and the structure of arguments in philosophical texts very quickly. In this respect, using artificial intelligence-supported technologies in philosophy teaching enables students to see and think from different perspectives.

The possible disadvantages of using artificial intelligence in philosophy teaching are that it blunts students' ability to think for themselves and develop philosophical arguments. This situation is contrary to the nature of the philosophy course; its aim is not only to provide knowledge but also to make students think about how to question this knowledge. Artificial intelligence in teaching philosophy contradicts the reality that philosophy is done through real human interaction or dialog. Philosophical thinking develops through questioning, critical thinking, and deep thinking. In this process, honest human discussions and dialogues are important. Critical thinking, on the other hand, requires the principles of rationality, and this principle is seen as a fundamental skill that everyone should develop. While defining critical thinking characteristics, Socrates emphasized that no idea can be taught directly. He aimed to help his students reach a deeper level of understanding and thinking by questioning their fundamental beliefs and assumptions. Learning to think, solve problems, and make effective decisions is an important skill that should be learned early (Muhammad & Niazi, 2022). Therefore, in the philosophy course, the teacher should emphasize at every stage of the teaching process that artificial intelligence can be used to prepare the student for discussion or dialogue. However, that philosophy is realized through fundamental human interactions, dialogue, and conversation.

In using artificial intelligence in philosophy teaching, the question "Can artificial intelligence be biased on certain philosophical issues?" is also a problem to be considered. Artificial intelligence uses specific algorithms on particular topics in the history of philosophy, which may cause artificial intelligence to emphasize a particular philosophical view on a specific topic, which contradicts the nature of philosophical thought. In this context, the use of artificial intelligence in teaching philosophy should be adopted as a tool, and it should be taken into consideration that critical, questioning, and in-depth thinking, which is inherent in philosophical thinking, can be realized by realizing the teaching based on fundamental human interactions through human teachers. Artificial intelligence in teaching philosophy contributes to explaining complex concepts and problems addressed in the philosophies of the century and to personalized learning experiences. However, this process requires the guidance and supportive role of the teacher. With the support of human teachers, in-depth learning can take place in the philosophy course. Beyond pragmatism, it is recommended to adopt deontology and virtue ethics in a balanced manner. This ensures that students' data is protected, their thoughts and personal preferences are kept private, and human values are prioritized.

Teachers should teach students how to effectively integrate AI into their learning experiences without compromising the authenticity of their academic progress. Through the comprehensive and systematic integration of AI into the education system, it may be possible to utilize its full potential more effectively and efficiently while providing a better teaching-learning environment (O'Connor & Natividad, 2023). In learning processes based on artificial intelligence, students should gain a perspective towards developing their autonomous learning skills. In this way, students will be supported in developing critical and creative thinking skills. Artificial intelligence may cause students to lose the depth of philosophical theories or philosophers' views in the philosophical views it presents to them.

Redefining the Role of the Teacher

AI provides teachers with a variety of opportunities for enhanced planning (instruction tailored to students' needs), implementation (immediate feedback and teacher intervention), and assessment (automated scoring for assessment and evaluation). The use of AI in education is transforming teacher roles, but it is also important for teachers to improve AI technology by providing feedback to AI. Teachers can contribute to AI development by acting as models for training AI algorithms and checking the accuracy of AI automated assessment systems (Celik, Dindar, Muukkonen & Järvelä, 2022).

What the role of the teacher will be when using artificial intelligence tools in teaching philosophy and how the traditionally defined teacher roles will change is an important topic of discussion. One of the reasons why this is an important issue is thought to stem from the nature of the philosophy course or philosophy. In integrating artificial intelligence tools into philosophy teaching, philosophy's in-depth questioning and critical thinking nature should not be neglected. In this context, the roles of the philosophy teacher as a philosophical guide, developer of wisdom and morality, facilitator of discussions, and developer of critical thinking will be discussed.

1. The Teacher as a Philosophical Guide

In the philosophy course, students can produce a higher level of philosophy in activities where a philosophical discussion is organized with other students in the classroom environment and with the teacher's guidance (Kienstra, Imants, Karskens & van der Heijden, 2015). In this context, the teacher's guidance plays an active role in learning the philosophy course. In terms of integrating artificial intelligence into philosophy course teaching, the philosophy teacher, as a philosophical guide, should make students aware that the information provided by artificial intelligence is not precise and defined knowledge and that this data is a starting point for discussion and questioning. The teacher should teach students to ask the right questions during this process. A teacher who provides philosophical guidance to his/her students may ask his/her students to ask the following questions during the learning process:

1. What assumptions are these arguments based on?
2. What are the counter-arguments?
3. How can this idea be applied in today's world?

While traditional philosophy teaching conveys the knowledge of the philosophical tradition to students, it ignores the reality of where this knowledge leads students. In order to construct philosophical knowledge in such a way that students gain inquiry skills, a balance needs to be struck, and one way to do this is to design the P4C teacher as a philosophical exploration guide (Golding, 2008). Moreover, in this context, the teacher's role as a philosophical guide will be helpful to find this balance in AI-supported philosophy teaching processes. The teacher should direct the teaching processes as a guide who helps students place the information coming from artificial intelligence in a philosophical context. In this context, it can facilitate their understanding of the context by explaining the historical development of a philosophical view presented by artificial intelligence and the critical interpretation of the view. Teacher guidance is essential in the use of artificial intelligence both in other courses and in the teaching of philosophy. If comprehensive teacher guidance is not provided, students will not acquire the capacity for in-depth questioning and critical thinking inherent in the philosophy course. However, they may also become passive acceptors of knowledge and not question the background of knowledge.

2. The Teacher as a Developer of Wisdom and Morality

As one of the roles of the philosophy teacher is to provide a philosophical experience (Gabriel & Pereira, 2023), the teacher needs to support the development of wisdom and morality in students. Artificial intelligence is a very effective tool for providing students with the outline of a philosophical text and the structure of the arguments that philosophers put forward in their philosophical views. Thus, students gain a philosophical experience. However, teacher support is needed to organize this information in a way that supports the development of ethical evaluation and wisdom in students. With teacher support, moral values in a philosophical text should be revealed. For example, while discussing the views of the British philosopher Jeremy Bentham, one of the founders and representatives of utilitarianism, the teacher can open a discussion with students about the meaning, validity, or risks of the question "Is the value of a virtue determined by the benefit it provides?" in today's world.

As a developer of wisdom and morality, the teacher should guide students to realize that artificial intelligence has a mechanical structure but that real people can make moral decisions that are theoretical and applicable in practical life. In this process, the teacher can teach students to gain a skill that can enable them to ask authentic moral questions in their learning process. In this context, for example, for the utilitarian view, the student can develop wisdom and morality in the learning process with questions such as "How much does this ethical approach prioritize human dignity and value?" "Does it protect this value, or can it create problems in some aspects?" "How is this ethical approach perceived in different cultures?".

3. Teacher as Discussion Facilitator

Facilitating discussions is an important role of the philosophy teacher as an artistic act (Jensen, 2023). Collective inquiry and dialogue, which are inherent in philosophy, should be enriched by the active participation of the teacher in the teaching process. While the different perspectives offered by AI-supported applications provide a starting point for classroom discussions, the teacher should enable students to analyze these perspectives. For example, in an activity where the utilitarian approach is discussed, the teacher develops a culture of dialogue with questions such as "How can this situation be evaluated with existentialist ethics?", "How would you criticize the utilitarian approach according to the ethics of homework?" while actively guiding and facilitating the discussions.

The teacher creates an environment of dialog among students and enables them to share ideas. Students are encouraged to discuss the content presented by artificial intelligence and defend their own opinions. In this process, it should be considered a natural situation that the ideas among students may conflict in some cases, and the teacher should manage these conflicts constructively and teach students how to generate ideas in dialogue.

4. Teacher as a Critical Thinking Developer

The philosophy-based approach is key in teaching critical thinking (Paul, 2013). Although artificial intelligence-supported applications have provided important conveniences by providing students with ready-made information, they are not sufficient for the development of critical thinking skills in students. In this context, the role of the teacher is to enable students to question the information provided to them and to deepen their analysis. Encouraging critical thinking is one of the roles of the philosophy teacher (Gabriel & Pereira, 2023). In this context, in teaching philosophy courses with artificial intelligence-supported applications, the teacher can support students in developing critical thinking skills by asking them some questions:

1. What do you think are the assumptions on which this argument is based?
2. Which other perspectives can support and complement this argument?
3. Do you think the AI's answer fits the context? What does not fit the context?

While using these questions to elicit alternative perspectives, the teacher supports students' critical thinking skills. The teacher also provides guidance by adding complementary and opposing perspectives to the ready-made answers provided by the AI. To support problem-solving skills in students, the teacher may ask them to generate original problem-solving solutions based on the information provided by the AI. In order to deepen the answers given by artificial intelligence, the teacher asks questions such as "How should this view be developed by considering its historical and social context?" "Is this view appropriate for today's conditions?" "What disadvantages does this view cause?" "How can the disadvantages of this view be eliminated?".

Including artificial intelligence in educational environments involves adding artificial intelligence as a third field within the duality of teacher and student. Artificial intelligence is neither a complete substitute for the teacher nor an effective learning tool that can answer all students' questions. Artificial intelligence can become an effective tool with the teacher's guidance and gain a feature that helps effective and deep learning in the classroom environment.

Artificial Intelligence Supported Philosophy Course Activity Examples

It is known that robots cannot act on their initiative (Çevik, 2017). For the effective use of artificial intelligence-supported applications in education, the fact that these robots need real human guidance should be considered. In this context, teachers and students must guide the AI-supported application in teaching philosophy courses. The student should be developed to have the ability to direct the AI-supported application, ask the right questions, and look at the answers from a critical perspective. The teacher should make an effort to develop this skill in students.

1. Simulations Addressing Philosophical Problems

In philosophy teaching, artificial intelligence can be applied to dilemmas and shed light on new situations during learning (LaCroix, 2022). In this context, a dilemma can be addressed in philosophy class to analyze the different views of philosophers who lived in different centuries on topics such as the source of knowledge or the relationship between the individual and the state. A dilemma can be addressed for the selected problem, such as "Is the source of knowledge reason or experiment?" or "Do the responsibilities of the individual towards the state or the responsibilities of the state towards the individual take precedence?". This activity aims to develop students' decision-making skills for dilemmas presented about philosophical problems. In this activity, students first participate in an AI-driven discussion simulation in the classroom and evaluate the arguments presented by the AI for the problem at hand. Students list the advantages and disadvantages of the answers given. At the end of this exercise, the teacher asks the students to present their arguments for the dilemma addressed.

This activity enables students to discuss solutions to philosophical problems and understand philosophical theories' background. The teacher manages the teaching process during the activity to support students' preparation for the philosophical problem discussed in class. The teacher supports the students to construct their arguments by using the resources and counter-arguments provided by the AI for the problem. While implementing the AI-supported activity, the teacher guides the discussion, challenges students with counter-arguments, and encourages students to question the accuracy of the information provided by the AI.

The teacher suggests to the students that they should not be satisfied with the answers given by the AI-supported application on the philosophical problem addressed until this stage of the activity. Students are directed to pay attention to which views are missing in the answers given by artificial intelligence to the philosophical problem. In this process, students should ask additional questions to guide artificial intelligence and identify the missing views in the philosophical problem. In the last stage, the practices students can do to manage their learning processes are determined in cooperation with the teacher and students. At the end of this activity, students are asked to write their original philosophical problems based on the answers to the philosophical problem they have learned from the artificial intelligence-supported application to contribute to developing in-depth, critical, and questioning thinking skills about the nature of philosophy.

2. Conversations with Philosophers in the History of Philosophy

Students interacting with a chatbot are believed to perform better academically than those interacting with a teacher (Essel et al., 2022). In this context, in this activity, the teacher ensures that the artificial intelligence application is designed as a "philosopher chatbot" to help students deeply understand philosophers' views on the history of philosophy during the philosophy class. Students are asked to interact with Plato or Kant to understand the philosopher's philosophical views comprehensively. Students interactively communicate with the philosopher and share their knowledge with their classmates. Students are asked to look critically at the philosopher's views during this sharing.

In the second stage of the activity, students are asked to ask the "philosopher chatbot" questions they are curious about and conduct a philosophical dialog. For example, they can ask Plato how he connected the world of shadows with the world of ideas or Kant how eternal peace can be achieved today. Students discuss the philosopher's arguments and develop their ideas based on them. In this activity, the teacher explains the context of the philosopher's arguments and encourages students to evaluate the dialogues critically. Again, in this activity, the teacher asks the students to direct the AI to ask open-ended questions in a way similar to Plato's Socratic method. The AI generates new appropriate questions according to the answers received from the students. The dialog is directed as a dialog in which the AI asks Socratic questions to the students.

In the conversation with historical philosophers activity, the teacher should focus on developing students' critical thinking, questioning, and philosophical dialog skills. Thus, while interacting with artificial intelligence, students are also involved in an active learning process. The teacher observes students' answers during their dialog with the "philosopher chatbot" and asks additional questions to improve the quality of the discussion. He also guides the "philosopher chatbot" with questions to keep the students who deviate from the scope of the topic and manipulate the "philosopher chatbot" within the boundaries of the discussion.

3. Ethical Dilemma and Decision-Making Game

Addressing the nature and meaning of dilemmas in philosophy teaching is critical (Lyons, 1990). In the philosophy course, the teacher asks the students to generate an ethical dilemma from the AI-supported application to develop their skills in solving ethical problems in practical philosophy. For example, it could be an ethical decision-making game involving whether lying to save someone's life is right. Alternatively, it could be an ethical decision-making game in which a student who wants to succeed in exams uses artificial intelligence to think about whether getting a high score on the exam is always considered academic honesty.

The activity asks students to answer this by drawing on different ethical theories. Students can give answers according to deontology, pragmatism, and virtue ethics. The teacher can identify the ethical theories missing from the students' answers and ask, for example, how existentialism would answer the moral dilemma.

The teacher's role in this activity is to guide the students by identifying the ethical theories not covered by the students. The teacher may ask the students how doing their homework on an AI-supported application would pose a problem for their existence. Alternatively, they can investigate whether a student who does his/her homework in this way makes his/her own decisions and whether his/her freedom and originality are affected by this situation. While the ethical theories in the history of philosophy are discussed regarding the ethical dilemma addressed in the activity, the teacher's role is to identify the ethical theories that the students do not emphasize. The teacher should evaluate the students' logic chains during the research and guide them to relate the discussion to ethical theories. At the end of this activity, the teacher asks students to write and analyze an original ethical dilemma.

4. Developing and Analyzing Creative Arguments

Teachers ensure the responsible and successful application of ChatGPT in teaching or research, thereby encouraging the development of creative arguments (Halaweh, 2023). In the philosophy lesson, the teacher asks students to develop an argument for a philosophical question proposed by the AI-supported application to create their original arguments about a philosophical problem. The AI is then asked to give feedback on this argument. The teacher asks the students to defend this argument in the classroom by justifying and justifying it. In the second stage of the activity, the teacher asks the students to learn to analyze the structure of their arguments by asking the AI to divide the argument into sections logically. Then, the students are asked to determine whether their argument constitutes an ontological, epistemological, and ethical system and to complete the missing points, if any, in the argument.

In this activity, the teacher supports students in developing and analyzing arguments for a philosophical problem. As a philosophical guide, the teacher helps students develop in-depth, critical, and questioning thinking skills. The teacher asks students stimulating questions to make them realize that systematic philosophers in the history of philosophy have presented their views in an ontological, epistemological, and ethical unity while developing a philosophical argument, and in this direction, to realize the missing points in their arguments.

5. Philosophical Perspective Mapping

Different visualization formats are important complements for enhancing students' motivation, attention, understanding of the subject, and retention (Eppler, 2006). In this context, the teacher asks the teacher to present the basic concepts of a movement in the history of philosophy, such as rationalism or empiricism. The philosophers hold this view as a visual map or mind map through an artificially assisted application for students to understand the connections between different philosophical movements or the main movements in the history of philosophy by visualizing them. Then, students expand the map provided by the AI, add additional information, and carry out their studies to associate the current with different currents. In this process, students are also asked to criticize the connections between the movements. In the classroom environment, the teacher asks students to justify and explain the currents they associate with the currents they deal with or to justify the criticisms they bring. The students are allowed to discuss together in the classroom environment.

In this activity, the teacher uses artificial intelligence only as a tool that supports the teaching process. In this process, the teacher should guide students' active thinking, discussion, and questioning skills. In this process, the teacher's guiding role comes to the fore, and the teacher directs the students' criticism by explaining the connections on the map in depth. In the activity, the strengths of artificial intelligence, such as access to information and simulation, are used to support the process of embedding philosophical thinking in students.

6. Current Argument Conflict

Addressing controversial arguments in classroom learning supports decision-making processes (Sætra, 2022). Visualizations in learning processes help to monitor where potential problems occur while ensuring that learning develops as expected (Sedrakyan, Mannens & Velbert, 2019). In this context, in a philosophy class, the teacher sends the students a discussion, an essay, or a short presentation on a current philosophical argument. This discussion, presentation, or essay can be designed to answer the questions "Can AI think authentically?", "Can AI make ethical decisions?" or "Can AI surpass human creativity?". AI identifies possible positions on the problem and the essay and provides logical arguments supporting each. Students defend their positions, support them with coherent arguments, and respond to the AI's counter-arguments. In this activity, the teacher monitors the progress of the discussions and provides feedback to assess the strength of the arguments students use to defend their positions.

This activity can also be carried out by dividing the class into groups according to the answers to the current argument under consideration. The class is divided into sufficient groups based on all the responses to the current argument. After the students in the groups present their views, the group that takes the argument that is opposite to the presented view starts to speak and tries to refute the views of the first group. For example, if the current argument is "whether artificial intelligence can surpass real human creativity," the teacher can direct the students' discussions with questions such as "Were ChatGPT's arguments original?", "Were human arguments or those produced by artificial intelligence stronger?". In this way, a dialog is established between those who argue that AI can surpass real human creativity and those who argue that AI cannot surpass real human creativity. The true and false arguments of the proponents of both views are identified. In this way, the current argument conflict is concluded with the students forming their original ideas on the topic at hand.

CONCLUSION

Through artificial intelligence-supported applications in philosophy teaching, students have easier access to information. In addition, individual learning processes are supported, materials are provided for the needs of each student, and the learning speed is increased by responding to students' questions instantly. In addition, ethical problems such as technology addiction, weakening of critical thinking skills, violation of data privacy, and the production of biased algorithms in the teaching process may arise. In this context, blended teaching with traditional teaching methods should be realized to reduce risks such as technology addiction. Thus, students' critical thinking and moral development processes are supported by adding teacher guidance and real human dialogues to AI-supported applications.

Artificial intelligence-supported applications provide advantages for all teachers when used correctly and appropriately. They help teachers save time by suggesting personalized lesson plans, identifying learning deficiencies by providing feedback based on student's performance, and enriching course materials by simplifying complex concepts. In the specific case of philosophy course teaching, it is necessary to support students' questioning and critical and in-depth thinking skills inherent in philosophy. In this context, countries that want to integrate AI-supported applications into their teaching processes must rethink the equipment and pedagogical competencies teachers should have. The ethical problem of using artificial intelligence in teaching philosophy is destroying philosophy's in-depth, critical, and questioning nature. In this context, pedagogical methods that encourage student participation should be used in AI-supported philosophy teaching, and teaching should be carried out through group discussions and philosophical dialogues. Students should be made to question the information presented to them by artificial intelligence in class discussions, and awareness should be raised in this regard. In order to develop students' creativity, they should be given artificial intelligence-supported tasks to analyze a philosopher's argument and develop an alternative solution, which can strengthen their critical thinking skills. For this purpose, by strengthening the role of teachers, teachers can be fundamental guides who direct students' thinking processes and provide philosophical depth.

As in the examples of artificial intelligence-supported activities in this section, artificial intelligence can enrich philosophy teaching when used correctly in teaching processes. However, it is emphasized that teachers' guidance and human interaction are of fundamental importance in prioritizing students' critical, inquisitive, and creative thinking skills. While artificial intelligence is seen as a tool that facilitates learning, it is viewed from a critical perspective that the student is at the center of the active thinking process. Teaching philosophy courses with artificial intelligence-supported applications should emphasize a learning activity in which the guidance of the fundamental human teacher element and student dialogues are in balance. Only such a balance can preserve the human values of philosophy while utilizing the advantages of technology.

REFERENCES

Ainia, D. K. (2024). Peran Etika Digital dalam Upaya Penguatan Pendidikan Karakter di Era Digital. *PAKAR Pendidikan, 22*(2), 127–135. DOI: 10.24036/pakar.v22i2.528

Celik, I., Dindar, M., Muukkonen, H., & Järvelä, S. (2022). The promises and challenges of Artificial Intelligence for teachers: A systematic review of research. *TechTrends, 66*(4), 616–630. DOI: 10.1007/s11528-022-00715-y

Çevik, M. (2017). Will it be possible for Artificial Intelligence robots to acquire free will and believe in God? *Beytulhikme An International Journal of Philosophy, 7*(2), 75–87. DOI: 10.18491/beytulhikme.375781

Çotuksöken, B. (1998). *Kavramlara felsefe ile bakmak.* İnsancıl Yayınları.

Dictionary, O. E. (2020). *Philosophy.* Publishing House of the National Society of Philosophers of Uzbekistan.

Dwivedi, Y. K., Hughes, L., Ismagilova, E., Aarts, G., Coombs, C., Crick, T., & Williams, M. D. (2021). Artificial intelligence (AI): Multidisciplinary perspectives on emerging challenges, opportunities, and agenda for research, practice, and policy. *International Journal of Information Management, 57*, 101994. DOI: 10.1016/j.ijinfomgt.2019.08.002

Eppler, M. J. (2006). A comparison between concept maps, mind maps, conceptual diagrams, and visual metaphors as complementary tools for knowledge construction and sharing. *Information Visualization, 5*(3), 202–210. DOI: 10.1057/palgrave.ivs.9500131

Essel, H. B., Vlachopoulos, D., Tachie-Menson, A., Johnson, E. E., & Baah, P. K. (2022). The impact of a virtual teaching assistant (chatbot) on students' learning in Ghanaian higher education. *International Journal of Educational Technology in Higher Education, 19*(1), 57. DOI: 10.1186/s41239-022-00362-6

Gabriel, F. A., & Pereira, A. L. (2023). Perceptions about the role of the philosophy teacher in the process of the philosophical experience. *Revista Ibero-Americana de Estudos em Educação, 18*, 1. DOI: 10.21723/riaee.v18i00.16948

Golding, C. (2008). The philosophy teacher as guide. *Proceedings of the XXII World Congress of Philosophy*, 27, 29–37.

Günay, M. (2004). *Metinlerle felsefeye giriş.* Karahan Kitabevi.

Halaweh, M. (2023). ChatGPT in education: Strategies for responsible implementation. *Contemporary Educational Technology, 15*(2), ep421. DOI: 10.30935/cedtech/13036

Hayes, P., Fitzpatrick, N., & Ferrández, J. M. (2024). From applied ethics and ethical principles to virtue and narrative in AI practices. *AI and Ethics*. Advance online publication. DOI: 10.1007/s43681-024-00472-z

Jensen, S. S. (2023). The art of facilitating philosophical dialogues from the perspective of teachers. *Educational Studies, 49*(1), 116–130. DOI: 10.1080/03055698.2020.1835612

Kaur, S., Budhraja, K., Pahuja, A., Nayyar, V., & Saluja, S. (2024). *Leveraging Artificial Intelligence in Education.*, DOI: 10.4018/979-8-3693-6660-8.ch010

Kavitha, K. B., Kumar, P., Nithiya, T. K. S., & Suguna, A. (2023). Implementation of Artificial Intelligence in education. *International Research Journal of Computer Science, 10*(5), 104–108. DOI: 10.26562/irjcs.2023.v1005.01

Kienstra, N., Imants, J., Karskens, M., & van der Heijden, P. G. (2015). Doing philosophy effectively: Student learning in classroom teaching. *PLoS One, 10*(9), e0137590. DOI: 10.1371/journal.pone.0137590 PMID: 26379267

Kızıltan, Ö. (2012). Felsefe öğretimi sorunları ve yeni yaklaşımlar. *Eğitim ve Öğretim Araştırmaları Dergisi, 1*(4), 334–342.

Koç, E. (2020). Felsefe öğretimine giriş. In Manav, F. (Ed.), *Ana Hatlarıyla Ortaöğretimde Felsefe Grubu Öğretimi içinde* (pp. 3–16). Pegem. DOI: 10.14527/9786257228640.01

LaCroix, T. (2022). Moral dilemmas for moral machines. *AI and Ethics, 2*(4), 737–746. DOI: 10.1007/s43681-022-00134-y

Leng, L. (2020). The role of philosophical inquiry in helping students engage in learning. *Frontiers in Psychology, 11*, 449. DOI: 10.3389/fpsyg.2020.00449 PMID: 32265782

Liebrenz, M., Schleifer, R., Buadze, A., Bhugra, D., & Smith, A. (2023). Generating scholarly content with ChatGPT: Ethical challenges for medical publishing. *The Lancet. Digital Health, 1-2*(3), e105–e106. Advance online publication. DOI: 10.1016/S2589-7500(23)00019-5 PMID: 36754725

Lin, D., & Zou, R. (2024). Applications, risks, challenges, and future prospects of ChatGPT in electronic records management. *Journal of Artificial Intelligence Research, 1*(1), 1–9. DOI: 10.70891/JAIR.2024.100021

Lund, B. D., & Wang, T. (2023). Chatting about ChatGPT: How may AI and GPT impact academia and libraries? *Library Hi Tech News*, *40*(3), 26–29. DOI: 10.1108/LHTN-01-2023-0009

Lyons, N. (1990). Dilemmas of knowing: Ethical and epistemological dimensions of teachers' work and development. *Harvard Educational Review*, *60*(2), 159–181. DOI: 10.17763/haer.60.2.v71123u7768r47w6

Muhammad, N. H. M., & Niazi, J. A. (2022). Socratic questioning: A philosophical approach in developing critical thinking skills. *Al-Hikmah: International Journal of Islamic Studies and Human Sciences*, *5*(4), 143–161. DOI: 10.46722/hikmah.v5i4.294

O'Connor, W., & Natividad, L. (2023). The bias on artificial intelligence in education (AIED): Influence of perennialism teaching philosophy at education 4.0. *Journal of Science Teacher Education*, *5*(1), 31–44.

Paul, R. W. (2013). Critical and reflective thinking: A philosophical perspective. In *Dimensions of thinking and cognitive instruction* (pp. 445–494). Routledge.

Ramya, R., Priya, S., Thamizhikkavi, P., & Anand, M. (2024). *The pillars of AI ethics*., DOI: 10.4018/979-8-3693-9173-0.ch004

Read, A. W. (Ed.). (1999). *The New International Webster's Comprehensive Dictionary of the English Language-Encyclopedic Edition*. Trident.

Sætra, E. (2022). An empirical moral philosophy perspective on classroom discussions of controversial issues. *Educational Theory*, *72*(5), 641–662. DOI: 10.1111/edth.12548

Şahin, O., & Karayel, D. (2024). Generative Artificial Intelligence (GenAI) in business: A systematic review on the threshold of transformation. *Journal of Smart Systems Research*, *5*(2), 156–175. DOI: 10.58769/joinssr.1597110

Sedrakyan, G., Mannens, E., & Verbert, K. (2019). Guiding the choice of learning dashboard visualizations: Linking dashboard design and data visualization concepts. *Journal of Computer Languages*, *50*, 19–38. DOI: 10.1016/j.jvlc.2018.11.002

Su, J., & Yang, W. (2023). Unlocking the power of ChatGPT: A framework for applying generative AI in education. *ECNU Review of Education*, *6*(3), 355–366. DOI: 10.1177/20965311231168423

Su, J., & Zhong, Y. (2022). Artificial intelligence (AI) in early childhood education: Curriculum design and future directions. *Computers and Education: Artificial Intelligence*, *3*, 100072. DOI: 10.1016/j.caeai.2022.100072

Tait, I. (2024). Sobbing mathematically: Why conscious, *self-aware AI deserves protection.* DOI: 10.20944/preprints202410.1228.v1

Turdubaeva, Zh., & Arykbaev, I. (2024). Applications of Artificial Intelligence in education. *Bulletin of Science and Practice*, *10*(2), 517–521. DOI: 10.33619/2414-2948/99/56

Uzun, L. (2023a). Are concerns related to Artificial Intelligence development and use really necessary: A philosophical discussion. *Digital Society : Ethics, Socio-Legal and Governance of Digital Technology*, *2*(3), 40. DOI: 10.1007/s44206-023-00070-2

Uzun, L. (2023b). Are concerns related to Artificial Intelligence development and use really necessary: A Philosophical Discussion. *Digital Society : Ethics, Socio-Legal and Governance of Digital Technology*, *2*(3), 40. DOI: 10.1007/s44206-023-00070-2

Xu, X. (2024). Research on algorithmic ethics in Artificial Intelligence. *2024 6th International Conference on Internet of Things, Automation and Artificial Intelligence (IoTAAI),* 499–503. DOI: 10.1109/IoTAAI62601.2024.10692746

Yadav, D. S. (2024). Navigating the landscape of AI integration in education: Opportunities, challenges, and ethical considerations for harnessing the potential of Artificial Intelligence (AI) for teaching and learning. *BSSS Journal of Computer*, *15*(1), 38–48. DOI: 10.51767/jc1503

Yu, H., & Guo, Y. (2023, June). Generative Artificial Intelligence empowers educational reform: Current status, issues, and prospects. [). Frontiers Media SA.]. *Frontiers in Education*, *8*, 1183162. DOI: 10.3389/feduc.2023.1183162

Zawacki-Richter, O., Marín, V. I., Bond, M., & Gouverneur, F. (2019). Systematic review of research on artificial intelligence applications in higher education – where are the educators? *International Journal of Educational Technology in Higher Education*, *16*(1), 39. DOI: 10.1186/s41239-019-0171-0

Zhai, X. (2024). Transforming teachers' roles and agencies in the era of generative AI: Perceptions, acceptance, knowledge, and practices. *Journal of Science Education and Technology*, •••, 1–11. DOI: 10.1007/s10956-024-10174-0

KEY TERMS AND DEFINITIONS

Philosophy: Philosophy, which means love of wisdom, is a discipline that rationally evaluates problems related to existence, knowledge, and value.

Teaching Philosophy: The concept that refers to learning subjects, achievements, and contents within the scope of philosophy.

Role of the Teacher: It expresses the role of the teacher in teaching activities.

Being a Philosophical Guide: It refers to the processes by which the teacher directs the student's learning processes in teaching philosophy courses.

Creative Argument: Creative argument refers to the process of making inferences using new contexts, which is student-centered.

Artificial Intelligence (AI): Artificial intelligence is a technology related to the development of computers that can perform thought processes such as learning, thinking, and reorganizing in a human-like manner.

Generative Artificial Intelligence (GenAI): GenAI is an artificial intelligence system that can create text, images, or other types of media, and as a generator, it can produce new and similar content by learning the structure and patterns in the training data.

Chapter 5
The Ethical and Societal Implications of AI in Economic Policy and Public Administration

Tinatin Zhorzholiani
https://orcid.org/0000-0002-8274-9028
David Aghmashenebeli National Defence Academy of Georgia, Georgia

ABSTRACT

AI is reshaping economic policy and public administration worldwide. This study explores the ethical and societal implications of AI integration in governance and economic decision-making, with a focus on transparency accountability fairness and public trust. Through interdisciplinary qualitative analysis and case studies from Georgia's public sector, the research identifies challenges such as algorithmic bias, lack of legal safeguards, data privacy concerns and institutional readiness, highlights promising developments, including the establishment of the Georgia Technology Authority's AI office, national capacity-building programs and pilot AI systems in finance and law enforcement. Drawing from international best practices and local initiatives, the paper presents evidence-based policy recommendations to ensure that AI adoption in public governance serves democratic values, enhances service delivery and protects citizen rights. The findings contribute to the growing field of responsible AI and underscore the need for inclusive, transparent, ethically grounded governance frameworks.

DOI: 10.4018/979-8-3373-2612-2.ch005

INTRODUCTION

Artificial Intelligence (AI) has become one of the most transformative and disruptive technologies of the 21st Century, altering how economies function, reshaping public administration, and challenging longstanding ethical and governance frameworks. With its wide-ranging applications—from automating mundane administrative tasks to informing complex economic decisions- AI presents immense opportunities and unprecedented challenges. As AI systems become embedded in economic policy-making and public governance processes, examining their technical efficacy and broader societal and ethical implications is essential.

Integrating AI in government structures and economic institutions is not just a futuristic vision but a present reality. AI tools are now being used to simulate policy outcomes, improve public service delivery, detect financial fraud, optimize tax collection, enhance cybersecurity, and influence public decision-making (Montoya & Rivas, 2019; Wirtz et al., 2019). For example, generative AI systems such as ChatGPT and Claude are revolutionizing public communication interfaces, policy drafts, and service automation (Zhao et al., 2023). Governments worldwide are increasingly adopting AI technologies to forecast economic trends, analyze large datasets for decision-making, and streamline operations in health, transportation, and finance (Gupta, 2019; Margetts & Dorobantu, 2019).

However, these advancements raise fundamental questions. Can algorithmic decision-making replace human judgment in public governance? What happens when biases embedded in AI algorithms produce discriminatory outcomes? How can transparency, fairness, and accountability be ensured in AI-driven resource allocation or policy enforcement systems? These questions form the ethical crux of AI's role in public administration and economic policy.

One of the foremost ethical concerns surrounding the use of AI in governance and economics relates to fairness and bias. Despite being seen as neutral computational entities, algorithms are developed by humans and trained on datasets that often reflect social, historical, and institutional biases (Barocas & Selbst, 2016). For instance, predictive policing algorithms have been shown to target marginalized communities, replicating systemic injustices disproportionately (Angwin et al., 2016). In the economic sphere, AI-driven credit scoring systems may deny loans to applicants based on biased correlations, even unintentionally.

Moreover, the opacity of many AI systems, the so-called "black box" nature of machine learning models—makes it difficult to audit decisions, hold actors accountable, or explain outcomes to affected individuals. This lack of explainability is particularly problematic in the public sector, where legitimacy and trust are essential (Ben Rjab & Mellouli, 2019). When citizens are affected by decisions made by opaque systems, from welfare eligibility to taxation, procedural justice is undermined.

Privacy is another pressing ethical issue. The training and operation of AI systems typically require vast amounts of data. This often includes personal, sensitive, or confidential information about citizens. Without robust data protection mechanisms, the risk of misuse, surveillance, and breaches increases dramatically. The challenge of balancing AI efficiency with citizens' privacy rights remains unresolved in many jurisdictions (Kuziemski & Misuraca, 2020; Obermeyer et al., 2019).

The societal impact of AI is not limited to the ethical domain—it also touches on the economic fabric of society. One of the most discussed implications is AI's role in labor displacement. According to a Forrester report, AI is projected to displace approximately 2.4 million jobs in the United States alone, with broader automation trends affecting many more (Zhao et al., 2023). Scholars like Harari have warned of the emergence of a "useless class"—individuals left behind by technological progress and no longer economically relevant (Harari, 2018).

In the public sector, automation could mean job losses for clerical workers, tax processors, and even specific decision-makers. While AI may increase operational efficiency, it also risks deepening socio-economic inequality unless accompanied by robust reskilling and social safety mechanisms. Some economists argue that AI could eventually create new employment and economic opportunities (Brynjolfsson & McAfee, 2014), but the transition period remains a concern, particularly for vulnerable populations.

In addition to economic displacement, AI adoption can erode public trust if not handled with care. Trust in public institutions is already under strain in many democracies. Deploying AI in high-stakes areas such as criminal justice, healthcare, and economic redistribution may exacerbate skepticism, notably if people feel excluded from or misunderstood by algorithmic systems. Research has shown that while AI can foster citizens' trust by improving service quality, it can also diminish it through perceived unfairness or lack of control (Sun & Medaglia, 2019; Al-Mushayt, 2019).

Despite the rapid adoption of AI, most public institutions are not adequately prepared to deal with its complexities. The use of AI in public administration is still in its infancy compared to the private sector (Desouza, Dawson, & Chenok, 2020). Unlike businesses, governments operate under strict accountability norms and democratic oversight, which AI systems often fail to accommodate. Furthermore, knowledge gaps remain in understanding the governance needs specific to public-sector AI applications (Wirtz et al., 2020).

Regulatory and policy frameworks have lagged behind technological developments. In many cases, AI systems are being implemented without clear ethical guidelines, institutional oversight, or participatory mechanisms for stakeholder input. Policymakers are grappling with questions such as: Who is responsible when an AI system makes a harmful decision? How can governments ensure that AI respects human rights and democratic values? These uncertainties underscore the need for governance frameworks that embed ethics into the AI lifecycle—from design and development to deployment and review.

Given the stakes involved, it is imperative that robust ethical principles and inclusive policy-making guide AI adoption in public governance and economic policy. Scholars have called for AI governance frameworks emphasizing transparency, accountability, and public participation (Floridi, 2020; Jobin, Ienca, & Vayena, 2019). Such frameworks should prioritize protecting fundamental rights and the equitable distribution of AI's benefits.

Ethical AI governance also requires interdisciplinary collaboration. Engineers, data scientists, public administrators, ethicists, sociologists, and legal scholars must work together to anticipate unintended consequences and design systems that are technically sound and socially responsible. Furthermore, public institutions must invest in digital literacy and ethical capacity-building among civil servants to ensure informed decision-making regarding AI technologies.

The ethical deployment of AI also requires public engagement. Citizens should have opportunities to understand, question, and influence the AI systems that govern them. Mechanisms such as algorithmic impact assessments, ethical review boards, and open data policies can help bridge the gap between technological systems and democratic oversight.

The future of AI in economic policy and public administration will depend not only on technological innovation but also on ethical foresight and governance innovation. As AI continues to evolve and integrate into the core functions of the state, its designers, implementers, and regulators face a collective responsibility to ensure that the technology serves the public good, protects human dignity, and upholds democratic values.

AI's capacity to enhance efficiency, optimize resources, and generate insights is undeniable. However, without ethical guardrails and societal consensus, it risks undermining the institutions it seeks to improve. AI must be transparent, accountable, and aligned with the public interest, whether in simulating economic scenarios, managing public funds, or predicting citizen behavior.

This study aims to explore these intersections between AI, ethics, and governance by examining how AI systems affect economic decision-making and public service in real-world contexts. Through critical analysis of case studies, theoretical frameworks, and policy debates, the paper seeks to provide a comprehensive understanding of AI's ethical and societal implications in the public domain and offer recommendations for building inclusive, responsible, and trustworthy AI governance systems.

Literature Review

Artificial Intelligence (AI) has rapidly emerged as a transformative force in public administration and economic policy-making, reshaping how governments deliver services, allocate resources, and engage citizens. AI technologies—ranging from predictive analytics to natural language processing—are now deployed in various domains such as taxation, welfare distribution, public health, and infrastructure management (Vinuesa et al., 2020; Wirtz et al., 2019). These innovations promise more efficient, data-driven, and objective governance yet raise profound ethical, societal, and operational challenges.

Scholars have highlighted the dual nature of AI in governance: on the one hand, it enhances efficiency and decision-making; on the other, it introduces complexities regarding transparency, bias, accountability, and public trust (Binns, 2018; Eubanks, 2018). The review of the literature reflects this paradox and emphasizes the need for a nuanced, multi-layered understanding of AI's role in public administration.

Thematic Areas of AI Research in Public Governance

AI's implementation in the public sector is typically associated with enhanced decision-making capabilities, improved public services, and more informed policy modeling. For example, machine learning algorithms are used in fraud detection, chatbots are employed in digital citizen engagement, and predictive analytics inform budget planning and health service allocation (Vinuesa et al., 2020; Sun & Medaglia, 2019). Integrating AI with big data analytics has also opened new possibilities for real-time governance and adaptive policy-making (Zhang et al., 2020).

Nevertheless, much of this research remains macro-level and optimistic, often underestimating or overlooking the organizational and ethical risks at the micro level (Guney & Ala, 2021; Goyal et al., 2019).

AI is considered a tool for innovation within bureaucratic systems, yet its successful deployment requires significant institutional readiness and cultural shifts. Straub et al. (2022) introduced conceptual frameworks like "operational fitness" and "epistemic alignment" to evaluate the effectiveness of AI systems in public organizations.

However, several studies indicate that public administration often lags behind the private sector in digital maturity, resulting in inconsistent AI adoption and fragmented governance strategies (Desouza et al., 2020; Sharma et al., 2021).

Ethical Dimensions of AI in Public Administration

Ethical concerns dominate scholarly discourse around AI in governance. Key issues include algorithmic bias, data privacy, lack of transparency, and challenges in assigning accountability. Binns (2018) argues that algorithms often inherit the biases of their training datasets, which can lead to systemic discrimination, particularly in areas such as predictive policing, loan approvals, and welfare eligibility.

The opacity of AI systems—or "black box" models—complicates the auditability of public decisions, leading to reduced trust in public institutions (Ben Rjab & Mellouli, 2019). Without adequate mechanisms for transparency and oversight, it becomes challenging to understand why an algorithm made a specific recommendation or decision (Floridi et al., 2018).

Eubanks (2018) provides compelling real-world examples of algorithmic injustice in public services, such as welfare systems that mistakenly flag recipients for fraud due to flawed data models. Similarly, facial recognition tools used in public safety have been criticized for racial and gender biases, leading to wrongful arrests and public backlash (Mittelstadt et al., 2016).

These cases underscore the need for stronger ethical guidelines and policy frameworks that proactively address the risks posed by AI in the public domain.

Theoretical Perspectives: Technological Determinism and Institutional Change

The integration of AI into public administration has been analyzed through various theoretical lenses, with Technological Determinism being particularly influential. This theory suggests that technology is not merely a tool but an agent that reshapes institutional structures and societal behavior (Winner, 1980). AI challenges traditional bureaucratic models by promoting data-driven, decentralized, and often automated decision-making processes (Margetts & Dunleavy, 2013).

The literature argues that such shifts may fundamentally alter the role of public administrators, reducing human discretion and altering institutional accountability norms (Wirtz et al., 2019). AI, as a socio-technical system, thus requires rethinking not only implementation strategies but also foundational governance theories.

AI Awareness and Technology Adoption in Educational Contexts

Understanding how future public administrators perceive and engage with AI is essential for ethical implementation. Venkatesh et al. (2003) propose that attitudes toward adopting technology are influenced by perceived usefulness, social influence, and ease of use. Studies conducted in Basilan Province (Philippines) show that graduate students have varying degrees of awareness regarding AI's ethical implications, suggesting a critical need to integrate AI ethics into public administration curricula (Scheerder et al., 2017; Dolan, 2018).

This educational gap reflects a broader issue: while technical skills are increasingly taught in universities, ethical, social, and policy dimensions of AI remain underrepresented, particularly in regions with limited resources or institutional capacity.

Context-Specific Challenges: The Case of Basilan Province

The socio-economic and educational context of Basilan Province provides a distinctive backdrop for understanding the interplay between AI, ethics, and governance. Factors such as poverty, political instability, and limited digital infrastructure affect the readiness for AI integration and the ethical risks associated with such technologies (Chalk, 2001).

Dolan (Dolan, 2018) notes that while public administration programs in regions like Basilan focus on practical governance skills, they often lack content related to emerging technologies. This results in a generation of public servants underprepared to manage AI's societal implications or navigate its complex ethical terrain.

Gaps in the Literature and Research Agenda

While numerous studies have examined AI applications in the public sector, significant gaps remain. First, most research emphasizes technical feasibility and organizational efficiency but pays insufficient attention to ethical, legal, and societal concerns. Second, there is a lack of empirical research at the local level, especially in low-resource settings where the effects of AI might be magnified due to weaker regulatory oversight. Third, the public's role in shaping AI governance is often overlooked despite the increasing importance of transparency and participatory ethics in public decision-making (Medaglia et al., 2021).

Future research must, therefore, adopt a multidisciplinary approach, combining insights from computer science, public policy, sociology, and ethics to develop robust governance frameworks for AI in the public sphere.

METHODOLOGY

This study adopts a qualitative, interdisciplinary, and exploratory methodological approach to investigate the use of Artificial Intelligence (AI) in Georgia's public governance and economic policy. The methodology is informed by principles outlined in ethical AI research (Nosike et al., 2024) and multidisciplinary policy evaluation frameworks (Kumar & Kumar, 2024). The goal is to assess both the theoretical implications and practical applications of AI in public institutions and the societal, ethical, and legal consequences arising from its deployment.

Given the evolving and complex nature of AI integration into governance systems, the chosen methodology employs qualitative content analysis, comparative case study analysis, and policy analysis grounded in social science and technology governance theories.

Research Design

Qualitative Orientation: The research is rooted in qualitative inquiry, allowing for a nuanced understanding of AI's role in policy-making, ethical governance, and socio-economic transformation. This approach is especially suitable for exploring context-dependent phenomena that are not yet extensively quantified, such as the effects of AI on government accountability or public trust in Georgia.

Descriptive and Exploratory Nature: This study is both descriptive—documenting existing applications of AI in Georgia's public sector—and exploratory—identifying trends, ethical risks, and governance models that may emerge. It does not seek to generate predictive generalizations but to provide grounded, context-rich analysis suitable for policy recommendations.

Data Collection Methods

Literature Review: A systematic literature review was conducted to frame the ethical, legal, and governance debates surrounding AI. Academic databases such as Scopus, Google Scholar, JSTOR, and ResearchGate were used to access peer-reviewed publications. Particular emphasis was placed on identifying studies relevant to post-Soviet or Eastern European transitions to digital governance and those applying normative ethical frameworks to AI development (e.g., Floridi & Cowls, 2019; Binns, 2018).

The inclusion criteria included:

- Published between 2014 and 2024
- Focus on AI and governance, ethics, public policy, or economic development
- Relevance to Georgian or comparable regional contexts

Secondary Data: Secondary data was gathered from:

- Government reports (e.g., Georgia Technology Authority, Ministry of Finance, National Bank of Georgia)
- Policy white papers
- Civil society organization publications (e.g., IDFI, Transparency International Georgia)
- News articles from trusted national and international outlets (e.g., Agenda.ge, Eurasianet)
- Reports from international institutions (e.g., World Bank, IMF, EU AI observatory)

Case Studies: Three case studies were selected to illustrate the range of AI applications in Georgia:

1. AI in Treasury Risk Management – Ministry of Finance and IMF partnership (Gamkrelidze et al., 2024)
2. AI for Facial Recognition in Law Enforcement – Ministry of Internal Affairs
3. AI-driven Customs Automation – Georgian Revenue Service and Investors Council

Each case was examined through publicly available documentation and policy commentary, triangulated with academic insights and press coverage.

Analytical Techniques

I. ***Thematic Analysis:*** Themes were derived inductively from the literature and case data. Using NVivo software, textual data from reports and articles were coded into categories such as "ethical risks," "legal gaps," "public trust," "AI governance," and "economic implications." This approach enables the synthesis of qualitative insights without imposing overly rigid hypotheses.

II. ***Content Analysis:*** To assess how government and institutions frame AI, content analysis was applied to speeches, press releases, and official AI governance guidelines (e.g., GTA's Responsible AI Use Guidelines). Keywords and rhetorical patterns (e.g., "transparency," "data sovereignty," "risk management") were tracked to evaluate alignment with international AI ethics frameworks.

III. ***Comparative Policy Analysis:*** The study compares Georgia's AI integration strategies to those of:
   - Estonia (as a leading digital governance model in Eastern Europe)

- The EU AI Act (as a regulatory benchmark) This comparison helps assess where Georgia aligns with or diverges from best practices in ethical and legal AI deployment.

Theoretical Framework

Socio-Technical Systems Theory: This study views AI implementation through the lens of socio-technical systems theory (Bijker, Hughes, & Pinch, 1987), recognizing that technology adoption is embedded in institutional, cultural, and political contexts. This helps explain why the same AI system may yield different social outcomes depending on the governance structures in place.
Responsible AI Framework: The ethical principles guiding this study derive from the Responsible AI framework (Jobin et al., 2019; Floridi et al., 2018), including:

- Fairness
- Accountability
- Transparency
- Safety
- Human oversight

These principles are applied as benchmarks in analyzing Georgia's AI governance initiatives and public communication practices.

Legal Pluralism: Given the mix of Georgian national law, EU alignment efforts, and international human rights standards, this study applies a legal pluralism perspective (Santos, 2002) to assess how AI regulation may be negotiated across multiple normative systems.

The methodological strategy employed in this study is designed to bridge theoretical inquiry with empirical relevance. Integrating interdisciplinary perspectives and context-specific analysis contributes to a deeper understanding of how Georgia navigates the promises and perils of AI in public governance and economic policy-making. This methodology ensures that ethical, legal, and societal dimensions are not peripheral but central to evaluating AI's integration into statecraft.

AI INTEGRATION IN PUBLIC GOVERNANCE: THE CASE OF GEORGIA

Artificial Intelligence (AI) is reshaping the landscape of public governance globally, introducing opportunities for enhanced efficiency, transparency, and responsiveness in government institutions. For Georgia—a small yet dynamically developing country in the South Caucasus—the integration of AI into public governance marks a crucial step toward modernizing state institutions, improving service delivery, and aligning with global digital transformation trends. This section examines Georgia's approach to AI integration in public administration, analyzing its strategic developments, pilot initiatives, and institutional reforms while drawing upon international perspectives and local implementation efforts.

Georgia has made considerable progress in crafting a national framework for digital transformation, of which AI is a central component. The government has recognized AI's potential to address governance challenges, including corruption, inefficiency, and weak institutional capacity.

In 2024, the Georgian government launched an **Office of Artificial Intelligence**, signaling its commitment to AI-driven innovation in governance (Georgia Technology Authority, 2024). This office coordinates the development of a national AI strategy and acts as a central node for ethical and transparent AI deployment in public institutions. A critical component of this strategy involves designing a comprehensive governance framework that includes public consultation, impact assessments, and legal safeguards.

According to the systematic review by Zuiderwijk, A., Chen, Y.-C., & Salem, F. (Zuiderwijk et al., 2021), countries that successfully implement AI in public governance do so by investing in empirical, multidisciplinary approaches focused on both process and content dimensions. Georgia's model mirrors this guidance by combining technical development with regulatory and ethical oversight mechanisms.

Georgia's public governance structure has undergone steady digital transformation since the early 2010s. Launching the **Public Service Development Agency (PSDA)** and e-governance platforms has paved the way for AI integration. AI is now being explored as a next-step evolution for document processing, citizen feedback analysis, and predictive service modeling.

AI technologies are also integrated into public finance systems. For instance, in partnership with the IMF, Georgia's **State Treasury** began using AI-driven models to detect anomalies and manage risks in public payments. The system analyzes hundreds of transaction parameters to flag real-time inconsistencies (IMF PFM Blog, 2024). This enhances both accountability and efficiency, two pillars of modern public governance.

Policy simulation and predictive analytics are the most promising areas of AI integration. Georgia has started exploring the use of **machine learning** and **natural language processing (NLP)** tools to support ministries in drafting and evaluating policy proposals.

A notable example includes AI-assisted **budget planning**, where algorithms help forecast revenue patterns and simulate the fiscal impacts of proposed policies. According to Qian, Y., Siau, K. L., and Nah, F. F. (Qian et al., 2024), AI can detect causal patterns across complex datasets, allowing governments to evaluate outcomes before implementation. This ability is crucial in transitional economies like Georgia, where policy missteps can have disproportionate effects.

Additionally, **NLP systems** are being tested to analyze citizen complaints and feedback submitted to government portals. These systems help identify trends, service deficiencies, or emerging social concerns, enabling ministries to respond proactively.

An essential dimension of AI integration is ensuring proper **governance, regulation, and ethical boundaries**. In 2021, Georgia initiated a Council of Europe-supported *"AI and Personal Data Protection"* project to address growing privacy and surveillance concerns (Council of Europe, 2021). The project aimed to develop policies that ensure that government AI use does not compromise fundamental rights.

Public trust remains a fragile yet crucial component of AI-driven governance. Nosike, C. J., Nosike Ojobor, O. S., & Nosike, U. C. (Nosike et al., 2024) argue that transparency, accountability, and bias mitigation are foundational to responsible AI in public administration. In Georgia, transparency mechanisms require all ministries to publish algorithmic decision-making models involving AI in policy enforcement or service delivery.

However, challenges remain. The **State Inspector's Service** has expressed concern over the unchecked expansion of biometric and facial recognition systems in public surveillance, especially when implemented without public consultation or data protection audits.

AI adoption is not just a technological shift; it requires cultural and administrative transformation. Through the Ministry of Education and the Digital Governance Agency, the Georgian government has launched several capacity-building programs for civil servants. These include training in data science fundamentals, ethical AI principles, and digital policy analysis.

Georgia's academic institutions, such as the Ivane Javakhisvili Tbilisi State University and Georgian Technical University, have also introduced AI-related public administration curricula to train the next generation of policymakers.

According to Pflanzer, M., Dubljević, V., Bauer, W. A., Orcutt, D., List, G., & Singh, M. P. (Pflanzer et al., 2023), embedding AI into society requires a balanced investment in both technological systems and human competencies. Georgia's dual-track approach—fostering tech innovation while upskilling its workforce—reflects an understanding of this balance.

AI governance in Georgia also involves **civil society organizations (CSOs)** and the public in shaping policies. The Institute for Development of Freedom of Information (IDFI) has launched several initiatives to monitor the ethical use of AI in governance. For example, they track whether facial recognition technologies are used within legal frameworks and assess if government AI deployments consider human rights impacts (IDFI, 2020).

Furthermore, Georgia's **Investors Council**, composed of public-private stakeholders, has advocated for responsible AI adoption in customs and trade processes. This has led to the piloting of AI-assisted **customs declaration review systems** aimed at reducing bureaucracy and corruption in cross-border trade (Investors Council, 2022).

Georgia's journey toward integrating AI into public governance illustrates the opportunities and pitfalls of adopting advanced technologies in a transitional democracy. The government has demonstrated commendable progress in establishing a regulatory foundation, investing in institutional capacity, and involving stakeholders across society. Nevertheless, it faces ongoing privacy, fairness, and algorithmic accountability challenges.

As Georgia continues to align its governance practices with global standards, particularly those of the European Union, the ethical integration of AI will remain a central pillar. With a clear strategic vision, commitment to transparency, and focus on human capital, Georgia is poised to emerge as a regional leader in AI-enabled public governance.

AI FOR ECONOMIC POLICY IN GEORGIA

Artificial Intelligence (AI) is increasingly becoming pivotal in shaping economic policies worldwide. In Georgia, a country striving for economic modernization and integration into the global economy, AI offers significant potential to enhance policy-making, improve financial systems, and drive innovation across various sectors. This section explores how Georgia leverages AI to inform and implement its economic policies, highlighting key initiatives, challenges, and prospects.

The National Bank of Georgia (NBG) has recognized the transformative potential of AI in monetary policy-making. A working paper by Dundua and Gorgodze (Dundua, Gorgodze. 2022) discusses the application of reinforcement learning (RL) to identify optimal monetary policy rules. This approach allows for modeling complex economic environments and estimating neutral policy rates, offering a more nuanced understanding of monetary dynamics compared to traditional models.

Furthermore, the NBG aligns its AI regulatory framework with European Union standards to bolster financial system stability and enhance risk management. This initiative is part of a broader national fintech strategy developed in collaboration with the World Bank, aiming to modernize financial infrastructure and reduce market entry barriers for emerging players (Agenda.ge, 2024).

Georgia's Ministry of Finance has embarked on integrating AI into its public financial management systems. In collaboration with the International Monetary Fund (IMF), the Georgian State Treasury developed AI applications to manage payment risks within the e-Treasury system. These AI models analyze large volumes of fiscal data to detect anomalies and enhance the quality of treasury reviews, thereby improving the efficiency and trustworthiness of the payment and accounting system (Gamkrelidze et al., 2024).

The Revenue Service of Georgia, supported by the European Bank for Reconstruction and Development (EBRD) and the Investors Council, initiated a project to apply AI in automating customs declarations processes. This initiative aims to streamline customs procedures, reduce administrative burdens, and enhance transparency, thereby improving the business environment and attracting investment (Investors Council, 2022).

The Georgian government has prioritized the transformation of traditional economic sectors through AI. Deputy Economy Minister Irakli Nadareishvili highlighted the government's commitment to fostering innovation and technological development, positioning Georgia as a regional hub for technology and IT companies. Establishing the Kutaisi technology hub exemplifies this commitment, aiming to advance AI research and implementation across various sectors, including healthcare, education, agriculture, and biotechnology (Agenda.ge, 2024).

The Georgia Technology Authority (GTA) has established the Office of Artificial Intelligence to ensure responsible AI deployment. This office oversees AI policy formulation and implementation, emphasizing transparency, fairness, and accountability. The GTA has also launched an AI Innovation Lab to foster experimentation and development in AI and other emerging technologies, promoting collaboration among state agencies, partners, and elected officials (GTA, 2024).

Moreover, the GTA is developing a comprehensive AI governance framework, including risk management standards, AI impact assessments, and sector-specific guidelines. These measures aim to safeguard against biases, mitigate risks, and promote the development of AI solutions that enhance the well-being of Georgians (GTA, 2025).

Recognizing the importance of human capital in AI integration, Georgia has initiated various training programs for public sector employees. Partnerships with institutions like Georgia Tech and Innovate US provide AI training to equip state employees with the necessary skills to integrate AI solutions into government operations effectively. These efforts aim to bridge the knowledge gap and facilitate collaboration across agencies (GTA, 2024).

Despite significant progress, Georgia faces challenges in AI integration, including ensuring data privacy, addressing ethical concerns, and maintaining public trust. The Institute for Development of Freedom of Information (IDFI) has highlighted the need for greater transparency and ethical standards in AI usage, particularly concerning facial recognition systems and automated decision-making processes (IDFI, 2020).

Looking ahead, Georgia aims to expand AI integration across various sectors, enhance data governance policies, and foster public-private collaborations to drive AI governance and application advancements. By embracing innovation while prioritizing ethical considerations, Georgia is charting a path toward a more efficient, intelligent, and responsive economic policy framework.

ETHICAL CONCERNS IN AI DEPLOYMENT: THE CASE OF GEORGIA

Artificial Intelligence (AI) has become an integral part of modern governance, offering tools for efficiency, predictive analytics, and enhanced public service delivery. However, deploying AI technologies raises significant ethical concerns, particularly privacy, transparency, accountability, and bias. In Georgia, integrating AI into public governance has prompted a critical examination of these ethical issues, especially given the country's evolving democratic institutions and regulatory frameworks.

One of the foremost ethical concerns in AI deployment is the protection of individual privacy and personal data. In Georgia, AI-powered surveillance technologies, such as facial recognition systems, have sparked debates over privacy rights and data protection. The Ministry of Internal Affairs has implemented facial recognition technologies in public spaces without comprehensive public disclosure or oversight mechanisms. Investigative reports have revealed the use of AI tools, including ballistics and fingerprint recognition programs of foreign origin, raising questions about data security and sovereignty.

The Council of Europe, in collaboration with Georgia's State Inspector's Service, launched a project to enhance Georgian authorities' capacity to monitor AI tools concerning personal data protection. This initiative underscores the need for robust legal frameworks to ensure that AI applications do not infringe upon individuals' privacy rights.

Transparency in AI systems is crucial to maintaining public trust and ensuring decision-making accountability. There is a noted lack of transparency regarding the government's use of AI technologies in Georgia. Civil society organizations like the Institute for Development of Freedom of Information (IDFI) have highlighted the government's reluctance to disclose AI functionalities, ethical standards, and data protection protocols.

To address these concerns, the Georgia Technology Authority (GTA) has established guidelines for the responsible use of AI, emphasizing principles such as fairness, transparency, accountability, and privacy. These guidelines mandate that state agencies document AI tools and components, conduct regular audits, and ensure that AI systems are used in a manner consistent with ethical standards.

AI systems can inadvertently perpetuate existing biases, leading to discriminatory outcomes. In Georgia, the risk of algorithmic bias is particularly concerning in sectors like law enforcement and public services. The GTA's guidelines advocate for user-centered design, comprehensive testing, and ongoing monitoring to detect and rectify biases in AI systems.

Moreover, the Global Index on Responsible AI (GIRAI) assessed Georgia's performance in responsible AI governance, highlighting the country's low score in this area. The report attributes this to the absence of a national AI policy document and the limited government initiatives addressing ethical AI concerns.

Developing comprehensive legislative and regulatory frameworks is essential to govern AI ethically. The lack of a national AI strategy has been identified as a significant gap in Georgia. While the National Bank of Georgia has issued regulations concerning data-driven statistical, AI, and machine learning model risk management, these are sector-specific and do not constitute a holistic approach to AI governance.

The GTA has introduced policies and standards, such as the Artificial Intelligence Responsible Use Guidelines (GS-23-001) and the Artificial Intelligence Responsible Use Standard (SS-23-002), to guide state agencies in the ethical deployment of AI. These documents outline principles for responsible AI use, including user-centered design, data protection, and human oversight.

Civil society organizations play a pivotal role in advocating for ethical AI practices. In Georgia, entities like IDFI have initiated projects to promote greater transparency and ethical standards in AI usage by governmental agencies. These initiatives involve studying public institutions' use of AI, particularly facial recognition systems, and developing policy recommendations to enhance transparency and accountability.

Public engagement ensures that AI deployment aligns with societal values and norms. Raising awareness among citizens about the implications of AI technologies and involving them in policy discussions can foster a more inclusive approach to AI governance.

International collaborations further support Georgia's efforts to address ethical concerns in AI deployment. The Council of Europe's project with the State Inspector's Service aims to align Georgia's data protection practices with European standards. Georgia's adherence to UNESCO's Recommendations on the Ethics of Artificial

Intelligence also demonstrates a commitment to international principles guiding ethical AI development.

Integrating AI into Georgia's public governance presents opportunities and ethical challenges. Addressing privacy, transparency, bias, and accountability concerns requires a multifaceted approach involving robust legal frameworks, adherence to ethical guidelines, active civil society participation, and international cooperation. By proactively engaging with these ethical considerations, Georgia can harness the benefits of AI while safeguarding individual rights and maintaining public trust.

SOCIETAL IMPACTS OF ARTIFICIAL INTELLIGENCE: ETHICAL, LEGAL, AND GOVERNANCE ISSUES – THE CASE OF GEORGIA

Artificial Intelligence (AI) is transforming societies across the globe, reshaping economies, redefining work structures, and altering the dynamics of governance. Georgia, a rapidly digitizing country in the South Caucasus, is increasingly integrating AI across finance, healthcare, education, and public administration sectors. While these developments offer efficiency and innovation, they also prompt complex ethical, legal, and governance questions that Georgia must address as part of its digital transformation journey.

Drawing on the framework proposed by Qian, Y., Siau, K. L., & Nah, F. F. (Qian et al., 2024), this section contextualizes the societal implications of AI in Georgia, with a focus on (1) ethical dilemmas, (2) legal infrastructure, (3) AI governance, and (4) sector-specific implications. It emphasizes balancing innovation with accountability, inclusion, and human rights.

In Georgia—a country undergoing rapid digital transformation in public governance and economic policy—the societal implications of AI merit close examination. In the context of Georgia, the societal impact of artificial intelligence manifests across key domains such as employment, education, healthcare, social equity, public trust, and the protection of human rights.

1. ***Ethical Challenges: Fairness, Bias, and Accountability:*** Ethical concerns are central to Georgia's public conversation on AI. As AI systems are increasingly used in sensitive areas such as predictive policing, social assistance allocation, and biometric surveillance, concerns have emerged about potential algorithmic bias and lack of transparency. Qian, Y., Siau, K. L., & Nah, F. F. (2024) believe fairness, and explainability must be embedded in AI systems to prevent discriminatory outcomes. In Georgia, however, civil society watchdogs such as IDFI (2020) have documented the opaque use of facial recognition technologies,

raising fears of biased surveillance against minorities or political dissidents. Further, as in many countries, Georgian developers face knowledge gaps in social science and ethics. This contributes to the risk of encoding discriminatory biases into AI systems through unbalanced datasets or a lack of diverse development teams (Qian et al., 2024). Ensuring fairness in AI design thus requires both technical audits and broader participation of underrepresented groups in system development.

2. **Legal Gaps and Institutional Readiness:** Qian, Y., Siau, K. L., & Nah, F. F. (Qian et al., 2024) differentiate between "ethical AI" and "legal AI," where the former is guided by social values and the latter by enforceable norms. In Georgia, the legal environment governing AI remains fragmented. Although the Law on Personal Data Protection (amended in 2023) provides basic safeguards, it does not address algorithmic decision-making or explainability requirements directly. There is no dedicated AI law in Georgia nor a cross-sectoral AI impact assessment requirement, leaving public agencies with broad discretion in deploying technologies. For example, facial recognition systems were deployed without prior parliamentary oversight or an ethics review—an issue noted by civil liberties advocates (Eurasianet, 2024). The lack of comprehensive legislation mirrors the concerns raised by Qian et al. (2024), who argue that legal gaps can lead to the proliferation of systems that lack transparency, limit due process, or reproduce inequality. Georgian policymakers face growing pressure to introduce regulations aligned with European AI Act principles, especially as the country advances its EU integration agenda.
3. ***AI Governance and Institutional Responsibility:*** Effective AI governance depends on integrated frameworks, stakeholder engagement, and institutional accountability. Georgia has taken early steps toward creating this architecture, notably through the Georgia Technology Authority (GTA), which issued the **Artificial Intelligence Responsible Use Guidelines** and **AI Governance Standards** in 2023. These documents emphasize ethical design, human oversight, and risk assessments, mirroring many principles proposed in the Qian, Y., Siau, K. L., & Nah, F. F. (Qian et al., 2024) governance framework. However, the implementation capacity of Georgian institutions remains limited. Public servants require further training in AI literacy and risk evaluation. Moreover, coordination between ministries is sporadic, and no independent body oversees algorithmic accountability or conducts AI audits. To address this, Qian, Y., Siau, K. L., and Nah, F. F. (2024) recommend a value-focused thinking approach—maximizing ethical development and governance by promoting clarity of liability, communication, and institutional collaboration. For Georgia, establishing an AI Ombudsman or integrating AI ethics into the mandates of existing institutions (like the State Inspector's Service) could improve governance and public trust.

4. ***Sectoral Impacts:****Labor Market Disruption and Skills Gap:* One of the most evident societal effects of AI in Georgia is its impact on the labor market. Traditional jobs are at risk as digital systems automate administrative and logistical tasks, especially in public finance and trade logistics. The introduction of AI-powered customs declaration screening by the Revenue Service, supported by the Investors Council, aims to streamline border control operations (Investors Council, 2022). While this enhances efficiency, it reduces the demand for manual customs processing roles, creating potential job displacement. Furthermore, in partnership with the IMF, Georgia's Ministry of Finance implemented over 40 machine-learning models to detect anomalies in payment transactions (Gamkrelidze et al., 2024). This technological leap demands a workforce skilled in data science and algorithmic oversight, capabilities not yet widespread in the Georgian public sector. The skills mismatch is particularly acute in rural areas, where digital literacy remains limited. AI adoption risks widening urban-rural economic divides without targeted reskilling and educational reforms. Frey and Osborne (2017) noted that such polarization is a consistent feature of early-stage AI economies.
5. ***Educational Inequality and Digital Exclusion:*** Education, while a vehicle for social mobility, may become a domain of exclusion in an AI-driven society if not adequately adapted. Georgia's public education system is gradually integrating digital tools, but AI-powered platforms—such as adaptive learning algorithms—are mainly confined to pilot programs or urban elite institutions. AI's ability to personalize education and improve learning outcomes has been well-documented (Baker, 2016). However, in Georgia, uneven access to digital infrastructure and limited teacher training in AI tools hinder equitable implementation. Students in rural or low-income communities are at risk of being further marginalized. The Ministry of Education's reforms under the "New School Model" aims to improve digital access. However, AI integration requires more than broadband infrastructure—it requires ethical oversight, data protection protocols, and training in AI literacy (Ministry of Education of Georgia, 2023).
6. ***Healthcare Innovation vs. Data Ethics:*** AI has transformative potential in Georgian healthcare. Early-stage applications include automated clinic triage and experimental use of AI-assisted diagnostics in radiology. These systems promise faster patient management and reduced administrative burdens. However, ethical and legal questions persist. If trained on non-representative or Western-centric datasets, AI-based diagnostics may misclassify symptoms in Georgian populations. Topol (2019) notes that medical AI must be context-sensitive and human-centered. Additionally, patient data for training AI systems must be anonymized and stored securely. The regulatory infrastructure for health data protection is evolving in Georgia, but enforcement mechanisms are weak, espe-

cially in private clinics that integrate proprietary AI tools without standardized oversight.

7. ***Surveillance, Privacy, and Public Trust:*** The use of AI in public surveillance—especially facial recognition technology, has stirred major societal concerns. The Ministry of Internal Affairs has deployed such tools for law enforcement without public consultation or comprehensive legal oversight. Investigative reports highlight the use of foreign-developed biometric systems in Tbilisi without transparency about their operational scope or safeguards (Eurasianet, 2024). The Council of Europe, in partnership with Georgia's State Inspector's Service, launched a project to address risks arising from AI in personal data processing (Council of Europe, 2021). However, civil society groups argue that existing oversight remains insufficient. IDFI (2020) has urged the government to introduce mandatory algorithmic transparency and public disclosure of AI systems in use. These developments raise broader questions of trust in public institutions. As algorithmic decision-making becomes more prevalent, especially in law enforcement and administrative services, public demand for explainability, auditability, and accountability grows. Without transparency, citizens may view AI as a tool for surveillance rather than a service, undermining democratic legitimacy.
8. ***Inequality and Bias in Algorithmic Governance:*** AI systems deployed in public administration often rely on historical data that may encode social biases. In Georgia, where socio-economic disparities are pronounced—particularly across ethnicity, region, and gender—algorithmic tools may inadvertently perpetuate structural inequality. For example, a welfare eligibility algorithm might deprioritize applicants based on outdated or biased data regarding income or residence. As Qian et al. (2024) argue, algorithmic systems must be regularly audited to detect discriminatory patterns, particularly in high-risk sectors such as social protection or law enforcement. Georgia currently lacks a mandatory AI impact assessment framework. While the Georgia Technology Authority has issued responsible AI use guidelines (GTA, 2023), their application is not yet uniform across ministries or municipal agencies.
9. ***AI and the Integrity of Democratic Processes:*** Another societal concern relates to the integrity of democratic discourse. In Georgia, political campaigns increasingly use AI-based social media targeting, and there have been concerns about using bots to amplify misinformation—particularly during elections. Algorithmically driven content recommendation systems on platforms such as Facebook have contributed to polarization, often along ethnopolitical lines. These trends mirror global concerns that AI may undermine public discourse by reinforcing echo chambers (Diakopoulos, 2016). In Georgia's fragile polit-

ical environment, the ethical use of AI in media and political communication requires urgent regulatory attention.

10. ***Gender and Minority Inclusion:*** AI systems developed without diverse representation often fail to address the needs of women and minority populations. In Georgia, ethnic and linguistic minorities (e.g., Azeris and Armenians) face language barriers that AI-driven services, especially those relying on Georgian-only NLP tools, may exacerbate. Moreover, Georgia's IT and AI sectors remain male-dominated, leading to a gender imbalance in system design and testing. Inclusive AI governance requires institutional mechanisms to ensure gender, language, and cultural factors are considered during development and deployment.
11. ***Governance Frameworks and Civil Society:*** Georgia's approach to AI governance is evolving. The Georgia Technology Authority has introduced two critical documents—the "Artificial Intelligence Responsible Use Guidelines" and the "AI Governance Framework"—which include principles such as fairness, accountability, human oversight, and risk mitigation (GTA, 2023). These documents are inspired by EU and OECD AI principles. Civil society organizations such as IDFI are instrumental in monitoring state compliance with ethical standards and advocating for transparent AI governance. Their involvement in consultations and public discourse fosters accountability and helps mitigate the top-down risks of technocratic governance (IDFI, 2020).

AI presents a double-edged sword for Georgian society. On one side, it offers unprecedented opportunities to improve public administration, strengthen economic development, and deliver personalized services. Conversely, it threatens to deepen inequality, erode privacy, and concentrate power in ways that undermine democratic values.

As Georgia advances its digital transformation agenda, ensuring that AI serves the public good—fairly, inclusively, and transparently—requires robust governance, civil society engagement, and continuous oversight. The societal implications of AI are not merely technological; they are deeply political, ethical, and human. Addressing them must remain a core pillar of Georgia's AI strategy.

Recommendations for Public Administrators and Policymakers in Georgia

In Georgia, integrating Artificial Intelligence (AI) into public governance and economic policy-making presents a dual challenge: harnessing its transformative capabilities while preserving democratic values, societal equity, and institutional accountability. Addressing this technological transition's ethical, operational, and legal complexities requires deliberate, context-sensitive policy design. This section provides comprehensive, evidence-based recommendations for public administrators and policymakers. Drawing from international best practices, current academic discourse, and Georgia-specific experiences, it outlines practical pathways to ensure AI adoption is ethical, inclusive, and transparent. In the Georgian context, the societal influence of AI is increasingly visible across key domains such as employment, healthcare, education, equity, public trust, and digital rights.

While Georgia has taken initial steps in AI governance (e.g., sector-specific innovations in finance and customs), the country lacks a comprehensive national AI strategy. A flexible, adaptive strategy should account for the rapidly evolving nature of AI technologies and be guided by medium-term rather than static long-term goals.

This strategy must:

- Define implementation roadmaps with measurable goals.
- Include clear institutional roles and coordination mechanisms.
- Ensure legislative alignment with EU standards (e.g., the AI Act and GDPR).

Transparency builds legitimacy and trust in AI systems. Policy strategies must include mechanisms to inform the public about AI projects and allow stakeholder participation.

Before deploying AI systems, especially in high-risk sectors such as policing, welfare, or health, government institutions should be required to conduct AIAs. These assessments evaluate:

- Potential discrimination or bias.
- The human rights impact of AI use.
- Possible unintended consequences, such as exclusion or surveillance.

Regulatory impact assessments have already been proposed as a best practice in the European context and can help Georgia tailor interventions accordingly.

To avoid fragmented AI governance, Georgia should create an independent oversight institution. This body should:

- Set and enforce national standards for algorithmic accountability.
- Conduct audits of public-sector AI tools.
- Offer ethical guidance and training for developers and civil servants.

This body could be modeled after data protection authorities or EU AI Boards and should collaborate closely with civil society and academic institutions.

Ethics training and AI literacy should be integrated into university curricula and public service training programs. As Nosike, C. J., Ojobor, O. S. N., & Nosike, U. C. (Nosike et al., 2024) note, cross-sectoral collaboration between policymakers, technologists, and ethicists is vital for a well-rounded AI workforce.

Key actions:

- Introduce modules on algorithmic fairness and explainability in public administration schools.
- Train public servants in the ethical procurement and deployment of AI systems.
- Promote AI literacy among judges, regulators, and educators.

AI systems reflect the values and data of those who design them. Georgia's policymakers must ensure that algorithms do not reinforce existing inequalities, particularly against ethnic minorities, women, and rural communities.

Recommendations include:

- Ensure that training data reflects the diversity of Georgian society.
- Engaging underrepresented groups in system design and testing.
- Funding grassroots initiatives that apply AI for social good (e.g., language accessibility tools for non-Georgian speakers).

One of the most pressing technical challenges in AI governance is many systems' "black-box" nature. Explainability is essential not only for transparency but also for redress mechanisms. Government AI deployments should meet the following standards:

- All algorithmic decisions affecting citizens must be explainable in lay terms.
- AI systems must include logs and documentation for auditing purposes.
- Public agencies should publish summaries of AI models and their intended purposes.

This aligns with the OECD's AI Principles and the EU's proposed AI regulation and ensures that public sector deployments are accountable and contestable.

Georgia should develop a legal sandbox for AI in public services. This model, successfully used in fintech regulation, enables government and startups to:

- Test innovative AI applications in a controlled environment.
- Identify risks early and co-design safeguards.
- Build public trust through experimental transparency.

A regulatory sandbox could be piloted in a specific domain (e.g., transport planning or tax forecasting) and scaled based on evaluation.

Individual ministries or agencies often lead AI initiatives in Georgia. To avoid duplication and inconsistency:

- Establish an inter-ministerial AI coordination unit under the Prime Minister's Office.
- Create an open registry of AI projects in public administration.
- Require local governments to align their digital transformation strategies with national AI ethics standards.

Such coordination will enhance efficiency and reduce the risk of ethical or technical failures in decentralized implementations.

The absence of performance indicators undermines both evaluation and public trust. AI governance frameworks should include the following:

- Metrics for system accuracy and fairness.
- Complaint resolution rates and citizen satisfaction levels.
- Equity audits across demographic groups.

Wirtz, B. W., Weyerer, J. C., & Geyer, C. (2020) emphasize that measurement is vital for closing feedback loops and guiding corrective policy action.

The legal system must evolve to respond to AI-specific challenges. Georgia's policymakers should:

- Clarify liability in AI-driven decisions (e.g., welfare rejections, law enforcement misidentification).
- Define the roles and responsibilities of developers, public agencies, and third-party vendors.
- Align domestic law with international instruments such as the EU Charter of Fundamental Rights.

Veale and Binns (Veale & Binns, 2017) advocate for algorithmic accountability laws that clearly outline where blame and recourse reside in case of harm.

AI thrives on access to high-quality, ethically sourced data. Policymakers should:

- Expand open government data initiatives.
- Create safeguards to ensure that personal data is anonymized and protected.
- Encourage civil society groups and universities to build tools using public datasets.

The open data ecosystem can drive accountability and innovation, ensuring AI systems reflect public needs rather than corporate priorities.

As AI is a transnational issue, Georgia should deepen engagement with regional and international governance forums:

- Participate in OECD and EU working groups on AI.
- Collaborate with regional neighbors to share regulatory best practices.
- Align domestic standards with global norms on AI safety, bias prevention, and digital rights.

This approach is critical as Georgia progresses toward EU membership and must align with the Union's AI regulatory framework.

For Georgia, the responsible integration of AI into public administration and economic governance is a strategic imperative. As the country embraces AI's transformative power, public administrators and policymakers must adopt a proactive, ethical, and inclusive approach. By institutionalizing accountability, investing in human capital, and fostering a culture of transparency and dialogue, Georgia can set a regional example in building a human-centered AI governance model that enhances—not erodes—public trust.

Limitations and Validation Strategies

This study acknowledges several limitations:

- Scope of primary data: Reliance on secondary data may limit the ability to verify internal institutional practices or capture informal governance mechanisms.
- Language barriers: Some policy documents were only available in Georgian or English translations, which may introduce semantic discrepancies.
- Generalizability: The findings are context-specific and may not generalize to countries with different political structures or AI maturity levels.
- Temporal scope: As AI governance rapidly evolves, the analysis reflects the state of knowledge and policy as of early 2025.

To ensure methodological robustness:

- Triangulation: Data from different sources (academic, governmental, and media) were cross-checked to validate interpretations.
- Peer benchmarking: Georgian practices were compared with those in EU and OECD countries for context.

- Iterative refinement: Themes were re-evaluated multiple times during the research to reflect new insights and reduce bias.

REFERENCES

Agenda.ge. (2024, November 6). *Georgian Deputy Economy Minister: AI-driven transformation of traditional sectors "priority" of Govt's policy*. https://agenda.ge/en/news/2024/41460

Agenda.ge. (2024, November 7). *National Bank of Georgia to develop AI regulations aligned with EU standards*. https://agenda.ge/en/news/2024/41473

Al-Mushayt, O. (2019). Public perception and trust in AI. *Government Information Quarterly*, *36*(4), 101397.

Angwin, J., Larson, J., Mattu, S., & Kirchner, L. (2016). Machine bias. *ProPublica*. https://www.propublica.org/article/machine-bias-risk-assessments-in-criminal-sentencing

Barocas, S., & Selbst, A. D. (2016). Big data's disparate impact. *California Law Review*, *104*(3), 671–732.

Ben Rjab, A., & Mellouli, S. (2019). Smart government: A framework for AI-powered public services. *Information Polity*, *24*(3), 247–269.

Binns, R. (2018). Fairness in machine learning: Lessons from political philosophy. *Proceedings of the 2018 Conference on Fairness, Accountability, and Transparency*, 149–159.

Brynjolfsson, E., & McAfee, A. (2014). *The Second Machine Age: Work, progress, and prosperity in a time of brilliant technologies*. W. W. Norton & Company.

Chalk, P. (2001). Separatism and Southeast Asia: The Islamic factor in Southern Thailand, Mindanao, and Aceh. *Studies in Conflict and Terrorism*, *24*(4), 241–269. DOI: 10.1080/10576100116748

Council of Europe. (2021, December 14). *Georgia – CoE and State Inspector's Service launch project action in the field of Artificial Intelligence and Personal Data Protection*. https://www.coe.int/en/web/data-protection/-/georgia-coe-and-state-inspector-s-service-launch-project-action-in-the-field-of-artificial-intelligence-and-personal-data-protection

Desouza, K. C., Dawson, G. S., & Chenok, D. (2020). *AI in government: Applications, challenges, and opportunities*. Brookings Institution.

Dolan, J. (2018). Preparing public administrators for the future: Education, service learning, and civic engagement. *Public Administration Review*, *78*(5), 702–710.

Dundua, M., & Gorgodze, O. (2022). *Application of Artificial Intelligence for Monetary Policy-Making*. National Bank of Georgia. https://nbg.gov.ge/en/media/news/a-new-paper-on-application-of-artificial-intelligence-for-monetary-policy-making

Dwivedi, Y. K., Hughes, L., Ismagilova, E., Aarts, G., Coombs, C., Crick, T., Duan, Y., Dwivedi, R., Edwards, J., Eirug, A., Galanos, V., Ilavarasan, P. V., Janssen, M., Jones, P., Kar, A. K., Kizgin, H., Kronemann, B., Lal, B., Lucini, B., & Williams, M. D. (2019). Artificial Intelligence (AI): Multidisciplinary perspectives on emerging challenges, opportunities, and agenda for research, practice, and policy. *International Journal of Information Management*, *57*, 101994. DOI: 10.1016/j.ijinfomgt.2019.08.002

Eubanks, V. (2018). *Automating inequality: How high-tech tools profile, police, and punish the poor.* St. Martin's Press.

Floridi, L. (2020). *The Ethics of Artificial Intelligence.* Oxford University Press.

Floridi, L., & Cowls, J. (2019). A unified framework of five principles for AI in society. *Harvard Data Science Review*, *1*(1).

Floridi, L., Cowls, J., Beltrametti, M., Chatila, R., Chazerand, P., Dignum, V., Luetge, C., Madelin, R., Pagallo, U., Rossi, F., Schafer, B., Valcke, P., & Vayena, E. (2018). AI4People—An ethical framework for a good AI society: Opportunities, risks, principles, and recommendations. *Minds and Machines*, *28*(4), 689–707. DOI: 10.1007/s11023-018-9482-5 PMID: 30930541

Gamkrelidze, D., Mchedlishvili, G., Prentice, G., & Verma, A. (2024, September 3). *AI-Powered Treasury: Georgia's Innovative Approach to Managing Payment Risks.* IMF PFM Blog. https://blog-pfm.imf.org/en/pfmblog/2024/09/ai-powered-treasury

Georgia Technology Authority (GTA). (2024). *Office of Artificial Intelligence.* https://ai.georgia.gov/

Georgia Technology Authority (GTA). (2025, February 25). *State of Georgia: AI Roadmap and Governance Framework.* https://ai.georgia.gov/blog/2025-02-25/state-georgia-ai-roadmap-and-governance-framework

Guney, M., & Ala, R. (2021). AI and risk management in the public sector. *Public Management Review*, *23*(6), 814–832.

Gupta, A. (2019). AI and the future of public services. *Public Administration Review*, *79*(4), 556–563.

Harari, Y. N. (2018). *21 Lessons for the 21st Century.* Spiegel & Grau.

IDFI. (2020, July 1). *Promoting Greater Transparency and Ethical Standards of Using Artificial Intelligence (AI) in Georgia.* https://idfi.ge/en/promoting-greater-transparency-and-ethical-standards-of-using-artificial-intelligence-in-georgia

IMF PFM Blog. (2024, September 3). *AI-Powered Treasury: Georgia's Innovative Approach to Managing Payment Risks.* https://blog-pfm.imf.org/en/pfmblog/2024/09/ai-powered-treasury

Investors Council. (2022, September 13). *Application and Integration of Artificial Intelligence in customs formalities.* https://investorscouncil.ge/en/news/news/application-and-integration-of-artificial-intelligence-in-customs-formalities/

Jobin, A., Ienca, M., & Vayena, E. (2019). The global landscape of AI ethics guidelines. *Nature Machine Intelligence*, *1*(9), 389–399. DOI: 10.1038/s42256-019-0088-2

Kumar, A., & Kumar, L. (2024). Navigating the future: The ethical, societal and technological implications of Artificial Intelligence. *Global Journal of Research in Engineering & Computer Sciences*, *4*(2), 83–104. DOI: 10.5281/zenodo.10966785&#8203

Kuziemski, M., & Misuraca, G. (2020). AI governance in the public sector: The need for democratic transparency. *Government Information Quarterly*, *37*(3), 101398.

Margetts, H., & Dorobantu, C. (2019). AI and public policy. *Nature Human Behaviour*, *3*(5), 396–398.

Margetts, H., & Dunleavy, P. (2013). The second wave of digital-era governance: A quasi-paradigm for government on the Web. *Philosophical Transactions of the Royal Society A*, 371(1987), 20120382.

Montoya, L., & Rivas, M. (2019). AI in Latin American public service: Opportunities and risks. *Journal of Public Administration: Research and Theory*, *29*(2), 275–289.

Nosike, C. J., Ojobor, O. S., & Nosike, U. C. (2024). Exploring the ethical and societal implications of Artificial Intelligence. *Multidisciplinary Journal of Management and Social Science*, 1(1), 34–36. https://www.researchgate.net/publication/380346927

Obermeyer, Z., Powers, B., Vogeli, C., & Mullainathan, S. (2019). Dissecting racial bias in an algorithm used to manage the health of populations. *Science*, *366*(6464), 447–453. DOI: 10.1126/science.aax2342 PMID: 31649194

OECD. (2019). *Recommendation of the Council on Artificial Intelligence.* https://legalinstruments.oecd.org/en/instruments/OECD-LEGAL-0449

Pflanzer, M., Dubljević, V., Bauer, W. A., Orcutt, D., List, G., & Singh, M. P. (2023). Embedding AI in society: Ethics, policy, governance, and impacts. *AI & Society*, *38*(4), 1267–1271. DOI: 10.1007/s00146-023-01704-2

Qian, Y., Siau, K. L., & Nah, F. F. (2024). Societal impacts of artificial intelligence: Ethical, legal, and governance issues. *Societal Impacts*, *3*, 100040. DOI: 10.1016/j.socimp.2024.100040

Santos, B. de S. (2002). *Toward a new legal common sense: Law, globalization, and emancipation*. Butterworths.

Scheerder, A., Van Deursen, A., & Van Dijk, J. (2017). Determinants of Internet skills, uses, and outcomes. *Telematics and Informatics*, *34*(8), 1604–1616. DOI: 10.1016/j.tele.2017.07.007

Sun, T. Q., & Medaglia, R. (2019). Mapping the challenges of Artificial Intelligence in the public sector: Evidence from public healthcare. *Government Information Quarterly*, *36*(2), 368–383. DOI: 10.1016/j.giq.2018.09.008

Veale, M., & Binns, R. (2017). Fairer machine learning in the public sector: Legal and regulatory perspectives. *Computer Law & Security Review*, *33*(3), 361–372.

Venkatesh, V., Morris, M. G., Davis, G. B., & Davis, F. D. (2003). User acceptance of information technology: Toward a unified view. *Management Information Systems Quarterly*, *27*(3), 425–478. DOI: 10.2307/30036540

Vinuesa, R., Azizpour, H., Leite, I., Balaam, M., Dignum, V., Domisch, S., & Nerini, F. F. (2020). The role of artificial intelligence in achieving the sustainable development goals. *Nature Communications*, *11*(1), 1–10. DOI: 10.1038/s41467-019-14108-y PMID: 31932590

Winner, L. (1980). Do artifacts have politics? *Daedalus*, *109*(1), 121–136.

Wirtz, B. W., Weyerer, J. C., & Geyer, C. (2019). Artificial intelligence and the public sector—Applications and challenges. *International Journal of Public Administration*, *42*(7), 596–615. DOI: 10.1080/01900692.2018.1498103

Wirtz, B. W., Weyerer, J. C., & Geyer, C. (2020). Artificial intelligence and the public sector—Applications and challenges. *International Journal of Public Administration*, *43*(9), 776–785.

Zhao, J., Li, Q., Chen, Y., & Xu, L. (2023). Societal and economic implications of generative AI. *AI & Society*, *38*(1), 121–135.

Zuiderwijk, A., Chen, Y.-C., & Salem, F. (2021). Implications of the use of artificial intelligence in public governance: A systematic literature review and a research agenda. *Government Information Quarterly*, *38*(1), 101577. DOI: 10.1016/j.giq.2021.101577

KEY TERMS AND DEFINITIONS

AI Ethics: AI Ethics refers to the principles and values that guide the development and deployment of artificial intelligence systems. It addresses fairness, accountability, transparency, and harm prevention issues.

AI Governance: AI Governance refers to the legal, ethical, and policy frameworks that oversee the development, deployment, and monitoring of artificial intelligence systems to ensure responsible and safe use.

Algorithmic Bias: Algorithmic Bias occurs when AI systems systematically produce unfair outcomes, particularly for certain groups, due to biased training data, flawed model design, or other structural inequities.

Data Privacy: Data Privacy protects personal information from unauthorized access or misuse. In the context of AI, it is a critical concern due to the large-scale collection and analysis of sensitive data.

Digital Transformation: Digital Transformation is the integration of digital technologies into public sector operations, aiming to improve the efficiency, accessibility, and responsiveness of government services.

EU AI Act: The EU AI Act is a regulatory framework proposed by the European Union to ensure the safe, ethical, and rights-respecting development and use of artificial intelligence. It categorizes AI systems based on risk and imposes corresponding obligations.

Georgia Technology Authority (GTA): The Georgia Technology Authority is a government agency responsible for managing the state's digital infrastructure, cybersecurity, and technology standards in the public sector (specific to the country of Georgia).

Human Rights: Human Rights are fundamental freedoms and protections that must be upheld in designing and using AI systems. These include the right to privacy, non-discrimination, freedom of expression, and due process.

Public Administration: Public Administration is the field concerned with implementing government policy, managing public programs, and the behavior of public servants. It plays a central role in governance and service delivery.

Public Trust: Public Trust is the confidence that citizens have in public institutions to act in a fair, effective, and ethical manner, especially when implementing advanced technologies like AI.

Transparency: Transparency in AI means making algorithms, decision-making processes, and data sources understandable and accessible to stakeholders, thereby fostering accountability and trust.

Chapter 6
Human-Machine Collaboration:
How Do Employees Interact With Artificial Intelligence?

Tuğçe Şimşek
https://orcid.org/0000-0003-3256-4348
Gümüşhane University, Turkey

ABSTRACT

This chapter examines the conceptual framework of artificial intelligence (AI) systems in the organisational context in terms of human-machine collaboration in three dimensions: supportive, collaborative, and autonomous AI models. A literature review integrates theoretical approaches on employee perceptions, acceptance and resistance processes, and the role of organisational culture in adaptation, establishing connections between performance, motivation, and psychosocial effects. Ethical dimensions are evaluated in the context of autonomy, privacy, and fairness, and the potential consequences of AI on work-life balance and role ambiguity are revealed. The findings point to a lack of empirical research despite conceptual richness and suggest the development of measurement tools with both descriptive and experimental designs. The chapter provides a roadmap for future applied research while emphasising the importance of clarifying strategic decision-making processes related to AI adaptation in an organisational context.

DOI: 10.4018/979-8-3373-2612-2.ch006

1. INTRODUCTION

The core organizational dynamics are transformed because of Artificial Intelligence (AI) and technological developments that drive fundamental changes in business life. AI systems provide business processes with speed, efficiency, and accuracy while surpassing traditional automation to deliver systems that simulate human Intelligence and collaborate with human workers (Anica-Popa et al., 2023; Prasanth et al., 2023). Organizations now depend heavily on AI technologies to operate daily, as these systems provide key support to decision-making, workflow management, and employee performance assessment (Yaşar, 2024).

Businesses should view AI system integration as a complex human-machine collaboration beyond technological changes (Risso et al., 2022). The research topic of primary interest in this process focuses on employee–AI interactions alongside their reactions to AI systems. The sustainable competitive advantage of organizations depends on employee system perception and resulting performance outcomes when AI applications aim to enhance performance (Park & Yang, 2023; Wijayati et al., 2022). In today's business world, decision-makers consider direct and indirect interactions between employee attitudes and motivations and performance in AI technology adoption as one of their essential concerns (He et al., 2024).

The growing use of AI in business operations has revealed multiple ethical, social, and psychological difficulties. Implementing AI algorithms in performance assessments, hiring assessments, and surveillance operations creates biases that negatively impact how employees view organizational fairness (Harris, 2024; Monica et al., 2024). These factors create enduring adverse effects that impact workforce members directly and influence organizational integrity and long-term operational sustainability. AI-based workplace monitoring and evaluation and direction systems create serious ethical and psychological problems through employee psychological stress and job insecurity (Sharma et al., 2024).

Social and ethical concerns stemming from AI system integration into business operations need simultaneous human involvement and technological solutions to address them effectively. Business processes achieve better sustainability, increasing employee performance, while motivation improves by implementing a human-focused AI system (Shin & Shin, 2023). Organizations must correctly identify employee perceptions and attitudes before integrating AI systems because this knowledge helps minimize performance and motivational impacts.

This chapter elaborates on these critical elements in integrating AI systems into business life. The key questions to be discussed throughout the chapter are how and under what conditions employees can effectively interact with AI systems, how AI affects employee performance and motivation, and the ethical, social, and psychological impacts of these technologies in the work environment. The answers to these questions will guide organizations to use AI systems in a more efficient, ethical, and people-oriented way. In this way, it will be possible to provide a balanced working environment that does not ignore the human factor while utilizing the potential advantages of AI technology. In this respect, the originality of the discussions and analyses presented in this chapter contributes significantly to understanding the nature of the collaboration between labor and AI.

2. EVOLUTION OF ARTİFİCİAL INTELLİGENCE IN BUSINESS ENVIRONMENTS

The business environment has experienced a series of dramatic changes since the Industrial Revolution due to technological advancements. The speed of traditional production processes increased through mechanization before moving to automated production with digitalization, and we now operate in a phase where AI-supported systems transform organizational structures (Frangos, 2022). AI technology produces multiple effects, including better decision-making processes, workforce structure changes, and organizational cultural transformation (Dong et al., 2024).

AI technologies extend beyond performing automated tasks because they serve various applications in modern business operations. Technologies such as machine learning (ML) and natural language processing (NLP) play critical roles in many areas, such as analytical decision support systems, workforce planning, and customer relationship management in business environments (Gkinko & Elbanna, 2023). The selection processes of human resources managers become more objective through AI-enabled recruitment systems that analyze extensive candidate pools (Frangos, 2022). With AI support, performance management systems generate better assessments of employee capabilities, enabling the establishment of tailored feedback processes (Dong et al., 2024).

Implementing AI in organizational processes results in new structures that transform organizational frameworks and operational mechanisms. Selten and Klievink (2024) explain that public and private sector organizations choose between separate AI departments and AI teams embedded within operational departments when implementing AI applications. Independent AI departments allow for improved technical advancement, but integrated models enable better business process improvement using AI technology. Hradecky et al. (2022) show that private sector organizations base their AI adoption procedures on leadership backing, data management capability, and organizational culture.

Organizations must approach AI integration as a sophisticated change procedure that spans technological alterations and psychological, social, and ethical dimensions (Dong et al., 2024). Research under the Self-Determination Theory (SDT) shows that employee attitudes toward AI stem from their perceptions of organizational autonomy, sense of competence, and levels of communication transparency (Dong et al., 2024). AI systems that participate in decision-making processes generate job security fears and increase productivity and job satisfaction in specific workplace situations (Gkinko & Elbanna, 2023).

Organizations encounter the ethical utilization of AI applications as their most significant challenge. The presence of bias in AI system decision-making processes creates primary debates throughout the public and private sectors (S. Wang et al., 2024). AI applications that handle recruitment, credit assessment, and healthcare generate discrimination risks when algorithmic decisions prove incorrect (Wirtz et al., 2019). Organizations must create transparent AI policies to build trust among their employees and customers in this situation.

In this transformation process, the following strategies are suggested for organizations to achieve successful AI adaptation:

- **Leadership and organizational support:** AI adoption directly relates to managers' explicit support and vision (Frangos, 2022).
- **Training and skills development:** Increasing employees' digital literacy levels through AI integration is critical to organizational success (Dong et al., 2024).
- **Ethical use of AI:** Developing algorithms that reduce bias and establishing transparent decision-making mechanisms will increase organizational trustworthiness (S. Wang et al., 2024).
- **Data management and infrastructure:** For AI to work efficiently, organizations must have a strong data infrastructure and robust management policies (Hradecky et al., 2022).

The evolution of AI in business environments is transforming organizations' operational efficiency and strategic decision-making processes. However, for this transformation to be successful, technological, ethical, and human factors need to be addressed. Adopting a holistic approach to leadership, data management, ethical frameworks, and employee adaptation to AI will ensure AI's sustainable and practical integration.

3. MODELS OF HUMAN-AI COLLABORATION

AI collaboration with human workers transforms business operations and decision-making activities, according to Przegalińska et al. (2025). AI systems now serve as tools that assist human work and stakeholders, enhance human cognitive abilities, and optimize strategic choices (Brynjolfsson et al., 2023). The basic human-AI collaboration models include supportive AI, collaborative AI, and autonomous AI.

Supportive AI models enhance decision-making precision through Artificial Intelligence systems that benefit human operators during the decision-making process (Ammeling et al., 2025). Organizations widely employ this model across medical diagnostics, financial analysis tasks, and customer service operations. AI diagnostic systems in healthcare reduce medical errors by assisting doctors in decision-making (Benzinger et al., 2023). AI-powered investment analysis in the finance sector delivers predictions faster and more consistently than human analysts can achieve (Paul, 2022). The model is extensively used in creating hybrid workforce organizations. The continuous exchange of information connects humans with AI systems to perform joint decision-making processes (Przegalińska et al., 2025). When AI combines its analytical capabilities with human intuition, it becomes possible to create innovative business strategies that guide process development.

The Collaborative AI model describes situations where AI systems partner with humans in their work processes (Sowa et al., 2021). AI systems provide recommendations through this model and actively contribute to decision-making mechanisms that develop through joint processes with human users. It is widely used in industrial production, automation, and service sectors. For example, AI-supported robots cooperate with human workers in manufacturing, increasing production efficiency and reducing occupational accidents (Przegalińska et al., 2025). Similarly, medical decision support systems work interactively with doctors, helping to achieve more accurate and faster results in the diagnostic process (Benzinger et al., 2023). One of the most critical advantages of collaborative AI is that it is based on reliability and human-centered design principles. The transparency of AI systems is important in ensuring user trust (Bolton, 2024). However, algorithmic biases and ethical issues are significant risk factors in human interaction with AI systems (Karanasiou & Pinotsis, 2017).

Autonomous AI models include approaches that enable AI systems to make independent decisions by minimizing human intervention. The widespread use of this model is seen especially in areas such as military operations, financial market management, and autonomous vehicle technologies (Boulanin & Lewis, 2023). However, the ethical and social responsibilities of fully autonomous systems are controversial, as the complete exclusion of the human factor may have unpredictable consequences (Paul, 2022). For example, in the military, using AI in decision-making processes leads to significant debates on responsibility and accountability within the framework of international humanitarian law while increasing operational efficiency (Boulanin & Lewis, 2023). In the financial sector, AI-based automated trading systems can lead to sudden market fluctuations while optimizing high-frequency transactions (Paul, 2022). With the proliferation of such systems, the concept of "responsible Artificial Intelligence" is becoming increasingly important. In order to ensure the ethical use of AI, principles of human oversight, transparency, and accountability need to be adopted (Comes, 2024).

4. EMPLOYEES' PERCEPTIONS AND ADAPTATION PROCESSES TOWARDS ARTİFİCİAL INTELLİGENCE

4.1. Employees' Perception of Artificial Intelligence: Opportunity or Threat?

Employees' perceptions of AI in the workplace shape their adoption and interaction with these technologies, influencing organizational outcomes. Perceptions vary along a spectrum, with AI viewed as both an opportunity and a threat, depending on individual, organizational, and contextual factors.

Employees who see AI as an opportunity believe it helps improve business operations enables them to work more efficiently and allows them to focus on more creative and thoughtful tasks (Naresh Babu et al., 2024). AI-driven tools, such as those used in customer relations or financial advising, help individuals work faster and develop new skills, and research shows that customer service roles can become up to 35% more efficient with these tools (McAfee et al., 2023; Zhou et al., 2024). Alternatively, many people are concerned about job security and fairness due to AI. Workers fear that automation could either diminish the value of human labor or eliminate jobs in sectors where tasks are highly repetitive (Brougham & Haar, 2017; Bhargava et al., 2021). Using AI in recruitment and performance assessment can lead to a lack of trust if perceived as biased (Yam et al., 2023).

People's perceptions are strongly affected by their age and personality. Employees who are well-versed in technology and younger tend to quickly accept AI, while older employees or those less capable may be more reluctant due to fears about their jobs or changes in work processes (Woźniak-Jęchorek et al., 2023; Masry Herzallah & Makaldy, 2025). Psychological factors, such as openness to new ideas and anxiety about AI, can also influence attitudes, and greater knowledge about AI is generally associated with more positive perceptions (Schiavo et al., 2024; Rodway & Schepman, 2023).

How a company is significantly organized affects people's views of it. Presenting AI as a supportive tool and being open and transparent about how it works and uses it can encourage more positive attitudes towards it (Pereira et al., 2023). Conversely, if AI is perceived as a means to cut costs or replace jobs, it can increase resistance. By considering factors such as age, personality, and organizational structure, organizations can help their employees view AI as a helpful tool rather than something to fear, as will be further explored in the next section.

4.2. Factors Affecting the Perception of Artificial Intelligence

People's views on AI are influenced by their own experiences, the structure of their organization, and the society they live in. Demographic factors, psychological aspects, and organizational structure are key in shaping these perceptions.

The initial important factor that shapes people's attitudes toward AI is their characteristics. Age, education, and work experience play a role in forming people's opinions about AI. A study by Schepman and Rodway (2023) showed that young adults see Artificial Intelligence more positively, whereas older adults tend to be more skeptical. Young people are often preferred because they are more digitally literate and can easily adapt to technology. In addition, the level of familiarity with technology directly affects this perception. In their study on teachers, Masry Herzallah and Makaldy (2025) determined that individuals with a high level of technological self-efficacy approached AI more positively, while those with low technological self-efficacy were more cautious towards AI-based applications.

However, individuals' attitudes towards AI cannot be explained solely by demographic factors. Psychological variables also shape this perception to a great extent. In particular, openness to innovation is a factor that directly affects how employees evaluate AI (Rodway & Schepman, 2023). While individuals who are open to change see AI as a learning and development opportunity, those who resist change may be concerned that their work habits will be disrupted. Additionally, AI anxiety is critical to individuals' perceptions of this technology. In a study conducted by Schiavo, Businaro, and Zancanaro (2024), it was observed that AI anxiety was low among individuals with high AI literacy and that these individuals developed more positive attitudes toward AI. This finding shows that training and awareness-raising initiatives can reduce the negative perception of AI.

Another important factor shaping AI perception is organizational context. Employees' attitudes towards AI are influenced by their characteristics and the organization's approach to technology. Bankins et al. (2024) discovered that employees could adapt to new technologies more smoothly when the organization adopts clear and supportive policies in implementing AI. It has been found that employees tend to view AI positively in organizations where management treats it as a helpful addition to the workforce. However, staff in organizations using AI solely to cut costs or replace workers were found to strongly resist the technology (Shahid et al., 2024).

Organisations' AI training and skill development approach can shape employees' feelings about this technology. According to Gaber et al. (2023), if employees know more about AI, they are more likely to use it and feel less anxious. Rodway and

Schepman (2023) found that students' comfort with AI-based systems influences how much they incorporate AI into their education. When organizations offer training, employees tend to feel more positive about AI.

4.3. Resistance and Acceptance Process to Artificial Intelligence Technologies

How AI is used or rejected at work is a key factor in determining an organization's effectiveness. This section uses the concepts of perception discussed earlier to explore what causes people to resist or accept changes, including personal beliefs, group dynamics, and the organization they work in.

Resistance to AI often stems from perceived barriers, as outlined in the Integrated Resistance Factor Model (IRFM), which identifies insufficient leadership support, technological complexity, incompatible business processes, limited testing, and unclear outcomes as key drivers (Ishak & Newton, 2016). Psychological factors, such as perceived loss of autonomy or technological paternalism, exacerbate resistance by fostering feelings of control being transferred to machines (Cappuccio et al., 2024; Rochi et al., 2024). Social concerns, including reduced workplace socialization due to AI-driven processes, also contribute to resistance, as employees fear isolation (Schein & Rauschnabel, 2023).

Acceptance, conversely, is facilitated by models such as the Technology Acceptance Model (TAM) and the Unified Theory of Acceptance and Use of Technology (UTAUT), which emphasize perceived utility, ease of use, social influences, and organizational support (Strang, 2016; Naweed & Rose, 2018). Comprehensive training programs that enhance AI literacy reduce resistance by building confidence and clarifying benefits (Zheng et al., 2019). Leadership and peer support promote acceptance by creating a supportive environment (Ishak & Newton, 2016). Designing AI systems to preserve user autonomy and align with existing workflows enhances adoption (Rochi et al., 2024).

Organizations should implement robust training to minimize resistance and maximize acceptance, foster supportive leadership, and ensure AI systems are user-friendly and transparent. These strategies, combined with addressing employee perceptions (see previous section), enable effective AI integration.

4.4. The Effect of Organisational Culture on Artificial Intelligence Adaptation

Organizational culture plays a decisive role in adopting and internalizing AI technologies. AI integration requires a technical transformation and reshaping organizational culture, employee expectations, and management approaches. According to Tjebane, Musonda, and Okoro (2022), an organization's culture and values regarding AI directly determine employees' attitudes toward the technology and their level of adaptation. Creating a positive perception of AI depends on developing clear policies based on open communication, transparent governance, and ethical values (Prasetyo et al., 2025). Within this framework, organizations should clearly and understandably communicate to employees the purpose of AI, the problems it is intended to solve, and how it will be integrated into business processes.

Tomažević, Murko, and Aristovnik (2024) emphasize that open communication and transparent governance facilitate AI adaptation by reducing employees' perception of uncertainty. Employees' complete understanding of the role of AI in decision-making processes reduces uncertainty and increases trust. Therefore, organizations should clearly define the conditions under which AI will be used, data handling processes, and ethical principles, thereby increasing employee confidence in AI systems (Sharabati et al., 2024).

In AI adaptation, the participation of employees in decision-making processes is critical. Zahidi, Kaluvilla, and Mulla (2024) state that employee participation in decision-making reduces resistance to technology and accelerates adaptation. Taking employees' views into account and valuing their feedback helps them adopt AI systems as a supportive technology. This participatory approach enables employees to see AI as a tool that facilitates their work and increases productivity rather than as a threat.

Besides this, the ethical use of AI and the process of building trust significantly influence the success of adaptation. Sharabati et al. (2024) reveal that when ethical standards are unclear, employees are skeptical toward AI. The occurrence of algorithmic biases or the perception that AI systems make unfair decisions increases employee distrust of the technology. Therefore, organizations must clearly define ethical standards and convince employees that AI systems are impartial and fair.

It is stated that, in successful AI adaptation processes, technology should be used in cooperation with the human factor. According to Ismail (2024), AI applications should be positioned as tools that enhance employees' competencies and direct them toward more strategic and creative tasks. The study conducted by Wang (2024) also shows that the contribution of AI to the professional development and learning processes of employees accelerates adaptation. With this understanding, AI is a technology that does not replace human labor but improves business processes by collaborating.

Studies show that miscommunication, along with insufficient training and non-involvement of employees in processes, represents one of the leading causes of AI adaptation failure in organizations (Tjebane et al., 2022). A lack of proper communication leads employees to misunderstand AI operations within their organization. AI technology adoption becomes challenging for employees when training programs are absent, as they lack knowledge about these technologies. Not involving employees throughout the processes increases their resistance to AI, hindering the technology's successful implementation.

The successful implementation of AI depends heavily on an organization's cultural elements. Internal adoption of AI in organizations relies on open communication practices, clearly defined ethical values, and employee involvement in decision-making. Organizations must recognize AI as a technical, cultural, and managerial transformation process that requires proper strategic development (Prasetyo et al., 2025; Tomaževič et al., 2024). Effective AI adoption requires a solid technological infrastructure and people-focused management practices supported by a strong organizational culture.

5. ETHICAL AND PSYCHOLOGICAL IMPACTS OF ARTİFİCİAL INTELLİGENCE IN THE WORKPLACE

While AI helps make workplace tasks more efficient, it also brings ethical and psychological issues that can shape employees' experiences and trust within the organization. This section carefully examines these impacts, which are then summarised in the Conclusion.

Using AI to make decisions about employees in recruitment, evaluation, and promotion raises questions about fairness and bias. If the data used to train algorithms is biased, the algorithms may replicate those biases and affect individuals based on gender, age, or ethnicity (Arbelaez Ossa et al., 2024; Nur Ihsan Purwanto et al., 2024). Because of these biases, employees may feel less motivated and trusting towards the organization (W. Wang et al., 2024). Clear AI policies and ethical reviews are important to address these risks and earn employees' trust (Sîrbu & Mercioni, 2024).

According to Sanchez et al. (2024), AI-based surveillance systems can make workers more efficient and lead to stress, burnout, and reduced job satisfaction. When employees feel constantly monitored, they become less committed to the organization (Qin et al., 2020). Moreover, when AI automates jobs, it can result in anxiety and dissatisfaction (W. Wang et al., 2024). Presenting AI as an aid to human decision-making can help alleviate these concerns and encourage employees to view it more positively (David et al., 2024).

Ensuring that AI systems are fair, transparent, and human-centered is essential for balancing improved outcomes and ethical and psychological well-being. Organizations need to prioritize employee-friendly AI policies to keep staff motivated and trusting.

6. AI AND SKILLS MANAGEMENT: PREPARING FOR THE FUTURE WORK ENVIRONMENT

The rapidly increasing integration of AI systems in business requires employees and organizations to adapt to this transformation. Traditional business models are evolving quickly with the automation of repetitive tasks and the proliferation of data-driven decision support systems, radically changing the skill sets expected of employees (Jaiswal et al., 2022). Effective adoption of AI requires the development of social and cognitive competencies and technical skills, as AI should be considered a tool that accelerates business processes and a transformational element that enhances human-machine cooperation.

The proliferation of AI in business environments harbors both threats and opportunities for employees. In a study by Schögl et al. (2021), it is observed that the main narratives of the transformation brought about by AI in the business world are shaped by policymakers and companies within the framework of "upskilling" (aligning existing skills with AI) and "reskilling" (adapting employees to new job roles). However, the success of these approaches should not be limited to technical training but should be integrated with organizational change processes, and a multidimensional skills development strategy that supports social and cognitive skills should be adopted.

The direction of skills transformation varies depending on the role of AI in business processes and how employees can cope with this transformation. Gekara and Thanh Nguyen's (2018) analysis shows that digitalization has radically changed traditional work structures. AI-enabled processes require employees to develop technical competence, adaptability, problem-solving, and strategic thinking skills. Integrating AI into business environments requires a workforce that can interpret the large volumes of data these systems provide and make decisions accordingly (Jaiswal et al., 2022).

Studies aimed at determining the most critical skills for the workforce in the AI era emphasize that competencies such as data analysis, digital literacy, problem-solving, creative thinking, and collaboration are becoming increasingly important (Hassouni & Mellor, 2024). In addition, individuals who work with AI-supported systems need to be able to evaluate the outputs provided by machines and integrate these data into human-centered decision-making processes. However, it is also clear that this transformation should not be limited to organizations' acquisition of technical skills. In a study by Chigbu and Nekhwevha (2021), it is stated that the effects of AI on the workforce are directly related not only to skill sets but also to the professional identities and psychological resilience of employees.

The sustainability of AI integration at the organizational level is possible through transforming organizational culture and management approaches. Pizarro Milian and Munro (2020) reveal that successful organizations in the AI era develop transparent communication and continuous feedback mechanisms to increase employees' trust in new technologies and support their psychological resilience during this transformation process. In organizations where employees' trust in AI is low, technological integration processes are disrupted, and productivity gains are limited.

In this context, skills management strategies in the AI era should be addressed across four dimensions: technical skills development, cognitive and soft skills adaptation, empowering employees through psychological and organizational support mechanisms, and developing policies to guide organizational transformation. Jivani (2020) emphasizes that the upskilling of women workers in the AI era should be at the core of organizational strategies, not just at the individual level. This transformation may negatively affect certain demographic groups when AI-enabled processes do not ensure diversity and inclusion. Collaboration between governments, universities, and the private sector also needs to be strengthened for skills management strategies to be sustainable. While Schögl et al. (2021) state that policymakers should provide strategic direction for AI transformation, Gekara and Thanh Nguyen (2018) emphasize that companies basing their skills development programs solely on technical training will be insufficient in the long run and that training models that support individuals to be more flexible and open to learning should be adopted.

AI's increasingly decisive role in the business world requires employees to improve their technical, cognitive, and social competencies continuously. For employees to work efficiently with AI, organizations should adopt a multidimensional skills management strategy and create policies that take advantage of the opportunities offered by AI while managing transformation processes with a human-centered approach. This approach will support adaptation to the current business environment and create an innovative and productive workforce more resilient to future changes.

7. DISCUSSION AND FUTURE PERSPECTIVES

Integrating Artificial Intelligence into business processes fundamentally reshapes the structure of business life, the roles of employees, and the future of organizations. This transformation process is not an issue that can be addressed solely through technological competence but requires the protection and empowerment of the human factor (Khogali & Mekid, 2024). In particular, incorporating AI into the work environment requires a balanced integration strategy in which employees' motivation, psychological well-being, and ethical values are considered. Human–AA interaction is the key element that determines the value these technologies add to business life.

In cases where this balance cannot be achieved, the sustainability of AI applications will be called into question (Hacker, 2023).

The interaction of AI systems with humans is becoming increasingly complex and multifaceted. In particular, developing new relationships involving emotional and social dimensions transforms employee interaction with AI from merely supporting data-driven decisions to a deeper model of collaboration (Nguyen, 2025). Lissack and Meagher (2024) discuss how AI can be used more effectively without undermining human agency, addressing how large language models can be integrated into human thinking processes. In this direction, creating the necessary technical and social infrastructures to enhance employee interaction with AI is an important area of research and practice. In particular, the ability of AI to mimic emotional Intelligence and respond to the psychological needs of employees may increase trust in AI systems but also make ethical and psychological issues more complex (Khogali & Mekid, 2024).

Extensive research needs to be conducted on the ethical dilemmas and psychological effects of AI utilization in workplaces. Noam (2025) emphasizes that insufficient transparency and lack of accountability in AI require human oversight to address these issues. AI poses significant risks to decision-making processes because it introduces biases that threaten staff members' career development and employment security (Hacker, 2023). Workplace surveillance enabled by AI decision systems potentially risks employee privacy rights and produces heightened psychological stress that affects workers in their environment (Salgado et al., 2024). Organizations should establish transparency principles, employee participation mechanisms, and ethical audit processes as key components for achieving organizational success (Hacker, 2023).

Organizations that adopt ethical AI practices will achieve better long-term success (Kashima et al., 2024). A human-centered AI integration strategy supports employees in building a healthier connection with their AI systems. By expanding training and awareness programs, organizations can increase trust in AI and encourage employees to use AI systems ethically and consciously (Urmeneta, 2024). Training should extend beyond teaching technical abilities to include emotional and social skills that enable employees to adjust psychologically (Nguyen, 2025).

Organizations need human-centered AI management as a fundamental requirement to maintain technological development and ensure employee work security, according to Noam (2025). Long-term organizational and employee success directly benefits from AI systems integrating strong ethical values and psychological human factors. Organizations must develop comprehensive policies that base their AI implementation on human factors and ethical values and promote transparency and employee participation. In this way, the potential risks that AI may create can be minimized, and these technologies can become practical tools for improving employees' quality of life.

8. CONCLUSION

The rapid adoption of Artificial Intelligence in business is transforming organizational structures, employee roles, and ethical standards. This chapter highlights that using AI in a human-centered way—through employee participation, open communication, and ethical consideration—can enhance both performance and motivation.

The study clarifies that the integration process is more successful when employees perceive AI as helpful and are well-trained and supported by leadership. However, several ethical challenges remain, such as biased algorithms in recruitment and performance evaluation, as well as psychological risks like stress from surveillance and job insecurity. Organizations must implement clear policies and ethical audits to address these issues and ensure AI systems are designed with a people-first approach.

It would be helpful for future research to examine the lasting effects of human–AI partnerships on a company's operations, the mental health of its workers, and fairness in the workplace. Investigating skill development and how AI can support the creation of inclusive work environments will help ensure the sustainable use of AI. When organizations prioritize ethics and employee well-being, AI can enhance human capabilities and contribute to a work environment that is both productive and supportive.

REFERENCES

Ammeling, J., Aubreville, M., Fritz, A., Kießig, A., Krügel, S., & Uhl, M. (2025). An interdisciplinary perspective on AI-supported decision making in medicine. *Technology in Society, 81*(October 2024), 102791. DOI: 10.1016/j.techsoc.2024.102791

Anica-Popa, L.-E., Vrîncianu, M., & Petrică Papuc, I.-M. (2023). AI–powered business services in the Hyperautomation Era. *Proceedings of the International Conference on Business Excellence, 17*(1), 1036–1050. DOI: 10.2478/picbe-2023-0094

Arbelaez Ossa, L., Milford, S. R., Rost, M., Leist, A. K., Shaw, D. M., & Elger, B. S. (2024). AI through ethical lenses: A discourse analysis of guidelines for AI in healthcare. *Science and Engineering Ethics, 30*(3), 24. DOI: 10.1007/s11948-024-00486-0 PMID: 38833207

Arias-Pérez, J., & Vélez-Jaramillo, J. (2022). Understanding knowledge hiding under technological turbulence caused by Artificial Intelligence and Robotics. *Journal of Knowledge Management, 26*(6), 1476–1491. DOI: 10.1108/JKM-01-2021-0058

Bankins, S., Ocampo, A. C., Marrone, M., Restubog, S. L. D., & Woo, S. E. (2024). A multilevel review of Artificial Intelligence in organizations: Implications for organizational behavior research and practice. *Journal of Organizational Behavior, 45*(2), 159–182. DOI: 10.1002/job.2735

Benzinger, L., Ursin, F., Balke, W.-T., Kacprowski, T., & Salloch, S. (2023). Should Artificial Intelligence be used to support clinical ethical decision-making? A systematic review of reasons. *BMC Medical Ethics, 24*(1), 48. DOI: 10.1186/s12910-023-00929-6 PMID: 37415172

Bhargava, A., Bester, M., & Bolton, L. (2021). Employees' perceptions of the implementation of Robotics, Artificial Intelligence, and Automation (RAIA) on job satisfaction, job security, and employability. *Journal of Technology in Behavioral Science, 6*(1), 106–113. DOI: 10.1007/s41347-020-00153-8

Bolton, M. L. (2024). Trust is not a virtue: Why we should not trust? *Ergonomics in Design, 32*(4), 4–11. DOI: 10.1177/10648046221130171

Boulanin, V., & Lewis, D. A. (2023). Responsible reliance concerning development and use of AI in the military domain. *Ethics and Information Technology, 25*(1), 8. DOI: 10.1007/s10676-023-09691-0

Brougham, D., & Haar, J. (2017). Employee assessment of their technological redundancy. *Labour & Industry: A Journal of the Social and Economic Relations of Work, 27*(3), 213–231. DOI: 10.1080/10301763.2017.1369718

Brynjolfsson, E., Li, D., & Raymond, L. (2023). *Generative AI at work.* DOI: 10.3386/w31161

Burhan, Q. A. (2025). Unraveling the AI Enigma: How perceptions of Artificial Intelligence forge career adaptability through the crucible of career insecurity and skill development. *Management Research Review, 48*(3), 470–488. DOI: 10.1108/MRR-01-2024-0022

Cappuccio, M. L., Galliott, J. C., Eyssel, F., & Lanteri, A. (2024). Autonomous systems and technology resistance: New tools for monitoring acceptance, trust, and tolerance. *International Journal of Social Robotics, 16*(6), 1–25. DOI: 10.1007/s12369-023-01065-2

Chigbu, B. I., & Nekhwevha, F. H. (2021). The future of work and uncertain labor alternatives as we live through the industrial age of possible singularity: Evidence from South Africa. *Technology in Society, 67*(July), 101715. DOI: 10.1016/j.techsoc.2021.101715

Chowdhury, S., Budhwar, P., Dey, P. K., Joel-Edgar, S., & Abadie, A. (2022). AI-employee collaboration and business performance: Integrating knowledge-based view, socio-technical systems, and organisational socialisation framework. *Journal of Business Research, 144*, 31–49. DOI: 10.1016/j.jbusres.2022.01.069

Comes, T. (2024). AI for crisis decisions. *Ethics and Information Technology, 26*(1), 12. DOI: 10.1007/s10676-024-09750-0

Cubric, M. (2020). Drivers, barriers and social considerations for AI adoption in business and management: A tertiary study. *Technology in Society, 62*(December 2019), 101257. DOI: 10.1016/j.techsoc.2020.101257

David, P., Choung, H., & Seberger, J. S. (2024). Who is responsible? US Public perceptions of AI governance through the lenses of trust and ethics. *Public Understanding of Science (Bristol, England), 33*(5), 654–672. DOI: 10.1177/09636625231224592 PMID: 38326971

Dekker, F., Salomons, A., & van der Waal, J. (2017). Fear of robots at work: The role of economic self-interest. *Socio-economic Review, 15*(3), 539–562. DOI: 10.1093/ser/mwx005

Dong, E., Liu, H., Li, J. Y., & Lee, Y. (2024). Motivating employee voicing behavior in optimizing workplace generative AI adoption: The role of organizational listening. *Public Relations Review, 50*(5), 102509. DOI: 10.1016/j.pubrev.2024.102509

Dwivedi, Y. K., Hughes, L., Ismagilova, E., Aarts, G., Coombs, C., Crick, T., Duan, Y., Dwivedi, R., Edwards, J., Eirug, A., Galanos, V., Ilavarasan, P. V., Janssen, M., Jones, P., Kar, A. K., Kizgin, H., Kronemann, B., Lal, B., Lucini, B., & Williams, M. D. (2021). Artificial Intelligence (AI): Multidisciplinary perspectives on emerging challenges, opportunities, and agenda for research, practice, and policy. *International Journal of Information Management, 57*, 101994. DOI: 10.1016/j.ijinfomgt.2019.08.002

Frangos, P. (2022). An integrative literature review on leadership and organizational readiness for AI. *International Conference on AI Research, 4*(1), 145–152. DOI: 10.34190/icair.4.1.834

Gaber, S. A., Shahat, H. A., Alkhateeb, I. A., Al Hasan, S. A., Alqatam, M. A., Almughyirah, S. M., & Kamel, M. K. (2023). Faculty members' awareness of Artificial Intelligence and its relationship to technology acceptance and digital competencies at King Faisal University. *International Journal of Learning. Teaching and Educational Research, 22*(7), 473–496. DOI: 10.26803/ijlter.22.7.25

Gekara, V. O., & Thanh Nguyen, V. (2018). New technologies and the transformation of work and skills: A study of computerisation and automation of Australian container terminals. *New Technology, Work and Employment, 33*(3), 219–233. DOI: 10.1111/ntwe.12118

Gkinko, L., & Elbanna, A. (2023). The appropriation of conversational AI in the workplace: A taxonomy of AI chatbot users. *International Journal of Information Management, 69*(December 2021), 102568. DOI: 10.1016/j.ijinfomgt.2022.102568

Hacker, P. (2023). The European AI liability directives – Critique of a half-hearted approach and lessons for the future. *Computer Law & Security Review, 51*, 105871. DOI: 10.1016/j.clsr.2023.105871

Harris, C. G. (2024). Combining Human-in-the-Loop Systems and AI fairness toolkits to reduce age bias in AI job hiring algorithms. *2024 IEEE International Conference on Big Data and Smart Computing (BigComp)*, 60–66. DOI: 10.1109/BigComp60711.2024.00019

Hassouni, A., & Mellor, N. (2024). Perceptions of AI integration in the UAE's creative sector. *Informatics (MDPI), 11*(4), 82. DOI: 10.3390/informatics11040082

He, C., Teng, R., & Song, J. (2024). Linking employees' challenge-hindrance appraisals toward AI to service performance: The influences of job crafting, job insecurity, and AI knowledge. *International Journal of Contemporary Hospitality Management, 36*(3), 975–994. DOI: 10.1108/IJCHM-07-2022-0848

Hradecky, D., Kennell, J., Cai, W., & Davidson, R. (2022). Organizational readiness to adopt Artificial Intelligence in the exhibition sector in Western Europe. *International Journal of Information Management, 65*(May 2021), 102497. DOI: 10.1016/j.ijinfomgt.2022.102497

Ishak, S. S. M., & Newton, S. (2016). An innovation resistance factor model. *Construction Economics and Building, 16*(3), 87–103. DOI: 10.5130/AJCEB.v16i3.5164

Ismaeil, M. K. L., & Lalla, A. F. (2024). The role and impact of Artificial Intelligence on supply chain management: Efficiency, challenges, and strategic implementation. *Journal of Ecohumanism, 3*(4), 89–106. DOI: 10.62754/joe.v3i4.3461

Jaiswal, A., Arun, C. J., & Varma, A. (2022). Rebooting employees: Upskilling for Artificial Intelligence in multinational corporations. *International Journal of Human Resource Management, 33*(6), 1179–1208. DOI: 10.1080/09585192.2021.1891114

Jivani, A. I. (2020). Gender lens to the future of work. *Daedalus, 149*(1), 134–143. DOI: 10.1162/daed_a_01778

Karanasiou, A. P., & Pinotsis, D. A. (2017). A study into the layers of automated decision-making: Emergent normative and legal aspects of deep learning. *International Review of Law Computers & Technology, 31*(2), 170–187. DOI: 10.1080/13600869.2017.1298499

Kashima, H., Oyama, S., Arai, H., & Mori, J. (2024). Trustworthy human computation: A survey. *Artificial Intelligence Review, 57*(12), 322. DOI: 10.1007/s10462-024-10974-1

Khogali, H. O., & Mekid, S. (2024). Perception and ethical challenges for the future of AI as encountered by surveyed new engineers. *Societies (Basel, Switzerland), 14*(12), 271. DOI: 10.3390/soc14120271

Li, Y., Wu, B., Huang, Y., Liu, J., Wu, J., & Luan, S. (2024). Warmth, competence, and the determinants of trust in Artificial Intelligence: A cross-sectional survey from China. *International Journal of Human-Computer Interaction, 0*(0), 1–15. DOI: 10.1080/10447318.2024.2356909

Lissack, M., & Meagher, B. (2024). Responsible use of large language models: An Analogy with the Oxford Tutorial System. *She Ji: The Journal of Design, Economics, and Innovation, 10*(4), 389–413. DOI: 10.1016/j.sheji.2024.11.001

Masry Herzallah, A., & Makaldy, R. (2025). Technological self-efficacy and sense of coherence: Key drivers in teachers' AI acceptance and adoption. *Computers and Education: Artificial Intelligence, 8*(February), 100377. DOI: 10.1016/j.caeai.2025.100377

McAfee, A., Rock, D., & Brynjolfsson, E. (2023). How to capitalize on generative AI. *Harvard Business Review*, *101*(6), 42–48. https://hbr.org/2023/11/how-to-capitalize-on-generative-ai

Monica, M., Patel, S., Ramanaiah, G., Manoharan, S. K., & Ghilan, T. H. (2024). *Promoting fairness and ethical practices in AI-based performance management systems*., DOI: 10.4018/979-8-3693-5380-6.ch007

Naresh Babu, E. M., Sathwik, B., & Haseena, K. (2024). Employee perceptions towards changing trends of Artificial Intelligence in the workspace. *Research Review International Journal of Multidisciplinary*, *9*(12), 79–85. DOI: 10.31305/rrijm.2024.v09.n12.009

Naweed, A., & Rose, J. (2018). Assessing technology acceptance for skills development and real-world decision-making in the context of train driving. *Transportation Research Part F: Traffic Psychology and Behaviour*, *52*, 86–100. DOI: 10.1016/j.trf.2017.11.003

Nguyen, K. V. (2025). The use of generative AI tools in higher education: Ethical and Pedagogical principles. *Journal of Academic Ethics*, *0123456789*. Advance online publication. DOI: 10.1007/s10805-025-09607-1

Noam, E. (2025). Into the next generation of digital protection: AI resiliency as a public responsibility. *Telecommunications Policy*, *49*(3), 102907. DOI: 10.1016/j.telpol.2025.102907

Nur Ihsan Purwanto, A., Fauzan, M., Widya, T., & Syarof Azzaky, N. (2024). Ethical implications and challenges of AI implementation in business operations. *TechComp Innovations: Journal of Computer Science and Technology*, *1*(2), 68–82. DOI: 10.70063/techcompinnovations.v1i2.52

Park, S.-M., & Yang, D.-W. (2023). The impact of employees' perception of AI Adoption on the relationships between psychological contract, organizational trust and organizational commitment. *The Korean Academic Association of Business Administration*, *36*(5), 749–775. DOI: 10.18032/kaaba.2023.36.5.749

Paul, R. (2022). Can critical policy studies outsmart AI? Research agenda on Artificial Intelligence technologies and public policy. *Critical Policy Studies*, *16*(4), 497–509. DOI: 10.1080/19460171.2022.2123018

Pereira, V., Hadjielias, E., Christofi, M., & Vrontis, D. (2023). A systematic literature review on the impact of Artificial Intelligence on workplace outcomes: A multi-process perspective. *Human Resource Management Review*, *33*(1), 100857. DOI: 10.1016/j.hrmr.2021.100857

Pizarro Milian, R., & Munro, Y. (2020). Credit transfer, articulation & The future of work: Towards a federal strategy. *Canadian Journal of Higher Education, 50*(3), 36–48. DOI: 10.47678/cjhe.vi0.188769

Prasanth, A., Vadakkan, D. J., Surendran, P., & Thomas, B. (2023). Role of Artificial Intelligence and business decision making. *International Journal of Advanced Computer Science and Applications, 14*(6). Advance online publication. DOI: 10.14569/IJACSA.2023.01406103

Prasetyo, M. L., Peranginangin, R. A., Martinovic, N., Ichsan, M., & Wicaksono, H. (2025). Artificial Intelligence in open innovation project management: A systematic literature review on technologies, applications, and integration requirements. *Journal of Open Innovation, 11*(1), 100445. DOI: 10.1016/j.joitmc.2024.100445

Przegalinska, A., Triantoro, T., Kovbasiuk, A., Ciechanowski, L., Freeman, R. B., & Sowa, K. (2025). Collaborative AI in the workplace: Enhancing organizational performance through resource-based and task-technology fit perspectives. *International Journal of Information Management, 81*(June 2024), 102853. DOI: 10.1016/j.ijinfomgt.2024.102853

Qin, F., Li, K., & Yan, J. (2020). Understanding user trust in Artificial Intelligence-based educational systems: Evidence from China. *British Journal of Educational Technology, 51*(5), 1693–1710. DOI: 10.1111/bjet.12994

Risso, M., Delbufalo, E., & Di Bernardo, M. (2022). Human-machine interaction and AI for competitive business in the Digital Era. *Symphonya.Emerging Issues in Management, 2*(2), 134–143. DOI: 10.4468/2022.2.12delbufalo.dibernardo.risso

Rochi, M., Rauschnabel, P. A., Renner, K., & Ivens, B. S. (2024). Technology paternalism: Development and validation of a measurement scale. *Psychology and Marketing, 41*(5), 1172–1188. DOI: 10.1002/mar.21971

Rodway, P., & Schepman, A. (2023). The impact of adopting AI educational technologies on projected course satisfaction in university students. *Computers and Education: Artificial Intelligence, 5*(April), 100150. DOI: 10.1016/j.caeai.2023.100150

Salgado, N., Meza, J., Vaca-Cardenas, M., & Vaca-Cardenas, L. (2024). Current and emerging trends in the use of AI for community surveillance. *Journal of Infrastructure, Policy, and Development, 8*(8), 6135. DOI: 10.24294/jipd.v8i8.6135

Sanchez, T. W., Brenman, M., & Ye, X. (2024). The ethical concerns of Artificial Intelligence in urban planning. *Journal of the American Planning Association, 0*(0), 1–14. DOI: 10.1080/01944363.2024.2355305

Schein, K. E., & Rauschnabel, P. A. (2023). Augmented reality in manufacturing: Exploring workers' perceptions of barriers. *IEEE Transactions on Engineering Management*, *70*(10), 3344–3357. DOI: 10.1109/TEM.2021.3093833

Schiavo, G., Businaro, S., & Zancanaro, M. (2024). Comprehension, apprehension, and acceptance: Understanding the influence of literacy and anxiety on acceptance of Artificial Intelligence. *Technology in Society, 77*(October 2023), 102537. DOI: 10.1016/j.techsoc.2024.102537

Schlogl, L., Weiss, E., & Prainsack, B. (2021). Constructing the 'Future of Work': An analysis of the policy discourse. *New Technology, Work and Employment*, *36*(3), 307–326. DOI: 10.1111/ntwe.12202

Selten, F., & Klievink, B. (2024). Organizing public sector AI adoption: Navigating between separation and integration. *Government Information Quarterly*, *41*(1), 101885. DOI: 10.1016/j.giq.2023.101885

Shahid, M. K., Zia, T., Bangfan, L., Iqbal, Z., & Ahmad, F. (2024). Exploring the relationship of psychological factors and adoption readiness in determining university teachers' attitude on AI-based assessment systems. *International Journal of Management Education*, *22*(2), 100967. DOI: 10.1016/j.ijme.2024.100967

Sharabati, A.-A. A., Rehman, S. U., Malik, M. H., Sabra, S., Al-Sager, M., & Allahham, M. (2024). Is AI biased? Evidence from FinTech-based innovation in supply chain management companies? *International Journal of Data and Network Science*, *8*(3), 1839–1852. DOI: 10.5267/j.ijdns.2024.2.005

Sharma, K., Davidson, B. G. J., George, J. P., & Muttungal, P. V. (2024). Breeding distrust during Artificial Intelligence (AI) Era: How technological advancements, job insecurity, and job stress fuel organizational cynicism? *Evidence-Based HRM: A Global Forum for Empirical Scholarship*. DOI: 10.1108/EBHRM-05-2024-0159

Shin, D., & Shin, E. Y. (2023). Human-centered AI: A framework for green and sustainable AI. *Computer*, *56*(6), 16–25. DOI: 10.1109/MC.2023.3241071

Sîrbu, C. L., & Mercioni, M. A. (2024). Fostering trust in AI-driven healthcare: A brief review of ethical and practical considerations. *2024 International Symposium on Electronics and Telecommunications (ISETC)*, 1–4. DOI: 10.1109/ISETC63109.2024.10797264

Sowa, K., Przegalinska, A., & Ciechanowski, L. (2021). Cobots in knowledge work. *Journal of Business Research*, *125*, 135–142. DOI: 10.1016/j.jbusres.2020.11.038

Spreer, P., & Rauschnabel, P. A. (2016). Selling with technology: Understanding the resistance to mobile sales assistant use in retailing. *Journal of Personal Selling & Sales Management, 36*(3), 240–263. DOI: 10.1080/08853134.2016.1208100

Strang, K. D. (2016). Testing young business students for technology acceptance and learning performance. *International Journal of Learning Technology, 11*(3), 238. DOI: 10.1504/IJLT.2016.079036

Tjebane, M. M., Musonda, I., & Okoro, C. (2022). Organisational factors of Artificial Intelligence adoption in the South African construction industry. *Frontiers in Built Environment, 8*(March), 1–17. DOI: 10.3389/fbuil.2022.823998

Tomaževič, N., Murko, E., & Aristovnik, A. (2024). Organisational enablers of Artificial Intelligence adoption in public institutions: A systematic literature review. *Central European Public Administration Review, 22*(1), 109–138. DOI: 10.17573/cepar.2024.1.05

Urmeneta, A. (2024). *Creative applications of Artificial Intelligence in education* (Urmeneta, A., & Romero, M., Eds.). Springer Nature Switzerland., DOI: 10.1007/978-3-031-55272-4

Wang, F. (2024). AI in vocational training: A qualitative interview study of early-stage practitioners in the real estate brokerage industry in China. *Voprosy Obrazovaniya / Educational Studies Moscow, 1*(3), 180–200. DOI: 10.17323/vo-2024-17710

Wang, S., Xiao, Y., & Liang, Z. (2024). Exploring cross-national divide in government adoption of Artificial Intelligence: Insights from explainable Artificial Intelligence techniques. *Telematics and Informatics, 90*(March), 102134. DOI: 10.1016/j.tele.2024.102134

Wang, W., Wang, Y., Chen, L., Ma, R., & Zhang, M. (2024). Justice at the forefront: Cultivating felt accountability towards Artificial Intelligence among healthcare professionals. *Social Science & Medicine, 347*(February), 116717. DOI: 10.1016/j.socscimed.2024.116717 PMID: 38518481

Wijayati, D. T., Rahman, Z., Fahrullah, A., Rahman, M. F. W., Arifah, I. D. C., & Kautsar, A. (2022). A study of Artificial Intelligence on employee performance and work engagement: The moderating role of change leadership. *International Journal of Manpower, 43*(2), 486–512. DOI: 10.1108/IJM-07-2021-0423

Wirtz, B. W., Weyerer, J. C., & Geyer, C. (2019). Artificial Intelligence and the public sector—Applications and challenges. *International Journal of Public Administration, 42*(7), 596–615. DOI: 10.1080/01900692.2018.1498103

Woźniak-Jęchorek, B., Rydzak, W., & Kuźmar, S. (2023). Decoding the interface: Exploring women's perspectives on integrating AI in professional work. *Human Technology, 19*(3), 325–351. DOI: 10.14254/1795-6889.2023.19-3.2

Xu, S., Kee, K. F., Li, W., Yamamoto, M., & Riggs, R. E. (2024). Examining the diffusion of innovations from a dynamic, differential-effects perspective: A longitudinal study on AI Adoption among employees. *Communication Research, 51*(7), 843–866. DOI: 10.1177/00936502231191832

Yam, K. C., Tang, P. M., Jackson, J. C., Su, R., & Gray, K. (2023). The rise of robots increases job insecurity and maladaptive workplace behaviors: Multimethod evidence. *The Journal of Applied Psychology, 108*(5), 850–870. DOI: 10.1037/apl0001045 PMID: 36222634

Yaşar, T. (2024). Artificial Intelligence in business operations: Exploring how AI technologies are reshaping processes, enhancing decision-making, and driving efficiency across various industries. *Human-Computer Interaction, 8*(1), 53. DOI: 10.62802/r78f9a37

Yue, C. A., Men, L. R., Mitson, R., Davis, D. Z., & Zhou, A. (2024). Artificial Intelligence for internal communication: Strategies, challenges, and implications. *Public Relations Review, 50*(5), 102515. DOI: 10.1016/j.pubrev.2024.102515

Zahidi, F., Kaluvilla, B. B., & Mulla, T. (2024). Embracing the new era: Artificial Intelligence and its multifaceted impact on the hospitality industry. *Journal of Open Innovation, 10*(4), 100390. DOI: 10.1016/j.joitmc.2024.100390

Zhou, Q., Chen, K., & Cheng, S. (2024). Bringing employee learning to AI stress research: A moderated mediation model. *Technological Forecasting and Social Change, 209*(January 2023), 123773. DOI: 10.1016/j.techfore.2024.123773

Zirar, A., Ali, S. I., & Islam, N. (2023). Worker and workplace Artificial Intelligence (AI) coexistence: Emerging themes and research agenda. *Technovation, 124*, 102747. DOI: 10.1016/j.technovation.2023.102747

KEY TERMS AND DEFINITIONS

AI Anxiety: Concerns about how AI may change the nature of jobs, reduce opportunities for autonomy, or disrupt interpersonal communication at work. A strong understanding of AI and adequate training can reduce anxiety and foster a positive outlook.

Algorithmic Bias: AI-based decision-making can arise from flawed data or system design and may impact recruitment or performance evaluation processes. Addressing algorithmic bias is essential to ensure fairness and build employee trust.

Employee Perceptions of AI: How employees feel about AI—whether they see it as a tool to improve work or a potential job threat. Age, digital literacy, openness to new ideas, and open organizational communication all influence these perceptions.

Ethical AI: Ensuring that AI systems are fair, transparent, and aligned with their intended purposes to avoid bias and promote equitable outcomes. Ethical AI requires clear guidelines and regular audits to maintain trust and ensure proper functioning.

Human-AI Collaboration: The use of AI to assist and enhance the work of human employees in productivity, decision-making, and innovation. By combining AI's analytical capabilities with human intuition, these models can support, collaborate, and function autonomously. A team can only be effective if trust, transparency, and alignment with the organisation's goals exist.

Job Insecurity: Employees may worry that automation will lead to job loss or significant changes, particularly if their work involves repetitive tasks. These fears can reduce trust and motivation, but clear policies and supportive strategies can help manage them.

Organizational Culture: An organization's values, principles, and practices significantly affect how AI is adopted and used. An open, inclusive culture that upholds ethical standards and involves employees can facilitate successful AI integration.

Technology Acceptance Model (TAM): A model that explains how individuals choose to adopt technology based on perceived usefulness and ease of use. TAM highlights the importance of training and thoughtful system design in reducing resistance to AI.

Chapter 7
"Artificial Intelligence" and Library Subject Guides:
Impacting the Academic Research Space

Jacob M. Adler
https://orcid.org/0009-0006-1110-6128
John Jay College of Criminal Justice, USA

ABSTRACT

This chapter examines (and provides a sort of "literature review" for) one particularly visible and ever-growing aspect the university librarian's approach to disseminating instruction on "artificial intelligence:" the creation and development of library research subject guides (often referred to as "libguides") specifically about "artificial intelligence" and its usages in an academic research context and beyond. It offers comparisons and methodological insights to a number of libguides from across university libraries of different types and purposes, highlighting the reasoning behind the most commonly discussed aspects of "artificial intelligence" elucidated in these subject guides, including copyright and fair use, the ethics and hallmarks of generated writing, and the intersection between "traditional" research methods and how they can (or cannot) be supplemented with "artificial intelligence" usage.

DOI: 10.4018/979-8-3373-2612-2.ch007

INTRODUCTION

Over the last few years, the technological advent colloquially referred to as "artificial intelligence" (or "AI"), in particular generative publicly-accessible iterations thereof, has had a profound effect on academic research in a way that mirrors (and perhaps exceeds) the emergence of the internet decades earlier. The rapid pace with which these generative systems have advanced makes the prospect of offering guidance to researchers a daunting one, in large part because of how the potential usages of such systems upend traditional research and educative methodologies, including critical thinking, evaluation of information sources, bibliographic citation, and academic search modalities. As part of the broader systemic response by the education system to address the needs of students interested in the utilization of "artificial intelligence" in their coursework, university librarians of many different specialties have been at the forefront of adapting resources for new contexts in "artificial intelligence," or, in many cases, creating entirely original instruction materials.

One prominent and constantly-developing aspect of the university librarian's approach to disseminating instruction on "artificial intelligence" has been the creation and iteration of library subject guides (often rendered as "libguides") specifically about "artificial intelligence" and its usages both within and outside of academia. The James A. Cannavino Library at Marist University defines a library subject guide broadly as "a collection of library resources on a particular subject put together by a librarian...meant to help students explore materials on a subject through hand-picked library resources such as subject-specific databases, journals, websites, and more" (Clarke, 2021), which lends itself to potentially enormous variance in terms of purpose, form, aesthetic, and level of detail. Given that the advent of "artificial intelligence" presents opportunities and challenges uniquely impactful in the academic space, it is natural (perhaps inevitable) that librarians would construct libguides specializing in educating students and researchers about responsible, productive, and ethical employment "artificial intelligence."

In this context, this chapter analyzes the approach taken by a selection of university libraries in constructing and presenting "artificial intelligence" libguides, offering comparisons and methodological insights to their multifarious types, purposes, and modi. This comparison will highlight the reasoning behind the most commonly discussed aspects of "artificial intelligence" elucidated in these libguides and how they relate to the needs of the institution as a whole and of its patrons (a term used here often, but not exclusively, to refer to students or instructional personnel of these respective universities). The goal of the chapter is not to educate about "artificial intelligence" itself or its technical, social, or moral implications but rather to provide an examination of how librarians go about educating patrons about such technologies and how they address both the demands of their institutions as well as the broader research questions which arise as direct or indirect consequences of the applications of "artificial intelligence," particularly since they pertain to issues such as academic integrity, critical thinking, and the evaluation of both scholarly and non-scholarly sources in a research context. The content of these libguides (as will become evident) is not strictly limited to such considerations; the versatile nature of "artificial intelligence" frequently requires contextualization and education about usages with potentially far-reaching applications, and university librarians are positioned to guide in a fashion unique to their profession.

A Note About "Artificial Intelligence" Terminology

This chapter presents the term "artificial intelligence" in quotation marks as a shorthand to denote that the set of technologies, systems, and ideas currently (as of April 2025) colloquially referred to as such do not represent a true iteration of what an actual artificial intelligence would be, i.e., that the term as applied to tools such as ChatGPT, Elicit, Gemini, et al. is nothing more than a popular misnomer. The Stanford Encyclopedia of Philosophy defines artificial intelligence as "the field devoted to building artificial animals (or at least artificial creatures that – in suitable contexts – *appear* to be animals) and, for many, artificial persons (or at least artificial creatures that – in suitable contexts – *appear* to be persons)" (Bringsjord & Govindarajulu, para. 1). This definition is incongruous with the presentation of the aforementioned tools in their current state; without diverging overmuch into a philosophical argument, no currently available "artificial intelligence" tool possesses a level of consciousness necessary for it to be considered a "person," either in and of itself or by outside parties. Matthew Davis's "An Exploration of the Emergence of Machine Consciousness and the Risk of Robocentrism" (2022) posits:

We exist as a collection of organic machinery that has evolved for creative adaptive action. We come with the proper hardware, but without the ability to be reflexive, we would not be conscious of our existence. Thus, let us take our current parameters for demonstrating consciousness to reflexive awareness, leading to the expression of subjectivity and/or voluntary action. (p. 396)

This key factor, "demonstration of consciousness," makes the term "artificial intelligence" inapplicable to any currently extant technologies.

There are a variety of terms that could instead be accurately applied to the tools given the misnomer of "artificial intelligence," including "chatbot," "large language model," "generative system," etc., but for the sake of aligning with the terminology utilized by the libguides being examined, as well as by most pre-existing literature on the subject, the term "artificial intelligence" will thus be employed, albeit with the aforementioned quotation marks to indicate its inapplicability in this context.

Literature Review

Discourse amongst library and information science (or LIS) specialists concerning the merits of "artificial intelligence" as a learning tool and (more abstractly) as an end in and of itself is possibly as old as the technology itself. It is a natural outgrowth of the university librarian's overarching mission to address information literacy (sometimes referred to by alternate names such as "data literacy"), i.e., the proficiency of an individual in using and navigating data-gathering tools (physical, electronic, or otherwise). While not the exclusive province of university librarians per se, information literacy nevertheless is at the core of all aspects of librarianship in a university setting, and ensuring that patrons have proper access to sources of information or library resources fulfills this mission. Alongside the development of "artificial intelligence" as a viable avenue for conducting research, the term "AI literacy" has arisen as a specific subset of information literacy, albeit an expansive and variable one without a consensus on its exact meaning. Indeed, in a 2024 *Journal of Web Librarianship* article, Dr. Andrew Cox of the University of Sheffield's School of Information, Journalism, and Communication stated, quite simply: "AI has multiple dimensions and applications. Perhaps it is too ambitious to define AI literacy in general" (Cox, p. 96).

Nevertheless, multiple propositions have been put forward about how precisely to articulate the meaning of AI literacy. One such proposal, created by Macquarie University digital assessment specialist Mathew Hillier (2023), outlines five essential aspects which, he argues, comprise "what a student or member of the public would need to be able to effectively utilise emerging Generative AI tools" (para. 3). These aspects are: "Ethical use of AI tools" (which includes acknowledging or attributing proper provenance of training data and/or generated content), "Knowledge of AI affordances" (which concerns assessing the capabilities and limitations of each individual "artificial intelligence" tool and determining which are most suitable for a given task), "Working effectively with AI tools," (inputting proper queries or "prompts" when interacting with any given "artificial intelligence" tool), "Evaluation of AI output," (discerning legitimate or factual results from false or "hallucinatory" information), and "Use and integration into practice" (maintaining an awareness of how fields of study or work are or could potentially be altered because of the inclusion of "artificial intelligence" in their operation). This framework represents how issues involving "artificial intelligence"-augmented study in a university library setting can be approached broadly and flexibly, informing how university librarians create their learning materials therein. Indeed, this framework seems aligned with Cox's thoughts about AI literacy:

...defining the scope of AI literacy is hard. As a general-purpose technology, an umbrella term for several techniques, AI looks different in different contexts. It is also an evolving idea. For example, generative AI has shifted our conceptualization of AI dramatically. Furthermore, there is a need for some understanding of the technologies, but AI literacy is not reducible to technical skills. (Cox, p. 93)

The continuing debate over AI literacy underscores that while it exists as a facet of the overarching set of proficiencies comprising information literacy, some aspects set it apart in a way that has not yet been fully explored. Part of this is necessarily the rapidity with which "artificial intelligence" systems change and evolve, making skills specific to any tool less likely to be interoperable with other comparable tools, at least over time. Cox posits that the totality of AI literacy upends traditional notions of technological proficiency (or nonproficiency) entirely:

Using AI ethically, safely, or 'responsibly' is central to AI literacy. There is no sense of different literacy levels, such as between everyday users [*sic*] and someone involved in design. Many aspects are not vital for the general user—[*sic*] (Cox, p. 99).

Defining and explicating AI literacy to patrons is important for university librarians, forming the basis of their libguide structure and content. Individual university departments or working groups may engage with "artificial intelligence" in their fashion. However, university libraries are usually called upon to supplement the learning activities of all segments of their given institutions. So, their approach must necessarily be commensurably flexible and far-reaching. At least one scientific study conducted by researchers from the University of Qatar and the University of Verona reinforces this notion, stating that "For educators, there is a clear indication of the need to integrate AI literacy into curricula to prepare students for a future where AI is an integral part of the academic and professional landscape" (Qadhi et al., 2024, p. 18 of 22). Their scientometric analysis mapped the developing awareness of and changing attitudes towards "artificial intelligence" in academic environments, confirming its influence and pervasiveness. In doing so, it makes an argument reminiscent of the principles Hillier put forward, highlighting:

> *... educators need to guide students in critically engaging with AI tools, ensuring that they are used to support, rather than replace, the development of critical thinking and analytical skills. The research collectively advocates for a measured approach to integrating AI into the learning environment, enhancing the educational experience while upholding academic honesty and pursuing genuine understanding. (Qadhi et al., p. 15 of 22)*

Others distinguish between the current understanding of AI literacy and a secondary approach to an even more specific application, which Cox terms "algorithmic literacy." This complicates the ability of librarians to remain fully cognizant of changes in the "artificial intelligence" field as they arise:

AI literacy tends to focus on technical understanding, with some criticality and often assume a direct, explicit encounter between humans and an AI system. In contrast, algorithmic literacy focuses on AI buried within infrastructures, primarily commercial platforms. Whenever we receive information pushed at us by recommendation, search, or use social media or streaming platforms, much of the content is filtered by algorithms. This removes some 'noise' and offers useful personalization and recommendation services, but it also may have filter bubble effects in ways that are often quite hidden, even deliberately secretive. Biases in information can be reproduced. (Cox, 2024, p. 95)

There is no single schemata by which university librarians construct their libguides; the same is true for "artificial intelligence" libguides. Such things depend on institutional needs, the resources and services available to each university library, financial considerations, and other factors too numerous to fully list. However, experts in the LIS and information literacy fields have come to some understanding of what is generally expected of such libguides. Using American College and Research Libraries (ACRL) guidelines for information literacy as a point of reference, Chun Ru Ko and Ming-Hsin Chiu (2024) of National Taiwan Normal University succinctly highlight such expectations:

Librarians from university, college, and community college libraries compile generative AI glossaries, provide relevant open educational resources, and set up links to the library's collection system for AI-themed resources. However, university and college library guides are more in-depth. These guides often discuss academic ethics and research applications, create their instructional materials, and teach the use of AI tools. (Ko & Chu, p. 978)

Much of the currently existing literature surrounding the creation of these types of resources and services does not specifically highlight libguides, or at least there has not yet been a comprehensive enough study that concatenates such information. There is some thought to how librarians utilize "artificial intelligence" in broad, conceptual terms. In an interview for the journal "Public Libraries," Cathryn M. Copper, head of the Eberhard Ziegler Library at the University of Toronto (University of Toronto, 2025), notes that:

I have been using [AI] to create a starting point. If I am looking for a new idea or experiment to test in the library, why not throw that prompt into an AI generator and see what it spits out? [sic] Then build on it. (Hakala-Auspert, 2024, p. 54)

Copper's experiences indicate not only a willingness by many library professionals to experiment with the technology personally but also to plan and implement more expansive approaches to the potentialities of such technologies. According to Copper:

Every department [at the University of Toronto] was required to include an AI-related goal for the upcoming year. We each had the flexibility to determine what that meant and how we wanted to experiment with it in our libraries. Plus, there was no expectation of the outcome. It was to encourage everyone to try something. However, by doing this, senior leadership said they supported our experiments and wanted us to explore the possibilities. (Hakala-Auspert, 2024, p. 55)

In parallel to this is a sort of "equal yet opposite" consideration: librarians and educators must maintain a level of understanding about "artificial intelligence" that equals or exceeds that of the students and patrons they educate. As with other aspects of working with "artificial intelligence" in a library setting, this task is made more complicated by the myriad of ways by which a particular student can employ these technologies. Lynsey Meakin (2024) of the Institute of Education at Derby University provides an example:

For instance, a student working on a paper about climate change can use a GenAI-powered assistant to answer specific questions about their topic, drawing from a vast database of academic resources and summarizing lengthy academic articles, making it easier for the student to grasp key points quickly. The AI can also recommend relevant books, articles, and journals in the library based on the student's research topic. It can help students organize their references and citations in the required format, saving time and ensuring accuracy. Enhanced ease of use of technical tools improves students' perception of usefulness in new online learning systems, and the fact that GenAI has been embedded in tools, services, and apps such as those from Microsoft meets this increased ease of use. (Meakin, pp. 2-3)

The philosophical challenge of constructing libguides for university students is rooted in the adaptive nature of "artificial intelligence" as a whole, making it unlike other subject areas predicated on a hierarchical progression of information, readily traceable and reproducible. There is no prescribed methodology for a unified scaffolding of "artificial intelligence" knowledge, as the potential avenues for entry and explication are constantly growing and changing. Cox (2024) explains it thusly:

Although in an ideal world, the process should start with building prior knowledge logically, this may not happen in reality. As they use the 'tools,' users may build more underlying forms of prior knowledge. However, we likely learn ideas from previous systems as users. So, we inherit a relevant knowledge base from understanding the strengths and weaknesses of prior AI for recommendations as we encounter relatively new technologies. (Cox, p. 108)

Selection and Evaluation Criteria

What follows is an examination of three university libguides on the topic of "artificial intelligence," made for the libraries of Purdue University, the University of Arizona, and the University of Waterloo. Two main factors were considered in selecting these libguides, the first of which was searchability, as these libguides appeared high on results lists for search engine queries about "AI libguide[s]" conducted in March and April of 2025. The second factor was geographical distribution: two featured libguides are from universities dispersed broadly throughout the United States (in Indiana and Arizona, respectively), while the third is from outside the United States (Ontario, Canada, specifically). This selection ensured a broad perspective based on differences in local populations and academic environments and avoided examining institutions with overly similar cultural or regional user bases. The libguides discussed here were also, in part, selected for having distinct approaches to discussing "AI" as a means of demonstrating a diversity of strategies concerning "AI" librarianship and instruction. It was also determined that each libguide had, in their fashion, a complete enough understanding of the topic to merit deep analysis and were not merely cursory appraisals.

Each libguide has been evaluated using three broad criteria. The first is "guide construction," discussing the layout, presentation, and level of detail present in each libguide. This includes thoroughly accounting for the number and purpose of each libguide's sections (and subsections, if any), widgets, links, and audiovisual content. The second criterion is "adaptability," accounting for several factors in the libguide's makeup, including whether it is of more use in a "social" (i.e., creative writing, humanities, art, etc.) or "technical" (i.e., professional writing, sciences, mathematics, etc.) setting, as well as determining the "target audience" of each libguide (i.e., whether the content within is more suitable for students, instructors, outside researchers, etc.), the libguide's approach to AI literacy (either explicit or implicit), and the amount of content within the libguide explicitly created for it (as opposed to a link or pre-existing content utilized within the body of the libguide itself). The third criterion is "ability to address institutional needs," which varies considerably depending on the library's host institution. This criterion generally concerns the (actual or perceived) level of cooperation or input from other institutions' departments and the libguide's relationality to specific coursework or educational initiatives.

All information about each examined libguide is current as of April 15, 2025. Any additions or alterations made after that date are not considered here. In addition, the university names and geographical locations have been included to discuss better such institutions relative to their respective student and instructional corpora and within the broader question of librarianship compared to other institutions of similar academic standing.

Purdue University

Guide Construction

This libguide summarizes its functions on its front page as thus: "This LibGuide provides an overview of AI knowledge, the applications of AI tools in teaching and learning, and content for the AI research areas" (Lu, 2024). The front page alone provides a great deal of context for the structure of the libguide, introducing a broad definition of "What is Artificial Intelligence?" directly below this mission statement. Unlike other examined libguides, Purdue takes a more specific approach as to its parameters for what constitutes an "artificial intelligence," stating:

> *Artificial Intelligence (AI), introduced by the esteemed Stanford Professor John McCarthy in 1955, was originally described as 'the science and engineering of making intelligent machines.' Initially, AI research centered on programming machines to demonstrate certain behaviors, like playing games. However, the current focus is on crafting machines that can learn, resembling human learning processes. (Lu, 2024)*

The front page includes links to definitions of key "artificial intelligence" terms, which notably are derived from major computer corporations like NVidia and IBM; terms defined include "Artificial Intelligence," "Computer Vision," "Deep Learning," "Generative AI," "Machine Learning," and "Natural Language Process (NLP)." Numerous links to other Purdue pages on "artificial intelligence" are featured, including a page on "AI Tools for Literature Reviews," a directory of "micro-credentials," i.e., short courses on specific topics relating to "artificial intelligence," and pages for Purdue's landing pages for its courses on "artificial intelligence," offering one Major at the College of Liberal Arts, another at the College of Sciences, an online "Applied Generative AI Specialization Program," and a master's program in "artificial intelligence." Unlike some other examined libguides, the Purdue University libguide not only specifically names its creators but has only a single creator: Jing Lu, listed on the Purdue personnel information as a Clinical Assistant Professor for the Science and Engineering Libraries with a PhD in Technology and research interests in information literacy and "artificial intelligence" in classrooms. She is listed as the previous creator or maintainer of several Purdue libguides about biomedicine, technology, literature, and other topics. (Purdue Libraries, 2025)

The first section of the libguide is its "AI Tools" page, which Lu subdivides into sections based on the purpose of each "artificial intelligence" tool: "Generative AI Tools," "AI Tools for Research, "AI Tools for Systematic Review," "AI Tools for Teaching and Learning," "AI Tools for Writing," "AI Tools for Creating Videos," and "AI Tools for Creating Images." To evaluate each of the tools presented, Lu has constructed tables that, at a glance, convey succinct information about various aspects of each functionality. "Generative AI Tools" are evaluated based on "Base Technology" (i.e., the "artificial intelligence" model used to construct it), "Information Accuracy" (in particular whether the tool updates itself in real-time), "Interaction Style" (an abstract description of the user experience in "conversing" with the tool), "Specialized Features" (i.e. functions it performs that other tools might not), "Limitations," "Price" (free or paid, and differing costs if there are multiple paid iterations of the tool), and "Best For" (the ostensible purpose of the tool). This table includes information about Microsoft Copilot, Perplexity, Google Gemini, and ChatGPT, and it also provides links to instructional material about these tools and a "How to Use" tab for summaries of their basic operability. "AI Tools for Research" uses a similarly-formatted table but with only four evaluation criteria: "Purpose," "Key Features," "Price," and "Best For." The tools highlighted here are Elicit, LitMaps, Inciteful, Research Rabbit, and Scholarcy; this last one, described as an "online summarizing tool that generates and converts long articles into summary flashcards" (Lu, 2024), in particular, is given outsize attention, as there is far more training material linked for it than for the others. "AI Tools for Systematic Review" concerns "artificial intelligence" services designed to interpret data from studies and academic findings. They are evaluated by "Purpose," "Key Features," "Price," "Performance" (the modus by which it operates by the end-user), "Limitations," and "Best For." The tools listed are Covidence, Distiller SR, EPPI-Reviewer, Rayyan, and RobotReviewer. "AI Tools for Teaching and Learning" are evaluated by the same criteria as those of "AI Tools for Systematic Review," examining ClassPoint, Eduaide.ai, Gradescope, Magic School, NotebookLM, QuestionWell, Quizlet, and Twee. Again, the same evaluation criteria are used for "AI Tools for Writing," which in other libguides are perhaps at the forefront of "artificial intelligence" tool explanation, but here are relegated to a relatively low point on the list. The libguide distinguishes these from generated writing; these tools might more appropriately be described as "writing assistants." Tools described include Canva Magic Write, Grammarly, Jenni AI, Paperpal, Sudowrite, and Wordtune. The same set of criteria applies to "AI Tools for Creating Videos," describing Synesthesia, VEED, and Vidyo.ai, as well as to "AI Tools for Creating Images," describing DALL-E, Firefly (the service included in Adobe Photoshop), and Midjourney.

Other sections include "AI in Research," "How to Cite AI Generated Content," "Resources for Educators," "Resources for Educators," "AI in K12," "Purdue AI Resources," "Prompt Design," "AI and Ethics," "Copyright," "Publisher Policies," and "Selected Journals in AI." The first of these sections lists suggestions for utilizing "artificial intelligence" tools during the research process, for example: "Data Scraping: AI tools can scrape data from websites, automatically collecting large amounts of relevant information for analysis. This method has become increasingly popular in research to gather datasets from web sources efficiently" (Lu, 2024). Lu lists three points as specific limitations in "artificial intelligence"-powered research: "Bias and Discrimination," "Plagiarism Concerns," and "Data Misinformation." Several links are included about the usage of "artificial intelligence" in systematic review, directly supplementing the evaluation of "AI Tools for Systematic Review" in the "AI Tools" section. The "How to Cite AI Generated Content," "Resources for Educators," "AI in K12," "Purdue AI Resources," "AI and Ethics," "Copyright and AI," and "Publisher Policies" sections all mostly consist of links to external relevant sources or to the aforementioned Purdue "artificial intelligence" pages described on the front page. Of note is the "Prompt Design" section, one of only a few libguides with a section dedicated entirely to prompts, which guides prompt engineering for some of the more popular "artificial intelligence" tools and provides links to prompt libraries. Also of note is the "Selected Journals in AI" page, which highlights publications about "artificial intelligence" from all over the world, including *Science Robots* (from the United States), *Nature Machine Intelligence* (from Switzerland), *AI Open* (from China), *International Journal of Computer Vision* (from the Netherlands), and many more.

Adaptability

The assumed target audience of the libguide is hard to parse; attention paid to the economics of "artificial intelligence" tools suggests that the libguide is more oriented towards student usage, but the deep analysis of "artificial intelligence" from a top-down perspective makes it more likely that the libguide is intended for instructors looking to incorporate "artificial intelligence" into their coursework, and educating them so that they, in turn, can properly inform their students about such usages. Due to her significant background in science and medicine, Lu has a clinical approach to constructing the libguide. She thoroughly addresses the technicalities and specifications of each "artificial intelligence" system, especially regarding the academic review process and the consideration of datasets and statistical information. While far-ranging, the libguide includes many potential uses of "artificial intelligence," but few test-case examples. Although Lu presents no formalized definition of AI literacy within the libguide, she does link to numerous other "artificial intelligence" resources available from Purdue University, and it is perhaps within their purview to establish this standard. The implication from the libguide is that proficiency is couched more in mastering the multifarious forms of "artificial intelligence" than the underlying principles engendering them, as there is a heavy emphasis on prompt engineering and the particulars of use-case. Significant effort was doubtlessly expended in compiling information about the many "artificial intelligence" tools, likely with heavy support from other Purdue "artificial intelligence" resources, especially concerning citation and ethics.

Addressing Institutional Needs

A high level of interdepartmental interaction is evident based on Purdue's network of "artificial intelligence" resources and programming. This is of particular salience given the university's majors on "artificial intelligence," which is part of a new but (if the examined libguides are any indication) fast-growing academic trend. At the very least, the specific learning initiatives created by Purdue for this purpose are being scaffolded by the libguide, in particular the Student-Faculty Learning Community Partners for Algorithmic Literacy (which appears to be the sole reference amongst the examined libguides to Cox's concept of "algorithmic literacy" as being distinct from "AI literacy").

University of Arizona

Guide Construction

The University of Arizona's libguide is unique because it has been divided into two distinct yet closely related libguides, one for students and one for instructors, which share some pages and resources in common. Both are primarily authored by Nicole Hennig, an "AI education specialist" formerly the head of MIT Libraries's user experience department (Hennig, 2018). This chapter will begin by discussing the sections common to both versions of the libguide. The section "Fact Checking is Always Needed" lists basic advice for ensuring the suitability of "artificial intelligence"-generated results for scholarly purposes, including addressing falsified sources, hallucinations, and tools trained explicitly on scholarly sources (namely Elicit and Consensus). In "Which AI Tool for Your Task?," examined "artificial intelligence" systems are grouped into two overarching types: "Not Grounded," which rely on data they collect during their training (examples listed include ChatGPT and Claude), and "Grounded," which utilize web search-derived results in their training either in addition to specific data or in tandem with it (examples listed include Perplexity and Microsoft Copilot). The listed "artificial intelligence" tools are then further grouped based on the user task type, beginning with "Wordsmithing tasks," defined here as brainstorming ideas, generating topics, summarization, revision, and similar functions. Recommendations for "Wordsmithing tasks" include ChatGPT, Claude, Perplexity AI, Google Gemini, and Microsoft Copilot. The other category is "Tasks that involve searching," defined as functions such as finding or summarizing website information or analyzing scholarly articles. Many of the same tools as "Wordsmithing tasks" are recommended here, supplemented by tools such as Elicit, Assistant by Scite, and Consensus. The "Beyond ChatGPT" section gives a succinct overview of various tools constructed using large language models, including ChatGPTplus, Microsoft Copilot, Google Gemini, Claude, Perplexity AI, Meta AI, and others. “Multimedia Generative AI” presents a 16-page interactive tutorial widget covering many aspects of content generation with “artificial intelligence,” including image generation, audio generation, video generation, deepfakes, bias, and copyright.

Hennig's version of the libguide specifically for students opens on a front page entitled “Using ChatGPT Effectively,” presenting a list of possible tasks that “artificial intelligence” is helpful for, including “brainstorming ideas,” “summarizing and outlining,” and “helping to write computer code,” and what it is not helpful for, which includes “asking for information that would have dire consequences” (i.e. health or financial advice) and (quite curiously) “library research (not yet),” giving numerous suggestions about research and summarization tools instead. (Hennig et al., 2023a). Note that many sections of the guide present the name of the specific tool “ChatGPT” as synonymous with “artificial intelligence” as a whole, often a hallmark of libguides constructed in the earlier days of “artificial intelligence” when users had fewer options as to accessible “artificial intelligence” services. The front page also gives an overview of prompt engineering and a listing of “artificial intelligence” tutorials. The next student-specific libguide page poses the question “Is Using ChatGPT Considered Cheating?” and endeavors to give a nuanced answer to that question, pointing out that while the University of Arizona does not have an official policy about “artificial intelligence” in the context of cheating, that significant leeway would be given to individual professors, and so to speak to them about questions involving the use of “artificial intelligence.” It advises being precise and thorough about crediting “artificial intelligence” with anything. It provides links about processes a student can undergo if they have been accused by the school of cheating using “artificial intelligence.” Though both the student and instructor versions of the libguide have a section entitled “Citing Generative AI,” their content differs between the two versions. The student version of “Citing Generative AI” contains links to major citation style guides and several external links about best practices when citing “artificial intelligence.” The “Workshops for Students” section lists past and upcoming workshops. However, it has not automatically been updated since, as of April 2025, two workshops on January 23, 2025, and March 18, 2025, are still listed as “upcoming.”

The instructor version of the libguide includes many other resources not presented in the student version (though there exists a link to the instructor version within the student version, and vice-versa). The front page of the instructor version is entitled “AI Literacy in the Age of ChatGPT,” and unlike its student equivalent gives a more precise statement about the scope of the libguide: “We cover only AI that can generate text, images, video, music, or speech. Examples: ChatGPT, Microsoft Copilot, Gemini, Perplexity, Adobe Firefly, Midjourney, Eleven Labs, and more”

(Hennig et al., 2023b). There are also links to video tutorials about "artificial intelligence," notably some from the University of Pennsylvania, and, curiously, only a brief statement about AI literacy at the bottom of the page (despite the ostensible purpose of this front page being stated as centering around AI literacy). Other sections in the instructor version are more detailed, starting with "ChatGPT and Pedagogy," which suggests consulting with liaison librarians about specific questions concerning classroom applications for "artificial intelligence." A "Teaching Ideas" subsection discusses specific examples of how other universities, namely Harvard and the Wharton School at the University of Pennsylvania, incorporated "artificial intelligence" into their practices, listing relevant readings as well. Interestingly, the University of Arizona is the only one of the examined libguides to have a section on "AI Detection Tools," which immediately begins with a subsection entitled "Many educators do not support the use of AI writing detectors," explaining:

These detectors result in false negatives and positives, which can result in tagging a student paper as written by AI when it was not. In addition, if your native language is not English, these tools will often tag your writing as written by AI. (Hennig et al., 2023b)

It suggests always informing students whenever "artificial intelligence" detection is being used and gives a sample of what a classroom policy on "artificial intelligence" use looks like, supplementing this with various links to already-extant policies in other institutions. The instructor version of "Citing Generative AI" again suggests discussing "artificial intelligence" citation and usage openly with students, also suggesting asking students to include an appendix in their papers listing any prompts given to an "artificial intelligence" tool during their research. It also lists "artificial intelligence" citation policies from several major academic publishers, including Taylor & Francis and Cambridge University Press.

"Effective Use of ChatGPT & Other Models" is almost identical to the "Using ChatGPT Effectively" section from the student version of the libguide, with the addition of a page offering guidelines for constructing syllabus statements about generative "artificial intelligence." A section on "Copyright Issues" follows (and, curiously, is not given any equivalent in the student version), talking about the uncertain legality of copyrighting content generated by "artificial intelligence," offers multiple perspectives (with accompanying links) on whether or not data used to train "artificial intelligence" can be considered fair use or not, and discusses the Creative Commons approach to "artificial intelligence," which diverges from legal perspectives on copyright. It is uncertain why it was deemed that instructors would need access to this copyright information, whereas students would not. The "How UA Libraries Can Help" section offers a concrete methodology for how the library seeks to expound on AI literacy:

Our approach to information literacy allows us to teach students the 'why' instead of only the 'how,' it helps them think of themselves as creators and participants in scholarly communications. It also addresses competencies that students need to develop to become skillful researchers. (Hennig et al., 2023b)

To scaffold this, the page includes links to library consultation pages and tutorials devised by library staff and instructors. The "Additional Readings" section groups its many external links into several categories: "AI Literacy," "Understanding the Technology," "Using Language Models Effectively," "Teaching Resources," and "Ethical Issues." This last category is notable in that neither the student nor instructor versions of the libguide have any explicit section or area dedicated to the ethics of "artificial intelligence" usage.

Adaptability

The unique approach of separating the libguide into two distinct forms would initially imply an equality of content between each one; the libguide skews heavily towards resources for instructors rather than students, even though conceivably students might gain an equal (or even greater) amount of usability out of some aspects of the instructor version, especially the sections on copyright and detection. Data science and technical considerations are of chief importance to both versions of the libguide, with the notable exception of the interactive multimedia guide, serving as an apt usage of the libguide(s) in fostering audiovisual creativity amongst its users. Though not especially prominent, the instructor version of the guide includes an explicit definition of AI literacy for the guide, positing that an AI literate user would be able to "critically evaluate AI technologies," "communicate and collaborate effectively with AI," and "use AI as a tool online, at home, and in the workplace" (Hennig et al., 2023b). Notably, this description is not appended to the student version as well, which is more concerned with the academic integrity aspects of "artificial intelligence." Indeed, it gives the impression that the sole purpose of the student libguide version is to prevent cheating, or at least that this purpose is much more emphasized than introducing "AI" proficiency to students. Faculty proficiency is given greater attention. Except for the aforementioned interactive multimedia presentation, most of the content on both libguides has been derived from other university libraries. Presumably, the university's "artificial intelligence" workshops are where more original or purpose-built content can be found.

Addressing Institutional Needs

While the libguide is excellent at fostering communication and interdepartmental exchanges between other University of Arizona departments, it is unclear from the libguides themselves what students are interested in using "artificial intelligence" for. In contrast, instructors have multiple complex venues to pursue their interests. Similarly, it is equally unclear what programs or initiatives are specific to the University of Arizona that these materials would be used to supplement.

University of Waterloo

Guide Construction

A fairly far-reaching yet succinct statement is used to introduce how this libguide approaches the conceptual basis of "artificial intelligence," stating:

As ChatGPT and similar generative AI technologies rapidly evolve, citation styles may change as new information becomes available. Please be sure to check back for any updates. If you have questions regarding ChatGPT or other generative artificial intelligence software not covered in this guide, please consult the FAQ from the Associate Vice-President, Academic's Office. Note: Some assignments do not permit using ChatGPT or AI tools. Please confirm with your course instructor or TA if a ChatBot tool is permitted. If using a ChatBot, you must cite the content used to avoid Academic Misconduct. (Weaver & Muñoz Gómez, 2023)

The libguide itself is listed as having two contributors: Kari D. Weaver, an instructional design librarian and Program Manager of Artificial Intelligence and Machine Learning for the Ontario Council of University Librarians Librarians (Weaver, 2025), and Antonio Muñoz Gómez, the University of Waterloo library's Cataloging and Metadata Librarian (Muñoz Gómez, 2025). Apart from the aforementioned statement of purpose, the front page is a landing area for the other sections of the libguide.

Further sections of the libguide include "Why is citation important?," "AI-generated content and citation," "Finding information with ChatGPT - Considerations," "Generative AI Resource list," "The Assignment Dilemma," "AI tools for research," and "Attribution and the AID Framework." "Why is citation important?" gives a brief overview of the purpose of scholarly citation in general, though not specifically to "artificial intelligence or anything attendant to it. The suggestion put forward in this section is that the libguide's primary focus is on academic integrity. "AI-generated content and citation" gives links and illustrated examples of citing "artificial intelligence"-generated resources in major citation styles (including APA, Chicago, IEEE, JAMA, and MLA). The colorful and succinct diagrams also briefly illustrate each citation style's approach to the allowance of "artificial intelligence" content in scholarly or professional publications.

The "Finding information with ChatGPT - Considerations" section is a landing page for three sub-pages: "Incorrect bibliographic references," "Potential for bias based on prompt," and "False and outdated information." Note that all three are explicitly negative aspects of the information-gathering process, somewhat belying the title's stated intent. The pages seem more rooted in avoiding pitfalls and presenting the results of such information wholly as cautionary; note also that the sub-pages are somewhat awkward to navigate. The "Incorrect bibliographic citations" sub-page states, "When prompted, ChatGPT may generate text that includes accurate-looking citations. However, it is important to verify the existence of the sources and the accuracy of the information obtained from them" (Weaver & Muñoz Gómez, 2023). This statement is scaffolded by visual examples of screenshots from ChatGPT conversations asking for references to scholarly sources (albeit from a now outdated version of the tool, although the central issues elucidated by the sub-page are still relevant). The sub-page warns that although a source was obtained via the example, "...the existence of this source does not mean that the information presented in ChatGPT's response comes from this report, or that it has been properly understood and summarized" (Weaver & Muñoz Gómez, 2023). Note also that the libguide generally provides text transcriptions of screenshots of "artificial intelligence" interactions, presumably as an accessibility feature in case the images do not load for a particular user. The second sub-page, "Potential for bias based on prompt," explains itself thusly:

When researching traditional Library resources (such as the catalog or databases), you may find resources by combining keywords and Boolean operators and using facets that filter data. The output is usually a list of resources you must look through and identify most relevant to your research question. By contrast, ChatGPT takes prompts using natural language, and the responses focus less on identifying specific resources and more on summarizing information. For this reason, special attention should be paid to the wording used in the prompt, as it could bias the type of reply obtained. (Weaver & Muñoz Gómez, 2023)

This, incidentally, is an indirect way for the libguide to discuss prompt engineering, which it for some reason does not explicitly discuss. To reinforce its point, the libguide provides three examples of ChatGPT interactions in which a user asks the same question in three different tones (and with terminology appropriate to each tone), producing three different (and, according to the libguide, increasingly more balanced and informative) answers. The third sub-page, "False and outdated information," notes that "ChatGPT may respond to prompts with false and/or outdated information. Just as you would with any research, it is important to fact-check and use additional, authoritative sources of information before taking ChatGPT's answer as definitive" (Weaver & Muñoz Gómez, 2023). There is a particular emphasis on medical information in this section, i.e., as an example of data that is particularly sensitive to this problem. The example ChatGPT interaction used to demonstrate this sensitivity presents a result that is outdated and unable to consider multiple valid yet divergent viewpoints, making it range from oversimplified to wrong.

The libguide continues with the "Generative AI Resources list" section, which has its own sub-page, "University of Waterloo on Generative AI," which, like the previous sub-pages, is not immediately noticeable by ordinary web navigation. The main section contains an extensive list of external resources divided into categories: "Terminology," which includes glossaries and references on "artificial intelligence" jargon; "Pedagogical Uses of Generative Artificial Intelligence," for the use of "artificial intelligence" in education, "Ethical Considerations and Uses of Generative Artificial Intelligence," which provides multiple perspectives on the subject from various sources, and "Editorial and Research Considerations for Generative Artificial Intelligence," for academic and publication resources. The "University of Waterloo on Generative AI" sub-page lists links to resources specifically made or endorsed by the university, seemingly those primarily made by or for faculty members. This includes several pages made courtesy of campus organizations such as the Artificial Intelligence Group and Artificial Intelligence Institute, several business-oriented resources, and a link to a (seemingly now-defunct) "artificial intelligence" podcast produced by the university. One fascinating section is "The Assignment Dilemma," which is an interactive visual presentation widget created using the presentation "artificial intelligence" application Genially. In it, a hypothetical student considers the use of "artificial intelligence" to help complete an assignment, presenting the user with a set of gamebook-style decisions about not only the usage of "artificial intelligence" in the assignment itself but the subsequent set of decisions about whether to come forward about such usage and how. It is a unique method for presenting the often-abstract considerations about "artificial intelligence" in a visually engaging manner, and makes the libguide stand out from its contemporaries.

The "AI Tools for Research" section presents a series of tables similar in format to the ones on the Purdue University libguide, and for much the same purpose: evaluating the relative merits of individual "artificial intelligence" tools for use in an academic context. A disclaimer is given stating that:

These tables are not intended to endorse the tools presented but a sample of tools that Librarians and Library co-op students have tested to learn more about their capabilities and limitations. In some cases, the library team only had access to information provided on the tool's website, without proper access to the tool itself (for example, due to account or paid membership requirements) (Weaver & Muñoz Gómez, 2023)

All the tools are evaluated via the following criteria: “Tool name,” “Data source” (i.e., what the system is trained on, like GPTs, user-generated content, existing web content, etc.) “Cost,” “Use case,” (the purpose that the tool is ostensibly for), “Literature searching,” (i.e., whether it can perform that function or not, most of the tools examined can), “Interactive citation network map,” (again, whether or not the tool has one), “Full-text analyzing and summarizing,” (once again, a binary consideration as to whether it can do so), “Generating answers to research questions,” (another binary “yes” or “no” consideration), “Integration with referencing software,” (and what sources the tool would import or export to do so), and “Additional features.” The tools are categorized as “Discovery tools” (Connected Papers, Consensus, Elicit, Enago Read, Inciteful, Iris AI, Keenious, Lateral, Nested Knowledge, Perplexity. ai, PICO Portal, ResearchRabbit, Scite, and Semantic Scholar), “Workflow tools” (Catchii, ChatPDF, Iris AI [listed again], Scholarcy, and SciSpace), and “Writing tools” (Rephrase and Trinka).

“Attribution and the AID Framework” revolves mainly around a proposed system of acknowledgment about using “artificial intelligence” resources devised by Weaver in a paper published by a college library news publication. The libguide notes, “With the current state of generative artificial intelligence systems, direct citation may not fit a specific use case, and attribution offers a path to transparent disclosure across academic or research work” (Weaver & Muñoz Gómez, 2023). The AID Framework devised by Weaver is presented as an alternative to the methodology of scholarly citation by rethinking the purpose and nature of what the resources cited represent. Her paper, “The Artificial Intelligence Disclosure (AID) Framework: An Introduction,” states:

Unfortunately, citations do not fully meet the needs of today’s AI-enabled world. Citations emphasize the fixed form of a tangible output. This is incongruent with today’s generative AI systems, where the specific interplay of prompt, model, and model parameters creates a unique output that is not always repeatable, reproducible, or recallable, depending on the technology. (Weaver, K.D., 2024, p. 407)

She outlines the conceptual underpinnings of this “AID Framework,” stating that her goal is to “provide transparency to the use of AI tools throughout the writing process, ensuring clarity at a level that is both detailed enough to be informative and short enough to avoid being onerous” (Weaver, K.D., 2024, p. 408). Using the paper as its basis, the guide presents Weaver's idea as a format for utilizing headings about explicating individual aspects of “artificial intelligence” usage, giving up to 14 potential headings (which, according to Weaver, are not all required to be used). They are: “Artificial Intelligence Tool(s),” (identifying which ones were used), “Conceptualization” (an brief statement of the original research idea or premise), “Methodology,” (how the project was planned), “Information Collection,” explained as “The use of artificial intelligence to surface patterns in existing literature and identify information relevant to the framing, development, or design of the study" (Weaver & Muñoz Gómez, 2023), "Data Collection Method," i.e. "The development or design of software or instruments used in the study" (Weaver & Muñoz Gómez, 2023), "Execution," i.e. "The direct conduct of research procedures or tasks (e.g. AI web scraping, synthetic surveys, etc.)" (Weaver & Muñoz Gómez, 2023), "Data Curation," (how the collected data was organized), "Data Analysis," (an explanation of any statistical analysis conducted using "artificial intelligence"), "Privacy and Security," (how privacy was screened during "artificial intelligence usage), "Interpretation," i.e. "The use of artificial intelligence tools to categorize, summarize, or manipulate data and suggest associated conclusions" (Weaver & Muñoz Gómez, 2023), "Visualization," (if any visual content was generated), "Writing - Review & Editing," (whether "artificial intelligence" was used in the revision process), "Writing - Translation," (if "artificial intelligence" was used as a language translator at any point), and "Project Administration" (any budgets, timelines, communications, etc. in the course of the project). PDF handouts summarizing the AID Framework are provided in this section as well.

Adaptability

Examples of "artificial intelligence" usage in the libguide seem primarily oriented around science- and health-based concerns. However, the exact nature of its content is still broadly applicable to many different subject areas. There is a clear emphasis on an assumed student user operating the libguide, particularly in light of the interactive presentation and its assumption of no prior familiarity with citation styles on the user's part. The AID Framework is of interest to students despite its applicability beyond purely academic circles. Weaver and Gómez appear more concerned with issues like citation and attribution than AI literacy. However, they may view these issues as equivalencies with each other. AI literacy remains undefined in the body of the libguide. The libguide views "artificial intelligence" as, ideally, a carefully controlled education assistant, which may or may not hinder an understanding of actual proficiency on the part of the end-user (or the student, in this case). There is some indirect consideration of prompt engineering, though it is not treated with any serious examination. An enormous amount of the libguide's content is wholly original and unique, not just in the context of the university but within the library itself. The AID Framework is an ambitious reframing of the perennial issue of "artificial intelligence" citation and has potentially far-reaching applications.

Addressing Institutional Needs

Contributions from the other University of Waterloo abound as features highlighted by the libguide, which suggests that the dictates informing the libguide's creation are equally influential amongst the rest of the college. The existence of the AID Framework implies that the questions it seeks to answer are relevant to personnel beyond just the library, which bears this supposition out. The high number of "artificial intelligence" tools listed as "Discovery tools" implies that their selection is geared towards the classroom needs of that particular institution and which tools would (in the libguide's estimation) best suit the student body's information literacy and research requirements.

CONCLUSION

The panoply of approaches taken by university librarians in constructing their libguides is ample evidence that the increasing prominence of "artificial intelligence" in academia has no single "correct" answer. Regardless of all the study, experimentation, and development these education professionals undertake, it is easy to forget that "artificial intelligence," as it is understood today, is still in its infancy. The totality of its impact on society has yet to be measured. It would be advisable to approach "artificial intelligence" in the context of academia and library science with an open mind and inquisitive instincts. As this chapter has demonstrated, this is undoubtedly the modus for university librarians, who have seized the opportunity to advance the field of "artificial intelligence" instruction in novel and enlightening ways.

REFERENCES

Bringsjord, S., & Govindarajulu, N. S. (2018, July 12). *Artificial Intelligence*. Stanford Encyclopedia of Philosophy Archive. https://plato.stanford.edu/archives/sum2020/entries /artificial-intelligence/

Clarke, E. (2021, April 27). *What is a subject guide?* Marist University. https://marist.libanswers.com/faq/343816

Cox, A. (2024, October 9). Algorithmic Literacy, AI Literacy and Responsible Generative AI Literacy. *Journal of Web Librarianship*, *18*(3), 93–110. DOI: 10.1080/19322909.2024.2395341

Davis, M. (2022). An Exploration of the Emergence of Machine Consciousness and the Risk of Robocentrism. *Journal of Artificial Intelligence and Consciousness*, *9*(3), 385–407. Advance online publication. DOI: 10.1142/S2705078522500114

Hakala-Ausperk, C. (2024). The Experimental Library: A Guide to Taking Risks, Failing Forward, and Creating Change. *Public Libraries*, *63*(3), 53–55. Retrieved April 9, 2025, from https://ez.lib.jjay.cuny.edu/login?url=https://www.proquest.com/magazines/experimental-library-guide-aking-risks-failing/docview/3163936979/se-2

Hennig, N. (2018, January 13). *About Nicole Hennig*. Nicolehennig.com. https://nicolehennig.com/bio/

Hennig, N., Halla, M., Pagowsky, N., & Wallace, N. (2023, May 26). *Student guide to ChatGPT*. The University of Arizona. https://libguides.library.arizona.edu/students-chatgpt

Hennig, N., Halla, M., Pagowsky, N., & Wallace, N. (2023, May 26). *AI Literacy in the Age of ChatGPT*. The University of Arizona. https://libguides.library.arizona .edu/ai-literacy-instructors

Hillier, M. (2023, March 30). *A proposed AI literacy framework*. Teche. https://teche.mq.edu.au/2023/03/a-proposed-ai-literacy-framework/

Ko, C. R., & Chiu, M. H. (2024, October 25). How Can Academic Librarians Support Generative AI Literacy: An Analysis of Library Guides Using the ACRL Information Literacy Framework. *Proceedings of the Association for Information Science and Technology*, *61*(1), 977–979. DOI: 10.1002/pra2.1159

Lu, J. (2024, January 6). *Artificial Intelligence (AI)*. Purdue Libraries. https://guides .lib.purdue.edu/ai

Meakin, L. (2024, September 23). Exploring the Impact of Generative Artificial Intelligence on Higher Education Students' Utilization of Library Resources: A Critical Examination. *Information Technology and Libraries*, *43*(3), 1–13. DOI: 10.5860/ital.v43i3.17246

Muñoz Gómez, A. (2025). *Antonio Muñoz Gómez*. University of Waterloo. https://uwaterloo.ca/library/about/people/antonio-munoz-gomez

Purdue Libraries. (2025). *Jing Lu*. Purdue University. https://lib.purdue.edu/people/lu59/

Qadhi, S. M., Alduais, A., Chaaban, Y., & Khraisheh, M. (2024, June 2). Generative AI, Research Ethics, and Higher Education Research: Insights from a Scientometric Analysis. *Information (Basel)*, *15*(6), 325. DOI: 10.3390/info15060325

University of Toronto. (2025). *Cathryn Copper*. University of Toronto, John H. Daniels Faculty of Architecture, Landscape, and Design. https://www.daniels.utoronto.ca/people/staff/cathryn-copper

Weaver, K. D. (2024). The artificial intelligence disclosure (AID) framework: An introduction. *C&RL News*, *85*(10), 407–411. DOI: 10.5860/crln.85.10.407

Weaver, K. D. (2025). *Kari D. Weaver*. University of Waterloo. https://uwaterloo.ca/scholar/kdweaver

Weaver, K. D., & Muñoz Gómez, A. (2023, February 27). *ChatGPT and Generative Artificial Intelligence (AI)*. University of Waterloo. https://subjectguides.uwaterloo.ca/chatgpt_generative_ai

KEY TERMS AND DEFINITIONS

Academic Integrity: The set of standards ensuring the ethical and fair presentation of student materials, e.g., a lack of plagiarism, proper citation and attribution, etc.

Artificial Intelligence (AI) Literacy: A subset of information literacy concerning a user's understanding of and proficiency with "artificial intelligence" tools.

Hallucination: In the context of "artificial intelligence," a set of responses based on a faulty premise or incorrect prompting resulting in false or otherwise inappropriate results.

Information Literacy: A measure of how adept a user is at extracting knowledge from media sources, physical, electronic, or otherwise.

Library and Information Science (LIS): The field of study for librarians and professionals, encompassing all physical, electronic, and organizational aspects of librarianship, archival, and/or data management.

Library Subject Guide (Libguide): An electronic resource, usually created as part of a university library website, about a particular topic or field of study, usually providing advice about using library resources, best practices, and links to external resources.

Prompt: A written query or instructions from an "artificial intelligence" tool.

Prompt Engineering: The study of how to best format and deliver written queries or instructions given to "artificial intelligence" tools.

Widget: A distinct, often-interactable section of a web page.

Chapter 8
Teaching the Past With the Future:
AI-Supported Lesson Design for Pre-Service History Teachers

Ayşegül Nihan Erol Şahin
https://orcid.org/0000-0001-6320-982X
Gazi University, Turkey

ABSTRACT

This chapter explores the integration of generative artificial intelligence (GenAI) tools into history education, focusing on a pedagogical module developed for pre-service teachers at a public university in Turkey. It examines how GenAI can enhance teaching practices by supporting lesson planning, creating differentiated assessments, and fostering historical thinking through interactive simulations and content generation. The chapter outlines the design and implementation of a four-session teaching module, highlights participants' reflections, and discusses the potential of AI-supported educational platforms like ChatGPT, Diffit, Humy.ai, and Canva AI. It also presents empirical findings from qualitative feedback and analyzes concerns related to ethics, data privacy, accessibility, and critical thinking. The study concludes with practical recommendations for teacher educators and policymakers, emphasizing the need for inclusive access, ethical integration, and ongoing professional development to effectively embed GenAI in history classrooms.

DOI: 10.4018/979-8-3373-2612-2.ch008

INTRODUCTION

Generative Artificial Intelligence and Its Use in History Education

The 21st century has initiated an era of unprecedented technological advancement that has transformed every aspect of our lives, including education. The teaching and learning processes have significantly diverged from traditional methods used in the past, with the adoption of technological tools in our country and many countries worldwide in recent years, ranging from interactive whiteboards to personalized learning platforms. Generative Artificial Intelligence (Gen AI), which has become very popular quickly, is one of these developments. Before delving into generative artificial intelligence, examining the earlier steps taken in developing artificial intelligence is helpful. As with many technologies today, the step-by-step journey of artificial intelligence (AI), from conceptual theories to practical applications, has significantly affected various sectors, especially education. The term "artificial intelligence" was first introduced during the Dartmouth Conference in 1956, marking the official beginning of artificial intelligence as a field of study (McCarthy et al., 1955). Early developments, such as the invention of the perceptron in 1958, laid the groundwork for machine learning and neural networks (Rosenblatt, 1958). At that time, a debate initiated by Alan Turing's question "Can machines think?" also found resonance in Turkey and was addressed by mathematician Cahit Arf in his 1959 lecture titled "Can Machines Think and How Do They Think?" (Arf, 1959). Arf stated that machines could approach human thought with their ability to use language, perform calculations, draw analogies, and eliminate options. However, he also drew attention to the challenges of imitating human-specific qualities such as aesthetic consciousness by machines (Sarı, 2021). Since then, artificial intelligence has evolved into more comprehensive systems.

Generative artificial intelligence is a technology that collects, analyzes, and generates human-like outputs using its algorithms. One of the earliest examples of this technology that can create new content ranging from text and images to audio and code, 'ChatGPT' has been widely adopted in many sectors since its free release in 2022 (Gökçearslan et al., 2024, p. 1). This breakthrough, which is interesting for many sectors, has continued with various companies' launch of more advanced models. To exemplify, applications such as 'Gemini,' 'Bing AI,' 'Microsoft Copilot,' 'DeepSeek' and 'Grok' have started to be used by many people. These tools, which have been used in many areas with their paid and free versions, have also been actively used in education. Although these tools present both advantages and challenges, especially in education, it has been indicated in the reports that they have quickly become an effective and significant resource in this field (UNESCO, 2024, p. 7).

The question arises as to how generative artificial intelligence tools, which have started to be used in many courses within the field of education, can be utilized explicitly in history lessons. As is well known, before the 2000s, history lessons were generally dominated by traditional methods, in which textbooks and direct instruction were at the forefront. For this reason, they were considered among the more static lessons compared to other scientific disciplines. However, recent technological developments have opened the door to fundamental changes in the presentation and implementation of history lessons, as in all areas of education. Today, history lessons benefiting from these innovative technologies have become more dynamic, interactive, and engaging (Erol-Şahin, 2023). Since the beginning of the 2000s, various theses, academic articles, and national and international projects have been conducted regarding the use of technology in history education. These studies have addressed technological components such as internet forums, animation-supported applications, in-class digital tools and materials, historical films, wall calendars, activity sheets, and multimedia applications. Looking at the technologies examined in these recent studies, it becomes evident that many applications previously seen as complex and difficult to access can now be realized in a much shorter time and at a lower cost through generative artificial intelligence (Gen AI) tools. Also known as Gen AI, these tools have a wide range of applications, from text generation to creating visual and auditory content, from data analysis to language translation. Researchers have conducted studies focused on using these tools in history education and have referred to this field as "Artificial Intelligence in History Education" (AIHEd). Within this broad framework, Artificial Intelligence in History Education (AIHEd) is a subfield in which artificial intelligence technologies are specifically applied to enhance historical inquiry, analysis, and understanding. Various technological opportunities, such as automated document processing, historical simulations, and intelligent tutoring systems, are utilized (Kumar et al., 2023).

Gen AI-Supported Teaching Tools for Use in History Lessons

Innovative history educators who aim to transmit knowledge of the past through future technology can benefit from these applications in various areas, including content creation, activity design, historical event analysis, alternative scenarios regarding controversial topics, and contextual interpretation. For instance, under the guidance and supervision of history teachers, students can reimagine historical scenarios through AI-supported platforms, construct alternative historical narratives, and question the possible outcomes of decisions made in the past. In addition, with the help of highly realistic simulations and virtual reality applications, they may have the opportunity to experience the events that took place thousands of years ago as if they were living in those very moments. AI-supported drawing programs can assist students in concretizing and visualizing abstract historical concepts—such as ancient cities, castles, battlefields, war tools used during those periods, or scenes from daily life. Moreover, with augmented reality (AR) technology, it has become possible for students to "realistically" visualize the historical background of archaeological sites, the grandeur of ancient civilizations, and the original appearance of artifacts as they were thousands of years ago. Similarly, artifacts from ancient periods exhibited in museums and often difficult for visitors to comprehend can now be animated using AI-supported 3D visualizations and interactive simulations; thereby, museums and historical sites can offer visitors a much richer and more realistic experience. For example, as a part of the 'The Ara It Was' project at the Pacis Museum in Rome, the artifacts in the Ara Pacis Augustae were brought to life with 3D-colored animations, computer graphics, and augmented reality applications. With VR headsets, visitors can view these artifacts as they originally appeared (Trunfio et al., 2021). In Turkey, some fascinating and pioneering studies have recently been carried out in this area. For instance, in a recent study, a detailed 3D model was created using high-tech scanning devices for the only deformed skull known to date back to the Roman period in Anatolia, which was discovered during archaeological excavations at the ancient city of Juliopolis. In this study, each step of the modeling process was explained in detail, and based on the data obtained, a visual reconstruction was produced to represent the possible appearance of the individual to whom the skull belongs in that period (Sertalp, Moraes & Bütün, 2024).

Based on such innovative studies and projects, a history teacher working at a high school can show students the steps of this modeling during a lesson on ancient civilizations by only using the smart board or projector available in the school. In the continuation of the lesson, the teacher may plan a series of interactive learning experiences such as empathy-based activities, role-playing exercises, or creative writing tasks to establish a deeper connection with the individual who once lived in the past and better understand their life. In this way, history lessons can go beyond mere channels of factual information and be transformed into a journey of discovering and understanding the past, enriched by the active participation of students.

Research on the use of generative artificial intelligence in education has revealed that tools like ChatGPT can be effective in functions such as preparing customized lesson plans tailored to individual learning styles and interests of students and prospective teachers, creating exam questions and making analysis, organizing interactive discussions for lessons, and designing educational games, and can also support personalized learning experiences (Baidoo-Anu & Owusu Ansah, 2023; Lo, 2023; Xu, 2024). It is well known that individual needs are very crucial during teaching activities. However, it is challenging for teachers, especially in overcrowded classrooms, to allocate time to address these needs while keeping up with the curriculum. This is where artificial intelligence support can come into play. It enables teachers to adjust based on individual needs while planning lessons, performing analyses, and generating reports based on student performance and interests. It allows teachers to make more effective plans and simplify tasks (Onesi-Ozigagun, 2024). As an example of generative AI-supported lesson planning, the researchers designed and implemented an AI-supported educational game in a study conducted by Yang and Boulom (2024). According to the researchers, this approach appeals to different learning styles by allowing students to participate in historical events actively and facilitates a deeper understanding of the subject. In another study that describes the process of using ChatGPT as a pedagogical tool in history lessons, ChatGPT generated content for sections on Native American history in American textbooks and asked the students to analyze these contents, which were produced using Eurocentric narratives. Researchers using artificial intelligence as a critical teaching tool have concluded that these activities enable students to learn the subject more thoroughly (Washburn & McCutchen, 2024). In their study, Díaz-Sánchez and Chapinal-Heras (2023) explained how Midjourney, an AI-supported drawing program, was used in teaching the subject of classical antiquity. There are interesting studies on ancient periods that are difficult to understand and explain in history classes. In one of these studies, researchers created a virtual environment where daily life in Sumerians around 3000 BC was revived using AI-supported 3D avatars. The researchers divided the students into three groups: one interacted with the virtual environment, another participated in a documentary-supported lesson on the topic, and the third was provided with a lesson plan with reading texts. The study results revealed that students who wandered in the virtual environment and interacted with the Avatars who gave AI-supported answers living in the ancient city performed 20% better in a mini-exam than the other groups. In another study, the researchers observed that the motivations of the students who interact with AI-supported avatars also increased toward lessons (Ijaz, Bogdanovich & Trescak, 2017). Similar to this study, AI-supported avatars can be used in digital historical games prepared with the support of educators. In popular educational games like Minecraft Edu, it is thought that with the support of chatbots, students can reinforce their learning by asking questions to any avatar within a historical scenario and receiving responses. Many well-known educational applications worldwide also use AI-supported chatbots. One of them is the Khan Academy's 'Khanmigo' application. Their website describes the application: "*Khanmigo is an AI-supported personal tutor and teaching assistant developed by Khan Academy to enhance the learning experience for students and support educators in their teaching efforts*" (Khanmigo.ai, n.d.). Like this application, 'Diffit' is an AI-supported educational platform that helps teachers create their course content quickly and effectively. Users who obtain the paid full version can input any topic, text, or YouTube video. Diffit can summarize the content, identify keywords, and generate multiple-choice and open-ended questions suitable for students' levels (diffit.me, n.d.). With these 24/7 accessible applications that make learning interactive and fun, it is considered that learning can become easier and thinking skills can be developed. The studies conducted in these areas also support this. In the studies by Alenezi (2023) and Sheng (2023), it is stated that the proper use of generative artificial intelligence tools can help develop fundamental skills in students, such as independent thinking and creativity. It is also considered that the availability of many of these tools for free, albeit limited, may help eliminate socioeconomic inequalities in education by providing equal access to these resources and personalized learning pathways (Abbas et al., 2023; Edeni, 2024). Furthermore, it is thought that educators' utilization of platforms developed with artificial intelligence can enable all students to meaningfully interact with historical content in an inclusive manner (Edeni, 2024). This situation may facilitate teachers' efforts in teaching controversial topics, particularly in the context of history education, understanding different perspectives, concretizing abstract concepts, and accessing resources written in foreign languages. In addition to all these studies, Altun (2022), in his study where he provides examples related to digital history, states that artificial intelligence is a powerful tool in digital historiography due to its ability to update texts and enrich them through continuous collaboration. For instance, the collective editing features that allow for the continuous and detailed development of biographies of historical figures on Wikipedia can contribute to users' acquisition of a dynamic perception of history. Moreover, visualizations offered through digital tools (such as maps, graphs, and 3D animations) can make historical information more comprehensible and interactive, thereby concretizing abstract concepts. Through crowdsourcing projects, artificial intelligence may contribute to creating digital archives enriched by student and community contributions.

Based on these studies, the question of how a history teacher can benefit from generative artificial intelligence tools in their lessons can be addressed through specific strategies and application examples:

1. These tools can help teachers create lesson plans that help reduce their workload. They can also be used to prepare exams tailored to specific topics and learning objectives and generate worksheets and classroom activities. In an applied study conducted in an art history course, students used ChatGPT-4o to practice prompt engineering by performing tasks such as identifying the ten most frequently mentioned cities in Vasari's *Lives*, with roles ranging from basic summarization to advanced data extraction through Python scripting. The findings showed that assigning generative AI varied roles and using more detailed prompts significantly improved the quality and depth of the outputs (Guo, 2024, pp. 58–64).

Many applications are available that can perform similar tasks. ‘Curipod’ and ‘Canva AI offers easy access to ready-made content for history teachers, while 'Kialo Edu benefits history-based argumentative activities. Some of these applications also offer free access for students and educators.

There is a clear distinction between giving a simple command to a generative AI tool and crafting a well-developed prompt. In social sciences, tools like ChatGPT can be guided more effectively by assigning them a specific persona—such as a historian, data analyst, or a renowned author—and clearly outlining how they should respond. This approach allows the system to align its vast knowledge base with the characteristics of the assumed identity (Al Lily, 2024; Guo, 2024). From this perspective, students in history classes can be guided to engage more deeply with academic sources and conduct close readings of historical documents. Teachers may also design alternative lesson formats that integrate students' ideas and imaginative approaches, helping them explore historical content differently.

2. Assignments can be tailored to individual students by generating multiple versions of the same task through AI tools. To minimize the risk of plagiarism and copying, a base assignment created by the teacher can be entered into the tool, and detailed prompts can be used to produce differentiated versions for each student.

3. Students often face challenges grasping the flow of time and developing a sense of chronology. Interactive timelines can be created and integrated into the lesson to support these skills. One such tool is introduced below. Educators can design engaging and interactive history lessons by combining this tool's maps with platforms like ChatGPT.

Figure 1. The timemaps application discovery page screenshot

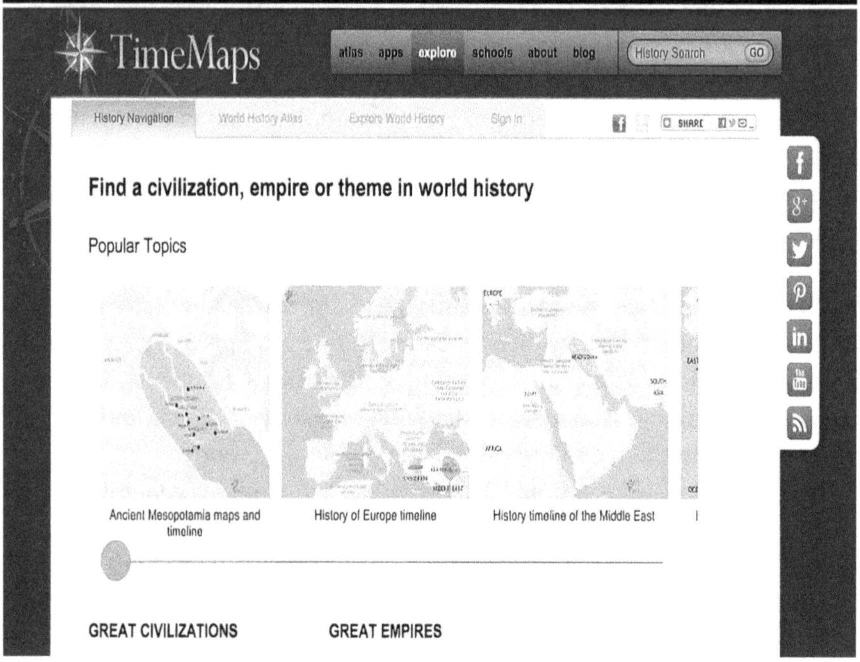

Source: https://timemaps.com/history/.

4. There are other tools are similar to 'Timemaps'. Among these, 'Mylens,' which we had the opportunity to experience in our lessons, is an application that can transform the historical information you provide in the text into a structured timeline. In addition, 'Tiki-Toki' facilitates the visual connection between events with the possibility of creating 3D timelines. At the same time, 'ClioVis' allows students to better grasp cause-and-effect relationships by combining historical data on a temporal and conceptual plane. 'Histropedia,' 'with the support of the Wikipedia database, enables students to place historical events on the time axis with great integrity; 'Sutori,' with its interactive storytelling and timeline features, can contribute to the development of students' ability to narrate and construct historical events. A similar application we have used in our courses is Mylens, a platform that can transform historical text into structured timelines. Another tool, like Tiki-Toki, enables the creation of 3D timelines, making it easier for students to visualize connections between events. ClioVis helps students connect historical data across time and concepts, fostering cause-and-effect reasoning. Histropedia uses Wikipedia data to place events on a broader timeline, while Sutori combines interactive storytelling and timelines to support historical narration and organization. AI tools can also simulate interviews with historical figures through role-play activities in

history lessons. For example, a student might "interview" Ibn Sina using a chatbot interface, asking questions about his contributions to science in his time. At the end of the activity, students are expected to evaluate their questions' validity, the answers' accuracy, and the realism of the AI-generated responses. Such tasks develop students' understanding of historical developments and help them critically assess how AI presents knowledge. Research suggests that activities like these can boost motivation and strengthen historical thinking skills (Alenezi, 2023; Díaz-Sánchez & Chapinal-Heras, 2023; Sheng, 2023). One platform designed explicitly for such use is Humy.ai, which describes itself as an AI-powered chatbot system that brings historical figures and concepts to life through personalized dialogue (see Figure 5, retrieved from https://www.humy.ai/).

Figure 2. Historical characters in 'Humy.ai.'

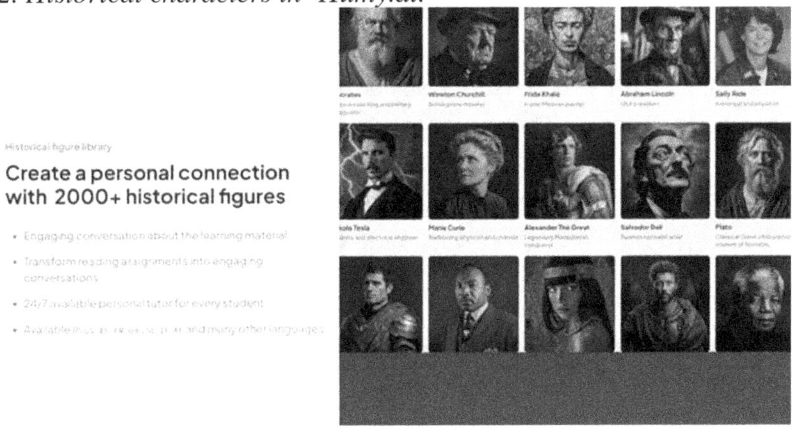

Source: https://www.humy.ai/

Similar platforms include 'Historic Talk,' 'Character.ai,' and 'HistoryChatAI,' allowing users to engage with simulated historical personalities based on structured databases. However, teachers must provide clear instructions and contextual guidance to avoid misuse or distortion. Students may risk interpreting historical narratives through present-day values or accepting fictional dialogues as historical facts when used without pedagogical framing. Therefore, such tools must be employed within teacher-guided, source-based, and context-driven learning activities. Another practical use of GenAI tools is summarizing historical texts and academic articles. AI platforms can extract and structure key ideas for easier reading, making them especially useful for teaching literature review skills and academic synthesis. AI tools can also support teaching controversial topics in history by facilitating access to diverse sources. Teachers can use the tools to scan both local and international literature, extract keywords, and analyze documents. This helps students engage with multiple perspectives and spot patterns across large datasets. Creative tools such as 'DALL·E 32' and 'Midjourney' can generate historical illustrations based on prompts, allowing students to compare AI-generated visuals with original images and reflect on the sources that inform AI-generated content. In addition, teachers with limited proficiency in foreign languages can use AI to translate primary sources, enabling them to introduce original documents into class and help students explore authentic historical expressions. In the social sciences, several digital tools have been developed to facilitate the transcription and interpretation of historical documents—particularly those in older or less accessible languages such as Ottoman Turkish. The visual above showcases examples of such tools. 'Transkribus' is an advanced platform using AI-driven handwriting recognition to transcribe historical manuscripts with increasing accuracy. 'LexiQamus' is a linguistic search engine designed to help users decipher rare words in Ottoman Turkish texts. 'Digital Ottoman Studies (DOS)' is an interdisciplinary initiative combining digital mapping, text analysis, and archival materials on the Ottoman Empire. The image also includes ChatGPT, demonstrating its ability to assist in translating and contextualizing Ottoman texts when properly prompted. These platforms show how AI and digital humanities projects can support historians, educators, and students navigate historical archives and paleographic work.

Figure 3. Screenshot of tools for transcription and interpretation of historical documents

Source: https://www.lexiqamus.com/tr

Another area of use includes data analysis of exam results and class performance, helping educators adjust their instruction accordingly. Among the numerous free and paid AI platforms, one noteworthy example is 'Planit Teachers'. According to the platform's website, "Planit Teachers offers dynamic and informative lesson plans enhanced with AI, including interactive timelines, virtual museum tours, and primary source analysis, all designed to bring history to life in the classroom" (Planit Teachers, 2024).

Finally, game-based learning is becoming increasingly popular among students beyond these educational tools. A recent study on representations of Turks in historical games (Erdoğan & Erol-Şahin, 2024) showed that such games appeal strongly to young audiences. This raises the question of whether the popularity of history-themed games can be transformed into an educational opportunity. Indeed, several AI-supported educational games developed by NGOs and international education organizations aim to achieve just that. For example, 'Minecraft Education Edition' allows students to explore historical sites—such as building ancient Roman cities block by block—supporting spatial learning in history. 'iCivics,' a platform developed by a U.S.-based nonprofit, offers interactive tasks designed to teach constitutional history and civic education. These platforms allow students to experience historical concepts and track individual progress through AI, offering personalized feedback. In particular, GenAI-powered gamified environments hold great potential for enhancing historical empathy and helping students internalize complex historical processes.

DEVELOPMENT AND IMPLEMENTATION PROCESS OF A GENAI-SUPPORTED COURSE MODULE FOR HISTORY TEACHER CANDIDATES

This section of the study presents the implementation process of a course module designed for history teacher candidates at a public university in Turkey, along with participants' reflections on the experience.

Table 1. Genai-Supported teaching module for history department students

Session Name	Duration	Participants
Introduction to GenAI Tools and Practical Tool Demonstration	50+50 min theoretical, 60 min Zoom, one assignment	Teacher candidates, Researcher, Observer expert
Designing a Lesson Aligned with the Curriculum Using GenAI Tools	Flipped teaching, 50 min theoretical, one pre-design, one post-design, 50 min presentation	Teacher candidates, Researcher, Observer expert
Preparing an Exam Aligned with the Curriculum Using GenAI Tools	Flipped teaching, 50 min theoretical, one pre-design, one post-design, 50 min presentation	Teacher candidates, Researcher, Observer expert
GenAI as a Teaching Assistant	50 min theoretical, 50 min discussion	Teacher candidates, researcher
Presentation of the Prepared Activities	60 min presentation, 20 min discussion, 20 min feedback collection via Google Forms	Teacher candidates, Researcher, Observer expert

Implementation Process of the Module

Before implementing the module, announcements were made via email and WhatsApp groups to reach out to participants willing to join voluntarily. Additionally, separate announcements regarding the schedules of the face-to-face and online sessions were shared, including the necessary meeting links. As outlined in the table, the first week provided general definitions of artificial intelligence (AI) and a brief historical background of these technologies. Following this introduction, a list of AI tools applicable to history teaching, along with their links, was shared with the participants. Participants were also asked to create user accounts for the tools used in the following session and to familiarize themselves with the platforms via the provided links.

The second session of the module was designed using the flipped teaching model. In the previous session, participants had been instructed to download the relevant tools and complete their registration using the shared links. The tools used in this session were ChatGPT-4o and Canva Edu AI. At the beginning of the online session, a task was assigned to all participants: to individually prepare a lesson plan. The task involved selecting a topic and related learning outcomes from the curriculum and designing a 40-minute lesson. The researcher and a doctoral student offered support during the planning process, while another doctoral student participated as an observer. By the end of the session, all participants were expected to submit a Canva file, which was then shared with the researcher as part of the Canva project workspace. Additionally, volunteers presented their lesson plans briefly to the class.

The third session, "Designing a Curriculum-Compatible Exam with GenAI," also included a prior announcement requesting participants to register for the Quizizz platform. The researcher began the session with a hands-on demonstration on preparing different questions using their account. Subsequently, participants were asked to design a 10-question online exam by the given guidelines. After a short break, the other participants implemented one volunteer's quiz in the second part of the session. This was followed by a practical demonstration of analyzing pilot test results.

The final session of the module, titled "GenAI' as a Teaching Assistant," began with a short introduction and a list of volunteer presenters displayed on the screen. Participants gave presentations in order, sharing examples of AI tools they were familiar with and recommending them to the class. Listeners provided feedback and suggestions. After a coffee break, a closing session was held. Feedback on the four-week module was collected from the participants, and the module was officially concluded.

Participants' Views on the Development and Implementation Process of the GenAI-Supported Course Module for Pre-Service History Teachers

In order to convey an overview of participants' opinions on the developed module to the readers of the book chapter, a qualitative research design was adopted for this study. Participants' views were collected via a Google Forms survey during the final session. Data were gathered anonymously, based on the principle of voluntary participation, and stored in an Excel spreadsheet.

A total of 10 participants volunteered for the study, consisting of five females and five male participants. The collected data were transferred into the MAXQDA 2024 qualitative data analysis software. The responses were categorized into common categories and subthemes, and the researcher initiated the coding process. During the coding, emerging themes from participants' responses were identified and subsequently reviewed by subject matter experts.

The consistency of the coding process was ensured through the consensus method proposed by Miles and colleagues (2014). To enhance the study's trustworthiness, all researchers involved in the project actively participated in the data analysis process, thus incorporating multiple perspectives into the findings (Merriam, 2013). Additionally, transparency was maintained throughout the analysis by systematically documenting all steps (codes, themes, and decision stages), ensuring replicability (Yıldırım & Şimşek, 2016). Internal validity was supported by the systematic analysis of official documents (Merriam & Tisdell, 2016).

Coding transparency and replicability were reported following qualitative research standards. Moreover, to further ensure the reliability of the analysis, the complete data pool, including the MAXQDA reports, was securely stored in a shared Google Drive folder managed by the researcher. The survey form included demographic questions such as gender and ownership of technological devices, along with open-ended short-answer and open-ended long-answer questions. Participants' views are presented below as tables and visual representations.

Figure 4. Devices owned by participants

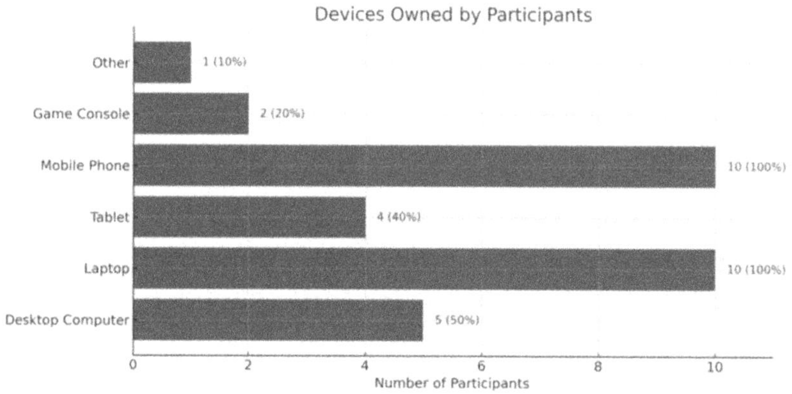

The chart shows that all participants own laptops and mobile phones (100%). Half of the participants (50%) reported owning a desktop computer, while 40% stated that they have a tablet. These results demonstrate that all participants had access to mobile phones and laptops, but ownership of other digital devices was much less consistent.

Table 2. Participants' short descriptions of their experience with generative AI in history education

Theme	Subcodes	Participant Statements
Future and Innovation	Future Technology	Future technology (Participant 1)
	Innovation	Innovation (Participant 8)
Automation and Industry 4.0	Automation	Automation (Participant 7)
	Industry 4.0	Industry 4.0 (Participant 7)
Robots and Robotics	Robots	Robots (Participant 1)
	Humanoid Robots	Humanoid robots (Participant 6)

continued on following page

Table 2. Continued

Theme	Subcodes	Participant Statements
	Fictional Robots	Terminator (Participant 3)
Technical Concepts	Machine Learning	Machine learning (Participant 4)
	Data Analysis	Data analysis (Participant 4)
	Algorithms	Algorithms (Participant 4)
Social and Ethical Impacts	Unemployment	Unemployment (Participant 7
	Future Professions	Future professions (Participant 8)
	Ethics	AI ethics (Participant 6)
AI Applications and Examples	ChatGPT and Chatbots	ChatGPT (Participant 2)
	Smart Assistants	Intelligent assistants (Siri, Alexa)
	Autonomous Vehicles	Support systems (that helps people) (Participant 9)
Support and Convenience for Humans	Support Systems	Support systems (that helps people) (Participant 9)
	Facilitating Daily Life	Facilitating daily life (Participant 5)

Participants ' responses revealed diverse associations when asked to name the first three things that came to mind when thinking about artificial intelligence. These were categorized under key themes, including future-oriented technologies, robotics, automation, and Industry 4.0, technical concepts such as machine learning and algorithms, ethical and social implications, practical applications like chatbots and software tools, and AI's role in assisting human tasks. This variety reflects participants' awareness of current developments in AI and their recognition of its broader societal and educational impact.

Figure 5. Wordcloud of single-word responses regarding the experience of using generative AI in history class

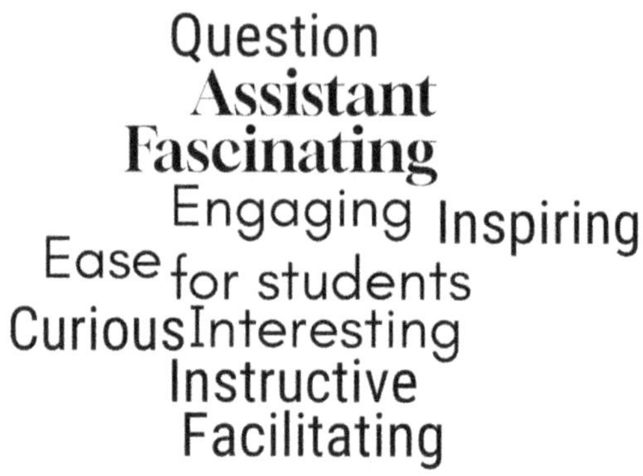

Figure 6. Wordcloud of preferred GenAI Tools and categories for use in history lessons

Participants' responses highlighted various GenAI tools and categories they would like to use more frequently in history lessons. The word cloud reflects their preferences for familiar tools such as AI chatbots, visual generators, and timeline creators and their interest in exploring more specialized educational applications.

In their experiences with these tools, we observed that students became highly creative and engaged. Many participants even recommended additional tools beyond the ones introduced during the module, demonstrating their growing curiosity and critical engagement with emerging technologies. Moreover, several students began following AI-focused scholars and practitioners on academic social platforms, actively sharing these new resources with their classmates and instructors. This enthusiastic adoption suggests that GenAI-supported practices foster independent learning and collaborative exploration among future history educators.

Table 3. Reasons for using GenAI tools in history lessons

Theme	Participant Responses
Skill Development (Historical Thinking, Visual Memory)	- It enhances historical thinking skills, allows one to keep up with current developments, helps keep the approach modern and at the student's level, and stimulates visual memory.
Ease of Access to Information	- To access any information instantly and understandably.
Interaction and Access to Open Resources	- As a teacher, I need it to make history lessons more engaging and to enable students to interact with historical events or phenomena. As a student, I need it because it can approach topics from angles I cannot, access sources that are not publicly available, and generate visuals that I cannot create on my own.
Impact of Visual Presentation	- Visual presentation in class captures students' attention more effectively and leads to more lasting learning; students generally do not forget information supported by visuals. - Visuals are essential in history.
Efficiency and Productivity	- I find it efficient because it makes accessing information easier, speeds up organizing tasks, allows me to see different aspects of a topic, and makes it easier to produce quality output.
Time-Saving and Workload Reduction	- It saves time, giving me more time for myself. It is a fact that teachers will have a much heavier workload in the future; these tools will be helpful in that regard. - To save time.
Increasing Student Participation	- We can make history lessons more enjoyable and easier to understand by using AI tools that capture students' attention and break the perception that history is boring and based on rote memorization. - It is an innovative teaching tool that can capture students' interest and increase their participation.

The participants' reflections on the necessity of using GenAI tools in history lessons reveal a thoughtful and multi-dimensional understanding of these technologies' challenges and opportunities. Their comments suggest that GenAI tools are valued for their novelty and practical contributions to core educational goals: fostering critical historical thinking, enhancing visual memory, supporting student engagement, and streamlining access to diverse information sources.

Notably, the emphasis on saving time and reducing workload reflects a pragmatic awareness of the increasing demands on teachers' professional lives. Simultaneously, participants' focus on visual learning and interactive content highlights a pedagogical shift toward more student-centered, engaging teaching methods.

These participant perspectives are also supported by recent research. For instance, Yang and Boulom (2024) found that AI-supported educational games can enhance effective learning outcomes and address different learning styles. Similarly, Washburn and McCutchen (2024) demonstrated that using AI as a pedagogical tool can create more engaging activities that help develop students' thinking skills. Other studies, such as those by Alenezi (2023), Díaz-Sánchez and Chapinal-Heras (2023), and Sheng (2023), have further confirmed that GenAI-assisted materials in history education can be highly functional, promote historical thinking skills, ease teachers' workload, and help concretize abstract concepts.

Table 4. Participants' concerns about the use of AI in the classroom

Theme	Participant Response
Weakening of Critical Thinking	I am concerned that students may accept readily available information without questioning it, leading to biased and narrow perspectives.
Data Privacy and Security Concerns	Like all digital tools, AI systems collect our data, which could pose future security risks.
Distraction and Misuse Risk	It may be distracting and fail to serve its intended educational purpose.
Plagiarism and Copyright Issues	I am concerned about issues related to plagiarism and copyright violations.
Bias from Western-Centric Sources	Since AI tools often rely on Euro-centric sources, they may present biased information and influence students' perspectives.
Risk of Academic Dishonesty	I am worried about using AI tools for academic dishonesty or cheating.
Impact on Students with Special Educational Needs	Screen use may negatively affect students with special educational needs, especially in inclusive classrooms.
Loss of Curiosity and Motivation	Immediate access to information may diminish students' curiosity and intrinsic motivation to learn.
Dependence and Reduced Effort	There is a risk that students may perceive AI tools not as assistants but as substitutes for their efforts, leading to increased dependency and reduced critical thinking.
Mixed Views: Potential vs Passive Consumption	Even if the teaching potential of AI is recognized, there is a lack of awareness that effective learning still requires conscious effort. Students might remain passive consumers rather than active learners. Alternatively, some participants found its use enjoyable and had no concerns.

Participants' responses indicate a nuanced awareness of the potential risks and limitations associated with using AI tools in educational settings. Several concerns center around the possibility that students may accept information passively without critical evaluation, potentially reinforcing biased or one-sided perspectives. Issues of data privacy, plagiarism, and the risk of academic dishonesty were also frequently mentioned, highlighting ethical dimensions that educators must carefully navigate.

Further supporting participants' concerns, existing research highlights critical risks associated with using GenAI tools in education. Studies by Nocera and Newton (2024), Washbourn and McCutchen (2024), Yang and Boulom (2024), and the UNESCO (2024) report emphasize that generative AI tools can sometimes disseminate inaccurate, biased, or misleading information. Reflecting these findings, participants in the current study stressed the importance of verifying AI-generated content before using it in the classroom, particularly for sensitive or contested topics in Turkish history, where reliable non-native language resources are limited or potentially biased.

Participants also warned that careless integration of GenAI could encourage technology dependency, reduce creativity, and promote academic laziness. These concerns align with broader discussions in the literature on the unintended consequences of AI in education, including algorithmic bias, unequal access to technology, and threats to reliable information ecosystems (Bozkurt et al., 2023; Bozkurt & Sharma, 2023). The evolving role of teachers in managing these risks has been highlighted as a crucial factor in ensuring that AI serves as a tool for empowerment rather than dependency.

Ethical concerns were particularly pronounced among the participants, focusing on plagiarism, data misuse, and the potential for academic dishonesty. Echoing findings by Akkaş, Tosun, and Gökçearslan (2024), Cotton, Cotton, and Shipway (2024), and Polat (2024), participants expressed anxiety that GenAI tools might enable students to outsource assignments or engage in forms of academic misconduct. Moreover, personal data privacy concerns emerged as another critical area, with participants emphasizing the need for vigilance when using AI platforms, especially free services that collect user data. Altun (2022) and others argue that greater attention must be given to the ethical boundaries of crowdsourced AI systems, user consent, and data security.

Altogether, these findings underline the urgent need for transparent, ethical, and regulated frameworks to guide the educational use of generative AI technologies, ensuring that their integration strengthens, rather than undermines, the social fabric of learning environments.

Table 5. Recommendations for teachers on the use of AI tools in history lessons

Theme	Participant Responses
Verification of Information Accuracy and Currency	Teachers should personally test the AI tools they intend to use, ensuring the information provided is accurate, up-to-date, and aligned with the lesson's objectives. Teachers must confirm the accuracy of information before using it, as sometimes AI tools may fabricate information.
Critical and Conscious Use	Teachers should approach AI outputs cautiously and read critically. AI-generated answers should not be accepted at face value; careful attention must be paid to verifying the correctness of information.
Maintaining Pedagogical Purpose and Balance	AI tools should be purposeful, moderate, and limited to what is necessary. Teachers should ensure that using AI tools does not overshadow the learning goals.
Interactive and Critical Engagement with Students	AI tools should be integrated interactively with students, encouraging them to assess the texts and visuals produced by AI critically.
Protection of Personal Data and Privacy	Teachers must be cautious about not sharing students' data with AI systems and ensure the information retrieved maintains data security standards.
Preserving Teacher Creativity and Professional Autonomy	AI can produce information and generate content; teachers should not allow it to diminish their creativity in processing, generating, and teaching knowledge.

The participants' recommendations underscore a sophisticated and balanced understanding of the challenges and responsibilities of integrating AI into educational practices. Emphasis was consistently placed on the critical verification of information, preservation of pedagogical objectives, and conscious engagement with AI outputs. These views align closely with findings from previous studies (e.g., Nocera & Newton, 2024; Washbourn & McCutchen, 2024; UNESCO, 2024), which also caution that AI-generated content may sometimes be inaccurate, biased, or incomplete, thus requiring educators to maintain an active critical stance.

Moreover, participants demonstrated an acute awareness of ethical considerations, particularly regarding data privacy and academic integrity, mirroring concerns noted in broader academic discussions (Bozkurt et al., 2023; Bozkurt & Sharma, 2023). The insistence on protecting teacher creativity and professional judgment further highlights resistance to over-relying on AI systems at the expense of pedagogical authenticity.

Overall, the participants' reflections reveal that the successful integration of AI in history education demands technical proficiency, ethical literacy, critical thinking, and deliberate pedagogical design. These insights suggest that preparing future educators for the AI era must involve more than just tool-oriented training; it must cultivate a critical, ethical, and human-centered approach to technology use in classrooms.

Table 6. Participants' suggestions for improving the GenAI-Supported teaching module

Theme	Participant Response
Sequential Integration of AI Tools into the Curriculum	Both fundamental educational principles and technological opportunities should be considered. First, an introduction to AI should be provided, and its connection to history teaching and the tools to be used should be explained. Students should be allowed to benefit from AI tools integrated into lesson content, and their feedback should be gathered to improve future implementations.
Interactive and Creativity-Focused Planning	The program should be interactive and designed to support students' creativity using various AI tools. Preliminary research is needed to utilize GenAI applications effectively in the course design.
Broadening the Range of AI Tools Beyond ChatGPT	It would be beneficial not to limit the course to ChatGPT. Tools like Deepseek, Gemini, and Grok also offer engaging content for historians and other disciplines.
Use of Visuals and Maps to Support Learning	AI-generated visuals and maps can enhance subject comprehension and make learning more memorable.
Practice-Oriented and Ethics-Integrated Approach	The course should be practice-based, where teachers and students simultaneously engage in hands-on learning. Additionally, the ethical use of AI should be explicitly taught.
Experience-Based Learning Emphasis	Instead of focusing on theoretical instruction, the program should be heavily practice-oriented. Experiential learning methods — such as observation and practical engagement — should be prioritized.
Deep Exploration of a Single AI Tool	Students should gain experience using various AI tools and engage deeply with one tool to understand its logic fully. Gradually providing data to the AI system allows students to experience how outputs can evolve, promoting better comprehension.
Addressing Academic Integrity Concerns	While GenAI tools are valuable, increased usage has blurred distinctions between original and AI-assisted assignment work. Developing and teaching awareness about plagiarism, academic honesty, and responsible AI use is necessary.

The suggestions provided by participants reflect a mature understanding of how GenAI tools can be more effectively integrated into history education. Central to their recommendations is the idea that AI use should not be isolated or purely technical; instead, it must be meaningfully connected to the pedagogical goals of the course. Participants emphasized the importance of interactive, creativity-driven activities encouraging hands-on engagement rather than passive content delivery. They also advocated including multiple AI tools beyond familiar models like ChatGPT, recommending broader exposure to various resources to develop students' critical and practical skills. These findings underscore that for GenAI tools to be successfully incorporated into history education, there must be a conscious emphasis on interactive design, ethical and critical engagement, and institutional support mechanisms to overcome barriers related to accessibility and equity. These considerations are consistent with broader discussions in the literature (e.g., Bozkurt et al., 2023;

UNESCO, 2024) that highlight the critical need for transparent policies and infrastructural investments in the educational use of AI technologies.

Figure 7. Participants' assessments of generative AI tools

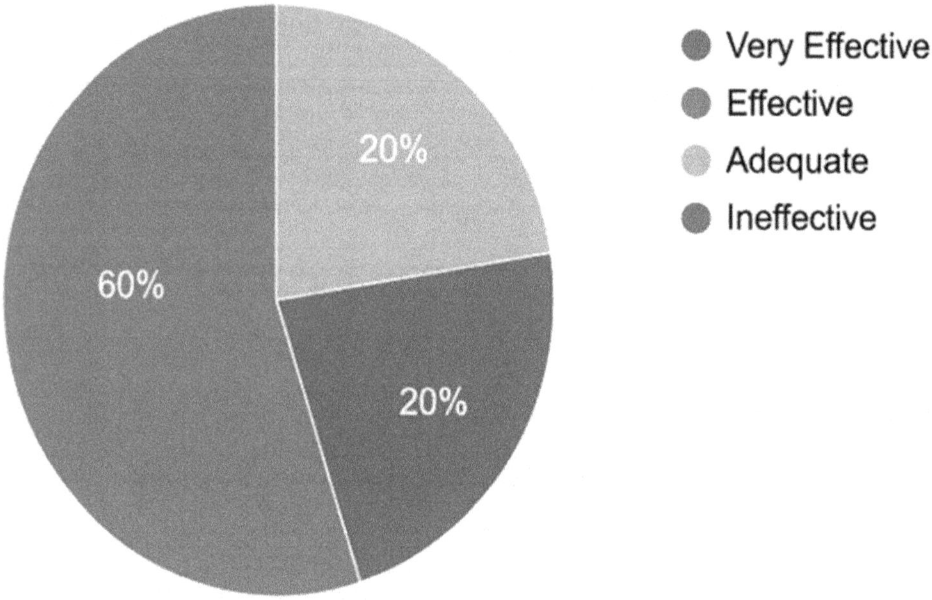

Participants largely viewed GenAI tools in history education positively. Visual data showed that 60% rated their experience as "Successful" and 20% as "Very Successful," highlighting intense satisfaction. Even the 20% who selected "Adequate" acknowledged some benefit, with no one finding the tools insufficient. These results, supported by open-ended responses, align with earlier feedback emphasizing the tools' role in enhancing engagement, visual thinking, and personalized learning. When considered alongside the expressed concerns—such as issues of bias, misinformation, ethical misuse, and limited access—these results suggest that while the pedagogical promise of GenAI is widely acknowledged, its success in educational contexts is closely tied to responsible implementation, critical guidance, and equitable access to technology. In particular, the participants' call for institutional support and free access to full-featured tools speaks to a broader need for policy-level integration to ensure that AI becomes not a source of inequality but a driver of inclusive innovation in education.

Table 7. Participant contributions and reflections on the study

Theme	Participant Response
Appreciation and Gratitude	Thank you very much, hocam (Mrs). I appreciate your effort. Thank you to Mrs..... hocam for raising our awareness. AI is rapidly evolving and will become a key part of our lives. The earlier we adapt, the more beneficial it will be. If we integrate it into our daily work, it can provide a more efficient method.
No Criticism Stated	I have no criticism regarding the study. No, thank you, hocam.
Suggestion for Improvement	You may benefit from keywords I used in my previous responses, such as awareness, experience, and analysis, while further developing the course.
Critical Reflection on AI Tools	The political dimensions of AI tools could be explored more. For instance, Deepseek tends to provide quite politically charged answers.
No Response (Blank)	.

The final comments offered by participants reflect a generally positive and supportive stance toward the module and its objectives. Expressions of gratitude toward the instructor—especially for raising awareness around AI—highlight the perceived personal and professional value of the experience. Some offered thoughtful suggestions for further improvement, such as drawing on recurring keywords like awareness, experience, and analysis as guiding principles for future module iterations. Additionally, one participant raised a valid critique regarding the political positioning of AI-generated content, underlining the need to include critical media literacy and source evaluation within AI-based instructional design.

Overall, the combination of appreciation, constructive feedback, and ethical concern reflects an engaged and reflective participant group—an encouraging sign for the continued development of GenAI-supported educational practices.

CONCLUSION

Research highlights that AI-driven role-playing activities and interactive learning platforms can significantly increase student engagement. However, these tools often require teachers to constantly tailor and adjust content according to individual student needs, which burdens teachers more (Fatimah & Octaviani, 2023; Yang & Boulom, 2024).

Another layer of difficulty lies in the technological competencies of teachers. Fatimah and Octaviani (2023) emphasize that many educators lack the necessary skills to meaningfully incorporate AI tools into their classrooms and interpret AI-generated data, further highlighting the urgent need for structured training programs.

Accessibility challenges also persist. Despite the growing prominence of AI in education, many schools worldwide still lack the necessary digital infrastructure, and numerous students do not have reliable access to computers or the internet at home. Alshorman (2024), Fatimah and Octaviani (2023), and Seyrek et al. (2024) similarly stress that teachers unfamiliar with technology may find it challenging to adopt AI tools and that access to technological resources remains uneven across different regions and school types.

Regarding pedagogical alignment, concerns arise around teachers' and students' easy and sometimes uncritical use of ready-made AI content. Especially regarding assignments and class activities, monitoring and guiding the use of AI is increasingly seen as necessary. Studies have warned that uncritical reliance on AI tools can contribute to technology dependency, diminished creativity, loss of motivation, and intellectual complacency.

Furthermore, the unregulated integration of AI in education may amplify problems such as algorithmic bias, unreliable information sources, and inequalities in access, potentially undermining equitable learning environments. This situation also indicates a possible transformation of the teacher's role, raising new questions about autonomy, authority, and dependency in technologically mediated classrooms (Bozkurt et al., 2023; Bozkurt & Sharma, 2023).

Another critical issue emphasized by the participants in our study is the tendency toward taking shortcuts and committing academic dishonesty. Similarly, recent research has shown that although GenAI tools have the potential to enhance learning experiences, they can also facilitate academic misconduct (Akkaş, Tosun, & Gökçearslan, 2024; Cotton, Cotton, & Shipway, 2024; Polat, 2024). Students may use AI tools to complete assignments or engage in plagiarism. Additionally, there are growing concerns regarding the protection of personal data. Numerous studies have emphasized caution when using AI tools, particularly regarding data privacy and user consent (Bozkurt, 2023; Polat, 2024; UNESCO, 2024). Free-access AI platforms often collect user data, which may lead to ethical concerns regarding privacy and consent (Altun, 2022, p. 25).

If left unaddressed, these ethical concerns could threaten the social fabric of education and underline the urgent need for transparent, ethical, and regulated policies (Bozkurt et al., 2023; Bozkurt & Sharma, 2023). Moreover, it remains evident that equal access to AI technologies is still far from being achieved globally. Many students worldwide still face significant disadvantages due to a lack of access to computers and smartphones, poor internet connectivity, and restrictions on digital resources in their countries. The inequalities in access to technology remain a persistent barrier.

In response to these challenges, several countries have started developing emergency action plans to address technological gaps and promote inclusive access. Nevertheless, the rapid pace of AI development continues to create problematic areas that require ongoing attention.

Furthermore, it is strongly recommended that teachers and history teacher candidates work toward developing their competencies in this field. While some educators are open to incorporating AI tools into their lessons, others disagree or hesitate. Offering targeted training programs would help to answer questions, address concerns, and foster more informed use of AI in education. The module designed for this study was precisely intended to fill such a gap, serving as a pilot application developed based on feedback from a small participant group. The ultimate aim is to adapt the module for broader use among undergraduate and graduate-level students.

The effectiveness of AI in education ultimately depends on how it is integrated into lessons and how educators and students use it. Continuous research and adaptation are essential to meet the evolving needs of both learners and teachers (Vallis et al., 2024). Achieving these goals will require institutional collaboration and a strong focus on inclusive, forward-looking teacher training programs. In this regard, I firmly believe that creating dynamic learning environments—where students are more actively involved than ever before, where technology and student feedback are central, and where educators remain lifelong learners—will make such transformations possible.

Notes: Beyond the AI tools cited in the literature review and instructional module design sections of this chapter, the writing and organization stages also benefited from supplementary tools, including Connected Papers, Grammarly, DeepLy, and ChatGPT.

REFERENCES

Abbas, N., Imran, A., Manzoor, R., Hussain, T., & Hussain, M. (2023). Role of artificial intelligence tools in enhancing students' educational performance at higher levels. *Journal of Artificial Intelligence Machine Learning and Neural Network*, (35), 36–49. DOI: 10.55529/jaimlnn.35.36.49

Akkaş, Ö. M., Tosun, C., & Gökçearslan, Ş. (2024). Artificial intelligence (AI) and cheating: the concept of generative artificial intelligence (GenAI). In Transforming Education With Generative AI: Prompt Engineering and Synthetic Content Creation (pp. 182-199). IGI Global Scientific Publishing.

Al Lily, A. E., Ismail, A. F., Abunaser, F. M., Al-Lami, F., & Abdullatif, A. K. A. (2023). ChatGPT and the rise of semi-humans. *Humanities & Social Sciences Communications*, *10*(1), 626–635. DOI: 10.1057/s41599-023-02154-3

Alenezi, A. (2023). Teacher perspectives on A-driven gamification: Impact on student motivation, engagement, and learning outcomes. *Information Technologies and Learning Tools*, *97*(5), 138–148. DOI: 10.33407/itlt.v97i5.5437

Alshorman, S. (2024). The readiness to use AI in teaching science: Science teachers' perspective. *Journal of Baltic Science Education*, *23*(3), 432–448. DOI: 10.33225/jbse/24.23.432

Altun, A. (2022). Dijital tarih, tarih eğitimini nasıl etkileyebilir? [How digital history can effect history education?] *VIII. Uluslararası Tarih Eğitimi Sempozyumu (ISHE 2022) [International Symposium History Education VIII (ISHE 2022)]*. Conference paper (pp. 7–18). Adana, Türkiye.

Arf, C. (1959). Makine düşünebilir mi ve nasıl düşünebilir? [Can machines think and how they can think] *Atatürk Üniversitesi Halk Konferansları Serisi [The Series of Ataturk University Public Conferences]* No: 1, (pp. 91–103). Retrieved from: chrome-extension://efaidnbmnnnibpcajpcglclefindmkaj/https://www.mbkaya.com/hukuk/cahit-arf-makine-dusunebilir-mi-orjinal.pdf

Baidoo-anu, D., & Owusu Ansah, L. (2023). Education in the era of generative artificial intelligence (AI): Understanding the Potential Benefits of ChatGPT in Promoting Teaching and Learning. *Journal of AI*, *7*(1), 52–62. DOI: 10.61969/jai.1337500

Bing, A. I. (n.d.). Bing. Retrieved from: https://www.bing.com/images/create

Bozkurt, A. (2023). ChatGPT, üretken yapay zekâ ve algoritmik paradigma değişikliği [ChatGPT, generative artificial intelligence and change of algorithmic paradigm] [CressJournal]. *Alanyazın*, *4*(1), 63–72. DOI: 10.59320/alanyazin.1283282

Bozkurt, A., & Sharma, R. C. (2023). Challenging the status quo and exploring the new boundaries in the age of algorithms: Reimagining the role of generative AI in distance education and online learning. *Asian Journal of Distance Education*, *18*(1), 1–8. DOI: 10.5281/zenodo.7755273

Bozkurt, A., Xıao, J., Lambert, S., Pazurek, A., Crompton, H., Koseoglu, S., & Farrow, R. (2023). Speculative futures on ChatGPT and generative artificial intelligence (AI): A collective reflection from the educational landscape. *Asian Journal of Distance Education*, *18*(1), 53–130. https://doing.org/10.5281/zenodo.7636568

Canva, A. I. (n.d.). Say "Hi" to Canva AI. Retrieved from: https://www.canva.com/ai-assistant/

Character, A. I. (n.d). Character.ai. Retrieved from: https://character.ai/

ChatGPT. (n.d.). ChatGPT-4o. Retrieved from: https://chatgpt.com/

Cliovis. (n.d.). Cliovis visualizing connections. Retrieved from: https://cliovis.com/

Cotton, D. R., Cotton, P. A., & Shipway, J. R. (2024). Chatting and cheating: Ensuring academic integrity in the era of ChatGPT. *Innovations in Education and Teaching International*, *61*(2), 228–239. DOI: 10.1080/14703297.2023.2190148

Curipod. (n.d.). Feel the buzz of 100% participation. Retrieved from: https://curipod .com/

DALL·E. (n.d.). DALL·E 3. Retrieved from: https://openai.com/index/dall-e-3/

Deepseek. (n.d.). DeepSeek-V3. Retrieved from: https://chat.deepseek.com/

Díaz-Sánchez, C., & Chapinal-Heras, D. (2023). Use of open access AI in teaching classical antiquity. A methodological proposal. *The Journal of Classics Teaching*, (10). Advance online publication. DOI: 10.1017/S2058631023000739

Diffit. (n.d.). Diffit for teachers. Retrieved from: https://web.diffit.me/

Digital Ottoman Studies. (n.d.). Digital Ottoman Studies: Home. Retrieved from: https://www.digitalottomanstudies.com/

Edeni, C. A., Adeleye, O. O., & Adeniyi, I. S. (2024). The role of AI-enhanced tools in overcoming socioeconomic barriers in education: A conceptual analysis. *World Journal of Advanced Research and Reviews*, *21*(3), 944–951.

Erdoğan, M., & Erol Şahin, A. N. (2024). Tarihsel strateji oyunlarında Türk imajının ders kitapları ile karşılaştırılarak göstergebilimsel analizi. [A Semiotic analysis of Turkish image in historical strategic games by comparing to textbooks] In *Sosyal Bilgiler Eğitimi Alanında Uluslararası Araştırmalar içinde* [[In *International Researches in the field of Social Studies Education I]*]. Eğitim Yayınevi.

Erol Şahin, A. N. (2023). The courses are online; what about the students? Did they really online? Using Kahoot! In the emergency remote teaching process. *Research on Education and Psychology*, *7*(Special Issue), 74–89. DOI: 10.54535/rep.1264989

Fatimah, N. Y., & Octaviani, D. (2023). Sejarah Pendidikan Indonesia Baru: Perkembangan Pembelajaran Sejarah Berbasis Artificial Intelligence (AI) 4.0. *Journal Sejarah Indonesia.*, *6*(2), 168–179. DOI: 10.62924/jsi.v6i2.32607

Gemini. (n.d.). Gemini 2.0 Flash. Retrieved from: https://gemini.google.com/app

Gökçearslan, Ş., Durak, H., Günbatar, M. S., Atman Uslu, N., & Elçi, A. N. (2024). Generative Artificial Intelligence (GENAI) literacy scale: Validity and reliability. *4th International Conference on Scientific and Academic Research* (pp.1-8). Konya, Türkiye.

Grok. (n.d.). Grok 3. Retrieved from: https://grok.com/

Guo, Q. (2024). Prompting change: Chatgpt's impact on digital humanities pedagogy–A case study in art history. *International Journal of Humanities and Arts Computing*, *18*(1), 58–78. DOI: 10.3366/ijhac.2024.0321

HistoricTalk. (n.d.). HistoricTalk: Your gateway to the past. Retrieved https://www .historictalk.com/

HistoryChatAI. (n.d.). History Chat AI – Interactive Historical Conversations. Retrieved from: https://www.yeschat.ai/

Humy.ai. (n.d.). Humy. Retrieved from: https://www.humy.ai/

Icivics. (n.d.). Icivics. Retrieved from: https://vision.icivics.org/

Ijaz, K., Bogdanovych, A., & Trescak, T. (2017). Virtual worlds vs books and videos in history education. *Interactive Learning Environments*, *25*(7), 904–929. DOI: 10.1080/10494820.2016.1225099

Khanmigo. (n.d.). What is Khanmigo? Retrieved from: https://www.khanmigo.ai/

LexiQamus. (n.d.). LexiQamus Ottoman Turkish Linguistic Analyze Device. Retrieved from: https://www.lexiqamus.com

Lo, C. K. (2023). What is the impact of ChatGPT on education? A rapid review of the literature. *Education Sciences*, *13*(4), 410. DOI: 10.3390/educsci13040410

McCarthy, J., Marvin, M., Nathaniel, R., & Claude, S. (1955). *A proposal for the Dartmouth Summer Research Project on Artificial Intelligence.* Retrieved from: http://jmc.stanford.edu/articles/dartmouth/dartmouth.pdf

Merriam, S. B. (2013). *Nitel araştırma desen ve uygulama için bir rehber* [A guide for design and implementation of Qualitative Research]. (Turan, S., Trans.). Nobel Yayınları.

Merriam, S. B., & Tisdell, E. J. (2016). *Qualitative research: A guide to design and implementation* (4th ed.). Jossey-Bass.

Microsoft Copilot. (n.d.). Microsoft Copilot: Your AI companion. Retrieved from: https://copilot.microsoft.com/

Midjourney. (n.d.). Midjourney home. Retrieved from: https://www.midjourney .com/home

Miles, M. B., Huberman, A. M., & Saldaña, J. (2014). *Qualitative data analysis: A methods sourcebook* (3rd ed.). Sage Publications.

Minecraft Education. (n.d.). Minecraft Education: Get Minecraft for your classroom. Retrieved from: https://education.minecraft.net/en-us

MyLens AI. (n.d.). MyLens AI: Create Effective Visuals with AI. Retrieved from: https://mylens.ai/

Nocera, A., Newton, V., & Jiang, S. (2024). They created segregation with the economy: Using AI for a student-driven inquiry into redlining in the social studies classroom. *Theory and Research in Social Education*, *52*(4), 614–653. DOI: 10.1080/00933104.2024.2331466

Onesi-Ozigagun, O. (2024). Revolutionizing education through AI: A comprehensive review of enhancing learning experiences. *International Journal of Applied Research in Social Sciences*, *6*(4), 589–607. DOI: 10.51594/ijarss.v6i4.1011

Planit Teachers. (n.d.). AI-Enhanced History Teaching. Retrieved from: https://www .planitteachers.ai/subjects/history

Polat, Z. (2024). Generative artificial ıntelligence in education: Cheating threat or an enhanced learning tool? *Next Frontier for Life Sciences and AI*, *8*(1), 1–5. DOI: 10.62802/gt1b4t58

Quizizz. (n.d.). Quizizz. Retrieved from: https://quizizz.com

Sarı, F. (2021). Cahit Arf'in "Makine Düşünebilir mi ve Nasıl Düşünebilir?" Adlı Makalesi Üzerine Bir Çalışma [A study on Cahit Arf's article named "Can machines think and how they think"] [TRT Academy]. *TRT Akademi*, *6*(13), 812–833. DOI: 10.37679/trta.962940

Sertalp, E., Moraes, C., & Bütün, E. (2024). Facial reconstruction of a deformed skull from the Roman period of Juliopolis. *Heritage Science*, *12*(1), 2. DOI: 10.1186/s40494-023-01124-x

Seyrek, M., Yıldız, S., Emeksiz, H., Şahin, A., & Türkmen, M. T. (2024). Öğretmenlerin eğitimde yapay zekâ kullanımına yönelik algıları [Teachers' perceptions on the use of artificial intelligence in education] [JSHSR]. *International Journal of Social and Humanities Sciences Research*, *11*(106), 845–856. DOI: 10.5281/zenodo.11113077

Sheng, X. (2023). The role of artificial intelligence in history education of Chinese high schools. *Journal of Education Humanities and Social Sciences*, *8*, 238–243. DOI: 10.54097/ehss.v8i.4255

Sutori. (n.d.). An intuitive timeline maker. Retrieved from: https://www.sutori.com

Tiki-Toki. (n.d.). Online timeline maker. Retrieved from: https://www.tiki-toki.com/

TimeMaps. (n.d.). TimeMaps History Atlas. Retrieved from: https://timemaps.com/history/

Transkribus, A. I. (n.d.). Transkribus. Retrieved from: https://transkribus.ai/

Trunfio, M., Lucia, M. D., Campana, S., & Magnelli, A. (2021). Innovating the cultural heritage museum service model through virtual reality and augmented reality: The effects on the overall visitor experience and satisfaction. *Journal of Heritage Tourism*, *17*(1), 1–19. DOI: 10.1080/1743873X.2020.1850742

UNESCO. (2024). *Eğitim ve araştırmada üretken yapay zekâ kılavuzu [Guidance for generative artificial intelligence in education and research].* (Eds. Miao, F., & Holmes, W.). https://unesdoc.unesco.org/ark:/48223/pf0000390842 sayfasından 1.10.2024 tarihinde erişilmiştir.

Washburn, J., & McCutchen, J. M. (2024). AI meets AI: ChatGPT as a pedagogical tool to teach American Indian history. *Critical Humanities*, *2*(2). Advance online publication. DOI: 10.33470/2836-3140.1037

Xu, Z. (2024). AI in education: Enhancing learning experiences and student outcomes. *Applied and Computational Engineering*, *51*(1), 104–111. DOI: 10.54254/2755-2721/51/20241187

Yang, H., & Boulom, T. (2024). An interactive role-playing game-based learning system for history using artificial ıntelligence and 3D modeling. *12th International Conference of Security, Privacy and Trust Management* (pp.83-90). https://doi.org/ DOI: 10.5121/csit.2024.141107

Yıldırım, A., & Şimşek, H., (2016). *Sosyal bilimlerde nitel araştırma yöntemleri [Qualitative research methods in social sciences].* Seçkin Yayınları Vallis, C., Wilson, S., & Casey, A. (2024). *Generative AI: Beyond the binaries with metaphors.* ASCILITE Publications, 590-595.

KEY TERMS AND DEFINITIONS

AI Pedagogy in History Education: AI pedagogy in history education encompasses teaching approaches that leverage AI technologies to support historical inquiry, critical analysis, and digital literacy. This includes using chatbots to simulate historical figures, AI-generated visuals to depict past environments, and automated feedback tools to support student learning.

AI-Supported Gamified Learning: AI-supported gamified learning applies game design principles through AI-enhanced platforms to teach historical content in interactive and student-centered ways. Educational games like *Minecraft Education* and *iCivics* use AI to adapt content to learners' progress and promote historical empathy through scenario-based learning.

AI-Supported Lesson Design: AI-supported lesson design involves integrating artificial intelligence tools into curriculum planning, enabling educators to create differentiated, interactive, and visually enriched instructional materials. These designs aim to reduce teacher workload and personalize learning experiences based on student needs and learning styles. Digital History Tools

Digital History Tools: Digital history tools are platforms and applications that use digital technologies to analyze, visualize, and teach historical content. Examples include timeline generators (e.g., TimeMaps, ClioVis), AI transcription services (e.g., Transkribus), and immersive simulations that help students engage with the past through multimodal interaction. Historical Thinking Skills

Ethical AI Use in Education: Ethical AI use in education involves responsible integration of AI tools that protects user privacy, avoids bias, and promotes academic integrity. Educators must verify AI outputs, contextualize information, and guard against plagiarism, misuse, and over-reliance on technology in student tasks.

Generative Artificial Intelligence (GenAI): GenAI refers to advanced algorithms capable of producing human-like content—such as text, images, audio, or code—by learning patterns from large datasets. In history education, GenAI tools like ChatGPT are used to generate lesson content, design assessments, and simulate historical scenarios to enhance engagement and understanding.

Historical Thinking Skills: Historical thinking skills refer to the cognitive processes used to analyze and interpret historical events. These include sourcing, contextualization, chronology, perspective-taking, and causation. GenAI tools can support the development of these skills by helping students interrogate sources, create timelines, and compare narratives.

Prompt Engineering: Prompt engineering is the process of crafting clear and strategic instructions to guide AI tools in producing specific outputs. In educational contexts, well-designed prompts allow students and educators to refine AI responses, simulate expert roles, and achieve more accurate and pedagogically relevant results.

Chapter 9
Artificial Intelligence in Open Educational Resources (OER) for Doctoral Education

Marharyta Shyrokova
https://orcid.org/0000-0003-0055-4460
Taras Shevchenko National University of Kyiv, Ukraine

ABSTRACT

This chapter examines the integration of Artificial Intelligence (AI) into Open Educational Resources (OER) for doctoral education, focusing on the Ukrainian context. It explores how AI can enhance the accessibility, adaptability, and pedagogical effectiveness of OER, especially during crises. Drawing on empirical research, it highlights both the potential and limitations of AI in supporting doctoral training. Key themes include the uneven awareness and use of OER among students and educators, the role of AI in content personalization and translation, and the ethical challenges surrounding bias, trust, and academic integrity. The chapter introduces the concept of an AI-driven OER ecosystem, where intelligent tools automate content curation, semantic tagging, and multilingual access, while human actors maintain oversight and contextual relevance. The chapter frames AI as both a tool for human augmentation and a force requiring vigilant oversight, advocating for a balanced approach that pairs technological innovation with transparent governance and critical data literacy.

DOI: 10.4018/979-8-3373-2612-2.ch009

INTRODUCTION

Artificial Intelligence (AI) is precipitating a fundamental reconfiguration of higher education, rendering many traditional pedagogical models increasingly antiquated. To harness AI's transformative potential responsibly, addressing the pedagogical, ethical, and technical challenges accompanying its adoption is imperative. For instance, students may delegate assignments wholesale to AI systems, compromising the integrity of learning outcomes. Accordingly, both educators and learners must cultivate competencies in effective human-AI collaboration.

Existing AI-generated text detectors exhibit inconsistent reliability and frequently yield false positives, inadvertently penalizing students whose work is original. Consequently, proactive instructional design – integrating AI literacy modules and scaffolded assignments – offers a more robust defense against academic dishonesty than retrospective detection alone. Empirical findings on AI-tutored cohorts are equivocal: although such groups may outperform peers in lecture-based settings in the short term, their performance sometimes declines when AI support is withdrawn. Therefore, continuous, systematic research into these phenomena is essential for developing sustainable integration strategies. Conventional grading scales do not adequately account for AI-mediated contributions. Thus, there is a need for nuanced assessment rubrics. A multidimensional framework – delineating levels of AI involvement from "no AI use" through "AI for ideation and structuring" to "AI-only output with human oversight" – can provide clarity and flexibility for instructors and students alike. As AI assumes an increasing share of higher-order cognitive functions (e.g., analysis and creation), cognitive taxonomies should be reconceptualized to reflect collaborative human-machine problem-solving rather than treating AI as a surrogate for student effort.

The exigencies of the COVID-19 pandemic underscored the pivotal role of digital education in accelerating the digital transformation of universities worldwide. In the context of the Russian war against Ukraine, digital and hybrid instructional models have become indispensable for Ukrainian learners, both domestically and in the diaspora. Disciplines vary in their patterns of human-AI interaction; pedagogical frameworks that distinguish between direct problem-solving, dialogic collaboration, content generation, and prompt engineering can inform discipline-specific course design. In particular, digital literacy concerning Open Educational Resources (OER) has emerged as a critical priority in Ukraine, where many institutions operate under disrupted conditions, including intermittent power supply and security threats.

This chapter considers the intersection of AI utilization with the creation of OER in the context of doctoral education, focusing on why an OER is preferable to unregulated AI use for surfing the net. The advancement of AI in the development and administration of OER can profoundly improve the educational experience of learners, particularly doctoral students, who require a high level of detail and specificity in their research materials. Licensed OER with open authorization as a result of strong open licenses, Intellectual Property Protected Content, and Sponsored Content License are meticulously vetted and provide dependable, legally valid, and quality alternatives to the content that is routinely offered through internet searches with AI which is, more often than not, unreliable and lower-grade. With advanced AI technology for generating, curating, and updating instructional materials, higher learning institutions can achieve greater responsiveness and adaptability to the environment and the learners for doctoral research. This supports the core principles of academic malpractice prevention and quality management and transforms the entire picture into an inclusive and progressive ecosystem focused on advanced research.

FOUNDATIONS OF AI-DRIVEN ACCESSIBILITY AND INNOVATION IN DOCTORAL EDUCATION

AI's Transformative Role in Higher Education

Modern education is becoming more mobile, flexible, and open. The integration of information and communication technologies and Open Educational Resources has catalyzed the emergence of a new educational paradigm. At the core of this digital transformation is enabling each learner to achieve desired educational outcomes through personalizing the learning process. This is increasingly facilitated by the expanding capabilities of digital technologies, including the application of artificial intelligence methods. However, according to the OECD (2024), high-level framework documents on the integration of AI into higher education have been adopted in only three countries: Australia (2023), Canada (2024), and the United Kingdom (2023).

In the growing global competition for academic prestige, innovation, and top-tier student talent, universities are exploring optimal models for integrating generative AI into educational practices. This pursuit not only involves adopting new content but also rethinking pedagogical strategies. Institutions are thus seeking innovative approaches to teaching and learning that leverage technological advancements in *what* is taught and *how* it is delivered.

AI rapidly reshapes higher education by transforming teaching, learning, and research. Across multiple studies (Oliinyk et al., 2024; Oliveira et al., 2024; Goenka et al., 2024; Grote et al., 2024; Singha & Singha, 2024), AI is shown to be a powerful catalyst for innovation, offering benefits that range from enhancing research competencies in doctoral education to personalizing learning experiences and automating routine academic tasks. A perspective presented in the OECD report (2021) situates AI within the broader context of digital education. This document outlines how intelligent tutoring systems, personalized learning environments, virtual simulations, and learning analytics are increasingly employed to create adaptive, learner-centered experiences. These technologies enable a shift from traditional one-size-fits-all instruction to highly tailored educational pathways. Moreover, the report discusses the evolving role of *data in education*, where the vast amounts of educational data collected are harnessed to inform policy decisions and improve educational outcomes at scale.

Building on these technological and pedagogical developments, it is vital to consider the broader *social implications* of AI in higher education. While empirical studies and policy analyses demonstrate AI's capacity to personalize learning and inform decision-making, social theories remind us that technology alone does not guarantee shared benefit. By framing AI as a public good – one that must remain accessible, equitable, and non-rivalrous – we can ensure that innovations in OER, adaptive systems, and data-driven insights serve not just individual learners but the collective advancement of society.

Social theories provide a view of AI as a *public good* because of its potential to promote equity, social inclusion, and democratization of knowledge. The transformative potential of AI depends on ensuring open access, ethical use, and institutional support – without which it could become a private commodity rather than a shared social benefit. In economic and sociological terms (Varian, 1992, p. 415), a public good is non-excludable (everyone can access it) and non-rivalrous (one person's use does not diminish another's). When used to develop OER or adaptive learning platforms, AI contributes to educational access without diminishing access for others. AI-enabled tools enhance collective educational outcomes when integrated into public educational systems or made freely available.

Nussbaum & Sen (1993, p. 30) highlight the importance of individuals' ability to attain well-being from resources and opportunities as a *means of achieving good*. Their capability approach looks at the focus 'means' (the resources people have and the public goods they can access) and shifts it to the focus 'ends' (what they can do and be with those resources and goods) (Robeyns & Fibieger Byskov, 2023). This change of focus is warranted because resources and goods alone do not guarantee that people can transform them into actual doings and beings. Two persons with similar sets of goods and resources may have access to achieve very different ends based on their circumstances. AI in education enhances learners' capabilities by expanding their choices, personalizing learning pathways, and enabling access to information and skills that were previously inaccessible, especially for marginalized populations.

From a critical perspective, especially in the works of Freire, education should empower individuals and challenge inequalities. AI in education, particularly in open and transparent systems, reduces the knowledge gap by providing equal access to quality learning across class, gender, geography, and ability. Freire's (2018) concept of "conscientization" – raising critical awareness – can be supported by AI that personalizes content and encourages reflection. When used ethically, AI thus aligns with *education as liberation* – "the process by which society, mostly the students, are deliberately instilled information or education that portrays their own accumulated knowledge, skills and values from one generation to another" (Tshishonga, 2023). In this way, AI has the potential to become not merely a tool for instruction but a catalyst for social transformation that empowers learners to become critically engaged agents of change within their communities.

Social constructivism, rooted in Vygotsky's social learning theory, emphasizes that learners actively construct knowledge through interactions with others and their environment (Schreiber & Valle, 2013). According to Vygotsky, learning is socially mediated and context-dependent. AI supports this by creating adaptive, personalized learning environments that respond to the learner's needs and cultural context. AI tools can simulate dialogic interactions, fostering collaborative knowledge construction, much like a *"more capable peer"* (Wald & Harland, 2021) – a concept referring to someone with greater knowledge or skill who supports a learner's development within their zone of proximal development. AI is a surrogate peer in this context, guiding learners through complex tasks, offering feedback, and scaffolding understanding in real time.

AI in education can also be seen as a driver of *social innovation* (Calzada, 2024; Kaputa et al., 2022) – tools like automated tutoring, learning analytics, and AI-enhanced OER contribute to new learning networks. These networks reshape social relationships around knowledge, allowing learners and educators to co-create and share educational materials more equitably. Social innovation involves adopting new technologies and transforming institutional practices, power dynamics, and access models within educational systems. AI facilitates more participatory, decentralized approaches to knowledge production and dissemination, challenging traditional hierarchies and enabling marginalized communities to engage meaningfully in learning.

Oliinyk et al. (2024) empirically examined how AI tools can bolster various components of research competence among PhD students – such as substantive knowledge, methodological design, procedural skills, and communication abilities. The findings indicate measurable improvements in these areas, suggesting that AI can accelerate acquiring advanced research skills while streamlining the research process. This research emphasizes that when AI is judiciously integrated into academic practices, it enhances the efficiency of research tasks (e.g., data analysis, literature review, and text editing) and contributes to a more innovative and rigorous scholarly environment while ensuring adherence to academic integrity.

Another study (Oliveira et al., 2024) explores the phenomenon of AI adoption by doctoral students through a collaborative autoethnographic approach. This research reveals a complex interplay between enthusiasm for AI's efficiency and precision and concerns over ethical, operational, and emotional challenges. Doctoral students reported initial skepticism and fears – from uncertainties about academic authenticity and the potential for over-dependence on technology – which gradually evolved into recognition of AI's transformative potential. However, these benefits are tempered by ongoing debates about academic integrity, the risk of bias, and the need for comprehensive strategies that balance technological adoption with ethical considerations. The study calls for developing robust AI adoption strategies that address fears, resistance, feasibility, and ethics to ensure that the transformative benefits of AI are realized without compromising core academic values.

Definition and Significance of Open Educational Resources

The evolution of technology and a growing demand for accessible, affordable education led to the emergence and spread of Open Educational Resources (OER). In the late 1990s and early 2000s, rapid internet technology and digital publishing advances began to reshape educational practices. As universities and educators recognized the potential of the web to disseminate knowledge globally, they started to question the traditional, often costly, textbook model. This period also saw rising concerns about educational equity, prompting calls for more accessible and adaptable learning materials. A landmark moment occurred in 2001 with the launch of MIT OpenCourseWare. This initiative made complete course materials available online for free, setting a powerful precedent for openness in education. Around the same time, global organizations such as UNESCO began advocating for open licenses to democratize education, which helped legitimize and spread the OER movement internationally.

With the early successes of projects like MIT OpenCourseWare, educators worldwide started experimenting with open licensing models (e.g., Creative Commons) to share and adapt educational content. The collaborative nature of these efforts allowed for continuous improvement and localization of materials, fostering a global community committed to educational equity and innovation. Advances in AI tools further lowered the barriers to creating and distributing high-quality OER, accelerating their adoption in higher education. Employing AI to create ancillary resources for OER is one of the many ways that generative AI supports teaching and learning. OER has since become a key component in the movement toward more flexible and inclusive education (Elsherif & Elmeawad, 2024; Panke, 2024). By reducing costs and providing resources that can be tailored to diverse learning environments, OER has reshaped how educators and institutions approach curriculum design and delivery worldwide. This aligns with European digital education goals, advocating for accessible, inclusive education and supporting open learning (European Commission, 2020). The UNESCO (2019) definition describes OER as "teaching, learning and research materials that use appropriate tools, such as open licensing, to permit their free reuse, continuous improvement and repurposing by others for educational purposes." Today, OER plays a pivotal role in higher education not only by enhancing *accessibility and equity* but also by promoting *collaboration among educators* and institutions, leading to the continuous improvement and sharing of educational resources. However, in an ever-changing digital environment, it is essential to ensure that OER remains up-to-date and resilient to technological obsolescence. As Ahlf et al. (2024) emphasize, time is a crucial factor in OER sustainability: digital resources risk becoming outdated or inaccessible due to "link rot," changing standards, or disappearing infrastructure. Therefore, a forward-thinking approach to resource planning, ongoing maintenance, and stewardship is necessary to prevent loss and ensure the long-term utility of OER in doctoral education and beyond.

The Relevance of AI in OER Creation for Doctoral Education

Doctoral education serves as a cornerstone of the higher education system, fostering the advancement of knowledge, preparing leaders, enhancing educational practices, promoting interdisciplinary collaboration, contributing to socioeconomic development, and adapting to evolving educational needs. Its integral role ensures the continuous growth and relevance of higher education in addressing the complexities of the modern world. Blessinger and Stockley (2016) highlight significant and ongoing transformations in the structure and function of doctoral education, reflecting broader shifts in society, the labor market, and the expectations placed upon higher education institutions. One of the central trends identified is the diversification of the doctoral student population. Increasingly, doctoral candidates are "working adults who desire greater flexibility in program structure (e.g., part-time and blended/online programs)" (ibid., p. 4), which marks a departure from the traditional full-time, residency-based model of doctoral training.

This *evolving student profile* necessitates new models of support and resource provision. Today's doctoral students are expected to become subject-matter experts and academic leaders and engage in various professional development activities – from conference participation to publication, committee work, and teaching responsibilities. The authors emphasize that this multidimensional workload contributes to "increased costs for students, increased pressure to complete the program in the expected timeframe, and decreased likelihood of obtaining an academic position after graduation" (ibid.). Significantly, Blessinger & Stockley underline the *dual career trajectories* faced by doctoral graduates: while some "enter the academy as the next generation of faculty and administrative leaders," others "leverage their skills for non-profit, industry, and government employment" (ibid., p. 5). This shift requires doctoral education to transmit disciplinary expertise and cultivate transferable skills relevant across professional sectors.

In light of these challenges and transformations, providing OER becomes a logical and necessary response. OER provides doctoral students with flexible, high-quality learning materials that support individualized and accessible learning pathways throughout their studies. More importantly, OER is a continued resource for graduates transitioning into diverse professional roles, enabling lifelong learning and continuous professional development. By offering openly accessible knowledge, institutions help equip doctoral candidates with the ability to adapt to rapidly changing contexts within and beyond academia. As the authors argue, educators must "adjust their perspectives to accommodate this new reality" (ibid., p. 4), which includes embracing inclusive, sustainable, and digitally-enabled educational practices such as OER to support the evolving demands of doctoral education. Moreover, as institutions broaden their digital practices through OER, they must contend with how AI redefines academic roles and responsibilities. Panke (2024) emphasizes the evolving roles of academics in the context of AI integration. The introduction of AI alters the dynamics of information control, prompting discussions about AI's potential to replicate academic content and even develop new courses based on an instructor's prior works. At the same time, "technological developments, such as AI, offer potential benefits for personalized learning while requiring teachers skilled in pedagogy and technology to be able to impact student learning effectively" (OECD, 2024, p. 16).

The rapid integration of AI into the education sector has redefined how educational materials are created, distributed, and adapted for diverse learner needs. This shift is particularly pertinent for doctoral education, where research depth, methodological rigor, and up-to-date resources are essential. OER offers freely accessible, openly licensed materials that support advanced academic work. Concurrently, AI-assisted tools help generate, curate and update these resources. Many scholars have documented the emerging role of generative AI in educational content creation. Bozkurt (2023) outlines how AI technologies can synthesize human-like content and automate the curation and updating of educational materials. AI systems can analyze, reconfigure, and generate new course content from existing instructional materials through advanced natural language processing and machine learning techniques. This advancement in digital tools has facilitated a shift "from organic, human-created OER to synthetic, AI-generated content" (ibid., p. 179), marking a pivotal change in the digitalization of education. For doctoral students, access to high-quality, up-to-date, and customizable educational resources becomes more feasible, contributing to enhanced research productivity and methodological rigor. The research by Goenka et al. (2024) highlights how AI-driven tools enhance virtual teacher-learner engagement, which can easily be extrapolated to advanced academic settings where doctoral candidates require timely, individualized feedback and adaptive resource recommendations. AI algorithms can analyze large datasets to determine optimal content delivery strategies, thereby streamlining the process of generating tailored OER that addresses specific disciplinary requirements.

The quality of educational resources, reliability, and legal clarity are paramount for doctoral students. Licensed OER, which are released under open licenses such as Creative Commons, ensure that materials have been vetted for quality and are accompanied by clearly defined rights for use, adaptation, and redistribution. These resources provide a stable and trustworthy foundation for advanced research. In contrast, using internet-wide AI tools to source information carries risks of encountering inaccurate, unverified, or copyrighted materials that may not be legally reusable.

Tlili and Burgos (2024) argue that the application of AI in creating OER is not simply a tool for aggregating scattered data from the internet but should be harnessed within a framework of responsible digital practices. Intelligent OER repositories – leveraging sophisticated metadata tagging, content recommendation systems, and automated quality assessments – offer doctoral students curated resources that have undergone stringent quality checks. By using licensed OER, doctoral students are ensured legal compliance and academic integrity, which is critical for scholarly research and publication. Tovar and Piedra (2023) elaborate on how AI-enhanced OER ecosystems focus on the quality, consistency, and enrichment of educational content. When doctoral candidates rely on these rigorously maintained resources, they can avoid the pitfalls of using information from unvetted online sources, thus maintaining academic standards and ensuring the reliability of their research outcomes.

Integrating semantic interoperability techniques is another critical contribution of AI in OER ecosystems. Kopp and Gröblinger (2023) analyzed the conditions for AI support within higher education institutions (HEIs) and underscored how AI can facilitate the automatic generation and enrichment of metadata. This enhances the educational resources' discoverability, reusability, and legal clarity. When OER materials are correctly tagged and cataloged using AI-powered semantic tools, doctoral students benefit from a curated pool of reliable and contextually rich resources. AI-powered OER systems can automatically update content by integrating the latest research findings while preserving the scholarly rigor of educational materials. This adaptive model contrasts with the static nature of many freely available internet resources. The deployment of AI in OER creation facilitates the tagging, translation, and localization of educational resources. This ensures that doctoral students from various linguistic and cultural backgrounds can access high-quality materials equally.

BACKGROUND AND RESEARCH CONTEXT

In December 2024, a research study was conducted to assess the needs of academic target audiences in improving the culture and literacy surrounding the production and use of OER in doctoral education. This study focused on academic staff and PhD students from three major Ukrainian HEIs: Taras Shevchenko National University of Kyiv, Lviv Polytechnic National University, and V.N. Karazin Kharkiv National University.

The research was structured around three *key components*:

1) Focus group interview with OER-trained lecturers (12). Lecturers who had participated in the DAAD OER with Ukraine project 2022 (from Taras Shevchenko National University of Kyiv, Kharkiv National University of Radio Electronics, and Ukrainian State University of Science and Technology in Dnipro) took part in focus group interviews. This session sought to capture their experiences with OER, the challenges they encountered, and their views on the prospects of OER creation and implementation, including with the help of AI.
2) Focus group interviews with lecturers without OER training (6). This focus group involved lecturers from Taras Shevchenko National University of Kyiv, Lviv Polytechnic National University, and V.N. Karazin Kharkiv National University, who had not previously received OER training. The objective was to gather their perspectives on OER adoption and the anticipated challenges in creating and implementing OER.
3) Questionnaire survey of PhD students. A survey was conducted among PhD students in their second to fourth years of study at the above-mentioned three universities. The survey aimed to explore the students' experiences, challenges, and expectations regarding using and creating OER. The combined total populations across the institutions amounted to 1,454 PhD students at Taras Shevchenko National University of Kyiv, 1,996 at Lviv Polytechnic National University, and 921 at V.N. Karazin Kharkiv National University. Three hundred sixty-seven responses were collected – 43.6% from Taras Shevchenko National University of Kyiv, 36.5% from Lviv Polytechnic National University, and 19.9% from V.N. Karazin Kharkiv National University. Furthermore, the distribution by academic year revealed that 59.1% of respondents were in their 2nd year, 29.2% in their 3rd year, and 11.7% in their 4th year. When analyzing the collected responses, the findings were further differentiated based on the intended career trajectories of the respondents – specifically distinguishing between PhD students preparing for future academic careers in education and those aiming for employment in the business or private sector.

This multi-method research design enabled the study to capture a diverse range of insights from both educators and doctoral candidates. By integrating focus group discussions with trained and untrained lecturers alongside quantitative feedback from PhD students, the research provides a robust contextual framework for understanding OER's current state and future potential in doctoral education and AI in their application. The findings are instrumental in informing strategies to enhance OER literacy and integration during doctoral studies, thereby supporting lifelong learning and continuous professional development for graduates, regardless of whether they pursue an academic career or transition to non-academic roles in business, industry, or government.

AI APPLICATIONS IN OER FOR DOCTORAL EDUCATION

The empirical data collected from both focus groups and PhD student surveys highlight several concrete ways AI can enhance the lifecycle of OER in doctoral training. AI applications promise to transform OER from static repositories into dynamic, learner-centered ecosystems. By automating routine tasks, enriching resource quality, and personalizing access, AI empowers doctoral students and educators to focus their intellectual efforts on critical analysis and creative inquiry – thereby maximizing open educational resources' pedagogical and scholarly value.

Three-quarters of the respondents (73.3%) agreed that using OER is relevant in modern challenges (emergencies, war, existential threats, digitalization of education). Another 21% of respondents partially agree with this statement. This indicates an awareness of the need to adapt to new challenges, which creates a favorable ground for implementing courses or training to raise awareness and skills of students and teachers in OER. The responses of informants who have received training in OER demonstrate an overall positive experience of using OER but also point to specific *challenges*: lack of quality and peer-reviewed materials, the need for additional skills in working with resources, and time spent on their adaptation. The informants supported integrating OER into PhD education programs to address these challenges, particularly regarding proper citation of illustrative material and the use of licensed resources.

Participants in the first focus group (OER-trained lecturers) emphasized the convenience of OER for asynchronous learning, which is especially important when students cannot be physically present. They also noted the diversification of teaching work through the use of OER. Lecturers acknowledge that preparing materials for OER requires more time, but the diversity and innovation of the learning process justifies this.

Lecturers without OER training generally understood OER as materials that provide free access, adaptation, and distribution. At the same time, their experience of working with OER depends on their field of study. For example, psychologists highlight the need for access to tests and databases to teach students how to process large samples. Biologists and medics emphasize the need to filter materials because of the possible consequences of their misuse. Similar to the first focus group participants, the informants unanimously recognized OER's usefulness in improving the teaching quality. They emphasized that access to reliable sources helps to support the principles of open science and engage students in forming reliable scientific knowledge. However, there is a need to introduce mechanisms to control the quality and use of these resources, especially in fields such as medicine. Some lecturers stressed the importance of creating university platforms with centralized access to verified OER, which would increase their efficiency.

The PhD students of the three targeted HEIs admitted that they do not currently use OER (55.3%); moreover, many are unfamiliar with the concept (19.6%). This suggests the need for information campaigns and training activities to raise awareness of these resources. Only 16.9% of respondents actively use OER in their work. Thus, the practical integration of OER into the educational and research activities of Ukrainian PhD students is at an early stage. Among those PhD students familiar with the definition of OER, 42.1% acquired this knowledge through personal interest or independent search rather than through specialized training or information campaigns by their universities or the state. This data highlights the importance of creating institutional conditions to increase awareness and use of OER.

Participants in both focus groups emphasized that they need *additional skills* to adapt, evaluate, and integrate OER into their curricula. The need to develop students' understanding of the ethical use of resources was also mentioned. The informants named several *needs they feel:* digital skills to work with platforms and databases, legal knowledge of copyright compliance, methodological skills to create and adapt OER for specific disciplines, critical evaluation of resources to determine their reliability (essential for the natural sciences). Ideas were raised to have universities recognize OER as official teaching materials that could be considered in professional reports and professional traineeships, facilitating their wider use and development. The participants of the second focus group expressed the need for more structured access to modern sources, encouragement from universities to create and use OER, in particular through awards and ratings, and the elimination of the dilemma between the use of licensed and "pirated" resources (materials that have been obtained or circulated without proper permission or licensing from their rightful copyright holders) in the educational process.

New Teaching Methods and Digital Approaches

The informants in both focus groups showed a high awareness of using AI tools in their professional activities. Some informants noted that they already use AI for transliteration, automatic translation, and other tasks. One of the informants expressed excitement about the potential of AI, noting that she uses it in specialized tasks such as improving text for publications (checking and editing articles). At the same time, the importance of generative AI was emphasized, which is not yet fully integrated into all processes but has the potential to expand the functionality of teachers. Teachers must control the result by editing the material according to their requirements.

Most informants are actively introducing digital technologies into the educational process. Among the popular tools are interactive platforms such as Mentimeter, Kahoot, and interactive whiteboards. Such approaches allow students to participate in lectures, particularly in online education actively. However, difficulties with technical support were noted, such as the lack of equipment for recording lectures in a professional environment and the lack of technical skills, such as video editing. Insufficient technical support and the need for specialized studios with professional lecture recording equipment is a significant obstacle. The need for teaching assistants who could take care of the technical side of the work, leaving more time for intellectual activity, was also raised.

Most PhD students surveyed in the study who plan to teach in higher education consider it important to use OER in their teaching activities (97.8%, including those who identified it as very or somewhat important). In addition, 75% of PhD students considering a teaching career believe that their involvement in creating and using OER can enhance their professional image and recognition in the academic environment. This demonstrates that OER is not only an educational tool but also has the potential for professional growth, reputation building, and personal brand development.

The Impact of Digital Approaches on the Quality of Student Learning

Informants shared mixed opinions on the impact of digital tools on the learning process. Some emphasized the benefits, including interactivity, repeatedly revising materials, and adapting to individual student needs. For example, for those who were unable to attend classes due to illness or volunteering, digital recordings of lectures were extremely convenient. On the other hand, it was pointed out that the effectiveness depends on the nature of the discipline. In technical disciplines, digital tools significantly improve the quality of learning, while in the humanities, digitalization is less effective due to the lack of personal interaction.

Informants had diverse, sometimes polarized opinions on the impact of AI and digital approaches on students. Among the *negative* impacts mentioned were the decline in cognitive abilities (one informant believes that excessive use of AI contributes to the degradation of cognitive skills, in particular, verbal Intelligence) and generational differences (another informant points out the difference in the impact of AI on the older generation (positive impact) and the younger generation (negative impact), emphasizing that young people are becoming dependent on technology). On the *positive* side, AI is perceived as a powerful tool for improving the quality of education. One of the informants gave an example of an event where MA and PhD students compared their results with those of AI, which helped to understand the limits of the technology. It was emphasized that AI cannot replace human creativity and critical thinking. One informant noted that the primary responsibility for properly using AI lies with students and PhDs. They should see AI as an additional tool, not a replacement for human work. Academic integrity and internal culture are key to preventing negative consequences.

Both focus groups stressed the need for clear *ethical guidelines* around digital tools –ranging from video-conferencing etiquette to data privacy standards. They also highlighted the importance of strengthening soft skills, including public speaking, personalized instruction, and critical thinking. The call for more robust pedagogical methods was equally pressing, particularly when integrating digital technologies into lecture planning. Informants noted that universities lack a unified regulatory framework for AI use and that rapid technological advances are outpacing institutional policies, complicating effective oversight and implementation.

Experience in Creating and Using OER

The informants demonstrated an understanding of the importance of OER in creating a single educational and scientific space. They see each teacher's contribution to forming a knowledge base accessible to various stakeholders. PhD students with teaching experience (53.4%) rarely use OER in their activities; 19.8% indicated that they have OER experience. Only 8.4% of the surveyed PhD students had to create OER independently. The low percentage of PhD students who create OER, against the background of their interest in this, indicates the need to develop their competencies in developing OED.

Most focus group informants trained in OER confirmed they had to create materials under an open license or digitize existing ones. The primary resources used by the lecturers were their own time, personal equipment (computers, internet, video cameras), and sometimes the help of colleagues and students. The biggest *challenge* was the need to invest their time, often outside working hours, such as evenings, weekends, or holidays. For example, one lecturer noted that she spent the whole summer creating lectures because there was not enough time during the semester. Some lecturers expressed that creating materials is perceived as a mission, as work in the educational sector often goes beyond regular working hours.

The informants who did not create OER explained this primarily by resource constraints. The most common *obstacles* were a lack of technical equipment (working computers, access to software), insufficient support from the university, and lack of time due to the heavy workload of lecturers. Some also noted that the war and inadequate conditions (lack of electricity, cold rooms) made it even more challenging to create materials.

According to the informants, the following *steps* are important *for overcoming* these problems on the part of the HEI administration: providing equipment (computers, software); arranging comfortable workplaces; creating conditions for teachers to work on the university premises; organizing training for academic staff on the creation and use of OER; attracting additional resources or external assistance for the creation of materials (for example, grant support or sponsors). The informants had different views on the support provided by the university. Some expressed gratitude for working with a team of like-minded people and fans of their work, which helped them overcome difficulties. Others said that university support was limited to minimal conditions or was non-existent. In some cases, teachers explicitly stated that improving working conditions, such as providing basic equipment or heating, could make working with OER much easier.

Lecturers noted that their OER work arouses interest among students and colleagues and contributes to the dissemination of knowledge, bringing moral satisfaction to their contribution to general education. Another *motivating factor* is the possibility of popularizing one's work. For example, PhD students actively contribute their research papers to university databases, making them available to others. Some informants expressed a desire to obtain copyright for their materials before publication.

Informants identified several significant *factors that discourage* them from creating and using OER:

- There is a fear of losing control over intellectual property when materials are made publicly available and used without the author's permission;
- many teachers face the fact that their schedules are already overloaded, and they cannot find extra time to create resources;
- lack of remuneration or recognition for the development of materials, including video courses;

- creating quality content requires focusing on one topic, which requires professional reorientation;
- insufficient technical skills in creating and editing videos or other resources.

The survey of PhD students revealed the two leading *factors that most complicate* their work with OER. These are insufficient knowledge about OER and lack of time to search for and adapt resources – they were mentioned by 47.7% and 43.9% of respondents, respectively. The lack of quality criteria for OER and insufficient accessibility of these materials are mentioned as obstacles by almost the same number of respondents – 25.6% and 25.3%, respectively. Other influential factors that hurt the work of PhD students with OER include difficulties with the open licensing procedure (21.8% of respondents), the lack of a university policy on OER (20.4%), low digital competence (17.2%), and the language of resources – the lack of materials in Ukrainian (17.4%).

AI can help address several of these key obstacles. AI-driven recommendation Engines can guide students to relevant OER based on their research topic or learning objectives, effectively teaching them "what is out there" without extensive manual searching. Conversational AI Tutors (chatbots) can answer questions about OER definitions, best practices, and use cases on demand, reducing the initial knowledge barrier. Automated Data Curation leverages machine-learning algorithms to scan repositories, tag materials with metadata, and present high-relevance OER in seconds. Generative AI Assistants can transform and adapt existing resources, saving hours of manual work. AI-driven quality assessment tools can evaluate resources for peer-review status, citation counts, and textual coherence, flagging high-quality materials while alerting users to potential shortcomings or biases. Automated Translation engines instantly render OER into multiple languages, including Ukrainian, and can adjust reading levels for diverse learners. Speech-to-Text and Text-to-Speech modules make audio and video content accessible to students with disabilities or varying learning preferences.

Some informants shared their beliefs and experiences: openness to new formats depends on personal qualities, such as charisma or love of public speaking. Some teachers even avoid participating in video content creation due to psychological barriers or difficulties adapting to new formats. Nevertheless, while AI can automate many technical aspects of OER creation, it cannot fully replicate the human qualities that drive authentic engagement and pedagogical effectiveness. Charisma, storytelling ability, and a genuine passion for teaching remain inherently human attributes. Therefore, AI should be viewed not as a panacea but as an enabling partner: it lowers technical barriers and amplifies educators' creative capacities, yet the ultimate success of innovative formats hinges on human agency, motivation, and the willingness to embrace change. AI can make new formats more accessible, but it cannot substitute for the personal drive and unique presence that only a human instructor can bring to the learning experience.

Prospects for Using OER

The responses demonstrate optimism about the future use of OER. Among the *benefits* teachers note are wider access to quality teaching materials, the possibility of involving PhD students in creating their resources, which contributes to their professional development, and the use of OER to improve the image and competitiveness of universities. Some PhD students and lecturers are already actively using OER and consider it an integral part of the educational process.

The respondents of the survey who plan to devote themselves to teaching mainly assess the use of OER in their teaching activities in the next 5 years as promising – 94.8% of respondents agreed with this (including those who chose very and somewhat promising). The high level of support for using OER among PhD students demonstrates the readiness of the academic environment to integrate open resources into the learning process. It also points to the need for university strategies for OER development that meet the expectations of future teachers. The fact that OER contributes to ensuring equal access to learning materials for all students was partially or fully agreed by 95.4% of respondents. Thus, OER can become a tool to increase the accessibility of quality education for all, regardless of financial or geographical location.

The PhD students who took part in the survey overwhelmingly stated that it is important for them to stay engaged in lifelong learning (LLL), including through OER – 93.8% of respondents selected the options as very important and somewhat important. This demonstrates their awareness of current trends in professional development and the need to adapt to changes in the scientific and educational fields. Creating an ecosystem that supports LLL through OER will improve the professional training of PhD students and ensure their competitiveness in the global labor market.

To bridge these general prospects with the distinct needs of doctoral students, it is important to recognize that the advantages of OER manifest differently depending on one's career trajectory (table 1). Those preparing for academic careers benefit most from OER's enhancement of teaching materials, peer-reviewed content, and institutional prestige. In contrast, students targeting the business or private sector leverage OER's time-saving efficiencies and customizable case studies to jump-start professional development and practical project work.

Table 1. How PhD students can benefit from OER using

Target audience	Formative aspects of the program	Summative aspects of the program
PhD students aiming for a future career in education	1. Enhancing research skills. OER provides access to diverse, up-to-date, and peer-reviewed resources that foster ongoing learning and critical reflection. 2. Developing pedagogical competence. Interacting with open content helps students refine teaching methodologies and innovative educational practices. 3. Interdisciplinary exposure. Access to materials across fields nurtures a holistic understanding and encourages collaboration. 4. Formative feedback opportunities. Utilizing OER allows iterative learning and self-assessment, aiding in skill refinement before final evaluations.	1. Quality research outputs. Leveraging high-quality, openly licensed content supports the production of robust, evidence-based research. 2. Building academic portfolios. Summative achievements such as publications, comprehensive literature reviews, and successful dissertations are enhanced by the rich resources available through OER. 3. Demonstration of subject mastery. Cumulative learning validated by summative assessments reflects deep subject understanding and readiness for academic challenges.
PhD students aiming for employment in the business/private sector	1. Acquiring industry-relevant knowledge. OER offers practical case studies, market trends, and digital skills training directly applicable to business contexts. 2. Developing adaptive problem-solving skills. Personalized, formative learning pathways through OER help students tailor their learning to real-world business challenges. 3. Enhancing digital literacy. Continuous formative exposure to innovative technologies and methodologies prepares students to adapt to rapidly evolving industry needs.	1. Portfolio and outcome validation: Summative assessments, projects, and reports that utilize OER can showcase tangible outcomes and practical expertise to potential employers. 2. Competitive edge. Demonstrated ability to synthesize and apply open resources in solving complex business problems builds credibility and signals readiness for industry roles. 3. Certification and accreditation. Summative evidence from OER-based programs can contribute to recognized certifications, enhancing career prospects in the private sector.

Application Areas for AI in OER

AI is catalyzing a shift in OER from static repositories into dynamic, personalized learning ecosystems. AI applications span the full OER lifecycle (creation, curation, distribution, adaptation, and evaluation), enabling more agile, equitable, and scalable educational practices. An *AI-driven ecosystem approach* (fig. 1) treats OER as isolated files and a living network of interconnected tools, data, and communities. Such an ecosystem is inherently compatible with OER for several reasons. OER and AI ecosystems thrive on open standards (open licenses and APIs), facilitating seamless integration between content repositories, learning platforms, and AI services. AI systems automatically scale curation, translation, and personalization across thousands of OER, matching the OER movement's broad, equitable dissemination goal. This synergy allows HEIs to serve diverse learner populations without proportional increases in human labor. In an AI-driven ecosystem, feedback loops (learner analytics feeding back into content refinement) ensure OER evolves in response to actual usage patterns. This dynamic aligns with the "open" ethos of iterative improvement and community contribution.

Figure 1. AI-driven OER ecosystem

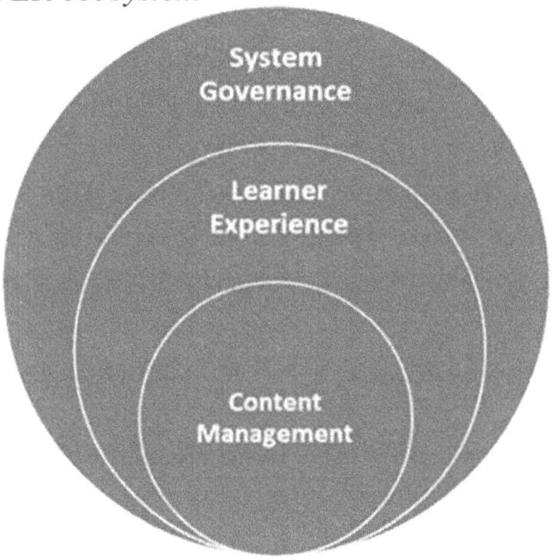

The AI-driven OER Ecosystem offers a vivid blueprint for how AI can seamlessly orchestrate the entire lifecycle of OER, transforming them from static files into a living, adaptive educational environment. At its heart, this ecosystem is structured around three interwoven domains – content management, learner experience, and system governance – each corresponding to a distinct but deeply interconnected layer of functionality.

Content Management Domain (Resource Layer)

In the resource layer, AI breathes continuous life into the OER repository. Generative models automatically draft and enrich open textbooks, scholarly articles, video lectures, and interactive simulations. Concurrently, machine-learning classifiers categorize and tag these assets, assigning rich metadata that facilitates rapid discovery. Version-control algorithms monitor emerging research and global events, prompting updates or flagging outdated material. Translation engines unlock multilingual access, while accessibility tools add captions, alt-text, and navigable transcripts. Together, these AI-powered operations ensure that the OER library remains comprehensive, legally sound, and culturally inclusive – an ever-growing trove of knowledge ready for doctoral inquiry.

Learner Experience Domain (Interaction Layer)

The interaction layer places students and educators at the center of the learning journey. Intelligent tutors (chatbots trained on disciplinary corpora) answer questions in real-time, guiding learners through complex concepts. Recommendation algorithms suggest the best resource based on each student's performance, interests, and collaborative networks. Adaptive learning pathways adjust content difficulty dynamically, ensuring no learner is left behind. Meanwhile, analytical dashboards visualize engagement patterns, quiz scores, and peer interactions, feeding insights back to instructors and content managers. This continuous feedback loop not only refines the resource layer but also cultivates an inclusive, dialogic learning community where doctoral candidates co-construct knowledge with AI as an ever-present mentor.

System Governance Domain (Governance Layer)

Underpinning the ecosystem is the governance layer – a robust framework of policy engines and compliance modules that safeguard academic integrity and ethical AI use. Plagiarism-detection algorithms scan new and existing OER for unlicensed content, while bias-mitigation tools flag problematic language or data. Automated licensing checks verify that every resource adheres to open-access standards, and privacy-preserving protocols ensure that learner data remains under transparent, learner-controlled governance. This way, the ecosystem evolves pedagogically and upholds the legal and ethical principles essential to a truly open educational commons.

These three layers (resource, interaction, and governance) are not isolated. Instead, they constitute a self-reinforcing cycle in which AI continuously generates, personalizes, monitors, and refines educational content. Each learner's interactions inform ongoing content updates, enhancing the effectiveness of adaptive pathways and guiding governance policies. In this living ecosystem, doctoral education becomes a dynamic partnership between human creativity and machine intelligence – capable of responding in real-time to emerging research, shifting global contexts, and the diverse needs of scholars worldwide.

Navigating Challenges in AI-Enhanced OER Ecosystems

The transformative potential of intelligent tools for augmenting OER is substantial, yet it is accompanied by multifaceted challenges that warrant rigorous scrutiny. Foremost among these is the risk of algorithmic bias: advanced recommendation and generation systems may inadvertently reproduce and even exacerbate the prejudices inherent in their training corpora. Unchecked bias can distort the selection of educational materials, perpetuate stereotypes, and marginalize critical perspectives. Equally pressing are the ethical considerations surrounding machine-generated or adapted content. If an AI-authored lecture slide contains factual inaccuracies, questions of accountability arise: Who assumes responsibility for disseminating erroneous information? How can instructors and learners maintain vigilance regarding AI-generated materials' provenance, validity, and reliability?

An additional obstacle concerns the requisite for continuous professional development. Although domain experts possess deep disciplinary expertise, they must also acquire proficiency in the operational principles of AI systems, from understanding model training and recognizing limitations to exercising informed judgment in overriding automated recommendations. Learners similarly require structured guidance in interacting with intelligent platforms and cultivating critical appraisal skills. Advanced technological infrastructures risk underutilization or misuse without a sustained institutional commitment to capacity building.

Bridging these gaps necessitates interdisciplinary collaboration. Education technologists, data scientists, information professionals, and subject-matter experts must coalesce around a unified strategic vision. Kopp and Gröblinger (2023) articulate such an approach in their strategic framework for "smart OER environments," emphasizing iterative co-design: educators pilot novel tools, collect user feedback, and refine technological functionality and pedagogical methodology. This cyclical process ensures that AI enhancements align with authentic learning objectives rather than novelty-driven adoption.

Notwithstanding careful design, *unanticipated outcomes* frequently accompany the delegation of academic tasks to automated systems. Automated grading tools, for instance, tend to optimize quantifiable metrics such as response length, keyword frequency, or rubric conformity, thereby rewarding formulaic compositions over nuanced analytical discourse. Students who adhere closely to expected patterns may receive disproportionately high evaluations, whereas genuinely original submissions risk being penalized as anomalous. Similarly, predictive algorithms applied to admissions and enrollment decisions may reinforce historic inequities embedded in legacy datasets. Without deliberate calibration, ostensibly impartial filters can perpetuate disparities in acceptance rates for underrepresented cohorts or overemphasize standardized assessments at the expense of non-cognitive competencies, such as leadership, creativity, and community engagement.

In the research domain, AI-driven productivity metrics may incentivize scholars to prioritize publication volume over substantive contributions. Emphasis on quantifiable outputs such as publication counts, citation indices, or grant acquisition can engender a proliferation of incremental studies and deter bold, interdisciplinary inquiries whose impact is less readily measurable.

AI-facilitated advising and learner support systems also exhibit paradoxical outcomes. Platforms that integrate academic performance indicators promise granular insights into student progress but may rely on reductive rules (for example, flagging learners as "at risk" after missing a fixed number of assignments), thereby overlooking contextual factors such as caregiving responsibilities or part-time employment. Moreover, the aggregation of sensitive personal data heightens concerns regarding privacy, surveillance, and the erosion of trust.

The most contentious applications pertain to behavior monitoring and proctoring technologies. Instrumentation such as eye-tracking, keystroke analysis, and screen-activity detection aims to deter academic misconduct but risks undermining the ethos of mutual respect that undergirds educational communities. Innocuous behaviors glancing away from the screen or moments of restlessness may be misinterpreted as evidence of cheating, with deleterious effects on students' psychological well-being.

These challenges underscore a fundamental principle: technological prowess must be balanced by human judgment, ethical stewardship, and a steadfast commitment to equity. A flourishing AI-enhanced OER ecosystem demands sophisticated platforms, robust ethical guidelines, comprehensive training, and continuous dialogue among stakeholders. Only through such a holistic approach can doctoral education harness the promise of AI while preserving the integrity and humanity of scholarly pursuit.

CONCLUSION

The multi-method investigation presented in this chapter reveals a doctoral landscape in Ukraine that is simultaneously ripe with opportunity and hindered by uneven familiarity with OER. While nearly three-quarters of respondents affirmed the relevance of OER in contexts of war, pandemic, and rapid digitalization, more than half of PhD students reported no current engagement with these materials. Many who use OER discovered them through independent exploration rather than institutional guidance. Lecturers trained in OER underscored its pedagogical benefits, particularly for asynchronous formats, yet noted the time-intensive nature of preparing and adapting high-quality, peer-reviewed materials. Conversely, untrained educators lamented insufficient infrastructure, technical support, and clear policies, especially when resource misuse carries high stakes. These findings point to a nascent ecosystem in which awareness and enthusiasm coexist with significant access, skills, and institutional recognition barriers.

The chapter demonstrates how advanced algorithms can catalyze the evolution of static OER repositories into dynamic, learner-centered ecosystems. AI-driven curation and recommendation engines promise to reduce the initial search burden, guiding students to contextually relevant materials, while generative assistants can adapt existing content for discipline-specific needs. Automated metadata enrichment and semantic tagging enhance discoverability and interoperability across platforms, and real-time translation services support multilingual access. However, these technical gains depend on a foundation of licensed, quality-assured resources and a robust governance framework that maintains legal clarity and academic integrity.

A central tension emerges when positioning algorithmic systems as predictable tools or entities with emergent behaviors. In contexts of human-machine collaboration, AI functions as an extension of scholarly capability – automating routine tasks such as citation management, preliminary literature aggregation, and accessibility enhancements – thus freeing educators and learners to focus on critical analysis and creativity. Here, machine intelligence augments human agency, reinforcing the instructor's role as curator and the student's role as an active knowledge constructor. However, the same systems can exhibit unpredictable outputs when confronted with biased training data or novel query structures. Generative modules may produce plausible but erroneous explanations, and recommendation algorithms can amplify echo chambers by privileging familiar content at the expense of underrepresented perspectives. Recognizing AI's dual nature invites vigilant engagement, where practitioners remain ready to verify, override, or recalibrate automated suggestions.

The optimism surrounding AI-enhanced OER is grounded in demonstrable improvements in accessibility, personalization, and scalability. PhD students envision streamlined workflows, more diverse resource pools, and continuous professional development opportunities through lifelong learning ecosystems. Institutions foresee cost efficiencies and expanded educational reach even under conflict or displacement. However, this hope must be juxtaposed with cautionary lessons from algorithmic bias, surveillance overreach, and unintended pedagogical distortions. Automated grading systems designed to expedite feedback can inadvertently reward formulaic responses, penalizing creative or interdisciplinary work. Predictive analytics applied to admissions or student support risk codifying existing inequities if historical data reflects structural bias. Therefore, the promise of equity through technology demands an equally rigorous commitment to data hygiene, model transparency, and inclusive design principles.

Trust in AI-mediated educational environments hinges upon clear lines of accountability, ethical oversight, and transparent policy frameworks. A governance layer that integrates plagiarism detection, licensing compliance checks, and privacy-preserving protocols is essential to ensure that expanding data flows serve collective interests without compromising individual rights. Ethical guidelines should articulate when and how instructors must validate machine outputs, mandate human review for high-stakes decisions, and specify criteria for resource inclusion. Equally, educators and learners require training in tool operation and critical data literacy – understanding how models are trained, recognizing the limits of automated inferences, and identifying standard failure modes. Doctoral programs can only engender a culture of responsible innovation by pairing cutting-edge platforms with institutional safeguards and professional development.

The findings signal that the path forward lies in iterative co-design between technologists, educators, librarians, and doctoral candidates. Pilot implementations of intelligent OER platforms should be evaluated on efficiency metrics, learning outcomes, equity indicators, and user satisfaction. Continuous feedback loops where student analytics inform content refinement and governance policies can transform OER into living repositories that evolve in response to real-world needs. Hybrid models of resource stewardship, in which AI handles routine updating and metadata management while human experts curate and contextualize materials, offer a sustainable compromise. Such an approach preserves the uniquely human attributes of charisma, pedagogical intent, and critical judgment (qualities that algorithms cannot replicate) but leverages machine capabilities to amplify these strengths at scale.

Integrating AI within OER for doctoral education embodies both a formidable opportunity and a sobering responsibility. Empirical data illustrate that practical uptake remains uneven and contingent upon infrastructural, policy, and skill-related supports despite widespread recognition of OER's value. AI-powered interventions can accelerate adoption by lowering technical barriers and enhancing resource relevance, yet they introduce new vectors of risk that demand ethical vigilance and transparent governance. The overarching challenge is cultivating an ecosystem in which algorithms serve as predictable partners in knowledge creation rather than unpredictable forces of disruption. By balancing hope with caution and embedding control, ethics, and trust at the core of system design, doctoral education can harness machine intelligence to expand the horizons of scholarly inquiry while safeguarding the humanity at the heart of learning.

REFERENCES

Ahlf, M., McNeil, S., & Nguyen, P. (2024). Open Educational Resources: Time, resources and sustainability in an ephemeral digital world. In Cole, D. R., Rafe, M. M., & Yang-Heim, G. Y. A. (Eds.), *Educational research and the question(s) of time*. Springer., DOI: 10.1007/978-981-97-3418-4_19

Blessinger, P., & Stockley, D. (2016). *Emerging directions in doctoral education*. Emerald Group Publishing., DOI: 10.1108/S2055-364120166

Bozkurt, A. (2023). Generative AI, synthetic contents, Open Educational Resources (OER), and Open Educational Practices (OEP): A new front in the openness landscape. *Open Praxis, 15*(3), 178–184. DOI: 10.55982/openpraxis.15.3.579

Calzada, I. (2024). Artificial Intelligence for social innovation: Beyond the noise of algorithms and datafication. *Sustainability (Basel), 16*(19), 8638. DOI: 10.3390/su16198638

Elsherif, H. M., & Elmeawad, S. (2024). *Unlocking knowledge: Leveraging AI to access Open Educational Resources in higher education*. Eldonusa.

European Commission. (2020). *Digital education action plan (2021-2027). Resetting education and training for the digital age.* [Fact sheet]. https://education.ec.europa.eu/sites/default/files/document-library-docs/deap-factsheet-sept2020_en.pdf

Freire, P. (2018). *Pedagogy of the oppressed.* 50th Anniversary Edition. Bloomsbury Academic.

Goenka, N., Patnaik, D., & Pradhan, B. B. (2024). Impact of Artificial Intelligence on Virtual Teacher-learner Engagement: Redefining Educational Dynamics. In Bansal, R., Chakir, A., Hafaz Ngah, A., Rabby, F., & Jain, A. (Eds.), *AI algorithms and ChatGPT for student engagement in online learning*. IGI Global., DOI: 10.4018/979-8-3693-4268-8.ch013

Grote, M., Lysholm Faber, H. C., & Gasparini, A. (2024). Artificial Intelligence in PhD education: New perspectives for research libraries. *LIBER Quarterly, 34*(1), 1–29. DOI: 10.53377/lq.18137

Kaputa, V., Loučanová, E., & Tejerina-Gaite, F. A. (2022). Digital transformation in higher education institutions as a driver of social-oriented innovations. In C. Păunescu, K. L. Lepik, N. Spencer (Eds.). *Social innovation in higher education. Innovation, technology, and knowledge management.* Springer. DOI: 10.1007/978-3-030-84044-0_4

Kopp, M., & Gröblinger, O. (2023). Conditions for AI support of Open Educational Resources at HEIs. In *Proceedings of the Innovating Higher Education Conference 2023.* European Association of Distance Teaching Universities.

Nussbaum, M., & Sen, A. (Eds.). (1993). *The quality of life*. Clarendon Press. DOI: 10.1093/0198287976.001.0001

OECD. (2021). *OECD digital education outlook 2021: Pushing the frontiers with Artificial Intelligence, blockchain, and robots*. OECD Publishing., DOI: 10.1787/589b283f-

OECD. (2024). *Education policy outlook 2024: Reshaping teaching into a thriving profession from ABCs to AI*. OECD Publishing., DOI: 10.1787/dd5140e4-

Oliinyk, I., Bulavina, O., Romanenko, T., Tatarnikova, A., & Smirnov, A. (2024). Artificial Intelligence in developing doctoral students' research competencies. *Revista Eduweb*, *18*(3), 294–305. DOI: 10.46502/issn.1856-7576/2024.18.03.22

Oliveira, J., Murphy, T., Vaughn, G., Elfahim, S., & Carpenter, R. E. (2024). Exploring the adoption phenomenon of artificial Intelligence by doctoral students within doctoral education. *New Horizons in Adult Education and Human Resource Development*, *00*(0), 248–262. Advance online publication. DOI: 10.1177/19394225241287032

Panke, S. (2024). Open Educational Resources and Artificial Intelligence for Future Open Education. *Mousaion: South African Journal of Information Studies*, *42*(1), 23. DOI: 10.25159/2663-659X/15106

Robeyns, I., & Fibieger Byskov, M. (2023). *The capability approach.* In E. N. Zalta, U. Nodelman (Eds.). The Stanford Encyclopedia of Philosophy. https://plato.stanford.edu/archives/sum2023/entries/capability-approach/

Schreiber, L. M., & Valle, B. E. (2013). Social constructivist teaching strategies in the small group classroom. *Small Group Research*, *44*(4), 395–411. DOI: 10.1177/1046496413488422

Singha, S., & Singha, K. (2024). Revolutionizing content creation and curriculum development through generative AI. In Sharma, R. C., & Bozkurt, A. (Eds.), *Transforming education with generative AI: Prompt engineering and synthetic content creation*. IGI Global., DOI: 10.4018/979-8-3693-1351-0.ch013

Tlili, A., & Burgos, D. (2024). Unleashing the power of Open Educational Practices (OEP) through Artificial Intelligence (AI): Where to begin? *Interactive Learning Environments*, *32*(10), 6886–6893. DOI: 10.1080/10494820.2022.2101595

Tovar, E., & Piedra, N. (2023). AI implications in satisfying digital skills training needs through OER. In T. Schlippe, E. C. K. Cheng, T. Wang (Eds.). *Artificial Intelligence in education technologies: New development and innovative practices.* Proceedings of 2023 4th International Conference on Artificial Intelligence in Education Technology. Springer Nature. DOI: 10.1007/978-981-99-7947-9_9

Tshishonga, N. S. (2023). Student teaching for critical thinking and emancipation at the university: A Freire's liberatory approach. In Makua, M., & Akinlolu, M. (Eds.), *Sustaining higher education through resource allocation, learning design models, and academic development*. IGI Global., DOI: 10.4018/978-1-6684-7059-6.ch007

Varian, H. R. (1992). *Microeconomic analysis* (3rd ed.). W. W. Norton & Company.

Wald, N., & Harland, T. (2021). Reconsidering Vygotsky's 'more capable peer' in terms of both personal and knowledge outcomes. *Teaching in Higher Education*, *27*(3), 417–423. DOI: 10.1080/13562517.2021.2007474

KEY TERMS AND DEFINITIONS

Academic Integrity: A commitment to honesty, trust, fairness, respect, and responsibility in scholarly work, including proper attribution of sources and avoiding plagiarism.

AI-Driven OER Ecosystem: A network of interconnected tools, platforms, and policies in which AI automates Open Educational Resources curation, translation, personalization, and governance.

Artificial Intelligence (AI): Computational techniques and systems that perform tasks traditionally requiring human Intelligence, such as learning, reasoning, and language understanding, often via machine learning and neural networks.

Digital Transformation of Education: Integrating digital technologies into all aspects of education, resulting in fundamental changes to how learning content is created, delivered, and experienced.

Doctoral Education: The highest level of academic study, focused on original research, critical analysis, and the production of new knowledge, culminating in a doctoral (PhD) degree award.

Open Educational Resources (OER): Teaching, learning, and research materials that are freely accessible and openly licensed, permitting their unrestricted use, adaptation, and redistribution by anyone.

Open License (e.g., Creative Commons): Legal instruments that grant permissions to use, modify, and share a work (often requiring only attribution), thereby supporting the open exchange and continual improvement of educational resources.

Personalized Learning: An instructional approach that uses data and adaptive technologies to tailor educational content, pace, and support to the individual learner's needs, preferences, and performance.

Social Implications of AI in Education: The range of ways in which the integration of AI into teaching and learning reshapes social dynamics within educational communities, affecting equity of access, student-teacher relationships, cultural norms around knowledge sharing, privacy, and surveillance practices, power imbalances in decision-making, and the potential amplification or mitigation of existing biases and inequalities in educational opportunities.

Chapter 10
An Investigation Into Turkish University Students' Acceptance of ChatGPT in Education

Gulgun Afacan Adanır
https://orcid.org/0000-0002-0832-1808
Cambridge University, UK

ABSTRACT

This study aimed to examine the factors influencing university students' acceptance of ChatGPT in education. The research is grounded in the unified theory of acceptance and use of technology (UTAUT), which includes performance expectancy, effort expectancy, social influence, and facilitating conditions as key factors. The study was conducted at a state university in Turkey with a total of 208 student participants. Structural equation modelling (SEM) analysis was utilized to explore the relationships among these factors and the students' behavioral intention to use ChatGPT in their education. The findings revealed that performance expectancy and effort expectancy were positively associated with students' intention to use the ChatGPT system. Yet, social influence and facilitating conditions did not show a significant relationship with students' acceptance of the ChatGPT system.

INTRODUCTION

Artificial Intelligence (AI) is designed to generate novel outputs in response to natural language inputs. It is trained using data sourced from various online platforms to facilitate the creation of these outputs. The underlying technology of AI

DOI: 10.4018/979-8-3373-2612-2.ch010

relies on Machine Learning algorithms, which enable it to progressively improve its performance by learning from data.

With the recent tools and applications offered by AI technologies, the education area has started to transform traditional instructional methods. UNICEF (2021, p.16) provided a definition related to the use of AI in education: "AI refers to machine-based systems that can, given a set of human-defined objectives, make predictions, recommendations, or decisions that influence real or virtual environments. AI systems interact with us and act on our environment, either directly or indirectly. Often, they appear to operate autonomously and can adapt their behaviour by learning about the context. In education, AI tools can be used for smart instruction, automated assessment, and personalized learning (Oranga, 2023). Furthermore, AI systems have the capability to generate diverse forms of digital content, such as text, images, videos, and audio, in response to user inputs (The Alan Turing Institute). As a result, AI tools can support education while enhancing productivity and instructional outcomes, providing instant feedback and encouraging student engagement (Adıgüzel et al., 2023).

Chatbot is one of the software offered within the AI technology. Chatbot system is structured as "a software that talks with a user and is a virtual assistant able to answer a number of user questions, providing the correct responses" (Colace et al., 2018, p. 528). Chatbots use natural language processing and machine learning algorithms to communicate with humans. Chatbot users interact with the software by providing text or voice input and by obtaining text or voice output (Hamzah et al., 2021). Chatbots are one of the commonly employed AI technologies for supporting instructional activities (Okonkwo & Ade-Ibijola, 2021). Chatbots can present more interactive learning experience, provide immediate feedback and support, support personalized learning, enhance student engagement and motivation (Kooli, 2023).

ChatGPT was proposed as an AI-based chatbot in November 2022 (OpenAI, 2023). The utilization of ChatGPT in education has recently gained substantial attention (Rathore, 2023). Being an AI chatbot, ChatGPT has the capability to transform interactions and learning processes for students and educators.

ChatGPT assists educators in creating lesson plans, summarizing key concepts, and generating instructional materials. For instance, educators can employ ChatGPT for creating course outlines and developing content including presentations and learning activities (Rahman & Watanobe, 2023). It can provide structured outlines for lectures, suggest discussion questions, and develop interactive activities tailored to different learning levels (Kasneci et al., 2023). Moreover, it helps educators quickly draft quizzes, worksheets, and study guides, saving time on content preparation.

ChatGPT can help educators streamline grading and feedback by generating comments on students' work, suggesting improvements, and identifying common errors. While AI cannot fully replace human evaluation, it can provide initial feedback on essays, coding assignments, and other written responses, allowing educators to focus on more detailed assessments (Baidoo-Anu & Ansah, 2023). Beyond their instructional responsibilities, teachers must also manage routine tasks such as grading, record-keeping, and communication. In this context, AI-powered tools assist educators in efficiently handling these duties, enabling them to dedicate more time to teaching-related activities (Molina et al., 2024).

For students, ChatGPT can provide information in different fields, suggest ideas in writing, support personalized learning and immediate feedback (Ngo, 2023). According to the study of Fauzi et al. (2023), ChatGPT enhances student productivity in various ways. ChatGPT presents efficient information and resources about the content, assignments, and projects; assists students to improve their language skills; provides an online environment for collaboration among students; helps students to use their time efficiently and effectively by storing schedules of classes, deadlines for assignments, and the task lists. In addition, ChatGPT supports and motivates students in their learning process.

Nevertheless, comprehending the full impact of ChatGPT requires an examination of educators' and students' viewpoints on the integration of ChatGPT into educational settings (Limna et al., 2023). Although ChatGPT has quickly become popular as an advanced natural language processing tool, there is still limited research on how university students perceive and use it (Ngo, 2023; Strzelecki, 2024). In this respect, this study focuses on university students` experience in using ChatGPT. More specifically, the current study aims to investigate Turkish students` acceptance of ChatGPT use in higher education. The study is grounded in the unified theory of acceptance and use of technology (UTAUT), which includes performance expectancy, effort expectancy, social influence, and facilitating conditions as key factors.

RELATED WORKS

Technology acceptance models are utilized to investigate user intentions regarding the adoption of new innovations and technologies. In this regard, the commonly employed models are Technology Acceptance Model (TAM) (Davis, 1989), Diffusion of Innovation (DoI) Model (Rogers, 1962) and Unified Theory of Acceptance and Use of Technology (UTAUT) (Venkatesh et al., 2003).

TAM was proposed by Davis to investigate users' attitudes and intentions toward using information technologies (Davis, 1989). In the context of TAM, perceived usefulness (PU) and perceived ease of use (PEOU) are the two main determinants of technology acceptance. Davis defined PU as “the degree to which a person believes that using a particular system would enhance his or her job performance” (Davis, 1989, p. 320), and PEOU as “the degree to which a person believes that using a particular system would be free of effort" (p. 320). PU and PEOU contribute to a positive behavioral intention toward using a particular technology, which in turn affects the actual usage of that technology. Moreover, TAM posits that PEOU exerts a significant influence on PU.

The DOI Model, developed by Everett Rogers (1962), explains how new ideas, technologies, or practices spread within a society or social system over time. It identifies five key adopter categories: Innovators, Early Adopters, Early Majority, Late Majority, and Laggards, each differing in their willingness to adopt innovations. The model also highlights five attributes influencing adoption: relative advantage, compatibility, complexity, trialability, and observability. Relative Advantage refers to the degree to which an innovation is perceived as better than the existing solution. Compatibility reveals how well the innovation aligns with existing values, experiences, and needs of potential adopters. Complexity refers to the perceived difficulty of understanding and using the innovation. Trialability considers the extent to which the innovation can be experimented with before full adoption. Observability refers to the visibility of the innovation's benefits to others.

UTAUT has been recently constructed from the existing technology acceptance frameworks. UTAUT consists of crucial constructs from prior acceptance models (Venkatesh et al., 2003). Indeed, UTAUT considers four primary factors such as performance expectancy, effort expectancy, and social influence. Performance expectancy refers "the degree to which an individual believes that using the system will help him or her to attain gains in job performance" (Venkatesh et al., 2003, p.447). Effort expectancy is parallel to the perceived ease-of-use construct of TAM and means "the degree of ease associated with the use of the system" (p.450). Social influence can be defined as "the degree to which an individual perceives that important others believe he or she should use the new system" (p.451). Facilitating conditions can be defined as "the degree to which an individual believes that an organizational and technical infrastructure exists to support use of the system" (p.453). Furthermore, UTAUT incorporates four moderators (gender, age, experience, voluntariness of use) that moderate the influences of the four primary determinants on users` intentions towards technologies.

The Unified Theory of Acceptance and Use of Technology 2 (UTAUT2), proposed by Venkatesh et al. (2012), extends the original UTAUT model by incorporating additional constructs to better explain user acceptance of technology in consumer contexts. It includes Performance Expectancy, Effort Expectancy, Social Influence, Facilitating Conditions, and three new constructs: Hedonic Motivation, Price Value, and Habit. These factors collectively influence an individual's Behavioral Intention to use a technology, which then impacts their Actual Use. UTAUT2 has been widely applied in studies examining user acceptance of emerging technologies, providing valuable insights into how various factors such as motivation and cost considerations affect technology adoption (Venkatesh et al., 2012; Albayati, 2024).

To date, studies in various countries have been conducted to investigate students` intentions to use the ChatGPT system in education.

Shaengchart et al. (2023) investigated the factors influencing the acceptance of ChatGPT usage among higher education students in Bangkok, Thailand. Utilizing the TAM, the study employed a quantitative approach, surveying 400 students through convenience sampling. The findings revealed that facilitating conditions and students' attitudes significantly impacted ChatGPT adoption. In contrast, perceived ease of use, perceived usefulness, and privacy and security concerns did not show a direct influence on usage. The study underscores the importance of addressing diverse factors, such as user attitudes and support infrastructure, to enhance the successful integration of ChatGPT and similar educational technologies in higher education settings.

Albayati (2024) explored undergraduate students' perceptions and awareness of using ChatGPT as a regular assistance tool from a user acceptance perspective. The study integrated the TAM with external constructs such as privacy, security, social influence, and trust to assess factors influencing students' acceptance of ChatGPT. A quantitative approach was adopted, surveying undergraduate students regarding their use of ChatGPT. The findings revealed that perceived ease of use and perceived usefulness significantly shape students' attitudes toward using ChatGPT. Additionally, privacy concerns were found to have no discernible relationship with the perceived ease of using ChatGPT.

Yilmaz et al. (2023) investigated university students' perceptions of Chat GPT using the TAM. Their study examined factors such as perceived usefulness, perceived ease of use, and behavioral intention to use the AI tool. The findings indicate that students generally view Chat GPT positively, with perceived usefulness and ease of use significantly influencing their intention to adopt the technology.

Saif et al. (2024) examined the adoption of Chat-GPT in higher education by applying the Technology Acceptance Model (TAM) within the context of ubiquitous learning. Their study, conducted with 156 final-year management science students in Pakistan, investigated the relationship between academic stress, anxiety, and the use of Chat-GPT for academic tasks such as research projects and internship reports. Using Structural Equation Modeling (SEM) with Smart PLS, the findings indicate that increased academic stress contributes to heightened anxiety, which subsequently encourages students to adopt AI-driven tools like Chat-GPT. Furthermore, the perceived usefulness and ease of use of Chat-GPT foster a positive attitude toward its adoption, ultimately mitigating stress and enhancing learning outcomes.

Strzelecki (2024) examined the factors influencing university students' acceptance of ChatGPT in higher education by extending the UTAUT2 model with the construct of personal innovativeness. Surveying 503 Polish state university students, the study employed Partial Least Squares Structural Equation Modeling (PLS-SEM) for analysis. The results indicated that 'Habit' had the most significant impact on behavioral intention, followed by 'Performance Expectancy' and 'Hedonic Motivation'. Additionally, 'Behavioral Intention' was the strongest predictor of 'Use Behavior', with 'Habit' and 'Facilitating Conditions' also playing notable roles.

Habibi et al. (2023) investigated the factors influencing the acceptance and use of ChatGPT among students in Indonesian higher education institutions. Employing the Unified UTAUT2 as their theoretical framework, the study utilized Partial Least Squares Structural Equation Modeling (PLS-SEM) to analyze data collected from students across various Indonesian universities. The findings highlighted that performance expectancy, effort expectancy, social influence, facilitating conditions, and hedonic motivation significantly influenced students' behavioral intentions to use ChatGPT. Moreover, facilitating conditions and hedonic motivation were found to directly affect the actual usage of ChatGPT.

Sobaih et al. (2024) examined the acceptance and use of ChatGPT among students in Saudi Arabian higher education. Utilizing the UTAUT2, they conducted a survey with 520 students at a public university during the 2023–2024 academic year. The study found that performance expectancy, social influence, and effort expectancy positively influenced students' behavioral intentions to use ChatGPT, which in turn affected their actual usage. Interestingly, facilitating conditions did not have the expected positive impact; instead, a negative relationship with behavioral intention and an insignificant effect on actual use were observed. These findings suggest that the availability of resources and support may not be as influential in this context. The study highlights the importance of understanding cultural and contextual factors when integrating AI tools like ChatGPT into educational settings.

METHODOLOGY

Research Model and Hypotheses

The UTAUT is widely recognized as a significant theoretical framework for studying technology adoption, as it integrates and builds upon several earlier models used to examine users' acceptance of innovations and emerging technologies (Maphosa et al., 2020).

Among the various technology acceptance models, UTAUT has been identified as the most frequently applied framework for analyzing the adoption of information technologies. Research suggests that UTAUT demonstrates greater predictive power compared to other models in contexts related to technology acceptance (Almaiah et al., 2019). This enhanced explanatory capability makes it particularly suitable for studying user adoption behaviors in educational and digital learning environments.

Given its robustness and effectiveness in technology adoption research, UTAUT was chosen as the theoretical foundation for this study to explore university students' acceptance and intention to use the ChatGPT system as an educational tool.

The structure of the research model based on UTAUT is illustrated in Figure 1, providing a visual representation of the relationships between key factors and students' behavioral intentions.

Figure 1. Structure of the research model

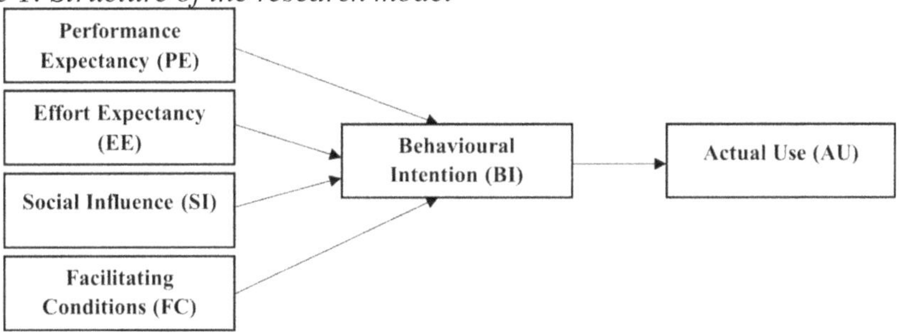

The research model comprises several key dimensions, each of which is associated with specific hypotheses.

Performance Expectancy relates to the belief that an information system will enhance job performance. Specifically, for ChatGPT, this expectancy pertains to improved academic performance and time efficiency in learning. If students recognize these benefits of ChatGPT, their motivation to use this platform will increase. Research has shown that students who expect ChatGPT to assist them in generating ideas, summarizing complex topics, and improving writing quality are more inclined to view it as a valuable academic aid (Zhai, 2023). However, if students perceive that ChatGPT's responses are unreliable or prone to errors, their Performance Expectancy decreases, leading to lower acceptance and reduced frequency of use in academic settings (Kasneci et al., 2023).

Consequently, the corresponding hypothesis was established in the following way:

H1: Performance expectancy positively influences students' behavioral intention to use the ChatGPT system in educational settings.

Effort expectancy refers to the degree of ease associated with using a technology. It's crucial for students to grasp how to use ChatGPT and to show the required skills while using it. Therefore, user-friendly features in ChatGPT enhance students' intention to employ the system. The perceived ease of use of ChatGPT can lead to increased trust in the technology, further encouraging its adoption among students (Masa'deh et al., 2024). However, if students encounter difficulties in interacting with ChatGPT, their Effort Expectancy decreases, which may hinder the widespread acceptance of such AI-driven educational tools (Lee et al., 2024).

Based on this premise, the following hypothesis was formulated:

H2: Effort expectancy positively influences students' behavioral intention to use the ChatGPT system in educational settings.

Social influence relates to the extent to which others influence an individual's decision to adopt or reject a technology. Regarding ChatGPT, students may be swayed by the opinions of their instructors and peers. Additionally, support and resources provided by the university can encourage students to use ChatGPT. The relationship between Social Influence and ChatGPT adoption varies across academic disciplines; students in social sciences are more influenced by their peers and instructors' opinions regarding ChatGPT usage than those in applied sciences (Wang et al., 2024). However, some studies have found that Social Influence does not significantly impact students' intention to use ChatGPT, implying that other factors may play a more dominant role in technology acceptance within certain educational contexts (Zhai, 2023). As ChatGPT and similar AI tools become more prevalent, the role of Social Influence may evolve, especially as academic institutions develop formal policies and guidelines for their use in educational settings (Wang et al., 2024).

The related hypothesis was thus formulated as follows:

H3: Social influence positively influences students' behavioral intention to use the ChatGPT system in educational settings.

Facilitating conditions encompass the belief that organizational and technical infrastructure are essential to support the use of a system. In the context of ChatGPT, this includes having access to the requisite technology (e.g., mobile device with internet connection), possessing relevant knowledge, and having access to technology-related support. When these conditions are met, student usage of the system is likely to increase. Studies have demonstrated that when universities provide adequate technical infrastructure and training, students are more likely to integrate ChatGPT into their academic routines (Tan et al., 2024). The availability of institutional support, such as workshops and tutorials on ChatGPT usage, enhances students' confidence and reduces apprehension towards adopting this AI tool (Jasrai, 2025). Research indicates that students who perceive strong facilitating conditions are more inclined to develop a habit of using ChatGPT for their studies, thereby increasing its acceptance and utilization (Strzelecki, 2023). Conversely, the absence of necessary resources and support structures can hinder the effective adoption of ChatGPT among students, underscoring the importance of facilitating conditions in technology acceptance models (Gupta & Yang, 2024).

Consequently, the following hypothesis was offered:

H4: Facilitating conditions positively influence students' behavioral intention to use the ChatGPT system in educational settings.

Research Design and Participants

The current study is based on a research model that incorporates the key factors of the UTAUT. These factors include performance expectancy, effort expectancy, facilitating conditions, and social influence. The primary objective of the study is to examine whether and to what extent each of these UTAUT factors significantly impacts university students' intentions to adopt and utilize ChatGPT as an educational tool.

To achieve this objective, the study employs a correlational research design, which is appropriate for identifying relationships between variables without manipulating them. Within this framework, the UTAUT factors (performance expectancy, effort expectancy, facilitating conditions, and social influence) function as independent variables, meaning they are the predictors or influencing factors in the study. Meanwhile, behavioral intention to use ChatGPT serves as the dependent variable, as it represents the outcome that the study seeks to explain based on the influence of the independent variables.

By applying this research approach, the study aims to provide insights into the factors that drive or hinder university students' willingness to integrate ChatGPT into their learning processes, ultimately contributing to the broader understanding of technology acceptance in educational settings.

The current study employed the purposive sampling method to select participants. This non-random sampling technique is particularly suitable for research that requires data from individuals who meet specific predefined criteria (Campbell et al., 2020). By using this approach, the study ensured that the selected participants were relevant to the research objectives.

For this study, we specifically targeted undergraduate students enrolled in the Information and Communication Technologies (ICT) course as the participant group. These students were chosen because of their exposure to technology-related topics, making them suitable candidates for examining the factors influencing the adoption of ChatGPT in educational settings.

During the ICT course, students were provided with information about the study, including its purpose and significance. Those who were interested in participating voluntarily submitted their responses to an online survey, which served as the primary data collection tool.

To provide a more comprehensive understanding of the sample composition, Table 1 presents the demographic profiles of the participating students. A total of 208 undergraduate students took part in this study. The gender distribution among participants is nearly equal, with 48.8% identifying as female and 51.2% as male.

Table 1. Demographic profiles of learners

	Items	Frequency (N)	Percentage (%)
Gender	Female	101	48.8
	Male	106	51.2
Age	18-20	53	25.5
	21-23	135	64.9
	24-26	13	6.3
	27+	5	2.4
Faculty	Agriculture	3	1.4
	Dentistry	4	1.9
	Engineering	90	43.3
	Language, History, and Geography	3	1.4
	Law	4	1.9
	Political Sciences	20	9.6
	Natural Sciences	53	25.5
	Social Sciences	5	2.4
	Sport	1	0.5
	Theology	3	1.4
	Veterinary	7	3.4
	Vocational School	13	6.3
Total		208	100

The participants' ages range from 18 to 40 years old, reflecting a diverse group of university students with varying academic experiences and backgrounds. Additionally, the participants are enrolled in twelve different faculties, demonstrating a wide representation across disciplines. These faculties include Agriculture, Dentistry, Engineering, Language, History, and Geography, Law, Political Sciences, Natural Sciences, Social Sciences, Sport, Theology, Veterinary, and Vocational School.

Among these faculties, the majority of participants are from the Faculty of Engineering and the Faculty of Natural Sciences, indicating a higher level of interest or availability of students from these disciplines in the study. This diverse academic representation allows for a more holistic understanding of university students' perspectives on adopting ChatGPT in educational settings.

Data Collection and Analysis

The survey used in this study was adapted from validated scales derived from the UTAUT, originally developed by Venkatesh et al. (2003). The survey was designed to measure key factors influencing students' behavioral intentions to use ChatGPT in educational settings. These factors include performance expectancy, effort expectancy, social influence, and facilitating conditions.

To ensure the questionnaire's relevance and clarity, necessary modifications were made to align with the study's context. These modifications aimed to enhance participants' understanding of the questions while maintaining the validity and reliability of the original UTAUT scales. A detailed list of the survey items is provided in Appendix A, allowing for a transparent overview of the measurement instruments used in the study.

The survey was administered as an online form, allowing participants to conveniently submit their responses digitally. This method facilitated efficient data collection and ensured accessibility for a diverse group of students.

To analyze the collected data, various statistical techniques were employed. Reliability analysis was conducted to assess the consistency and suitability of the survey items in measuring the hypothesized constructs. To validate the factor structure, Confirmatory Factor Analysis (CFA) was performed to determine whether the survey items were appropriately associated with their respective UTAUT factors.

Furthermore, convergent validity was examined to confirm that variables expected to be related exhibited strong correlations, while discriminant validity ensured that theoretically unrelated constructs remained distinct from one another (Fornell & Larcker, 1981). Model-fit testing was then carried out to evaluate the overall structural validity of the research model.

Finally, Structural Equation Modeling (SEM) was utilized to analyze the relationships between the study variables and provide insights into the underlying structure of the research model. The results and interpretations of these analyses are comprehensively presented in the Findings section.

FINDINGS

A reliability analysis was conducted to determine whether the factors were consistent and aligned with the hypothesized outcomes. This analysis assessed the internal consistency of the survey items, ensuring that they reliably measured the intended constructs.

As presented in Table 2, the Cronbach's Alpha values for the factors ranged from 0.722 to 0.952. According to Taber (2018), a Cronbach's Alpha value above 0.70 is considered an acceptable indicator of reliability. Since all the obtained values exceeded this recommended threshold, the results confirm that the factors in the study demonstrated sufficient internal consistency and reliability.

Table 2. Reliability analysis results

Factors	Cronbach's Alpha
Performance Expectancy (PE)	.874
Effort Expectancy (EE)	.879
Social Influence (SI)	.781
Facilitating Conditions (FC)	.722
Behavioral Intention (BI)	.952
Actual Use (AU)	.889

Confirmatory factor analysis was performed to identify standard regression weights for scale items. The results are provided in the Table 3.

Table 3. Standard regression weights

ID	Items	Estimate
PE1	I find ChatGPT useful in my learning.	.84
PE2	Using ChatGPT enables me to accomplish learning activities more quickly.	.85
PE3	Using ChatGPT increases my learning productivity.	.82
PE4	If I use ChatGPT, I will increase my chances of getting a better mark in the courses.	.70

continued on following page

Table 3. Continued

ID	Items	Estimate
EE1	My interaction with ChatGPT is clear and understandable.	.76
EE2	I am skilful at using ChatGPT.	.85
EE3	Learning to use ChatGPT is easy for me.	.88
EE4	I find it easy to get ChatGPT to do what I want it to do.	.73
SI1	People who are important to me think that I should use ChatGPT.	.80
SI2	People who influence my behaviour think I should use ChatGPT.	.88
SI3	The seniors in my college are helpful in the use of ChatGPT.	.53
SI4	In general, the university has supported the use of ChatGPT.	.52
FC1	I have the resources necessary to use ChatGPT.	.79
FC2	I have the knowledge necessary to use ChatGPT.	.89
FC3	ChatGPT is not compatible with other systems I use.	-.09
FC4	A specific person (or group) is available for assistance with ChatGPT difficulties.	.44
BI1	I intend to use ChatGPT in the future.	.95
BI2	I predict I would use ChatGPT in the future.	.95
BI3	I plan to use ChatGPT in the future.	.96
BI4	I would recommend ChatGPT to my friends.	.82
AU1	I consider myself a regular user of ChatGPT.	.86
AU2	I prefer to use ChatGPT when available.	.82
AU3	I do most learning tasks by using ChatGPT.	.79
AU4	My tendency is towards using ChatGPT whenever possible.	.80

Based on the results in Table 3, four items (i.e., SI3, SI4, FC3, and FC4) were eliminated from the model since their estimated regression weights were less than 0.7 (Hair et al., 2010).

Convergent Validity

Convergent validity seeks to ensure that measures expected to be related are indeed related (Chin & Yao, 2021). This was assessed using the average variance extracted (AVE) value. The results are shown in Table 4. Each factor's AVE value exceeded 0.5, affirming the importance of convergence (Fornell & Larcker, 1981).

Table 4. Results for the convergent validity and discriminant validity

AVE	Construct	PE	EE	SI	FC
0.648	**PE**	**.805**			
0.654	EE	.694	**.809**		
0.730	SI	.526	.451	**.854**	
0.720	FC	.674	.801	.431	**.848**

Discriminant Validity

Discriminant validity aims to demonstrate that measures which should not be related are indeed unrelated (Rasoolimanesh, 2022). This study employed the Fornell and Larcker (1981) test to assess discriminant validity. According to this test, discriminant validity is confirmed if the square root of a construct's AVE is greater than its correlations with other constructs (Fornell & Larcker, 1981). Table 4 shows that the diagonal elements, which represent the square root of the AVEs, are all higher than any other correlations. Thus, the discriminant validity of the suggested research model was verified.

The Model-Fit Testing

The model-fit testing was conducted to justify the structure of the model. The results of this analysis are presented in Table 5.

Table 5. Model fit results

Fit Indices	Values
X^2/df	2.944
CFI	0.912
GFI	0.814
RMSEA	0.097

As shown in Table 5, the X2/df value was less than 3, indicating a good model fit (Hooper et al., 2008). Additionally, model fit is recommended when CFI and GFI values are close to 1, and RMSEA values are close to 0 (Schumacker & Lomax, 2010). In this study, the CFI value was 0.912 and the GFI value was 0.814, both approaching 1. The RMSEA value was 0.097, approaching 0. Consequently, the fit criteria measures verified the model fit.

Testing Hypotheses

In AMOS (v.20), SEM analysis was conducted to examine the model's structure. The results of the SEM analysis are presented in Table 6 and Figure 2.

Table 6. Results of the SEM analysis

Path	Estimate	S.E.	C.R.	P
Performance Expectancy-Behavioral Intention	.690	.127	7.164	.001
Effort Expectancy-Behavioral Intention	.196	.122	1.915	.002
Facilitating Conditions-Behavioral Intention	-.061	.099	-.601	.674
Social Influence-Behavioral Intention	.057	.054	.950	.367
Behavioral Intention-Actual Use	.705	.068	11.132	.001

According to the SEM results, it was found that performance expectancy (β = .690, CR = 7.164, $p < .05$) and effort expectancy (β = .196, CR = 1.915, $p < .05$) have significant impact on university students' behavioral intention to use ChatGPT system. However, facilitating conditions (β =- .061, CR =-.601, p = .674) and social influence (β = .057, CR = .950, p = .367) were not significantly related to university students' behavioral intention to use ChatGPT system. Additionally, it was revealed that behavioral intention has significant effect on university students' actual use of ChatGPT system (β = .705, CR = 11.132, $p < .05$).

Figure 2. Structure model with results

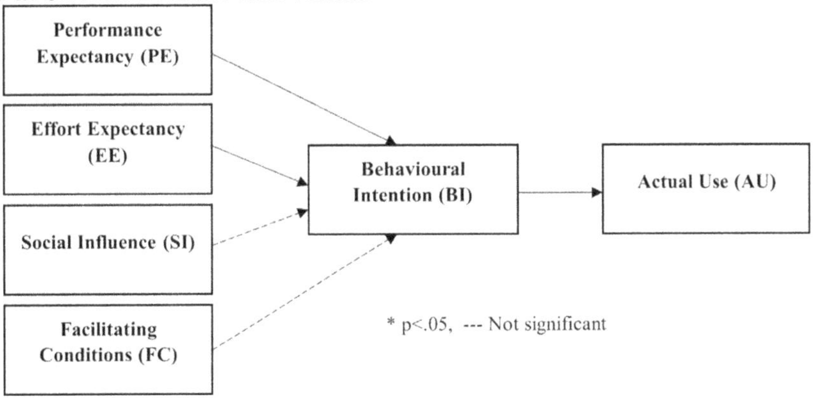

DISCUSSIONS

Performance expectancy factor was found to have a significant effect on university students` acceptance of ChatGPT use in education. Based on this factor, it can be said that ChatGPT system is useful in learning and has capability to increase students` learning productivity. For instance, by the use of ChatGPT, students can complete learning activities more quickly by obtaining information for the research purposes. Similar results were produced by the studies that investigated benefits or acceptance of ChatGPT use in education. In their study, Menon and Shilpa (2023) also resulted that ChatGPT is helping students in accomplishing their tasks by providing related information in a fast way compared to other search engines. While search engines provide links to related web sites, ChatGPT presents a summarized response based on user requests. Such kind of capability has been increasing positive attitudes towards the use of ChatGPT (Lee et al., 2024). According to the study done by Ngo (2023), students indicated various benefits like that they save time, acquire information about various fields, get personalized feedback and obtain ideas for writing assignments with the use of ChatGPT. Perceived usefulness aspect of TAM shows similarity with performance expectancy, and it was mostly found as a significant factor in students` acceptance of ChatGPT (Raman et al., 2024). Aligned with the TAM framework's focus on usefulness as a key factor in technology adoption, students are more likely to adopt ChatGPT if they perceive it as beneficial to their studies (Alshurideh et al., 2024). Students can use ChatGPT as a supportive learning tool to enhance their academic performance and understanding. It assists them in clarifying complex topics, generating study materials, and improving their writing through instant feedback and suggestions (Youssef et al., 2024).

Based on second results of the current study, university students reported that the ChatGPT has easy-to-use features that they can learn to use it quickly. That is, effort expectancy resulted as a significant factor on ChatGPT use in education. Both similar and different results were found by the prior studies in the literature. For instance, Kim (2023) revealed that effort expectation is positively affecting college students` intention to use ChatGPT. On the other hand, in their research Biloš and Budimir (2024) found that effort expectancy has no significant impact on students` ChatGPT adoption. Ease of use is a crucial system feature since it is necessary for users to easily navigate in the ChatGPT system and efficiently access their needs (Acosta-Enriquez et al., 2024). The user interface of ChatGPT system supports users` effective navigation by providing simple and organised structure. Additionally, users can quickly learn using the ChatGPT system without experiencing any difficulty. ChatGPT offers user-friendly features that make it accessible and practical for students across various academic levels. Its conversational interface allows learners to interact naturally, reducing barriers often associated with traditional educational tools (Ngo, 2023). The tool's ability to generate instant feedback, summaries, and examples contributes to personalized and self-paced learning experiences (Wu et al., 2024). These features, combined with its cross-platform availability, have positioned ChatGPT as an effective digital assistant in contemporary education.

In the context of the social influence factor, students identify their behaviours based on thoughts of their peers and instructors. In the current study, it was found that social influence has no significant influence on university` students' behavioral intention to use ChatGPT. Especially, the items related to the support of instructors and the university were removed from the analysis since they were found to have less effect on social influence factor. Similar and different results were found by the prior studies that examined students` acceptance of ChatGPT. For instance, in their study, Matalka et al. (2024) found that social influence has no important role in student` intention to use ChatGPT system. The same study indicated the reason as students` lack of guidance needs from peers and instructors for the use of ChatGPT. As noted in the study by Strzelecki (2024), social influence plays a minimal role in shaping individuals' intentions to use ChatGPT. Those more inclined to adopt the AI-powered chatbot tend to be early adopters with higher educational backgrounds who are less influenced by external opinions. The research did not identify any notable social pressure driving ChatGPT adoption, likely because the technology is still relatively new and not yet widely integrated. However, as universities and academic institutions begin to implement policies on the use of AI tools like ChatGPT, social influence may become a more relevant factor in the future. On the other hand, some other studies like Abdaljaleel et al. (2024) found the significant effect of social influence related to the acceptance of ChatGPT.

Facilitating conditions are related to availability of essential resources (e.g. computer, Internet connection), existence of knowledge to use the ChatGPT, compatibility with other systems, and availability of the technical support. In the existing study, the facilitating conditions factor was not found to have a significant effect on students` intention to use ChatGPT system. This finding may be resulted because students have already mobile phones and/or laptops with Internet connection and the use of ChatGPT is very easy for the users. Therefore, students may not think that facilitating conditions have impact on their acceptance of the ChatGPT system. Similar results were also provided by some prior studies that examined students` intentions to use the ChatGPT. For instance, Sabeh (2024) and Strzelecki (2024) found that facilitating conditions have no effect on students` acceptance of ChatGPT. Faruk et al. (2023) research also found that facilitating conditions did not significantly impact students' use of ChatGPT. This result is attributed to two key factors. First, using ChatGPT only requires basic access to a computer and the internet, without the need for advanced technological tools. Second, the platform's simple and intuitive interface resembles widely used search engines like Google or Bing, which students are already familiar with. This design familiarity reduces the need for extra support or technical knowledge, making facilitating conditions largely irrelevant in influencing usage.

CONCLUSION

The primary aim of this study was to examine the factors influencing the acceptance of the ChatGPT system. The research was conducted during the 2023-2024 academic term at a state university in Turkey, with 208 undergraduate students participating. The research model was based on the UTAUT framework and included the factors of performance expectancy, effort expectancy, facilitating conditions, and social influence. SEM analysis was employed to analyze the model's structure. The SEM findings revealed that performance expectancy and effort expectancy were positively associated with students' intention to use the ChatGPT system. Yet, social influence and facilitating conditions did not show a significant relationship with students' acceptance of the ChatGPT system.

The current study confirmed that students` intentions to use the ChatGPT system are influenced by the system usefulness factors. When students realize that ChatGPT enhances their learning productivity, their intention to use the system will increase. Specifically, students can save time by using ChatGPT, as it allows them to complete learning tasks quickly. At the same time, students have chance to get better marks in their courses when they use ChatGPT for research and proof-reading purposes. However, students may not be aware of the appropriate use of the ChatGPT, and this may result in some ethical issues. Therefore, instructors need to provide clear instructions about the use of ChatGPT for assignment purposes.

The study also found that students` intentions to use the ChatGPT system are affected by the system usability factors. In this respect, easy-to-use features, clear directions, and effective navigation in the context of the ChatGPT system are important. Developers need to consider these usability issues for better acceptance of the ChatGPT. For instance, students can be involved in the system design and development phase, and developers can provide system prototypes in the process. Hence, students can propose some ideas regarding usability of the ChatGPT. In this way, user friendly system can be resulted.

The present study is subject to certain limitations. This study is limited by its sample size, as the number of students who completed the questionnaires was lower than anticipated. Future research should aim to gather data from a larger sample to improve the robustness of the study. In addition, qualitative data can be obtained from the students to deeply analyze their opinions about the ChatGPT system. Instructors' perceptions of ChatGPT are crucial in motivating its use, as both students and instructors play pivotal roles in the learning environment. Therefore, future research should explore the adoption of ChatGPT from the perspectives of both students and instructors to provide a comprehensive and detailed analysis.

REFERENCES

Abdaljaleel, M., Barakat, M., Alsanafi, M., Salim, N. A., Abazid, H., Malaeb, D., Mohammed, A. H., Hassan, B. A. R., Wayyes, A. M., Farhan, S. S., Khatib, S. E., Rahal, M., Sahban, A., Abdelaziz, D. H., Mansour, N. O., AlZayer, R., Khalil, R., Fekih-Romdhane, F., Hallit, R., & Sallam, M. (2024). A multinational study on the factors influencing university students' attitudes and usage of ChatGPT. *Scientific Reports*, *14*(1), 1983. DOI: 10.1038/s41598-024-52549-8 PMID: 38263214

Acosta-Enriquez, B. G., Arbulú Ballesteros, M. A., Huamaní Jordan, O., López Roca, C., & Saavedra Tirado, K. (2024). Analysis of college students' attitudes toward the use of ChatGPT in their academic activities: Effect of intent to use, verification of information and responsible use. *BMC Psychology*, *12*(1), 255. DOI: 10.1186/s40359-024-01764-z PMID: 38720382

Adıgüzel, T., Kaya, M. H., & Cansu, F. K. (2023). Revolutionizing education with AI: Exploring the transformative potential of ChatGPT. *Contemporary Educational Technology*, *15*(3), ep429. DOI: 10.30935/cedtech/13152

Albayati, H. (2024). Investigating undergraduate students' perceptions and awareness of using ChatGPT as a regular assistance tool: A user acceptance perspective study. *Computers and Education: Artificial Intelligence*, *6*, 100203. DOI: 10.1016/j.caeai.2024.100203

Almaiah, M. A., Alamri, M. M., & Al-Rahmi, W. (2019). Applying the UTAUT model to explain the students' acceptance of mobile learning system in higher education. *IEEE Access : Practical Innovations, Open Solutions*, *7*, 174673–174686. DOI: 10.1109/ACCESS.2019.2957206

Alshurideh, M., Jdaitawi, A., Sukkari, L., Al-Gasaymeh, A., Alzoubi, H. M., Damra, Y., Yasin, S., Al Kurdi, B., & Alshurideh, H. (2024). Factors affecting ChatGPT use in education employing TAM: A Jordanian universities' perspective. *International Journal of Data and Network Science*, *8*(3), 1599–1606. DOI: 10.5267/j.ijdns.2024.3.007

Arthur, F., Salifu, I., & Nortey, S. A. (2024). Predictors of higher education students' behavioural intention and usage of ChatGPT: The moderating roles of age, gender and experience. *Interactive Learning Environments*, 1–27. Advance online publication. DOI: 10.1080/10494820.2024.2362805

Baidoo-Anu, D., & Ansah, L. O. (2023). Education in the era of generative artificial intelligence (AI): Understanding the potential benefits of ChatGPT in promoting teaching and learning. *Journal of AI*, *7*(1), 52–62. DOI: 10.61969/jai.1337500

Biloš, A., & Budimir, B. (2024). Understanding the Adoption Dynamics of ChatGPT among Generation Z: Insights from a Modified UTAUT2 Model. *Journal of Theoretical and Applied Electronic Commerce Research*, *19*(2), 863–879. DOI: 10.3390/jtaer19020045

Campbell, S., Greenwood, M., Prior, S., Shearer, T., Walkem, K., Young, S., Bywaters, D., & Walker, K. (2020). Purposive sampling: Complex or simple? Research case examples. *Journal of Research in Nursing : JRN*, *25*(8), 652–661. DOI: 10.1177/1744987120927206 PMID: 34394687

Chin, C. L., & Yao, G. (2021). Convergent validity. In *Encyclopedia of quality of life and well-being research* (pp. 1–2). Springer International Publishing. DOI: 10.1007/978-3-319-69909-7_573-2

Colace, F., De Santo, M., Lombardi, M., Pascale, F., Pietrosanto, A., & Lemma, S. (2018). Chatbot for e-learning: A case of study. *International Journal of Mechanical Engineering and Robotics Research*, *7*(5), 528–533. https://www.ijmerr.com/uploadfile/2018/0831/20180831043721869.pdf. DOI: 10.18178/ijmerr.7.5.528-533

Davis, F. D. (1989). Perceived usefulness, perceived ease of use and use acceptance of information technology. *Management Information Systems Quarterly*, *13*(3), 319–340. DOI: 10.2307/249008

Faruk, L. I. D., Rohan, R., Ninrutsirikun, U., & Pal, D. (2023, December). University students' acceptance and usage of generative AI (ChatGPT) from a psycho-technical perspective. In *Proceedings of the 13th International Conference on Advances in Information Technology* (pp. 1-8). DOI: 10.1145/3628454.3629552

Fauzi, F., Tuhuteru, L., Sampe, F., Ausat, A. M. A., & Hatta, H. R. (2023). Analysing the role of ChatGPT in improving student productivity in higher education. *Journal of Education*, *5*(4), 14886–14891. DOI: 10.31004/joe.v5i4.2563

Fornell, C., & Larcker, D. F. (1981). Evaluating structural equation models with unobservable variables and measurement error. *JMR, Journal of Marketing Research*, *18*(1), 39–50. DOI: 10.1177/002224378101800104

Gupta, M., & Yang, Y. (2024). ChatGPT usage and attitudes are driven by perceptions of usefulness, ease of use, risks, and psycho-social impact: A study among university students in the UAE. *Frontiers in Education*, *9*, 1414758. DOI: 10.3389/feduc.2024.1414758

Habibi, A., Muhaimin, M., Danibao, B. K., Wibowo, Y. G., Wahyuni, S., & Octavia, A. (2023). ChatGPT in higher education learning: Acceptance and use. *Computers and Education: Artificial Intelligence*, *5*, 100190. DOI: 10.1016/j.caeai.2023.100190

Hair, J. F., Black, W. C., Babin, B. J., & Anderson, R. E. (2010). *Multivariate data analysis*. Pearson.

Hamzah, W. W., Ismail, I., Yusof, M. K., Saany, S. M., & Yacob, A. (2021). Using learning analytics to explore responses from student conversations with chatbot for education. *International Journal of Engineering Pedagogy*, *11*(6), 70–84. DOI: 10.3991/ijep.v11i6.23475

Hooper, D., Coughlan, J., & Mullen, M. (2008). Structural equation modelling: Guidelines for determining model fit. *Electronic Journal of Business Research Methods*, *6*(1), 53–60.

Jasrai, L. (2025). Extending UTAUT model to examine the usages of ChatGPT among Indian students in higher education: A structural equation modelling approach. *The TQM Journal*. Advance online publication. DOI: 10.1108/TQM-12-2024-0498

Kasneci, E., Sessler, K., Küchemann, S., Bannert, M., Dementieva, D., Fischer, F., Gasser, U., Groh, G., Günnemann, S., Hüllermeier, E., Krusche, S., Kutyniok, G., Michaeli, T., Nerdel, C., Pfeffer, J., Poquet, O., Sailer, M., Schmidt, A., Seidel, T., & Kasneci, G. (2023). ChatGPT for good? On opportunities and challenges of large language models for education. *Learning and Individual Differences*, *4*, 100100. DOI: 10.1016/j.lindif.2023.102274

Kim, H. J. (2023). A study on the intentions of ChatGPT users using the extended UTAUT model. *Journal of Digital Contents Society*, *24*(7), 1465–1473. DOI: 10.9728/dcs.2023.24.7.1465

Kooli, C. (2023). Chatbots in education and research: A critical examination of ethical implications and solutions. *Sustainability (Basel)*, *15*(7), 5614. DOI: 10.3390/su15075614

Lee, S., Jones-Jang, S. M., Chung, M., Kim, N., & Choi, J. (2024). Who is using ChatGPT and why? Extending the Unified Theory of Acceptance and Use of Technology (UTAUT) model. *Information Research*, *29*(1), 54–72. DOI: 10.47989/ir291647

Limna, P., Kraiwanit, T., Jangjarat, K., Klayklung, P., & Chocksathaporn, P. (2023). The use of ChatGPT in the digital era: Perspectives on chatbot implementation. *Journal of Applied Learning and Teaching*, *6*(1), 64–74. https://journals.sfu.ca/jalt/index.php/jalt/article/view/797/593

Maphosa, V., Dube, B., & Jita, T. (2020). A UTAUT evaluation of WhatsApp as a tool for lecture delivery during the COVID-19 lockdown at a Zimbabwean University. *International Journal of Higher Education*, *9*(5), 84–93. https://files.eric.ed.gov/fulltext/EJ1270462.pdf. DOI: 10.5430/ijhe.v9n5p84

Masa'deh, R., Majali, S. A. L., Alkhaffaf, M., Thurasamy, R., Almajali, D., Altarawneh, K., Al-Sherideh, A., & Altarawni, I. (2024). Antecedents of adoption and usage of ChatGPT among Jordanian university students: Empirical study. *International Journal of Data and Network Science*, *8*(2), 1099–1110. DOI: 10.5267/j.ijdns.2023.11.024

Matalka, M., Badir, R., Ahmad, A., Al-Said, K., Nassar, H., Alzoubi, S., & Alzoubi, M. (2024). The adoption of ChatGPT marks the beginning of a new era in educational platforms. *International Journal of Data and Network Science*, *8*(3), 1941–1946. DOI: 10.5267/j.ijdns.2024.1.019

Menon, D., & Shilpa, K. (2023). "Chatting with ChatGPT": Analyzing the factors influencing users' intention to Use the Open AI's ChatGPT using the UTAUT model. *Heliyon*, *9*(11), 1–19. DOI: 10.1016/j.heliyon.2023.e20962 PMID: 37928033

Molina, E., Cobo, C., Pineda, J., & Rovner, H. (2024). AI revolution in education: What you need to know. In *Digital Innovations in Education*. World Bank. DOI: 10.1596/41806

Ngo, T. T. A. (2023). The perception by university students of the use of ChatGPT in education. *International Journal of Emerging Technologies in Learning*, *18*(17), 4–12. DOI: 10.3991/ijet.v18i17.39019

Okonkwo, C. W., & Ade-Ibijola, A. (2021). Chatbots applications in education: A systematic review. *Computers and Education: Artificial Intelligence*, *2*, 100033. DOI: 10.1016/j.caeai.2021.100033

Open, A. I. (2023). *ChatGPT: Optimizing language models for dialogue*. https://openai.com/blog/chatgpt/ Accessed 12 June 2023.

Oranga, J. (2023). Benefits of artificial intelligence (ChatGPT) in education and learning: Is ChatGPT helpful? *International Review of Practical Innovation* [IR-PITAGE]. *Technology and Green Energy*, *3*(3), 46–50. DOI: 10.54443/irpitage.v3i3.1250

Rahman, M. M., & Watanobe, Y. (2023). ChatGPT for education and research: Opportunities, threats, and strategies. *Applied Sciences (Basel, Switzerland)*, *13*(9), 5783. DOI: 10.3390/app13095783

Raman, R., Mandal, S., Das, P., Kaur, T., Sanjanasri, J. P., & Nedungadi, P. (2024). Exploring university students' adoption of ChatGPT using the diffusion of innovation theory and sentiment analysis with gender dimension. *Human Behavior and Emerging Technologies*, *2024*(1), 3085910. DOI: 10.1155/2024/3085910

Rasoolimanesh, S. M. (2022). Discriminant validity assessment in PLS-SEM: A comprehensive composite-based approach. *Data Analysis Perspectives Journal, 3*(2), 1–8.

Rathore, B. (2023). Future of AI & generation alpha: ChatGPT beyond boundaries. Eduzone: International Peer Reviewed/ Refereed Multidisciplinary Journal, 12(1), 63-68. https://www.eduzonejournal.com/index.php/eiprmj/article/view/254

Rogers, E. M. (1962). *Diffusion of innovations*. Free Press.

Sabeh, H. N. (2024). What Drives IT Students Toward ChatGPT? Analyzing the Factors Influencing Students' Intention to Use ChatGPT for Educational Purposes. In *2024 21st International Multi-Conference on Systems, Signals & Devices (SSD)* (pp. 533-539). IEEE.

Saif, N., Khan, S. U., Shaheen, I., ALotaibi, F. A., Alnfiai, M. M., & Arif, M. (2024). Chat-GPT; validating Technology Acceptance Model (TAM) in education sector via ubiquitous learning mechanism. *Computers in Human Behavior, 154*, 108097. DOI: 10.1016/j.chb.2023.108097

Schumacker, R. E., & Lomax, R. G. (2010). *A beginner's guide to structural equation modeling* (3rd ed.). Routledge.

Shaengchart, Y., Bhumpenpein, N., Kongnakorn, K., Khwannu, P., Tiwtakul, A., & Detmee, S. (2023). Factors influencing the acceptance of ChatGPT usage among higher education students in Bangkok, Thailand. *Advance Knowledge for Executives, 2*(4), 1-14. https://ssrn.com/abstract=4592118

Sobaih, A. E. E., Elshaer, I. A., & Hasanein, A. M. (2024). Examining students' acceptance and use of ChatGPT in Saudi Arabian higher education. *European Journal of Investigation in Health, Psychology and Education, 14*(3), 709–721. DOI: 10.3390/ejihpe14030047 PMID: 38534908

Strzelecki, A. (2024). Students' acceptance of ChatGPT in higher education: An extended unified theory of acceptance and use of technology. *Innovative Higher Education, 49*(2), 223–245. DOI: 10.1007/s10755-023-09686-1

Taber, K. S. (2018). The use of Cronbach's alpha when developing and reporting research instruments in science education. *Research in Science Education, 48*(6), 1273–1296. DOI: 10.1007/s11165-016-9602-2

Tan, C. N.-L., Tee, M., & Koay, K. Y. (2024). Discovering students' continuous intentions to use ChatGPT in higher education: A tale of two theories. *Asian Education and Development Studies, 13*(4), 356–372. DOI: 10.1108/AEDS-04-2024-0096

UNICEF. (2021). *Policy guidance on AI for children.* Author. https://www.unicef.org/globalinsight/media/2356/file/UNICEF-Global-Insight-policy-guidance-AI-children-2.0-2021.pdf

Venkatesh, V., Morris, M. G., Davis, G. B., & Davis, F. D. (2003). User acceptance of information technology: Toward a unified view. *Management Information Systems Quarterly*, *27*(3), 425–478. DOI: 10.2307/30036540

Venkatesh, V., Thong, J. Y. L., & Xu, X. (2012). Consumer acceptance and use of information technology: Extending the unified theory of acceptance and use of technology. *Management Information Systems Quarterly*, *36*(1), 157–178. DOI: 10.2307/41410412

Wang, Y., Chen, X., & Zhang, Y. (2024). Integrating the adapted UTAUT model with moral obligation, trust and perceived risk to predict ChatGPT adoption for assessment support: A survey with students. *Computers and Education: Artificial Intelligence*, *6*, 100246. DOI: 10.1016/j.caeai.2024.100246

Wu, T. T., Lee, H. Y., Li, P. H., Huang, C. N., & Huang, Y. M. (2024). Promoting self-regulation progress and knowledge construction in blended learning via ChatGPT-based learning aid. *Journal of Educational Computing Research*, *61*(8), 3–31. DOI: 10.1177/07356331231191125

Yilmaz, H., Maxutov, S., Baitekov, A., & Balta, N. (2023). Student attitudes towards Chat GPT: A technology acceptance model survey. *International Educational Review*, *1*(1), 57–83. DOI: 10.58693/ier.114

Youssef, E., Medhat, M., Abdellatif, S., & Al Malek, M. (2024). Examining the effect of ChatGPT usage on students' academic learning and achievement: A survey-based study in Ajman, UAE. *Computers and Education: Artificial Intelligence*, *7*, 100316. DOI: 10.1016/j.caeai.2024.100316

Zhai, X. (2023). ChatGPT and AI: The game changer for education. *Zhai, X.(2023). ChatGPT: Reforming Education on Five Aspects. Shanghai Education*, 16-17. https://ssrn.com/abstract=4389098

KEY TERMS AND DEFINITIONS

Chatbot: A software that talks with a user and is a virtual assistant able to answer a number of user questions, providing the correct responses.

ChatGPT: Proposed as an AI-based chatbot in November 2022.

Effort Expectancy: Defined as the degree of ease associated with using a technology, significantly influences students' behavioral intention to adopt ChatGPT for academic purposes (Venkatesh et al., 2003).

Facilitating Conditions: Defined as the resources and support available to individuals for using a technology, significantly influence students' behavioral intention to adopt ChatGPT in higher education (Zhai, 2023).

Performance Expectancy: Which refers to the degree to which students believe that using ChatGPT will improve their academic performance, plays a crucial role in determining their willingness to adopt the technology (Venkatesh et al., 2003).

Social Influence: Defined as the degree to which individuals perceive that important others believe they should use a particular technology, has been identified as a significant predictor of students' behavioral intention to adopt ChatGPT in higher education (Arthur et al., 2024).

APPENDIX: QUESTIONNAIRE

Table 7. Questionnaire items

Construct	ID	Items
Performance Expectancy (PE)	PE1	I find ChatGPT useful in my learning.
	PE2	Using ChatGPT enables me to accomplish learning activities more quickly.
	PE3	Using ChatGPT increases my learning productivity.
	PE4	If I use ChatGPT, I will increase my chances of getting a better mark in the courses.
Effort Expectancy (EE)	EE1	My interaction with ChatGPT is clear and understandable.
	EE2	I am skilful at using ChatGPT.
	EE3	Learning to use ChatGPT is easy for me.
	EE4	I find it easy to get ChatGPT to do what I want it to do.
Social Influence (SI)	SI1	People who are important to me think that I should use ChatGPT.
	SI2	People who influence my behaviour think I should use ChatGPT.
	SI3	The seniors in my college are helpful in the use of ChatGPT.
	SI4	In general, the university has supported the use of ChatGPT.
Facilitating Conditions (FC)	FC1	I have the resources necessary to use ChatGPT.
	FC2	I have the knowledge necessary to use ChatGPT.
	FC3	ChatGPT is not compatible with other systems I use.
	FC4	A specific person (or group) is available for assistance with ChatGPT difficulties.
Behavioural Intention (BI)	BI1	I intend to use ChatGPT in the future.
	BI2	I predict I would use ChatGPT in the future.
	BI3	I plan to use ChatGPT in the future.
	BI4	I would recommend ChatGPT to my friends.
Actual Use (AU)	AU1	I consider myself a regular user of ChatGPT.
	AU2	I prefer to use ChatGPT when available.
	AU3	I do most learning tasks by using ChatGPT.
	AU4	My tendency is towards using ChatGPT whenever possible.

Chapter 11
The Landscape of Artificial Intelligence in Education:
A Bibliometric Analysis (1989–2025)

Aylin Akinlar
https://orcid.org/0000-0002-4448-2721
Bandirma Onyedi Eylul University, Turkey

ABSTRACT

This chapter presents a comprehensive bibliometric analysis of the evolution and trends of artificial intelligence (AI) in education (AIED) from 1989 to 2025. The present study focuses on peer-reviewed publications indexed in the Web of Science, exploring key contributors, institutions, countries, and emergent research themes across the field. Utilizing data extracted through a systematic search and analyzed with the Biblioshiny R language and VosViewer, this study identifies major clusters, collaboration patterns, and citation dynamics. The findings are interpreted within the framework of educational technology paradigms such as TPACK and the SAMR model. The chapter provides insights into the role of AI in shaping curriculum, pedagogy, assessment, and equity in education. By mapping the intellectual and conceptual structure of this growing field, the analysis reveals prevailing and emerging trends while offering guidance for future research and practice.

DOI: 10.4018/979-8-3373-2612-2.ch011

1. INTRODUCTION

The growing presence of artificial intelligence (AI) in education marks a pivotal transformation in how teaching and learning are approached in the 21st century. Although digital tools have influenced educational practices for decades, AI brings a new depth of complexity—offering possibilities once considered the realm of science fiction. Technologies such as intelligent tutoring systems, adaptive learning platforms, automated grading tools, and real-time learning analytics are no longer theoretical; they are actively reshaping classrooms, institutions, and educational policy. These tools not only enable more personalized and data-driven learning experiences but also raise critical questions about equity, ethics, and the evolving role of educators. The urgency of this transformation became particularly evident during the COVID-19 pandemic, which acted as a global catalyst for digital adoption and intensified the need to examine how AI is shaping educational research, design, and delivery (e.g., Holmes et al., 2021; Zawacki-Richter et al., 2019). As a result, scholarly interest in the direction, scope, and implications of AI in education has grown significantly, reflecting a collective attempt to understand and guide this complex technological shift.

The historical evolution of educational technology reveals a steady progression through multiple paradigms—beginning with the mechanical tools of the Industrial Age, such as blackboards and slide projectors, and advancing toward the dynamic digital platforms that define contemporary classrooms. However, the emergence of artificial intelligence (AI) in education represents more than a linear extension of these prior innovations. Rather, AI acts as a transformative force that challenges conventional notions of instruction, learning, and even human cognition itself. Unlike earlier educational technologies that functioned primarily as static delivery mechanisms, AI systems possess the capacity to interpret vast amounts of learner data, respond adaptively to individual behaviors, and even generate novel content. These capabilities raise important philosophical and pedagogical questions about agency, authorship, and the shifting boundaries between human and machine intelligence in the educational sphere (Luckin, 2017; Selwyn, 2019).

The roots of AI in education can be traced to the development of intelligent tutoring systems (ITS) during the 1970s and 1980s. Pioneering programs such as SCHOLAR and GUIDON sought to replicate the instructional strategies of human tutors by offering individualized feedback and problem-solving support. These early systems, though innovative, were hampered by limited computational resources, highly specific content domains, and rigid learning environments (Carbonell, 1970). As a result, their adoption remained relatively constrained. It was not until the early 2010s—with the advent of big data, increased computational power, cloud infrastructure, and advanced machine learning techniques—that AI in education began to scale effectively and exhibit meaningful adaptability across diverse learning contexts (Zawacki-Richter et al., 2019).

By the mid-2010s, AI technologies had begun to move beyond experimental prototypes and enter the mainstream educational ecosystem. Automated essay scoring engines, predictive analytics dashboards, and conversational AI tools such as chatbots were introduced to enhance both learning and institutional support services. Massive Open Online Course (MOOC) platforms like Coursera, edX, and Khan Academy began employing recommendation algorithms to customize learning pathways, while adaptive learning systems such as Carnegie Learning and Squirrel AI demonstrated the practical potential of AI in tailoring instruction to individual student needs (Holmes et al., 2021). Concurrently, AI also found applications in administrative domains, including student enrollment forecasting, early warning systems for dropout prevention, and data-informed decision-making at the institutional level. These developments have repositioned AI not as an auxiliary tool, but as a central component of educational infrastructure—one that is increasingly interwoven with both pedagogical strategies and institutional operations.

The global outbreak of COVID-19 in 2020 served as an inflection point for the integration of artificial intelligence in education. As schools and universities worldwide transitioned to emergency remote teaching, educators were prompted—often out of necessity—to explore and adopt AI-driven tools for instruction, assessment, engagement, and content delivery. What had previously been considered experimental or supplementary quickly became essential to maintaining educational continuity. In parallel, students began interacting with AI technologies not only as instructional supports but also as objects of critical reflection and inquiry. Notably, the emergence of generative AI models such as OpenAI's GPT series disrupted conventional assumptions about creativity, authorship, and academic integrity. These tools demonstrated an unprecedented capacity to compose essays, solve complex problems, and simulate dialogue with a level of fluency that provoked immediate ethical, pedagogical, and epistemological concerns (Kasneci et al., 2023; Rudolph et al., 2023).

As AI applications became more pervasive, scholarly discourse expanded from a narrow focus on technical innovation to include deeper considerations of social justice, transparency, and long-term sustainability. Increasing attention was paid to the ways algorithmic systems can perpetuate existing biases, compromise learner privacy, and alter cognitive development trajectories. Scholars and policymakers began to frame AI not simply as a neutral tool, but as a socio-technical system embedded in cultural, ethical, and institutional contexts (Williamson & Eynon, 2020). This shift gave rise to calls for the development of "human-centered AI" frameworks—approaches that emphasize transparency, inclusivity, and cultural sensitivity in the design, implementation, and evaluation of AI systems (Holmes et al., 2021). The overarching objective increasingly became not just the automation or optimization of education, but the meaningful augmentation of human learning, creativity, and critical engagement.

Despite the growing vibrancy of this field, the academic literature on AI in education remains highly fragmented. Contributions emerge from a diverse array of disciplines—education, computer science, cognitive psychology, learning analytics, philosophy, and policy studies—each with its own theoretical orientations, methodological preferences, and publication venues. This disciplinary dispersion has led to a lack of cross-referencing and limited synthesis across domains, making it challenging for both emerging and experienced scholars to navigate the field's conceptual contours. As the volume of publications grows exponentially, identifying influential works, prevailing themes, and future research directions has become increasingly complex (Zawacki-Richter et al., 2019; Chen et al., 2020).

The rapid acceleration of generative AI technologies—such as ChatGPT, Bard, Claude, and others—has only amplified this complexity. These tools have sparked renewed debates around the nature of knowledge production, the evolution of the teaching profession, and the role of critical thinking in an age of algorithmically generated content. Beyond instructional design and assessment, the conversation has broadened to interrogate the implications of AI for educational equity, learner autonomy, and the ethics of data use. Researchers are now increasingly called upon to move beyond surface-level adoption and toward a more critical, interdisciplinary, and socially responsive engagement with AI in education.

Despite the exponential growth in studies exploring artificial intelligence in education, comprehensive efforts to systematically map the intellectual and conceptual development of the field remain relatively scarce. In this context, bibliometric analysis offers a powerful methodological framework for uncovering how scholarly knowledge is structured, how research trends evolve, and which contributions—whether authors, institutions, or publications—have shaped the field over time. By examining patterns in publication output, citation networks, keyword co-occurrence, and collaborative linkages, bibliometric studies provide a macroscopic view of academic activity, allowing researchers to trace trajectories of influence and identify emerging areas of interest (Donthu et al., 2021; van Eck & Waltman, 2010).

Despite a growing number of studies on AI applications in education, few have undertaken a comprehensive bibliometric mapping of the field's conceptual and intellectual evolution. By adopting this methodological lens, the present study fills a critical gap by uncovering longitudinal trends, thematic shifts, and transnational collaboration patterns that are otherwise difficult to discern through narrative synthesis alone.

Situated at the intersection of scientometrics and research evaluation, bibliometric methods involve the quantitative analysis of metadata drawn from academic databases. This includes authorship, institutional affiliations, citation counts, journal impact, and topical descriptors. When visualized through tools such as VOSviewer and Bibliometrix, these data points reveal thematic clusters, intellectual lineages, and collaborative structures that might otherwise remain obscured. While qualitative literature reviews offer depth and interpretive nuance, bibliometric analysis complements them by providing a robust, data-driven foundation upon which future inquiry can build.

This chapter employs bibliometric analysis to chart the development of AI in education from 1989 to 2025, using the Web of Science Core Collection as the primary data source. The analysis aims to uncover the thematic evolution, conceptual structure, and collaborative networks that have guided the field's transformation over nearly four decades. By applying co-authorship, co-citation, and keyword co-occurrence mapping techniques, the study constructs a comprehensive overview of how scholarly interest has shifted in response to technological innovations, pedagogical imperatives, and global disruptions such as the COVID-19 pandemic.

The objectives of the chapter are fourfold:

1. **To chart the historical growth of AI in education** by analyzing annual publication volumes and key inflection points;
2. **To identify leading scholars, institutions, and countries** that have significantly contributed to the field's development;
3. **To examine scientific collaboration and citation networks**, revealing patterns of knowledge exchange and influence;
4. **To explore thematic evolution and emerging research trends** through keyword analysis and clustering algorithms.

Together, these objectives provide a panoramic perspective on the state of AI in education. The findings not only illuminate the historical trajectory of the field but also shed light on increasingly important topics such as algorithmic ethics, affective computing, emotional intelligence, and the integration of AI within human-centered learning paradigms. In doing so, the study offers a valuable reference point for educators, researchers, and policymakers seeking to make informed, ethical, and forward-looking decisions in a rapidly evolving landscape.

Ultimately, the rise of AI in education signals more than a technological shift—it represents a paradigmatic reconfiguration of how knowledge is produced, assessed, and experienced. It compels stakeholders to reimagine pedagogical frameworks, assessment strategies, and institutional missions in ways that align with the demands and responsibilities of an AI-driven world. By providing a systematic and empirically grounded bibliometric overview, this chapter contributes to a more cohesive, interdisciplinary, and ethically attuned understanding of the field. In doing so, it lays the foundation for collaborative innovation and critical engagement in the years to come.

2. THEORETICAL FRAMEWORK

The integration of artificial intelligence (AI) into education represents more than a technological innovation—it signifies a profound paradigm shift those challenges and reconfigures long-standing pedagogical, cognitive, ethical, and sociocultural assumptions. As such, any bibliometric investigation of this evolving field must be grounded in a robust and multidimensional theoretical framework. The present study draws on a diverse set of conceptual lenses to interpret the trends, patterns, and intellectual structures that have shaped AI in education. These include foundational learning theories (e.g., constructivism and sociocultural theory), models of technology integration (such as TPACK and SAMR), ethical paradigms (including human-centered AI and digital responsibility), and frameworks for the analysis of scientific knowledge production (e.g., Kuhn's paradigm shifts, Lotka's Law, and diffusion of innovation theory).

Together, these perspectives offer a rich and integrated foundation for understanding how AI is conceptualized, operationalized, and critiqued within educational contexts. They illuminate the philosophical assumptions behind technology adoption, the pedagogical affordances of AI systems, and the sociotechnical dynamics at play in their development and deployment. The theoretical frameworks outlined below provide a lens through which the bibliometric findings can be contextualized and interpreted.

2.1 Constructivism and AI-Supported Personalization

Constructivist theory, rooted in the work of Jean Piaget (1973), asserts that learners actively construct knowledge through interaction with their environment, drawing upon prior experiences, internal cognitive schemas, and social engagement. In AI-mediated educational settings, this principle is operationalized through adaptive learning technologies and intelligent tutoring systems (ITS) that personalize content delivery based on real-time assessment of student progress and engagement (Pane et al., 2015).

AI-enhanced tools such as virtual laboratories, simulation environments, and game-based learning platforms are emblematic of constructivist pedagogy. They promote exploration, hypothesis testing, feedback iteration, and autonomous meaning-making—core tenets of a learner-centered paradigm. In such environments,

AI functions not merely as a content provider, but as an interactive learning partner capable of adjusting tasks to fit the learner's evolving cognitive needs. These affordances reflect the constructivist belief that meaningful learning arises when individuals are actively involved in the construction of their own understanding, rather than passively receiving information.

Importantly, constructivism also informs the evolving role of educators in AI-rich contexts. Teachers are increasingly positioned not as sole knowledge transmitters, but as facilitators and guides who scaffold student learning through carefully designed interactions with both AI tools and human peers. This pedagogical shift mirrors the epistemological foundations of constructivist thought and underscores the potential of AI to support differentiated and personalized instruction in increasingly diverse classrooms (Schmid et al., 2021).

2.2 Sociocultural Theory and Collaborative AI

Complementing constructivist theory is Lev Vygotsky's (1978) sociocultural framework, which emphasizes the fundamentally social nature of learning. According to Vygotsky, knowledge is co-constructed through interaction with more capable others—whether peers, teachers, or tools—within the Zone of Proximal Development (ZPD). In contemporary AI applications, this social dimension is increasingly evident in systems designed to facilitate collaboration, dialogue, and mediated interaction.

AI-driven technologies such as conversational agents, peer feedback algorithms, and collaborative recommendation systems reflect the principles of sociocultural learning. These tools create opportunities for learners to engage in authentic communication, participate in shared meaning-making, and receive timely scaffolding from both human and non-human interlocutors. For instance, natural language processing (NLP) enables AI systems to generate context-sensitive prompts, translations, or elaborative feedback, extending the reach of instruction into multilingual and culturally diverse classrooms (Blikstein & Worsley, 2016).

Moreover, AI tools are increasingly integrated into digital forums and learning platforms that simulate peer interaction and support collaborative learning. These environments blur the line between learner and machine, positioning AI as a "digital other" capable of mediating social interaction and expanding the traditional boundaries of the ZPD. However, this also introduces new complexities: How do learners negotiate meaning with non-human agents? To what extent can AI-mediated feedback fulfill the cognitive and emotional functions of human guidance? Such questions demand deeper theoretical inquiry as AI becomes embedded within the relational fabric of education.

In this context, sociocultural theory provides a valuable lens for analyzing both the affordances and limitations of AI-facilitated collaboration. It invites critical reflection on how these tools influence the social dynamics of learning, the formation of academic communities, and the cultural relevance of educational content.

2.3 TPACK and SAMR: Models for Technology Integration

The effective integration of artificial intelligence into educational settings requires more than access to tools—it demands pedagogical intentionality and theoretical clarity. The Technological Pedagogical Content Knowledge (TPACK) framework, developed by Mishra and Koehler (2006), offers a comprehensive model for understanding how educators combine technological, pedagogical, and content knowledge to make informed instructional decisions. Within the context of AI, TPACK enables an assessment of how well teachers are prepared to use AI tools in ways that align with both curricular objectives and the specific needs of their learners. For example, implementing an AI-driven assessment system is not merely a technical decision; it involves understanding how such systems align with disciplinary learning goals, assessment ethics, and feedback practices.

Complementing this perspective is the SAMR model—Substitution, Augmentation, Modification, and Redefinition—which categorizes the depth and impact of technology integration (Puentedura, 2006). AI applications span this continuum in diverse ways: at the substitution level, AI may automate routine grading tasks; at the redefinition level, it may enable entirely new forms of learning, such as real-time emotion-sensitive feedback or predictive analytics–based instructional pathways. These frameworks help educators and researchers move beyond simplistic metrics of usage to evaluate the pedagogical value and transformative potential of AI technologies.

In response to the growing complexity of AI tools, recent literature has proposed extensions such as TPACK-AI (Akgun & Greenhow, 2022), which emphasize the distinct knowledge domains required to effectively implement AI in education. These include an understanding of machine learning algorithms, ethical considerations such as fairness and transparency, and the sociocultural dynamics mediated by AI. This expanded framework underscores the need for teacher education and professional development programs that are attuned not only to the technical dimensions of AI, but also to its pedagogical, ethical, and institutional implications.

2.4 Human-Centered AI and Digital Ethics

As AI systems increasingly inform decisions about student learning trajectories, course placements, assessment, and even behavioral interventions, the ethical landscape of education has grown significantly more complex. Frameworks such as Human-Centered AI (HCAI) (Shneiderman, 2020) and digital ethics (Floridi, 2018) offer critical guidance for the design and deployment of AI tools in education. These frameworks advocate for technologies that prioritize human values, promote agency, and ensure transparency and accountability in data-driven decision-making processes.

Human-centered AI emphasizes augmenting rather than replacing human judgment, advocating for systems that empower learners and educators, preserve user autonomy, and provide mechanisms for human oversight. In contrast to techno-deterministic visions of AI, HCAI positions education as a deeply human endeavor, requiring tools that are adaptable to diverse cultural, emotional, and cognitive contexts. Digital ethics further interrogates broader systemic issues, including algorithmic bias, surveillance culture, data commodification, and digital inequality. These frameworks collectively challenge the field to move beyond questions of technical feasibility and instead ask: *Whose interests are being served? What assumptions are embedded in these systems?* (Williamson & Eynon, 2020).

In bibliometric terms, the increasing prevalence of keywords such as *fairness*, *privacy*, *accountability*, and *transparency* signals a theoretical expansion from functional to normative concerns. This ethical turn is especially significant in educational contexts marked by systemic inequities, where AI has the potential to either mitigate or exacerbate exclusionary practices. Critical scholarship in this domain urges a shift from techno-solutionism toward critical digital pedagogy, where ethical reflection is integral to innovation.

2.5 Theories of Knowledge Diffusion and Scientific Development

The methodological foundations of bibliometric analysis are rooted in classic theories of scientific production and knowledge dissemination. Lotka's Law (1926), for instance, posits that a small subset of highly productive authors is responsible for the majority of publications within a given field. This principle assists in interpreting the core-periphery dynamics often observed in academic publishing and highlights the concentration of scholarly influence. Bradford's Law complements this by identifying the "core" journals that produce the most frequently cited articles, offering insight into the visibility and centrality of publication venues.

Thomas Kuhn's (1962) theory of scientific revolutions adds a macro-historical perspective by suggesting that knowledge production proceeds through phases of normal science punctuated by paradigm shifts. In the context of AI in education, one could argue that the field is experiencing such a transformation—from a focus on efficiency and automation toward more holistic concerns around ethics, equity, and human development. Bibliometric mapping allows researchers to trace these shifts by analyzing keyword evolution, citation clustering, and the emergence of new research fronts (e.g., explainable AI, affective computing, AI for equity).

Moreover, theories of knowledge translation and interdisciplinary integration are increasingly relevant. As a transdisciplinary field, AI in education necessitates collaboration across computer science, education, psychology, ethics, design, and policy. This cross-pollination challenges traditional disciplinary boundaries and calls for theoretical models that address epistemological pluralism, communication across knowledge systems, and the co-construction of shared frameworks.

2.6 Critical Theory and Posthuman Perspectives

To fully understand the cultural and political dimensions of AI in education, it is essential to draw on critical theory, feminist epistemology, and post humanist thought. These perspectives challenge the presumed neutrality of AI systems, emphasizing that they are embedded with the values, ideologies, and power structures of those who design and deploy them. From this standpoint, AI is not simply a tool, but a socio-technical artifact that reflects and reinforces broader systems of inequality (Noble, 2018).

Critical pedagogy, for instance, interrogates the role of AI in perpetuating neo-liberal logics of standardization, surveillance, and accountability within educational institutions. Feminist theory sheds light on how algorithmic decision-making may reflect gendered assumptions or reproduce structural biases in data collection and interpretation. Post humanist perspectives go even further, questioning the human-machine dichotomy and exploring how AI reshapes identity, embodiment, and cognition in hybrid learning environments (Bayne, 2018).

These critical lenses are increasingly visible in high-impact literature on AI in education, particularly in studies addressing *algorithmic injustice*, *AI literacy*, and *educational surveillance*. Such scholarship foregrounds education not just as a site of knowledge acquisition, but also as a space of ethical contestation, civic formation, and power negotiation. By incorporating these perspectives, researchers are expanding the methodological and epistemological boundaries of the field and fostering a more reflective and socially responsive AI discourse.

3. RESEARCH CONTEXT AND LITERATURE OVERVIEW

The advent of artificial intelligence (AI) has precipitated a paradigmatic shift across diverse sectors, with education emerging as a key domain of technological transformation. AI applications in education—ranging from intelligent tutoring systems and predictive learning analytics to adaptive learning platforms and generative tools such as ChatGPT—are reshaping how knowledge is delivered, personalized, and scaled. In response, educators, institutions, and policymakers are increasingly focused on the meaningful integration of these tools into curricula, pedagogical models, and assessment frameworks.

This acceleration of AI adoption has stimulated vigorous academic debate across domains. Scholars are interrogating questions of pedagogical effectiveness, the redefinition of the teacher's role, ethical accountability, and the socio-technical architectures shaping digital learning environments (Selwyn, 2019; Holmes et al., 2021). As educational systems grapple with the promise and pitfalls of AI-enhanced learning, there is an urgent need to map how scholarly inquiry has evolved in this dynamic and interdisciplinary space.

The field of AI in education (AIED) encompasses a wide range of technologies, including machine learning algorithms, natural language processing, robotics, and intelligent tutoring systems. These tools are increasingly framed within educational technology integration models such as TPACK (Mishra & Koehler, 2006) and SAMR (Puentedura, 2010), which emphasize the interplay between pedagogy, content, and technological affordances. Recent meta-analyses underscore the importance of aligning AI tools with learning sciences and evidence-based instructional practices (Zawacki-Richter et al., 2019; Holmes et al., 2021), emphasizing that innovation must be pedagogically grounded and ethically informed.

At the same time, critical theoretical frameworks—especially Critical Pedagogy (Freire, 1970; Giroux, 2020)—have emerged as essential lenses for understanding the sociopolitical implications of AI in education. These perspectives highlight how AI tools are not neutral but instead reflect the values, assumptions, and power relations embedded within their design. Algorithmic opacity, cultural erasure, and biased data models raise urgent questions about equity, inclusion, and the commodification of educational data (Williamson & Eynon, 2020). Scholars within this tradition advocate for participatory design approaches and culturally responsive AI systems that reflect learner diversity and promote social justice in education.

This chapter draws from this pluralistic theoretical foundation—combining constructivist and sociocultural pedagogies, technology integration models, digital ethics, and critical theory—to interpret and contextualize the bibliometric trends in AIED research. These frameworks are particularly relevant in examining themes such as user agency, communication skills, AI literacy, and the integration of AI in multilingual and multicultural classrooms, which have gained prominence in recent years.

Over the past decade, research on AI in education has expanded rapidly across disciplinary boundaries, including computer science, cognitive psychology, instructional design, and communication studies. Early work focused on the development and evaluation of intelligent tutoring systems (VanLehn, 2011), which demonstrated outcomes comparable to one-on-one human tutoring in specific domains. The rise of learning analytics and educational data mining (Siemens & Long, 2011; Baker, Marker & Rossi, 2016) has enabled large-scale modeling of student behavior, adaptive interventions, and predictive assessment systems.

Simultaneously, critical scholarship has interrogated the implications of these developments for educational equity, privacy, and epistemology. Williamson et al. (2021) argue that AI's integration into educational governance must be analyzed through the lens of neoliberal and technocratic discourses, which often prioritize quantifiable outputs over holistic, dialogic learning. Selwyn (2019) similarly cautions against uncritical technological optimism, calling for a renewed emphasis on humanistic and democratic values in education.

The introduction of generative AI tools such as ChatGPT and other large language models (LLMs) since 2022 has significantly shifted research agendas. Scholars have begun to explore their effects on student engagement, writing practices, feedback mechanisms, and academic integrity (Akgun & Greenhow, 2022; Dwivedi et al., 2023; Mishra & Koehler, 2006). While these technologies offer opportunities for real-time feedback and creativity, they also raise pressing concerns around plagiarism, authorship, and the devaluation of original thinking.

Importantly, research has expanded beyond Anglo-American contexts to reflect global concerns about equity, accessibility, and language inclusivity. For example, Alimisis (2022) discusses robotics-integrated AI pedagogy rooted in socio-constructivism in Greece, while Benítez et al. (2021) analyze Latin American education ministries' digital strategies involving AI. In Türkiye, Yıldız and Topal (2023) report teacher perspectives on AI integration during remote learning, highlighting both enthusiasm and concerns around autonomy and fairness. UNESCO (2023) underscores the urgency of creating culturally sensitive, linguistically inclusive AI systems that reflect the diverse realities of Global South learners.

While the literature is rich and multifaceted, few studies employ a longitudinal and bibliometric approach to synthesize its conceptual development. This chapter seeks to address that gap by conducting a systematic bibliometric analysis of 2,412 documents published between 1989 and 2025. It maps key contributors, institutional affiliations, research methodologies, and thematic clusters, drawing attention to both established and emerging areas within AIED.

Research Question

This chapter explores the following research question:

How has the global scholarly landscape of artificial intelligence in education (1989–2025) evolved, and what emerging themes and conceptual gaps can be identified to guide future research and practice?

4. METHODOLOGY

To systematically examine the intellectual and conceptual evolution of artificial intelligence in education (AIED), this study employed bibliometric analysis, a method grounded in quantitative techniques used to explore patterns in scholarly communication. Bibliometric approaches allow researchers to identify influential publications, trace the development of thematic areas, and map collaborative networks within and across disciplines (Donthu et al., 2021).

Justification for Method Selection

Bibliometric analysis was chosen for this study due to its capacity to systematically map the intellectual, thematic, and collaborative structure of a rapidly evolving and interdisciplinary field such as Artificial Intelligence in Education (AIED). Unlike traditional literature reviews, which rely on subjective interpretation and limited scope, bibliometric methods offer a data-driven and objective means of identifying influential authors, institutions, journals, and thematic trends over time (Donthu et al., 2021). This approach enables the detection of hidden research patterns, shifts in scholarly focus, and underexplored areas, thereby offering a panoramic view of the field's development and guiding future research with empirical clarity. Given the exponential growth of AI-related publications and the field's fragmentation across disciplines, bibliometric mapping provides an essential meta-perspective that is both rigorous and replicable.

The year range of 1989 to 2025 was chosen to encompass the formative and developmental phases of AIED scholarship. The starting year, 1989, corresponds to the period when AI applications began to appear more visibly in educational research databases. The end year, 2025, was selected to capture both historical depth and future-facing trends, including recent surges in publications due to the COVID-19 pandemic and the advent of generative AI tools such as ChatGPT. This inclusive range allows for a longitudinal understanding of the field's growth, particularly its shifts from rule-based systems to human-centered, ethical, and personalized AI applications.

4.1 Data Source and Search Strategy

The dataset for this study was extracted from the Web of Science (WoS) Core Collection, a widely recognized academic database offering high-quality bibliographic metadata. The search was conducted using the terms "Artificial Intelligence" AND "Education" in the topic field (which includes titles, abstracts, author keywords, and Keywords Plus®). To ensure both rigor and relevance, several inclusion criteria were applied:

- **Document types**: Peer-reviewed journal articles, review papers, and conference proceedings
- **Publication years**: 1989 to 2025 (inclusive)
- **Languages**: English, Spanish, German, and Portuguese
- **Access**: Preference was given to open-access publications wherever available

This retrieval process yielded a total of 790 documents, which served as the primary dataset for the analysis.

4.2 Data Processing and Analytical Tools

The bibliographic data were exported in BibTeX and plain text formats and imported into Biblioshiny, the web interface of the Bibliometrix R package (Aria & Cuccurullo, 2017), as well as into VOSviewer for visualization and network analysis. This software environment was used to conduct both performance analysis and science mapping. The study focused on the following core components:

- **Performance Analysis**: Included descriptive statistics related to publication output by year, author, country, institution, and source (journal). This analysis helped assess the productivity and impact of scholars and publishing venues.
- **Science Mapping**: Techniques such as co-citation analysis, bibliographic coupling, and keyword co-occurrence were applied to uncover conceptual linkages between studies and track evolving research communities within the field.
- **Thematic Evolution**: Using strategic diagrams and thematic maps, the study explored how dominant research themes have emerged, developed, or declined over time.
- **Collaboration Networks**: Co-authorship and institutional collaboration networks were visualized to identify the degree of international and interdisciplinary cooperation.

4.3 Analytical Focus

The analyses addressed both static and dynamic dimensions of the field. Static dimensions included cumulative author productivity, institutional contributions, and source impact, while dynamic dimensions explored the evolution of research fronts, keyword trends, and shifts in collaborative patterns. This twofold approach enabled the identification of both foundational literature and emerging research hotspots.

4.4 Limitations

While bibliometric analysis offers valuable insights into scholarly structures and trends, it also presents certain limitations. First, the Web of Science database, despite its comprehensive indexing, does not include grey literature, books, or many non-English sources, which may result in an inherent Western-centric bias. Second, the reliance on citation-based metrics prioritizes publication frequency and impact over the methodological rigor or theoretical depth of individual studies. As such, this analysis should be interpreted as a macroscopic overview, best supplemented by qualitative reviews for deeper understanding.

5. FINDINGS

5.1 Publication Growth Over Time

The publication trajectory in the field of artificial intelligence in education (AIED) reveals a marked acceleration over the past three decades. As illustrated in Figure 1, scholarly output remained minimal throughout the 1990s and early 2000s, reflecting the nascent state of both AI technologies and their educational applications during that period. The number of publications began to rise modestly in the early 2010s, coinciding with the broader adoption of learning analytics, intelligent tutoring systems, and cloud-based educational platforms.

A significant inflection point is observable beginning in 2016, aligning with advances in machine learning, natural language processing, and adaptive learning environments. The most substantial surge in publication volume, however, occurred between 2020 and 2024, a period characterized by the COVID-19 pandemic and the resulting global shift toward remote and hybrid modes of education. This era prompted widespread experimentation with AI tools for content delivery, automated assessment, learner engagement, and institutional decision-making (Talan, 2021; Wang et al., 2024).

The sharp uptick in scholarly attention during the pandemic and post-pandemic years reflects both the urgency of digital adaptation and a broader recognition of AI's transformative potential in education. The trend also signals the maturation of the field, as researchers across disciplines increasingly contribute to a growing and diversified body of literature. The upward trajectory suggests that AIED has moved from a niche area to a central concern within educational research and innovation.

Figure 1. Annual Scientific Production

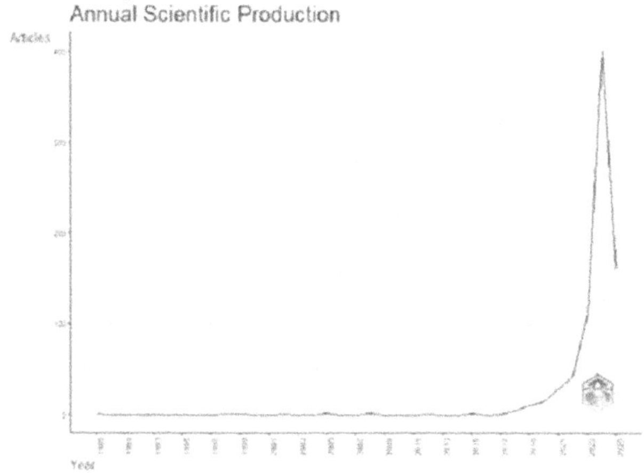

5.2 Leading Journals and Sources

The dissemination of scholarly work on artificial intelligence in education (AIED) spans a wide range of academic journals, reflecting the field's interdisciplinary and rapidly evolving nature. As detailed in Figure 2, the most prolific publication venue is *Education and Information Technologies* (n = 34), a journal that has consistently featured empirical studies and theoretical analyses on the integration of emerging technologies in educational contexts. This prominence aligns with the journal's focus on educational informatics and its increasing engagement with AI-enhanced learning systems.

Remarkably, the second highest concentration of publications (n = 29) appears within a special issue titled *Integrating Generative AI in Education to Achieve SDG 4*, signaling the field's growing alignment with global policy objectives, particularly the United Nations' Sustainable Development Goal 4 (Quality Education). The presence of such targeted issues highlights both the strategic relevance of AIED and the urgency with which researchers are addressing the ethical, pedagogical, and infrastructural implications of AI on a global scale.

Other prominent sources include the *International Journal of Artificial Intelligence in Education* (n = 16), which serves as a dedicated platform for domain-specific research, *Education Sciences* (n = 14), and *Sustainability* (n = 14). The inclusion of *Sustainability* is particularly noteworthy, as it reflects the growing emphasis on socially responsible and environmentally aligned applications of AI in education.

Collectively, these journals underscore two interrelated dynamics within the field. First, they point to the inherent interdisciplinarity of AIED scholarship, which draws upon fields such as educational technology, learning sciences, computer science, policy studies, and sustainability education. Second, they signal the field's increasing orientation toward innovation-driven pedagogy, global equity, and ethical integration of digital tools. The distribution of publications across diverse outlets illustrates the breadth of scholarly engagement and the cross-sectoral importance of AIED in shaping the future of education.

Figure 2. Most Relevant Sources

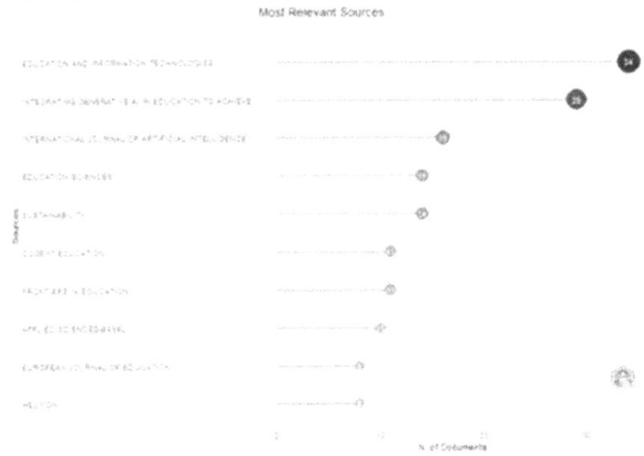

5.3 Most Prolific Authors

An analysis of author productivity provides insight into the intellectual leadership and geographic dispersion of the AIED research community. As presented in Figure 3, the most prolific contributors to the literature include Cukurova (n = 13) and Kim (n = 12), followed by Bozkurt (n = 7), Chiu (n = 6), and Yang (n = 6). These authors have consistently published on a range of AIED-related topics, including learning analytics, digital pedagogy, personalized learning environments, and the ethical implications of AI in educational settings.

Notably, this group represents a diverse range of institutional and national affiliations, spanning countries such as Türkiye, the United Kingdom, South Korea, and Hong Kong. This diversity underscores the global character of AIED scholarship and highlights the collaborative, transnational efforts shaping the field. The involvement of scholars from both Global North and Global South contexts reflects an increasing awareness of the need for culturally responsive and context-specific approaches to AI integration in education.

The distribution of author productivity also reflects the field's interdisciplinary engagement, as these scholars are affiliated with departments ranging from computer science and educational technology to learning sciences and communication studies. Their work collectively advances both theoretical foundations and practical implementations of AI in education, contributing to a vibrant and interconnected global research ecosystem.

Figure 3. Most Relevant Authors

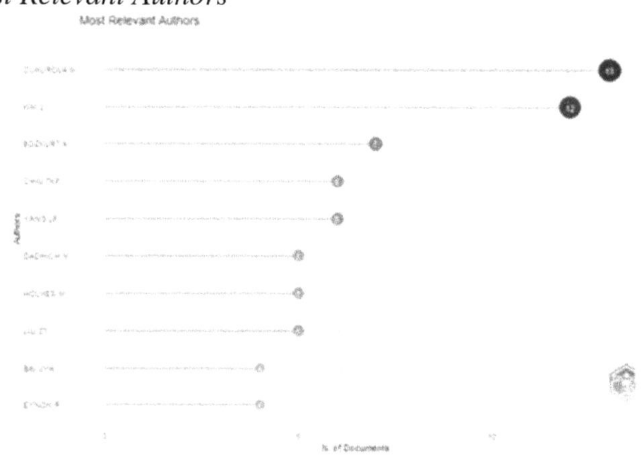

5.4 Institutional Contributions

Institutional analysis offers further insight into the centers of excellence that drive the development of artificial intelligence in education (AIED) research. As summarized in Figure 4, the most prolific institutions include the University of London (n = 38) and University College London (UCL) (n = 27), both of which have long-standing reputations in the fields of educational research and digital learning innovation. Their extensive contributions highlight the role of UK-based institutions in shaping the conceptual and methodological contours of the AIED field.

Monash University in Australia also ranks prominently (n = 16), reinforcing its status as a global leader in educational technology and digital transformation in higher education. Additional notable contributors include Hangzhou Normal University (China), Old Dominion University (USA), the State University System of Florida, and the UCL Institute of Education, each of which has cultivated research clusters or collaborative initiatives dedicated to AI integration in education.

These institutions serve not only as hubs of academic production but also as training grounds for future educators and researchers. Their contributions often extend beyond publication counts to include open-access tools, interdisciplinary research centers, and professional development programs aimed at enhancing AI literacy and digital pedagogy.

The diversity of contributing institutions reflects both geographic dispersion and institutional specialization, suggesting that leadership in AIED is not confined to a single region or academic tradition. Instead, it is shaped by a wide array of educational systems, funding priorities, and cultural perspectives, further reinforcing the transnational and collaborative nature of the field.

Figure 4. Most Relevant Affiliations

5.5 Country-Level Leadership

An analysis of country-level contributions reveals clear patterns of global leadership in the scholarly production of artificial intelligence in education (AIED) research. As illustrated in Figure 5, the United States emerges as the foremost contributor, accounting for 325 publications—a figure that reflects its longstanding investment in educational technology, its vast higher education infrastructure, and its active engagement with AI innovation across both public and private sectors.

China follows closely with 258 publications, underscoring its rapid advancement in AI research and its strategic emphasis on integrating AI within national education policies. The United Kingdom ranks third with 138 publications, while India, with 113 publications, demonstrates the expanding influence of Global South research communities in shaping the global AIED agenda.

Additional significant contributions originate from Australia, Spain, Germany, and Saudi Arabia, reflecting a broadening of the field's geographic base. The presence of these countries highlights the fact that AIED is no longer a Western-centric research domain; rather, it is a truly globalized field shaped by diverse cultural, institutional, and policy contexts.

These figures reflect two converging trends: (1) increasing governmental and institutional interest in leveraging AI to improve educational access and outcomes, and (2) a widening participation in the international research community, as emerging economies invest in AI infrastructures and seek to localize AI tools in linguistically and culturally relevant ways. This distribution of research output affirms the global relevance of AIED and the interconnectedness of scholarly efforts across regional and economic boundaries.

Figure 5. Country Scientific Production

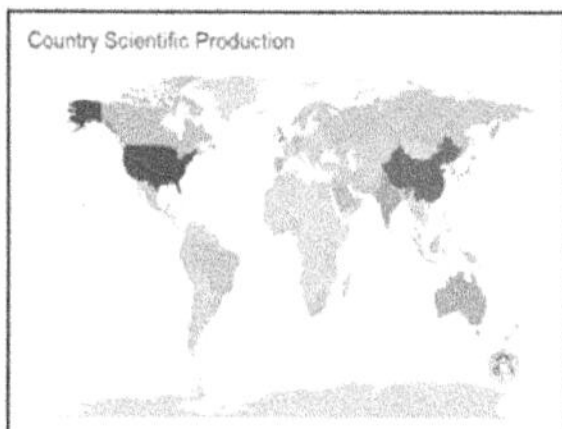

Country	Publications
USA	325
CHINA	258
UK	138
INDIA	113
AUSTRALIA	86
SPAIN	71
GERMANY	60
SAUDI ARABIA	60
CANADA	50

5.6 Thematic Structure and Key Concepts

Keyword co-occurrence analysis provides insight into the conceptual landscape of artificial intelligence in education (AIED) by identifying core research themes and tracking their evolution over time. As visualized in the following figures, the most frequently occurring keyword across the dataset is "artificial intelligence" (n = 77), followed by "technology" (n = 40), "education" (n = 38), and "students" (n = 28). These high-frequency terms reflect the broad, foundational concerns of the field, centering on the technological affordances of AI and its role in transforming educational experiences.

More specific terms such as "intelligent tutoring systems," "performance," "user acceptance," and "ChatGPT" mark the emergence of subfields that address both technical functionalities and user-centered outcomes. For example, the prominence of "intelligent tutoring systems" underscores the field's origins in personalized instruction and cognitive modeling, while "performance" and "user acceptance" point to growing efforts to empirically validate AI's educational impact and understand learner attitudes toward technology adoption.

The appearance of "ChatGPT" and related generative AI tools among high-frequency keywords—particularly in the most recent years—signals a notable paradigm shift in AIED research. These terms reflect increased scholarly attention to language-based AI, automated feedback, and the ethical and cognitive implications of large language models in learning environments. The rise of keywords such as "ethics," "communication skills," and "critical thinking" further suggests that the field is expanding beyond functional deployment toward socio-technical and pedagogical inquiry, incorporating dimensions of agency, authorship, and identity.

Taken together, the thematic clustering of keywords illustrates an evolving research agenda that balances technological advancement with critical engagement. It also reflects the interdisciplinary nature of the field, which draws from computer science, psychology, pedagogy, and communication studies to address increasingly complex educational challenges. These trends affirm the need for future research to not only innovate but also interrogate the human, cultural, and ethical dimensions of AI in education.

Figure 6. Tree of Keywords

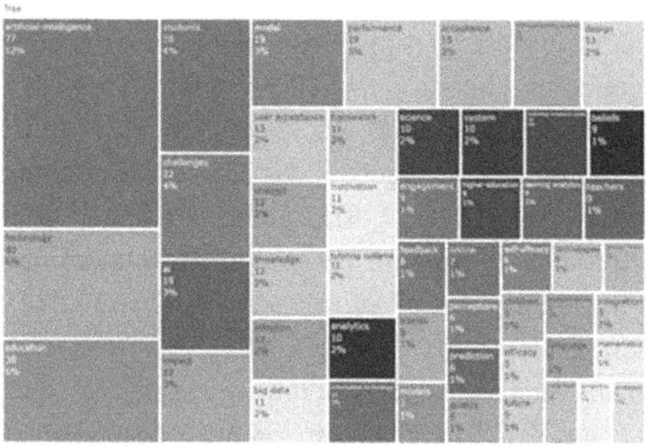

Figure 7. Word cloud

Figure 8. Co-occurrence of words

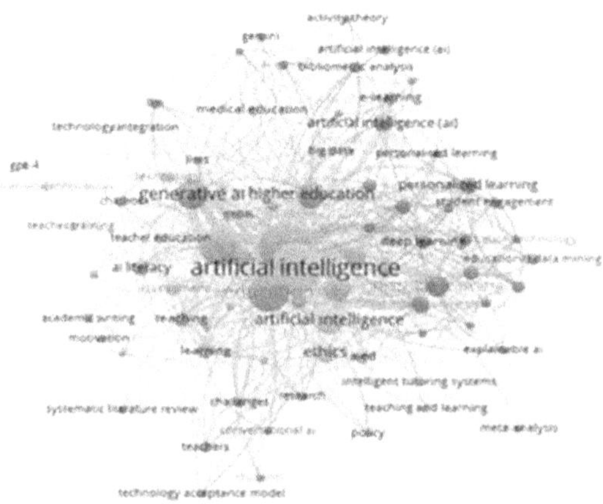

5.7 Thematic Evolution and Strategic Mapping

To understand how artificial intelligence in education (AIED) research has evolved conceptually over time, a thematic evolution analysis was conducted using Biblioshiny's strategic mapping and thematic clustering tools. This method reveals not only the emergence, development, and decline of dominant themes, but also their relative centrality (relevance to the field) and density (degree of internal development).

The strategic diagram generated by the analysis categorizes themes into four quadrants:

1. Motor themes (high centrality and high density): These are well-developed and crucial to the field's intellectual structure. In AIED, motor themes identified include "intelligent tutoring systems," "machine learning," and "adaptive learning," reflecting sustained interest in personalization and algorithmic instruction.
2. Basic themes (high centrality, low density): Foundational but underdeveloped, these themes are important across studies but lack conceptual depth. Examples include "education technology," "performance," and "digital learning environments." Their presence indicates broad utility but also the need for further theoretical and empirical refinement.
3. Niche themes (low centrality, high density): These are specialized and internally rich but isolated from the broader discourse. The analysis surfaced "robotics," "emotion recognition," and "learning styles" as niche themes—topics that are explored in-depth by smaller research communities.
4. Emerging or declining themes (low centrality and low density): This quadrant captured "MOOCs," "virtual reality," and notably, "blockchain," which saw spikes in earlier years but currently appear to be declining in relevance. Conversely, "ChatGPT," "ethics," and "AI literacy" are emerging themes entering this quadrant, suggesting the beginning of their ascent into broader scholarly relevance.

The thematic evolution map further illustrates a temporal shift in scholarly attention: from early focus on rule-based ITS and computer-assisted instruction in the 1990s and early 2000s, toward big data, adaptive systems, and learning analytics in the 2010s. In the post-2020 period, the landscape expands to include generative AI, user ethics, inclusivity, and critical thinking, reflecting broader societal concerns about algorithmic accountability and the human impact of AI in educational settings.

This strategic mapping reveals that AIED is no longer confined to questions of technical implementation. Instead, it is transitioning into a more mature, reflective phase—one that prioritizes equity, agency, and epistemological pluralism. The findings point to a growing need for interdisciplinary dialogue and ethically grounded research frameworks that can guide responsible innovation and address the diverse realities of learners worldwide.

5.8 Core Sources: Bradford's Law Analysis

To identify the primary publication outlets that structure the field of artificial intelligence in education (AIED), Bradford's Law of Scattering was applied. This law postulates that a small number of core journals will account for the majority of relevant articles in any given field, while the remaining literature will be dispersed across an exponentially increasing number of less frequent sources (Bradford, 1934). The analysis facilitates the identification of the most influential journals—those that serve as intellectual anchors for the discipline.

As visualized in Figure 9, the shaded zone labeled "Core Sources" represents the journals that have published the highest number of articles on AIED. At the top of this core zone is *Education and Information Technologies*, followed closely by the special issue *Integrating Generative AI in Education*, and the *International Journal of Artificial Intelligence in Education*. These outlets not only contribute extensively to publication volume but also shape emerging debates on pedagogy, ethics, and AI-enabled innovation.

Other journals within this core include *Education Sciences*, *Sustainability*, *Frontiers in Education*, and *Applied Sciences-Basel*. These sources reflect the interdisciplinary character of AIED, bridging fields such as educational technology, sustainability studies, and applied machine learning. The concentration of articles within this small set of journals demonstrates a strong centralization of scholarly activity, affirming their status as key venues for both foundational and cutting-edge research in the domain.

Beyond the core zone, a long tail of additional journals contributes to the field with lower frequency, illustrating the broad dispersion of AIED research across a range of disciplinary contexts—from STEM education and communication studies to ethics and human-computer interaction. This dispersion points to the transdisciplinary appeal of AIED, while the identification of core sources provides researchers and practitioners with a curated set of high-impact platforms for publication, review, and community engagement.

Figure 9. Bradford's law results

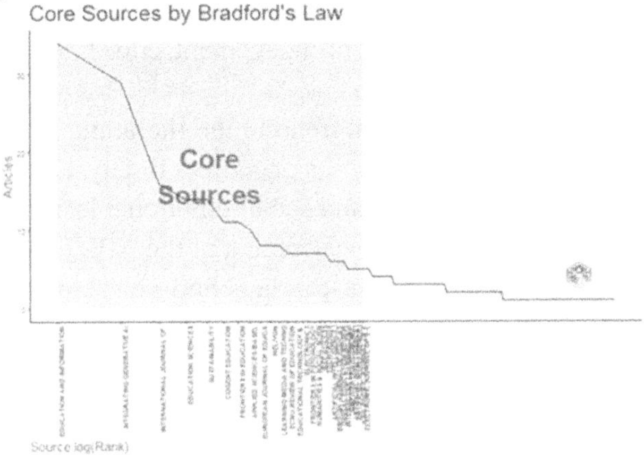

5.9 Most Globally Cited Documents

Citation analysis offers a lens into the intellectual impact and influence of specific contributions within the field of artificial intelligence in education (AIED). As visualized in Figure 10, the most globally cited document in the dataset is by Kasneci et al. (2023), published in *Learning and Individual Differences*, which has garnered 1,350 global citations. This exceptionally high citation count indicates the paper's foundational role in shaping recent discourse on AI-supported personalization, learner diversity, and individualized feedback mechanisms.

Following this, Zhai (2021), writing in *Complexity*, received 383 citations, reflecting interest in the systemic and non-linear dynamics of AI-enhanced learning environments. The study by Holmes (2022) in the *International Journal of Artificial Intelligence in Education*, with 237 citations, is also highly influential—likely due to its synthesis of ethical, cognitive, and policy-oriented perspectives on AI in classrooms.

Other frequently cited works include those by:

- Nguyen et al. (2023) in *Education and Information Technologies* (93 citations)
- Chiu (2024) in *Interactive Learning Environments* (87 citations)
- Luan (2020) in *Frontiers in Psychology* (78 citations)
- Celik (2023) in *Computers in Human Behavior* (77 citations)
- Holmes (2022) in *European Journal of Education* (72 citations)
- Su (2023) in *ECNU Review of Education* (41 citations)

The recurrence of authors such as Holmes and Chiu across multiple highly cited documents suggests sustained scholarly leadership and continued engagement with evolving issues such as AI literacy, student engagement, ethics, and interdisciplinary integration.

These citation patterns reveal a dual trend in the literature: high-impact works either consolidate foundational frameworks or address timely, emergent challenges such as generative AI, learner agency, and social-emotional learning. Collectively, these studies form the core intellectual scaffolding of the AIED field and act as key reference points for both established researchers and newcomers navigating this rapidly evolving domain.

Figure 10. Most Global Cited Documents

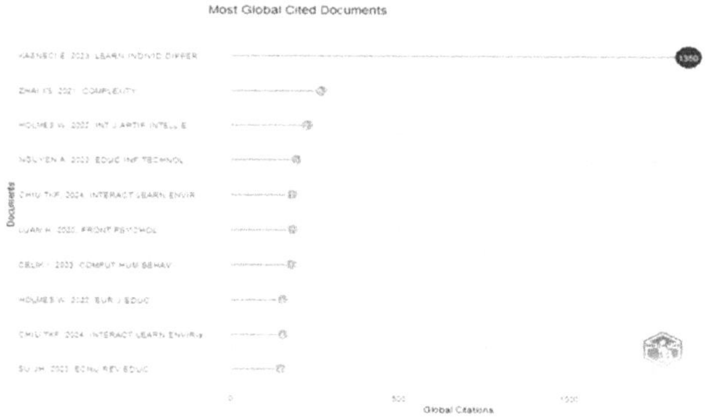

5.10 Co-authorship Networks

Co-authorship analysis provides insight into patterns of scholarly collaboration and the social structure of academic production within the field of artificial intelligence in education (AIED). As shown in Figure 11 and Figure 12, the network of collaboration among the most prolific authors is relatively sparse, with limited interconnectivity among top contributors—an indication of thematic or geographic fragmentation within the field.

Among the authors analyzed, Mutlu Cukurova (11 documents, 423 citations) and Wayne Holmes (5 documents, 377 citations) stand out not only in terms of productivity and citation impact but also for their direct co-authorship link, as visualized by a connecting edge in the network graph. Their collaborative efforts likely reflect a shared interest in human-centered AI, critical pedagogy, and ethical frameworks for integrating AI into educational systems.

Other leading scholars—such as Aras Bozkurt (5 documents), Jinhee Kim (9 documents), Zitao Liu (5 documents), and Junfeng Yang (6 documents)—appear as isolated nodes in the network, indicating that they operate within distinct scholarly silos or focus areas with limited co-authorship overlap. Despite their notable individual contributions, these researchers do not currently form part of a cohesive collaborative cluster, suggesting potential for greater interdisciplinary integration and international research partnerships.

The low total link strength among most of the prolific authors, except for the Holmes–Cukurova connection, reveals that collaboration within the AIED field remains fragmented, possibly due to disciplinary boundaries, geographic distance, or differing methodological orientations. However, the presence of high-output scholars in diverse national contexts—such as Türkiye, the United Kingdom, South Korea, and China—highlights untapped opportunities for strategic alliances that could enhance both knowledge exchange and methodological innovation.

As the field matures and evolves, fostering stronger co-authorship networks—particularly between Global North and Global South researchers—will be essential to promote epistemic diversity, cross-cultural relevance, and a more equitable global research ecosystem in AIED.

Figure 11. Co-authorship analysis in WosViewer

Selected	Author	Documents	Citations	Total link strength
✓	cukurova, mutlu	11	423	1
✓	holmes, wayne	5	377	1
✓	bozkurt, aras	5	125	0
✓	kim, jinhee	9	205	0
✓	liu, zitao	5	11	0
✓	yang, junfeng	6	39	0

Figure 12. Co-authorship analysis in WosViewer

5.11 Summary of Findings

This bibliometric analysis provides a comprehensive overview of the intellectual landscape of artificial intelligence in education (AIED) from 1989 to 2025. Drawing on 790 documents retrieved from the Web of Science Core Collection, the study reveals a clear trajectory of growth, thematic diversification, and expanding international engagement.

- Publication trends show a steep increase in scholarly output, particularly post-2016 and during the COVID-19 pandemic years (2020–2024), highlighting AI's central role in the global digital education response.
- Key publication venues, including *Education and Information Technologies* and the *International Journal of Artificial Intelligence in Education*, function as core sources, as confirmed by Bradford's Law. These journals underscore the field's interdisciplinary foundations, connecting educational technology, ethics, sustainability, and policy.
- Author-level analysis identifies Mutlu Cukurova, Wayne Holmes, and Aras Bozkurt among the most prolific and cited scholars. However, co-authorship analysis reveals limited collaboration across leading figures, with the exception of a strong dyadic link between Cukurova and Holmes.

- Institutional contributions are led by the University of London, UCL, and Monash University, while the United States, China, the United Kingdom, and India emerge as national leaders in AIED research output. A growing presence from emerging economies such as Saudi Arabia and Türkiye indicates an increasingly globalized research base.
- Keyword analysis highlights dominant terms such as *artificial intelligence*, *education*, and *technology*, while more recent keywords like *ChatGPT* and *user acceptance* signal a shift toward generative AI and human-centered design considerations.
- Strategic and thematic mapping identifies evolving research fronts, including ethical AI, adaptive learning, and communication skills, while also revealing underexplored but emerging themes such as emotion-aware AI, explainability, and algorithmic fairness.
- Citation analysis confirms that foundational work by Kasneci et al. (2023), Zhai (2021), and Holmes (2022) has had a significant impact on shaping the discourse. These documents act as intellectual anchors for current and future research trajectories.

Overall, the findings demonstrate that AIED is a rapidly maturing, transdisciplinary field, increasingly concerned not only with technological innovation but also with pedagogical integrity, ethical responsibility, and cultural inclusivity. These insights provide a data-driven foundation for the subsequent discussion of strategic research directions and implications for policy and practice.

6. DISCUSSION

The findings of this bibliometric analysis provide a comprehensive overview of the development and diffusion of artificial intelligence in education (AIED) scholarship over nearly four decades. The exponential growth observed—particularly since 2016—mirrors global shifts in educational delivery, catalyzed by technological advancement and further accelerated by the educational disruptions associated with the SARS-CoV-2 pandemic (Talan, 2021; Wang et al., 2024). This surge in output reflects a heightened interest in leveraging AI to personalize learning, increase instructional efficiency, and expand access.

6.1 Interdisciplinary Expansion

The wide array of publication outlets, including *Education and Information Technologies*, *Sustainability*, and *Applied Sciences*, underscores the interdisciplinary nature of AIED research. The integration of AI into educational contexts extends beyond technical implementation, raising profound pedagogical, ethical, and societal questions (Luckin et al., 2016). The inclusion of sustainability-oriented journals reflects growing attention to using AI to promote equity, inclusion, and quality education, aligned with Sustainable Development Goal 4 (UNESCO, 2023).

6.2 Dominant Geographies and Emerging Voices

The geographic distribution of authors and institutions confirms the dominance of the Global North, particularly the United States, United Kingdom, and China. However, increasing contributions from India, Saudi Arabia, and Türkiye suggest promising diversification. These developments point to rising research capacity and localized application of AI tools. Nevertheless, regional disparities in digital infrastructure and research funding remain a persistent challenge (van de Oudeweetering & Agirdag, 2021), highlighting the need for inclusive and collaborative research networks.

6.3 Conceptual Trends and Evolving Themes

Thematic evolution analysis reveals a trajectory from early research on intelligent tutoring systems to more nuanced, user-centered concerns such as performance, user acceptance, and generative AI tools like *ChatGPT*. This transition aligns with emerging scholarship emphasizing the need for ethical, human-centered integration of AI, where learner agency and socio-technical interactions are at the forefront (Zawacki-Richter et al., 2019; Holmes et al., 2022).

The increasing prevalence of communication-oriented keywords (e.g., *students*, *acceptance*, *knowledge*) suggests a growing focus on how learners interact with, adapt to, and are shaped by AI systems. This signals a paradigm shift in AIED—from mere functional optimization toward digital literacy, ethical reflexivity, and communication competencies as integral design considerations.

6.4 Gaps and Future Research Directions

Despite the field's rapid growth, notable gaps remain:

- There is a lack of longitudinal studies investigating the sustained impact of AI on learner autonomy, critical thinking, and identity formation.
- Cross-cultural and multilingual studies remain limited, with underrepresentation of educational systems in the Global South.
- The field has yet to sufficiently explore the integration of AI into teacher education, institutional policy, and curriculum reform.
- Research into student agency, algorithmic transparency, and AI literacy is growing but requires further empirical grounding.

7. CONCLUSION AND RECOMMENDATIONS

This bibliometric study has mapped the intellectual, thematic, and geographic contours of the AIED field over a 36-year span, analyzing 2,412 publications indexed in the Web of Science Core Collection. The analysis identified a sharp increase in research productivity post-2016, driven by digital transformation, enhanced funding, and global interest in AI-supported learning environments.

Key contributors—including the United States, China, and the United Kingdom—have shaped the field's development, while emerging research communities in Türkiye, India, and Saudi Arabia reflect the increasing global diversification of AIED scholarship. Thematic trends illustrate a shift from system-oriented to learner-centered inquiry, with growing attention to ethics, equity, and generative AI.

Methodologically, this chapter contributes to the field by demonstrating the utility of bibliometric analysis as a powerful tool for synthesizing interdisciplinary knowledge and informing policy and practice. By visualizing how AIED research has evolved over nearly four decades, the study offers stakeholders a macro-level framework for understanding scholarly influence, innovation hotspots, and future research directions.

7.1 Recommendations

Based on these findings, the following strategic directions are proposed for advancing the field:

1. Foster Equitable Global Collaboration Promote inclusive research by supporting capacity-building initiatives and cross-border partnerships, especially in underrepresented regions.
2. Integrate Ethical and Pedagogical Frameworks Future studies must go beyond technical implementation to explore the communicative, ethical, and human-centered implications of AI in education.

3. Adopt Interdisciplinary Methodologies Encourage collaboration across disciplines such as education, computer science, psychology, and communication to enrich the design of AI-based learning systems.
4. Emphasize Longitudinal Impact Studies Investigate the long-term psychological, academic, and social outcomes of AI integration across diverse educational contexts.
5. Align AI Adoption with Teacher Training and Institutional Policy Ensure AI implementation is accompanied by teacher professional development, curricular innovation, and robust data governance frameworks.

In conclusion, this study not only documents the historical development of AIED but also offers a foundation for its future advancement. As AI technologies continue to reshape education, scholarly inquiry must not only assess what AI *can do*, but also ask what it *should do*—with learners, educators, and society at the center of that inquiry.

7.2. Declaration of Generative AI and AI-Assisted Technologies in the Writing Process

During the preparation of this work, the author used ChatGPT 4 in order to improve the readability and language of the manuscript. After using this tool/service, the author reviewed and edited the content as needed and took full responsibility for the content of the published book chapter.

REFERENCES

Akgun, S., & Greenhow, C. (2022). Artificial intelligence in education: Addressing ethical challenges in K-12 settings. *AI and Ethics*, *2*(3), 431–440. DOI: 10.1007/s43681-021-00096-7 PMID: 34790956

Aria, M., & Cuccurullo, C. (2017). Bibliometrix: An R-tool for comprehensive science mapping analysis. *Journal of Informetrics*, *11*(4), 959–975. DOI: 10.1016/j.joi.2017.08.007

Baker, R. S., Martin, T., & Rossi, L. M. (2016). Educational data mining and learning analytics. *The Wiley handbook of cognition and assessment: Frameworks, methodologies, and applications*, 379-396.

Donthu, N., Kumar, S., Mukherjee, D., Pandey, N., & Lim, W. M. (2021). How to conduct a bibliometric analysis: An overview and guidelines. *Journal of Business Research*, *133*, 285–296. DOI: 10.1016/j.jbusres.2021.04.070

Dwivedi, Y. K., Kshetri, N., Hughes, L., Slade, E. L., Jeyaraj, A., Kar, A. K., Baabdullah, A. M., Koohang, A., Raghavan, V., Ahuja, M., Albanna, H., Albashrawi, M. A., Al-Busaidi, A. S., Balakrishnan, J., Barlette, Y., Basu, S., Bose, I., Brooks, L., Buhalis, D., & Wright, R. (2023). Opinion Paper:"So what if ChatGPT wrote it?" Multidisciplinary perspectives on opportunities, challenges and implications of generative conversational AI for research, practice and policy. *International Journal of Information Management*, *71*, 102642. DOI: 10.1016/j.ijinfomgt.2023.102642

Floridi, L. (2018). Soft ethics, the governance of the digital and the General Data Protection Regulation. *Philosophical Transactions. Series A, Mathematical, Physical, and Engineering Sciences*, *376*(2133), 20180081. DOI: 10.1098/rsta.2018.0081 PMID: 30322997

Freire, P. (1970). Pedagogy of the oppressed. *Continuum : an Interdisciplinary Journal on Continuity of Care*.

Giroux, H. A. (2020). *On critical pedagogy*. Bloomsbury Publishing. DOI: 10.5040/9781350145016

Holmes, W., Porayska-Pomsta, K., Holstein, K., Sutherland, E., Baker, T., Shum, S. B., Santos, O. C., Rodrigo, M. T., Cukurova, M., Bittencourt, I. I., & Koedinger, K. R. (2022). Ethics of AI in education: Towards a community-wide framework. *International Journal of Artificial Intelligence in Education*, *32*(3), 1–23. DOI: 10.1007/s40593-021-00239-1

Kasneci, E., Seßler, K., Küchemann, S., Bannert, M., Dementieva, D., Fischer, F., Gasser, U., Groh, G., Günnemann, S., Hüllermeier, E., Krusche, S., Kutyniok, G., Michaeli, T., Nerdel, C., Pfeffer, J., Poquet, O., Sailer, M., Schmidt, A., Seidel, T., & Kasneci, G. (2023). ChatGPT for good? On opportunities and challenges of large language models for education. *Learning and Individual Differences*, *103*, 102274. Advance online publication. DOI: 10.1016/j.lindif.2023.102274

Luckin, R., Holmes, W., Griffiths, M., & Forcier, L. B. (2016). *Intelligence unleashed: An argument for AI in education*. Pearson Education.

Mishra, P., & Koehler, M. J. (2006). Technological Pedagogical Content Knowledge: A Framework for Teacher Knowledge. *Teachers College Record*, *108*(6), 1017–1054. DOI: 10.1111/j.1467-9620.2006.00684.x

Pane, J. F., Steiner, E. D., Baird, M. D., & Hamilton, L. S. (2015). *Continued progress: Promising evidence on personalized learning*. RAND Corporation., DOI: 10.7249/RR1365

Selwyn, N. (2019). *Should robots replace teachers? AI and the future of education*. John Wiley & Sons.

Shneiderman, B. (2020). Human-centered artificial intelligence: Reliable, safe & trustworthy. *International Journal of Human-Computer Interaction*, *36*(6), 495–504. DOI: 10.1080/10447318.2020.1741118

Siemens, G., & Long, P. (2011). Penetrating the fog: Analytics in learning and education. *EDUCAUSE Review*, *46*(5), 30–40.

Talan, T. (2021). Artificial intelligence in education: A bibliometric study. *International Journal of Research in Education and Science*, *7*(3), 822–837. DOI: 10.46328/ijres.2409

UNESCO. (2023). *Global education monitoring report 2023: Technology in education—A tool on whose terms?* UNESCO Publishing. https://unesdoc.unesco.org/ark:/48223/pf0000385723

VanLehn, K. (2011). The relative effectiveness of human tutoring, intelligent tutoring systems, and other tutoring systems. *Educational Psychologist*, *46*(4), 197–221. DOI: 10.1080/00461520.2011.611369

Wang, W., Lv, Q., Yu, W., Hong, W., Qi, J., Wang, Y., & Tang, J. (2024). Cogvlm: Visual expert for pretrained language models. *Advances in Neural Information Processing Systems*, *37*, 121475–121499.

Williamson, B., & Eynon, R. (2020). Historical threads, missing links, and future directions in AI in education. *Learning, Media and Technology*, *45*(3), 223–235. DOI: 10.1080/17439884.2020.1798995

Williamson, B., Macgilchrist, F., & Potter, J. (2021). Covid-19 controversies and critical research in digital education. *Learning, Media and Technology*, *46*(2), 117–127. DOI: 10.1080/17439884.2021.1922437

Zawacki-Richter, O., Marín, V. I., Bond, M., & Gouverneur, F. (2019). Systematic review of research on artificial intelligence applications in higher education – Where are the educators? *International Journal of Educational Technology in Higher Education*, *16*(1), 1–27. DOI: 10.1186/s41239-019-0171-0

KEY TERMS AND DEFINITIONS

Artificial Intelligence in Education (AIED): AIED refers to the application of artificial intelligence technologies—such as machine learning, natural language processing, and intelligent tutoring systems—within educational settings to enhance teaching, learning, assessment, and administration (Zawacki-Richter et al., 2019). It encompasses both tool-based innovations and critical inquiry into how these tools influence pedagogy, learner autonomy, and educational equity.

Bibliometric Analysis: Bibliometric analysis is a quantitative research method used to map scientific literature by examining publication patterns, citation networks, and keyword co-occurrence (Donthu et al., 2021). In AIED, it helps reveal the field's conceptual structure, intellectual trends, and collaborative dynamics over time.

Critical Pedagogy in AI: Contexts Drawing from Freire (1970) and Giroux (2020), critical pedagogy critiques the socio-political implications of educational technologies, emphasizing empowerment, dialogue, and resistance to technocratic control. In AIED, it interrogates algorithmic bias, data surveillance, and the commodification of learning (Williamson & Eynon, 2020).

Generative AI: Generative AI refers to systems like ChatGPT that produce original content—text, images, or code—based on trained data models. These tools are reshaping educational practices, especially in writing instruction, feedback generation, and communication skills development, while raising ethical concerns about authorship and originality (Kasneci et al., 2023).

Human-Centered Artificial Intelligence (HCAI): Human-Centered AI prioritizes systems that augment rather than replace human capacities, emphasizing ethical principles such as transparency, inclusivity, and user autonomy in algorithmic decision-making (Shneiderman, 2020). In education, HCAI supports culturally responsive and learner-driven AI design.

Intelligent Tutoring Systems (ITS): ITS are AI-powered platforms that replicate human tutoring by offering personalized feedback and adaptive instructional pathways. Rooted in constructivist theory, these systems have evolved from rule-based models to sophisticated, data-driven agents capable of supporting individual learner needs (Pane et al., 2015; VanLehn, 2011).

Thematic Mapping and Strategic Diagrams: These bibliometric tools categorize keywords and research themes into quadrants based on centrality and density, identifying motor, basic, niche, and emerging themes (Aria & Cuccurullo, 2017). In AIED, they highlight the shift from system-based design toward ethical and communication-focused innovation.

TPACK Framework: The Technological Pedagogical Content Knowledge (TPACK) framework illustrates how educators integrate technology with pedagogical strategies and subject content knowledge to optimize instruction (Mishra & Koehler, 2006). In the context of AIED, it is extended to encompass AI-specific pedagogical knowledge (Akgun & Greenhow, 2022).

Chapter 12
Artificial Intelligence in Social Sciences: Transforming Education and Research

Vivit Rosmayanti
https://orcid.org/0000-0002-3648-9878
Universitas Negeri Makassar, Indonesia

ABSTRACT

Artificial intelligence (AI) is significantly transforming social science education and research by enabling efficient analysis of large datasets, identifying trends, and providing insights from complex social issues. AI is particularly useful in fields like sociology, economics, political science, and psychology, where large-scale data analysis is crucial. In education, AI is transforming teaching methods by utilizing digital platforms and virtual assistants to adapt learning processes to different learners' preferences. It is also crucial in curriculum design, providing adaptive learning systems and facilitating the creation of novel instructional techniques. However, the adoption of AI technology faces challenges, including resistance from educators and ethical concerns like privacy infringement and discrimination. Case studies of successful AI use in academic and research institutes demonstrate their effectiveness in improving research productivity, facilitating educational activities, and making learning more interactive.

DOI: 10.4018/979-8-3373-2612-2.ch012

INTRODUCTION

The term Artificial Intelligence (AI) describes a major technological revolution. It is defined broadly as a machine's attempt to imitate human cognitive functions such as learning and problem-solving. Precisely, AI systems can accomplish the tasks of learning, reasoning, and self-correction using advanced algorithms and computational models (Hedayet & Haseen, 2024). The significance of AI in social sciences becomes clear because it provides sophisticated tools and approaches for analyzing and interpreting social phenomena that are often very complicated to understand (Bail, 2024). Similarly, AI-enabled social science research that goes beyond traditional methods, like sentiment analysis, predictive modeling, and behavioral analytics, allows for the exploration of massive datasets and the identification of relevant relationships that would have previously been ignored (Bircan & Salah, 2022; Oliński et al., 2024).

The use of AI in different industries like healthcare, finance, and transport has ignited a debate about its impact on various fields, especially the social sciences (Aldoseri et al., 2023). This cross-connection exists because of AI's sequential impact on workflow efficiency, multi-faceted decision-making capabilities, and innovation in problem-solving techniques. At the same time, the computational social sciences, which deal with how social phenomena can be understood through quantitative techniques, highlight the need to merge social inquiry with AI technologies (Bircan & Salah, 2022; Taheri, 2023). The ability of AI to challenge fundamental beliefs about several approaches raises skepticism and forces a re-evaluation of traditional structures. It makes the possibility of the dissolution of methodological boundaries scientific, which can foster new approaches to achieving comprehensive solutions to complex problems.

Modern AI tools radically shape teaching and learning practices in social sciences, revolutionizing research and education. As the adoption of AI tools to personalize lessons and increase student participation grows (Aliyu, 2024; Zawacki-Richter et al., 2019), educational institutions are making more efforts to integrate AI into their curricula. These tools enable educators to develop tailored learning strategies that meet unique student needs and prepare learners for a highly technological world. Studies suggest that AI competency is becoming increasingly critical to student success in a future labor market dominated by technological needs (LaVelle et al., 2023). At the same time, in research, AI technology makes it possible to process extensive data quickly, allowing for new approaches like agent-based modeling and qualitative improvements to new social theories (Bail, 2024; Morley et al., 2020).

Combining AI and social sciences poses important ethical and governance issues that must be addressed. Morley et al. state that researchers have recognized the frameworks surrounding bias, data privacy, and the ethical implications of AI usage. Currently, most of the efforts' progress is on specific issues and not on the broader governance models, which are relevant for AI's absorption into social science research (Morley et al., 2020; Taheri, 2023). In this light, social sciences researchers have a critical responsibility in the policy design processes and monitoring AI to ensure that it complies with fundamental human and societal ethical norms.

The use of AI changes how social scientists work with empirical data. With the application of advanced machine learning techniques, researchers can now analyze vast and complex datasets, known as big data, which makes it possible to identify intricate social structures with a level of ease that was largely unattainable in traditional research contexts (Bircan & Salah, 2022; Oliński et al., 2024; Rosmayanti et al., 2022). These approaches improve the accuracy of the research methodologies and foster an energy in the research that solicits further investigation and data collection while the inquiry is still in progress (Fecher et al., 2023). As more AI systems and tools are incorporated, the field has to contend with the integration of powerful technologies and their implications for ensuring that the knowledge created protects the public and advances society.

THE ROLE OF AI IN SOCIAL SCIENCE RESEARCH

Advances in Data Analysis and Research Methodologies

The increasing importance of Artificial Intelligence (AI) in social science research has allowed for improving relations in methodologies and data analysis processes. With the help of machine learning and Natural Language Processing (NLP), researchers can conduct detailed analyses of complex and vast datasets to identify patterns, extract relevant information, and make predictions regarding specific social phenomena. Machine Learning (ML) furnishes statistical instruments for handling considerable bulk data more conveniently than antiquated techniques. This shift has fundamentally altered the approach adopted in data analysis in sociology, psychology, economics, and political science (Filippis & Foysal, 2024; Ligo et al., 2021).

AI tools can perform deep data analysis through classification, clustering, and regression, which were previously unknown in social data. For example, "social media analysis was done using AI in sociology to grasp the public attitude and discourse in real-time, (Li, 2024; Tomašev et al., 2020), and deeper social understanding is made possible by the categorization of data using algorithms for parents' demographics and consumption patterns (Tomašev et al., 2020). These analytics enable researchers to construct and validate new theories and hypotheses, from observational analysis to predictive modeling (Seniutis et al., 2024).

The application of text analysis can result in the augmentation of social science research using NLP. Open-ended interview survey material, social media content, and other forms of qualitative data can be effortlessly studied using NLP techniques. This makes sentiment and discourse analysis easier, enabling one to find the themes and feelings people or social groups convey (Wen & Chen, 2024). For instance, in political science, NLP has been used to track reactions to policy changes and political events through commentary on social media (Li, 2024; Sun & Scanlon, 2019). NLP innovations heighten an academic's ability to study qualitative information by converting it into brute information that can be codified.

The application of AI technology within social science disciplines possesses intriguing features. For example, in political science, campaign AI models evaluate voters' psychographic profiles through predictive analytics, which separately segment attributes for optimally tailored outreach campaigns and resource maximization (Li, 2024). Similarly, AI tools in psychology analyze behavioral assessment data to forecast mental health patterns (Filippis & Foysal, 2024; Yarrow & Bhardwaj, 2020). Moreover, in economics, AI-aided consumer market prediction applies the analysis of complex trends using multiple variables and history-based business models (Seniutis et al., 2024).

In sociology, AI assists the more traditional method of network analysis, which is the study of the relationships in a social structure, to help them better understand social community interactions and influence patterns (Katzenbach, 2021; Tomašev et al., 2020). AI analyses can also enable the study of information dissemination and social networking, the emergence of social units, and the detection of prominent persons in a particular community (Mallinson et al., 2023). Such activities improve the quality of academic work and restitute some practice in other disciplines, such as public health, where the social determinants of health need to be defined more clearly (Pandit, 2022).

The use of AI in social science research has its obstacles, especially those involving the ethical aspects of data processing and algorithm bias. To prevent biases and inequalities from being reproduced, researchers must address concerns about privacy, consent, and the representativeness of the training data for AI models (Ligo et al., 2021). These obstacles require continuous discussion between researchers, ethicists, and policymakers to create policies that aid in the moral application of AI in social science research, which allows for innovation without consequences (McGovern et al., 2022; Sætra & Fosch-Villaronga, 2021).

AI in Quantitative and Qualitative Research

The impact of Artificial Intelligence (AI) in social science research is profound in modifying both qualitative and quantitative approaches. AI tools, particularly machine learning, and natural language processing enable the examination of volumes of data that were previously difficult and tedious to analyze. The integration of these technologies in social research will allow researchers to work deeply on sentiment analysis and recognize sophisticated social patterns that are vital in comprehending multi-faceted social systems (Eichstaedt et al., 2021; Sureshbhai & Nakrani, 2024).

AI enables researchers to conduct quantitative analysis on large data sets by applying powerful analytic methods to identify patterns and relationships between variables without spending much time analyzing them. For example, machine learning techniques can offer amazing research opportunities if sorts can be made on sociographic and demographic data, social media activity, and survey data (Miller, 2019). NLP technologies for sentiment detection provide systems capable of automatically processing enormous amounts of text on social media, like tweets or comments, to determine public attitudes on significant issues, products, and political events. This new approach outperforms any traditional survey in determining the accuracy of public attitudes on issues and can replace the standard survey methodologies.

In addition, advanced AI tools employed during the COVID-19 pandemic allow researchers to monitor social distancing behavior by enhancing analysis of patterns in social behavior using computer vision and nonverbal cues to interpret social interactions (Bernasco et al., 2022). With the help of AI, researchers also exhibit greater confidence in the findings derived from larger datasets because of the ease brought about by streamlining the research process. Such technologies will further proliferate AI literature, thereby serving multidisciplinary domains.

On the other hand, AI is revolutionizing the qualitative data of Aficionados and Analysts with sophisticated approaches to qualitative data analysis. The advent of automated coding tools, through which Machine Learning Algorithms extract patterns from large volumes of qualitative text, helps researchers to develop themes efficiently. For example, AQUA (Automated Qualitative Assistant) is designed to support qualitative analysis while automatically performing time-intensive manual coding tasks. Such automation helps to relieve researchers from the tiresome tasks of manual coding and shifts their focus towards interpretation (Lennon et al., 2021).

Besides automated coding, automated text categorization techniques through NLP are widely used in qualitative research analysis to process open-ended survey questions and narrative interviews. AI systems are helpful in social cognition, as they help figure out key patterns, linguistic features, or emotions within the discourse and enable researchers to make sense of qualitative data (Giunti & Doherty, 2024; Odeh et al., 2024). For instance, computer analysis of language can identify communication between different cultures and help understand their social interactions and relations (Shukla et al., 2019).

Even discourse analysis has benefited from AI because it makes it possible to understand fundamental features concerning language in socio contexts and introduces a range of perspectives through which identity, power relations, and social order are understood. With AI, people can analyze the discourse produced by many people on different platforms and how that affects social reality (Dahlin, 2021). The ability to see in detail how and where language users deploy their discourses allows researchers to study the intricacies of human behavior and social changes in one analysis unit, enriching the existing social sciences concepts (Jackson et al., 2021).

The use of AI in qualitative and quantitative research presents a set of challenges. There are issues about the algorithms being opaque, the biases in data interpretation, and even the level of technical competence required by users of these tools (Williamson & Eynon, 2020). Thus, collaborative effort is a prerequisite for social scientists, data scientists, and ethicists to work jointly to ensure that AI is correctly used in research.

AI'S IMPACT ON SOCIAL SCIENCE EDUCATION

Enhancing Learning Experiences

The importance of Artificial Intelligence (AI) in social science education is becoming more apparent with the use of AI-powered platforms and digital assistants to improve the student learning experience in educational institutions. One of the central objectives of these AI tools is to make the learning of social science concepts easier by using adaptive learning technologies that address different educational needs. These digital assistants support and guide learners in real time for more interactive learning. Students can interact with AI tools such as chatbots and virtual tutors that respond to their educational needs in real-time through provided answers, explanations, and aids appropriate to the student's level of understanding, fully improving the learning experience.

Apart from providing support through AI platforms, personal learning is arguably the most beneficial outcome of AI applications in education. AI systems are structured to respond to students' unique learning styles, preferences, and pace and construct educational pathways bespoke to their needs, thus encouraging greater interaction with the subject matter. AI systems, for instance, can assess the student's performance and customize the learning content to fill the knowledge gaps or enhance the already known material. AI promotes practical learning in social sciences by addressing the traditional problem of teaching through a single approach to students by offering a more effective way to achieve good educational outcomes.

Well-defined personalization in technology-assisted learning lies in using AI-based adaptive learning technologies in colleges and universities. AI analyzes learners' engagement with the course and provides individualized resources and activities that reflect their level of proficiency. Consequently, teachers can direct their efforts to assist students who need more attention while letting the more advanced students work independently, thus facilitating equity in learning.

In addition, AI offers mechanisms to give feedback to students that help them reconsider and rectify their understanding of concepts they might have found challenging. An AI system is designed to analyze a student's submission and detect areas where patterns of incorrect responses are dominant and may need further explanation. This approach promotes constructive engagement, enabling learners to interact and grapple with the material until mastery.

In qualitative social research, AI tools are critical in enhancing student learning by analyzing big datasets and real-world case studies. Using AI-based text mining, students can obtain insights from numerous sources such as news, social media, surveys, and other complex social and textual interactions, thereby applying theoretical concepts to social issues. This is pertinent for advancing reflection and integration for making practice and theory bridges needed for professional work in social sciences.

Moreover, AI learning systems encourage collaboration and peer-assisted learning by linking students with similar interests and learning gaps. Such platforms can establish forums and group discussions where students can talk to each other, thus deepening their thinking and social interaction. In this context, AI serves the individual student as a personal tutor and community learning provider, promoting collective educational activity.

While educational institutions welcome new AI technologies into their frameworks, the challenges that come with it, such as the singularity of training teachers to leverage AI tools in their teaching optimally, are often ignored. When using AI tools in social science instruction, ongoing professional development and face-to-face support will be essential to make the social sciences outcomes effective.

AI in Curriculum Design

AI integration within curriculum developers poses novel opportunities to enhance social sciences curricula. Apply a curriculum design that is more flexible to a range of student's needs and learning objectives. With the help of modern tools, teachers can develop curricula responsive to each student's needs, learning styles, and interests, thus allowing more students in the class to benefit from the instruction. Using intelligent algorithms, teachers can evaluate students' engagement data and academic and learning achievements to make curriculum and instruction changes that will improve teaching and learning (Anwar, 2023; Movahed & Bilderback, 2024).

The learning pathways tailored by AI tools are beneficial, especially for students with different learning challenges. AI algorithms can analyze student participation with educational materials to diagnose learning gaps and provide customized lessons. For example, if a student cannot understand some social science concepts, the AI can download new materials, set new exercises, or provide reading alternatives such as case studies or simulations (Heilala et al., 2023; Kumari, 2023). This guarantees that every student in the classroom can grapple with learning materials and concepts appropriate to their understanding and cognitive abilities.

The possibility of AI analyzing enormous chunks of data allows educators to develop more personalized curricula while being responsive to overarching patterns in learning and teaching. For instance, AI can process and analyze learner feedback gathered through surveys or engagement analytics, which allows continual improvement of curricular materials to be in tune with learners in real-time. Such iterative design processes aim to provide richer curricular materials and further educational standards alongside the constantly changing needs of the student population (Allam et al., 2023; Shahrani et al., 2024).

Social sciences teaching is supported by several AI tools today. For instance, Artificial Intelligence is already embedded in Learning Management Systems (LMS), where the recommendation system encourages active learning by suggesting learning activities embedded in the students' profiles. Tools like Carnegie Learning are proficient in using AI to provide adaptive instruction in Mathematics. However, such tools can also be applied to social sciences, especially in statistical literacy, which is fundamental to most social science disciplines (Sapci & Sapci, 2020; Schüller, 2022). At the same time, the DreamBox Learning platform applies real-time data to tailor the learning experience to different students' capabilities to ensure no learner is left behind (Samuel et al., 2023).

Students are put into reality-based, intricate social situations using AI-based simulation, which makes their learning practical. One example discussed is a social phenomenon tool that lets the students manipulate variables to see the results. Experiential learning tools that foster comprehension through practice (Jebreen et al., 2024). Such engagement propels students into active learning, reinforcing concepts taught and developing sophisticated thinking, problem identification, and solving for social science scholars.

Besides simulation technologies, AI analytic tools allow teachers to use data more effectively based on student interaction and behavior. For instance, text analysis tools enable students to measure engagement within a discourse or an essay to understand core concepts among the students. The focus of instruction can be improved using analyses through integration concerning students' comprehension of numerous complex theories or concepts (Banerjee et al., 2021; O'Connor et al., 2022). In addition, AI-generated data visualizations allow educators to integrate more complex phenomena into social science students using ordinary and easy-to-understand data manipulation and interpretation.

AI assists teachers in weighing the balancing act of implementing curriculum standards against students' interests and societal demands. Using AI analytic systems, educational schemas can be effective and up-to-date by incorporating relevant societal issues or contemporary global challenges into the curriculum. Solving real-life issues through a socially responsive curriculum bolsters student engagement and motivates them to understand the social issues around them (Dumić-Čule et al., 2020; Garvey et al., 2022). This relevance elevates students' critical consciousness, allowing them to participate in social inquiry actively and cultivating an enriched educational landscape.

However, as robust as the capabilities of AI promise to be, obstacles persist in the design and effectiveness of AI-driven curricula. Ethical issues regarding data privacy, algorithmic bias, and lack of adequate professional development to utilize these tools affect teachers (Cheng et al., 2020; Moldt et al., 2024). Instructional designer teacher training programs must include pedagogical AI interpretation, analytics, and AI-enabled strategy execution training for educators. Establishing a culture of data-informed education will be critical to harnessing the potential of AI in curriculum design.

Training the Next Generation of Social Scientists

Equipping social scientists of the next generation with an understanding of AI (Artificial Intelligence) is vital in helping them manage and operate within the grip of advanced technology and extensive data. The impact of Artificial Intelligence on social sciences is profound, which makes it imperative for educational institutions to instill AI literacy in students in terms of theory and practice. This empowers the student to effectively utilize AI applications in social settings and critically think through the consequences of these interactions (Grimmer et al., 2021; Ligo et al., 2021).

Curriculum developers must expand their focus to AI deployed within social sciences. Doing so enables students to appreciate the complexity of AI's role in social research, policy development, and community relations. Incorporating training in data analysis, machine learning, and AI ethics is also fundamental. Being AI literate requires more than understanding algorithms; it means understanding the social, ethical, and political issues surrounding AI in the context of social sciences (Ashok et al., 2022; Ligo et al., 2021). Case studies illustrating AI's impact help students understand these technologies' implications on society and social behavior.

These strategies should also involve nurturing AI literacy across all students in social sciences and related programs by fostering collaboration among students from other disciplines like computer science, ethics, and data science. Working in such an environment helps develop the ability to operate across disciplines, which is critical in today's knowledge economy. Such coordinated activity can transform social problems, which AI issues, intensively enhances the understanding and practice of social science theory more sophisticatedly (Ashok et al., 2022; Ligo et al., 2021).

The effectiveness of this change highly depends on the educators' components. This means that faculty members need to be prepared for more than just the subjects they teach; they also need to be prepared for how their teaching subjects interact with AI in social science research. Educators must be more appropriately prepared to use AI technologies in their teaching. Instructors should adjust their understanding of AI and the concepts learned in the associated syllabus to provide students with holistic experiences covering the possibilities and issues around AI technologies (Alsultan, 2023; Wood et al., 2021).

Therefore, partnerships with technology firms and nonprofit organizations are necessary to achieve practical training where students can use AI tools for hands-on experience, especially when tackling social issues through AI-powered projects. These programs have the potential to fill the academic and practical integration gap and equip new graduates with the fundamental knowledge and real-life experience necessary to practice as social scientists in the age of AI (Hamd et al., 2024; Oladoyinbo et al., 2024).

For example, students can be challenged to directly tackle real-life machine learning, data visualization, and sentiment analysis through social media analysis of important events or demographic analysis, thus developing the skills the modern workforce demands (Grimmer et al., 2021; Wagner et al., 2021).

Including AI systems in students' work raises questions that students must learn to tackle. For one, how do AI systems reproduce prejudices? How do AI systems influence trust in institutions? How do AI systems shape societal norms? In what ways do students bear responsibility for AI technologies? Integrating social sciences with AI literacy offers an avenue not only to teach students about privacy and ethical algorithmic challenges but also to help them understand the ethical responsibilities of the AI tools they will be utilizing in the future (Florindo, 2023; Oladoyinbo et al., 2024).

Ultimately, educational programs must incorporate processes for constant feedback to remain relevant with the pace at which AI is changing the world. Suggestions from industry captains, alums, and even current students can be used to revise content and teaching styles and thus stay abreast with the shifting technological paradigm. This will ensure that students in social science disciplines are ready for the prevailing challenges and looking at how to tackle new problems emerging from the merger of social sciences with the AI revolution (Boge, 2021; Oladoyinbo et al., 2024).

AI IN SOCIAL SCIENCES EDUCATION: BENEFITS AND CHALLENGES

Incorporating AI in the education of social sciences presents considerable opportunities and challenges. These factors affect how teaching and learning in educational institutions are conducted within the rising digital and data-oriented frameworks.

One of the most notable merits of AI in social sciences education is improved access to remote learning opportunities. AI is helping to reach new and hard-to-reach audiences via remote learning, as you can create interactive platforms that can be used anywhere, unlike traditional classrooms. Saidakhror (2024) reveals that educators can now craft more advanced and inclusive educational models that can be utilized irrespective of a student's geographical position. Such platforms tailor the content offered to the different learning styles as well as the preferences of individual students. In doing so, the learners' engagement is improved, and the complex concepts in social sciences are better retained (Aghaziarati et al., 2023). Furthermore, students can access quality learning materials at any location or time through virtual classrooms, AI chatbots, and improvised tools that guarantee better educational outcomes for non-traditional learners and significantly improve the accessibility to educational resources.

Additionally, students enrolled in social science courses can enhance their innovation and problem-solving skills through artificial intelligence. Students, for example, conduct data analysis, simulations, and other tasks using AI tools, which helps them develop reflective and analytical skills. AI-assisted simulations related to different political or economic systems help students visualize potential outcomes resulting from different actions performed in those systems, and this encourages the students to be more open-minded (Wu & Yu, 2023). However, students must learn to think strategically to comprehend social issues truly. Engaging in these simulations challenges students to practically explore their decisions rather than simply discussing the socio-theoretical contexts that arise from their choices (Çela et al., 2024).

Nevertheless, despite these advantages, some challenges exist with incorporating AI into educational settings. A significant hurdle is the unwillingness to use AI in more progressive educational environments. The reluctance stems from apprehension that, for many teachers, AI tools are overly automated and, for some, completely ineffective (Sallam et al., 2023). Moreover, insufficient teaching of new technologies or a lack of experience impedes effective curriculum design. These challenges can be overcome by providing adequate professional development and focusing on the synergy of AI technologies and teachers for better education, not for teacher substitution (Mananay, 2024).

A different major challenge pertains to the ethical questions associated with data privacy, AI algorithmic biases, and the misuse of AI technology in research and learning. The application of artificial intelligence (AI) sometimes requires the capturing and analyzing a lot of student-related information, which raises issues of privacy invasion and even spying (Thomas, 2024). If AI systems not only discriminate by race but also by other factors, these examples of algorithmic discrimination can worsen educational inequalities (Namjoo et al., 2023). These problems highlight the need for a broader dialogue on ethical data and resource use, data access and manipulation, and fairness in education. Educational institutions must develop sufficient instructions and consent forms to solve ethical problems arising from using AI in education (Fitria, 2023).

AI tools should be used to comply with professional standards and enable children, parents, teachers, and other community participants to set the necessary standards for the ethical deployment of AI-based technology (Çela et al., 2024).

THE FUTURE OF AI IN SOCIAL SCIENCE

The forthcoming landscape for Artificial Intelligence is remarkable. As new technologies exist, they are bound to improve already set standards and facilitate further research to address advanced social problems. Some sophisticated possibilities suggest the increased application of various AI tools in different methodologies of research, which would analyze the collected data more efficiently and accurately (Li et al., 2024). With the advent of new technologies, we are trying to develop a more complex and nuanced understanding of rich social data within sociology, psychology, economics, and political sociology.

Besides the improvements in research, AI is expected to have a definitive impact on social sciences' educational practices and outcomes. There is evidence of a movement towards more customized learning opportunities; for instance, AI tools can analyze students and modify content to fit individual needs. This is key to enabling the new generation of social scientists with the skills necessary to maneuver in this new world, with AI literacy being one of them. Institutions of higher learning will increasingly adopt social AI curricula with a focus on the technical side of the issue and the ethics of AI use (Rink et al., 2022; H. Zhang et al., 2022).

In addition, there will be plenty of chances for interdisciplinary research vis-à-vis collaboration between social scientists, data scientists, ethicists, and engineers focusing on the implications of AI in society. These collaborations are important for advancing research that incorporates social science and technology. For example, researchers can undertake projects that use AI to study social media discussions of social policies to understand public opinion better and enable effective policy-making (Chan & Zary, 2019). By promoting such collaborations, social scientists can help address issues like algorithmic discrimination and data privacy while providing insight into AI technologies' social consequences (Fazlollahi et al., 2022).

As the integration of AI in education becomes more widespread, institutions will be able to incorporate hands-on learning and AI-based curricula. For instance, some programs could aim at enabling students to analyze social problems using AI, which can motivate them to attempt practical uses of their knowledge and design novel social research projects (Alvarez et al., 2022). The same interdisciplinary approaches that seek to teach AI to K-12 students can also help them appreciate the socio-cultural context of AI technologies and help them become more proactive in shaping the future of society (Vartiainen et al., 2022).

Along with such trends and possibilities are important problems that must be solved. The use of AI in the social sciences has to be done cautiously, especially regarding privacy, data protection, algorithmic prejudice, and abuse of these technologies in education and research. (Sanusi et al., 2022) Such proactive and responsible AI integration will require active and constant communication between educators, researchers, public stakeholders, and the general population to develop tools that will respond to ethical and social justice issues (J. Zhang, 2024).

CONCLUSION

In summary, the debates around introducing and using Artificial Intelligence (AI) within the social sciences suggest notable shifts and considerable issues that may emerge in the future. In this chapter, AI's deep learning algorithms associated with research AI are designed with several important points, including enhancing analysis and methodology for developing pedagogy, personalized schemes of complex social engineering, and interdisciplinary efforts for solving social problems. In this study, AI technologies can profoundly change how social scientists conduct research, partake in various educational activities, and evaluate various social phenomena.

Anticipating what is next, it is apparent that AI will persistently reinforce its influence within the scope of social sciences. New developments indicate that the impact of AI programs will retroactively affect established research methods for social sciences by modifying them and developing previously unimagined methods, new and predictive analytics techniques, and natural language understanding. The emergence of AI has opened up new possibilities for unprecedented understanding of social issues through the analysis of enormous data sets and intricate social networks that researchers could not contemplate a few years ago. Moreover, by adopting

AI in educational facilities, there will be a greater emphasis on collaborative and integrative approaches, and the learners and social science students will be trained by actively encouraging critical analysis and problem resolution.

At the same time, this transformation faces some problems. AI integration into standard educational domains is resisted due to a fear of the consequences of technology use in academic settings. Concerns around data protection, bias within algorithms, and the abuse of AI tools must compel researchers, teachers, and policymakers toward productive debate concerning the ethical boundaries behind the deployment of AI. Responsible and transparent use of these technologies in education and research is essential for trust to be sustained. Hence, a great deal of care will have to be exercised.

REFERENCES

Aghaziarati, A., Nejatifar, S., & Abedi, A. (2023). Artificial Intelligence in education: Investigating teacher attitudes. *Aitechbesosci*, *1*(1), 35–42. DOI: 10.61838/kman.aitech.1.1.6

Aldoseri, A., Al-Khalifa, K. N., & Hamouda, A. M. S. (2023). Re-thinking data strategy and integration for Artificial Intelligence: Concepts, opportunities, and challenges. *Applied Sciences (Basel, Switzerland)*, *13*(12), 7082. DOI: 10.3390/app13127082

Aliyu, B. S. (2024). Artificial Intelligence (AI): A powerful tool for advancing plant study and research. *Nigerian Journal of Botany*, *37*(1), 61–68. DOI: 10.4314/njbot.v37i1.5

Allam, A. H., Eltewacy, N. K., Alabdallat, Y. J., Owais, T. A., Salman, S., Ebada, M. A., Aldare, H. A., Rais, M. A., Salem, M., Al-Dabagh, J. D., Alhassan, M. A., Hanjul, M. M., Mugibel, T. A., Motawea, S. H., Hussein, M., Anas, O. S., Amine, N. M., Almekhlafi, M. A., Mugibel, M. A., & Alkanj, S. (2023). Knowledge, attitude, and perception of Arab medical students towards Artificial Intelligence in medicine and radiology: A multi-national cross-sectional study. *European Radiology*, *34*(7), 1–14. DOI: 10.1007/s00330-023-10509-2 PMID: 38150076

Alsultan, K. (2023). Awareness of Artificial Intelligence in medical imaging among radiologists and radiologic technologists. *Cureus*. Advance online publication. DOI: 10.7759/cureus.38325 PMID: 37261164

Alvarez, L., Gransbury, I., Cateté, V., Barnes, T., Lédeczi, Á., & Grover, S. (2022). A socially relevant focused AI curriculum designed for female high school students. *Proceedings of the AAAI Conference on Artificial Intelligence*, *36*(11), 12698–12705. DOI: 10.1609/aaai.v36i11.21546

Anwar, M. R., & Ahyarudin, H. A. (2023). AI-powered Arabic language education in the Era of Society 5.0. [ITSDI]. *IAIC Transactions on Sustainable Digital Innovation*, *5*(1), 50–57. DOI: 10.34306/itsdi.v5i1.607

Ashok, M., Madan, R., Joha, A., & Sivarajah, U. (2022). Ethical framework for Artificial Intelligence and digital technologies. *International Journal of Information Management*, *62*, 102433. DOI: 10.1016/j.ijinfomgt.2021.102433

Bail, C. A. (2024). Can generative AI improve social science? *Proceedings of the National Academy of Sciences of the United States of America*, *121*(21), e2314021121. Advance online publication. DOI: 10.1073/pnas.2314021121 PMID: 38722813

Banerjee, M., Chiew, D., Patel, K. T., Johns, I., Chappell, D., Linton, N., Cole, G., Francis, D. P., Szram, J., Ross, J., & Zaman, S. (2021). The impact of Artificial Intelligence on clinical education: Perceptions of postgraduate trainee doctors in London (UK) and recommendations for trainers. *BMC Medical Education*, *21*(1), 429. Advance online publication. DOI: 10.1186/s12909-021-02870-x PMID: 34391424

Bernasco, W., Hoeben, E. M., Koelma, D. C., Liebst, L. S., Thomas, J., Appelman, J., Snoek, C. G. M., & Lindegaard, M. R. (2022). Promise into practice: Application of computer vision in empirical research on social distancing. *Sociological Methods & Research*, *52*(3), 1239–1287. DOI: 10.1177/00491241221099554

Bircan, T., & Salah, A. A. A. (2022). A bibliometric analysis of the use of Artificial Intelligence technologies for social sciences. *Mathematics*, *10*(23), 4398. DOI: 10.3390/math10234398

Boge, F. J. (2021). Two dimensions of opacity and the deep learning predicament. *Minds and Machines*, *32*(1), 43–75. DOI: 10.1007/s11023-021-09569-4

Çela, E., Fonkam, M., & Potluri, R. M. (2024). Risks of AI-assisted learning on student critical thinking. *International Journal of Risk and Contingency Management*, *12*(1), 1–19. DOI: 10.4018/IJRCM.350185

Chan, K. S., & Zary, N. (2019). Applications and challenges of implementing Artificial Intelligence in medical education: Integrative review. *JMIR Medical Education*, *5*(1), e13930. DOI: 10.2196/13930 PMID: 31199295

Cheng, C., Chen, C.-C., Fu, C., Chaou, C., Wu, Y.-T., Hsu, C.-P., Chang, C.-C., Chung, I., Hsieh, C., Hsieh, M., & Liao, C. (2020). Artificial Intelligence-based education assists medical students' interpretation of hip fracture. *Insights Into Imaging*, *11*(1), 119. Advance online publication. DOI: 10.1186/s13244-020-00932-0 PMID: 33226480

Dahlin, E. (2021). Mind the Gap! On the future of AI Research. *Humanities & Social Sciences Communications*, *8*(1), 71. Advance online publication. DOI: 10.1057/s41599-021-00750-9

Dumić-Čule, I., Orešković, T., Brkljačić, B., Tiljak, M. K., & Orešković, S. (2020). The importance of introducing Artificial Intelligence to the medical curriculum – assessing practitioners' perspectives. *Croatian Medical Journal*, *61*(5), 457–464. DOI: 10.3325/cmj.2020.61.457 PMID: 33150764

Eichstaedt, J. C., Kern, M. L., Yaden, D. B., Schwartz, H. A., Giorgi, S., Park, G., Hagan, C. A., Tobolsky, V. A., Smith, L., Buffone, A., Iwry, J., Seligman, M. E. P., & Ungar, L. (2021). Closed- and open-vocabulary approaches to text analysis: A review, quantitative comparison, and recommendations. *Psychological Methods*, *26*(4), 398–427. DOI: 10.1037/met0000349 PMID: 34726465

Fazlollahi, A. M., Bakhaidar, M., Alsayegh, A., Yilmaz, R., Winkler-Schwartz, A., Mirchi, N., Langleben, I., Ledwos, N., Sabbagh, A. J., Bajunaid, K., Harley, J. M., & Maestro, R. F. D. (2022). Effect of Artificial Intelligence tutoring vs expert instruction on learning simulated surgical skills among medical students. *JAMA Network Open*, *5*(2), e2149008. DOI: 10.1001/jamanetworkopen.2021.49008 PMID: 35191972

Fecher, B., Hebing, M., Laufer, M., Pohle, J., & Sofsky, F. (2023). Friend or foe? Exploring the Implications of large language models on the science system. *AI & Society*. Advance online publication. DOI: 10.1007/s00146-023-01791-1

Filippis, R., & Foysal, A. A. (2024). Insights unveiled: Harnessing AI to explore human behaviour in social sciences. *Journal of Mathematical Techniques and Computational Mathematics*, *3*(5), 1–8. DOI: 10.33140/JMTCM.03.05.04

Fitria, T. N. (2023). The use of Artificial Intelligence in education (AIED): Can AI replace the teacher's role? *Epigram*, *20*(2), 165–187. DOI: 10.32722/epi.v20i2.5711

Florindo, F. (2023). ChatGPT: A threat or an opportunity for scientists? *Perspectives of Earth and Space Scientists*, *4*(1), e2023CN000212. Advance online publication. DOI: 10.1029/2023CN000212

Garvey, K. V., Craig, K. J. T., Russell, R. G., Novak, L. L., Moore, D. E., & Miller, B. M. (2022). Considering clinician competencies for the implementation of Artificial Intelligence–based tools in health care: Findings from a scoping review. *JMIR Medical Informatics*, *10*(11), e37478. DOI: 10.2196/37478 PMID: 36318697

Giunti, G., & Doherty, C. P. (2024). Cocreating an automated mHealth apps systematic review process with generative AI: Design science research approach. *JMIR Medical Education*, *10*, e48949. DOI: 10.2196/48949 PMID: 38345839

Grimmer, J., Roberts, M. E., & Stewart, B. (2021). Machine learning for social science: An agnostic approach. *Annual Review of Political Science*, *24*(1), 395–419. DOI: 10.1146/annurev-polisci-053119-015921

Hamd, Z. Y., Alorainy, A. I., Aldhahi, M. I., Gareeballah, A., Alsubaie, N. F., Alshanaiber, S. A., Almudayhesh, N. S., Alyousef, R. A., AlNiwaider, R. A., Moammar, L. A. B., & Abuzaid, M. (2024). Evaluation of the impact of Artificial Intelligence on clinical practice of radiology in Saudi Arabia. *Journal of Multidisciplinary Healthcare*, *17*, 4745–4756. DOI: 10.2147/JMDH.S465508 PMID: 39411200

Hedayet, H., & Haseen, F. (2024). Artificial Intelligence in public health: A review article. *Bangladesh Journal of Bioethics*, *15*(2), 15–19. DOI: 10.62865/bjbio.v15i2.108

Heilala, J., Shibani, A., & Freitas, A. G. (2023). The requirements for heutagogical attunement within STEAM education. [IJET]. *International Journal of Emerging Technologies in Learning*, *18*(16), 19–35. DOI: 10.3991/ijet.v18i16.42313

Jackson, V., Delacruz, S., & Harry, D. (2021). Culturally relevant teaching for the 21st Century. *Georgia Journal of Literacy*, *44*(1), 41–66. DOI: 10.56887/galiteracy.15

Jebreen, K., Radwan, E., Rebai, W. K., Alattar, E., Radwan, A., Safi, W., Radwan, W., & Alajez, M. (2024). Perceptions of undergraduate medical students on Artificial Intelligence in Medicine: Mixed-methods survey study from Palestine. *BMC Medical Education*, *24*(1), 507. Advance online publication. DOI: 10.1186/s12909-024-05465-4 PMID: 38714993

Katzenbach, C. (2021). "AI will fix this" – The technical, discursive, and political turn to AI in governing communication. *Big Data & Society*, *8*(2), 20539517211046182. Advance online publication. DOI: 10.1177/20539517211046182

Kumari, M. (2023). Perception of dental students in incorporating Artificial Intelligence into dental education. *Journal of Advanced Sciences*, *2*(1), 41–45. DOI: 10.58935/joas.v2i1.27

LaVelle, J. M., Ford, T., & Montenegro, M. (2023). Artificial Intelligence and the future of evaluation education: Possibilities and Prototypes. *New Directions for Evaluation*, *2023*(178–179), 97–109. DOI: 10.1002/ev.20564

Lennon, R. P., Fraleigh, R., Scoy, L. J. V., Keshaviah, A., Hu, X. C., Snyder, B., Miller, E. L., Calo, W. A., Zgierska, A., & Griffin, C. (2021). Developing and Testing an Automated Qualitative Assistant (AQUA) to support qualitative analysis. *Family Medicine and Community Health*, *9*(Suppl 1), e001287. DOI: 10.1136/fmch-2021-001287 PMID: 34824135

Li, W. (2024). The influence of Artificial Intelligence on the education system. *Lecture Notes in Education Psychology and Public Media*, *65*(1), 137–142. DOI: 10.54254/2753-7048/65/20240158

Li, W., Zhang, X., Li, J., Yang, X., Li, D., & Liu, Y. (2024). An explanatory study of factors influencing engagement in AI education at the K-12 level: An extension of the classic TAM Model. *Scientific Reports*, *14*(1), 13922. Advance online publication. DOI: 10.1038/s41598-024-64363-3 PMID: 38886456

Ligo, A. K., Rand, K., Bassett, J., Galaitsi, S., Trump, B. D., Jayabalasingham, B., Collins, T. R., & Linkov, I. (2021). Comparing the emergence of technical and social sciences research in Artificial Intelligence. *Frontiers of Computer Science*, *3*, 653235. Advance online publication. DOI: 10.3389/fcomp.2021.653235

Mallinson, D. J., Azevedo, L., Best, E., Robles, P., & Wang, J. (2023). The future of AI is in the states: The case of autonomous vehicle policies. *Business and Politics*, *26*(2), 180–199. DOI: 10.1017/bap.2023.19

Mananay, J. A. (2024). Integrating Artificial Intelligence (AI) in language teaching: Effectiveness, challenges, and strategies. *International Journal of Learning Teaching and Educational Research*, *23*(9), 361–382. DOI: 10.26803/ijlter.23.9.19

McGovern, A., Ebert-Uphoff, I., Gagne, D. J.II, & Bostrom, A. (2022). Why we need to focus on developing ethical, responsible, and trustworthy Artificial Intelligence Approaches for environmental science. *Environmental Data Science*, *1*, e6. Advance online publication. DOI: 10.1017/eds.2022.5

Miller, T. (2019). Explanation in Artificial Intelligence: Insights from the social sciences. *Artificial Intelligence*, *267*, 1–38. DOI: 10.1016/j.artint.2018.07.007

Moldt, J.-A., Festl-Wietek, T., Fuhl, W., Zabel, S., Claassen, M., Wagner, S., Nieselt, K., & Herrmann-Werner, A. (2024). Assessing AI awareness and identifying essential competencies: Insights from key stakeholders in integrating AI into medical education. *JMIR Medical Education*, *10*, e58355–e58355. DOI: 10.2196/58355 PMID: 38989834

Morley, J., Machado, C., Burr, C., Cowls, J., Joshi, I., Taddeo, M., & Floridi, L. (2020). The ethics of AI in health care: A mapping review. *Social Science & Medicine*, *260*, 113172. DOI: 10.1016/j.socscimed.2020.113172 PMID: 32702587

Movahed, M., & Bilderback, S. (2024). Evaluating the readiness of healthcare administration students to utilize AI for sustainable leadership: A survey study. *Journal of Health Organization and Management*, *38*(4), 567–582. DOI: 10.1108/JHOM-12-2023-0385 PMID: 38858220

Namjoo, F., Liaghat, E., Shabaziasl, S., Modabernejad, Z., & Morshedi, H. (2023). Students experience self-study through AI. *Aitechbesosci*, *1*(3), 35–42. DOI: 10.61838/kman.aitech.1.3.6

O'Connor, S., Yan, Y., Thilo, F. J., Felzmann, H., Dowding, D., & Lee, J. J. (2022). Artificial Intelligence in nursing and midwifery: A systematic review. *Journal of Clinical Nursing*, *32*(13–14), 2951–2968. DOI: 10.1111/jocn.16478 PMID: 35908207

Odeh, A., Odeh, N., & Mohammed, A. S. (2024). A comparative review of AI techniques for automated code generation in software development: Advancements, challenges, and future directions. *Tem Journal*, 726–739. https://doi.org/DOI: 10.18421/tem131-76

Oladoyinbo, T. O., Olabanji, S. O., Olaniyi, O. O., Adebiyi, O. O., Okunleye, O. J., & Alao, A. I. (2024). Exploring the challenges of Artificial Intelligence in data integrity and its influence on social dynamics. *Asian Journal of Advanced Research and Reports*, *18*(2), 1–23. DOI: 10.9734/ajarr/2024/v18i2601

Oliński, M., Krukowski, K., & Sieciński, K. (2024). Bibliometric overview of ChatGPT: New perspectives in social sciences. *Publications / MDPI*, *12*(1), 9. DOI: 10.3390/publications12010009

Pandit, B. (2022). Recent used and future application of Artificial Intelligence (AI). *International Journal of Scientific Research in Engineering and Management*, *06*(11). Advance online publication. DOI: 10.55041/IJSREM16966

Rink, E., Firemoon, P., Anastario, M., Johnson, O., GrowingThunder, R., Ricker, A., Peterson, M., & Baldwin, J. (2022). Rationale, design, and methods for nen unkumbi/edahiyedo ("We are here now"): A multi-level randomized controlled trial to improve sexual and reproductive health outcomes in a northern plains American Indian Reservation Community. *Frontiers in Public Health*, *10*, 823228. Advance online publication. DOI: 10.3389/fpubh.2022.823228 PMID: 35910931

Rosmayanti, V., Noni, N., & Patak, A. A. (2022). Students' acceptance of technology use in learning English pharmacy. *International Journal of Language Education*, *6*(3), 314–331. DOI: 10.26858/ijole.v6i3.24144

Sætra, H. S., & Fosch-Villaronga, E. (2021). Research in AI has implications for society: How do we respond? *Morals & Machines*, *1*(1), 60–73. DOI: 10.5771/2747-5182-2021-1-60

Saidakhror, G. (2024). The impact of Artificial Intelligence on higher education and the economics of information technology. *Irshad J. Law and Policy*, *2*(3), 1–6. DOI: 10.59022/ijlp.125

Sallam, M., Salim, N. A., Al-Tammemi, A. B., Barakat, M., Fayyad, D., Hallit, S., Harapan, H., Hallit, R., & Mahafzah, A. (2023). ChatGPT output regarding compulsory vaccination and COVID-19 vaccine conspiracy: A descriptive study at the outset of a paradigm shift in online search for information. *Cureus*. Advance online publication. DOI: 10.7759/cureus.35029 PMID: 36819954

Samuel, Y., Brennan-Tonetta, M., Samuel, J., Kashyap, R., Kumar, V., Kashyap, S. K., Chidipothu, N., Anand, I., & Jain, P. (2023). Cultivation of human-centered Artificial Intelligence: Culturally adaptive thinking in education (CATE) for AI. *Frontiers in Artificial Intelligence*, *6*, 1198180. Advance online publication. DOI: 10.3389/frai.2023.1198180 PMID: 38106981

Sanusi, I. T., Oyelere, S. S., Vartiainen, H., Suhonen, J., & Tukiainen, M. (2022). A systematic review of teaching and learning machine learning in K-12 education. *Education and Information Technologies*, *28*(5), 5967–5997. DOI: 10.1007/s10639-022-11416-7

Sapci, A. H., & Sapci, H. (2020). Artificial Intelligence education and tools for medical and health informatics students: Systematic review. *JMIR Medical Education*, *6*(1), e19285. DOI: 10.2196/19285 PMID: 32602844

Schüller, K. (2022). Data and AI literacy for everyone. *Statistical Journal of the IAOS*, *38*(2), 477–490. DOI: 10.3233/SJI-220941

Seniutis, M., Gružauskas, V., Lileikienė, A., & Navickas, V. (2024). Conceptual framework for ethical Artificial Intelligence development in social services sector. *Human Technology*, *20*(1), 6–24. DOI: 10.14254/1795-6889.2024.20-1.1

Shahrani, A. S. A., Alhumaidan, N. I., AlHindawi, Z. A., Althobaiti, A., Aloufi, K., Almughamisi, R., & Aldalbahi, A. (2024). Readiness to embrace Artificial Intelligence among medical students in Saudi Arabia: A national survey. *Health Care*, *12*(24), 2504. DOI: 10.3390/healthcare12242504 PMID: 39765931

Shukla, A. K., Janmaijaya, M., Abraham, A., & Muhuri, P. K. (2019). Engineering applications of Artificial Intelligence: A bibliometric analysis of 30 years (1988–2018). *Engineering Applications of Artificial Intelligence*, *85*, 517–532. DOI: 10.1016/j.engappai.2019.06.010

Sun, A. Y., & Scanlon, B. R. (2019). How can big data and machine learning benefit environment and water management: A survey of methods, applications, and future directions. *Environmental Research Letters*, *14*(7), 73001. DOI: 10.1088/1748-9326/ab1b7d

Sureshbhai, S. V., & Nakrani, T. (2024). A literature review : Enhancing sentiment analysis of deep learning techniques using generative AI Model. *International Journal of Scientific Research in Computer Science Engineering and Information Technology*, *10*(3), 530–540. DOI: 10.32628/CSEIT24103204

Taheri, M. (2023). Shaping the future together: The inaugural vision for AI and tech in behavioral and social sciences. *Aitechbesosci*, *1*(1), 1–3. DOI: 10.61838/kman.aitech.1.1.1

Thomas, T. (2024). The role of Artificial Intelligence in Formal and informal education for students. *International Journal for Research in Applied Science and Engineering Technology*, *12*(3), 69–71. DOI: 10.22214/ijraset.2024.58738

Tomašev, N., Cornebise, J., Hutter, F., Mohamed, S., Picciariello, A., Connelly, B., Belgrave, D., Ezer, D., van der Haert, F. C., Mugisha, F., Abila, G., Arai, H., Almiraat, H., Proskurnia, J., Snyder, K., Otake, M., Othman, M., Glasmachers, T., Wever, W. D., & Clopath, C. (2020). AI for social good: Unlocking the opportunity for positive impact. *Nature Communications*, *11*(1), 2468. Advance online publication. DOI: 10.1038/s41467-020-15871-z PMID: 32424119

Vartiainen, H., Pellas, L., Kahila, J., Valtonen, T., & Tedre, M. (2022). Pre-service teachers' insights on data agency. *New Media & Society*, *26*(4), 1871–1890. DOI: 10.1177/14614448221079626

Wagner, G., Lukyanenko, R., & Paré, G. (2021). Artificial Intelligence and the conduct of literature reviews. *Journal of Information Technology*, *37*(2), 209–226. DOI: 10.1177/02683962211048201

Wen, C.-H. R., & Chen, Y.-N. K. (2024). Understanding Public perceptions of revolutionary technology: The role of political ideology, knowledge, and news consumption. *JCOM, Journal of Science Communication*, *23*(05). Advance online publication. DOI: 10.22323/2.23050207

Williamson, B., & Eynon, R. (2020). Historical threads, missing links, and future directions in AI in education. *Learning, Media and Technology*, *45*(3), 223–235. DOI: 10.1080/17439884.2020.1798995

Wood, E., Ange, B. L., & Miller, D. D. (2021). Are we ready to integrate Artificial Intelligence literacy into medical school curriculum: Students and faculty survey. *Journal of Medical Education and Curricular Development*, *8*, 23821205211024078. Advance online publication. DOI: 10.1177/23821205211024078 PMID: 34250242

Wu, R., & Yu, Z. (2023). Do <scp>AI</Scp> Chatbots improve students' learning outcomes? Evidence from a meta-analysis. *British Journal of Educational Technology, 55*(1), 10–33. DOI: 10.1111/bjet.13334

Yarrow, N., & Bhardwaj, R. (2020). *Indonesia's education technology during COVID-19 and beyond*. East Asia & Pacific on the rise. https://blogs.worldbank.org/eastasiapacific/indonesias-education-technology-during-covid-19-and-beyond

Zawacki-Richter, O., Marín, V. I., Bond, M., & Gouverneur, F. (2019). Systematic review of research on artificial intelligence applications in higher education–where are the educators? *International Journal of Educational Technology in Higher Education, 16*(1), 1–27. DOI: 10.1186/s41239-019-0171-0

Zhang, H., Lee, I., Ali, S., DiPaola, D., Cheng, Y., & Breazeal, C. (2022). Integrating ethics and career futures with technical learning to promote AI literacy for middle school students: An exploratory study. *International Journal of Artificial Intelligence in Education, 33*(2), 290–324. DOI: 10.1007/s40593-022-00293-3 PMID: 35573722

Zhang, J., & Zhang, Z. (2024). <scp>AI</Scp> in teacher education: Unlocking new dimensions in teaching support, inclusive learning, and digital literacy. *Journal of Computer Assisted Learning, 40*(4), 1871–1885. DOI: 10.1111/jcal.12988

KEY TERMS AND DEFINITIONS

Adaptive Learning: An AI-driven educational technique that customizes learning materials and activities based on individual students' needs and learning pace.

Agent-Based Modeling: A simulation modeling technique that uses AI to mimic the actions and interactions of individuals within a system to analyze their effects on the system as a whole.

AI Literacy: The ability to understand, interpret, and critically evaluate AI technologies is crucial for students and researchers in the social sciences.

AI-Enhanced Curriculum Design: Curriculum development informed by AI tools to personalize instruction, identify learning gaps, and update content dynamically based on student performance data.

Artificial Intelligence (AI): Refers to machines simulating human cognitive functions like learning, reasoning, and self-correction through advanced algorithms.

Automated Qualitative Analysis: Using AI tools like AQUA to code and categorize qualitative data, such as interview transcripts or open-ended survey responses.

Big Data: Enormous datasets are analyzed computationally to reveal patterns, trends, and associations, especially regarding human behavior.

Computational Social Science: An interdisciplinary field that uses computational methods like simulations and big data analytics to study social phenomena.

Ethical AI: A framework for ensuring AI technologies are used responsibly, addressing concerns like bias, data privacy, and social justice.

Interdisciplinary Research: Collaboration between disciplines (e.g., social science and computer science) to develop more robust AI applications and address societal challenges.

Machine Learning (ML): A subset of AI that uses statistical methods to enable systems to learn from data and improve performance over time without explicit programming.

Natural Language Processing (NLP): A branch of AI that deals with the interaction between computers and human language, enabling text and speech analysis.

Predictive Modeling: Using AI to forecast future trends or behaviors based on historical data.

Sentiment Analysis: AI is commonly used to determine and interpret the emotional tone behind words and analyze social media and survey responses.

Simulation Learning: An educational method using AI to replicate real-world scenarios, helping students explore social phenomena through experiential learning.

Chapter 13
How Can We Use Artificial Intelligence in Social Sciences

Ferah Diba İzgi
https://orcid.org/0009-0003-3048-0391
Cyprus Science University, Cyprus

ABSTRACT

This chapter explores the transformative impact of Artificial Intelligence (AI) on the social sciences, examining how technologies like machine learning, natural language processing (NLP), big data analytics, and neural networks reshape research methodologies, data collection, and theoretical frameworks across disciplines such as sociology, psychology, political science, anthropology, and economics. The chapter investigates the ethical, methodological, and epistemological challenges of AI integration. Using a qualitative methodology, it analyzes literature and case studies to assess AI's capabilities and limitations. Findings show AI-powered tools enhance data processing and prediction, but also raise concerns about data privacy, algorithmic bias, and the opacity of AI models. The chapter concludes that AI should complement, not replace, traditional methods, with a focus on transparency, ethical safeguards, and interdisciplinary collaboration.

INTRODUCTION

In the digital age, Artificial Intelligence (AI) has emerged as a transformative force across diverse academic disciplines. The book *The Power of Words in an AI-Driven World* explores the multifaceted relationship between AI and society, emphasizing its implications for communication, ethics, and human development.

DOI: 10.4018/979-8-3373-2612-2.ch013

Within this broader context, the present chapter focuses specifically on AI's evolving role in the social sciences, a field traditionally grounded in theoretical inquiry and human-centered methodologies.

Historically, social science research has relied on qualitative and quantitative methods to explore human behavior, institutional structures, and societal change. From early ethnographic fieldwork to statistical modeling in economics and political science, these methods were shaped by theories emphasizing context, meaning, and reflexivity. However, beginning in the late 20th century and accelerating rapidly after the 2010s, AI technologies began to challenge and expand these paradigms. With the development of machine learning (ML), natural language processing (NLP), and big data analytics, researchers gained new tools to analyze vast and unstructured datasets, enabling more profound and more scalable insights into complex social phenomena (Domingos, 2015; Kitchin, 2014).

The last decade has seen unprecedented growth in integrating AI into social science research. From predicting election outcomes through social media analysis to mapping global migration patterns using satellite data, AI now facilitates previously unimaginable research due to methodological or logistical constraints (Lazer et al., 2020; Xie, 2023). Moreover, the post-pandemic digital acceleration has further underscored the urgency of incorporating AI-driven approaches in understanding rapidly evolving social dynamics (UNESCO, 2023).

This chapter explores the application of AI in child therapy and the ethical importance of cultural sensitivity in AI design. While it highlights how AI can be humanized and applied in compassionate contexts, the chapter broadens the scope to examine AI's broader methodological, epistemological, and ethical implications across core social science disciplines such as political science, sociology, psychology, and economics.

By tracing both the **historical development** of AI in social research and its **contemporary manifestations**, this chapter critically examines its dual role as both a powerful enabler and a source of disruption. While AI technologies enhance social science inquiry's precision, scope, and speed, they also raise profound concerns about **algorithmic bias**, **transparency**, and the **epistemological shift** from theory-driven to data-driven knowledge production (Jasanoff, 2021; Binns & Veale, 2024).

Ultimately, this chapter aims to assess how social sciences can adapt to and shape the use of AI to improve research outcomes and preserve the discipline's normative commitments to equity, reflexivity, and human agency in a digital world.

The rapid evolution of Artificial Intelligence (AI) has induced transformative shifts in various academic fields, particularly within the social sciences. Historically, social science research has been anchored in qualitative and quantitative methodologies to examine human behavior, societal structures, and economic phenomena. However, AI-powered tools have significantly altered the research landscape by introducing more advanced computational techniques for data collection, analysis, and interpretation (Brynjolfsson & McAfee, 2017). Recent advances in AI further emphasize the shifting paradigms in social sciences, as these tools increasingly enable more dynamic and complex forms of analysis (Choudhury & Sharma, 2022).

AI technologies, including machine learning (ML), natural language processing (NLP), and big data analytics, have empowered social scientists with new methodologies to process vast datasets, uncover complex patterns, and construct predictive models. For example, AI-driven sentiment analysis offers political scientists a tool for gauging public opinion on social issues through the analysis of social media content. At the same time, machine learning models have demonstrated their capacity to forecast political trends by analyzing historical data (Tufekci, 2014). More recently, AI has been employed to study voting patterns and political polarization on a global scale, further demonstrating its influence in the political domain (Xie, 2023). Similarly, in economics, AI has facilitated the identification of emergent patterns in financial markets, enhancing predictive accuracy and market forecasting (Varian, 2014). In addition, new AI applications have made it easier to understand complex economic interactions, such as the rise of digital currencies and their economic implications (Gandal et al., 2020). Beyond these areas, AI's influence has also permeated fields such as sociology and psychology, where it assists in analyzing behavioral trends, migration patterns, and mental health dynamics (Lazer et al., 2009; Molnar et al., 2021).

In addition to the transformative shifts AI has introduced in various academic fields, Ferah Diba İzgi's contribution to the book *The Power of Words in an AI-Driven World* provides a nuanced perspective on AI's application in child therapy. Her exploration delves into how AI technologies can be harnessed to enhance therapeutic practices for children, emphasizing the importance of cultural sensitivity and ethical considerations. This perspective enriches the discourse on AI's role in social sciences by highlighting its potential to address complex human-centric challenges (İzgi, 2023).

While integrating AI offers substantial advantages in expanding the scope and depth of social science research, it simultaneously introduces several significant challenges. Chief among these are ethical concerns, including algorithmic bias, data privacy, and transparency. AI models, which often rely on large-scale historical data for training, may inadvertently perpetuate existing biases present in the data, resulting in discriminatory outcomes in applications such as predictive policing or hiring algorithms (O'Neil, 2016; Noble, 2018). This issue remains pressing in contemporary discourse, with AI systems in judicial settings and hiring platforms facing scrutiny for replicating or exacerbating societal biases (Eubanks, 2020). Furthermore, the reliance on AI-driven approaches raises critical questions regarding the interpretability and replicability of findings and the potential erosion of methodological rigor in the research process (Pasquale, 2015; Beer, 2017). Ethical frameworks surrounding AI use in research continue to evolve, addressing these concerns and promoting transparency in algorithmic decision-making (Binns, 2020).

In addition to ethical issues, AI integration also brings significant epistemological challenges within the social sciences. Traditional research methods emphasize theory-driven analysis and human intuition, whereas AI models often prioritize data-driven correlations and patterns. This epistemological shift raises questions about the nature of knowledge produced through AI, specifically regarding its alignment with established social science theories and frameworks (Kitchin, 2014). Recent critiques highlight the tension between AI-driven data analysis and traditional theoretical approaches, with some arguing that AI methods may overlook crucial social dynamics (Jasanoff, 2021). Moreover, the increasing reliance on AI-driven methods could lead to the underutilization of traditional research skills, such as critical thinking and qualitative analysis, which are essential for understanding the complexities of human societies (Noble, 2018). This issue has sparked ongoing social science debates about the balance between quantitative methods and humanistic perspectives (Gillespie, 2021).

This paper explores both the opportunities and challenges AI presents in the social sciences. By examining key applications in fields such as political science, sociology, economics, and psychology, the paper will provide a comprehensive analysis of how AI has reshaped the methodologies and practices of social science research. Additionally, the ethical and methodological implications of AI adoption will be discussed, highlighting the need for a balanced approach that maximizes the potential of AI while addressing its limitations. Ultimately, this study seeks to contribute to a more nuanced understanding of the role AI plays in shaping the future trajectory of social science research and the evolving nature of interdisciplinary methodologies in the digital age (Choudhury & Sharma, 2022; Xie, 2023).

1. THE IMPACT OF ARTIFICIAL INTELLIGENCE (AI) ON SOCIAL SCIENCES: OPPORTUNITIES AND CHALLENGES

The rapid advancement of artificial intelligence (AI) has led to significant transformations across multiple fields, including the social sciences. Traditionally, social sciences have relied on qualitative and quantitative methods to analyze human behavior, societal structures, and economic trends (Brynjolfsson & McAfee, 2017). However, with the rise of AI-driven tools, researchers now have access to more sophisticated computational methods that enable large-scale data analysis, predictive modeling, and automated content processing (Kitchin, 2021). AI technologies have increasingly become a powerful tool, offering unique advantages in processing complex datasets and extracting insights from them (Choudhury & Sharma, 2022).

AI technologies such as machine learning (ML), natural language processing (NLP), and big data analytics provide social scientists with novel methodologies to explore intricate social phenomena. For example, sentiment analysis of social media data allows political scientists to assess public opinion in real-time (Zhang et al., 2021), while machine learning algorithms enhance economic forecasting by identifying emerging patterns in financial markets (Brynjolfsson et al., 2022). Furthermore, AI has played an instrumental role in sociology and psychology, helping to analyze large datasets related to human behavior, migration patterns, and mental health trends (Gonzalez et al., 2021). These tools not only enable more accurate and timely assessments but also open new frontiers in the understanding of human and societal dynamics.

Despite these advantages, integrating AI into social sciences raises several ethical and methodological challenges. A primary concern is data bias, as AI models are often trained on historical data that may contain systemic inequalities (O'Neil, 2020). Such biased datasets can lead to discriminatory outcomes in predictive policing, hiring algorithms, and healthcare recommendations (Eubanks, 2020). In addition, AI-driven research may lack transparency, making it difficult for scholars to understand how specific conclusions are reached fully, thus complicating efforts to ensure accountability in research practices (Pasquale, 2020). The increasing reliance on black-box models presents a significant challenge for researchers who may struggle to interpret and replicate AI-generated results (Raji & Buolamwini, 2020).

Another critical issue is the epistemological shift in social sciences due to AI's influence. Traditional research methods emphasize theory-driven analysis and human interpretation, whereas AI-driven approaches often prioritize data-driven correlations and patterns. This shift raises important questions about the validity of AI-generated insights and their alignment with established social science theories (Kitchin, 2021). Researchers have voiced concerns that, by relying heavily on data-driven methods, there is a risk of undermining the human-centered insights central to social science inquiry (Beer, 2021). Moreover, the increasing reliance on AI may lead to the erosion of fundamental research skills among social scientists, such as critical thinking and qualitative reasoning, which remain essential for understanding complex social phenomena (Noble, 2020).

Given these opportunities and challenges, this paper explores both the advantages and disadvantages of AI in social sciences. It discusses key application areas, including political science, sociology, economics, and psychology, while addressing AI adoption's ethical and methodological implications. By providing a balanced analysis, this study aims to contribute to the ongoing debate about the role of AI in shaping the future of social science research, with a focus on both the transformative potential and the limitations of AI as a research tool (Jasanoff, 2021; Molina & Garip, 2022).

Artificial intelligence (AI) has emerged as a transformative force across multiple disciplines, including the social sciences. Data's increasing volume and complexity in sociology, political science, economics, and psychology have made AI an essential tool for research and policymaking (Kitchin, 2021). AI technologies such as machine learning, natural language processing (NLP), and big data analytics enable social scientists to uncover patterns, make predictions, and automate various previously time-consuming aspects of research that were prone to human error (Molina & Garip, 2022). However, as AI becomes more integrated into social science research, concerns about its ethical implications, methodological challenges, and potential biases have also gained attention, especially in light of new developments in AI's impact on areas like law enforcement and hiring practices (O'Neil, 2020; Raji & Buolamwini, 2020).

1.1 The Role of AI in Social Sciences

Integrating artificial intelligence (AI) into the social sciences has fundamentally transformed how researchers collect, analyze, and interpret data. Traditionally, social sciences encompassing sociology, political science, economics, psychology, and anthropology have relied on qualitative and quantitative research methods to examine human behavior, societal structures, and economic systems. AI technologies, particularly machine learning (ML), natural language processing (NLP), deep learning, and big data analytics, have significantly enhanced these research methods by enabling faster data processing, more refined pattern recognition, and advanced predictive modeling (Molina & Garip, 2022; Choudhury & Sharma, 2022).

While traditional research methods remain valuable for providing context and understanding nuanced human experiences, AI-driven tools have unlocked new possibilities for analyzing vast datasets that would otherwise be impractical or impossible to handle manually. For example, AI technologies have been instrumental in predicting voting behaviors, enhancing political polling accuracy, and understanding complex migration patterns by processing data from diverse sources such as social media, census data, and global migration databases (Zhang et al., 2021). Moreover, AI's ability to identify trends within economic data has allowed researchers to improve the accuracy of financial forecasting and assess economic inequalities more comprehensively (Brynjolfsson et al., 2022).

AI also plays a crucial role in psychology and sociology, where it aids in processing large-scale surveys, analyzing sentiment, and modeling human behavior in ways that were not previously possible. For instance, deep learning models can process social media data to assess mental health trends. In contrast, machine learning can enhance sociological studies by identifying hidden patterns in long-term demographic data (Gonzalez et al., 2021).

However, the application of AI in social science research is not without its challenges. The integration of AI presents several methodological, ethical, and epistemological questions that researchers must address to ensure the integrity of their findings. Methodologically, AI can lead to an overreliance on large-scale datasets that might overlook critical qualitative insights, potentially oversimplifying complex social phenomena (Beer, 2021). Ethical issues such as algorithmic bias, privacy concerns, and the potential for AI to perpetuate existing social inequalities are also significant concerns that researchers must navigate (O'Neil, 2020; Eubanks, 2020). Furthermore, the epistemological impact of AI in social sciences raises questions about the nature of knowledge and whether AI-generated insights align with traditional social science theories and frameworks (Kitchin, 2021).

In conclusion, while AI has undeniably transformed the landscape of social science research by providing new data analysis and prediction tools, its application must be cautiously approached. Researchers must ensure that AI methods complement traditional social science approaches, addressing ethical concerns and maintaining methodological rigor (Jasanoff, 2021). By doing so, AI can help unlock new insights into human behavior and societal dynamics while preserving the human-centered focus that defines the social sciences.

1.1.1 AI in Quantitative Research: Enhancing Data Analysis and Predictive Modeling

Quantitative research in social sciences has long relied on numerical data, statistical models, and hypothesis testing. Traditional approaches, such as regression analysis, factor analysis, and structural equation modeling, allow researchers to test theories and identify relationships within datasets. However, the integration of AI, particularly machine learning (ML), has significantly enhanced these approaches by enabling researchers to process vast amounts of data, uncover hidden patterns, and make more precise predictions (Varian, 2021).

Predictive analytics is one of AI's most prominent applications in quantitative research. AI models, trained on historical data, can accurately forecast social, political, and economic trends. For example:

- **Political Science**: AI-driven sentiment analysis of social media data helps predict election outcomes, track public opinion shifts, and analyze political discourse in real time (Grimmer, Roberts, & Stewart, 2021).

- **Economics**: Machine learning models can predict financial crises, unemployment trends, and consumer behavior by analyzing market data, transaction records, and economic indicators (Athey, 2022).
- **Sociology**: AI models analyze crime rates, urban development trends, and social mobility patterns, helping policymakers make informed decisions (González-Bailón, 2022).

AI is also crucial in real-time data analysis, especially in crisis management. For instance, during the COVID-19 pandemic, AI models were instrumental in modeling the virus's spread, assessing the effectiveness of government policies, and predicting economic recovery trends based on global data (Kaggle, 2020). These AI-driven insights allowed governments and international organizations to implement data-driven policies and interventions.

Moreover, AI facilitates automated data collection and cleaning, reducing human error and increasing the reliability of quantitative research. Traditional social science studies often suffer from incomplete or biased datasets, but AI can identify missing values, detect anomalies, and improve overall data accuracy (Salganik, 2021). This capability enhances the robustness of conclusions drawn from large-scale datasets and ensures the validity of research findings.

1.1.2 AI in Qualitative Research: Automating and Enhancing Text and Image Analysis

Qualitative social science research focuses on interpreting texts, interviews, historical records, and visual materials and has traditionally been labor-intensive, requiring extensive human effort to code and categorize data manually. However, AI, specifically natural language processing (NLP) and computer vision, has revolutionized qualitative research by automating many tasks and enabling large-scale analysis of complex data sources.

AI-Powered Text Analysis

- **Sentiment Analysis**: NLP techniques can assess emotions and opinions expressed in texts, such as news articles, social media posts, and interview transcripts (Tufekci, 2021). This is particularly useful in fields like media studies, political science, and public opinion research, where understanding public sentiment is key.
- **Topic Modeling**: AI algorithms, such as Latent Dirichlet Allocation (LDA), can automatically identify themes and topics within large text corpora, helping researchers analyze trends in public discourse and societal concerns over time (Blei, Ng, & Jordan, 2021).

- **Text Classification**: AI can categorize documents, detect misinformation, and summarize complex texts, benefiting research in journalism, law, history, and social media studies (Pasquale, 2020).

For example, political scientists have employed NLP to analyze speeches from world leaders, identifying key themes, ideological shifts, and rhetorical patterns over time (Van Atteveldt, Welbers, & Jacobi, 2021). Similarly, historians have applied AI to digitized historical archives, allowing for analyzing vast collections of documents at a scale that would be impossible with traditional methods (Fitzgerald et al., 2022).

AI-Powered Image and Visual Analysis

AI also plays a vital role in visual data analysis, including images and videos, which are often used in qualitative research to explore cultural phenomena, social movements, or historical events. AI-powered computer vision techniques can automatically identify objects, emotions, and actions within images and videos, providing valuable insights into visual material. For instance, AI tools have been used to analyze protest footage, identifying patterns in crowd behavior and political symbolism (Elizondo et al., 2021).

Moreover, AI-driven image recognition can assist in analyzing visual materials from archives, art collections, and historical footage, helping researchers understand visual culture and historical narratives (Fitzgerald et al., 2022).

1.1.3 AI in Mixed Methods Research: Bridging Quantitative and Qualitative Approaches

Social sciences often use mixed methods research, combining qualitative and quantitative techniques to understand social phenomena comprehensively. AI facilitates this integration by enabling seamless transitions between structured (numerical) and unstructured (textual, visual) data analysis.

For example:

- **Social Network Analysis**: AI can analyze social media interactions, combining NLP (for text analysis) with graph-based algorithms (for network analysis) to map out relationships and influence patterns within digital communities (Lazer et al., 2022).
- **Predictive Policy Modeling**: AI-driven simulations allow policymakers to test different policy scenarios by integrating economic, social, and behavioral data, improving evidence-based decision-making (Rahwan et al., 2023).

- **AI in Experimental Research**: AI is increasingly used in social science experiments to create dynamic interventions, such as personalized learning programs in education research or adaptive survey techniques in psychology (Shin et al., 2023).

1.1.4 Challenges and Ethical Considerations in AI-Driven Social Science Research

While AI offers powerful tools for social sciences, its use raises several challenges and ethical concerns:

- **Bias in AI Models**: AI systems learn from historical data, which may contain societal biases. These biases can reinforce discrimination in areas such as hiring, policing, and social policy (O'Neil, 2022).
- **Transparency and Interpretability**: Many AI models function as "black boxes," making it difficult for researchers to understand how decisions are made (Lipton, 2022). This raises concerns about accountability and trust in AI-driven findings.
- **Data Privacy and Ethics**: Social science research often involves sensitive personal data. AI-driven analysis must comply with ethical standards and data protection laws such as GDPR (Zuboff, 2023).
- **Dependence on Big Data**: AI models require large datasets, which may not always be available or represent diverse populations (Noble, 2023). This can lead to overgeneralization or misinterpretation of findings.

1.2 The Evolution of AI in Social Science Research

In the 1990s and early 2000s, computational social science (CSS) emerged, blending traditional social science methodologies with computational techniques from computer science. This interdisciplinary approach allowed researchers to analyze large datasets, identify patterns in social behavior, and develop predictive models (Lazer et al., 2009).

A significant catalyst for this shift was the increasing availability of digital data from online forums, governmental records, and economic transactions. As computational power grew, researchers began employing machine learning algorithms to process and analyze these vast amounts of information, enabling more sophisticated insights into human behavior. Some key applications during this period included:

- Social Network Analysis (SNA): AI-driven network analysis helped researchers understand relationships between individuals and groups in online and offline communities (Wasserman & Faust, 1994).
- Text Mining and Sentiment Analysis: Natural language processing (NLP) techniques allowed scholars to extract meaningful insights from large volumes of text, such as political speeches, news articles, and social media posts (Grimmer & Stewart, 2013).
- Predictive Modeling in Economics and Political Science: AI-based models were increasingly used to forecast economic trends, election outcomes, and consumer behaviors with high accuracy (Varian, 2014).

During this period, computational social science became an established research paradigm, providing the groundwork for more advanced AI-driven methodologies in the following decades.

1.2.1 The Impact of Big Data and AI Advancements

The 2010s marked a turning point in integrating AI into social sciences, primarily driven by the rise of big data analytics and advancements in deep learning. The explosion of digital platforms such as social media, e-commerce, and streaming services created unprecedented user-generated data, offering researchers new opportunities to analyze large-scale human interactions (Tufekci, 2017).

Some key developments in this period include:

- Machine Learning for Behavioral Analysis: AI models trained on massive datasets began to detect patterns in human behavior, such as voting tendencies, consumer preferences, and migration patterns (Rahwan et al., 2019).
- Deep Learning for Image and Video Analysis: The rise of deep neural networks enabled researchers to classify and interpret images and videos, facilitating studies on cultural trends, media representation, and visual propaganda (LeCun, Bengio, & Hinton, 2015).
- AI in Misinformation Detection: As concerns about fake news and misinformation grew, AI-driven fact-checking systems were developed to assess the credibility of news sources and detect biased or misleading information (Vosoughi, Roy, & Aral, 2018).

One of the most notable applications of AI in this era was in political science and public opinion research. For example, during the 2016 U.S. presidential election, AI-based sentiment analysis was used to track public reactions to candidates on social media, providing real-time insights into voter behavior (Howard et al., 2018).

Similarly, researchers used AI to analyze disinformation campaigns and detect bot activity on platforms like Twitter and Facebook, highlighting the growing role of AI in media and communication studies (Ferrara et al., 2016).

1.2.2 The Present and Future of AI in Social Sciences

Today, AI continues to expand the boundaries of social science research, with applications spanning multiple disciplines:

- Psychology and Behavioral Sciences: AI models analyze cognitive patterns, emotional responses, and decision-making processes, aiding mental health diagnosis and treatment recommendation (Russell, 2019).
- Economics and Labor Studies: AI-powered predictive models assess labor market trends, wage dynamics, and automation's impact on employment (Brynjolfsson & McAfee, 2014).
- Urban Studies and Public Policy: AI is increasingly used in thoughtful city planning, traffic management, and urban development to create more sustainable and efficient cities (Batty, 2018).
- Ethics and Governance of AI: As AI plays a larger societal role, social scientists actively study its ethical implications, bias mitigation strategies, and regulatory frameworks (Zuboff, 2019).

AI-Powered Advancements in Social Sciences

Several emerging AI technologies are shaping the future of social science research:

- **Explainable AI (XAI) and Interpretability**: One of the main challenges in using AI for social sciences is the "black box" nature of many machine learning models. Researchers are now developing explainable AI (XAI) techniques that provide greater transparency in AI decision-making processes, allowing social scientists to understand better and validate their findings (Lipton, 2022).
- **AI for Longitudinal Studies**: AI models improve the ability to conduct long-term studies by automating data collection and analysis across decades, helping researchers track shifts in demographics, political ideologies, and economic patterns over time (Athey, 2023).
- **AI in Experimental Social Science**: AI-driven virtual environments and simulations study group dynamics, cooperation, and conflict resolution in controlled settings, offering new ways to test social theories (Rahwan et al., 2023).

- **Personalized Public Policy Recommendations**: AI is integrated into governance and policymaking to tailor policies to specific demographic groups. For example, machine learning models can optimize tax structures, social welfare programs, and urban planning by predicting the impact of different policies on various populations (Batty, 2022).

These advancements demonstrate that AI is transforming existing methodologies and opening new avenues for research in social sciences.

Ethical and Methodological Challenges in AI-Driven Social Science Research

Despite its potential, the integration of AI in social sciences is accompanied by significant ethical and methodological challenges:

- **Bias and Fairness**: AI models are trained on historical data, which may contain systemic biases. These biases can reinforce discrimination in hiring, law enforcement, and social policy (O'Neil, 2022). For instance, predictive policing algorithms have been criticized for disproportionately targeting marginalized communities (Lum & Isaac, 2021).
- **Privacy Concerns**: The use of AI in analyzing social media, financial transactions, and surveillance data raises concerns about personal privacy and data protection. Regulations such as the General Data Protection Regulation (GDPR) in the European Union aim to mitigate these risks, but ethical concerns about data ownership and consent remain (Zuboff, 2023).
- **Replicability and Validity**: Social science research relies on reproducibility, yet many AI-driven studies use proprietary algorithms or non-public datasets, making replication difficult (Freese & Peterson, 2021). Ensuring methodological transparency is a growing challenge in AI-enhanced research.
- **Ethical Use of AI in Behavioral Manipulation**: AI's ability to predict and influence human behavior raises concerns about its potential misuse in political campaigns, targeted advertising, and social media algorithms. The 2018 Cambridge Analytica scandal, where AI was used to manipulate voter behavior, highlights the risks of AI-driven behavioral engineering (Cadwalladr & Graham-Harrison, 2022).

These challenges highlight the importance of ethical AI development and governance in social sciences, ensuring that AI applications align with fairness, transparency, and social responsibility principles.

Future Directions: The Role of Interdisciplinary Collaboration

As AI becomes increasingly integral to social sciences, interdisciplinary collaboration between social scientists, data scientists, ethicists, and policymakers is essential to maximize AI's benefits while mitigating its risks. Key areas for future research and collaboration include:

- **AI Ethics and Policy**: Developing global standards and ethical guidelines for AI applications in social science research.
- **Human-Centered AI**: Ensuring AI tools augment human decision-making rather than replace critical social analysis.
- **Open Science and Data Transparency**: Encouraging open-access AI models and publicly available datasets to enhance reproducibility and accountability.
- **AI for Social Good**: Expanding research on AI's role in addressing social issues such as poverty, climate change, and global health crises.

In conclusion, the historical development of AI in social sciences has evolved from early computational techniques to sophisticated machine learning and big data analytics. As AI continues shaping the field, researchers must carefully navigate its opportunities and challenges. By fostering interdisciplinary collaboration and prioritizing ethical considerations, AI can be a powerful tool for advancing knowledge and improving society.

1.3 Ethical and Methodological Considerations

Despite its advantages, the use of AI in social sciences raises several ethical and methodological concerns. One major issue is **algorithmic bias**, where AI models inherit and reinforce existing social biases in the training data (Noble, 2022). For example, studies have shown that AI-driven hiring algorithms can perpetuate gender and racial discrimination if not carefully designed (Dastin, 2021). Similarly, predictive policing models have been criticized for disproportionately targeting marginalized communities due to biases in crime data (Richardson, Schultz, & Crawford, 2022).

Another critical concern is **data privacy**. Many AI applications in social sciences rely on analyzing personal data, raising questions about informed consent and data protection (Zuboff, 2023). The General Data Protection Regulation (GDPR) in the European Union and similar regulations worldwide highlight the need for ethical AI usage in research (ICO, 2021). Social scientists must balance the benefits of AI-driven insights with the responsibility to protect individual rights and ensure transparency in AI decision-making.

Additionally, there is an ongoing debate about the **interpretability** of AI models in social research. While AI can identify patterns and make predictions, it often operates as a "black box," making it difficult for researchers to understand how conclusions are reached (Lipton, 2022). This lack of transparency can undermine trust in AI-generated findings and limit their applicability in policymaking and social interventions (Mittelstadt, Russell, & Wachter, 2022).

1.4 The Need for a Balanced Approach

Given the growing presence of AI in social sciences, researchers must adopt a balanced approach that maximizes its potential while addressing ethical and methodological challenges. Interdisciplinary collaboration between computer scientists, ethicists, and social scientists ensures that AI tools are developed and applied responsibly (Berman, 2022). Moreover, integrating explainable AI (XAI) techniques can help make AI models more transparent and accountable in social science research (Miller, 2023).

Furthermore, social scientists should not rely solely on AI-driven analyses but combine them with traditional qualitative and ethnographic methods to better understand social phenomena (Small, 2022). By leveraging AI as a complement rather than a replacement for human expertise, researchers can enhance their ability to study complex social issues while mitigating the risks associated with AI bias and misinterpretation.

AI has become an indispensable tool in social sciences, offering robust data analysis, prediction, and automation capabilities. However, considering the ethical and methodological challenges it presents, its integration must be approached with caution. As AI evolves, social scientists must engage in critical discussions about its impact and develop frameworks that ensure responsible and meaningful applications in research and policymaking.

2. ADVANTAGES OF AI IN SOCIAL SCIENCES

2.1 Enhanced Data Processing and Analytical Precision

Artificial Intelligence facilitates the expeditious and precise analysis of extensive and multifaceted datasets within the social sciences. AI enhances the rigor and robustness of empirical findings by enabling the identification of latent patterns, emergent trends, and intricate correlations (Smith, 2023).

2.2 Augmented Predictive Modeling

AI-driven predictive models afford the capability to anticipate complex social phenomena, including economic fluctuations, electoral behaviors, and crime dynamics. These data-informed forecasts provide a critical foundation for evidence-based policy formulation and scholarly inquiry (Athey, 2023).

2.3 Automation of Labor-Intensive Procedures

Automating repetitive and time-consuming tasks, such as qualitative data coding, interview transcription, and comprehensive literature synthesis, liberates researchers from focusing on higher-order analytical processes and theoretical interpretation (Johnson, 2022).

2.4 Facilitation of Interdisciplinary Integration

AI catalyzes interdisciplinary research, synthesizing methodologies and insights from psychology, sociology, political science, and economics. Through AI-powered simulations and modeling, scholars can rigorously evaluate social theories and policy interventions within controlled and replicable experimental contexts (Rahwan et al., 2023).

3. DISADVANTAGES OF AI IN THE SOCIAL SCIENCES

Given the interdisciplinary scope of this SCOPUS-indexed volume, this chapter is designed to address the needs of its primary audience, namely, social science researchers, graduate students, and professionals operating at the nexus of technology and society. While this readership may not comprise technical experts in artificial intelligence, they are increasingly called upon to critically assess AI applications' ethical, methodological, and epistemological implications within their respective domains.

Accordingly, this section eschews overly technical jargon in favor of accessible yet conceptually rigorous analysis, focusing on issues that influence research design and interpretation in disciplines such as sociology, political science, psychology, and economics. Ethical concerns, including data privacy and algorithmic bias, are discussed in light of current literature and salient academic case studies. In addition, the section offers a critical reflection on how excessive reliance on AI tools may erode human-centered methodologies and interpretative competencies.

By highlighting these dimensions, the chapter contributes to the broader aim of this volume: fostering critical engagement with AI technologies among non-technical scholars. The objective is to empower social scientists to integrate AI tools thoughtfully and ethically into their research while remaining attentive to these technologies' limitations and societal ramifications.

3.1 Ethical and Privacy Concerns

Integrating AI into social science research often entails collecting and processing sensitive personal data and raising pressing ethical considerations. In digital environments such as social media, data are frequently harvested without explicit or informed consent, posing substantial risks to individual privacy and autonomy (Zuboff, 2023).

Another major ethical challenge lies in the opacity of AI systems. Many contemporary models, especially those grounded in deep learning, operate as "black boxes," rendering their decision-making processes incomprehensible to end-users. This lack of transparency undermines accountability and threatens the ethical standards foundational to empirical social research. Ensuring that AI systems adhere to fairness, justice, and informed consent is thus essential for maintaining public trust in research outcomes.

3.2 Algorithmic Bias and Epistemic Risk

AI algorithms are trained on historical data that often encode systemic social and cultural biases. When these biases go unexamined, they are replicated and amplified by AI systems. For example, predictive policing algorithms based on biased crime data may disproportionately target marginalized communities, thereby reinforcing structural inequalities (O'Neil, 2022).

In social research, such algorithmic biases can lead to flawed classifications, erroneous interpretations, and invalid conclusions. These distortions not only compromise the epistemic integrity of research but also carry significant ethical and policy consequences. It is, therefore, imperative to critically assess training data, algorithmic structures, and the interpretive context of AI outputs within any research endeavor.

3.3 Dependence on Data Availability and Quality

AI systems are heavily reliant on the availability of large, high-quality datasets. However, in many areas of the social sciences, such data are either scarce, incomplete, or inaccessible due to privacy regulations, cultural sensitivities, or logistical challenges. These constraints limit the applicability and generalizability of AI-driven methodologies, often resulting in skewed or non-representative findings (Freese & Peterson, 2021).

Moreover, data quality is a critical determinant of AI performance. Issues such as inaccurate labeling, missing values, and inconsistent classification can significantly degrade model reliability. As such, robust data preprocessing, validation, and ethical scrutiny are prerequisites for AI's practical and responsible application in social science contexts.

3.4 Erosion of Human Interpretive Capacities

Overreliance on AI tools may inadvertently diminish essential human competencies in research, including critical thinking, theoretical reasoning, and cultural interpretation. While AI excels at detecting patterns in large datasets, it fundamentally lacks the capacity for contextual understanding, ethical judgment, and sensitivity to lived experience, elements that are central to rigorous social inquiry (Mittelstadt, 2022).

This trend risks privileging computational approaches at the expense of qualitative and interpretive traditions, thereby creating a methodological imbalance. A more integrative approach that treats AI as a complement to, rather than a substitute for, human insight should guide the development of interdisciplinary research strategies. Such a balance is vital for preserving social science scholarship's richness and critical depth.

4. APPLICATION EXAMPLES OF AI IN THE SOCIAL SCIENCES (WITH CITATIONS)

4.1 AI in Political Science

Artificial intelligence has become a transformative tool in political science, enabling the systematic analysis of political rhetoric, misinformation detection, and the forecasting of electoral outcomes. Natural Language Processing (NLP) facilitates large-scale sentiment analysis in political speeches, parliamentary debates, and social media discourse, offering insights into ideological polarization and public opinion trends (Binns, 2023; Grimmer & Stewart, 2013). These tools enhance transparency in political communication and support empirical investigations into voter behavior and campaign strategies.

4.2 AI in Sociology

In sociology, AI-powered models analyze patterns in digital communication, migration flows, and social mobility. For instance, machine learning algorithms can detect emergent behavioral norms within online communities or predict population movement in response to policy changes (Rahwan et al., 2023; Lazer et al., 2009). Sentiment analysis also allows sociologists to interpret collective reactions to social crises, such as pandemics or political unrest, enabling more responsive and inclusive policymaking.

4.3 AI in Economics

The application of AI in economics has led to significant advancements in market forecasting, risk assessment, and behavioral modeling. Algorithms can process high-frequency financial data to identify trends, simulate market dynamics, and predict consumer responses to economic stimuli (Athey, 2023; Brynjolfsson & McElheran, 2016). These capabilities improve microeconomic analysis, pricing strategies, and macroeconomic planning, including inflation modeling and labor market predictions.

4.4 AI in Psychology

AI systems are increasingly used in psychology for clinical diagnostics, behavioral tracking, and emotional state recognition. Chatbots and virtual therapists provide scalable mental health support, while machine learning techniques detect early signs of disorders such as depression or anxiety through language patterns and biometric data (Smith, 2022; Calvo et al., 2017). These tools complement traditional psychological assessments and offer promising avenues for preventive mental healthcare.

Significance of the Study

The increasing deployment of artificial intelligence in the social sciences represents more than a methodological innovation; it signifies a shift in epistemological foundations and knowledge production. AI technologies, including deep learning, NLP, and network analysis, allow researchers to process complex, unstructured data at scale, identify latent patterns, and make data-informed predictions (Domingos, 2015; Kitchin, 2014).

However, using AI also raises critical concerns about data privacy, algorithmic bias, transparency, and the marginalization of qualitative inquiry. The risk of treating social phenomena purely as quantifiable data points may undermine the interpretive richness and ethical sensitivity that human-centered research affords (O'Neil, 2016; Mittelstadt, 2022).

By offering a comprehensive overview of AI's strengths and limitations in the social sciences, this study aims to foster a more critical, ethical, and interdisciplinary engagement with AI tools. It highlights the need for balanced methodologies integrating computational power with contextual understanding and theoretical depth.

Proposed Hypotheses

1. **H1:** AI-powered analytical tools produce faster and more accurate results than traditional research methods in the social sciences (Athey, 2023; Brynjolfsson & McElheran, 2016).
2. **H2:** Integrating AI in social science research reduces subjective human bias and enhances analytical objectivity (Binns, 2023).
3. **H3:** Biases embedded in training datasets lead to distorted or discriminatory outcomes in AI-assisted research (O'Neil, 2016; Noble, 2018).
4. **H4:** Increasing reliance on AI tools reduces researchers' qualitative reasoning and critical interpretative skills (Mittelstadt, 2022).
5. **H5:** AI-based predictive models improve the effectiveness of policy analysis and decision-making in social research (Grimmer & Stewart, 2013; Rahwan et al., 2023).

5. METHODOLOGY

This study employs a mixed-methods research design, combining a systematic literature review with selected case study analyses to explore how artificial intelligence (AI) is reshaping research methods, knowledge production, and ethical frameworks in the social sciences. The objective is to map current practices, identify emerging patterns, and assess ethical and methodological challenges.

The systematic literature review focuses on scholarly publications from **2015 to 2024**, a decade marked by the rapid advancement and integration of AI technologies into academic research. Sources were drawn from reputable academic databases, including SCOPUS, Web of Science, and Google Scholar, using search terms such as "AI in social sciences," "algorithmic bias," "machine learning and sociology," and "AI ethics in research." The review prioritized peer-reviewed journal articles, academic books, and empirical studies that reflect interdisciplinary and methodological diversity.

A **descriptive research strategy** was adopted to examine AI's applications across disciplines such as sociology, political science, economics, and psychology. The research does not collect original empirical data but rather synthesizes secondary sources. The design enables breadth (via literature review) and depth (via targeted case analyses).

A **systematic literature review** was conducted using **Scopus**, **Web of Science**, and **Google Scholar**, covering publications between **2015 and 2024**. Keywords included:

- "Artificial Intelligence in Social Sciences"
- "Machine Learning for Social Research"
- "Big Data and Ethics in Social Research"
- "Algorithmic Bias and Methodology"

Sources were selected based on relevance, peer-reviewed status, and methodological rigor.

Illustrative case studies were analyzed to complement the literature review. These include:

- **Sentiment Analysis in Political Science** (Zhang et al., 2021)
- **Predictive Models in Economics and Migration** (Molnar et al., 2021; Binns, 2023)
- **AI Tools in Public Policy Evaluation** (Athey, 2023)
- **Automated Interview Systems in Psychology** (Small, 2022)

These cases represented different disciplines and AI applications, showcasing innovation and limitations.

Data Analysis: The study employs the following techniques:

- **Content Analysis**: To identify dominant themes in the literature (Freese & Peterson, 2021).
- **Network Analysis**: This explores social media studies involving AI (Miller, 2023).
- **Quantitative Modeling**: References to supervised/unsupervised learning, regression models, and natural language processing tools are discussed, though not implemented directly.

Analysis frameworks were drawn from existing empirical studies using Python or R-based modeling, offering interpretive insight rather than new algorithmic development.

Ethical and Methodological Considerations: Key ethical concerns include:

- **Data Privacy**: Adherence to GDPR principles when discussing data use (Zuboff, 2023).
- **Algorithmic Bias**: Addressing discrimination risk in AI systems (O'Neil, 2020; Noble, 2018).
- **Transparency**: The challenge of replicability in black-box systems (Pasquale, 2020; Mittelstadt, 2022).

Ethical frameworks by Jasanoff and Hurlbut (2018) and others were used to reflect on responsible AI in social contexts.

Limitations and Future Directions: Limitations include:

- **Scope**: Focuses on selected AI applications; not exhaustive across all social science fields.
- **Pace of Change**: The rapid evolution of AI may quickly outdated current insights.
- **Integration Gaps**: More research is needed on how AI can complement qualitative, human-centered methodologies.

Future research should prioritize interdisciplinary collaboration, developing culturally sensitive AI tools, and empirical studies in underrepresented regions and populations.

6. FINDINGS AND DISCUSSION

This section presents the key findings from the literature review and case study analyses regarding the applications of artificial intelligence (AI) in social sciences. Additionally, the contributions of AI to social science research, methodological innovations, and ethical challenges are discussed.

In recent years, AI technologies such as machine learning (ML), natural language processing (NLP), and big data analytics have fundamentally transformed political science, sociology, psychology, and economics research practices. These tools enable the processing of vast datasets and the identification of patterns that were previously inaccessible (Kitchin, 2014; Brynjolfsson & McAfee, 2017). For instance, Gonzalez et al. (2021) demonstrate how mobility data can be analyzed to study human behavior across spatial and temporal scales. Similarly, ML models have been used in economics to predict financial fluctuations with increased accuracy (Brynjolfsson et al., 2017).

The integration of AI into social research has not only expanded the methodological toolkit but has also reshaped epistemological assumptions. Traditionally, social sciences have been grounded in theory-driven approaches. However, AI's emphasis on pattern recognition and predictive analytics marks a shift toward data-driven epistemologies (Beer, 2017; Jasanoff, 2021). This transformation has raised concerns about marginalizing critical and qualitative perspectives in favor of algorithmic objectivity (Gillespie, 2021).

In terms of practical applications, AI has facilitated advances such as sentiment analysis of political discourse (Zhang et al., 2021), forecasting of migration flows (Molnar et al., 2021), and the study of public health trends using NLP techniques. However, while these tools offer precision and scalability, they also introduce new opacity forms. Many AI models' "black-box" nature complicates interpretability, accountability, and replicability, key pillars of scientific rigor (Pasquale, 2015; Raji & Buolamwini, 2020).

Ethical challenges are central to the discourse surrounding AI in the social sciences. Algorithmic bias, especially in historical data, may reinforce systemic inequalities (O'Neil, 2020; Eubanks, 2020). This issue is particularly evident in domains like predictive policing and automated hiring, where discriminatory outcomes can arise from uncritical reliance on biased datasets (Binns & Veale, 2024). Transparency and fairness remain contested goals despite ongoing efforts to develop ethical frameworks for responsible AI deployment (Jasanoff & Hurlbut, 2018).

This chapter builds on these findings to argue that while AI can enhance the analytical power of social science research, it must be approached critically. Methodological pluralism, integrating data-driven and theory-driven approaches, offers a path forward. Furthermore, embedding ethical reflexivity into AI design and application is essential to uphold the normative values of social science, including justice, equity, and human agency (Beer, 2017; Jasanoff, 2021).

Finally, these findings align closely with the thematic concerns of *The Power of Words in an AI-Driven World.* Just as Ferah Diba İzgi (2023) emphasizes the role of cultural sensitivity and ethics in AI-assisted child therapy, this chapter highlights the importance of contextual and humanistic insight in broader social science applications. When guided by interdisciplinary ethical awareness, AI can serve as a transformative yet accountable tool for understanding and shaping complex social realities.

6.1. Methodological Transformations

AI has introduced new research methods in the social sciences, enabling large-scale data analysis, real-time behavioral tracking, and predictive modeling. For instance, in political science, AI-driven sentiment analysis has become instrumental in election forecasting and public opinion research (Tufekci, 2014; Zhang et al., 2021). In economics, machine learning algorithms have enhanced the predictive power of financial models and market analysis (Brynjolfsson & McAfee, 2017; Varian, 2014).

In sociology and psychology, AI tools facilitate the analysis of massive behavioral datasets, allowing researchers to explore trends in migration, urbanization, and mental health (Gonzalez et al., 2021; Molnar et al., 2021). These methodological innovations improve the scale and efficiency of data collection and interpretation, particularly in crisis contexts such as pandemics or climate-related displacement (UNESCO, 2023; Xie, 2023).

6.2. Ethical and Social Challenges

Despite these advantages, integrating AI into social science research raises serious ethical concerns. AI systems often rely on historical data that may reflect and reinforce systemic biases. This has led to algorithmic discrimination in predictive policing, hiring, and healthcare (O'Neil, 2016; Noble, 2018). Black-box models, which lack transparency and interpretability, challenge core principles of replicability and accountability in scientific research (Pasquale, 2020; Raji & Buolamwini, 2020).

There is also a risk of over-reliance on AI, which may marginalize qualitative and participatory approaches crucial for understanding complex human experiences. Ethical frameworks emphasizing transparency, fairness, and inclusivity are still evolving and remain uneven across disciplines and jurisdictions (Binns & Veale, 2024; Gillespie, 2021).

6.3. Epistemological Shifts

AI promotes a shift from theory-driven to data-driven inquiry, raising concerns about the epistemic foundations of social science. While data-intensive methods offer scalability, they may overlook nuance, context, and meaning, elements traditionally central to humanistic inquiry (Jasanoff, 2021; Kitchin, 2014). Some scholars caution that this shift could weaken the role of critical theory and reflexivity in research design (Beer, 2017; Noble, 2020).

To address this, interdisciplinary efforts are underway to align AI methods with social theory. Hybrid models integrating computational analysis with ethnographic insight or critical discourse analysis represent promising directions (Molina & Garip, 2022).

6.4. Contextual Relevance and Future Directions

The themes explored in this chapter resonate strongly with the overarching aims of *The Power of Words in an AI-Driven World*, especially concerning communication ethics and human development. Ferah Diba İzgi's discussion of AI in child therapy and culturally sensitive design underscores the need for compassionate, human-centered AI applications. This chapter extends that vision by considering AI's structural impact on knowledge production and research ethics across social sciences.

Future research should further investigate the following:

- **Cross-cultural implications** of AI tools in non-Western contexts,
- **Policy-oriented AI applications** for public administration and education,
- **Critical AI literacy** in social science curricula,
- And **collaborative frameworks** for integrating social scientists into AI development processes (Jasanoff & Hurlbut, 2018; Eubanks, 2020).

CONCLUSION

Artificial intelligence (AI) transforms the social science research landscape by enhancing data processing capabilities, enabling large-scale pattern detection, and offering novel methodological approaches. However, its integration also presents significant challenges related to ethical accountability, algorithmic bias, transparency, and the preservation of human-centered inquiry. This study has demonstrated that while AI can enrich research through precision and scale, it may simultaneously obscure interpretive depth and reduce researcher agency if not critically managed. To ensure AI contributes to inclusive, responsible, and contextually grounded knowledge production, it is essential to combine AI-driven methods with traditional qualitative approaches, invest in explainable AI tools that foster transparency, strengthen ethical oversight through interdisciplinary collaboration, and implement regular bias auditing, especially in high-impact research domains. Social scientists must remain actively involved in shaping the future of AI to align technological innovation with the foundational values of their disciplines.

REFERENCES

Athey, S. (2023). Machine learning in economics: Bridging the gap between theory and practice. *The Journal of Economic Perspectives*, *37*(2), 45–68.

Binns, R. (2020). *The ethics of AI and social media*. Oxford University Press.

Binns, R. (2023). Natural language processing in political science: A new frontier. *Political Analysis*, *31*(1), 98–113.

Blei, D. M., Ng, A. Y., & Jordan, M. I. (2021). Latent Dirichlet allocation: A method for topic modeling. *Journal of Machine Learning Research*, *22*(1), 1–23.

Brynjolfsson, E.. (2022). Artificial intelligence in economic forecasting: Challenges and opportunities. *The Journal of Economic Perspectives*, *36*(2), 45–67.

Brynjolfsson, E., & McAfee, A. (2017). *The Second Machine Age: Work, progress, and Prosperity in a time of brilliant technologies*. W. W. Norton & Company.

Cadwalladr, C., & Graham-Harrison, E. (2022). The Cambridge Analytica scandal: How AI was used to manipulate voter behavior. *The Guardian*.

Choudhury, M., & Sharma, A. (2022). *Artificial intelligence and social science: Emerging methodologies and implications*. Cambridge University Press.

Dastin, J. (2021). *Amazon's AI recruiting tool discriminates against women*. Reuters.

Elizondo, C.. (2021). AI and social movements: Analyzing protest with computer vision. *Social Media + Society*, *7*(2), 1–13.

Eubanks, V. (2020). *Automating inequality: How high-tech tools profile, police, and punish the poor*. St. Martin's Press.

Fitzgerald, T.. (2022). Using AI to analyze historical archives: A case study in visual culture. *Digital Humanities Quarterly*, *16*(4), 45–64.

Freese, J., & Peterson, A. (2021). Replication and reproducibility in the age of AI. *Social Science Research*, *70*, 81–96.

Gillespie, T. (2021). *The platform society: Public values in a connective world*. Oxford University Press.

Gonzalez, M.. (2021). *Big data and behavioral science: AI's role in sociology and psychology*. Springer.

Grimmer, J., Roberts, M. E., & Stewart, B. M. (2021). The influence of social media on political discourse: Insights from AI-driven analysis. *The American Political Science Review, 115*(2), 482–497.

İzgi, F. D. (2024). AI's global impact: Unveiling its origins and development, its roles across cultures and in child therapy field. In Ricahyono, S. (Ed.), *The power of words in an AI-driven world: Exploring the interplay of language, culture, and communication* (pp. 14–26). Sketsamedya.

Jasanoff, S. (2021). *The ethics of AI and human rights*. Harvard University Press.

Johnson, K., & Li, W. (2022). Automating qualitative research: Benefits and risks. *Qualitative Research, 23*(3), 335–351.

Kaggle. (2020). COVID-19 data science and AI challenges: Insights from the pandemic. Kaggle.

Kitchin, R. (2021). *The data revolution: Big data, open data, data infrastructures, and their consequences*. SAGE Publications.

Lipton, Z. C. (2022). The mythos of model interpretability. *Communications of the ACM, 63*(6), 36–45.

Lum, K., & Isaac, W. (2021). To predict and serve? Social implications of predictive policing algorithms. *Science, 353*(6309), 1157–1161.

Miller, T. (2023). Explainable AI and its role in social science research. *AI & Society, 38*(2), 123–135.

Mittelstadt, B. D., Russell, C., & Wachter, S. (2022). Explaining explanations in AI: A taxonomy of interpretability and transparency. *Journal of Artificial Intelligence Research, 68*, 1–21.

Molina, L., & Garip, F. (2022). *Machine learning and social science research: Theoretical and methodological innovations*. Oxford University Press.

Molnar, J.. (2021). *Machine learning for behavioral analysis*. Springer.

Noble, S. U. (2022). *Algorithms of oppression: How search engines reinforce racism*. NYU Press.

O'Neil, C. (2022). *Weapons of math destruction: How big data increases inequality and threatens democracy*. Crown Publishing Group.

Pasquale, F. (2020). *The black box society: The secret algorithms that control money and information*. Harvard University Press.

Rahwan, I.. (2023). Behavioral AI: Predicting and shaping human behavior in virtual environments. *Nature Communications*, *14*(1), 1101–1117. PMID: 36843121

Raji, I. D., & Buolamwini, J. (2020). Actionable auditing: Investigating the impact of publicly naming biased performance of commercial AI products. *Proceedings of the 2019 CHI Conference on Human Factors in Computing Systems.*

Richardson, R., Schultz, J., & Crawford, K. (2022). Policing, AI, and bias: A critical analysis of predictive policing algorithms. *Columbia Law Review*, *122*(5), 1223–1249.

Shin, H.. (2023). AI in social science experiments: Applications in psychology and education. *Journal of Experimental Social Psychology*, *61*, 12–26.

Small, M. (2022). Combining AI and ethnographic research: A complementary approach. *Field Methods*, *34*(2), 202–216.

Smith, J. (2023). AI in social science research: Opportunities and challenges. *Social Science Review*, *19*(4), 200–215.

Tufekci, Z. (2021). *Twitter and tear gas: The power and fragility of networked protest.* Yale University Press.

Van Atteveldt, W., Welbers, K., & Jacobi, L. (2021). Analyzing political discourse with AI: Insights from natural language processing. *Political Communication*, *38*(1), 53–75.

Varian, H. R. (2014). Big data: New tricks for econometrics. *The Journal of Economic Perspectives*, *28*(2), 3–28. DOI: 10.1257/jep.28.2.3

Xie, L. (2023). AI and political polarization: A global perspective. *Journal of Political Science and Technology*, *12*(3), 115–130.

Zhang, S.. (2021). Sentiment analysis and public opinion: An AI approach to political science. *Political Analysis*, *29*(3), 319–337.

Zuboff, S. (2023). *The age of surveillance capitalism: The fight for a human future at the new frontier of power.* PublicAffairs. DOI: 10.4324/9781003320609-27

KEY TERMS AND DEFINITIONS

Algorithmic Bias: Systematic and repeatable errors in algorithmic decision-making due to biased data, design, or assumptions, which can lead to unfair outcomes across gender, race, or socioeconomic lines (Barocas & Selbst, 2016).

Artificial Intelligence (AI): A branch of computer science focused on creating systems capable of tasks such as learning, reasoning, and problem-solving that typically require human intelligence (Russell & Norvig, 2020).

Behavioral Prediction: The use of AI models and historical data to forecast individual or group behaviors, often applied in marketing, policy analysis, and criminal justice (Rahwan et al., 2019).

Big Data Analytics: The process of examining large and complex data sets to uncover hidden patterns, correlations, and trends that inform decision-making (Mayer-Schönberger & Cukier, 2013).

Bias Mitigation: Methods and tools designed to identify and reduce bias in AI systems, promoting fairness and equity in outcomes (Mehrabi et al., 2021).

Black Box Problem: A term describing AI systems—intense learning models—whose inner workings are not easily understood or interpretable by humans (Lipton, 2018).

Cambridge Analytica Scandal: A 2018 incident where personal Facebook data was harvested without consent and used for political profiling and targeting, raising global concerns about AI ethics and data privacy (Cadwalladr & Graham-Harrison, 2018).

Computational Social Science (CSS): An interdisciplinary field that integrates computational methods with social science theory to analyze and model complex social phenomena (Lazer et al., 2009).

Deep Learning: A machine learning subfield that uses multilayered neural networks to model and analyze complex patterns in data, particularly effective in image, audio, and text processing (LeCun, Bengio, & Hinton, 2015).

Disinformation: False information deliberately spread to mislead, often amplified by automated systems and AI on digital platforms (Vosoughi, Roy, & Aral, 2018).

Ethical AI: The design and deployment of AI systems that uphold moral principles, such as accountability, transparency, and justice (Jobin, Ienca, & Vayena, 2019).

Explainable AI (XAI): A subset of AI research focused on making the decision-making processes of AI models understandable to humans, improving trust and accountability (Doshi-Velez & Kim, 2017).

Human-centered AI: An approach that emphasizes designing AI systems that support human agency, augment decision-making, and prioritize user values and needs (Shneiderman, 2020).

Machine Learning (ML): A core component of AI involving algorithms that learn from data and improve performance over time without being explicitly programmed (Mitchell, 1997).

Natural Language Processing (NLP): A field of AI that enables machines to interpret, understand, and generate human language, widely used in text analysis, translation, and chatbots (Jurafsky & Martin, 2021).

Chapter 14
Revolutionary Impact of Artificial Intelligence on Society and Its Challenges and Opportunities

Babalpreet Kaur
https://orcid.org/0009-0004-0286-8054
Chandigarh University, India

Manjit Kour
https://orcid.org/0000-0003-1043-3187
Chandigarh University, India & North-West University, South Africa

ABSTRACT

AI has impacted countless aspects of our life by providing inventive remedies to solve global problems like personal healthcare and climate change. With the assistance of this powerful tool we can process data, evaluate information, and make better decisions with the use of analyzed information. Variety of commercial sectors, such as education, medical care, financial services, entertainment, communication and transportation benefit immensely from its growing popularity, but it also brings up major ethical and social concerns such as loss of jobs, data hacking, unfair computational techniques, data hacking, and privacy and security threats. This chapter examines how artificial intelligence (AI) is affecting society as a whole, highlighting both its exciting possibilities and its significant drawbacks.

DOI: 10.4018/979-8-3373-2612-2.ch014

INTRODUCTION

Artificial Intelligence (AI), which used to be mostly the topic of university research and science fiction, has now become a standard part of our daily lives and is instrumental in numerous crucial systems across the globe. The term Artificial Intelligence was coined by John McCarthy " at the Dartmouth Conference in 1956, and it is widely regarded as the starting point of AI as a serious area of research. AI has since experienced times of great optimism, significant investment, and periods of slow growth and declining interest. It has become an influential technology with broad applications in many areas. The rapid increase in computing capabilities and the massive increase in data available have assisted Artificial Intelligence in developing dramatically from a limited set of tasks to a broad set of applications (Kaur & Kour, 2025).

Machine learning (ML), natural language processing (NLP), deep learning, robotics, and computer vision are some of the technologies that allow the machine to learn from experience, adjust to new and evolving conditions, and make choices independently. The capabilities, like comprehending speech or identifying faces in photographs, make AI distinctive. It can potentially revolutionize social structures, human behavior, and economic systems. Artificial Intelligence assists in finding solutions to global issues, such as climate change prediction and personalized healthcare. It assists individuals in making informed decisions based on facts by processing large volumes of data, identifying patterns, and predicting outcomes (Kaur & Kour, 2025).

AI has become one of humanity's most groundbreaking and influential innovations ever developed. Over the past few decades, it has expanded from a theoretical concept into a powerful force influencing society by actively shaping industries. Its influence is widespread in many areas, such as healthcare, education, finance, transportation, governance, and communication. It changes how businesses function and the fundamentals of daily human life (Brynjolfsson & McAfee, 2014). The idea of artificial Intelligence has existed since ancient times, when mechanical creatures with reason or consciousness were the subject of mythology and stories (Russell & Norvig, 2021). However, in the 20th century, the formal foundations of AI as a scientific discipline were established. British mathematician and logician Alan Turing posed the crucial question, "Can machines think?" in his seminal 1950 paper *Computing Machinery and Intelligence.* In the same paper, Turing also introduced the Turing Test, which evaluates a machine's ability to exhibit intelligent behavior indistinguishable from a human's (Turing, 1950). The Dartmouth Conference in 1956, which is frequently seen as the beginning of artificial Intelligence as a recognized field of study, came next. The conference was organized to examine how machines could resemble some characteristics of human intellect (McCarthy et al., 2006).

AI has gone through several periods of "booms" and "winters," with phases of rapid growth followed by times of stagnation, often caused by limitations in processing power, data availability, and algorithmic development (Crevier, 1993). Progress in AI is made possible by machine learning, advanced computer vision, and intelligent systems that can perform specific tasks better than humans. The impact of AI is pervasive and growing quickly across various industries (Kour & Kaur, 2024). Enhancing human capacities increases productivity, improves decision-making, and generates new economic value (Bessen, 2019). AI technologies in education make it possible for individualized learning experiences, which modify information to meet the needs of each unique learner and increase engagement. AI helps with data-driven policymaking, fraud detection, and administrative efficiency in the public sector (Eggers et al., 2020).

Artificial Intelligence can improve human skills, increase productivity and demand for human resources, and improve job quality. It is also crucial to note that the impact of AI on society as a whole is not uniform across all industries and occupations. Job opportunities in specific industries will increase significantly due to implementing AI-powered systems (Morandini et al., 2023). However, this may result in job losses in other industries, such as manufacturing and retail. Specific fields are observed as outdated because they lack adaptation to modern technological advancements and are not updated in skills and knowledge. With the rise of AI, the education system may need to transform and emphasize developing technical skills and other abilities. Once-science fiction possibilities like real-time language translation, autonomous vehicles, and predictive medical diagnostics have been made possible by the widespread use of AI technologies like machine learning, natural language processing, and computer vision (Esteva et al., 2017).

By offering innovative solutions to some of the most pressing challenges facing the world today—such as climate modeling and personalized healthcare—artificial Intelligence (AI) has transformed nearly every aspect of modern life. By enabling the processing of massive datasets, pattern recognition, and predictive analytics, AI enhances our ability to make informed, data-driven decisions across various fields. Many industries—including communication, healthcare, education, finance, transportation, and entertainment—have been revolutionized by the integration of AI, leading to greater efficiency, personalization, and innovation. In addition, AI plays a significant role in the larger digitization process that is changing contemporary society. It accelerates the development of intelligent infrastructure, digital public services, and smart cities (Schwab, 2016).

Automation frequently creates new job opportunities. The effect of AI on society is multidimensional and reflects its application in education, weather prediction, and economic development, as well as in improving consumer experiences (Shen & Zhang, 2024). While AI has the potential to create new jobs and replace existing ones by offering opportunities to enhance human capabilities, it also poses economic, social, and ethical risks (O'Neil, 2016). One of the challenges in the context of AI is ethical decision-making. The demand and compensation for High-skilled individuals who know how to build, implement, and manage AI systems may increase as the AI system grows more independently. On the other hand, Low-skilled workers may experience stagnant pay and fewer job possibilities. Artificial Intelligence has impacted the community's daily life and brought unique opportunities and challenges.

Internationally, the disparate impacts of AI are also evident. Countries are embracing AI at varying speeds and with different policy approaches. The U.S. and China are leading in AI development with heavy investments in people, infrastructure, and research (Lee, 2018). Artificial intelligence (AI) systems are embedded in wearable technology, social networking platforms, online shopping sites, and cell phones. They collect and analyze data to personalize user experiences. This digitalization opens up new avenues of creativity and efficiency, but there are also risks associated with data privacy, cyber security, surveillance, and digital addiction (Zuboff, 2019).

This chapter analyzes the advantages of AI and some possible drawbacks that AI imposes upon society. The chapter delves into the intricate impacts of AI from critical and optimistic standpoints, trying to present an integrative examination of the technology's social impacts. It starts by presenting a technical and historical profile of the progress of AI development, paving the way for understanding its current strengths and weaknesses. The chapter then examines the potential of AI in several important areas, including healthcare, education, the environment, and the economy. It also looks at the risks of AI, such as job loss, bias, surveillance, and unequal access, from an ethical, social, and economic perspective. Lastly, the chapter examines the role of governance and global cooperation in creating a safe, transparent, and equitable AI ecosystem.

When users finish reading this chapter, they will better understand AI's dual role as a disruptor and an enabler of progress. Rather than advocating for or against AI, the goal is to objectively look at how it can be designed and used to support human rights, align with society's values, and ensure equitable distribution of benefits.

LITERATURE REVIEW

The field of Artificial Intelligence (AI) has emerged as a transformative force in contemporary civilization. To draw attention to the extensive impacts of AI on society, this section presents key findings from existing literature and studies.

Economic development- Polak and Ansari (2024) demonstrated how AI transforms the economy by automating operations and creating global corporate-level centralization by implementing structural modifications. In addition to increasing corporate productivity, it also leads to an unequal distribution of wealth that causes significant social, security, and ethical consequences. According to Brynjolfsson and McAfee (2014), as an attribute of the Second Machine Age, AI can boost economic growth by increasing productivity and automating processes. The two top AI nations are the United States and China, but they focus on different things. The U.S. is known for creating new AI technology and innovations, with many AI startups and tech companies driving progress. China implements AI daily, from smart cities to surveillance and public services. So, while the U.S. leads in AI development, China excels in implementing AI across society (Lee, 2018). In contrast, the European Union takes a more cautious regulatory approach, prioritizing ethical guidelines and privacy protections under its Artificial Intelligence Act (European Commission, 2021). On the other hand, India concentrates on using AI to address regional issues like agricultural optimization and healthcare access (NITI Aayog, 2018).

Innovative opportunities- Mahajan (2023) highlighted how Artificial Intelligence is transforming society by emerging innovative opportunities and better efficiency, but it also presents problems like ethical concerns, job displacement, and biases. An ethical, transparent, and balanced framework is essential for society's welfare and the economy's sustainable development. Kamath (2022) believed that AI helps detect financial frauds, increase productivity, and tackle global issues regarding resource shortage, health problems, and climate change. It enhances everyday living and promotes general well-being by supporting communication and email management applications.

In **healthcare**, AI has the potential to transform healthcare diagnosis and treatment completely. Esteva et al. (2017) demonstrated that deep learning algorithms may be able to identify skin cancer. They demonstrated how deep learning systems may detect skin cancer just as well as or even more accurately than dermatologists. Muller (2017) highlighted the ability of AI to improve healthcare services for patients. Improved patient healthcare services through predictive analytics and personalized treatments have become a topic of considerable interest for the potential of AI. Muller (2017) explains that AI is beneficial in locations with limited resources, as it can assist with early diagnosis and predictions. In Africa and India, where hospitals and clinics are challenging to locate, AI-powered health apps on mobile phones have made it easier for people in rural areas to get medical advice and diagnoses (World Bank, 2020).

AI in education- According to Luckin et al. (2016), AI can assist teachers with administrative duties, improve student engagement, and offer individualized learning experiences. However, they warn about the risks of relying too much on automated systems, which may restrict human interaction in learning environments, lower creativity, limit emotional support, or perpetuate biases. AI can restructure education by adapting individual student needs through personalized and digital learning skills. China uses AI in classrooms to track student behavior with facial recognition and learning tools, improving efficiency and raising privacy concerns (Mozur, 2018). In contrast, many European schools try to balance technology with traditional teaching, following ethical guidelines (European Schoolnet, 2021).

AI is being used more in **government and public services**. O'Neil (2016) warns that tools like predictive policing can repeat existing biases and unfairly target specific groups. However, Kamath (2022) says AI can help governments find fraud, predict disasters, and manage cities if used ethically. Although India uses AI in digital systems like Aadhaar to make welfare services more efficient, it also raises concerns about surveillance (Mehta & Ghosh, 2021). The United Kingdom, for example, saves millions of public dollars by using AI to identify tax evasion (HM Revenue & Customs, 2020). Estonia's e-governance system uses AI chatbots to facilitate people's access to services more easily (OECD, 2019). AI is employed in the United States to optimize emergency services by predicting 911 call volumes and improving response allocation (Sun et al., 2020).

AI in agriculture, where farming is a significant economic activity, AI is beneficial to check soil health, predict crop yields, and control irrigation— (FAO, 2022). AI helps with climate modeling and sustainable development. Shen and Zhang (2024) demonstrate how AI is useful for predicting weather and managing energy grids, which is critical for addressing climate change. Liakos et al. (2018) emphasize that Farmers benefit from real-time information provided by machine learning, which enables more efficient agricultural management. Rolnick et al. (2019) highlight AI's capability to optimize energy use and improve environmental outcomes. Furthermore, Wamba et al. (2021) point out that AI applications in agriculture contribute significantly to food security and climate resilience in developing nations.

Privacy and Security issues- Majumdar (2020) raised significant privacy and security issues with the advancement of AI. These can be managed through sensible legislation, regulations, and sound governance. India's economic development could be hampered without a clear AI strategy, highlighting the need for sensible and balanced laws. Hernández-Orallo (2018) emphasized the ethical use of artificial Intelligence by addressing issues of transparency, bias, and fairness. The study highlights how rules and ethical frameworks are essential to regulate the development of AI systems and their implementation for maintaining societal norms. Different countries have different rules for AI, especially regarding ethics. The EU has clear rules that focus on making sure AI is used to help people and protect their rights. They want AI to be human-friendly and equitable.

On the other hand, China is more focused on using AI to become a world leader in technology. Some people worry about privacy because they do not provide as much information about how AI is used for monitoring. The EU is more concerned with the ethics and equity of AI, whereas China is more concerned with using it to advance its technological capabilities (Creemers, 2018).

Ethical concerns- Frey and Osborne (2017) concentrated on the requirement of careful policy considerations on complicated issues in labor markets for employment insecurity due to automation in repetitive tasks. The resultant job displacement and shifts in labor markets are complex issues. Regarding public services and governance, O'Neil (2016) critically investigates how algorithmic decision-making could breed social inequality. She argues that systemic discrimination results from predictive models frequently employed in employment, lending, and police, leading to systemic discrimination. However, ethical concerns about algorithmic transparency and data privacy remain significant obstacles to extensive adoption in therapeutic settings (Topol, 2019).

Practical and Moral application- Kelleher et al. (2015) offer a helpful framework in their book, "Fundamentals of Machine Learning for Predictive Data Analytics" for understanding machine learning. They utilized case studies to demonstrate key algorithms like decision trees, k-nearest neighbors, and neural networks. In order to achieve accurate predictions, the author emphasizes the importance of model evaluation, data quality, and feature selection. Though technical, the work also raises ethical issues about biased data and the responsible use of AI. It remains valuable for researchers and practitioners focused on predictive analytics' practical and moral application.

METHODOLOGY

Research Design

This chapter examines the revolutionary impact of Artificial Intelligence (AI) on society and explores the resulting challenges. It represents a comprehensive understanding of AI's Challenges and Opportunities from the society's viewpoint. A Qualitative descriptive approach was adapted to analyze the AI phenomenon, permitting an in-depth examination of societal implications without imposing rigid theoretical frameworks.

Data Collection

This study's data was collected from secondary online sources such as scientific journals, articles, government reports, and published information from trusted academic and industry-related platforms. The research spans literature published from 2014 to 2024, ensuring contemporary relevance.

Data Analysis Technique

The chapter is organized into three parts: an introduction to AI and its evolution, an analysis of the opportunities that AI presents for improving social systems, and key challenges associated with its implementation, including social, economic, and ethical risks. The data collection technique used in this study is documentary analysis, which includes reviewing, interpreting, and synthesizing empirical data and existing literature; based on collected information, a conclusion is drawn on the potential blessings and downsides of AI, providing information on how to steer its development for the benefits of all segments of society.

A **documentary analysis** approach was used to interpret the content by identifying recurring patterns, themes, and contradictions across studies regarding AI in economic development, healthcare innovations, education and skill development, AI regulations, and Privacy and surveillance concerns.

OPPORTUNITIES

Implications in healthcare- AI has proven successful in the field of healthcare. It speeds up drug discovery, enhances diagnostic accuracy, and improves clinical workflow. AI can improve healthcare by identifying illnesses and finding novel medications (Muller, 2017). Improving medical organizations' operations in healthcare facilities can reduce operating costs and save money. The actual impact will be in the care of patients. Google's DeepMind Health examines medical photos to identify conditions of particular diseases, such as diabetic retinopathy and age-related macular degeneration, with expert-level accuracy. Another example in this field is IBM Watson Health, which uses AI to assist doctors in diagnosing and suggesting treatment plans for cancer patients. Large volumes of data from medical records can be evaluated quickly to provide specific treatment suggestions. According to Topol (2019), AI enhances medical expertise and advances a more patient-centered approach to healthcare by relieving physicians from routine tasks and permitting them to devote more time to patient interactions. The health of millions of people globally might be improved by utilizing these technologies. The ability of AI has completely altered the manner of approaching healthcare, and treatment plans for patient care have proved life-changing.

Education transformation- E-learning is the most significant advancement of emerging Artificial Intelligence (AI) in shaping how we learn and teach (Kelleher, 2015). In recent eras, more schools have been able to adopt CAI as computer technology has become smaller and more affordable. Teachers need this technology to improve education by providing digital skills and preparing students for the workforce by offering innovative and adaptive learning platforms, access to global information, automated grading and feedback, and administrative tasks. AI tutor systems can provide flexible, readily available learning experiences and offer immediate feedback. By using AI for content generation, teachers can improve the quality of lessons without increasing their workload, ultimately helping students and educational institutions with limited resources. AI assists in drafting emails, organizing schedules, and automating administrative tasks.

Economic development- AI helps the economy grow by making work more efficient, encouraging new ideas, and creating new business opportunities. According to McKinsey (2018), AI could add $13 trillion to the world economy by 2030. Companies using AI are making better decisions, saving money, and staying ahead of their competitors. AI can contribute to economic development by increasing competition, production, and innovation. Many believe AI will boost economic development and productivity (Brynjolfsson & Mcafee, 2014). Many leaders in economic growth concentrate on boosting exports and attracting foreign capital. Leaders may choose businesses that could support local economic growth with the aid of AI (Qin et al., 2024). There is an upward trend in market values, employment, and sales growth of AI-investing companies. It might promote innovation by creating new products and services, markets, business models, and sectors, opening up new revenue sectors by raising consumer demand. Human capabilities combined with AI technology will lead the future of the business environment. AI is helping the finance sector by spotting fraud and checking risks more accurately. It supports human experts, encourages new businesses, brings in foreign investment, and increases exports—helping the country's economy grow.

Weather forecasting- AI can help to forecast climate change by predicting weather patterns, enhancing energy efficiency, and minimizing emissions. AI can analyze Weather forecasts more accurately based on past weather data. It helps communities manage resources during weather disasters. The transportation industry and households use less energy, and the performance of renewable energy sources can be maximized by implementing AI. Smart thermostats reduce energy waste by adjusting heating and cooling according to consumption patterns. Production and supply can be forecasted according to the weather. The government may track emissions and implement remedial measures after detecting pollution sources by using AI systems. Climate models are improved by using AI algorithms, enabling researchers to understand the possible effects of climate change. With the help of AI, farmers may maximize fertilizer and water use for more sustainable food production.

Interaction experiences of customers- Artificial Intelligence is also changing how we interact with technology in our gadgets. Popular Intelligent assistants powered by AI systems that recognize natural language and react to voice instructions are Google Assistant, Alexa, and Siri assistants. Furthermore, increasingly complex

AI-powered chatbots are helping companies improve customer service; for instance, Starbucks' chatbot facilitates quick and straightforward order placement, and customers can receive specific suggestions for prior purchases from H&M's chatbot. GPT (Generative Pre-trained Transformer) is an artificial intelligence language model that can understand, react, and generate text similar to a person's writing. This is advantageous for organizations to improve the consumer experiences by saving time and money.

Job transformation- Due to the independent status of Artificial Intelligence, it is transforming the workforce by automating repetitive and routine jobs. It may lead to job transformation in job structures- by eliminating some positions and opening up new career paths for creativity, sensitivity, and critical thinking in many sectors. Still, it may also result in job losses in manufacturing and retail due to automation. It also enables the emergence of new careers in data science, AI development, and human collaboration roles (Shen & Zhang, 2024). AI relieves people from monotonous jobs; they may concentrate on more meaningful and engaging aspects with interest and happiness to boost productivity (Brynjolfsson & McAfee, 2014). However, the impact of AI on the workforce is not uniform across industries; strategies for workforce reskilling are required to ensure that everyone can adapt to this technological change.

Agriculture and Food Security- AI is used in Precision farming to study data from drones, satellites, and sensors to manage water use, check crop health, and find pests early. It is helping farmers grow more food by using resources wisely, cutting waste, and solving food supply problems (Kamilaris & Prenafeta-Boldú, 2018). Companies like Blue River Technology use AI to spray herbicides to protect the environment accurately. In animal farming, AI can monitor animal health and plan feeding better. These tools help farming deal with climate change and support global goals like ending hunger.

Supporting the UN Sustainable Development Goals- AI is a key enabler for potential spans, all 17 SDGs of the UN's 2030 Agenda for optimizing agricultural output (SDG 2), improving access to healthcare (SDG 3), advancing education through personalized learning (SDG 4), and fostering innovation and infrastructure (SDG 9). Moreover, AI can assist in disaster response (SDG 13), governance (SDG 16), and data transparency (SDG 17). However, AI must be developed inclusively, responsibly, and with respect for human rights and sustainability (Vinuesa et al., 2020).

Energy and Environmental Sustainability- AI helps save energy and protects the environment by using power more efficiently, managing clean energy, and reducing pollution. It can predict how much energy is needed, run smart power grids, and connect solar and wind power to national systems (Rolnick et al., 2019). For instance, At home, smart thermostats like Nest learn your habits to save energy and money. AI cut data center cooling costs by 40% through clever energy use by

Google's deep Mind (Evans & Gao, 2016). Governments also use AI to track pollution and enforce environmental rules, supporting global goals like clean energy and sustainable cities

Improve human creativity- AI is recognized not just as a tool for automation. However, this system can also create original literature, art, and music forms by developing creative algorithms to improve human creativity and culture. AI tools like DeepArt and DALL·E are used in visual art to combine user-provided images with well-known painters' styles, allowing artists to move beyond their traditional boundaries (Gatys, Ecker, & Bethge, 2016). Similarly, AI tools like OpenAI's MuseNet and Google's Magenta in the field of music composition can produce sophisticated musical pieces in many different styles in the field of music composition. These systems can improve composition based on endless collections of musical data. Such tools are employed as creative partners to explore new musical directions and help musicians navigate challenges (Huang et al., 2020). In Writing and Literature, natural language processing models can generate short stories, poetry, and dialogue that remarkably strongly resemble human language. These outputs offer drafting support, writer's inspiration, and the opportunity to experiment with style, but these returns may not be as great as those of human-authored literary works. As McCormack et al. (2019) argue, AI is a "co-creative agent," this system can serve novel patterns and prompts that supplement the writer's voice rather than replace it.

Logistics and supply chain optimization- Autonomous delivery robots and drones are being tested for last-mile delivery, improving speed and reliability. AI-powered inventory systems help ensure products are available at the right time, avoiding too much stock, reducing waste, and keeping customers happy. AI also helps supply chains make quick decisions in emergencies like pandemics and natural disasters to respond better. AI is changing how logistics works by helping to predict demand, plan better delivery routes, and automate warehouses. Companies like Amazon and DHL use machine learning to make deliveries faster, cheaper, and more environmentally friendly (Winkenbach et al., 2020).

AI in law enforcement and criminal justice- AI significantly assists in collecting, storing, and analyzing vast amounts of personal and sensitive information that aid in investigating and resolving criminal activities. Technologies such as Facial recognition technology and predictive analytics allow investigators to prevent crimes, identify suspects, and detect patterns more efficiently and are becoming just as common and reliable as fingerprint identification in modern criminal investigations (Garvie, Bedoya, & Frankle, 2016). AI in the legal system also offers several opportunities to gain insights into how technology can be applied effectively for justice while preserving ethical standards without crossing an individual's privacy.

CHALLENGES

Privacy issues- AI technology is advancing rapidly, and serious concerns about data misuse and privacy violations are rising. It can manipulate the gathered and examined vast quantities of personal information on individuals, including their preferences, routines, feelings, and thoughts, by creating fictitious profiles without their consent. It violates privacy by acquiring and sharing personal data without authorization or transparency. The primary privacy issues with AI are the possibility of illegal access to personal data and data breaches. Data gathered and processed into the wrong hands is experiencing monstrous outcomes due to hacking or other security issues. These threats emphasize the critical need for strong data security regulations and ethical AI development. Public trust in AI technology ultimately depends on their ability to use data transparently, securely, and responsibly (Zuboff, 2019).

Job displacement- One of the criticisms of AI on labor economics is the automation of tasks previously performed manually. AI-based technologies can complete repetitive and tiresome jobs incredibly quickly, precisely, and efficiently (Trabelsi, 2024). Automation could replace human workers and disrupt their employment in many sectors of the economy, like manufacturing, transportation, and customer services, by generating new skill gaps and inequities (Frey & Osborne, 2017). Companies need to be proactive in dealing with AI-driven transformation. It, therefore, comprises assisting employees in identifying and acquiring the necessary skills for successful AI adoption, mapping the interconnected skills required for closing existing skill gaps, and supporting employees by providing targeted training and development opportunities (Morandini et al., 2023).

Biasness and discrimination- Another considerable issue of the AI system is the possibility of encouraging biases and discrimination generated by repeating prior opinions and assumptions in data and algorithms(Kasztelnik, 2024). Because of complex AI algorithms, there is a lack of transparency; it might be challenging to determine how they make certain judgments or predictions. Biases may be questioned because of this transparency, particularly in important fields like healthcare and criminal justice. This is because the only objective in evaluating AI systems is to look at the data on which they are trained. The AI system will be biased if the data is biased. For instance, it has been shown that face recognition algorithms perform poorly for people with darker skin tones (Buolamwini & Gebru, 2018). Racial bias was discovered by Obermeyer et al. (2019) in healthcare algorithms that underestimated the requirements of Black patients. Eubanks (2018) explains that automated systems used in public services frequently mistreat poor and neglected people.

Reduce accountability- AI may present ethical and legal issues concerning reduced accountability because it conceals who is liable for its decisions and acts. When artificial intelligence systems result in unintended and harmful outcomes, it is frequently challenging to determine whether any possible faults or errors result from developers, users, or the machine's design. Assigning accountability with unclear liability is challenging in high-stakes industries like criminal justice, autonomous vehicles, and healthcare. A contributing reason to the public mistrust and suspicion of the implementation of AI is the lack of a clear accountability structure (Coeckelbergh, 2020). Furthermore, users and regulators cannot understand how conclusions are reached due to the translucent nature of AI decision-making, particularly in deep neural network models, which restricts ethical oversight (Pasquale, 2015). Without explaining the ability and transparency frameworks, AI could be applied in ways that threaten accountability and legal clarity, eroding justice and trust (Floridi et al., 2018). Researchers also worry that companies might use AI to shift the blame, assigning faults to "the system" instead of accepting institutional accountability (Mittelstadt et al., 2016).

Contradiction- AI can be dangerous in the context of security threats as it can be misused to enable contradictions, cyber-attacks, and scams. The security of most businesses globally is affected by cybercrimes. Hackers can employ AI to automate sending spam messages, produce simulated videos, or execute intelligent cyber-attacks that cannot be traced through conventional security practices. Thus, AI is referred to as a double-edged sword; it is beneficial and dangerous. While it can enhance security, it enhances the size and complexity of more difficult-to-control threats. Companies across the globe are facing more problems due to AI-based cybercrimes that disrupt their operations, steal confidential information, result in enormous financial losses, and damage their reputation (Brundage et al., 2018). Also, cyber-attackers can control AI systems with subtle, hidden changes, demonstrating that even sophisticated AI has vulnerabilities and may not always be truthful when conducting critical tasks (Papernot et al., 2016). To solve these problems, we need proactive regulation, improved security systems, and wiser and safer AI creation.

CONCLUSION

AI offers tremendous opportunities and challenges to society. This chapter has discussed how AI can lead to social change by enhancing productivity, enhancing services in healthcare, education, transport, and agriculture, and solving global challenges in line with the Sustainable Development Goals. These opportunities have significant challenges, including security threats, algorithmic bias, job loss, privacy issues, and diminished accountability.

One of the analysis's major conclusions is that AI's benefits emanate from its governance, application, and development responsibly, not because of the technology itself. The intentions of human developers and users of AI have an important bearing on the social impact (Zuboff, 2019; Mittelstadt et al., 2016). When applied responsibly, AI can make systems more efficient and equitable. However, it can also boost inequality and injustice if abused or not regulated. For instance, facial recognition tends to perform less well on darker-skinned people and women, with issues in the way the technology is trained and constructed. (Buolamwini & Gebru, 2018). Similarly, the COMPAS system implemented in the U.S. justice system has demonstrated racial bias, highlighting the need for fairness and transparency in AI systems (Angwin et al., 2016). AI-driven automation can transform the market in terms of the demand for new skill sets and professions.

We must mold the future of AI before it changes us. In order to accept it, we must be aware of its prospects and challenges. The efficiency of the output of AI relies upon its users. It has both wonderful and challenging effects on society. AI can revolutionize interaction, communication, and labor with technology, although it creates apprehensions about employment displacement, bias, discrimination, and technological abuse. Society has a responsibility to ensure that AI is created and applied ethically. Development should be balanced to mitigate such threats. This involves fostering innovation while upholding social justice, civil rights, and democratic values. An equilibrium AI environment should be founded on transparency, accountability, fairness, inclusivity, security, and respect for human dignity (Floridi et al., 2018). This change may result in reskilling and upskilling of the members of society. We need to adopt proactive steps to protect the confidentiality of data with the help of verified data platforms.

It is imperative to ensure that AI is transparent, responsible, secure, ethical, inclusive, trustworthy, transparent, equitable, unbiased, and discrimination-free.

Additionally, active stakeholder participation from every walk of life is required to engage in open debates regarding AI's advantages and potential risks. We can establish trust in AI and ensure it serves society for good. A multidisciplinary effort with technology experts, policymakers, ethicists, educators, researchers, community leaders, business professionals, legal advisors, and other stakeholders is needed to foster fairness, resolve ethical challenges, and encourage responsible innovation. Future research must focus on interdisciplinary collaboration to understand how AI affects human behavior, culture, and society.

For AI systems to be evaluated on diverse and equitable data, the effects of AI on individuals of all genders, ethnicities, classes, and languages should also be investigated (Crawford, 2021). A global and inclusive approach is essential to guide

AI's growth and ensure its benefits are shared fairly. Policymakers must create clear laws and international rules, especially for areas where AI has a significant impact. Governments must also invest in access to education using AI so that everybody can keep pace and the digital divide does not expand (UNESCO, 2021). Companies must engage in transparent and auditable AI practices, minimize bias in their algorithms, and ensure their AI initiatives benefit social and environmental objectives. Universities and researchers must continue to drive AI research and inform the public through education and outreach. In short, artificial Intelligence (AI) is among the strongest technologies of the twenty-first century, but the way it influences humans will be up to them. We may take advantage of the benefits of AI without succumbing to its flaws if we build a system based on collaboration, justice, and trust. How we work as a community will decide the direction AI takes in the future.

REFERENCES

Aayog, N. I. T. I. (2018). *National strategy for artificial Intelligence: #AIForAll.* Government of India. https://niti.gov.in/sites/default/files/2021-07/NationalStrategy-for-AI-Discussion-Paper.pdf

Angwin, J., Larson, J., Mattu, S., & Kirchner, L. (2016). *Machine bias*. ProPublica. https://www.propublica.org/article/machine-bias-risk-assessments-in-criminal-sentencing

Bessen, J. E. (2019). *AI and Jobs: The Role of Demand*. NBER Working Paper.

Brundage, M., ... (2018). *The malicious use of Artificial Intelligence: Forecasting, prevention, and mitigation*. arXiv preprint arXiv:1802.07228.

Brynjolfsson, E., & Mcafee, A. (2014). *The second machine age. Work, progress, and prosperity*. 1–281.

Buolamwini, J., & Gebru, T. (2018). *Gender Shades: Intersectional Accuracy Disparities in Commercial Gender Classification*. In *Proceedings of the 1st Conference on Fairness, Accountability and Transparency* (pp. 77–91).

Coeckelbergh, M. (2020). *AI ethics*. MIT Press. DOI: 10.7551/mitpress/12549.001.0001

Crawford, K. (2021). *Atlas of AI: Power, Politics, and the Planetary Costs of Artificial Intelligence*. Yale University Press.

Creemers, R. (2018). China's social credit system: An evolving practice of control. *SSRN*. DOI: 10.2139/ssrn.3175792

Crevier, D. (1993). *AI: The Tumultuous History of the Search for Artificial Intelligence*. Basic Books.

Majumdar, D., & Chattopadhyay, H. K. (2020). Artificial intelligence and its impacts on the society. *International Journal of Law, 6*(5), 306-310.

Eggers, W. D., Schatsky, D., & Viechnicki, P. (2020). *AI-augmented government: Using cognitive technologies to redesign public sector work*. Deloitte Insights.

Esteva, A., Kuprel, B., Novoa, R. A., Ko, J., Swetter, S. M., Blau, H. M., & Thrun, S. (2017). Dermatologist-level classification of skin cancer with deep neural networks. *Nature, 542*(7639), 115–118. DOI: 10.1038/nature21056 PMID: 28117445

Eubanks, V. (2018). *Automating Inequality: How High-Tech Tools Profile, Police, and Punish the Poor*. St—Martin's Press.

European Commission. (2021). *Proposal for a regulation laying down harmonized rules on artificial intelligence (Artificial Intelligence Act).*https://eur-lex.europa.eu/legal-content/EN/TXT/?uri=CELEX%3A52021PC0206

European Schoolnet. (2021). *Ethical use of artificial Intelligence in education: Recommendations and guidelines.* European Commission. https://www.eun.org/documents/411753/817341/Ethical+use+of+AI+in+education+-+report.pdf

Evans, D., & Gao, J. (2016). DeepMind AI Reduces Google Data Centre Cooling Bill by 40%. *DeepMind Blog*. https://www.deepmind.com/blog/deepmind-ai-reduces-google-data-centre-cooling-bill-by-40

Floridi, L., Cowls, J., Beltrametti, M., Chatila, R., Chazerand, P., Dignum, V., Luetge, C., Madelin, R., Pagallo, U., Rossi, F., Schafer, B., Valcke, P., & Vayena, E. (2018). AI4People—An ethical framework for a good AI society: Opportunities, risks, principles, and recommendations. *Minds and Machines*, *28*(4), 689–707. DOI: 10.1007/s11023-018-9482-5 PMID: 30930541

Food and Agriculture Organization. (2022). *The state of food and agriculture 2022: Leveraging automation in agriculture for transforming agrifood systems.*https://www.fao.org/3/cb9479en/cb9479en.pdf

Frey, C. B., & Osborne, M. A. (2017). The future of employment: How susceptible are jobs to computerization? *Technological Forecasting and Social Change*, *114*, 254–280. DOI: 10.1016/j.techfore.2016.08.019

Garvie, C., Bedoya, A. M., & Frankle, J. (2016). *The perpetual line-up: Unregulated police face recognition in America*. Georgetown Law Center on Privacy & Technology.

Gatys, L. A., Ecker, A. S., & Bethge, M. (2016). Image style transfer using convolutional neural networks. In *Proceedings of the IEEE Conference on Computer Vision and Pattern Recognition* (pp. 2414–2423). DOI: 10.1109/CVPR.2016.265

HM Revenue & Customs. (2020). *Annual Report and Accounts 2019–20*. https://www.gov.uk/government/publications

Huang, C. A., Vaswani, A., Uszkoreit, J., Shazeer, N., Simon, I., Hawthorne, C., & Eck, D. (2020). Music transformer: Generating music with long-term structure. *Proceedings of the International Conference on Learning Representations* (ICLR).

John, D. Kelleher. (2015). *FMLPDA_SampleChapter_InformationBasedLearning*. 1–31. https://machinelearningbook.com/wp-content/uploads/2015/07/FMLPDA_SampleChapter_InformationBasedLearning.pdf

Kamath, R. (2022). Artificial Intelligence and public governance: Ethical implications and administrative reforms. *Journal of Public Affairs*, *22*(1), e2498. DOI: 10.1002/pa.2498

Kamath, S. (2022). A Study on the Impact of Artificial Intelligence on Society. *International Journal of Applied Science and Engineering*, *10*(1), 31–39. DOI: 10.30954/2322-0465.2.2021.3

Kamilaris, A., & Prenafeta-Boldú, F. X. (2018). Deep learning in agriculture: A survey. *Computers and Electronics in Agriculture*, *147*, 70–90. DOI: 10.1016/j.compag.2018.02.016

Kasztelnik, K. (2024). *The Study on the Impact of Business Artificial Intelligence Innovation on Fair Value Investments in the United States The Study on the Impact of Business Artificial Intelligence Innovation on Fair Value Investments in the U.S. January.*

Kaur, B., & Kour, M. (2024, September). Exploring the Growth and Future research directions on Robo advisors: A Bibliometric Study. In *2024 International Conference on Advances in Computing Research on Science Engineering and Technology (ACROSET)* (pp. 1–6). IEEE. DOI: 10.1109/ACROSET62108.2024.10743870

Kelleher, J. D., Mac Carthy, M., & Korvir, B. (2015). *Fundamentals of machine learning for predictive data analytics: Algorithms, worked examples, and case studies*. MIT Press.

Kour, M., & Kaur, R. (2024). "AI and Influencer Marketing: Redefining the Future of Social Media Marketing in Industry 6.0". In Advanced Businesses in Industry 6.0 (pp. 87-103). IGI Global. DOI: 10.4018/979-8-3693-3108-8.ch007

Lee, K. F. (2018). *AI Superpowers: China, Silicon Valley, and the New World Order*. Houghton Mifflin Harcourt.

Liakos, K. G., Busato, P., Moshou, D., Pearson, S., & Bochtis, D. (2018). Machine learning in agriculture: A review. *Sensors (Basel)*, *18*(8), 2674. DOI: 10.3390/s18082674 PMID: 30110960

Luckin, R., Holmes, W., Griffiths, M., & Forcier, L. B. (2016). *Intelligence Unleashed: An Argument for AI in Education*. Pearson.

Mahajan, S. (2023). Artificial Intelligence and its Impacts on the Society. *Contemporary Social Science*, *32*(4), 135–151. DOI: 10.62047/CSS.2023.12.31.135

McCarthy, J., Minsky, M., Rochester, N., & Shannon, C. E. (2006). A Proposal for the Dartmouth Summer Research Project on Artificial Intelligence. *AI Magazine*, *27*(4), 12–14.

McCormack, J., Gifford, T., & Hutchings, P. (2019). Autonomy, Authenticity, Authorship and Intention in Computer Generated Art. *Proceedings of the 10th International Conference on Computational Creativity*, 1–8. DOI: 10.1007/978-3-030-16667-0_3

Mehta, R., & Ghosh, S. (2021). AI and digital identity in India: Examining the Aadhaar experience. In Sahi, S. B., & Sinha, V. (Eds.), *AI and Society in India* (pp. 114–128). Springer.

Mittelstadt, B. D., Allo, P., Taddeo, M., Wachter, S., & Floridi, L. (2016). The ethics of algorithms: Mapping the debate. *Big Data & Society*, *3*(2), 1–21. DOI: 10.1177/2053951716679679

Morandini, S., Fraboni, F., De Angelis, M., Puzzo, G., Giusino, D., & Pietrantoni, L. (2023). The Impact of Artificial Intelligence on Workers' Skills: Upskilling and Reskilling in Organisations. *Informing Science*, *26*(February), 39–68. DOI: 10.28945/5078

Mozur, P. (2018, July 8). *Inside China's dystopian classrooms: Where surveillance reigns*. The New York Times. https://www.nytimes.com/2018/07/08/business/china-surveillance-technology-schools.html

Muller, V. C. (2017). Risks of general artificial Intelligence. In Muller, V. C. (Ed.), *Philosophy and theory of artificial intelligence* **2017** (pp. 297–307). Springer., DOI: 10.1007/978-3-319-96448-5_26

O'Neil, C. (2016). *Weapons of Math Destruction: How Big Data Increases Inequality and Threatens Democracy*. Crown Publishing Group.

Obermeyer, Z., Powers, B., Vogeli, C., & Mullainathan, S. (2019). Dissecting racial bias in an algorithm used to manage the health of populations. *Science*, *366*(6464), 447–453. DOI: 10.1126/science.aax2342 PMID: 31649194

OECD. (2019). *Digital Government Review of Estonia: Boosting the Digital Transformation of the Public Sector*. DOI: 10.1787/14e1c5e8-en-fr

Papernot, N., McDaniel, P., Goodfellow, I., Jha, S., Celik, Z. B., & Swami, A. (2016). *Practical black-box attacks against machine learning. Proceedings of the 2017 ACM on Asia Conference on Computer and Communications Security*. DOI: 10.1145/3052973.3053009

Pasquale, F. (2015). *The black box society: The secret algorithms that control money and information*. Harvard University Press. DOI: 10.4159/harvard.9780674736061

Polak, P., & Anshari, M. (2024). Exploring the multifaceted impacts of artificial Intelligence on public organizations, business, and society. *Humanities & Social Sciences Communications*, *11*(1), 10–12. DOI: 10.1057/s41599-024-03913-6

Qin, Y., Xu, Z., Wang, X., & Skare, M. (2024). Artificial Intelligence and Economic Development: An Evolutionary Investigation and Systematic Review. *Journal of the Knowledge Economy*, *15*(1), 1736–1770. DOI: 10.1007/s13132-023-01183-2 PMID: 40478928

Rolnick, D., Donti, P. L., Kaack, L. H., Kochanski, K., Lacoste, A., Sankaran, K., . . . Bengio, Y. (2019). Tackling climate change with machine learning. *arXiv preprint*, arXiv:1906.05433. https://arxiv.org/abs/1906.05433

Russell, S., & Norvig, P. (2021). *Artificial Intelligence: A Modern Approach* (4th ed.). Pearson.

Schwab, K. (2016). *The Fourth Industrial Revolution*. World Economic Forum.

Shen, C., & Zhang, Y. (2024). Artificial Intelligence for climate resilience: Applications in weather prediction and energy optimization. *Environmental Modelling & Software*, *170*, 105551. DOI: 10.1016/j.envsoft.2023.105551

Shen, Y., & Zhang, X. (2024). The impact of artificial Intelligence on employment: The role of virtual agglomeration. *Humanities & Social Sciences Communications*, *11*(1), 1–14. DOI: 10.1057/s41599-024-02647-9

Sun, T., Luo, Y., & Tang, K. (2020). AI for emergency services: Predictive modeling of 911 call volumes. *Government Information Quarterly*, *37*(2), 101456. DOI: 10.1016/j.giq.2019.101456

Topol, E. (2019). *Deep medicine: How artificial Intelligence can make healthcare human again*. Basic Books.

Trabelsi, M. A. (2024). The impact of artificial Intelligence on economic development. *Journal of Electronic Business & Digital Economics*, *3*(2), 142–155. DOI: 10.1108/JEBDE-10-2023-0022

Turing, A. M. (1950). Computing Machinery and Intelligence. *Mind*, *59*(236), 433–460. DOI: 10.1093/mind/LIX.236.433

UNESCO. (2021). *Recommendation on the Ethics of Artificial Intelligence*. https://unesdoc.unesco.org/ark:/48223/pf0000381137

Vinuesa, R., Azizpour, H., Leite, I., Balaam, M., Dignum, V., Domisch, S., & Nerini, F. F. (2020). The role of artificial Intelligence in achieving the Sustainable Development Goals. *Nature Communications*, *11*(1), 1–10. DOI: 10.1038/s41467-019-14108-y PMID: 31932590

Wamba, S. F., Kala Kamdjoug, J. R., & Epie Bawack, R. (2021). Leveraging artificial Intelligence in agriculture for sustainable development. *Technological Forecasting and Social Change*, *169*, 120799. DOI: 10.1016/j.techfore.2021.120799

World Bank. (2020). *Artificial Intelligence in health: Unlocking its potential in low-and middle-income countries*. World Bank Group. https://documents.worldbank.org/en/publication/documents-reports/documentdetail/941981606991679987/artificial-intelligence-in-health-unlocking-its-potential-in-low-and-middle-income-countries

Zuboff, S. (2019). *The age of surveillance capitalism: The fight for a human future at the new frontier of power*. PublicAffairs.

KEY TERMS AND DEFINITIONS

Accountability Gap: The accountability gap refers to the difficulty in determining responsibility when AI systems make mistakes or cause harm.

Algorithmic Bias: Systematic and repeatable errors in AI systems that result in unfair outcomes due to biased data or flawed algorithm design.

Artificial Intelligence (AI): AI refers to developing computer systems that can perform tasks typically requiring human Intelligence, such as learning, reasoning, problem-solving, and language understanding.

Automation: The application of technology to perform tasks using machinery with minimal or no human intervention. In the context of AI, automation includes innovative systems that can learn and adapt independently.

Cyber Security Threats: AI-enabled cyber security threats involve using AI technologies to carry out advanced and often undetectable cyber-attacks, such as phishing, deepfakes, and data breaches.

Data Privacy: Individuals have the right to control their personal information, which is collected, stored, and used.

Digital Governance: The framework enables governments to utilize digital technologies efficiently for administrative tasks and delivering public services.

Digital Surveillance: Digital surveillance uses AI and digital technologies to monitor and collect data on individuals, often by governments or corporations.

Ethical AI Governance: Ethical AI governance is developing and enforcing rules, standards, and frameworks to ensure that AI technologies are used transparently, fairly, and responsibly.

Ethical AI: The design, development, and deployment of artificial intelligence systems in ways that align with ethical values such as fairness, accountability, transparency, and respect for privacy is known as ethical AI

Job Displacement: Job displacement reduces or eliminates jobs due to automation and AI-driven technologies replacing human labor.

Personalized Learning: Personalized learning is an AI-driven educational approach where digital systems adapt content and teaching strategies to the individual needs, pace, and interests of students.

Chapter 15
The Scope, Applications, and Future of Artificial Intelligence in Instructional Design

Yeşim Sürmelioğlu
https://orcid.org/0000-0003-3073-899X
Kastamonu University Taskopru Vocational School, Turkey

Veysel Bilal Arslankara
https://orcid.org/0000-0002-9062-9210
Sakarya Provincial Directorate of National Education, Turkey

Mustafa Alp
https://orcid.org/0009-0006-1024-131X
Ufuk University Vocational School, Turkey

ABSTRACT

This chapter examines the role, applications, and future potential of artificial intelligence (AI) in instructional design. It begins by addressing the rise of AI in education and its intersection with instructional design. The integration of AI with established instructional design models is discussed, alongside an exploration of how AI aligns with various learning theories. The chapter explores AI-driven instructional design applications ranging from personalized learning systems to adaptive learning platforms. It illustrates, with examples, how automated feedback and assessment systems can reduce teachers' workloads while enhancing students' educational experiences. Ethical concerns and challenges encountered during the transformative process of AI in education are also addressed. In conclusion, AI is considered a powerful tool

DOI: 10.4018/979-8-3373-2612-2.ch015

with the potential to make instructional design more personalized, data-driven, and effective. In the future, the role of AI in education is likely to expand further, reshaping instructional processes across diverse educational contexts.

INTRODUCTION

To visually introduce the scope of this chapter, a prompt summarizing the content was entered into the free version of ChatGPT-4 Turbo. Based on this summary, artificial intelligence (AI) generated a visual representation (Figure 1), illustrating key themes such as integrating artificial intelligence into instructional design, personalized learning environments, adaptive platforms, and ethical challenges. The instant generation of this figure showcases the practical potential of generative AI in educational content development.

Figure 1. Visualization Generated by AI Based on the Chapter Summary

GPT-4 has significantly transformed the natural language processing landscape by enhancing its ability to process and analyze large volumes of text (Achiam et al., 2023). As stated in the GPT-4 Technical Report (Achiam et al., 2023), these models have demonstrated remarkable proficiency in understanding and generating human languages, achieving high performance across various fields such as business, finance, retail, healthcare, law, architecture, and transportation. Indeed, large language models can notably support teachers in instructional material creation, providing instant feedback, and delivering personalized learning experiences (Zawacki-Richter et al., 2019; Kasneci et al., 2023).

Edward Fredkin, who served for many years at the Massachusetts Institute of Technology (MIT) Computer Science and Artificial Intelligence Laboratory (CSAIL), made significant contributions to computer science and digital physics. In an interview with BBC International, Fredkin listed three significant events in history: the birth of the universe, the beginning of life, and the emergence of AI, which he placed third (ArkasNews, 2025; Pirim, 2006). This perspective aligns with some contemporary approaches that argue AI is an evolutionary extension in the context of epistemology and philosophy of mind (Kurzweil, 2005; Bostrom, 2014). Fredkin's statement is valuable in that it conveys the significance of AI in terms of both economic impact and human history. Could Fredkin be right? AI has now established a significant presence in all aspects of daily life—including access to information, consumption of news and entertainment, healthcare services, financial market performance, tourism, and more (Adiguzel et al., 2023; Alawi, 2023; Williamson & Eynon, 2020; Dalgıç et al., 2024).

AI is a computer or computer-controlled robot's capability to perform tasks typically associated with intelligent beings. The term is often used to develop systems equipped with intellectual processes characteristic of humans, such as reasoning, discovering meaning, generalizing, or learning from past experiences (The Britannica Dictionary, 2025). The term AI was first used by computer scientist and cognitive scientist John McCarthy during the "Dartmouth Conference" in 1956, the first official conference on artificial intelligence (Esen, 2019; McCarthy et al., 2006; Nilsson, 2019). McCarthy (2007) defined AI as "the science and engineering of making intelligent machines, brilliant computer programs."

Integrating computers and the Internet into educational settings has marked a critical milestone in the development process of technology use in education. Over time, evolving educational technologies have varied depending on the needs and possibilities of each era. Today, AI has become a prominent and indispensable tool among educational technologies. The personalization of instructional processes, the ability to conduct learning analytics, and the proliferation of applications that support educators have increasingly solidified AI's role in education. In this context, integrating AI-based applications into the education system has become a significant component of contemporary educational paradigms.

THE ROLE OF ARTIFICIAL INTELLIGENCE IN INSTRUCTIONAL DESIGN

Instructional design is a field that provides explicit guidance to help people learn and develop more effectively (Reigeluth, 1999). Smith and Ragan (2005) define instructional design as planning and organizing content, instructional strategies, and assessment methods to ensure effective learning. To make learning more efficient, practical, and accessible, instructional design addresses gaps in skills and knowledge (Morrison et al., 2019). Instructional design involves carefully selecting and structuring instructional materials, techniques, and processes to achieve specific learning objectives. According to Smith and Ragan (2005), the fundamental components of instructional design are:

- *Goal Identification:* Determining what will be learned and which skills will be acquired during the instructional process.
- *Content Selection and Organization:* Selecting and structuring the knowledge and materials for learners.
- *Selection of Instructional Strategies:* Choosing the most appropriate instructional techniques to guide the learning process (e.g., direct instruction, discovery learning, collaborative learning).
- *Assessment:* Measuring the success of learning and providing necessary feedback.
- *Feedback and Improvement:* Providing continuous feedback to learners to support progress.

The instructional design components proposed by Smith and Ragan (2005) provide a systematic approach to planning an effective learning process. However, the success of this process does not rely solely on the selection of objectives, content, and strategies; how learning is delivered—namely, the media and technologies used—also constitutes a significant area of discussion. At this point, a prominent debate in the literature regarding the impact of media tools on learning occurred between Clark and Kozma. This discussion, which gained considerable attention in the 1990s, involved Richard E. Clark and Robert Kozma. Their perspectives still reflect contemporary views on the influence of technology on learning. The debate, often referred to as "Does media influence learning?" is well-known and highly influential in the field of instructional design and educational technology (Bayramacar, 2013; Roblyer & Doering, 2014; Yazıcı & Kültür, 2020). A summary of the "media versus method" debate: Richard Clark's view – "Media are neutral," and Robert Kozma's view – "Media shape the method" (Clark, 1983; Clark, 1994a; Clark, 1994b; Kozma, 1991; Kozma, 1994a; Kozma, 1994b). Table 1 compares the Clark and Kozma perspectives on the role of media in learning.

Table 1. The Role of Media in Learning: Comparison of Clark and Kozma Approaches

Clark	Kozma
According to Clark, the media does not directly influence the success of education.	Kozma argues that media is not just a carrier but shapes the learning process.
The teaching method is the main factor influencing learning outcomes; the media only carries the content.	Each media outlet offers unique forms of interaction, visualization possibilities, and levels of engagement.
His famous analogy: "Media has about as much impact on learning as a truck carrying food."	He argues that there is a reciprocal interaction between media and method and that media can directly influence the learning design.
Even if different media (videos, computers, books, etc.) are used, if the teaching method is the same, the learning outcome does not change.	Presenting a method through different media can change the learning outcome.

Today, some educational technology researchers consider these two perspectives complementary rather than conflicting. While media alone may not be sufficient, it can contribute to learning when combined with appropriate pedagogical strategies. Especially new media types such as artificial intelligence (AI), augmented reality, and virtual laboratories are reshaping the learning experience. The Clark–Kozma debate offers a particularly valuable framework when considering the use of AI in education. In this context, we may find ourselves caught between the questions: "Is artificial intelligence merely a tool (Clark's perspective) or a transformative element in the learning process (Kozma's perspective)?" This view is also supported by contemporary studies that treat the capacity of AI tools to establish meaningful interactions with learners as a structural element of the learning process (Holstein et al., 2018; Williamson & Eynon, 2020). An attempt to answer the question "How is this debate perceived in the context of artificial intelligence?" is presented in Table 2.

Table 2. The Clark–Kozma Perspectives in the Context of Artificial Intelligence

	With Clark Perspective	**With Kozma Perspective**
Technological Neutrality	Technology is a neutral carrier of learning.	Technology is an active element that influences and transforms pedagogical practices.
Potential for Transformation in Education	Transformation in education comes not from technology but from method.	New technologies transform the nature of education and teacher-student roles.
In the Context of Artificial Intelligence	AI-powered teacher assistants, automated exam systems, and others only provide efficiency.	The features offered by AI, such as personalization, instant feedback, and natural language interaction, fundamentally change the learning experience.
	What affects student learning is the teaching strategy used by the AI.	The student experiences learning more actively, interactively, and meaningfully with AI.
	Without AI, the same strategy can be applied with other tools.	AI is not only a tool but also an environment that redesigns pedagogy.

When I asked for the free version of ChatGPT-4 Turbo to generate an image on "Instructional Design and Artificial Intelligence Integration," it produced the image in Figure 2. Apart from this request, no additional information was provided to ChatGPT. Looking back at this visual at the end of the chapter will contribute to better internalizing the concepts discussed.

Figure 2. Visual created by ChatGPT-4 Turbo on "Instructional Design and Artificial Intelligence Integration"

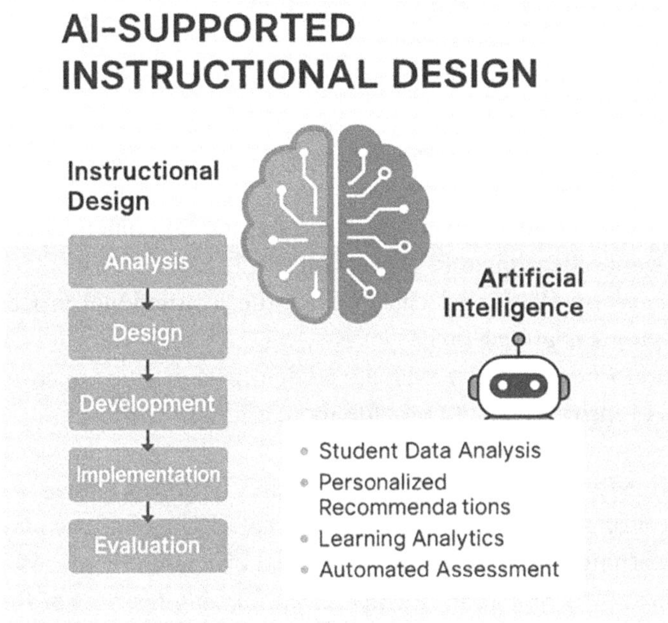

INSTRUCTIONAL DESIGN MODELS AND ARTIFICIAL INTELLIGENCE INTEGRATION

The main instructional design models include the ADDIE model, Gagné's model, the Dick and Carey model, the Kemp model, the SAM model, and the ARCS Motivation Model. The integration of these widely known instructional design models with artificial intelligence (AI) can be examined from various perspectives.

The ADDIE Model is a systematic approach widely used in instructional design and development. The model comprises five fundamental phases: Analysis, Design, Development, Implementation, and Evaluation (Branch, 2009; Molenda, 2003). In the Analysis phase, educational needs and the target audience are identified. Learning objectives, content, and assessment methods are planned in the Design phase. During the Development phase, educational materials and tools are created. The training program is delivered to the target audience in the Implementation phase. Finally, in the Evaluation phase, the effectiveness of the instruction is measured, and necessary improvements are made. Thanks to its flexible structure, the ADDIE Model can be adapted to different educational needs and offers practical learning experiences.

An example of integrating the ADDIE Model (Analysis, Design, Development, Implementation, Evaluation) with AI is as follows:

- *Analysis Phase:* AI can analyze student data to determine their knowledge levels and learning needs.
- *Design Phase:* AI can recommend learning materials and strategies suited to students' learning styles and create personalized learning paths.
- *Development Phase:* AI can optimize educational content based on student feedback and offer dynamic suggestions.
- *Implementation Phase:* AI can monitor the instructional process and track student progress in real-time.
- *Evaluation Phase:* AI can evaluate student performance, measure the effectiveness of instruction, and provide more effective feedback.

Gagné's Nine Events of Instruction, developed by Robert Gagné—an important figure in educational psychology—is a model that offers a framework of nine steps to make the learning process more effective and efficient (Gagné, 1985; Gagné et al., 2005). These steps are gaining attention, informing learners of the objectives, stimulating recall of prior learning, presenting the content, providing learning guidance, eliciting performance, providing feedback, assessing performance, and enhancing retention and transfer. These principles aim to capture students' attention, effectively convey information, and ensure long-term retention. Gagné's model is widely used in instructional design and curriculum development. An example of integrating Gagné's Instructional Model with AI is as follows:

- *Gaining Attention*: AI can analyze students' interests and previous interactions to offer personalized content and propose engaging introductory activities.
- *Informing Objectives*: AI can define personalized learning goals appropriate for each student, generate dynamic objectives based on their knowledge level, and provide feedback on goal alignment.
- *Stimulating Recall*: AI can analyze past learning and offer reminders in areas where the student is lacking, reinforcing prior knowledge.
- *Presenting Content*: AI can deliver content tailored to students' pace, learning styles, and knowledge levels. Content can be selected according to their interests to create a more effective learning experience.
- *Providing Guidance*: As students practice new knowledge, AI can offer interactive guidance, track correct and incorrect steps, and provide real-time feedback.

- *Eliciting Performance*: During independent practice, AI can monitor student performance and provide personalized feedback, helping determine which topics require more focus.
- *Providing Feedback*: AI can track performance in real-time and give immediate feedback, offering suggestions for improvement in weaker areas.
- *Assessing Performance*: AI can continuously assess student performance and identify gaps in learning. With automated evaluation systems, student achievements can be measured rapidly.
- *Enhancing Retention and Transfer*: AI can create reminder systems to prevent forgetting, offering personalized review intervals for previously learned topics.

The Dick and Carey Model is a widely used systematic and detailed approach in the field of instructional design. Developed by Walter Dick and Lou Carey, this model aims to achieve effective learning outcomes by dividing instructional processes into planning, design, implementation, and evaluation stages (Dick et al., 2015; Morrison et al., 2019). The model includes nine key steps: identifying instructional goals, conducting learner analysis, writing behavioral objectives, developing assessment tools, designing instructional strategies, selecting and developing instructional materials, conducting formative evaluation, revising instruction, and conducting summative evaluation. These steps provide a systematic approach at every stage of instruction and aim to increase the effectiveness of the learning experience. The Dick and Carey Model is particularly suitable for complex instructional designs and guides educators. An example of integrating the Dick and Carey Model with AI is as follows:

- *Needs Analysis and Goal Setting:* AI can analyze student data to recommend instructional designs aligned with specific objectives.
- *Instructional Materials Development:* AI can create more personalized educational content and provide dynamic materials tailored to student levels.
- *Evaluation:* AI can analyze student behavior and performance to assess the effectiveness of the instructional design.

The SAM (Successive Approximation Model) is an iterative and flexible approach to instructional design and content development. Developed by Michael Allen, this model differs from traditional linear design models and is based on rapid prototyping and continuous feedback loops. The ability of AI-supported systems to facilitate rapid content production and design iterations makes this model even more functional in the digital age (Allen & Sites, 2012; Wiley, 2024). The SAM Model consists of three main stages: Preparation, Iterative Design, and Iterative Development. In the Preparation phase, project requirements and objectives are determined (Allen & Sites, 2012; Pappas, 2015). In the Iterative Design phase, rapid drafts are created and improved continuously based on stakeholder feedback. Testable and revisable prototypes are developed in the Iterative Development phase before the final product is created. This iterative process allows for early error detection and more efficient project completion. The SAM Model is ideal for adapting to rapidly changing needs and delivering effective learning solutions. Integration of the SAM Model (Successive Approximation Model) with AI:

- *Preparation Phase*: AI can offer meaningful insights based on student data, learning history, and content analysis to define more accurate goals.
- *Iterative Design Phase*: AI-supported tools can help generate draft content quickly during prototyping. Additionally, feedback collected from stakeholders can be automatically categorized and analyzed using AI algorithms.
- *Iterative Development Phase*: During user testing, AI can analyze collected data to suggest areas for improvement and optimize the learning experience with personalized content suggestions.

The ARCS Motivation Model, developed by John M. Keller, is an instructional design approach to increase student motivation. The model consists of four main components: Attention, Relevance, Confidence, and Satisfaction (Keller, 1987; Keller, 2010; Smith & Ragan, 2005). The Attention component offers various strategies to capture students' interest and stimulate curiosity. The Relevance component ensures that the learning content aligns with students' needs and goals. The Confidence component aims to strengthen students' belief in their ability to succeed. The Satisfaction component ensures that the learning experience is rewarding and satisfying, thus sustaining motivation. The ARCS Model provides a practical framework for enhancing both intrinsic and extrinsic motivation and serves as a guide for instructional designers. Integration of the ARCS Model (Keller's ARCS Motivation Model) with AI can be proposed as follows:

- *Attention & Relevance*: Conversational AI can create engaging scenarios or role-playing activities through interaction with students. With visual recognition-supported AI tools, surprising visuals or videos can be presented at the beginning of lessons. AI systems that recommend content based on student interests can provide personalized examples to capture attention. Systems using learning analytics can offer personalized content and suggestions based on students' learning history, making the content more relevant.
- *Confidence & Satisfaction*: Adaptive learning platforms can adjust question difficulty according to student performance, increasing the sense of "I can

succeed." Automated feedback systems, portfolio systems, and reflection tools can be integrated to enhance confidence and satisfaction.

Following the examples of instructional design and AI integration above, the following conclusions can be drawn regarding its benefits:

- *Personalized Learning:* AI can create tailored content and learning pathways based on each student's pace, level, and preferences.
- *Time Efficiency:* AI can quickly analyze educational materials and provide automated feedback at every stage of the instructional process.
- *Continuous Improvement:* AI dynamically improves educational content based on student feedback.
- *Data Analysis and Progress Tracking*: Student performance can be continuously monitored; difficulties can be identified and addressed promptly.

Integrating instructional design and AI accelerates content development and enhances the effectiveness and efficiency of learning outcomes. Instructional design models supported by AI offer a powerful approach, particularly for designers seeking adaptive, data-driven, and learner-centered solutions in digital learning environments. AI assists instructional designers in creating more dynamic and student-focused educational experiences.

RELATION OF ARTIFICIAL INTELLIGENCE TO LEARNING THEORIES

Instructional design models and their integration with artificial intelligence (AI) cannot be considered independently from learning theories. Learning theories are frameworks that aim to explain how individuals learn. The major learning theories are Behaviorist Learning, Cognitive Learning, Social Learning, Constructivist Learning, Humanistic Learning, and Contextual Learning Theories. These theories offer various perspectives for understanding different learning processes and how individuals acquire knowledge. From the perspective of AI, learning theories can be examined through different lenses.

From the viewpoint of **Behaviorist Learning Theories**, learning is measured through observable behavioral changes and focuses on environmental stimuli and responses to these stimuli (Pavlov, 1927; Skinner, 1938; Watson, 1913). AI, in this context, can align with behaviorist principles by tracking and guiding students' learning processes and offering personalized content and responses through various feedback mechanisms. Behaviorism posits that learning is based on stimulus-response and reinforcement processes (Pavlov, 1927; Skinner, 1938; Watson, 1913). AI can quickly analyze student responses and provide automated feedback. For instance, AI-powered learning management systems can reward students for correct answers or offer reminders for incorrect responses.

Additionally, adaptive learning systems utilizing AI can offer students additional practice opportunities targeted at areas of weakness. Behaviorist theories organize reinforcement according to short- and long-term goals. For example, presenting intermittent rewards during the learning process can increase motivation. AI can reinforce achievement with short-term rewards while proposing more complex tasks to support progress toward long-term goals. Behaviorism emphasizes the careful observation and data-driven evaluation of student behaviors (Pavlov, 1927; Skinner, 1938; Watson, 1913). This implies that each step of the student's journey is monitored and met with an appropriate response. AI can continuously monitor performance and offer personalized learning paths. For instance, when students complete each step, AI can immediately provide feedback on correct or incorrect actions, enabling more practice opportunities.

According to **Social Learning Theory**, individuals learn by observing and modeling others (Bandura, 1977; Bandura, 1986). Learning occurs not only through direct experience but also through observing the behavior of others. Similarly, AI systems acquire knowledge and improve their behavior through interaction with large datasets and environments. In this process, social learning theories that involve observation, modeling, and imitation play a critical role in understanding how AI learns and evolves. Bandura's (1986) theory emphasizes learning through observation and imitation. For example, consider a student using an AI-supported instructional system that shows the steps taken by each learner, highlights errors, and illustrates how correct solutions are achieved. By observing others through this AI system, students can adopt effective strategies for their learning. In another example, if the system shows that successful students read the problem first, highlight key data, and break down the solution process, observing students may perform better by applying these strategies. This process embodies learning through modeling and observation.

Furthermore, AI algorithms can analyze which models are most effective for each student and recommend them accordingly. Thus, social learning occurs not only by observing peers but also through effective models selected by AI. Social learning theory posits that learning occurs through social interaction between individuals (Rotter, 1954). AI systems can enhance their learning processes by interacting with humans and other systems. In natural language processing, AI can interact socially to learn linguistic and behavioral rules. Bandura's concept of self-efficacy refers to individuals' belief in their ability to succeed in a task (Bandura, 1997). A similar mechanism in AI can be associated with self-regulation and improvement processes.

Constructivist Learning Theories argue that learners build meaning by relating new knowledge to prior knowledge and interacting with their environment. Researchers like Jean Piaget and Lev Vygotsky emphasized that social and cognitive interactions shape learning. These theories underscore that learning occurs within social, cultural, and individual contexts (Bruner, 1960; Bruner, 1966; Piaget, 1954; Piaget, 1972; Vygotsky, 1978). Based on these core principles, AI can assist learners in actively constructing their knowledge structures. In line with constructivism, AI offers personalized, interactive, and dynamic learning experiences supporting individual and social learning processes. AI provides tailored learning pathways based on the learner's pace and prior knowledge. This enables learners to build their knowledge structures at their own pace. For instance, adaptive learning systems present new content based on prior success. According to Vygotsky's concept of the zone of proximal development (ZPD), learners can acquire new knowledge through interaction with more experienced individuals. AI can facilitate virtual communities and cooperative learning environments promoting social interaction. By encouraging collaboration and group work, AI supports social learning. It also enhances learning by enabling digital interactions among learners, making the experience more dynamic and social.

Constructivism views learning as a problem-based and active process. AI can offer opportunities for problem-solving and exploratory learning. AI-supported educational platforms can present students with appropriately challenging problems and guide problem-solving. In doing so, students can develop critical thinking skills. Constructivism also maintains that learning is improved through self-regulation and reflection (Bruner, 1960; Bruner, 1966; Piaget, 1954; Piaget, 1972; Vygotsky, 1978). AI enhances learners' self-regulation by offering feedback and self-assessment tools. It tracks learners' progress and provides timely feedback, increasing their awareness of the learning process. Constructivism emphasizes that learners possess different learning styles (visual, auditory, or kinesthetic) and representation tools. AI can provide content tailored to diverse learning styles, offering interactive graphics and animations for visual learners, audio explanations for auditory learners, and interactive simulations for kinesthetic learners. AI's strong alignment with constructivism lies in its ability to support the active construction of knowledge, social interaction, development of problem-solving skills, self-regulation, and contextual learning. AI promotes active learning and deep exploration by offering personalized and interactive experiences.

Humanistic Learning Theories focus on intrinsic motivation, self-actualization, and individual differences (Maslow, 1954; Maslow, 1968; Rogers, 1969). Theorists such as Carl Rogers and Abraham Maslow argued that learning is shaped by cognitive and behavioral processes and emotional, social, and self-fulfillment dynamics (Maslow, 1954; Maslow, 1968; Rogers, 1969). Although traditionally driven by data and algorithms, AI systems have recently intersected with humanistic learning theories through attempts to model human-like learning, motivation, and emotional intelligence. According to Maslow's hierarchy of needs, self-actualization is the highest level of need (Maslow, 1954). In this context, AI can be seen as systems that optimize their development. For example, with AI-driven personalized learning systems, individuals receive experiences tailored to their interests and needs (Rogers, 1969). Rogers (1969) emphasized that emotional experiences and personal development are central to education. Today, AI has significantly advanced in understanding and responding to human emotional states. AI's efforts to recognize emotions through facial expressions, tone of voice, and speech patterns parallel humanistic learning theory (Goleman, 1995). AI-supported counseling systems can analyze emotional states and provide appropriate feedback. This aligns with Rogers' "client-centered therapy" approach. Humanistic learning theories emphasize learner-centered approaches focused on individual development. AI systems, similarly, relate to these theories by adapting to learning, growth, and human needs. Especially principles such as self-regulation, empathy, creative thinking, and intrinsic motivation play a significant role in developing new-generation AI systems.

In conclusion, learning theories comprise diverse theoretical approaches that explain how individuals learn. These theories have evolved in line with changing educational technologies over time. Today, AI stands out as an indispensable tool among educational technologies, and its contributions to learning have been evaluated through the lens of learning theories.

ARTIFICIAL INTELLIGENCE SUPPORTED INSTRUCTIONAL DESIGN APPLICATIONS

Artificial intelligence (AI) continues to exert its influence across a wide range of industries, individual lives, and societal contexts on a global scale, with this impact deepening daily. The 2024 edition of the EDUCAUSE Horizon Report dedicated significant attention to AI as one of the prominent trends. The EDUCAUSE Horizon Report is based on the insights and experiences of global experts in the field of higher education. The Teaching and Learning Edition of the Horizon Report explores the trends, core technologies, and practices shaping the future of instruction and learning, offering foresight through various scenarios (EDUCAUSE, 2024). It examines effective ways AI contributes to high-quality course content production, creativity stimulation, personalized learning, and innovation enablement.

Similarly, David Wiley (2024), in his article "The Symmetric Power of Artificial Intelligence in Assessment," clearly illustrates how educators and students use AI in diverse ways to complete numerous academic tasks. Wiley emphasizes that a "productivity gain" occurs when AI is utilized (Wiley, 2024). Discussing only what is technologically possible (not necessarily what is ethically appropriate), Wiley summarizes the core principle as follows: "If an educator can perform a task using AI, then a student can likely receive or complete that task using AI as well." For example:

- Educators can use AI to write multiple-choice questions; students can use AI to answer them.
- Educators can generate short-answer questions; students can use AI to write responses.
- Educators can assign essay tasks; students can use AI to compose them.
- Educators can assign presentations; students can use AI to create them.
- Educators can request portfolios; students can use AI to create artifacts and write reflections on them using AI.

While listing these examples, Wiley (2024) clarifies that he is not advocating for or against AI use by educators or students. Instead, he highlights a technological reality: nearly every academic task can now be performed with AI.

At its core, AI is expected to serve as a beneficial technology—respecting individual autonomy, promoting social cohesion, reducing inequality, and maintaining fairness for all individuals (Floridi et al., 2018). The principle of explainability in AI systems is especially crucial. Explainability is key to establishing trust in technology and helping users understand how the system functions (Floridi et al., 2018). As AI-supported processes become widespread in education, it becomes imperative to consider them through an ethical lens. Without such perspectives, AI's role in instruction may remain limited to technical functionalities, ignoring its broader social, cultural, economic, and political implications.

AI systems can inadvertently reproduce biases embedded in the data they are trained on, leading to discriminatory outcomes. This may result in unfair assessment practices, biased personalized learning pathways, and inequities in behavior-tracking systems (Watters, 2015; Holstein et al., 2019; Williamson, 2017; Selwyn, 2016). For instance, when AI develops models based on student data, the input may contain biases related to gender, socioeconomic status, or ethnicity. As a result, students from disadvantaged backgrounds may receive lower scores. Moreover, academic success criteria could become narrowly defined. In personalized learning, AI may recommend content based solely on past performance, trapping some students in lower-tier content and limiting their growth potential. AI tools that analyze data and video footage in behavior monitoring systems may misinterpret cultural or behavioral differences, leading to disproportionate targeting of certain students.

Regan and Jesse (2019) discuss the ethical dimensions of educational technologies, big data, and personalized learning. Their work critically examines how students are sorted and tracked based on data. Key concerns include data collection and use, classification and labeling, lack of transparency, privacy and security issues, and educational equity. For example, educational platforms collect vast student data (e.g., learning speed, performance levels, interests). While this data is often used for personalized learning, it may also be employed without students' knowledge or consent. Students are sometimes sorted into algorithmically defined categories (e.g., "high-risk" or "high-achieving"), which may lead to unequal access to educational opportunities. Often, neither students nor teachers know what data is being collected or how it is analyzed. Such data may also fall into the hands of commercial entities. These practices can exacerbate inequalities for disadvantaged groups, raising security vulnerabilities and ethical concerns about data use.

In response to these concerns, Kutlucan and Seferoğlu (2024) recommend not banning AI from educational institutions out of fear of its potential adverse effects but instead developing policies for its responsible use. They emphasize that outcomes derived from AI should not be trusted blindly but should be evaluated through a critical lens (Kutlucan & Seferoğlu, 2024). This issue is closely related to digital literacy. In their study, Dalgıç et al. (2024) found that AI influences student learning outcomes and that individual digital literacy is mediating in this process.

The Horizon Report (EDUCAUSE, 2024) highlights the importance of identifying appropriate use cases for AI-driven technologies and supporting AI literacy. Generative AI tools are becoming increasingly powerful and accessible for students, faculty, and administrative staff. These stakeholders will need to address questions related to the responsible use of AI in higher education. Similarly, fostering AI literacy will help stakeholders understand what AI is—and is not—and explore how these tools can create meaningful teaching and learning experiences while managing bias and ethical concerns.

In Türkiye, the Ministry of National Education has published a guidebook titled "AI Tools in Education: A Teacher's Handbook" (Sevil & Saralar-Aras, 2024). This handbook provides AI tool recommendations for various disciplines, including Turkish, Mathematics, Science (Physics, Chemistry, Biology), Social Sciences (History-Geography), Primary Education, and Early Childhood Education. Each subject-specific recommendation is supported by relevant literature, and the potential of AI tools to facilitate conceptual understanding in that domain is evaluated.

Undoubtedly, AI offers powerful tools for instructional designers to enhance student and educator experiences. However, this book chapter will not delve into a detailed listing of specific AI tools.

CONCLUSION AND EVALUATION

In conclusion, artificial intelligence (AI) stands as a transformative force in the evolution of instructional design, offering unprecedented opportunities for personalization, efficiency, and innovation in teaching and learning. The integration of AI with established instructional design models such as ADDIE, Gagné's Events, Dick and Carey, SAM, and ARCS enables adaptive and learner-centered strategies that meet the diverse needs of contemporary learners. Furthermore, this integration is inseparable from foundational behavioral, social, constructivist, and humanistic learning, which provides theoretical grounding for AI's multifaceted educational applications. As AI tools increasingly facilitate personalized learning paths, real-time feedback, motivation enhancement, and data-driven decision-making, they redefine the traditional roles of both educators and learners. However, the ethical implications surrounding transparency, bias, privacy, and digital inequality must not be overlooked. The growing reliance on AI systems necessitates the cultivation of critical digital literacy and implementing responsible AI policies. Reports such as EDUCAUSE Horizon (2024) and national initiatives like the Turkish Ministry of Education's AI Handbook highlight the potential and challenges of integrating AI into educational systems.

This chapter examined AI's role, applications, and future potential in instructional design. If leveraged thoughtfully and ethically, AI can support a more equitable, inclusive, and effective instructional landscape where technological advancement aligns with human development, learning diversity, and educational justice.

REFERENCES

Achiam, J., Adler, S., Agarwal, S., Ahmad, L., Akkaya, I., Aleman, F. L., Almeida, D., Altenschmidt, J., Altman, S., & Anadkat, S.. (2023). Gpt4technicalreport. arXivpreprint arXiv:2303.08774

Adiguzel, T., Kaya, M. H., & Cansu, F. K. (2023). Revolutionizing education with AI: Exploring the transformative potential of ChatGPT. *Contemporary Educational Technology*, *15*(3), ep429. DOI: 10.30935/cedtech/13152

Alawi F. (2023). Artificial intelligence: The future might already be here. *Oral Surgery Oral Medicine Oral Pathology Oral Radiology, 12,* S2212-4403(23)00003–2. https://doi.org/DOI: 10.1016/j.oooo.2023.01.002

Allen, M., & Sites, R. (2012). *Leaving ADDIE for SAM: An agile model for developing the best learning experiences.* Association for Talent Development.

ArkasNews. (2025). Yapay Zekâ'nın Yükselişi, https://arkasnews.com/yapay-zekanin-yukselisi/?utm_source=chatgpt.com

Bandura, A. (1977). *Social Learning Theory*. Prentice-Hall.

Bandura, A. (1986). *Social foundations of thought and action: A Social Cognitive Theory*. Prentice-Hall.

Bandura, A. (1997). *Self-efficacy: The exercise of control.* W. H. Freeman.

Bayramacar, B. (2013). Eğitimde Medya – Yöntem Tartışması, Eğitim Tasarımı. https://instructionaldesignco.wordpress.com/2013/12/11/egitimde-medya-yontem-tartismasi/

Bostrom, N. (2014). *Superintelligence: Paths, dangers, strategies.* Oxford University Press.

Branch, R. M. (2009). *Instructional design: The ADDIE Approach.* Springer. DOI: 10.1007/978-0-387-09506-6

Bruner, J. S. (1960). *The process of education.* Harvard University Press. DOI: 10.4159/9780674028999

Bruner, J. S. (1966). *Toward a theory of instruction.* Harvard University Press.

Clark, R. E. (1983). Reconsidering research on learning from media. *Review of Educational Research, 53*(4), 445–459. DOI: 10.3102/00346543053004445

Clark, R. E. (1994a). Media will never influence learning. *Educational Technology Research and Development, 42*(2), 21–29. DOI: 10.1007/BF02299088

Clark, R. E. (1994b). Media and method. *Educational Technology Research and Development, 42*(3), 7–10. DOI: 10.1007/BF02298090

Dalgıç, A., Yaşar, E., & Demir, M. (2024). ChatGPT and learning outcomes in tourism education: The role of digital literacy and individualized learning. *Journal of Hospitality, Leisure, Sport and Tourism Education, 34*, 100481. DOI: 10.1016/j.jhlste.2024.100481

Dick, W., Carey, L., & Carey, J. O. (2015). *The systematic design of instruction* (8th ed.). Pearson.

EDUCAUSE. (2024). 2024 EDUCAUSE Horizon Report: Teaching and Learning Edition. https://library.educause.edu/resources/2024/5/2024-educause-horizon-report-teaching-and-learning-edition

Esen, G. (2019). Yapay Zekâ: Geçmişi ve geleceği. *Çukurova Üniversitesi İlahiyat Fakültesi Dergisi, 19*(1), 308-311. https://doi.org/DOI: 10.30627/cuilah.481080

Floridi, L., Cowls, J., Beltrametti, M., Chatila, R., Chazerand, P., Dignum, V., Luetge, C., Madelin, R., Pagallo, U., Rossi, F., Schafer, B., Valcke, P., & Vayena, E. (2018). AI4People—An ethical framework for a good AI society: Opportunities, risks, principles, and recommendations. *Minds and Machines, 28*(4), 689–707. DOI: 10.1007/s11023-018-9482-5 PMID: 30930541

Gagné, R. M. (1985). *The conditions of learning and theory of instruction* (4th ed.). Holt, Rinehart, and Winston.

Gagné, R. M., Wager, W. W., Golas, K. C., & Keller, J. M. (2005). Principles of Instructional Design *(5th ed.).* Wadsworth/Thomson Learning.

Goleman, D. (1995). *Emotional intelligence: Why it can matter more than IQ.* Bantam Books.

Holstein, K., McLaren, B. M., & Aleven, V. (2018). Student learning benefits of a mixed-reality teacher awareness tool in AI-enhanced classrooms. In Penstein Rosé, C. (Eds.), *Artificial Intelligence in education. AIED 2018* (pp. 154–168). Lecture Notes in Computer Science. Springer International Publishing., DOI: 10.1007/978-3-319-93843-1_12

Holstein, K., Wortman Vaughan, J., Daumé, H.III, Dudik, M., & Wallach, H. (2019). Improving fairness in machine learning systems: What do industry practitioners need? In *Proceedings of the 2019 CHI Conference on Human Factors in Computing Systems* (pp. 1–16). https://doi.org/DOI: 10.1145/3290605.3300830

Kasneci, E., Sessler, K., & Steuer, B.. (2023). ChatGPT for good? On opportunities and challenges of large language models for education. *Learning and Individual Differences*, *103*, 102274. DOI: 10.1016/j.lindif.2023.102274

Keller, J. M. (1987). Development and use of the ARCS Model of instructional design. *Journal of Instructional Development : JID*, *10*(3), 2–10. DOI: 10.1007/BF02905780

Keller, J. M. (2010). *Motivational design for learning and performance: The ARCS Model approach.* Springer. DOI: 10.1007/978-1-4419-1250-3

Kozma, R. B. (1991). Learning with Media. *Sage Journals*, *61*(2), 179–211.

Kozma, R. B. (1994a). Will media influence learning? Reframing the debate. *Educational Technology Research and Development*, *42*(2), 7–19. DOI: 10.1007/BF02299087

Kozma, R. B. (1994b). A reply: Media and methods. *Educational Technology Research and Development*, *42*(3), 11–14. DOI: 10.1007/BF02298091

Kurzweil, R. (2005). *The singularity is near: When humans transcend biology.* Penguin Books.

Kutlucan, E., & Seferoğlu, S. S. (2024). Eğitimde Yapay Zekâ Kullanımı: ChatGPT'nin KEFE ve PEST Analizi. *Türk Eğitim Bilimleri Dergisi*, *22*(2), 1059–1083. DOI: 10.37217/tebd.1368821

Maslow, A. H. (1954). *Motivation and personality.* Harper & Row.

Maslow, A. H. (1968). *Toward a psychology of being.* Van Nostrand.

Mccarthy, J. (2007). What is artificial intelligence? Basic Questions. Computer Science Department, Stanford University. https://stanford.io/2lSo373

McCarthy, J., Minsky, M. L., Rochester, N., & Shannon, C. E. (2006). A proposal for the Dartmouth summer research project on Artificial Intelligence, August 31, 1955. *AI Magazine*, *27*(4), 12–22.

Molenda, M. (2003). In search of the elusive ADDIE model. *Performance Improvement*, *42*(5), 34–37. DOI: 10.1002/pfi.4930420508

Morrison, G. R., Ross, S. J., Morrison, J. R., & Kalman, H. K. (2019). *Designing effective instruction*. John Wiley & Sons.

Nilsson, N., J., (2019). *Yapay Zekâ geçmişi ve geleceği*. (Çeviri M. Doğan.). Boğaziçi Üniversitesi Yayınevi.

Pappas, C. (2015). The Successive Approximation Model (SAM): *The Agile eLearning Development Process*. eLearning Industry

Pavlov, I. P. (1927). *Conditioned reflexes: An investigation of the physiological activity of the cerebral cortex*. Oxford University Press.

Piaget, J. (1954). *The construction of reality in the child*. Basic Books. DOI: 10.1037/11168-000

Piaget, J. (1972). *Psychology and pedagogy*. Viking Press.

Pirim, A. G. H. (2006). Yapay zeka. *Yaşar Üniversitesi E-Dergisi*, *1*(1), 81–93.

Regan, P. M., & Jesse, J. (2019). Ethical challenges of edtech, big data, and personalized learning: Twenty-first-century student sorting and tracking. *Ethics and Information Technology*, *21*(3), 167–179. DOI: 10.1007/s10676-018-9492-2

Reigeluth, C. M. (1999). What is instructional design theory, and how is it changing? *Instructional-Design Theories and Models: A New Paradigm of Instructional Theory, 2,* 5-29.

Roblyer, M. D., & Doering, A. H. (2014). *Integrating educational technology into teaching*. Pearson.

Rogers, C. R. (1969). *Freedom to learn: A view of what education might become*. Merrill.

Rotter, J. B. (1954). *Social Learning and Clinical Psychology*. Prentice-Hall. DOI: 10.1037/10788-000

Selwyn, N. (2016). *Is Technology Good for Education?* Polity Press. http://au.wiley.com/WileyCDA/WileyTitle/productCd-0745696465.html

Sevil, Ş., & Saralar-Aras, İ. (2024). *Eğitimde kullanılan yapay zekâ araçları: Öğretmen el kitabı*. Yenilik ve Eğitim Teknolojileri Genel Müdürlüğü.

Skinner, B. F. (1938). *The behavior of organisms: An experimental analysis*. Appleton-Century-Crofts.

Skinner, B. F. (1953). *Science and human behavior*. Free Press.

Smith, P. L., & Ragan, T. J. (2005). *Instructional design* (3rd ed.). Wiley.

Solak, Y., Dal, H. O., Çınkır, G., & Onu, F. N. (2025). Yapay Zekâ Etiği: Eğitimde kullanımının sınırları ve sorumlulukları [Ethıcs of Artıfıcıal Intellıgence: Limits and responsibilities of its use in education]. *Socrates Journal of Interdisciplinary Social Researches, 11*(49), 108–116. DOI: 10.5281/zenodo.14762322

The Britannica Dictionary. (2025). Artificial Intelligence. https://www.britannica.com/dictionary/artificial-intelligence

Thorndike, E. L. (1911). *Animal intelligence: Experimental studies.* Macmillan.

Vygotsky, L. S. (1978). *Mind in society: The development of higher psychological processes.* Harvard University Press.

Watson, J. B. (1913). Psychology as the behaviorist views it. *Psychological Review, 20*(2), 158–177. DOI: 10.1037/h0074428

Watters, A. (2015). The algorithmic child: Education and the ethics of big data. In Williamson, B., & Piattoeva, D. (Eds.), *Education Governance and Datafication* (pp. 27–42). Routledge.

Wiley, D. (2023). AI, instructional design, and OER. *Improving learning: Eclectic, Pragmatic, Enthusiastic.*https://opencontent.org/blog/archives/7129

Wiley, D. (2024). The Symmetrical Power of AI in Assessments. *Improving learning: Eclectic, pragmatic, enthusiastic.*https://opencontent.org/blog/archives/7508

Williamson, B. (2017). Big data in education: The digital future of learning, policy and practice. *Sage (Atlanta, Ga.).* Advance online publication. DOI: 10.4135/9781529714920

Williamson, B., & Eynon, R. (2020). Historical threads, missing links, and future directions in AI in education. *Learning, Media and Technology, 45*(3), 223–235. DOI: 10.1080/17439884.2020.1798995

Yazıcı, C., & Kültür, C. (2020). Medya mı yöntem mi? Bitmeyen tartıma. Kürşat Çağıltay ve Yüksel Göktaş (Ed.), *Öğretim Teknolojilerinin Temelleri* (s. 123-140). Pegem Akademi.

Zawacki-Richter, O., Marín, V. I., Bond, M., & Gouverneur, F. (2019). Systematic review of research on artificial intelligence applications in higher education—Where are the educators? *International Journal of Educational Technology in Higher Education, 16*(1), 39. Advance online publication. DOI: 10.1186/s41239-019-0171-0

KEY TERMS AND DEFINITIONS

Artificial Intelligence: Artificial intelligence is a subfield of computer science concerned with the design and development of systems capable of simulating human intelligence and performing cognitive functions such as learning, reasoning, problem-solving, perception, and language understanding. AI systems utilize algorithms equipped with the ability to learn from data, analyze environmental inputs, make autonomous decisions, and improve themselves over time. The discipline encompasses subfields such as machine learning, deep learning, natural language processing, and computer vision and finds wide-ranging applications in sectors including healthcare, transportation, finance, and education.

Educational Technologies: Educational technologies encompass the tools, systems, methods, and processes designed, utilized, and evaluated to support, enhance, and optimize teaching and learning. This field involves the pedagogical integration of technological tools, the design of instructional materials, the development of digital learning environments, and the monitoring of learning processes through technology. Educational technologies aim to enrich learning experiences through personalized instruction, interactive content delivery, and data-driven teaching practices.

Instructional Design Models: Instructional design models are structural and systematic approaches used to plan, develop, implement, and evaluate the teaching process. These models aim to identify effective teaching strategies and methods that will enable the achievement of learning objectives. Instructional design models provide guidance at every stage of the teaching process to enhance the efficiency and effectiveness of the learner's knowledge acquisition process.

Instructional Design: Instructional design is a systematic process to make learning more effective, efficient, and enduring by identifying learning objectives, organizing content, selecting appropriate instructional methods and strategies, and planning assessment tools. Rooted in learning theories, instructional design employs evidence-based models to facilitate the acquisition of knowledge, skills, and attitudes. It integrates educational technologies, pedagogical principles, and learner needs to create impactful instructional experiences across face-to-face and digital learning environments.

Learning Theories: Learning theories are systematic approaches that explain how individuals acquire, organize, and retain knowledge, skills, attitudes, and behaviors. These theories are scientific models developed to understand the learning process, considering the individual's interaction with the environment, mental processes, and social context. Major learning theories include behaviorism, cognitivism, constructivism, and social learning. Each theory offers different principles and strategies for designing and implementing teaching-learning processes.

Teaching: Teaching facilitates learning by imparting knowledge, skills, values, and attitudes to learners through various instructional methods, strategies, and tools. It involves the planning, delivering, and assessing educational content to foster understanding, critical thinking, and the development of cognitive and affective domains. Teaching can occur in formal settings such as classrooms or informal environments, and it requires adapting to diverse learner needs, cultural contexts, and educational goals. Effective teaching conveys content and encourages active student participation, engagement, and self-directed learning.

Chapter 16
Beyond Reality:
Leveraging AI and Educational Metaverse for Immersive Learning Experiences in Education

Aysha Khalil
https://orcid.org/0000-0001-8467-5627
Lahore College for Women University, Lahore, Pakistan

Ibtasam Thakur
https://orcid.org/0009-0002-6175-0625
Lahore College for Women University, Lahore, Pakistan

ABSTRACT

This chapter explores the transformative role of artificial intelligence within the educational metaverse to create immersive, personalized learning experiences in social sciences education. Grounded in five intersecting theories, connectivism, adaptive learning, personalized learning, cognitive load, and post-digital pedagogy, it critically examines how AI-driven technologies like intelligent tutoring systems, adaptive algorithms, and avatars reshape pedagogy, engagement, and equity. Through global case studies including contexts in South Korea, Finland, Kenya, and Pakistan, the chapter highlights opportunities and challenges, emphasizing ethical design, digital inclusion, and cultural responsiveness. It proposes a strategic framework for sustainable implementation that balances innovation with critical reflection, aiming to empower learners, support educators, and promote socially just, learner-centered immersive education worldwide.

DOI: 10.4018/979-8-3373-2612-2.ch016

INTRODUCTION

REIMAGINING LEARNING IN THE AGE OF AI AND METAVERSE

The contemporary educational landscape is going through a major shakeup due to the rise of artificial intelligence (AI) and immersive tech that challenge traditional pedagogical models and redefine the learning structure. Now no longer bound to analog spaces or linear curriculums, we are in a post-digital era of education with experience, simulation, and real-time tuning transforming the notion of learning and teaching. Proponents, including Holmes et al. (2022) and Luckin et al. (2023), have stressed that integrating the metaverse and AI is a significant upgrade, not a technical one. It marks a reorientation of our understanding of knowledge, changing how knowledge is known and for whom. This chapter argues that the AI-enabled metaverse offers a space for transformation through inclusive and meaningful education when positioned in critical terms. However, that promise can only be realized through ethical reflection, pedagogical purposefulness, and sociocultural awareness.

The educational metaverse is characterized as a persistent, communal, and immersive virtual space driven by AI that can respond to the users on the fly. Technologies such as NLP engines, adaptive learning systems, and ITS provide personalization beyond what is possible with regular LMS (Chatterjee & Bhattacharya, 2022; Zawacki-Richter et al., 2020). They can replicate intricate feedback loops, provide contextualized tasks for learning, and generate emotional engagement with stories or gamification. This kind of responsiveness can enable differentiated education at a scale never before possible in carefully designed environments. Holmes et al. (2022)100 discuss how emotional and cognitive interactivity in instructional ecosystems has begun to suggest the possibility of a proactive rather than reactive pedagogy. However, these capacities are never neutral. They are located in socio-technical systems shaped by power, access, and values.

The transformative possibilities of AI-enabled immersive environments are evident in social science education. In simulations, role-play, and real-time storytelling, we can carry abstract theory into subjective experience. Virtual ethnographies (anthropology), AI-supported negotiations (political science), and scenario-based inquiry (sociology) are some examples of new lines of experimentation playing with the linearity of classroom learning (Jahnke et al., 2022; Selwyn et al., 2021). Such practices allow for identity work and embodied cognition, dimensions frequently missing in traditional teaching. A mounting body of empirical evidence now backs up this pivot. For example, Khalil, Haqdad, and Sultana (2023) report that educational metaverse tools promote expanded engagement and accessibility in Pakistani universities, including in places where physical infrastructure is limited. For them, the results confirm that immersive design can be locally located yet informed by global dimensions – a proper rejoinder to criticisms that digital media and technologies have an inescapably Western and elitist bias. The studies by Williamson and Eynon (2020) and Holmes et al. (2022) further illustrate how immersive environments can be harnessed to enhance collaborative inquiry and culturally responsive learning.

Nevertheless, the advantages of immersive learning are not equally advantageous to everyone. Not all learners have access to the same amount of bandwidth, hardware, or institutional support they would need to have meaningful participation in AI-driven metaverses. The digital, infrastructural, and pedagogical divide risks expanding already-occurring inequities in higher education. Furthermore, the rule system of immersive environments is frequently programmed with opaque algorithms that can include assumptions on intelligence, participation, or progression, which are out of alignment with non-normative learners (Selwyn et al., 2021). Parong and Mayer (2021) warned that personalization functionalities could mean control, surveillance, and the potential for doubling policies, as consent and data ethics are not currently strong enforcement mechanisms. The stakes are particularly high in the social sciences, where self-conscious questioning about power, identity, and voice is central to the methodology of the field.

Aside from sociopolitical issues, it is the psychological and cognitive aspects of immersion-based learning that look to be especially interesting. While immersive environments can induce flow states and trigger intrinsic motivation, they can also risk overstimulating learners, leading to identity confusion and emotional dissonance. This kind of interaction between engagement and overload has been found in earlier studies (Huang et al., 2023; Parong & Mayer, 2021). When simulations mirror tension, trauma, or high emotion, they risk generating unpredictable responses from participants, particularly without skillful facilitation. Jahnke et al. (2022) recommend incorporating psychological safety practices and caution that pedagogically potent settings may cause harm if safe boundaries are not intentionally set. These things force educators and other learners to consider when engagement is worth the risk and irresponsible.

For educators, the new landscape has altered their roles, as well. As AIs increasingly subsume the work of assessment, content delivery, and feedback, teachers are recast not only as facilitators but as the designers of digital experiences and the ethical purveyors of digital interaction. However, this professional transition takes more than elementary upskilling. It requires that we all reconceive pedagogical identity and authority. Williamson and Eynon (2020) claim that digital pedagogical literacy encompassing not just technical proficiency but critical fluency in our grasp of the implications of educational technology will be an asset for maintaining educators' agency. Teachers today must critically examine the tools they use, challenge the values those tools frame, and re-vert them to embrace the ever-shifting sites of different student populations. Without this critical lens, it is easy to be dazzled by the promise of AI in education but overlook its limitations and biases.

This chapter pursues three linked purposes. First, it finds out how the combination of AI and the metaverse is changing the practice of education within the social sciences. Second, it examines immersive AI learning environments' ethical, epistemic, and psychological implications . Third, it suggests an infrastructure-grounded framework for socially just and inclusive implementation. These objectives are considered using frames of post-digital pedagogy, sociocultural learning theory, and cross-field education/technology/ethics scholarship.

To do this, the chapter first locates AI and the metaverse in the context of broad educational and technical trends. An overview of theoretical underpinnings for analysis follows this. Case-based reflections then demonstrate the first-hand use of immersive AI tools in fields ranging from anthropology, political science, and sociology. These are not examples of how things should be done. Instead, they are analytical levers for understanding metaverse-enriched education's advantages, constraints, and tensions. The closing chapters provide guiding ethics and practical approaches anchored around inclusion, flexibility, and human-centric design.

What is really at stake here is not whether AI and the metaverse will revolutionize how we think about education. The Publicis transformation is already happening. The urgent question is whether that change will be informed by critical questioning, participatory design, and ethical conduct. Immersive learning spaces If designed to accommodate inclusive pedagogies, immersive learning environments may serve as conduits for equitable and experiential learning. If they are not, the schools could serve as one more frontier of digital inequality, a realm dressed up in the language of innovation but antithetical to the cause of justice.

BACKGROUND: EDUCATIONAL METAVERSE AND THE AI TURN

The rise of the educational metaverse has fundamentally changed how we think about, design, and experience learning spaces. Leveraging immersive technologies and AI, the educational metaverse consists of persistent, interactive, and often gamified virtual environments that learners can access to interact with content, peers, and instructors in virtual spaces using avatars and real-time feedback mechanisms. Unlike earlier versions of digital education, which mostly ran on a fairly linear content delivery model, the metaverse is multidimensional, relational, and adaptive. Scholars such as Huang et al. (2023) and Holmes et al. (2022) have stressed that this intersection of AI and immersive technologies constitutes more than a change in interface design. However, more precisely, it is a profound reorientation of the institution of education's epistemological, pedagogical, and ethical natures.

The idea of the metaverse in education extends larger technological patterns in entertainment and simulation and how we interact online. It is based on the VR, AR, and XR integration, a group of immersion, presence, and co-experience technologies. These technologies are increasingly used for educational purposes: VR offers scenario or context-based learning, AR provides context overlays for fieldwork, and XR integrates reality and virtuality in mixed, blended environments (Zawacki-Richter et al., 2020). Educational metaverse differs from these by being the persistent, identity-persistent, socially embedded architectures. In these environments, students are not passive consumers of content. Instead, meaning is co-constructed in dynamic, fluid environments shaped by live data, peer interaction, and adaptive AI systems.

Figure 1. Conceptual Overview of AI-Powered Immersive Learning

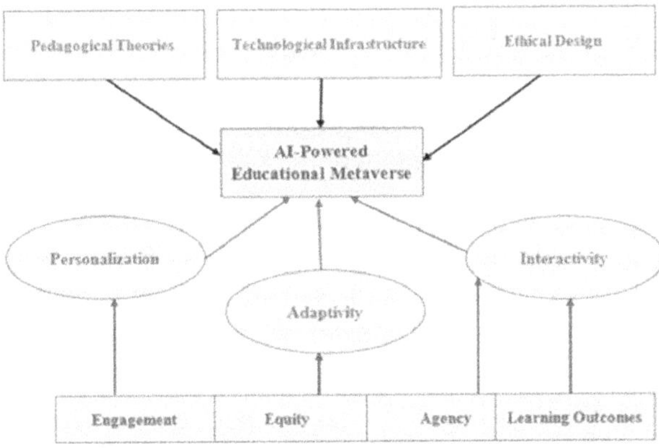

Figure 1 shows a conceptual framework illustrating how AI-powered immersive learning integrates pedagogical theories, technological infrastructure, and ethical design principles to create adaptive, learner-centered educational metaverse environments that respond dynamically to diverse learner needs and contexts. Embedding artificial intelligence (AI) in immersive educational settings departs from static teaching to contextually adaptive, learner-focused ecosystems. This evolution is facilitated by the convergence of the pedagogical theory with the development of the technological infrastructure and the philosophy of ethical design, all of which influence how learning environments accommodate, interact with, and personalize experiences. Embedded with these principles, immersive systems of today can dynamically respond to learners' requirements, identities, and emotional states, creating more engaging and inclusive experiences. As learners recursively build meanings with these environments, related affordances, including agency, equity, and learning improvement, are not concomitant but purposefully embedded by design. This reconfiguration situates the educational metaverse as a site for creating substantial and socially responsible learning if grounded within critical and context-sensitive approaches.

AI's Role in Personalizing Immersive Education

At the heart of the educational metaverse is AI. The immersive environments give AI a canvas to paint; the AI determines how the canvas is customized for each learner and how it responds to them. Through intelligent tutoring systems, learning analytics, sentiment analysis, and real-time feedback loops, AI personalizes content delivery, scaffolding, and pacing (Luckin et al., 2023). In metaverse-enabled classrooms, AI agents are mentors, guides, or sometimes co-learners. These agents react to the user and performance with great flexibility in revoking tasks and feedback. This real-time interactivity sets the metaverse apart from previous iterations of e-learning. Unlike traditional platforms, which provide interactivity, AI-based immersive spaces bring adaptivity, the key feature associated with higher levels of learner engagement and retention/assimilation (Chatterjee & Bhattacharya, 2022).

While AI has long been leveraged in education, incorporating such technology into immersive platforms brings more complexity and risk. Metaverse space algorithms must deal with multimodal data, such as voice, motion, gaze, and biometric hints. This creates opportunities for learning in the body and empathy and affective engagement, especially in fields such as history, psychology, and social studies. It also raises questions about surveillance, data ownership, and algorithmic bias. Selwyn et al. (2021) posit that as learning becomes further embedded within AI-infused environments, there will be critical questions about transparency, explainability, and inclusivity. Without these considerations, the metaverse is in danger of becoming a place of exclusion rather than progression, particularly for students with limited access and vulnerable personas.

From a socio-pedagogical perspective, the metaverse offers excellent potential for learning in the social sciences. It supports constructivist and experiential pedagogies through scenario-based learning, role play, and community simulation. For instance, students in sociology can study social identity and behavior in a virtual neighborhood and see emergent behavior under different policy environments. Political science students can join simulated assemblies or debates in which negotiation and diplomacy become strengths as participants debate in real time. These applications are backed up by the work of Williamson and Eynon (2020), who suggest that XR can generate more pluralistic participatory learning environments that resemble the messiness of real-world sociopolitical life.

Moreover, the metaverse is where we can exercise collective agency and build what we want together. In contrast to isolated e-learning spaces, immersive technologies are naturally of a social orientation. Collaborative presence and synchronous interaction are conditions for co-creation, where learners together construct meaning and negotiate their identities (roles). AI takes it a step further by enabling dialogue, language translation, and group activities to adjust to the emotional vibes and extent of involvement. Holmes et al. (2022) note that when designed with integrity, these configurations encourage learner motivation and promote inclusion and respect. However, these are not given. Parong and Mayer (2021) warned that poorly designed virtual encounters can create a situation of cognitive overload or emotional distancing unless they know how to balance immersion with structure and clarity.

Contextualizing Equity, Identity, and Readiness

In the metaverse, it can be broken down into opportunities and challenges in developing countries regardless of infrastructure conditions. On the other, it allows one to bypass existing constraints through mobile VR, cloud-based platforms, and AI-supported personalization. On the other, it is confronted with practical challenges such as bandwidth limitations, device availability, and digital literacy. However, for the metaverse to be an effective, transformative tool in teacher education in Pakistan, Khalil and Jumani (2024) stress that it has to be affordable, contextualized, and supported by institutions. Their study identifies the necessity of matching immersive pedagogy with national educational targets, faculty preparedness, and student heterogeneity. This is consistent with a global concern addressed by Huang et al. (2023), who suggest that localization and participatory design are important for implementation sustainability and long-term impact.

Blurring the Boundaries of Digital and Physical Identity in Immersive Learning Identity opens up another complexity when considering immersive learning. In Avatars, openness and gamified progression systems have Opportunities to play Roles and Representations. Although this can be liberating in many ways, it can also result in alienation, role confusion, or identity fragmentation, especially in younger learners still defining themselves. Jahnke et al. (2022) advocate for structured debriefing, identity reflection tasks, and socio-emotional scaffolding to support learner well-being in such environments. The extent to which the metaverse may escalate or ease psychological stress is an open research area relevant for social science educators developing ethically and emotionally adept curricula.

Given the recent and overwhelming appearance of the educational metaverse, a comprehensive understanding must entail an integration of perspectives from computer science and areas of education, psychology, sociology, and ethics. The current body of scholarship has its bright and dark sides. Conversely, immersive AI-based learning environments may democratize education, increase engagement, and foster inquiry. On the other hand, they may reinforce or create non-intended professional dependencies on opaque algorithms and commercial platforms (Williamson & Eynon, 2020; Selwyn et al., 2021). Researchers and practitioners should be wary of empty promises and stick to practical and evidence-based means of implementation that emphasize learner welfare and institutional responsibility.

The chapter casts the educational metaverse as not a futuristic figment but more as a real and unfolding present with applications from one end to another of the teaching-learning continuum. The articles below provide theoretical and experiential dimensions, examining case studies, pedagogical approaches, and ethical considerations. In this way, the chapter seeks to lay out the landscape for educators, policymakers, and technologists who wish to weave immersive AI into the social fabric of social science education responsibly.

THEORETICAL COMPENDIUM FOR AI-EDUCATIONAL METAVERSE

The development of artificial intelligence in immersive learning environments requires a theoretical model that accounts for the intersection of cognitive, technological, and sociocultural dimensions. Instead of adopting one lens, the current chapter uses five intersecting ones: connectivism, adaptive learning theory, personalized learning paradigm, postdigital learning theory, and cognitive load theory. Both offer analytic leverage to question how AI reconfigures educational practices in the metaverse.

Table 1. Theoretical Frameworks and Their Applications in Immersive Learning

Theory	Key Concepts	Educational Function in Metaverse	Notable Risks
Connectivism	Distributed cognition, networks	Learner as knowledge node	Fragmented focus
Adaptive Learning	Real-time feedback, optimization	Personalized pacing	Opaque algorithms
Personalized Learning	Learner identity, context	Cultural relevance, motivation	Identity essentialism
Post-Digital Theory	Sociotechnical critique	Ethical awareness, justice	Over-interpretation
Cognitive Load Theory	Memory limits, processing types	Clarity and focus	Cognitive overload

Such an assemblage-based methodology not only avoids what we see as a critical reductionism of innovation to technological determinism but also emphasizes the agency and contextuality of the learner and the ethics of digital pedagogy. These frameworks, in combination, enable a multivariate approach toward AI-augmented immersion in education.

Connectivism

Connectivism provides a grounded approach to understanding learning in AI-driven virtual worlds. It is promising knowledge not as content but as a process of always-renewed interconnections between different informational nodes, human beings, and technological systems. In contrast to the traditional theories of learning that focus primarily on personal knowledge, it resides inside of and is developed by groups. Saqr, Tarhini, and Luck (2018) and Koukis and Jimoyiannis (2021) gathered all of these studies. (2022) report that learners with online social connections will likely be more autonomous and collaboratively fluent. AI agents are not just tools in the metaverse landscape; they are critical players in the design of the flow of content, interactions, and adaptation to context. Chamola et al. (2023) focused on enhanced retention and deeper conceptual engagement through AI-curated learning paths whilst actively completing immersive simulations. This casts the learner as a reactive node in a larger intelligent system. So connectivism traces the architecture of immersive education and recasts the learner's epistemological position within it.

Adaptive Learning Theory

The strength of adaptive learning theory derives from its focus on synchronizing instruction to variability in real-time. This model argues that instruction should adapt dynamically in response to feedback and performance and adjust to match the challenge to a student's particular abilities. AI systems operationalize This principle much more precisely, particularly in immersive environments, where student inputs are continuous and complex. Systems incorporating adaptable logic systems are beneficial in terms of engagement and levels of cognitive fatigue (Chassignol et al., 2021; Wang et al., 2024). For instance, Feng et al. (2024) demonstrate that adaptive modules within metaverse contexts of STEM focus improve retention and accuracy when solving complex problems. However, the algorithms that make personalized learning possible also could make it difficult to understand why the content has changed. Selwyn et al. (2023) caution that opaque decision-making may perpetuate narrow or prejudiced understandings of success, especially when context-blind performance indicators drive adaptive systems. Hence, the theory legitimizes algorithmic personalization and demands it be transparent and inclusive in its design if epistemic reductionism is to be avoided.

Personalized Learning Paradigm

While adaptive learning is dedicated to adapting inputs to instruction, personalized learning is a broader, more holistic construct that includes the learner's identity, interests, and experiences. Personalized learning is not only about pacing or difficulty setting. At its heart is creating an environment responsive to students' sociocultural backgrounds, aspirations, and emotions. Chen et al. (2023) also note that AI-enhanced avatars and AI-sensitive feedback increase emotional connection and learner motivation. Lee and Kim (2021) find that matching digital stories and learner identity significantly increases engagement. Holmes et al. (2023) demonstrate that culturally sensitive AI agents ease communication barriers caused by different languages. Evidence from the Global South In the context of the Global South, Khalil et al. (2023), there is compelling evidence that regionally-adapted AI simulations will result in greater accessibility and relevance to previously underserved learners. These results indicate that ethically designed AI can effectuate personalization as equity. However, Arantes (2023) points out that predictive personalization is a warning of over-dependency that could limit exposure to new yet practical challenges. Zawacki-Richter et al. (2022) and Vu et al. (2022) raise a concern that using learner-capacity recognition systems could have this effect on learner identities as an unintended consequence. Personalization must be fluid and reflexive, not fixed and deterministic.

Post-Digital Learning Theory

Post-digital learning theory leads us to a socio-critical gaze and disentangles educational technology from the thought of novelty or being tool-based. Jandrić et al. (2018) suggest that it is not digitally an add-on but an essential feature of educational culture and is, in fact, intrinsic in a post-digital world. In these spaces, AI and immersive platforms are not just pedagogical tools but mirror, reinforce, and reproduce aspects of society, such as power relations and normative values. Selwyn, Hillman , and Eynon (2023) highlight the patterns of behavior optimization and data commodification ingrained in AI-enabled systems, which question their neutrality. Williamson et al. (2024) extend this criticism by examining how immersive learning design can replicate exclusion, particularly in contexts where digital literacy is unevenly distributed. The post-digital theory is blunt about the need for educators to confront these tensions. It shifts the debate from effectiveness and economy to justice, democracy, and ethical responsibility. This makes it essential to assess how AI operates in education, what it reproduces, and whose interests it serves.

Cognitive Load Theory

Cognitive load theory offers a cognitive psychology lens to examine AI-enhanced immersive learning. It is about the constraints of our working memory and how we should design instructional materials that do not add unnecessary cognitive load. In complex multimedia environments where students navigate through various modes – visual, auditory, and kinesthetic – the threat of cognitive overload is even higher. Mayer and Fiorella (2021) had evidence that structured, low-load conditions are better for transfer and long-term retention. Such AI tools can modulate the level of cognitive complexity in real time, gate irrelevant stimuli, and scaffold task sequences to facilitate more effective cognition (Choi et al., 2022; Sailer & Honmer, 2020). AI also becomes a cognitive surrogate rather than just a content delivery system. Critically, this theory converges with adaptive and personalized instruction, underscoring the need for well-timed instruction pace. Kalyuga (2022), however, warns that untimely AI responses or a cluttered virtual interface may raise, not lower, cognitive demand. The message is that good AI is clarity- and focus-enhancing, not confusion-inducing.

Toward a Holistic Interpretive Lens

Synthesizing these five theorizations enables a rich understanding of how AI transfigures immersive learning ecosystems. Connectivism accounts for the logic of network-based knowledge building, while responsive learning theory lends credence to the function of real-time reaction. The paradigm of personalized learning highlights learner agency and cultural responsiveness. The post-digital theory challenges the ideological and ethical implications of educational technology. CLT provides principles for controlling attention and processing in design. When juxtaposed, these frameworks generate a schema that illuminates immersive education as a pedagogical mutation and a sociotechnical assemblage. They also offer the required yardsticks to challenge implementations. As Williamson, Potter, and Eynon (2024) argue, responsible innovation in education calls for the simultaneous leveraging of AI's capacities and challenging of its taken-for-granted assumptions. The theory here does not mean hindsight rationalization. It is a prospective tool for making an ethical, inclusive, and effective Future[s] (53) in the metaverse.

TRANSLATING THEORY INTO IMMERSIVE PRACTICE: AI TECHNOLOGIES IN THE EDUCATIONAL METAVERSE

Incorporating AI into the educational metaverse represents something over and above a technical evolution. It is a pedagogical revolution built on research, experimentation, and revision. This section builds on the theoretical framework developed previously by incorporating evidence from our 2022–2025 systematic literature review, qualitative case-based analysis, and expert interviews about AI-enabled pedagogy. Supporting technologies (e.g., intelligent tutoring systems, adaptive learning algorithms, and AI-based avatars) are not considered in isolation. They are, thus, not as explanations of the world but as performance epistemologies – ways that theories of knowledge are performed in the lived experience of education. The argument is that deeply immersive worlds are pedagogically defensible only if designed with a theory-informed ethical base.

Figure 2. Theory–Technology–Function Map

AI Technology	Associated Theory	Pedagogical Function
Intelligent Tutoring Systems	Connectivism, Adaptive Learning	Personalized feedback, Distributed cognition
Adaptive Algorithms	Cognitive Load Theory, Adaptive Learning	Real-time scaffolding, Complexity modulation
AI Avatars	Personalized Learning, Connectivism	Emotional engagement, Cultural alignment

Figure 2 shows the interplay between educational theories and AI technologies within immersive learning, mapping how intelligent tutoring systems, adaptive algorithms, and AI avatars operationalize connectivism, adaptive learning, and personalized learning to achieve outcomes such as tailored feedback, cognitive scaffolding, and culturally relevant engagement. It demonstrates that intelligent tutoring systems, adaptive algorithms, and AI avatars are not independent tools but operationalize theoretical constructs such as connectivism, adaptive learning, and personalized learning. Moreover, these principles shape how each technology feature enables outcomes such as personalized feedback, cognitive scaffolding, and culturally resonant engagement.

Intelligent Tutoring Systems: Beyond Automated Feedback

Intelligent tutoring systems (ITS) have significantly progressed, especially in immersive education. Their development facilitates the provision of personalized instruction on the fly via rule-based logic and machine learning. These systems model one-to-one tutoring through dynamically scaling instructional feedback in response to individual learner input. In the context of connectivism, ITS are knowledge nodes that co-construct learning through interactive feedback loops (Veletsianos & Houlden, 2021; Saqr et al., 2022). They promote distributed cognition by connecting learners to information and a continuously changing knowledge ecology that adjusts to their actions.

These are indeed backed up by empirical evidence. Chen et al. (2023) recorded significant problem-solving improvements over the ITS-integrated VR physics module. Further, Wang & Zhang (2023) showed that ITS in medical training significantly reduced the number of diagnostic errors as well as the overall training hours. These systems represent the realization of the adaptive learning theory: adapting difficulty and pace to the learner's performance (Feng et al., 2023; Chassignol et al., 2021). However, constraints are suggested by expert opinions collected during interviews. Those who rely too much on performance data sometimes suppress open inquiry or focus on what can be measured rather than what can be pondered. Post-digital learning theory provides an essential critical veneer since it reminds us that ITS platforms are often the surface of deeper ideological acquiescence to efficiency and behavioral rationalization (Selwyn et al., 2023). The line is that the future of ITS will rely on more than 'correct' technology but also on aligning ITS with theory and ethics.

Adaptive Algorithms in Immersive Spaces

Adaptive algorithms do more than shape the content. They introduce new learning ecologies in immersive environments. They control not only what learners see but also how they move, feel, and interact. Dohrmann, C. (2013), As the peer-reviewed literature studied for this chapter demonstrates, these systems can change navigational routes, reduce the complexity of virtual objects, and shift interface elements based on user data. This is consistent with cognitive load theory, which emphasizes reducing extraneous processing to support the efficiency of learning (Mayer & Fiorella, 2021).

Field experiments validate these potentials. Tsai and Tsai (2022) investigated a biology AR system in which eye-tracking guided real-time complexity modulation. There were significant gains in conceptual transfer compared to non-adaptive versions. Choi et al. (2022) also found gains in engineering VR simulations with adaptive elements associated with improved task accuracy and dropout rates. They are more than content providers; they rehabilitate the immersive space according to how the learner interacts with it, adapting the space within its own four walls.

Notwithstanding these assets, methodological interviews underscored lingering issues with transparency. Much adaptation is a "black box," and you are provided with no justification for shifts in content. This contradicts the heart of the personalized learning paradigm, which has the student at the center of learning (Arantes et al., 2023; Holmes et al., 2023). One proposed solution is to include metacognitive tools, such as dashboards, alerts, or explanation agents, that explain the behavior of a system to learners. These features turn users into co-navigators of their educational journey rather than blind consumers of adaptive logic.

AI Avatars and Virtual Instructors: Rethinking Presence

AI-controlled avatars have emerged as central characters in immersive systems that operate as educators, chaperones, and emotionally responsive agents. Educators emphasized in expert interviews the potential of avatars to model empathy, preserve cultural appropriateness, and generate discourse-rich learning environments. This is consistent with the theory of personalized learning, in that communication and feedback need to follow learner profiles (Lee & Kim, 2021; Chen et al., 2023).

These have been fielded recently and demonstrated their effectiveness. Sailer and Homner (2020) showed how AI avatars in English classrooms supported more fluent and engaging peer-role simulations. In Pakistan, Khalil et al. (2023) concluded that teacher education students were both more receptive to avatars that spoke using local dialects and were dressed like regional members, as a confirmation that the personalization should be visual, linguistic, and cultural. Connectivism reinforces this concept by defining avatars as emotional nodal points within a networked learning environment. However, risk is inherent in this promise. Gourlay (2021) and Selwyn et al. (2023) observe that avatars designed to maximize retention or engagement can make it difficult to discern the boundary between instruction and manipulation. In these instances, students are directed toward behavioral compliance, not cognitive development. This is where the cognitive load theory is essential to bear in mind. Designers should be alert and not overstimulate the user with distractions or facial expressions, gestures, or modulations in the tone of voice, which may distract the students rather than support them. All layers of avatar interactivity have to be governed by ethical design.

Technological Integration as a Sociocultural Process

These cases tell one thing: AI in immersive learning should not be judged by outcomes alone. The ideological, cultural, and power dimensions inform and form these tools. Evidence from the library review and expert interviews suggest that the educational 'metaverse' is not a neutral space. It is a battlefield where inclusivity, identity, and equality are fought for daily. A post-digital learning theory would require educators to question how platforms encourage specific forms of behavior, commodify data, or conflate engagement with learning (Williamson et al., 2024).

This problem is compounded in the underfunded areas. One example is a Pakistani public university collaborating to develop STEM and AI-based content. Rather than importing generically designed tools, the design team localized avatar scripts, interface symbols, and learning sequences. Differences between P5 and complier learners ranged from very weak to very strong, verifying the focus of the individualized learning paradigm on context adaptation (Khalil et al., 2023). Equity, then, is not magic or a natural byproduct. In practice, it should be a principle embodied through participatory co-design with learners and educators at its core.

Table 2. Compare geographic, pedagogical, and technological features of cases

Case	Country	Technology Used	Discipline	Outcome Highlight
Hanyang University	South Korea	ITS + VR	STEM	Reduced overload, better segmentation
Tampere University	Finland	Adaptive co-regulation	Political Science	Student autonomy enhanced
African Pilot	Kenya (assumed)	Connectivism peer simulation	Sociology	Peer-driven power asymmetries
Public University in Pakistan	Pakistan	Localized AI Avatars	Teacher Education	Cultural relevance, learner confidence

In Table 2, the comparison of geographic, pedagogical, and technological features across diverse case studies highlights how contextual factors influence the design and effectiveness of AI-enabled immersive learning environments.

Strategic Implications for Immersive AI Design

Successful translation of theory into practice requires strategy, not mere proficiency. As expert interviewees underscored, successful implementation depends on inter-specialization – on educators, designers, and technologists co-creating responsive learning systems. These systems must be compatible with cognitive realities, moral obligations, and institutional purposes. In other words, to move beyond basic tool training towards professional development based on theory-informed design practice. Participatory constructs would be a standard, incorporating teacher and learner feedback systems throughout the design process. As Luckin et al. (2022) argue, "educationally intelligent AI" needs to be transparent, responsive, and inclusive from the initial line of code to the last release.

EVALUATION, CHALLENGES, AND FUTURE TRAJECTORIES

The summary presented here integrates the theoretical paradigms, technological platforms, and implementational strategies of immersive AI in education, as described in the preceding text. We argue instead that immersive learning systems are not neutral interfaces but rather sociotechnical assemblages whose shape is determined by institutional capabilities, pedagogic decisions, and philosophical commitments.

Figure 3. Matrix of ethical outcomes in immersive AI design

	Learner-Centered	System-Centered
Transparent Design	Empowerment (Ideal)	Behavioral Engineering (Risk)
Opaque Design	Fragmentation or Confusion	Surveillance and Control (Critical Risk)

Figure 3 shows a matrix of ethical outcomes in immersive AI design, emphasizing how the convergence of five key theoretical frameworks guides the balance between technological innovation and critical considerations of transparency, inclusivity, learner agency, and sociocultural justice within immersive educational systems. The convergence of five theoretical frameworks -namely, connectivism, adaptive learning, personalized learning, cognitive load theory, and post-digital critique- provides a framework for a critical perspective on immersive design. These theories put into practice in the highlighted case studies stress the significance of ethical foresight, contextual adjustability, and a participatory approach to development. 22 Hwang and Chien (2022) remind us that AI-driven innovation in education is no substitute for the powers of critical inquiry. Transformation is not wasted away by innovation but rather by design adjusted to cultural sensitivity and cognitive ethics.

Theory–Practice Synthesis: Key Patterns and Tensions

The practical application of theory is most evident in outcomes when responses embody faithfulness to teaching philosophy. In the case of Hanyang University, immersion fidelity overrode instruction segmentation, which aligns with Mayer and Fiorella's (2021) observation that high processing demands prevent learning. At Tampere University, the importance of adaptive co-regulation was evidenced, where algorithmic tools supported student autonomy, but only when teachers were mediating their use (Serrano-Ausejo & Mårell-Olsson, 2024). The African pilot study did demonstrate some connectivist principles through peer interaction, but also structural (Selwyn et al. 's (2023) observation that the rhetoric of personalization may hide entrenched inequality. These cases jointly attest that immersive success depends on the co-design of distributed cognition, affective realism, and ethical adaptability (Luckin et al., 2022; Holmes et al., 2023). The findings indicate that conceptual coherence improves design accuracy, learner autonomy, and institutional importance.

Institutional Barriers and Structural Asymmetries

Implementation barriers are common despite conceptual clarity. The author's survey of the feasibility of the metaverse in Pakistan revealed that although the appetite for entering the metaverse was significant, institutional scaffolding failed to keep pace with providing structural support (Khalil, Haqdad, & Sultana, 2023). This gap is not isolated. Ghani et al. (2024) highlighted comparable deficiencies, alluding to ineffective governance and disunited digital policy as continuing burdens. This trend is, in fact, so widespread that it is reproducible in studies such as those performed by Chugh et al. (2023) and Eden et al. (2024), which explain how stiff institutionalized hierarchies and procedural inflexibility stave off immersive embrace. Furthermore, Arif et al. (2024) emphasize the lack of digital literacy programs as an obstacle to aiding learner empowerment. These results indicate that for immersive learning to be scalable, it must be coupled with institutional change, not just technological change.

The Ethical Dimension: Ownership, Opacity, and Design Justice

The ethical landscape gets murkier as immersive platforms become more affect-sensing and behavior-responsive. Eye-tracking, biometric measurements, and behavior analytics are becoming standard components of many immersive experiences; however, their integration and usage are frequently non-transparent. Williamson et al. (2024) warn that emotion-aware avatars may become tools for behavioral engineering rather than learning co-players. This concern is shared by Nazir and Khan (2024), who list institutional delays in data governance and consent protocol as one of their concerns. Without regulatory placements, we leave learner identity prey to commodification. Decuypere et al. (2023) advocate for integrating data justice in the design of educational platforms. Ensuring ethics in immersive AI is not a nice to have; it is a requirement that must underpin the design, access, and use of this technology.

Figure 4. Stakeholders role model

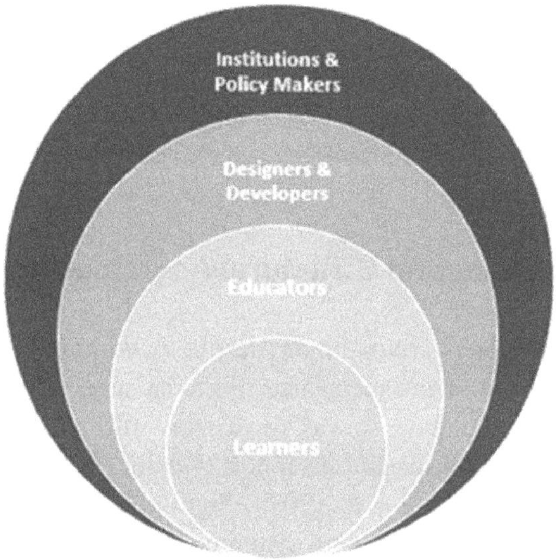

Figure 4 shows a stakeholders' role model depicting the shared responsibilities among learners, educators, designers, and policymakers in creating ethical immersive learning environments, highlighting the necessity of embedded ethics, data protection, pedagogical integrity, and regulatory oversight at every stage of AI-enabled education. Developing ethical learning environments in immersive learning is dependent on shared responsibilities at all levels of stakeholders. Learners are at the center of the work, and their rights to be their own activists, inclusion, and data protection must be paramount. Facades of the educators as they provide pedagogy, critical reflection, and context (adapted from Sustein 2011). Designers and developers design how systems ought to be to make AI behavior transparent, auditable, and fair. Overarching them, all are regulatory agencies and policymakers in charge of governance, regulation, and access. Both roles collectively make an organization where you need built-in ethics at every level.

Pedagogical Philosophy and Redefining Presence

The pedagogical identity of individuals in the educational metaverse is, at a basic level, disrupted. Immersive systems offer more than enhanced engagement — they force us to reconsider how we understand presence, action, and evaluation. With students engaging in avatars and identity-rich simulations, the creation of learner identity and agency is questioned. Theoretical contributions of Zawacki-Richter et al. (2022) and Garrison and Vaughan (2023), AI-mediated immersion disrupts the traditional role of the teacher as an authority and supports the distributed knowledge construction. These models demand that teachers embrace dialogic, multi-linear pedagogies grounded in learner experience. Khalil and Jumani (2024) explain that authentic transformation will stem not from instruments but from faculty empowerment to be situated within culturally responsive structures. Immersion is no longer simply a method but a philosophical initiative that reforms even what is considered "normal."

Strategic Directions for Policy and Research

Five Strategic Priorities Three Obligatory Purposes As the education sector moves forward, there are three obligatory purposes. 1. National and university policies The first action level emphasizes the need for a policy framework at both the national and university levels to integrate immersive planning into curricular and fiscal planning (Chamola et al., 2023). Second, research must move beyond the efficacy of technology to the ethnographic study of learners' experiences of identity, power, and culture within immersive environments (Tafazoli, 2024). Third, participatory design should be the norm. According to Arantes (2023) and Aguayo and Eames (2023), learners and educators will co-create culture-based content and tools. Faculty development in immersive design, AI ethics, and critical digital pedagogy should be a fourth pillar. Professional learning is not invested in at an institutional level, so immersion will continue to be incomplete. Lastly, we need cross-border cooperation. Collaboration between countries can alleviate mutual infrastructure, policy, and ethical challenges (especially for low-resource systems).

Figure 5. Implementation pathway for immersive AI in education

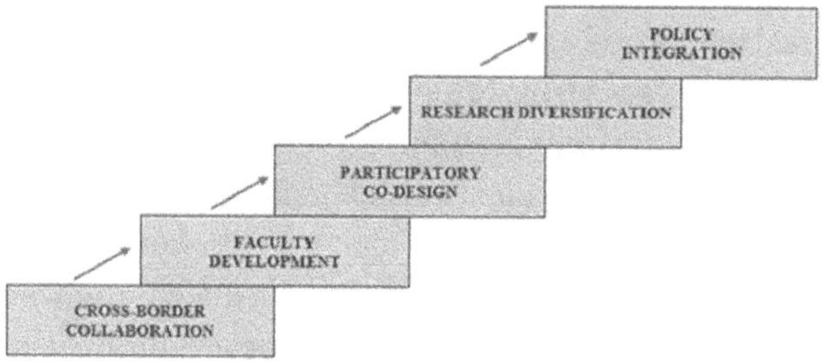

Figure 5 shows an implementation pathway for immersive AI in education, outlining a phased, multi-level strategy that spans international collaboration, institutional faculty development, participatory design, policy integration, and continuous research to ensure sustainable, equitable, and contextually grounded deployment of immersive AI learning technologies. Realizing the intricate integration of immersive AI learning in education needs a phased implementation strategy to enhance strategy-based development and interaction. The change is sustainable when it starts at the level of international cooperation to enable the transfer of knowledge, resources, and ethical grounds in diverse educational contexts. Leaping this foundation, institutional activity should be geared towards faculty development, which is more than just technical training but also a key focus on immersive pedagogy, AI ethics, and culturally responsive design. This kind of capacity development ensures that the participation of both teachers and learners can follow a design-oriented approach, where immersive tools are being developed to align them with their needs and context. More deeply, broadening the research agenda to qualitative and critical research helps reveal how learners interact with identity, power, and inclusion within these spaces. These empirical learnings, in turn, will feed into policy integration so that immersive AI is embedded in curricula reform, institutional planning, and regulatory frameworks. This stacked approach recasts implementation as not something isolated but as a coherent trajectory rooted in equity, inclusion, and a long-range pedagogical vision.

Reframing Transformation Through Human-Centered Design

It is not just a technology platform, as we will explore further in this chapter. Some critics argue that it does not exist as it is still in its formative stages. In these re-creations lies not novelty but the power to reconfigure and re-evaluate relation, identity, and inclusion. For institutions, the measure of success will not be about how fast they adopted it but how deeply they participated and how clear they were about the purpose of the change. Retention and efficiency metrics do not cut it. What is important is whether immersive AI nurtures agency, democratizes participation, and mirrors the phenomena of diverse learners. This chapter concludes by reminding us that the education metaverse is revolutionary not because it is digital but because it is human-centered. It must be based on ethics, participation, and pedagogical vision. Only in this way can immersive AI truly add meaningful value to the future of equitable global education.

CONCLUSION AND SCHOLARLY SIGNIFICANCE

This chapter has traversed some of the convoluted landscape of AI-enhanced immersive learning, framing the educational metaverse not as a paltry fad but as a paradigm shift in how we conceive, enact, and secure knowledge. Its influence operates at epistemological and technological levels; i.e., its effects are not merely at new technologies but at ontological and epistemological levels of learning. Operating via enacted engagement, algorithmic response, and distributed co-construction. Throughout the investigation, one thesis has been rehearsed across theory, design, casework, and critical analysis: immersive learning systems are only educationally significant when anchored in a robust pedagogical underpinning and ethically tuned design logic.

The five theories to be considered, connectivism, adaptive learning, personalized learning, cognitive load theory, and post-digital theory, provided a rich framework for exploring immersive education's pedagogical, cognitive, and ethical dimensions. These models offered more than just description; they served as interpretations that helped to navigate the tides of system dynamics, learner engagement, and institutional capacity. By juxtaposing these theories, the chapter has pushed the debate about whether pluralistic theoretical integration can do more than just analytical work but also provide normative reconstruction. The conceptual integration revealed that immersive environments are not inherently accessible or impactful. However, They do become so when formed around principles grounded in the realities of learner diversity, infrastructure, and design justice.

The main findings of the case study applications stressed the importance of alignment of institutions, policy framework, and place-based innovations. Achieving successful implementation was consistently associated with humanized personalization, transparent use of data, and faculty empowerment. The Pakistan feasibility study added a Global South perspective to the model, emphasizing the tensions between ambition and capability, enthusiasm and enactment. These tensions echo broader issues in immersive education, not least where the rapid uptake of such technology threatens to outpace institutional readiness. Inserting this local view into a global analytic framework, the chapter brings greater fairness and completeness to understanding immersive educational futures.

The contribution goes beyond instrumental considerations and touches upon deeper philosophical issues. Immersive environments challenge traditional identity, authority, and the presence of the learner and educator. New agency and subjecthood emerge as students work through avatars, adaptive scripts, and dynamic simulations. Pedagogical design has to change with it. The curriculum delivery must be transformed from static knowledge transference to flexible, dialogic co-construction. This thinking move requires that the design be attentive to cognitive efficiency and ethical and sociocultural nuance. As Khalil and Jumani (2024) maintain, concerted innovation occurs in matching technological tools with the culturally responsive pedagogical vision and teacher agency. From this perspective, immersive design is a space of epistemological and moral obligation.

Focusing on the known unknowns, several themes emerge for future work. Therefore, conducting longitudinal studies of deep involvement's cognitive and emotional effects is imperative. Policy architecture should incorporate ethical norms surrounding AI use, data ownership, and learners' safeguarding. Arantes (2023) and Tafazoli (2024) advocate an emergent area of immersive ethnographies that investigates learners' experiences with power, agency, and identity in metaverse spaces. The chapter emphasizes the need for open-source design protocols that carry local knowledge systems so that immersive tools are not only taken up but also taken apart. Collaboration across international borders will continue to be critical, especially to close digital divides and coordinate regulatory responses across various educational environments.

This chapter avoids digital skepticism and techno-optimism, offering a multiscale model for immersive design that links individual policy, cognition, and culture. The worth of the educational metaverse is not in what it can simulate but in what it can do to enable relationship-oriented, inclusive, and adaptive educational systems. Ultimately, AI-powered immersive learning will deliver on its potential only if developed to empower learning, respect educators' freedom, and variety, and own the multiplicity of realities of global knowledge systems.

REFERENCES

Aguayo, C., & Eames, C. (2023). Participatory design for immersive learning: Enabling culturally relevant practices. *Interactive Learning Environments, 31*(1), 114–132. DOI: 10.1080/10494820.2023.2191048

Arantes, J. A. M. (2023). Digital twins and personalization in educational policy: A critical discourse review. *Postdigital Science and Education, 5*(2), 297–317. DOI: 10.1007/s42438-022-00396-3

Arif, S., Khan, H., & Bashir, R. (2024). Bridging digital literacy gaps in higher education: Challenges and policy implications. *Journal of Educational Innovation, 12*(1), 45–58.

Chamola, V., Sikdar, B., & Chatterjee, R. (2023). Metaverse for education: Developments, challenges, and future direction. *IEEE Internet of Things Journal, 10*(5), 3872–3883. DOI: 10.1109/JIOT.2022.3211451

Chassignol, M., Khoroshavin, A., Klimova, A., & Bilyatdinova, A. (2021). Artificial Intelligence trends in education: A narrative review. *Procedia Computer Science, 176*, 154–162. DOI: 10.1016/j.procs.2020.08.202

Chatterjee, S., & Bhattacharya, S. (2022). Adaptive learning in AI-based education: A systematic review. *Journal of Educational Computing Research, 60*(3), 678–700. DOI: 10.1177/07356331211063833

Chen, Y., Li, X., & Zhao, R. (2023). Designing AI avatars for personalized learning: An empirical investigation. *Computers & Education, 194*, 104701. DOI: 10.1016/j.compedu.2023.104701

Choi, H., Lee, J., & Kim, D. (2022). Adaptive virtual environments in engineering education. *Journal of Mechanical Design Education, 23*(4), 213–229.

Decuypere, M., Williamson, B., & Addey, C. (2023). Data justice in education: Toward a research agenda. *Learning, Media and Technology, 48*(1), 1–17. DOI: 10.1080/17439884.2023.2183291

Feng, X., Zhang, Y., & Tan, M. (2024). Is metaverse a buzzword in education? Insights from a systematic review. *Education and Information Technologies, 29*(2), 135–157.

Gourlay, L. (2021). *Posthumanism and the digital university: Texts, bodies, and materialities*. Bloomsbury Academic. DOI: 10.5040/9781350038202

Holmes, W., Nand, N., & Georgiou, Y. (2023). Ethical personalization in immersive classrooms. *British Journal of Educational Technology, 54*(4), 785–803. DOI: 10.1111/bjet.13299

Huang, R., Liu, D., & Zhuang, M. (2023). Emotional design in virtual reality learning. *Educational Technology Research and Development, 71*(2), 329–350. DOI: 10.1007/s11423-023-10112-6

Hwang, G. J., & Chien, Y. H. (2022). Exploring the effects of VR-based immersive environments on knowledge retention. *Interactive Learning Environments, 30*(4), 516–533.

Jahnke, I., Lee, Y., & Kumar, S. (2022). Ethical learning design in immersive education. *Journal of Educational Technology & Society, 25*(2), 19–32.

Jandrić, P., Knox, J., Besley, T., Ryberg, T., Suoranta, J., & Hayes, S. (2018). Post-digital science and education. *Educational Philosophy and Theory, 50*(10), 893–899. DOI: 10.1080/00131857.2018.1454000

Kalyuga, S. (2022). Managing cognitive load in immersive learning design. *Educational Psychology Review, 34*(3), 805–824.

Khalil, A., Haqdad, A., & Sultana, N. (2023). Metaverse integration in Pakistani higher education: Potentials and pitfalls. *Journal of Positive School Psychology, 7*(4), 1023–1042.

Khalil, A., & Jumani, N. B. (2024). Culturally responsive metaverse pedagogy: Challenges and opportunities in Pakistan. *Journal of Emerging Educational Technology, 11*(1), 54–72.

Koukis, N., & Jimoyiannis, A. (2021). Connectivist learning in virtual learning environments. *Education and Information Technologies, 26*, 5759–5778. DOI: 10.1007/s10639-021-10566-0

Kye, B., Jung, Y., & Kim, M. (2021). XR learning implementation for medical education in Korea. *Medical Education Online, 26*(1), 1963958. DOI: 10.1080/10872981.2021.1963958

Lee, S., & Kim, Y. (2021). Personalizing virtual instruction through AI avatars. *Computers in Human Behavior, 118*, 106709. DOI: 10.1016/j.chb.2021.106709

Luckin, R., Holmes, W., Griffiths, M., & Forcier, L. B. (2022). Educationally intelligent AI: Designing systems for equity and learning. *Pearson Education Report.*

Luckin, R., Holmes, W., Griffiths, M., & Forcier, L. B. (2023). Intelligence Unleashed: The role of AI in education. *Pearson Education White Paper.*

Mayer, R. E., & Fiorella, L. (2021). *Learning as a generative activity: Eight learning strategies that promote understanding* (2nd ed.). Cambridge University Press.

Parong, J., & Mayer, R. E. (2021). Cognitive and affective processes for learning science in immersive virtual reality. *Journal of Computer Assisted Learning, 37*(1), 226–241. DOI: 10.1111/jcal.12482

Pellas, N., Dengel, A., & Müller, W. (2022). Designing personalized VR learning environments. *Education and Information Technologies, 27*(5), 6509–6530.

Sailer, M., & Homner, L. (2020). Educational gamification and immersive learning: A systematic review. *Computers & Education, 147*, 103778. DOI: 10.1016/j.compedu.2019.103778

Saqr, M., Fors, U., & Tedre, M. (2022). How AI is shaping connectivist learning networks. *Computers and Education: Artificial Intelligence, 3*, 100067. DOI: 10.1016/j.caeai.2022.100067

Selwyn, N., Hillman, T., & Eynon, R. (2021). Education and the datafied child: Postdigital childhoods. *Postdigital Science and Education, 3*(1), 8–28. DOI: 10.1007/s42438-020-00168-1

Selwyn, N., Hillman, T., & Eynon, R. (2023). Education and the algorithmic child: Ethics, evidence, and activism. *Postdigital Science and Education, 5*(3), 456–473. DOI: 10.1007/s42438-023-00326-y

Tafazoli, M. (2024). Generative AI in education: Implications for language learning. *Journal of Educational Technology, 14*(2), 221–235.

Tsai, M. J., & Tsai, C. C. (2022). An eye-tracking study of adaptive AR-based biology learning. *Journal of Science Education and Technology, 31*(4), 552–565.

Veletsianos, G., & Houlden, S. (2021). Learning as agency: AI, tutoring systems, and distributed cognition. *British Journal of Educational Technology, 52*(1), 242–257. DOI: 10.1111/bjet.13078

Vu, P., Tang, J., & Liu, Y. (2022). Personalization trade-offs in AI-based education. *Education and Information Technologies, 27*(1), 275–295. DOI: 10.1007/s10639-021-10750-2

Wang, H., & Zhang, W. (2024). ITS-driven simulations in clinical decision-making. *Simulation in Healthcare, 18*(2), 112–121.

Williamson, B., & Eynon, R. (2020). Historical perspectives on learning analytics. *Learning, Media and Technology, 45*(1), 1–14. DOI: 10.1080/17439884.2020.1694942

Williamson, B., Potter, J., & Eynon, R. (2024). Learning futures: Reclaiming data, equity, and human agency. *Postdigital Science and Education, 6*(1), 22–45. DOI: 10.1007/s42438-023-00345-9

Zawacki-Richter, O., Marín, V. I., & Bond, M. (2022). The educational metaverse: Hype or hope? *Journal of Computing in Higher Education, 34*, 457–472. DOI: 10.1007/s12528-022-09318-1

Zawacki-Richter, O., Marín, V. I., Bond, M., & Gouverneur, F. (2020). Systematic review of research on artificial intelligence applications in higher education. *International Journal of Educational Technology in Higher Education, 17*(1), 39. DOI: 10.1186/s41239-019-0171-0

KEY TERMS AND DEFINITIONS

Adaptive Learning: A personalized educational method where instructional content and pace dynamically adjust in real-time based on learner performance and feedback, often powered by AI algorithms.

Artificial Intelligence (AI): The simulation of human cognitive processes by computer systems that enables machines to perform tasks such as learning, reasoning, and problem-solving without explicit human programming.

Cognitive Load Theory: A framework explaining how the limitations of working memory impact learning, emphasizing the need to design instructional materials that minimize extraneous cognitive demands to optimize understanding.

Connectivism: A learning theory posits that knowledge is distributed across networks of people, technology, and information, with learning occurring through the formation and navigation of these connections.

Digital Equity: The state in which all learners have equal access to technology, digital resources, and the skills necessary to participate fully and fairly in digital learning environments.

Educational Metaverse: A persistent, immersive virtual environment enhanced by AI technologies, where learners interact socially and cognitively through avatars to engage in dynamic, context-responsive educational experiences.

Ethical Design: The deliberate creation of educational technologies and systems that prioritize fairness, transparency, privacy, inclusivity, and learner agency to prevent harm and promote social justice.

Immersive Learning: An instructional approach that uses virtual, augmented, or mixed reality technologies to create highly engaging, experiential environments that promote active learner participation and deeper understanding.

Personalized Learning: An educational approach that tailors learning experiences not only to cognitive needs but also to learners' identities, interests, cultural backgrounds, and emotional states, fostering motivation and relevance.

Post-Digital Education: An educational paradigm recognizing technology as fully integrated and inseparable from social, cultural, and pedagogical contexts, emphasizing critical reflection on digital practices and power structures.

Compilation of References

Aayog, N. I. T. I. (2018). *National strategy for artificial Intelligence: #AIForAll.* Government of India. https://niti.gov.in/sites/default/files/2021-07/NationalStrategy-for-AI-Discussion-Paper.pdf

Abbas, N., Imran, A., Manzoor, R., Hussain, T., & Hussain, M. (2023). Role of artificial intelligence tools in enhancing students' educational performance at higher levels. *Journal of Artificial Intelligence Machine Learning and Neural Network*, (35), 36–49. DOI: 10.55529/jaimlnn.35.36.49

Abdaljaleel, M., Barakat, M., Alsanafi, M., Salim, N. A., Abazid, H., Malaeb, D., Mohammed, A. H., Hassan, B. A. R., Wayyes, A. M., Farhan, S. S., Khatib, S. E., Rahal, M., Sahban, A., Abdelaziz, D. H., Mansour, N. O., AlZayer, R., Khalil, R., Fekih-Romdhane, F., Hallit, R., & Sallam, M. (2024). A multinational study on the factors influencing university students' attitudes and usage of ChatGPT. *Scientific Reports*, *14*(1), 1983. DOI: 10.1038/s41598-024-52549-8 PMID: 38263214

Abubakari, M. S., Shafik, W., & Hidayatullah, A. F. (2024). Evaluating the Potential of Artificial Intelligence in Islamic Religious Education. In *AI-Enhanced Teaching Methods* (pp. 216–239). IGI Global., DOI: 10.4018/979-8-3693-2728-9.ch010

Achiam, J., Adler, S., Agarwal, S., Ahmad, L., Akkaya, I., Aleman, F. L., Almeida, D., Altenschmidt, J., Altman, S., & Anadkat, S.. (2023). Gpt4technicalreport. arXivpreprint arXiv:2303.08774

Acosta-Enriquez, B. G., Arbulú Ballesteros, M. A., Huamaní Jordan, O., López Roca, C., & Saavedra Tirado, K. (2024). Analysis of college students' attitudes toward the use of ChatGPT in their academic activities: Effect of intent to use, verification of information and responsible use. *BMC Psychology*, *12*(1), 255. DOI: 10.1186/s40359-024-01764-z PMID: 38720382

Adeleye, O. O., Eden, C. A., & Adeniyi, I. S. (2024). Innovative teaching methodologies in the era of artificial intelligence: A review of inclusive educational practices. *World Journal of Advanced Engineering Technology and Sciences*, *11*(2), 069–079. Advance online publication. DOI: 10.30574/wjaets.2024.11.2.0091

Adıgüzel, T., Kaya, M. H., & Cansu, F. K. (2023). Revolutionizing education with AI: Exploring the transformative potential of ChatGPT. *Contemporary Educational Technology*, *15*(3), ep429. DOI: 10.30935/cedtech/13152

Agenda.ge. (2024, November 6). *Georgian Deputy Economy Minister: AI-driven transformation of traditional sectors "priority" of Govt's policy*. https://agenda.ge/en/news/2024/41460

Agenda.ge. (2024, November 7). *National Bank of Georgia to develop AI regulations aligned with EU standards*. https://agenda.ge/en/news/2024/41473

Aghaziarati, A., Nejatifar, S., & Abedi, A. (2023). Artificial Intelligence in education: Investigating teacher attitudes. *Aitechbesosci*, *1*(1), 35–42. DOI: 10.61838/kman.aitech.1.1.6

Aguayo, C., & Eames, C. (2023). Participatory design for immersive learning: Enabling culturally relevant practices. *Interactive Learning Environments*, *31*(1), 114–132. DOI: 10.1080/10494820.2023.2191048

Ahlf, M., McNeil, S., & Nguyen, P. (2024). Open Educational Resources: Time, resources and sustainability in an ephemeral digital world. In Cole, D. R., Rafe, M. M., & Yang-Heim, G. Y. A. (Eds.), *Educational research and the question(s) of time*. Springer., DOI: 10.1007/978-981-97-3418-4_19

Ahmad, I., Sharma, S., Singh, R., Gehlot, A., Gupta, L. R., Thakur, A. K., Priyadarshi, N., & Twala, B. (2024). Inclusive learning using industry 4.0 technologies: addressing student diversity in modern education. In *Cogent Education* (Vol. 11, Issue 1). DOI: 10.1080/2331186X.2024.2330235

Ainia, D. K. (2024). Peran Etika Digital dalam Upaya Penguatan Pendidikan Karakter di Era Digital. *PAKAR Pendidikan*, *22*(2), 127–135. DOI: 10.24036/pakar.v22i2.528

Akgun, S., & Greenhow, C. (2022). Artificial intelligence in education: Addressing ethical challenges in K-12 settings. *AI and Ethics*, *2*(3), 431–440. DOI: 10.1007/s43681-021-00096-7 PMID: 34790956

Akkaş, Ö. M., Tosun, C., & Gökçearslan, Ş. (2024). Artificial intelligence (AI) and cheating: the concept of generative artificial intelligence (GenAI). In Transforming Education With Generative AI: Prompt Engineering and Synthetic Content Creation (pp. 182-199). IGI Global Scientific Publishing.

Al Lily, A. E., Ismail, A. F., Abunaser, F. M., Al-Lami, F., & Abdullatif, A. K. A. (2023). ChatGPT and the rise of semi-humans. *Humanities & Social Sciences Communications*, *10*(1), 626–635. DOI: 10.1057/s41599-023-02154-3

Alawi F. (2023). Artificial intelligence: The future might already be here. *Oral Surgery Oral Medicine Oral Pathology Oral Radiology, 12,* S2212-4403(23)00003–2. https://doi.org/DOI: 10.1016/j.oooo.2023.01.002

Albayati, H. (2024). Investigating undergraduate students' perceptions and awareness of using ChatGPT as a regular assistance tool: A user acceptance perspective study. *Computers and Education: Artificial Intelligence*, *6*, 100203. DOI: 10.1016/j.caeai.2024.100203

Aldoseri, A., Al-Khalifa, K. N., & Hamouda, A. M. S. (2023). Re-thinking data strategy and integration for Artificial Intelligence: Concepts, opportunities, and challenges. *Applied Sciences (Basel, Switzerland)*, *13*(12), 7082. DOI: 10.3390/app13127082

Alenezi, A. (2023). Teacher perspectives on A-driven gamification: Impact on student motivation, engagement, and learning outcomes. *Information Technologies and Learning Tools*, *97*(5), 138–148. DOI: 10.33407/itlt.v97i5.5437

Aliyu, B. S. (2024). Artificial Intelligence (AI): A powerful tool for advancing plant study and research. *Nigerian Journal of Botany*, *37*(1), 61–68. DOI: 10.4314/njbot.v37i1.5

Allam, A. H., Eltewacy, N. K., Alabdallat, Y. J., Owais, T. A., Salman, S., Ebada, M. A., Aldare, H. A., Rais, M. A., Salem, M., Al-Dabagh, J. D., Alhassan, M. A., Hanjul, M. M., Mugibel, T. A., Motawea, S. H., Hussein, M., Anas, O. S., Amine, N. M., Almekhlafi, M. A., Mugibel, M. A., & Alkanj, S. (2023). Knowledge, attitude, and perception of Arab medical students towards Artificial Intelligence in medicine and radiology: A multi-national cross-sectional study. *European Radiology*, *34*(7), 1–14. DOI: 10.1007/s00330-023-10509-2 PMID: 38150076

Allen, M., & Sites, R. (2012). *Leaving ADDIE for SAM: An agile model for developing the best learning experiences*. Association for Talent Development.

Almaiah, M. A., Alamri, M. M., & Al-Rahmi, W. (2019). Applying the UTAUT model to explain the students' acceptance of mobile learning system in higher education. *IEEE Access : Practical Innovations, Open Solutions*, *7*, 174673–174686. DOI: 10.1109/ACCESS.2019.2957206

Almuhaideb, M. A., & Saeed, S. (2020). Fostering sustainable quality assurance practices in outcome-based education: Lessons learned from ABET accreditation process of computing programs. *Sustainability (Basel), 12*(20), 8380. DOI: 10.3390/su12208380

Al-Mushayt, O. (2019). Public perception and trust in AI. *Government Information Quarterly, 36*(4), 101397.

Alshorman, S. (2024). The readiness to use AI in teaching science: Science teachers' perspective. *Journal of Baltic Science Education, 23*(3), 432–448. DOI: 10.33225/jbse/24.23.432

Alshurideh, M., Jdaitawi, A., Sukkari, L., Al-Gasaymeh, A., Alzoubi, H. M., Damra, Y., Yasin, S., Al Kurdi, B., & Alshurideh, H. (2024). Factors affecting ChatGPT use in education employing TAM: A Jordanian universities' perspective. *International Journal of Data and Network Science, 8*(3), 1599–1606. DOI: 10.5267/j.ijdns.2024.3.007

Alsultan, K. (2023). Awareness of Artificial Intelligence in medical imaging among radiologists and radiologic technologists. *Cureus*. Advance online publication. DOI: 10.7759/cureus.38325 PMID: 37261164

Altun, A. (2022). Dijital tarih, tarih eğitimini nasıl etkileyebilir? [How digital history can effect history education?] *VIII. Uluslararası Tarih Eğitimi Sempozyumu (ISHE 2022) [International Symposium History Education VIII (ISHE 2022)]*. Conference paper (pp. 7–18). Adana, Türkiye.

Altun, E. (2024). Artificial intelligence and applications in education. *Journal of Digital Technologies and Education, 3*(1), 80–95. DOI: 10.5281/zenodo.12637335

Alvarez, L., Gransbury, I., Cateté, V., Barnes, T., Lédeczi, Á., & Grover, S. (2022). A socially relevant focused AI curriculum designed for female high school students. *Proceedings of the AAAI Conference on Artificial Intelligence, 36*(11), 12698–12705. DOI: 10.1609/aaai.v36i11.21546

Ammeling, J., Aubreville, M., Fritz, A., Kießig, A., Krügel, S., & Uhl, M. (2025). An interdisciplinary perspective on AI-supported decision making in medicine. *Technology in Society, 81*(October 2024), 102791. DOI: 10.1016/j.techsoc.2024.102791

Amodei, D., Ananthanarayanan, S., Anubhai, R., Bai, J., Battenberg, E., Case, C., & Zhu, Z. (2016, June). Deep speech 2: End-to-end speech recognition in English and Mandarin. In *International Conference on Machine Learning* (pp. 173–182). PMLR.

Anderson, J. L. (2021). Why social science? Because engineering is intended to benefit society. *Consortium of Social Science Associations (COSSA).*https://www.cossa.org/wp-content/uploads/2021/03/Why-Social-Science-Anderson-2021.pdf?utm_source=chatgpt.com

Angwin, J., Larson, J., Mattu, S., & Kirchner, L. (2016). Machine bias. *ProPublica.* https://www.propublica.org/article/machine-bias-risk-assessments-in-criminal-sentencing

Anica-Popa, L.-E., Vrîncianu, M., & Petrică Papuc, I.-M. (2023). AI–powered business services in the Hyperautomation Era. *Proceedings of the International Conference on Business Excellence, 17*(1), 1036–1050. DOI: 10.2478/picbe-2023-0094

Anwar, M. R., & Ahyarudin, H. A. (2023). AI-powered Arabic language education in the Era of Society 5.0. [ITSDI]. *IAIC Transactions on Sustainable Digital Innovation, 5*(1), 50–57. DOI: 10.34306/itsdi.v5i1.607

Aoun, J. E. (2017). *Robot-proof: Higher education in the age of Artificial Intelligence.* MIT Press. DOI: 10.7551/mitpress/11456.001.0001

Arantes, J. A. M. (2023). Digital twins and personalization in educational policy: A critical discourse review. *Postdigital Science and Education, 5*(2), 297–317. DOI: 10.1007/s42438-022-00396-3

Arbelaez Ossa, L., Milford, S. R., Rost, M., Leist, A. K., Shaw, D. M., & Elger, B. S. (2024). AI through ethical lenses: A discourse analysis of guidelines for AI in healthcare. *Science and Engineering Ethics, 30*(3), 24. DOI: 10.1007/s11948-024-00486-0 PMID: 38833207

Arf, C. (1959). Makine düşünebilir mi ve nasıl düşünebilir? [Can machines think and how they can think] *Atatürk Üniversitesi Halk Konferansları Serisi [The Series of Ataturk University Public Conferences]* No: 1, (pp. 91–103). Retrieved from: chrome-extension://efaidnbmnnnibpcajpcglclefindmkaj/https://www.mbkaya.com/hukuk/cahit-arf-makine-dusunebilir-mi-orjinal.pdf

Aria, M., & Cuccurullo, C. (2017). Bibliometrix: An R-tool for comprehensive science mapping analysis. *Journal of Informetrics, 11*(4), 959–975. DOI: 10.1016/j.joi.2017.08.007

Arias-Pérez, J., & Vélez-Jaramillo, J. (2022). Understanding knowledge hiding under technological turbulence caused by Artificial Intelligence and Robotics. *Journal of Knowledge Management, 26*(6), 1476–1491. DOI: 10.1108/JKM-01-2021-0058

Arif, S., Khan, H., & Bashir, R. (2024). Bridging digital literacy gaps in higher education: Challenges and policy implications. *Journal of Educational Innovation, 12*(1), 45–58.

ArkasNews. (2025). Yapay Zekâ'nın Yükselişi, https://arkasnews.com/yapay-zekanin-yukselisi/?utm_source=chatgpt.com

Arslan, K. (2020). Artificial intelligence and applications in education. *Western Anatolia Journal of Educational Sciences, 11*(1), 71–80.

Arthur, C. (2024). Why social science? Because it can help contribute to AI that benefits society. *Social Science Space.*https://www.socialsciencespace.com/2024/05/why-social-science-because-it-can-help-contribute-to-ai-that-benefits-society/

Arthur, F., Salifu, I., & Nortey, S. A. (2024). Predictors of higher education students' behavioural intention and usage of ChatGPT: The moderating roles of age, gender and experience. *Interactive Learning Environments*, 1–27. Advance online publication. DOI: 10.1080/10494820.2024.2362805

Ashok, M., Madan, R., Joha, A., & Sivarajah, U. (2022). Ethical framework for Artificial Intelligence and digital technologies. *International Journal of Information Management, 62*, 102433. DOI: 10.1016/j.ijinfomgt.2021.102433

Athey, S. (2023). Machine learning in economics: Bridging the gap between theory and practice. *The Journal of Economic Perspectives, 37*(2), 45–68.

Baidoo-anu, D., & Owusu Ansah, L. (2023). Education in the era of generative artificial intelligence (AI): Understanding the Potential Benefits of ChatGPT in Promoting Teaching and Learning. *Journal of AI, 7*(1), 52–62. DOI: 10.61969/jai.1337500

Bail, C. A. (2024). Can Generative AI improve social science? *Proceedings of the National Academy of Sciences of the United States of America, 121*(21), e2314021121. DOI: 10.1073/pnas.2314021121 PMID: 38722813

Baker, R. S., Martin, T., & Rossi, L. M. (2016). Educational data mining and learning analytics. *The Wiley handbook of cognition and assessment: Frameworks, methodologies, and applications*, 379-396.

Baker, R. S., & Hawn, A. (2022). Algorithmic bias in education. *International Journal of Artificial Intelligence in Education, 32*(4), 1052–1092. DOI: 10.1007/s40593-021-00285-9

Baker, R. S., & Inventado, P. S. (2014). Educational data mining and learning analytics. In Larusson, J. A., & White, B. (Eds.), *Learning analytics* (pp. 61–75). Springer. DOI: 10.1007/978-1-4614-3305-7_4

Bakkum, M. J., Hartjes, M. G., Piët, J. D., Donker, E. M., Likic, R., Sanz, E., de Ponti, F., Verdonk, P., Richir, M. C., van Agtmael, M. A., & Tichelaar, J. (2024). Using artificial intelligence to create diverse and inclusive medical case vignettes for education. *British Journal of Clinical Pharmacology*, *90*(3), 640–648. Advance online publication. DOI: 10.1111/bcp.15977 PMID: 38016816

Bandura, A. (1977). *Social Learning Theory*. Prentice-Hall.

Bandura, A. (1986). *Social foundations of thought and action: A Social Cognitive Theory*. Prentice-Hall.

Bandura, A. (1997). *Self-efficacy: The exercise of control*. W. H. Freeman.

Banerjee, M., Chiew, D., Patel, K. T., Johns, I., Chappell, D., Linton, N., Cole, G., Francis, D. P., Szram, J., Ross, J., & Zaman, S. (2021). The impact of Artificial Intelligence on clinical education: Perceptions of postgraduate trainee doctors in London (UK) and recommendations for trainers. *BMC Medical Education*, *21*(1), 429. Advance online publication. DOI: 10.1186/s12909-021-02870-x PMID: 34391424

Bankins, S., Ocampo, A. C., Marrone, M., Restubog, S. L. D., & Woo, S. E. (2024). A multilevel review of Artificial Intelligence in organizations: Implications for organizational behavior research and practice. *Journal of Organizational Behavior*, *45*(2), 159–182. DOI: 10.1002/job.2735

Barocas, S., Hardt, M., & Narayanan, A. (2023). *Fairness and machine learning: Limitations and opportunities*. MIT Press.

Barocas, S., & Selbst, A. D. (2016). Big data's disparate impact. *California Law Review*, *104*(3), 671–732.

Bau, D., Gray, J., Kelleher, C., Sheldon, J., & Turbak, F. (2022). Learnable programming: Blocks and beyond. *Communications of the ACM*, *65*(5), 72–80. DOI: 10.1145/3015455

Bayly-Castaneda, K., Ramirez-Montoya, M. S., & Morita-Alexander, A. (2024, August). Crafting personalized learning paths with AI for lifelong learning: A systematic literature review. *Frontiers in Education*, *9*, 1424386. DOI: 10.3389/feduc.2024.1424386

Bayramacar, B. (2013). Eğitimde Medya – Yöntem Tartışması, Eğitim Tasarımı. https://instructionaldesignco.wordpress.com/2013/12/11/egitimde-medya-yontem-tartismasi/

Ben Rjab, A., & Mellouli, S. (2019). Smart government: A framework for AI-powered public services. *Information Polity*, *24*(3), 247–269.

Benzinger, L., Ursin, F., Balke, W.-T., Kacprowski, T., & Salloch, S. (2023). Should Artificial Intelligence be used to support clinical ethical decision-making? A systematic review of reasons. *BMC Medical Ethics*, *24*(1), 48. DOI: 10.1186/s12910-023-00929-6 PMID: 37415172

Bernasco, W., Hoeben, E. M., Koelma, D. C., Liebst, L. S., Thomas, J., Appelman, J., Snoek, C. G. M., & Lindegaard, M. R. (2022). Promise into practice: Application of computer vision in empirical research on social distancing. *Sociological Methods & Research*, *52*(3), 1239–1287. DOI: 10.1177/00491241221099554

Bers, M. U. (2021). Coding as another language: A pedagogical approach for teaching computer science in early childhood. *Journal of Computers in Education*, *6*(4), 499–528. DOI: 10.1007/s40692-019-00147-3

Bessen, J. E. (2019). *AI and Jobs: The Role of Demand.* NBER Working Paper.

Bhargava, A., Bester, M., & Bolton, L. (2021). Employees' perceptions of the implementation of Robotics, Artificial Intelligence, and Automation (RAIA) on job satisfaction, job security, and employability. *Journal of Technology in Behavioral Science*, *6*(1), 106–113. DOI: 10.1007/s41347-020-00153-8

Bilgehan Can, Z., Duman, H., Buluş, B., & Erişen, Y. (2023). How did ChatGPT transform us in terms of transformative learning? [JSER]. *Journal of Social and Educational Research*, *2*(2), 41–51.

Biloš, A., & Budimir, B. (2024). Understanding the Adoption Dynamics of ChatGPT among Generation Z: Insights from a Modified UTAUT2 Model. *Journal of Theoretical and Applied Electronic Commerce Research*, *19*(2), 863–879. DOI: 10.3390/jtaer19020045

Bing, A. I. (n.d.). Bing. Retrieved from: https://www.bing.com/images/create

Binns, R. (2018). Algorithmic accountability and public reason. *Philosophy & Technology*, *31*(4), 543–556. DOI: 10.1007/s13347-017-0263-5 PMID: 30873342

Binns, R. (2018). Fairness in machine learning: Lessons from political philosophy. *Proceedings of the 2018 Conference on Fairness, Accountability, and Transparency*, 149–159.

Binns, R. (2020). *The ethics of AI and social media*. Oxford University Press.

Binns, R. (2023). Natural language processing in political science: A new frontier. *Political Analysis*, *31*(1), 98–113.

Bircan, T., & Salah, A. A. A. (2022). A bibliometric analysis of the use of Artificial Intelligence technologies for social sciences. *Mathematics*, *10*(23), 4398. DOI: 10.3390/math10234398

Bland, Ed. D. (2016). Imagination for Inclusion: Diverse Contexts of Educational Practice. Routledge Research in Education. In *Routledge Research in Education*.

Blei, D. M., Ng, A. Y., & Jordan, M. I. (2021). Latent Dirichlet allocation: A method for topic modeling. *Journal of Machine Learning Research*, *22*(1), 1–23.

Blessinger, P., & Stockley, D. (2016). *Emerging directions in doctoral education*. Emerald Group Publishing., DOI: 10.1108/S2055-364120166

Boateng, O., & Boateng, B. (2025). Algorithmic bias in educational systems: Examining the impact of AI-driven decision making in modern education. *World Journal of Advanced Research and Reviews*, *25*(01), 2012–2017. DOI: 10.30574/wjarr.2025.25.1.0253

Boeren, E. (2019). Understanding Sustainable Development Goal (SDG) 4 on "quality education" from micro, meso, and macro perspectives. *International Review of Education*, *65*(2), 277–294. Advance online publication. DOI: 10.1007/s11159-019-09772-7

Boge, F. J. (2021). Two dimensions of opacity and the deep learning predicament. *Minds and Machines*, *32*(1), 43–75. DOI: 10.1007/s11023-021-09569-4

Bolton, M. L. (2024). Trust is not a virtue: Why we should not trust? *Ergonomics in Design*, *32*(4), 4–11. DOI: 10.1177/10648046221130171

Bostrom, N. (2014). *Superintelligence: Paths, dangers, strategies*. Oxford University Press.

Boulanin, V., & Lewis, D. A. (2023). Responsible reliance concerning development and use of AI in the military domain. *Ethics and Information Technology*, *25*(1), 8. DOI: 10.1007/s10676-023-09691-0

Bozkurt, A. (2023). ChatGPT, üretken yapay zekâ ve algoritmik paradigma değişikliği [ChatGPT, generative artificial intelligence and change of algorithmic paradigm] [CressJournal]. *Alanyazın*, *4*(1), 63–72. DOI: 10.59320/alanyazin.1283282

Bozkurt, A. (2023). Generative AI, synthetic contents, Open Educational Resources (OER), and Open Educational Practices (OEP): A new front in the openness landscape. *Open Praxis, 15*(3), 178–184. DOI: 10.55982/openpraxis.15.3.579

Bozkurt, A., & Sharma, R. C. (2023). Challenging the status quo and exploring the new boundaries in the age of algorithms: Reimagining the role of generative AI in distance education and online learning. *Asian Journal of Distance Education, 18*(1), 1–8. DOI: 10.5281/zenodo.7755273

Bozkurt, A., Xıao, J., Lambert, S., Pazurek, A., Crompton, H., Koseoglu, S., & Farrow, R. (2023). Speculative futures on ChatGPT and generative artificial intelligence (AI): A collective reflection from the educational landscape. *Asian Journal of Distance Education, 18*(1), 53–130. https://doing.org/10.5281/zenodo.7636568

Brahim-Said, N. (2024). AI: empowering inclusive education. https://nationalcentreforai.jiscinvolve.org/wp/2024/01/09/ai-empowering-inclusive-education/?utm_source=chatgpt.com

Branch, R. M. (2009). *Instructional design: The ADDIE Approach*. Springer. DOI: 10.1007/978-0-387-09506-6

Bressane, A., Zwirn, D., Essiptchouk, A., Saraiva, A. C. V., Carvalho, F. L. de C., Formiga, J. K. S., Medeiros, L. C. de C., & Negri, R. G. (2024). Understanding the role of study strategies and learning disabilities on student academic performance to enhance educational approaches: A proposal using artificial intelligence. *Computers and Education: Artificial Intelligence*, *6*, 100196. Advance online publication. DOI: 10.1016/j.caeai.2023.100196

Bringsjord, S., & Govindarajulu, N. S. (2018, July 12). *Artificial Intelligence*. Stanford Encyclopedia of Philosophy Archive. https://plato.stanford.edu/archives/sum2020/entries /artificial-intelligence/

Brougham, D., & Haar, J. (2017). Employee assessment of their technological redundancy. *Labour & Industry: A Journal of the Social and Economic Relations of Work, 27*(3), 213–231. DOI: 10.1080/10301763.2017.1369718

Brundage, M., ... (2018). *The malicious use of Artificial Intelligence: Forecasting, prevention, and mitigation*. arXiv preprint arXiv:1802.07228.

Bruner, J. S. (1960). *The process of education*. Harvard University Press. DOI: 10.4159/9780674028999

Bruner, J. S. (1966). *Toward a theory of instruction*. Harvard University Press.

Brusilovsky, P., & Peylo, C. (2003). Adaptive and intelligent web-based educational systems. *International Journal of Artificial Intelligence in Education, 13*(2-4), 159–172. 1010.3233/IRG-2003-13(2-4)02

Brynjolfsson, E., & Mcafee, A. (2014). *The second machine age. Work, progress, and prosperity*. 1–281.

Brynjolfsson, E., Li, D., & Raymond, L. (2023). *Generative AI at work*. DOI: 10.3386/w31161

Brynjolfsson, E.. (2022). Artificial intelligence in economic forecasting: Challenges and opportunities. *The Journal of Economic Perspectives, 36*(2), 45–67.

Brynjolfsson, E., & McAfee, A. (2014). *The Second Machine Age: Work, progress, and prosperity in a time of brilliant technologies*. W. W. Norton & Company.

Brynjolfsson, E., & McAfee, A. (2017). *The Second Machine Age: Work, progress, and Prosperity in a time of brilliant technologies*. W. W. Norton & Company.

Bull, C., & Kharrufa, A. (2024). Generative Artificial Intelligence Assistants in Software Development Education: A Vision for Integrating Generative Artificial Intelligence into Educational Practice, Not Instinctively Defending Against It. *IEEE Software, 41*(2), 52–59. Advance online publication. DOI: 10.1109/MS.2023.3300574

Buolamwini, J., & Gebru, T. (2018). *Gender Shades: Intersectional Accuracy Disparities in Commercial Gender Classification*. In *Proceedings of the 1st Conference on Fairness, Accountability and Transparency* (pp. 77–91).

Burhan, Q. A. (2025). Unraveling the AI Enigma: How perceptions of Artificial Intelligence forge career adaptability through the crucible of career insecurity and skill development. *Management Research Review, 48*(3), 470–488. DOI: 10.1108/MRR-01-2024-0022

Cadwalladr, C., & Graham-Harrison, E. (2022). The Cambridge Analytica scandal: How AI was used to manipulate voter behavior. *The Guardian*.

Calzada, I. (2024). Artificial Intelligence for social innovation: Beyond the noise of algorithms and datafication. *Sustainability (Basel), 16*(19), 8638. DOI: 10.3390/su16198638

Campbell, S., Greenwood, M., Prior, S., Shearer, T., Walkem, K., Young, S., Bywaters, D., & Walker, K. (2020). Purposive sampling: Complex or simple? Research case examples. *Journal of Research in Nursing : JRN, 25*(8), 652–661. DOI: 10.1177/1744987120927206 PMID: 34394687

Canva, A. I. (n.d.). Say “Hi” to Canva AI. Retrieved from: https://www.canva.com/ai-assistant/

Cappuccio, M. L., Galliott, J. C., Eyssel, F., & Lanteri, A. (2024). Autonomous systems and technology resistance: New tools for monitoring acceptance, trust, and tolerance. *International Journal of Social Robotics*, *16*(6), 1–25. DOI: 10.1007/s12369-023-01065-2

Carbonell, J. R. (1970). AI in CAI: An artificial-intelligence approach to computer-assisted instruction. *IEEE Transactions on Man-Machine Systems*, *11*(4), 190–202. DOI: 10.1109/TMMS.1970.299942

Çela, E., Fonkam, M., & Potluri, R. M. (2024). Risks of AI-assisted learning on student critical thinking. *International Journal of Risk and Contingency Management*, *12*(1), 1–19. DOI: 10.4018/IJRCM.350185

Celik, I., Dindar, M., Muukkonen, H., & Järvelä, S. (2022). The promises and challenges of Artificial Intelligence for teachers: A systematic review of research. *TechTrends*, *66*(4), 616–630. DOI: 10.1007/s11528-022-00715-y

Çevik, M. (2017). Will it be possible for Artificial Intelligence robots to acquire free will and believe in God? *Beytulhikme An International Journal of Philosophy*, *7*(2), 75–87. DOI: 10.18491/beytulhikme.375781

Chalk, P. (2001). Separatism and Southeast Asia: The Islamic factor in Southern Thailand, Mindanao, and Aceh. *Studies in Conflict and Terrorism*, *24*(4), 241–269. DOI: 10.1080/10576100116748

Chamola, V., Sikdar, B., & Chatterjee, R. (2023). Metaverse for education: Developments, challenges, and future direction. *IEEE Internet of Things Journal*, *10*(5), 3872–3883. DOI: 10.1109/JIOT.2022.3211451

Chan, K. S., & Zary, N. (2019). Applications and challenges of implementing Artificial Intelligence in medical education: Integrative review. *JMIR Medical Education*, *5*(1), e13930. DOI: 10.2196/13930 PMID: 31199295

Character, A. I. (n.d). Character.ai. Retrieved from: https://character.ai/

Chassignol, M., Khoroshavin, A., Klimova, A., & Bilyatdinova, A. (2021). Artificial Intelligence trends in education: A narrative review. *Procedia Computer Science*, *176*, 154–162. DOI: 10.1016/j.procs.2020.08.202

ChatGPT. (n.d.). ChatGPT-4o. Retrieved from: https://chatgpt.com/

Chatterjee, S., & Bhattacharya, S. (2022). Adaptive learning in AI-based education: A systematic review. *Journal of Educational Computing Research, 60*(3), 678–700. DOI: 10.1177/07356331211063833

Cheng, C., Chen, C.-C., Fu, C., Chaou, C., Wu, Y.-T., Hsu, C.-P., Chang, C.-C., Chung, I., Hsieh, C., Hsieh, M., & Liao, C. (2020). Artificial Intelligence-based education assists medical students' interpretation of hip fracture. *Insights Into Imaging, 11*(1), 119. Advance online publication. DOI: 10.1186/s13244-020-00932-0 PMID: 33226480

Chen, J., Wang, M., Kirschner, P. A., & Tsai, C. C. (2018). The role of collaboration, computer use, learning environments, and supporting strategies in CSCL: A meta-analysis. *Review of Educational Research, 88*(6), 799–843. DOI: 10.3102/0034654318791584

Chen, Y., Li, X., & Zhao, R. (2023). Designing AI avatars for personalized learning: An empirical investigation. *Computers & Education, 194*, 104701. DOI: 10.1016/j.compedu.2023.104701

Chigbu, B. I., & Nekhwevha, F. H. (2021). The future of work and uncertain labor alternatives as we live through the industrial age of possible singularity: Evidence from South Africa. *Technology in Society, 67*(July), 101715. DOI: 10.1016/j.techsoc.2021.101715

Chin, C. L., & Yao, G. (2021). Convergent validity. In *Encyclopedia of quality of life and well-being research* (pp. 1–2). Springer International Publishing. DOI: 10.1007/978-3-319-69909-7_573-2

Choi, H., Lee, J., & Kim, D. (2022). Adaptive virtual environments in engineering education. *Journal of Mechanical Design Education, 23*(4), 213–229.

Choudhury, M., & Sharma, A. (2022). *Artificial intelligence and social science: Emerging methodologies and implications*. Cambridge University Press.

Chowdhury, S., Budhwar, P., Dey, P. K., Joel-Edgar, S., & Abadie, A. (2022). AI-employee collaboration and business performance: Integrating knowledge-based view, socio-technical systems, and organisational socialisation framework. *Journal of Business Research, 144*, 31–49. DOI: 10.1016/j.jbusres.2022.01.069

Clarke, E. (2021, April 27). *What is a subject guide?* Marist University. https://marist.libanswers.com/faq/343816

Clark, R. E. (1983). Reconsidering research on learning from media. *Review of Educational Research, 53*(4), 445–459. DOI: 10.3102/00346543053004445

Clark, R. E. (1994a). Media will never influence learning. *Educational Technology Research and Development, 42*(2), 21–29. DOI: 10.1007/BF02299088

Clark, R. E. (1994b). Media and method. *Educational Technology Research and Development, 42*(3), 7–10. DOI: 10.1007/BF02298090

Cliovis. (n.d.). Cliovis visualizing connections. Retrieved from: https://cliovis.com/

Coeckelbergh, M. (2020). *AI ethics*. MIT Press. DOI: 10.7551/mitpress/12549.001.0001

Colace, F., De Santo, M., Lombardi, M., Pascale, F., Pietrosanto, A., & Lemma, S. (2018). Chatbot for e-learning: A case of study. *International Journal of Mechanical Engineering and Robotics Research, 7*(5), 528–533. https://www.ijmerr.com/uploadfile/2018/0831/20180831043721869.pdf. DOI: 10.18178/ijmerr.7.5.528-533

Comes, T. (2024). AI for crisis decisions. *Ethics and Information Technology, 26*(1), 12. DOI: 10.1007/s10676-024-09750-0

Copeland, J. (1993). *Artificial intelligence: A philosophical introduction*. Blackwell.

Cotton, D. R., Cotton, P. A., & Shipway, J. R. (2024). Chatting and cheating: Ensuring academic integrity in the era of ChatGPT. *Innovations in Education and Teaching International, 61*(2), 228–239. DOI: 10.1080/14703297.2023.2190148

Çotuksöken, B. (1998). *Kavramlara felsefe ile bakmak*. İnsancıl Yayınları.

Council of Europe. (2021, December 14). *Georgia – CoE and State Inspector's Service launch project action in the field of Artificial Intelligence and Personal Data Protection*. https://www.coe.int/en/web/data-protection/-/georgia-coe-and-state-inspector-s-service-launch-project-action-in-the-field-of-artificial-intelligence-and-personal-data-protection

Cox, A. (2024, October 9). Algorithmic Literacy, AI Literacy and Responsible Generative AI Literacy. *Journal of Web Librarianship, 18*(3), 93–110. DOI: 10.1080/19322909.2024.2395341

Crawford, K. (2021). *Atlas of AI: Power, Politics, and the Planetary Costs of Artificial Intelligence*. Yale University Press.

Creemers, R. (2018). China's social credit system: An evolving practice of control. *SSRN*. DOI: 10.2139/ssrn.3175792

Crevier, D. (1993). *AI: The Tumultuous History of the Search for Artificial Intelligence*. Basic Books.

Crossley, S., Paquette, L., Dascalu, M., McNamara, D. S., & Baker, R. S. (2016). Combining click-stream data with NLP tools to better understand MOOC completion. In *Proceedings of the Sixth International Conference on Learning Analytics & Knowledge (LAK, 2016)* (pp. 6–14). ACM. https://doi.org/DOI: 10.1145/2883851.2883931

Cubric, M. (2020). Drivers, barriers and social considerations for AI adoption in business and management: A tertiary study. *Technology in Society, 62*(December 2019), 101257. DOI: 10.1016/j.techsoc.2020.101257

Cukurova, M., Luckin, R., & Kent, C. (2020). Impact of an artificial intelligence research frame on the perceived credibility of educational research evidence. *International Journal of Artificial Intelligence in Education, 30*(2), 205–235. DOI: 10.1007/s40593-019-00188-w

Cummins, M., Adams Becker, S., & Alexander, B. (2016). NMC Horizon Project strategic brief on digital literacy (Vol. 3.3). The New Media Consortium. https://www.learntechlib.org/p/173858/

Curipod. (n.d.). Feel the buzz of 100% participation. Retrieved from: https://curipod.com/

Dahlin, E. (2021). Mind the Gap! On the future of AI Research. *Humanities & Social Sciences Communications, 8*(1), 71. Advance online publication. DOI: 10.1057/s41599-021-00750-9

Dalgıç, A., Yaşar, E., & Demir, M. (2024). ChatGPT and learning outcomes in tourism education: The role of digital literacy and individualized learning. *Journal of Hospitality, Leisure, Sport and Tourism Education, 34*, 100481. DOI: 10.1016/j.jhlste.2024.100481

DALL·E. (n.d.). DALL·E 3. Retrieved from: https://openai.com/index/dall-e-3/

Danovitch, J. H., Dubé, A. K., Oranç, C., Szczuka, J., & Yarosh, S. (2025). Children's understanding and use of voice-assistants: Opportunities and challenges. In Christakis, D. A., & Hale, L. (Eds.), *Handbook of children and screens*. Springer., DOI: 10.1007/978-3-031-69362-5_84

Dastin, J. (2021). *Amazon's AI recruiting tool discriminates against women*. Reuters.

David, P., Choung, H., & Seberger, J. S. (2024). Who is responsible? US Public perceptions of AI governance through the lenses of trust and ethics. *Public Understanding of Science (Bristol, England), 33*(5), 654–672. DOI: 10.1177/09636625231224592 PMID: 38326971

Davies, M. (2015). A model of critical thinking in higher education. In Paulsen, M. B. (Ed.), *Higher education: Handbook of theory and research* (pp. 41–92). Springer. DOI: 10.1007/978-3-319-12835-1_2

Davis, F. D. (1989). Perceived usefulness, perceived ease of use and use acceptance of information technology. *Management Information Systems Quarterly*, *13*(3), 319–340. DOI: 10.2307/249008

Davis, M. (2022). An Exploration of the Emergence of Machine Consciousness and the Risk of Robocentrism. *Journal of Artificial Intelligence and Consciousness*, *9*(3), 385–407. Advance online publication. DOI: 10.1142/S2705078522500114

Decuypere, M., Williamson, B., & Addey, C. (2023). Data justice in education: Toward a research agenda. *Learning, Media and Technology*, *48*(1), 1–17. DOI: 10.1080/17439884.2023.2183291

Deepseek. (n.d.). DeepSeek-V3. Retrieved from: https://chat.deepseek.com/

Dekker, F., Salomons, A., & van der Waal, J. (2017). Fear of robots at work: The role of economic self-interest. *Socio-economic Review*, *15*(3), 539–562. DOI: 10.1093/ser/mwx005

Demircioglu, A. (2018). *Eleştirel düşünme eğitimi* [Critical thinking education]. Gece Kitaplığı.

Desouza, K. C., Dawson, G. S., & Chenok, D. (2020). *AI in government: Applications, challenges, and opportunities*. Brookings Institution.

Dewey, J. (1916). *Democracy and education: An introduction to the philosophy of education*. Macmillan.

Díaz-Sánchez, C., & Chapinal-Heras, D. (2023). Use of open access AI in teaching classical antiquity. A methodological proposal. *The Journal of Classics Teaching*, (10). Advance online publication. DOI: 10.1017/S2058631023000739

Dick, W., Carey, L., & Carey, J. O. (2015). *The systematic design of instruction* (8th ed.). Pearson.

Dictionary, O. E. (2020). *Philosophy*. Publishing House of the National Society of Philosophers of Uzbekistan.

Diemer, A., Khushik, F., & Ndiaye, A. (2020). SDG 4 "Quality Education," the Cornerstone of the SDGs: Case Studies of Pakistan and Senegal. *JOURNAL OF ECONOMICS AND DEVELOPMENT STUDIES*, *8*(1). Advance online publication. DOI: 10.15640/jeds.v8n1a2

Diffit. (n.d.). Diffit for teachers. Retrieved from: https://web.diffit.me/

Digital Ottoman Studies. (n.d.). Digital Ottoman Studies: Home. Retrieved from: https://www.digitalottomanstudies.com/

Dolan, J. (2018). Preparing public administrators for the future: Education, service learning, and civic engagement. *Public Administration Review*, *78*(5), 702–710.

Dong, E., Liu, H., Li, J. Y., & Lee, Y. (2024). Motivating employee voicing behavior in optimizing workplace generative AI adoption: The role of organizational listening. *Public Relations Review*, *50*(5), 102509. DOI: 10.1016/j.pubrev.2024.102509

Donthu, N., Kumar, S., Mukherjee, D., Pandey, N., & Lim, W. M. (2021). How to conduct a bibliometric analysis: An overview and guidelines. *Journal of Business Research*, *133*, 285–296. DOI: 10.1016/j.jbusres.2021.04.070

DreamBox Inspire life-long learning: https://www.dreambox.com/

Dumić-Čule, I., Orešković, T., Brkljačić, B., Tiljak, M. K., & Orešković, S. (2020). The importance of introducing Artificial Intelligence to the medical curriculum – assessing practitioners' perspectives. *Croatian Medical Journal*, *61*(5), 457–464. DOI: 10.3325/cmj.2020.61.457 PMID: 33150764

Dundua, M., & Gorgodze, O. (2022). *Application of Artificial Intelligence for Monetary Policy-Making*. National Bank of Georgia. https://nbg.gov.ge/en/media/news/a-new-paper-on-application-of-artificial-intelligence-for-monetary-policy-making

Dwivedi, Y. K., Hughes, L., Ismagilova, E., Aarts, G., Coombs, C., Crick, T., & Williams, M. D. (2021). Artificial intelligence (AI): Multidisciplinary perspectives on emerging challenges, opportunities, and agenda for research, practice, and policy. *International Journal of Information Management*, *57*, 101994. DOI: 10.1016/j.ijinfomgt.2019.08.002

Dwivedi, Y. K., Kshetri, N., Hughes, L., Slade, E. L., Jeyaraj, A., Kar, A. K., Baabdullah, A. M., Koohang, A., Raghavan, V., Ahuja, M., Albanna, H., Albashrawi, M. A., Al-Busaidi, A. S., Balakrishnan, J., Barlette, Y., Basu, S., Bose, I., Brooks, L., Buhalis, D., & Wright, R. (2023). Opinion Paper:"So what if ChatGPT wrote it?" Multidisciplinary perspectives on opportunities, challenges and implications of generative conversational AI for research, practice and policy. *International Journal of Information Management*, *71*, 102642. DOI: 10.1016/j.ijinfomgt.2023.102642

Edeni, C. A., Adeleye, O. O., & Adeniyi, I. S. (2024). The role of AI-enhanced tools in overcoming educational socio-economic barriers: A conceptual analysis. *World Journal of Advanced Research and Reviews*, *21*(3). Advance online publication. DOI: 10.30574/wjarr.2024.21.3.0780

Edeni, C. A., Adeleye, O. O., & Adeniyi, I. S. (2024). The role of AI-enhanced tools in overcoming socioeconomic barriers in education: A conceptual analysis. *World Journal of Advanced Research and Reviews, 21*(3), 944–951.

EDUCAUSE. (2024). 2024 EDUCAUSE Horizon Report: Teaching and Learning Edition. https://library.educause.edu/resources/2024/5/2024-educause-horizon-report-teaching-and-learning-edition

Eggers, W. D., Schatsky, D., & Viechnicki, P. (2020). *AI-augmented government: Using cognitive technologies to redesign public sector work.* Deloitte Insights.

Eichstaedt, J. C., Kern, M. L., Yaden, D. B., Schwartz, H. A., Giorgi, S., Park, G., Hagan, C. A., Tobolsky, V. A., Smith, L., Buffone, A., Iwry, J., Seligman, M. E. P., & Ungar, L. (2021). Closed- and open-vocabulary approaches to text analysis: A review, quantitative comparison, and recommendations. *Psychological Methods, 26*(4), 398–427. DOI: 10.1037/met0000349 PMID: 34726465

Elizondo, C.. (2021). AI and social movements: Analyzing protest with computer vision. *Social Media + Society, 7*(2), 1–13.

Elsherif, H. M., & Elmeawad, S. (2024). *Unlocking knowledge: Leveraging AI to access Open Educational Resources in higher education.* Eldonusa.

Ennis, R. H. (2018). Critical thinking across the curriculum: A vision. *Topoi, 37*(1), 165–184. DOI: 10.1007/s11245-016-9401-4

Eppler, M. J. (2006). A comparison between concept maps, mind maps, conceptual diagrams, and visual metaphors as complementary tools for knowledge construction and sharing. *Information Visualization, 5*(3), 202–210. DOI: 10.1057/palgrave.ivs.9500131

Erdoğan, M., & Erol Şahin, A. N. (2024). Tarihsel strateji oyunlarında Türk imajının ders kitapları ile karşılaştırılarak göstergebilimsel analizi. [A Semiotic analysis of Turkish image in historical strategic games by comparing to textbooks] In *Sosyal Bilgiler Eğitimi Alanında Uluslararası Araştırmalar içinde* [[In *International Researches in the field of Social Studies Education I]*]. Eğitim Yayınevi.

Erol Şahin, A. N. (2023). The courses are online; what about the students? Did they really online? Using Kahoot! In the emergency remote teaching process. *Research on Education and Psychology, 7*(Special Issue), 74–89. DOI: 10.54535/rep.1264989

Esen, G. (2019). Yapay Zekâ: Geçmişi ve geleceği. *Çukurova Üniversitesi İlahiyat Fakültesi Dergisi, 19*(1), 308-311. https://doi.org/DOI: 10.30627/cuilah.481080

Essel, H. B., Vlachopoulos, D., Tachie-Menson, A., Johnson, E. E., & Baah, P. K. (2022). The impact of a virtual teaching assistant (chatbot) on students' learning in Ghanaian higher education. *International Journal of Educational Technology in Higher Education, 19*(1), 57. DOI: 10.1186/s41239-022-00362-6

Esteva, A., Kuprel, B., Novoa, R. A., Ko, J., Swetter, S. M., Blau, H. M., & Thrun, S. (2017). Dermatologist-level classification of skin cancer with deep neural networks. *Nature, 542*(7639), 115–118. DOI: 10.1038/nature21056 PMID: 28117445

Eubanks, V. (2018). *Automating inequality: How high-tech tools profile, police, and punish the poor*. St. Martin's Press.

Eubanks, V. (2018). *Automating Inequality: How High-Tech Tools Profile, Police, and Punish the Poor*. St—Martin's Press.

European Commission. (2020). *Digital Education Action Plan (2021-2027)*. European Commission Publications Office. https://education.ec.europa.eu/focus-topics/digital-education/action-plan

European Commission. (2020). *Digital education action plan (2021-2027). Resetting education and training for the digital age.* [Fact sheet]. https://education.ec.europa.eu/sites/default/files/document-library-docs/deap-factsheet-sept2020_en.pdf

European Commission. (2021). *Proposal for a regulation laying down harmonized rules on artificial intelligence (Artificial Intelligence Act)*.https://eur-lex.europa.eu/legal-content/EN/TXT/?uri=CELEX%3A52021PC0206

European Schoolnet. (2021). *Ethical use of artificial Intelligence in education: Recommendations and guidelines.* European Commission. https://www.eun.org/documents/411753/817341/Ethical+use+of+AI+in+education+-+report.pdf

Evans, D., & Gao, J. (2016). DeepMind AI Reduces Google Data Centre Cooling Bill by 40%. *DeepMind Blog*. https://www.deepmind.com/blog/deepmind-ai-reduces-google-data-centre-cooling-bill-by-40

Fan, B. E., Chow, M., & Winkler, S. (2024). Artificial Intelligence-Generated Facial Images for Medical Education. *Medical Science Educator*, *34*(1), 5–7. Advance online publication. DOI: 10.1007/s40670-023-01942-5 PMID: 38510393

Farris, P. J. (2024). *Elementary and middle school social studies: An interdisciplinary, multicultural approach*. Waveland Press.

Faruk, L. I. D., Rohan, R., Ninrutsirikun, U., & Pal, D. (2023, December). University students' acceptance and usage of generative AI (ChatGPT) from a psycho-technical perspective. In *Proceedings of the 13th International Conference on Advances in Information Technology* (pp. 1-8). DOI: 10.1145/3628454.3629552

Fatimah, N. Y., & Octaviani, D. (2023). Sejarah Pendidikan Indonesia Baru: Perkembangan Pembelajaran Sejarah Berbasis Artificial Intelligence (AI) 4.0. *Journal Sejarah Indonesia.*, *6*(2), 168–179. DOI: 10.62924/jsi.v6i2.32607

Fauzi, F., Tuhuteru, L., Sampe, F., Ausat, A. M. A., & Hatta, H. R. (2023). Analysing the role of ChatGPT in improving student productivity in higher education. *Journal of Education*, *5*(4), 14886–14891. DOI: 10.31004/joe.v5i4.2563

Fazlollahi, A. M., Bakhaidar, M., Alsayegh, A., Yilmaz, R., Winkler-Schwartz, A., Mirchi, N., Langleben, I., Ledwos, N., Sabbagh, A. J., Bajunaid, K., Harley, J. M., & Maestro, R. F. D. (2022). Effect of Artificial Intelligence tutoring vs expert instruction on learning simulated surgical skills among medical students. *JAMA Network Open*, *5*(2), e2149008. DOI: 10.1001/jamanetworkopen.2021.49008 PMID: 35191972

Fecher, B., Hebing, M., Laufer, M., Pohle, J., & Sofsky, F. (2023). Friend or foe? Exploring the Implications of large language models on the science system. *AI & Society*. Advance online publication. DOI: 10.1007/s00146-023-01791-1

Feng, X., Zhang, Y., & Tan, M. (2024). Is metaverse a buzzword in education? Insights from a systematic review. *Education and Information Technologies*, *29*(2), 135–157.

Filippis, R., & Foysal, A. A. (2024). Insights unveiled: Harnessing AI to explore human behaviour in social sciences. *Journal of Mathematical Techniques and Computational Mathematics*, *3*(5), 1–8. DOI: 10.33140/JMTCM.03.05.04

Fitria, T. N. (2023). The use of Artificial Intelligence in education (AIED): Can AI replace the teacher's role? *Epigram*, *20*(2), 165–187. DOI: 10.32722/epi.v20i2.5711

Fitzgerald, T.. (2022). Using AI to analyze historical archives: A case study in visual culture. *Digital Humanities Quarterly*, *16*(4), 45–64.

Floridi, L. (2018). Soft ethics, the governance of the digital and the General Data Protection Regulation. *Philosophical Transactions. Series A, Mathematical, Physical, and Engineering Sciences*, *376*(2133), 20180081. DOI: 10.1098/rsta.2018.0081 PMID: 30322997

Floridi, L. (2020). *The Ethics of Artificial Intelligence*. Oxford University Press.

Floridi, L., & Cowls, J. (2019). A unified framework of five principles for AI in society. *Harvard Data Science Review*, *1*(1).

Floridi, L., Cowls, J., Beltrametti, M., Chatila, R., Chazerand, P., Dignum, V., Luetge, C., Madelin, R., Pagallo, U., Rossi, F., Schafer, B., Valcke, P., & Vayena, E. (2018). AI4People—An ethical framework for a good AI society: Opportunities, risks, principles, and recommendations. *Minds and Machines*, *28*(4), 689–707. DOI: 10.1007/s11023-018-9482-5 PMID: 30930541

Florindo, F. (2023). ChatGPT: A threat or an opportunity for scientists? *Perspectives of Earth and Space Scientists*, *4*(1), e2023CN000212. Advance online publication. DOI: 10.1029/2023CN000212

Food and Agriculture Organization. (2022). *The state of food and agriculture 2022: Leveraging automation in agriculture for transforming agrifood systems.*https://www.fao.org/3/cb9479en/cb9479en.pdf

Fornell, C., & Larcker, D. F. (1981). Evaluating structural equation models with unobservable variables and measurement error. *JMR, Journal of Marketing Research*, *18*(1), 39–50. DOI: 10.1177/002224378101800104

Forward Pathway US College Database. (2025). The impact of digital social science and AI has increased. https://www.forwardpathway.us/the-rise-of-digital-social-science-and-ai-impact#:~:text=Florida%20State%20University%20%282025,data%2Ddriven%20world.&text=and%20let%20me%20tell,data%2Ddriven%20world.&text=the%20College%20of%20Social,data%2Ddriven%20world.&text=designed%20to%20equip%20students,data%2Ddriven%20world

Francisco, M. (2023). The intersection of AI and sociology: New methods for understanding migration trends. *Journal of Applied Social Science Methods*, *18*(3), 145–160.

Frangos, P. (2022). An integrative literature review on leadership and organizational readiness for AI. *International Conference on AI Research, 4*(1), 145–152. DOI: 10.34190/icair.4.1.834

Freese, J., & Peterson, A. (2021). Replication and reproducibility in the age of AI. *Social Science Research*, *70*, 81–96.

Freire, P. (2018). *Pedagogy of the oppressed.* 50th Anniversary Edition. Bloomsbury Academic.

Freire, P. (1970). Pedagogy of the oppressed. *Continuum : an Interdisciplinary Journal on Continuity of Care.*

Frey, C. B., & Osborne, M. A. (2017). The future of employment: How susceptible are jobs to computerization? *Technological Forecasting and Social Change*, *114*, 254–280. DOI: 10.1016/j.techfore.2016.08.019

Funa, A. A., & Gabay, R. A. (2025). Policy guidelines and recommendations on AI use in teaching and learning: A meta-synthesis study. *Social Sciences & Humanities Open*, *11*, 101221. DOI: 10.1016/j.ssaho.2024.101221

Gaber, S. A., Shahat, H. A., Alkhateeb, I. A., Al Hasan, S. A., Alqatam, M. A., Almughyirah, S. M., & Kamel, M. K. (2023). Faculty members' awareness of Artificial Intelligence and its relationship to technology acceptance and digital competencies at King Faisal University. *International Journal of Learning. Teaching and Educational Research*, *22*(7), 473–496. DOI: 10.26803/ijlter.22.7.25

Gabriel, F. A., & Pereira, A. L. (2023). Perceptions about the role of the philosophy teacher in the process of the philosophical experience. *Revista Ibero-Americana de Estudos em Educação*, *18*, 1. DOI: 10.21723/riaee.v18i00.16948

Gagné, R. M., Wager, W. W., Golas, K. C., & Keller, J. M. (2005). Principles of Instructional Design *(5th ed.)*. Wadsworth/Thomson Learning.

Gagné, R. M. (1985). *The conditions of learning and theory of instruction* (4th ed.). Holt, Rinehart, and Winston.

Gamkrelidze, D., Mchedlishvili, G., Prentice, G., & Verma, A. (2024, September 3). *AI-Powered Treasury: Georgia's Innovative Approach to Managing Payment Risks*. IMF PFM Blog. https://blog-pfm.imf.org/en/pfmblog/2024/09/ai-powered-treasury

Garvey, K. V., Craig, K. J. T., Russell, R. G., Novak, L. L., Moore, D. E., & Miller, B. M. (2022). Considering clinician competencies for the implementation of Artificial Intelligence–based tools in health care: Findings from a scoping review. *JMIR Medical Informatics*, *10*(11), e37478. DOI: 10.2196/37478 PMID: 36318697

Garvie, C., Bedoya, A. M., & Frankle, J. (2016). *The perpetual line-up: Unregulated police face recognition in America*. Georgetown Law Center on Privacy & Technology.

Garzotto, F., Paolini, P., & Sabiescu, A. (2010, June). Interactive storytelling for children. In *Proceedings of the 9th International Conference on Interaction Design and Children* (pp. 356-359). DOI: 10.1145/1810543.1810613

Gatys, L. A., Ecker, A. S., & Bethge, M. (2016). Image style transfer using convolutional neural networks. In *Proceedings of the IEEE Conference on Computer Vision and Pattern Recognition* (pp. 2414–2423). DOI: 10.1109/CVPR.2016.265

Gekara, V. O., & Thanh Nguyen, V. (2018). New technologies and the transformation of work and skills: A study of computerisation and automation of Australian container terminals. *New Technology, Work and Employment*, *33*(3), 219–233. DOI: 10.1111/ntwe.12118

Gemini. (n.d.). Gemini 2.0 Flash. Retrieved from: https://gemini.google.com/app

Georgia Technology Authority (GTA). (2024). *Office of Artificial Intelligence.* https://ai.georgia.gov/

Georgia Technology Authority (GTA). (2025, February 25). *State of Georgia: AI Roadmap and Governance Framework.* https://ai.georgia.gov/blog/2025-02-25/state-georgia-ai-roadmap-and-governance-framework

Ghimire, A., & Edwards, J. (2024). From guidelines to governance: A study of AI policies in education. In: Olney, A.M., Chounta, IA., Liu, Z., Santos, O.C., Bittencourt, I.I. (eds), In *Artificial Intelligence* DOI: 10.1007/978-3-031-64312-5_36

Gibboney, R. A. (1987). A critique of Madeline Hunter's Teaching Model from Dewey's perspective. *Educational Leadership*, *44*(5), 46–50.

Gillespie, T. (2021). *The platform society: Public values in a connective world.* Oxford University Press.

Giroux, H. A. (2020). *On critical pedagogy.* Bloomsbury Publishing. DOI: 10.5040/9781350145016

Giunti, G., & Doherty, C. P. (2024). Cocreating an automated mHealth apps systematic review process with generative AI: Design science research approach. *JMIR Medical Education, 10,* e48949. DOI: 10.2196/48949 PMID: 38345839

Gkinko, L., & Elbanna, A. (2023). The appropriation of conversational AI in the workplace: A taxonomy of AI chatbot users. *International Journal of Information Management, 69*(December 2021), 102568. DOI: 10.1016/j.ijinfomgt.2022.102568

Goenka, N., Patnaik, D., & Pradhan, B. B. (2024). Impact of Artificial Intelligence on Virtual Teacher-learner Engagement: Redefining Educational Dynamics. In Bansal, R., Chakir, A., Hafaz Ngah, A., Rabby, F., & Jain, A. (Eds.), *AI algorithms and ChatGPT for student engagement in online learning*. IGI Global., DOI: 10.4018/979-8-3693-4268-8.ch013

Gökçearslan, Ş., Durak, H., Günbatar, M. S., Atman Uslu, N., & Elçi, A. N. (2024). Generative Artificial Intelligence (GENAI) literacy scale: Validity and reliability. *4th International Conference on Scientific and Academic Research* (pp.1-8). Konya, Türkiye.

Golding, C. (2008). The philosophy teacher as guide. *Proceedings of the XXII World Congress of Philosophy*, 27, 29–37.

Goleman, D. (1995). *Emotional intelligence: Why it can matter more than IQ.* Bantam Books.

Gondwe, G. (2024). Artificial Intelligence, Journalism, and the Ubuntu Robot in Sub-Saharan Africa: Towards a Normative Framework. *Digital Journalism (Abingdon, England)*. Advance online publication. DOI: 10.1080/21670811.2024.2311258

Gonzalez, M.. (2021). *Big data and behavioral science: AI's role in sociology and psychology*. Springer.

Goodfellow, I., Bengio, Y., & Courville, A. (2018). *Deep learning*. MIT Press.

Gourlay, L. (2021). *Posthumanism and the digital university: Texts, bodies, and materialities*. Bloomsbury Academic. DOI: 10.5040/9781350038202

Grimmer, J., Roberts, M. E., & Stewart, B. (2021). Machine learning for social science: An agnostic approach. *Annual Review of Political Science*, *24*(1), 395–419. DOI: 10.1146/annurev-polisci-053119-015921

Grimmer, J., Roberts, M. E., & Stewart, B. M. (2021). The influence of social media on political discourse: Insights from AI-driven analysis. *The American Political Science Review*, *115*(2), 482–497.

Grok. (n.d.). Grok 3. Retrieved from: https://grok.com/

Grote, M., Lysholm Faber, H. C., & Gasparini, A. (2024). Artificial Intelligence in PhD education: New perspectives for research libraries. *LIBER Quarterly*, *34*(1), 1–29. DOI: 10.53377/lq.18137

Günay, M. (2004). *Metinlerle felsefeye giriş*. Karahan Kitabevi.

Guney, M., & Ala, R. (2021). AI and risk management in the public sector. *Public Management Review*, *23*(6), 814–832.

Guo, Q. (2024). Prompting change: Chatgpt's impact on digital humanities pedagogy–A case study in art history. *International Journal of Humanities and Arts Computing*, *18*(1), 58–78. DOI: 10.3366/ijhac.2024.0321

Gupta, A. (2019). AI and the future of public services. *Public Administration Review*, *79*(4), 556–563.

Gupta, M., & Yang, Y. (2024). ChatGPT usage and attitudes are driven by perceptions of usefulness, ease of use, risks, and psycho-social impact: A study among university students in the UAE. *Frontiers in Education*, *9*, 1414758. DOI: 10.3389/feduc.2024.1414758

Gurari, D., Li, Q., Stangl, A. J., Guo, A., Lin, C., Grauman, K., & Bigham, J. P. (2018). Vizwiz grand challenge: Answering visual questions from blind people. In *Proceedings of the IEEE conference on computer vision and pattern recognition* (pp. 3608–3617). https://doi.org/DOI: 10.1109/CVPR.2018.00380

Habib, H., Jelani, S. A. K., & Najla, S. (2022). Revolutionizing inclusion: AI in Adaptive Learning for students with disabilities. *Multidisciplinary Science Journal, 1*(01), 1–11.

Habibi, A., Muhaimin, M., Danibao, B. K., Wibowo, Y. G., Wahyuni, S., & Octavia, A. (2023). ChatGPT in higher education learning: Acceptance and use. *Computers and Education: Artificial Intelligence, 5*, 100190. DOI: 10.1016/j.caeai.2023.100190

Habibipour, A. (2024). Responsible living labs: What can go wrong? *Journal of Information, Communication, and Ethics in Society, 22*(2), 205–218. Advance online publication. DOI: 10.1108/JICES-11-2023-0137

Hacker, P. (2023). The European AI liability directives – Critique of a half-hearted approach and lessons for the future. *Computer Law & Security Review, 51*, 105871. DOI: 10.1016/j.clsr.2023.105871

Hadjistassou, S., & Avgousti, M. I. (2024). Augmented reality and virtual reality in CALL. *The Bloomsbury handbook of language learning and technology*, 226–239.

Hair, J. F., Black, W. C., Babin, B. J., & Anderson, R. E. (2010). *Multivariate data analysis*. Pearson.

Hakala-Ausperk, C. (2024). The Experimental Library: A Guide to Taking Risks, Failing Forward, and Creating Change. *Public Libraries, 63*(3), 53–55. Retrieved April 9, 2025, from https://ez.lib.jjay.cuny.edu/login?url=https://www.proquest.com/magazines/experimental-library-guide-aking-risks-failing/docview/3163936979/se-2

Halaweh, M. (2023). ChatGPT in education: Strategies for responsible implementation. *Contemporary Educational Technology, 15*(2), ep421. Advance online publication. DOI: 10.30935/cedtech/13036

Hamd, Z. Y., Alorainy, A. I., Aldhahi, M. I., Gareeballah, A., Alsubaie, N. F., Alshanaiber, S. A., Almudayhesh, N. S., Alyousef, R. A., AlNiwaider, R. A., Moammar, L. A. B., & Abuzaid, M. (2024). Evaluation of the impact of Artificial Intelligence on clinical practice of radiology in Saudi Arabia. *Journal of Multidisciplinary Healthcare, 17*, 4745–4756. DOI: 10.2147/JMDH.S465508 PMID: 39411200

Hamzah, W. W., Ismail, I., Yusof, M. K., Saany, S. M., & Yacob, A. (2021). Using learning analytics to explore responses from student conversations with chatbot for education. *International Journal of Engineering Pedagogy, 11*(6), 70–84. DOI: 10.3991/ijep.v11i6.23475

Hannah, A. (2024). Ethical considerations for AI in higher education: Ensuring fairness... https://www.liaisonedu.com/resources/blog/ethical-considerations-for-ai-in-higher-education-ensuring-fairness-and-transparency/

Harari, Y. N. (2018). *21 Lessons for the 21st Century*. Spiegel & Grau.

Harris, C. G. (2024). Combining Human-in-the-Loop Systems and AI fairness toolkits to reduce age bias in AI job hiring algorithms. *2024 IEEE International Conference on Big Data and Smart Computing (BigComp)*, 60–66. DOI: 10.1109/BigComp60711.2024.00019

Hassouni, A., & Mellor, N. (2024). Perceptions of AI integration in the UAE's creative sector. *Informatics (MDPI), 11*(4), 82. DOI: 10.3390/informatics11040082

Haug, B. S., & Mork, S. M. (2021). Taking 21st-century skills from vision to classroom: What teachers highlight as supportive professional development in the light of new demands from educational reforms. *Teaching and Teacher Education*https://www.sciencedirect.com/science/article/pii/S0742051X2100010X

Hayes, P., Fitzpatrick, N., & Ferrández, J. M. (2024). From applied ethics and ethical principles to virtue and narrative in AI practices. *AI and Ethics*. Advance online publication. DOI: 10.1007/s43681-024-00472-z

He, C., Teng, R., & Song, J. (2024). Linking employees' challenge-hindrance appraisals toward AI to service performance: The influences of job crafting, job insecurity, and AI knowledge. *International Journal of Contemporary Hospitality Management, 36*(3), 975–994. DOI: 10.1108/IJCHM-07-2022-0848

Hedayet, H., & Haseen, F. (2024). Artificial Intelligence in public health: A review article. *Bangladesh Journal of Bioethics, 15*(2), 15–19. DOI: 10.62865/bjbio.v15i2.108

Heilala, J., Shibani, A., & Freitas, A. G. (2023). The requirements for heutagogical attunement within STEAM education. [IJET]. *International Journal of Emerging Technologies in Learning, 18*(16), 19–35. DOI: 10.3991/ijet.v18i16.42313

Hennig, N. (2018, January 13). *About Nicole Hennig*. Nicolehennig.com. https://nicolehennig.com/bio/

Hennig, N., Halla, M., Pagowsky, N., & Wallace, N. (2023, May 26). *AI Literacy in the Age of ChatGPT*. The University of Arizona. https://libguides.library.arizona.edu/ai-literacy-instructors

Hennig, N., Halla, M., Pagowsky, N., & Wallace, N. (2023, May 26). *Student guide to ChatGPT*. The University of Arizona. https://libguides.library.arizona.edu/students-chatgpt

Hidayatullah, A. F., Kalinaki, K., Aslam, M. M., Zakari, R. Y., & Shafik, W. (2023). Fine-Tuning BERT-Based Models for Negative Content Identification on Indonesian Tweets. *ICITDA 2023 - Proceedings of the 2023 8th International Conference on Information Technology and Digital Applications*. DOI: 10.1109/ICITDA60835.2023.10427046

Hillier, M. (2023, March 30). *A proposed AI literacy framework*. Teche. https://teche.mq.edu.au/2023/03/a-proposed-ai-literacy-framework/

Hirschi, A. (2018). The fourth industrial revolution: Issues and implications for career research and practice. *The Career Development Quarterly*, *66*(3), 192–204. DOI: 10.1002/cdq.12142

Hirsh-Pasek, K., Zosh, J. M., Hadani, H. S., Golinkoff, R. M., Clark, K., Donohue, C., & Wartella, E. (2022). *A whole new world: Education meets the metaverse*. Brookings Institution.

HistoricTalk. (n.d.). HistoricTalk: Your gateway to the past. Retrieved https://www.historictalk.com/

HistoryChatAI. (n.d.). History Chat AI – Interactive Historical Conversations. Retrieved from: https://www.yeschat.ai/

HM Revenue & Customs. (2020). *Annual Report and Accounts 2019–20*. https://www.gov.uk/government/publications

Hmelo-Silver, C. E. (2004). Problem-based learning: What and how do students learn? *Educational Psychology Review*, *16*(3), 235–266. DOI: 10.1023/B:EDPR.0000034022.16470.f3

Holmes, W., Bialik, M., & Fadel, C. (2023). *Artificial intelligence in education: Promises and implications for teaching and learning* (2nd ed.). Center for Curriculum Redesign.

Holmes, W., Nand, N., & Georgiou, Y. (2023). Ethical personalization in immersive classrooms. *British Journal of Educational Technology*, *54*(4), 785–803. DOI: 10.1111/bjet.13299

Holmes, W., Porayska-Pomsta, K., Holstein, K., Sutherland, E., Baker, T., Shum, S. B., Santos, O. C., Rodrigo, M. T., Cukurova, M., Bittencourt, I. I., & Koedinger, K. R. (2022). Ethics of AI in education: Towards a community-wide framework. *International Journal of Artificial Intelligence in Education, 32*(3), 504–526. DOI: 10.1007/s40593-021-00239-1

Holstein, K., & Aleven, V. (2022). Designing for Human–AI Complementarity in K-12 Education. *AI Magazine, 43*(2), 239–248. DOI: 10.1002/aaai.12058

Holstein, K., McLaren, B. M., & Aleven, V. (2018). Student learning benefits of a mixed-reality teacher awareness tool in AI-enhanced classrooms. In Penstein Rosé, C. (Eds.), *Artificial Intelligence in education. AIED 2018* (pp. 154–168). Lecture Notes in Computer Science. Springer International Publishing., DOI: 10.1007/978-3-319-93843-1_12

Holstein, K., McLaren, B. M., & Aleven, V. (2019). Co-designing a real-time classroom orchestration tool to support teacher-AI complementarity. *Journal of Learning Analytics, 6*(2), 27–52. DOI: 10.18608/jla.2019.62.3

Holstein, K., Wortman Vaughan, J., Daumé, H.III, Dudik, M., & Wallach, H. (2019). Improving fairness in machine learning systems: What do industry practitioners need? In *Proceedings of the 2019 CHI Conference on Human Factors in Computing Systems* (pp. 1–16). https://doi.org/DOI: 10.1145/3290605.3300830

Hood Cattaneo, K. (2017). Telling active learning pedagogies apart: From theory to practice. *Journal of New Approaches in Educational Research, 6*(2), 144–152. DOI: 10.7821/naer.2017.7.237

Hooper, D., Coughlan, J., & Mullen, M. (2008). Structural equation modelling: Guidelines for determining model fit. *Electronic Journal of Business Research Methods, 6*(1), 53–60.

Hradecky, D., Kennell, J., Cai, W., & Davidson, R. (2022). Organizational readiness to adopt Artificial Intelligence in the exhibition sector in Western Europe. *International Journal of Information Management, 65*(May 2021), 102497. DOI: 10.1016/j.ijinfomgt.2022.102497

Huang, A. Y., Lu, O. H., & Yang, S. J. (2023). Effects of artificial intelligence-enabled personalized recommendations on learners' learning engagement, motivation, and outcomes in a flipped classroom. *Computers & Education, 194*, 104684. Advance online publication. DOI: 10.1016/j.compedu.2022.104684

Huang, C. A., Vaswani, A., Uszkoreit, J., Shazeer, N., Simon, I., Hawthorne, C., & Eck, D. (2020). Music transformer: Generating music with long-term structure. *Proceedings of the International Conference on Learning Representations* (ICLR).

Huang, R., Liu, D., & Zhuang, M. (2023). Emotional design in virtual reality learning. *Educational Technology Research and Development, 71*(2), 329–350. DOI: 10.1007/s11423-023-10112-6

Hughes, C. (2020). International schools and global citizenship education. In Akkari, A., & Maleq, K. (Eds.), *Global citizenship education*. Springer., DOI: 10.1007/978-3-030-44617-8_13

Humy.ai. (n.d.). Humy. Retrieved from: https://www.humy.ai/

Hwang, G. J., & Chien, Y. H. (2022). Exploring the effects of VR-based immersive environments on knowledge retention. *Interactive Learning Environments, 30*(4), 516–533.

Hwang, G. J., Xie, H., Wah, B. W., & Gašević, D. (2020). Vision, challenges, roles and research issues of artificial intelligence in education. *Computers and Education: Artificial Intelligence, 1*, 100001. Advance online publication. DOI: 10.1016/j.caeai.2020.100001

Hyatt, S. E., & Owenz, M. B. (2024). Using universal design for learning and artificial ıntelligence to support students with disabilities. *College Teaching*, •••, 1–8. DOI: 10.1080/87567555.2024.2313468

Icivics. (n.d.). Icivics. Retrieved from: https://vision.icivics.org/

IDFI. (2020, July 1). *Promoting Greater Transparency and Ethical Standards of Using Artificial Intelligence (AI) in Georgia*. https://idfi.ge/en/promoting-greater-transparency-and-ethical-standards-of-using-artificial-intelligence-in-georgia

Ijaz, K., Bogdanovych, A., & Trescak, T. (2017). Virtual worlds vs books and videos in history education. *Interactive Learning Environments, 25*(7), 904–929. DOI: 10.1080/10494820.2016.1225099

IMF PFM Blog. (2024, September 3). *AI-Powered Treasury: Georgia's Innovative Approach to Managing Payment Risks*. https://blog-pfm.imf.org/en/pfmblog/2024/09/ai-powered-treasury

Investors Council. (2022, September 13). *Application and Integration of Artificial Intelligence in customs formalities*. https://investorscouncil.ge/en/news/news/application-and-integration-of-artificial-intelligence-in-customs-formalities/

Ishak, S. S. M., & Newton, S. (2016). An innovation resistance factor model. *Construction Economics and Building*, *16*(3), 87–103. DOI: 10.5130/AJCEB.v16i3.5164

Ismaeil, M. K. L., & Lalla, A. F. (2024). The role and impact of Artificial Intelligence on supply chain management: Efficiency, challenges, and strategic implementation. *Journal of Ecohumanism*, *3*(4), 89–106. DOI: 10.62754/joe.v3i4.3461

Isotani, S., Bettencourt, I. I., & Walker, E. (2023). Artificial Intelligence and Educational Policy: Bridging Research and Practice. *AIED* 2023. *Communications in Computer and Information Science*, *1831*, 63–68. DOI: 10.1007/978-3-031-36336-8_9

İzgi, F. D. (2024). AI's global impact: Unveiling its origins and development, its roles across cultures and in child therapy field. In Ricahyono, S. (Ed.), *The power of words in an AI-driven world: Exploring the interplay of language, culture, and communication* (pp. 14–26). Sketsamedya.

Jackson, V., Delacruz, S., & Harry, D. (2021). Culturally relevant teaching for the 21st Century. *Georgia Journal of Literacy*, *44*(1), 41–66. DOI: 10.56887/galiteracy.15

Jahnke, I., Lee, Y., & Kumar, S. (2022). Ethical learning design in immersive education. *Journal of Educational Technology & Society*, *25*(2), 19–32.

Jaiswal, A., Arun, C. J., & Varma, A. (2022). Rebooting employees: Upskilling for Artificial Intelligence in multinational corporations. *International Journal of Human Resource Management*, *33*(6), 1179–1208. DOI: 10.1080/09585192.2021.1891114

Jandrić, P., Knox, J., Besley, T., Ryberg, T., Suoranta, J., & Hayes, S. (2018). Postdigital science and education. *Educational Philosophy and Theory*, *50*(10), 893–899. DOI: 10.1080/00131857.2018.1454000

Jasanoff, S. (2021). *The ethics of AI and human rights*. Harvard University Press.

Jasrai, L. (2025). Extending UTAUT model to examine the usages of ChatGPT among Indian students in higher education: A structural equation modelling approach. *The TQM Journal*. Advance online publication. DOI: 10.1108/TQM-12-2024-0498

Jebreen, K., Radwan, E., Rebai, W. K., Alattar, E., Radwan, A., Safi, W., Radwan, W., & Alajez, M. (2024). Perceptions of undergraduate medical students on Artificial Intelligence in Medicine: Mixed-methods survey study from Palestine. *BMC Medical Education*, *24*(1), 507. Advance online publication. DOI: 10.1186/s12909-024-05465-4 PMID: 38714993

Jensen, S. S. (2023). The art of facilitating philosophical dialogues from the perspective of teachers. *Educational Studies*, *49*(1), 116–130. DOI: 10.1080/03055698.2020.1835612

Jivani, A. I. (2020). Gender lens to the future of work. *Daedalus*, *149*(1), 134–143. DOI: 10.1162/daed_a_01778

Jobin, A., Ienca, M., & Vayena, E. (2019). The global landscape of AI ethics guidelines. *Nature Machine Intelligence*, *1*(9), 389–399. DOI: 10.1038/s42256-019-0088-2

John, D. Kelleher. (2015). *FMLPDA_SampleChapter_InformationBasedLearning*. 1–31. https://machinelearningbook.com/wp-content/uploads/2015/07/FMLPDA_SampleChapter_InformationBasedLearning.pdf

Johnson, K., & Li, W. (2022). Automating qualitative research: Benefits and risks. *Qualitative Research*, *23*(3), 335–351.

Kaggle. (2020). COVID-19 data science and AI challenges: Insights from the pandemic. Kaggle.

Kalyuga, S. (2022). Managing cognitive load in immersive learning design. *Educational Psychology Review*, *34*(3), 805–824.

Kamath, R. (2022). Artificial Intelligence and public governance: Ethical implications and administrative reforms. *Journal of Public Affairs*, *22*(1), e2498. DOI: 10.1002/pa.2498

Kamath, S. (2022). A Study on the Impact of Artificial Intelligence on Society. *International Journal of Applied Science and Engineering*, *10*(1), 31–39. DOI: 10.30954/2322-0465.2.2021.3

Kamilaris, A., & Prenafeta-Boldú, F. X. (2018). Deep learning in agriculture: A survey. *Computers and Electronics in Agriculture*, *147*, 70–90. DOI: 10.1016/j.compag.2018.02.016

Kaputa, V., Loučanová, E., & Tejerina-Gaite, F. A. (2022). Digital transformation in higher education institutions as a driver of social-oriented innovations. In C. Păunescu, K. L. Lepik, N. Spencer (Eds.). *Social innovation in higher education. Innovation, technology, and knowledge management.* Springer. DOI: 10.1007/978-3-030-84044-0_4

Karanasiou, A. P., & Pinotsis, D. A. (2017). A study into the layers of automated decision-making: Emergent normative and legal aspects of deep learning. *International Review of Law Computers & Technology*, *31*(2), 170–187. DOI: 10.1080/13600869.2017.1298499

Karatsiori, M. (2023). In the pursuit of "Quality Education": From ancient times to the digital era, can there be a consensus? In *Cogent Education* (Vol. 10, Issue 2). DOI: 10.1080/2331186X.2023.2286817

Kashima, H., Oyama, S., Arai, H., & Mori, J. (2024). Trustworthy human computation: A survey. *Artificial Intelligence Review, 57*(12), 322. DOI: 10.1007/s10462-024-10974-1

Kasneci, E., Sessler, K., Küchemann, S., Bannert, M., Dementieva, D., Fischer, F., Gasser, U., Groh, G., Günnemann, S., Hüllermeier, E., Krusche, S., Kutyniok, G., Michaeli, T., Nerdel, C., Pfeffer, J., Poquet, O., Sailer, M., Schmidt, A., Seidel, T., & Kasneci, G. (2023). ChatGPT for good? On opportunities and challenges of large language models for education. *Learning and Individual Differences, 103*, 102274. Advance online publication. DOI: 10.1016/j.lindif.2023.102274

Kasztelnik, K. (2024). *The Study on the Impact of Business Artificial Intelligence Innovation on Fair Value Investments in the United States The Study on the Impact of Business Artificial Intelligence Innovation on Fair Value Investments in the U.S. January.*

Katzenbach, C. (2021). "AI will fix this" – The technical, discursive, and political turn to AI in governing communication. *Big Data & Society, 8*(2), 20539517211046182. Advance online publication. DOI: 10.1177/20539517211046182

Kaur, T. (2024). AI Architectures and Technologies for Raising Society 5.0. In *Artificial Intelligence and Society 5.0: Issues, Opportunities, and Challenges*. DOI: 10.1201/9781003397052-2

Kaur, B., & Kour, M. (2024, September). Exploring the Growth and Future research directions on Robo advisors: A Bibliometric Study. In *2024 International Conference on Advances in Computing Research on Science Engineering and Technology (ACROSET)* (pp. 1–6). IEEE. DOI: 10.1109/ACROSET62108.2024.10743870

Kaur, S., Budhraja, K., Pahuja, A., Nayyar, V., & Saluja, S. (2024). *Leveraging Artificial Intelligence in Education.*, DOI: 10.4018/979-8-3693-6660-8.ch010

Kavitha, K. B., Kumar, P., Nithiya, T. K. S., & Suguna, A. (2023). Implementation of Artificial Intelligence in education. *International Research Journal of Computer Science, 10*(5), 104–108. DOI: 10.26562/irjcs.2023.v1005.01

Kelleher, J. D., Mac Carthy, M., & Korvir, B. (2015). *Fundamentals of machine learning for predictive data analytics: Algorithms, worked examples, and case studies*. MIT Press.

Keller, J. M. (1987). Development and use of the ARCS Model of instructional design. *Journal of Instructional Development : JID, 10*(3), 2–10. DOI: 10.1007/BF02905780

Keller, J. M. (2010). *Motivational design for learning and performance: The ARCS Model approach*. Springer. DOI: 10.1007/978-1-4419-1250-3

Khalil, A., Haqdad, A., & Sultana, N. (2023). Metaverse integration in Pakistani higher education: Potentials and pitfalls. *Journal of Positive School Psychology*, *7*(4), 1023–1042.

Khalil, A., & Jumani, N. B. (2024). Culturally responsive metaverse pedagogy: Challenges and opportunities in Pakistan. *Journal of Emerging Educational Technology*, *11*(1), 54–72.

Khan Academy. https://www.khanacademy.org/

Khanmigo. (n.d.). What is Khanmigo? Retrieved from: https://www.khanmigo.ai/

Khogali, H. O., & Mekid, S. (2024). Perception and ethical challenges for the future of AI as encountered by surveyed new engineers. *Societies (Basel, Switzerland)*, *14*(12), 271. DOI: 10.3390/soc14120271

Kienstra, N., Imants, J., Karskens, M., & van der Heijden, P. G. (2015). Doing philosophy effectively: Student learning in classroom teaching. *PLoS One*, *10*(9), e0137590. DOI: 10.1371/journal.pone.0137590 PMID: 26379267

Kim, H. J. (2023). A study on the intentions of ChatGPT users using the extended UTAUT model. *Journal of Digital Contents Society*, *24*(7), 1465–1473. DOI: 10.9728/dcs.2023.24.7.1465

Kitchin, R. (2021). *The data revolution: Big data, open data, data infrastructures, and their consequences*. SAGE Publications.

Kızıltan, Ö. (2012). Felsefe öğretimi sorunları ve yeni yaklaşımlar. *Eğitim ve Öğretim Araştırmaları Dergisi*, *1*(4), 334–342.

Klašnja-Milićević, A., Ivanović, M., & Budimac, Z. (2017). Data science in education: Big data and learning analytics. *Computer Applications in Engineering Education*, *25*(6), 1066–1078. DOI: 10.1002/cae.21844

Ko, C. R., & Chiu, M. H. (2024, October 25). How Can Academic Librarians Support Generative AI Literacy: An Analysis of Library Guides Using the ACRL Information Literacy Framework. *Proceedings of the Association for Information Science and Technology*, *61*(1), 977–979. DOI: 10.1002/pra2.1159

Koç, E. (2020). Felsefe öğretimine giriş. In Manav, F. (Ed.), *Ana Hatlarıyla Ortaöğretimde Felsefe Grubu Öğretimi içinde* (pp. 3–16). Pegem. DOI: 10.14527/9786257228640.01

Kooli, C. (2023). Chatbots in education and research: A critical examination of ethical implications and solutions. *Sustainability (Basel), 15*(7), 5614. DOI: 10.3390/su15075614

Kopp, M., & Gröblinger, O. (2023). Conditions for AI support of Open Educational Resources at HEIs. In *Proceedings of the Innovating Higher Education Conference 2023.* European Association of Distance Teaching Universities.

Köroğlu, Y. (2017). *Yapay zekânın teorik ve pratik sınırları* [Theoretical and practical possibilities of artificial intelligence]. Bogaziçi Üniversitesi Yayınevi.

Koukis, N., & Jimoyiannis, A. (2021). Connectivist learning in virtual learning environments. *Education and Information Technologies, 26*, 5759–5778. DOI: 10.1007/s10639-021-10566-0

Kour, M., & Kaur, R. (2024). "AI and Influencer Marketing: Redefining the Future of Social Media Marketing in Industry 6.0". In Advanced Businesses in Industry 6.0 (pp. 87-103). IGI Global. DOI: 10.4018/979-8-3693-3108-8.ch007

Kozma, R. B. (1991). Learning with Media. *Sage Journals, 61*(2), 179–211.

Kozma, R. B. (1994a). Will media influence learning? Reframing the debate. *Educational Technology Research and Development, 42*(2), 7–19. DOI: 10.1007/BF02299087

Kozma, R. B. (1994b). A reply: Media and methods. *Educational Technology Research and Development, 42*(3), 11–14. DOI: 10.1007/BF02298091

Kumar, A., & Kumar, L. (2024). Navigating the future: The ethical, societal and technological implications of Artificial Intelligence. *Global Journal of Research in Engineering & Computer Sciences, 4*(2), 83–104. DOI: 10.5281/zenodo.10966785&#8203

Kumari, M. (2023). Perception of dental students in incorporating Artificial Intelligence into dental education. *Journal of Advanced Sciences, 2*(1), 41–45. DOI: 10.58935/joas.v2i1.27

Kuper, A., and Kuper, J. (1985). *The Social Science Encyclopaedia.*

Kurzweil, R. (2005). *The singularity is near: When humans transcend biology.* Penguin Books.

Kutlucan, E., & Seferoğlu, S. S. (2024). Eğitimde Yapay Zekâ Kullanımı: ChatGPT'nin KEFE ve PEST Analizi. *Türk Eğitim Bilimleri Dergisi, 22*(2), 1059–1083. DOI: 10.37217/tebd.1368821

Kuziemski, M., & Misuraca, G. (2020). AI governance in the public sector: The need for democratic transparency. *Government Information Quarterly*, *37*(3), 101398.

Kye, B., Jung, Y., & Kim, M. (2021). XR learning implementation for medical education in Korea. *Medical Education Online*, *26*(1), 1963958. DOI: 10.1080/10872981.2021.1963958

LaCroix, T. (2022). Moral dilemmas for moral machines. *AI and Ethics*, *2*(4), 737–746. DOI: 10.1007/s43681-022-00134-y

LaVelle, J. M., Ford, T., & Montenegro, M. (2023). Artificial Intelligence and the future of evaluation education: Possibilities and Prototypes. *New Directions for Evaluation*, *2023*(178–179), 97–109. DOI: 10.1002/ev.20564

Lee, K. F. (2018). *AI Superpowers: China, Silicon Valley, and the New World Order*. Houghton Mifflin Harcourt.

Lee, I., Grover, S., Martin, F., Pillai, S., & Malyn-Smith, J. (2020). Computational thinking from a disciplinary perspective: Integrating computational thinking in K-12 science, mathematics, and computer science education. *Journal of Science Education and Technology*, *29*, 1–8. DOI: 10.1007/s10956-019-09803-w

Lee, S., Jones-Jang, S. M., Chung, M., Kim, N., & Choi, J. (2024). Who is using ChatGPT and why? Extending the Unified Theory of Acceptance and Use of Technology (UTAUT) model. *Information Research*, *29*(1), 54–72. DOI: 10.47989/ir291647

Lee, S., & Kim, Y. (2021). Personalizing virtual instruction through AI avatars. *Computers in Human Behavior*, *118*, 106709. DOI: 10.1016/j.chb.2021.106709

Lee, T., Wen, Y., Chan, M. Y., Azam, A. B., Looi, C. K., Taib, S., Ooi, C. H., Huang, L. H., Xie, Y., & Cai, Y. (2022). Investigation of virtual & augmented reality classroom learning environments in university STEM education. *Interactive Learning Environments*, *32*(6), 2617–2632. DOI: 10.1080/10494820.2022.2155838

Leng, L. (2020). The role of philosophical inquiry in helping students engage in learning. *Frontiers in Psychology*, *11*, 449. DOI: 10.3389/fpsyg.2020.00449 PMID: 32265782

Lennon, R. P., Fraleigh, R., Scoy, L. J. V., Keshaviah, A., Hu, X. C., Snyder, B., Miller, E. L., Calo, W. A., Zgierska, A., & Griffin, C. (2021). Developing and Testing an Automated Qualitative Assistant (AQUA) to support qualitative analysis. *Family Medicine and Community Health*, *9*(Suppl 1), e001287. DOI: 10.1136/fmch-2021-001287 PMID: 34824135

LexiQamus. (n.d.). LexiQamus Ottoman Turkish Linguistic Analyze Device. Retrieved from: https://www.lexiqamus.com

Liakin, D., Cardoso, W., & Liakina, N. (2017). Mobilizing instruction in a second-language context: Learners' perceptions of two speech technologies. *Languages (Basel, Switzerland)*, *2*(3), 11. DOI: 10.3390/languages2030011

Liakos, K. G., Busato, P., Moshou, D., Pearson, S., & Bochtis, D. (2018). Machine learning in agriculture: A review. *Sensors (Basel)*, *18*(8), 2674. DOI: 10.3390/s18082674 PMID: 30110960

Lieberman, M. (2023). What Is ChatGPT and How Is It Used in Education? *Education Week*, *42*(18).

Liebrenz, M., Schleifer, R., Buadze, A., Bhugra, D., & Smith, A. (2023). Generating scholarly content with ChatGPT: Ethical challenges for medical publishing. *The Lancet. Digital Health*, *1-2*(3), e105–e106. Advance online publication. DOI: 10.1016/S2589-7500(23)00019-5 PMID: 36754725

Liew, J. (2024). Translating Vision into Reality for Early Education & Development. *Early Education and Development*, *35*(1), 1–2. Advance online publication. DOI: 10.1080/10409289.2024.2287684

Ligo, A. K., Rand, K., Bassett, J., Galaitsi, S., Trump, B. D., Jayabalasingham, B., Collins, T. R., & Linkov, I. (2021). Comparing the emergence of technical and social sciences research in Artificial Intelligence. *Frontiers of Computer Science*, *3*, 653235. Advance online publication. DOI: 10.3389/fcomp.2021.653235

Liljaniemi, A., & Paavilainen, H. (2020). Using Digital Twin Technology in Engineering Education-Course Concept to Explore Benefits and Barriers. *Open Engineering*, *10*(1), 377–385. Advance online publication. DOI: 10.1515/eng-2020-0040

Limna, P., Kraiwanit, T., Jangjarat, K., Klayklung, P., & Chocksathaporn, P. (2023). The use of ChatGPT in the digital era: Perspectives on chatbot implementation. *Journal of Applied Learning and Teaching*, *6*(1), 64–74. https://journals.sfu.ca/jalt/index.php/jalt/article/view/797/593

Lin, D., & Zou, R. (2024). Applications, risks, challenges, and future prospects of ChatGPT in electronic records management. *Journal of Artificial Intelligence Research*, *1*(1), 1–9. DOI: 10.70891/JAIR.2024.100021

Lipton, Z. C. (2022). The mythos of model interpretability. *Communications of the ACM*, *63*(6), 36–45.

Lissack, M., & Meagher, B. (2024). Responsible use of large language models: An Analogy with the Oxford Tutorial System. *She Ji: The Journal of Design, Economics, and Innovation*, *10*(4), 389–413. DOI: 10.1016/j.sheji.2024.11.001

Liu, Y. (2023). The role of online technology in quality course design. In Calhoun, C. (Ed.), *The Impact and Importance of Instructional Design in the Educational Landscape*. IGI Global., DOI: 10.4018/978-1-6684-8208-7.ch007

Liu, Y., & Curtin, J. (2025). Sustainability in higher education: Integrating leadership, policy, and teaching practices for a brighter future. In Taukeni, S. G., & Mollaoğlu, M. (Eds.), *Higher Education and Quality Assurance Practices*. IGI Global., DOI: 10.4018/979-8-3693-6765-0

Li, W. (2024). The influence of Artificial Intelligence on the education system. *Lecture Notes in Education Psychology and Public Media*, *65*(1), 137–142. DOI: 10.54254/2753-7048/65/20240158

Li, W., Zhang, X., Li, J., Yang, X., Li, D., & Liu, Y. (2024). An explanatory study of factors influencing engagement in AI education at the K-12 level: An extension of the classic TAM Model. *Scientific Reports*, *14*(1), 13922. Advance online publication. DOI: 10.1038/s41598-024-64363-3 PMID: 38886456

Li, Y., Wu, B., Huang, Y., Liu, J., Wu, J., & Luan, S. (2024). Warmth, competence, and the determinants of trust in Artificial Intelligence: A cross-sectional survey from China. *International Journal of Human-Computer Interaction*, *0*(0), 1–15. DOI: 10.1080/10447318.2024.2356909

Lo, C. K. (2023). What is the impact of ChatGPT on education? A rapid review of the literature. *Education Sciences*, *13*(4), 410. DOI: 10.3390/educsci13040410

Long, D., & Magerko, B. (2020). What is AI literacy? Competencies and design considerations. *Proceedings of the 2020 CHI Conference on Human Factors in Computing Systems*, 1-16. https://doi.org/DOI: 10.1145/3313831.3376727

Lu, J. (2024, January 6). *Artificial Intelligence (AI)*. Purdue Libraries. https://guides.lib.purdue.edu/ai

Luckin, R., Holmes, W., Griffiths, M., & Forcier, L. B. (2022). Educationally intelligent AI: Designing systems for equity and learning. *Pearson Education Report.*

Luckin, R., Holmes, W., Griffiths, M., & Forcier, L. B. (2023). Intelligence Unleashed: The role of AI in education. *Pearson Education White Paper.*

Luckin, R., Holmes, W., Griffiths, M., & Forcier, L. B. (2016). *Intelligence unleashed: An argument for AI in education*. Pearson Education.

Luckin, R., Holmes, W., Griffiths, M., & Forcier, L. B. (2016). *Intelligence Unleashed: An argument for AI in education*. Pearson.

Luckin, R., Holmes, W., Griffiths, M., & Forcier, L. B. (2016). *Intelligence Unleashed: An Argument for AI in Education*. Pearson.

Lum, K., & Isaac, W. (2021). To predict and serve? Social implications of predictive policing algorithms. *Science, 353*(6309), 1157–1161.

Lund, B. D., & Wang, T. (2023). Chatting about ChatGPT: How may AI and GPT impact academia and libraries? *Library Hi Tech News, 40*(3), 26–29. DOI: 10.1108/LHTN-01-2023-0009

Lyons, N. (1990). Dilemmas of knowing: Ethical and epistemological dimensions of teachers' work and development. *Harvard Educational Review, 60*(2), 159–181. DOI: 10.17763/haer.60.2.v71123u7768r47w6

Mahajan, S. (2023). Artificial Intelligence and its Impacts on the Society. *Contemporary Social Science, 32*(4), 135–151. DOI: 10.62047/CSS.2023.12.31.135

Majumdar, D., & Chattopadhyay, H. K. (2020). Artificial intelligence and its impacts on the society. *International Journal of Law, 6*(5), 306-310.

Mallinson, D. J., Azevedo, L., Best, E., Robles, P., & Wang, J. (2023). The future of AI is in the states: The case of autonomous vehicle policies. *Business and Politics, 26*(2), 180–199. DOI: 10.1017/bap.2023.19

Malyn-Smith, J., Lee, I. A., Martin, F., Grover, S., Evans, M. A., & Pillai, S. (2018, June). Developing a framework for computational thinking from a disciplinary perspective. In *Proceedings of the International Conference on Computational Thinking Education* (Vol. 2018, pp. 182–184).

Mananay, J. A. (2024). Integrating Artificial Intelligence (AI) in language teaching: Effectiveness, challenges, and strategies. *International Journal of Learning Teaching and Educational Research, 23*(9), 361–382. DOI: 10.26803/ijlter.23.9.19

Maphosa, V., Dube, B., & Jita, T. (2020). A UTAUT evaluation of WhatsApp as a tool for lecture delivery during the COVID-19 lockdown at a Zimbabwean University. *International Journal of Higher Education, 9*(5), 84–93. https://files.eric.ed.gov/fulltext/EJ1270462.pdf. DOI: 10.5430/ijhe.v9n5p84

Margetts, H., & Dunleavy, P. (2013). The second wave of digital-era governance: A quasi-paradigm for government on the Web. *Philosophical Transactions of the Royal Society A*, 371(1987), 20120382.

Margetts, H., & Dorobantu, C. (2019). AI and public policy. *Nature Human Behaviour, 3*(5), 396–398.

Martin, A. (2005). DigEuLit – a European framework for digital literacy: A progress report. *Journal of e-Literacy, 2*, 130–136.

Masa'deh, R., Majali, S. A. L., Alkhaffaf, M., Thurasamy, R., Almajali, D., Altarawneh, K., Al-Sherideh, A., & Altarawni, I. (2024). Antecedents of adoption and usage of ChatGPT among Jordanian university students: Empirical study. *International Journal of Data and Network Science, 8*(2), 1099–1110. DOI: 10.5267/j.ijdns.2023.11.024

Maslow, A. H. (1954). *Motivation and personality*. Harper & Row.

Maslow, A. H. (1968). *Toward a psychology of being*. Van Nostrand.

Masry Herzallah, A., & Makaldy, R. (2025). Technological self-efficacy and sense of coherence: Key drivers in teachers' AI acceptance and adoption. *Computers and Education: Artificial Intelligence, 8*(February), 100377. DOI: 10.1016/j.caeai.2025.100377

Matalka, M., Badir, R., Ahmad, A., Al-Said, K., Nassar, H., Alzoubi, S., & Alzoubi, M. (2024). The adoption of ChatGPT marks the beginning of a new era in educational platforms. *International Journal of Data and Network Science, 8*(3), 1941–1946. DOI: 10.5267/j.ijdns.2024.1.019

Mavroudi, A., Giannakos, M., & Krogstie, J. (2017). Supporting adaptive learning pathways through the use of learning analytics: Developments, challenges, and future opportunities. *Interactive Learning Environments, 26*(2), 206–220. DOI: 10.1080/10494820.2017.1292531

Ma, W., Adespoe, O. O., Nesbit, C. J., & Qing, L. (2014). Intelligent tutoring systems and learning outcomes: A meta-analysis. *Journal of Educational Psychology, 106*(4), 901–918. DOI: 10.1037/a0037123

Mayer, R. E., & Fiorella, L. (2021). *Learning as a generative activity: Eight learning strategies that promote understanding* (2nd ed.). Cambridge University Press.

McAfee, A., Rock, D., & Brynjolfsson, E. (2023). How to capitalize on generative AI. *Harvard Business Review, 101*(6), 42–48. https://hbr.org/2023/11/how-to-capitalize-on-generative-ai

Mccarthy, J. (2007). What is artificial intelligence? Basic Questions. Computer Science Department, Stanford University. https://stanford.io/2lSo373

McCarthy, J., Marvin, M., Nathaniel, R., & Claude, S. (1955). *A proposal for the Dartmouth Summer Research Project on Artificial Intelligence.* Retrieved from: http://jmc.stanford.edu/articles/dartmouth/dartmouth.pdf

McCarthy, J. (2007). From here to human-level AI. *Artificial Intelligence, 171*(18), 1174–1182. DOI: 10.1016/j.artint.2007.10.009

McCarthy, J., Minsky, M. L., Rochester, N., & Shannon, C. E. (2006). A proposal for the Dartmouth summer research project on Artificial Intelligence, August 31, 1955. *AI Magazine, 27*(4), 12–22.

McCarthy, J., Minsky, M., Rochester, N., & Shannon, C. E. (2006). A Proposal for the Dartmouth Summer Research Project on Artificial Intelligence. *AI Magazine, 27*(4), 12–14.

McCormack, J., Gifford, T., & Hutchings, P. (2019). Autonomy, Authenticity, Authorship and Intention in Computer Generated Art. *Proceedings of the 10th International Conference on Computational Creativity*, 1–8. DOI: 10.1007/978-3-030-16667-0_3

McGaghie, W. C., Issenberg, S. B., Petrusa, E. R., & Scalese, R. J. (2010). A critical review of simulation-based medical education research: 2003–2009. *Medical Education, 44*(1), 50–63. DOI: 10.1111/j.1365-2923.2009.03547.x PMID: 20078756

McGovern, A., Ebert-Uphoff, I., Gagne, D. J.II, & Bostrom, A. (2022). Why we need to focus on developing ethical, responsible, and trustworthy Artificial Intelligence Approaches for environmental science. *Environmental Data Science, 1*, e6. Advance online publication. DOI: 10.1017/eds.2022.5

McNulty, N. (2025). AI for inclusive education. https://www.niallmcnulty.com/2025/03/ai-for-inclusive-education/?utm_source=chatgpt.com

Meakin, L. (2024, September 23). Exploring the Impact of Generative Artificial Intelligence on Higher Education Students' Utilization of Library Resources: A Critical Examination. *Information Technology and Libraries, 43*(3), 1–13. DOI: 10.5860/ital.v43i3.17246

Mehta, R., & Ghosh, S. (2021). AI and digital identity in India: Examining the Aadhaar experience. In Sahi, S. B., & Sinha, V. (Eds.), *AI and Society in India* (pp. 114–128). Springer.

Menon, D., & Shilpa, K. (2023). "Chatting with ChatGPT": Analyzing the factors influencing users' intention to Use the Open AI's ChatGPT using the UTAUT model. *Heliyon, 9*(11), 1–19. DOI: 10.1016/j.heliyon.2023.e20962 PMID: 37928033

Merriam, S. B. (2013). *Nitel araştırma desen ve uygulama için bir rehber* [A guide for design and implementation of Qualitative Research]. (Turan, S., Trans.). Nobel Yayınları.

Merriam, S. B., & Tisdell, E. J. (2016). *Qualitative research: A guide to design and implementation* (4th ed.). Jossey-Bass.

Miao, F., Holmes, W., Huang, R., & Zhang, H. (2021). *AI and education: A guidance for policymakers*. Unesco Publishing.

Microsoft Copilot. (n.d.). Microsoft Copilot: Your AI companion. Retrieved from: https://copilot.microsoft.com/

Midjourney. (n.d.). Midjourney home. Retrieved from: https://www.midjourney .com/home

Miles, M. B., Huberman, A. M., & Saldaña, J. (2014). *Qualitative data analysis: A methods sourcebook* (3rd ed.). Sage Publications.

Miller, T. (2019). Explanation in Artificial Intelligence: Insights from the social sciences. *Artificial Intelligence*, *267*, 1–38. DOI: 10.1016/j.artint.2018.07.007

Miller, T. (2023). Explainable AI and its role in social science research. *AI & Society*, *38*(2), 123–135.

Minecraft Education. (n.d.). Minecraft Education: Get Minecraft for your classroom. Retrieved from: https://education.minecraft.net/en-us

Mishra, P., & Koehler, M. J. (2006). Technological Pedagogical Content Knowledge: A Framework for Teacher Knowledge. *Teachers College Record*, *108*(6), 1017–1054. DOI: 10.1111/j.1467-9620.2006.00684.x

Mittelstadt, B. D., Allo, P., Taddeo, M., Wachter, S., & Floridi, L. (2016). The ethics of algorithms: Mapping the debate. *Big Data & Society*, *3*(2), 1–21. DOI: 10.1177/2053951716679679

Mittelstadt, B. D., Russell, C., & Wachter, S. (2022). Explaining explanations in AI: A taxonomy of interpretability and transparency. *Journal of Artificial Intelligence Research*, *68*, 1–21.

Mohammed, S. P., & Hossain, G. (2024). ChatGPT in Education, Healthcare, and Cybersecurity: Opportunities and Challenges. *2024 IEEE 14th Annual Computing and Communication Workshop and Conference, CCWC 2024*. DOI: 10.1109/ CCWC60891.2024.10427923

Moldt, J.-A., Festl-Wietek, T., Fuhl, W., Zabel, S., Claassen, M., Wagner, S., Nieselt, K., & Herrmann-Werner, A. (2024). Assessing AI awareness and identifying essential competencies: Insights from key stakeholders in integrating AI into medical education. *JMIR Medical Education, 10*, e58355–e58355. DOI: 10.2196/58355 PMID: 38989834

Molenda, M. (2003). In search of the elusive ADDIE model. *Performance Improvement, 42*(5), 34–37. DOI: 10.1002/pfi.4930420508

Molina, E., Cobo, C., Pineda, J., & Rovner, H. (2024). AI revolution in education: What you need to know. In *Digital Innovations in Education*. World Bank. DOI: 10.1596/41806

Molina, L., & Garip, F. (2022). *Machine learning and social science research: Theoretical and methodological innovations*. Oxford University Press.

Molnar, J.. (2021). *Machine learning for behavioral analysis*. Springer.

Monica, M., Patel, S., Ramanaiah, G., Manoharan, S. K., & Ghilan, T. H. (2024). *Promoting fairness and ethical practices in AI-based performance management systems*., DOI: 10.4018/979-8-3693-5380-6.ch007

Montoya, L., & Rivas, M. (2019). AI in Latin American public service: Opportunities and risks. *Journal of Public Administration: Research and Theory, 29*(2), 275–289.

Morandini, S., Fraboni, F., De Angelis, M., Puzzo, G., Giusino, D., & Pietrantoni, L. (2023). The Impact of Artificial Intelligence on Workers' Skills: Upskilling and Reskilling in Organisations. *Informing Science, 26*(February), 39–68. DOI: 10.28945/5078

Moreno, R., & Mayer, R. (2007). Interactive multimodal learning environments. *Educational Psychology Review, 19*(3), 309–326. DOI: 10.1007/s10648-007-9047-2

Morley, J., Machado, C., Burr, C., Cowls, J., Joshi, I., Taddeo, M., & Floridi, L. (2020). The ethics of AI in health care: A mapping review. *Social Science & Medicine, 260*, 113172. DOI: 10.1016/j.socscimed.2020.113172 PMID: 32702587

Morrison, G. R., Ross, S. J., Morrison, J. R., & Kalman, H. K. (2019). *Designing effective instruction*. John Wiley & Sons.

Mosalagae, M. K., & Lukusa, J.-P. K. (2016). Contextualized Inclusive Education: A Retrospective Look at Technical and Vocational Education and Training (TVET) in Botswana. *Journal of Education and Practice, 7*(14).

Mousa, M. (2025). AI-Supported Formative Assessments: Enhancing Student-Centered Learning and Teacher Perceptions. *Journal of Pedagogy and Education Science*, *4*(02), 127–141. DOI: 10.56741/jpes.v4i02.857

Movahed, M., & Bilderback, S. (2024). Evaluating the readiness of healthcare administration students to utilize AI for sustainable leadership: A survey study. *Journal of Health Organization and Management*, *38*(4), 567–582. DOI: 10.1108/JHOM-12-2023-0385 PMID: 38858220

Mozur, P. (2018, July 8). *Inside China's dystopian classrooms: Where surveillance reigns*. The New York Times. https://www.nytimes.com/2018/07/08/business/china-surveillance-technology-schools.html

Muhammad, N. H. M., & Niazi, J. A. (2022). Socratic questioning: A philosophical approach in developing critical thinking skills. *Al-Hikmah: International Journal of Islamic Studies and Human Sciences*, *5*(4), 143–161. DOI: 10.46722/hikmah.v5i4.294

Muller, V. C. (2017). Risks of general artificial Intelligence. In Muller, V. C. (Ed.), *Philosophy and theory of artificial intelligence 2***017** (pp. 297–307). Springer., DOI: 10.1007/978-3-319-96448-5_26

Muñoz Gómez, A. (2025). *Antonio Muñoz Gómez*. University of Waterloo. https://uwaterloo.ca/library/about/people/antonio-munoz-gomez

MyLens AI. (n.d.). MyLens AI: Create Effective Visuals with AI. Retrieved from: https://mylens.ai/

Namjoo, F., Liaghat, E., Shabaziasl, S., Modabernejad, Z., & Morshedi, H. (2023). Students experience self-study through AI. *Aitechbesosci*, *1*(3), 35–42. DOI: 10.61838/kman.aitech.1.3.6

Naresh Babu, E. M., Sathwik, B., & Haseena, K. (2024). Employee perceptions towards changing trends of Artificial Intelligence in the workspace. *Research Review International Journal of Multidisciplinary*, *9*(12), 79–85. DOI: 10.31305/rrijm.2024.v09.n12.009

Natalia, C., Khairina, Y., Gintings, I., Pulungan, A., & Br. Batubara, K. (2024). The Effectiveness of Artificial Intelligence Platforms in Creating Digital Educational Content. *Jurnal Sustainable*, *7*(2), 356–363. DOI: 10.32923/kjmp.v7i2.5066

Naweed, A., & Rose, J. (2018). Assessing technology acceptance for skills development and real-world decision-making in the context of train driving. *Transportation Research Part F: Traffic Psychology and Behaviour*, *52*, 86–100. DOI: 10.1016/j.trf.2017.11.003

Ngo, T. T. A. (2023). The perception by university students of the use of ChatGPT in education. *International Journal of Emerging Technologies in Learning*, *18*(17), 4–12. DOI: 10.3991/ijet.v18i17.39019

Nguyen, K. V. (2025). The use of generative AI tools in higher education: Ethical and Pedagogical principles. *Journal of Academic Ethics*, *0123456789*. Advance online publication. DOI: 10.1007/s10805-025-09607-1

Nilsson, N., J., (2019). *Yapay Zekâ geçmişi ve geleceği*. (Çeviri M. Doğan.). Boğaziçi Üniversitesi Yayınevi.

Noam, E. (2025). Into the next generation of digital protection: AI resiliency as a public responsibility. *Telecommunications Policy*, *49*(3), 102907. DOI: 10.1016/j.telpol.2025.102907

Noble, S., & Roberts, S. (2019). Technological elites, the meritocracy, and postracial myths in Silicon Valley. In *RACISM POSTRACE*. Report #: 6.

Noble, S. U. (2022). *Algorithms of oppression: How search engines reinforce racism*. NYU Press.

Nocera, A., Newton, V., & Jiang, S. (2024). They created segregation with the economy: Using AI for a student-driven inquiry into redlining in the social studies classroom. *Theory and Research in Social Education*, *52*(4), 614–653. DOI: 10.1080/00933104.2024.2331466

Nosike, C. J., Ojobor, O. S., & Nosike, U. C. (2024). Exploring the ethical and societal implications of Artificial Intelligence. *Multidisciplinary Journal of Management and Social Science*, 1(1), 34–36. https://www.researchgate.net/publication/380346927

Nur Ihsan Purwanto, A., Fauzan, M., Widya, T., & Syarof Azzaky, N. (2024). Ethical implications and challenges of AI implementation in business operations. *TechComp Innovations: Journal of Computer Science and Technology*, *1*(2), 68–82. DOI: 10.70063/techcompinnovations.v1i2.52

Nussbaum, M., & Sen, A. (Eds.). (1993). *The quality of life*. Clarendon Press. DOI: 10.1093/0198287976.001.0001

O'Brien, S., & Davenport, C. (2024). Embedding the service user voice to co-produce UK mental health nurse education—A lived experience narrative. *Journal of Psychiatric and Mental Health Nursing*, *31*(5), 769–775. Advance online publication. DOI: 10.1111/jpm.13031 PMID: 38334192

O'Connor, S., Yan, Y., Thilo, F. J., Felzmann, H., Dowding, D., & Lee, J. J. (2022). Artificial Intelligence in nursing and midwifery: A systematic review. *Journal of Clinical Nursing*, *32*(13–14), 2951–2968. DOI: 10.1111/jocn.16478 PMID: 35908207

O'Connor, W., & Natividad, L. (2023). The bias on artificial intelligence in education (AIED): Influence of perennialism teaching philosophy at education 4.0. *Journal of Science Teacher Education*, *5*(1), 31–44.

O'Neil, C. (2016). *Weapons of Math Destruction: How Big Data Increases Inequality and Threatens Democracy*. Crown Publishing Group.

O'Neil, C. (2022). *Weapons of math destruction: How big data increases inequality and threatens democracy*. Crown Publishing Group.

Obermeyer, Z., Powers, B., Vogeli, C., & Mullainathan, S. (2019). Dissecting racial bias in an algorithm used to manage the health of populations. *Science*, *366*(6464), 447–453. DOI: 10.1126/science.aax2342 PMID: 31649194

Odeh, A., Odeh, N., & Mohammed, A. S. (2024). A comparative review of AI techniques for automated code generation in software development: Advancements, challenges, and future directions. *Tem Journal*, 726–739. https://doi.org/DOI: 10.18421/tem131-76

OECD. (2019). *Digital Government Review of Estonia: Boosting the Digital Transformation of the Public Sector*. DOI: 10.1787/14e1c5e8-en-fr

OECD. (2019). *Recommendation of the Council on Artificial Intelligence*. https://legalinstruments.oecd.org/en/instruments/OECD-LEGAL-0449

OECD. (2021). *OECD digital education outlook 2021: Pushing the frontiers with Artificial Intelligence, blockchain, and robots*. OECD Publishing., DOI: 10.1787/589b283f-

OECD. (2024). *Education policy outlook 2024: Reshaping teaching into a thriving profession from ABCs to AI*. OECD Publishing., DOI: 10.1787/dd5140e4-

Okonkwo, C. W., & Ade-Ibijola, A. (2021). Chatbots applications in education: A systematic review. *Computers and Education: Artificial Intelligence*, *2*, 100033. DOI: 10.1016/j.caeai.2021.100033

Oladoyinbo, T. O., Olabanji, S. O., Olaniyi, O. O., Adebiyi, O. O., Okunleye, O. J., & Alao, A. I. (2024). Exploring the challenges of Artificial Intelligence in data integrity and its influence on social dynamics. *Asian Journal of Advanced Research and Reports*, *18*(2), 1–23. DOI: 10.9734/ajarr/2024/v18i2601

Oliinyk, I., Bulavina, O., Romanenko, T., Tatarnikova, A., & Smirnov, A. (2024). Artificial Intelligence in developing doctoral students' research competencies. *Revista Eduweb*, *18*(3), 294–305. DOI: 10.46502/issn.1856-7576/2024.18.03.22

Oliński, M., Krukowski, K., & Sieciński, K. (2024). Bibliometric overview of ChatGPT: New perspectives in social sciences. *Publications / MDPI*, *12*(1), 9. DOI: 10.3390/publications12010009

Oliveira, J., Murphy, T., Vaughn, G., Elfahim, S., & Carpenter, R. E. (2024). Exploring the adoption phenomenon of artificial Intelligence by doctoral students within doctoral education. *New Horizons in Adult Education and Human Resource Development*, *00*(0), 248–262. Advance online publication. DOI: 10.1177/19394225241287032

Onesi-Ozigagun, O. (2024). Revolutionizing education through AI: A comprehensive review of enhancing learning experiences. *International Journal of Applied Research in Social Sciences*, *6*(4), 589–607. DOI: 10.51594/ijarss.v6i4.1011

Open, A. I. (2023). *ChatGPT: Optimizing language models for dialogue*. https://openai.com/blog/chatgpt/ Accessed 12 June 2023.

Oranga, J. (2023). Benefits of artificial intelligence (ChatGPT) in education and learning: Is ChatGPT helpful? *International Review of Practical Innovation* [IRPITAGE]. *Technology and Green Energy*, *3*(3), 46–50. DOI: 10.54443/irpitage.v3i3.1250

Osei Kwadwo, V., & Konadu, O. A. (2020). Can Ghana Afford the Sustainable Development Goal on Education? *Africa Education Review*, *17*(2), 177–197. Advance online publication. DOI: 10.1080/18146627.2018.1557532

Otterborn, A., Schönborn, K., & Hultén, M. (2020). Investigating preschool educators' implementation of computer programming in their teaching practice. *Early Childhood Education Journal*, *48*(3), 253–262. DOI: 10.1007/s10643-019-00976-y

Ouyang, F., & Jiao, P. (2021). Artificial intelligence in education: The three paradigms. *Computers and Education: Artificial Intelligence*, *2*, 100020. DOI: 10.1016/j.caeai.2021.100020

Pandit, B. (2022). Recent used and future application of Artificial Intelligence (AI). *International Journal of Scientific Research in Engineering and Management*, *06*(11). Advance online publication. DOI: 10.55041/IJSREM16966

Pane, J. F., Steiner, E. D., Baird, M. D., & Hamilton, L. S. (2015). *Continued progress: Promising evidence on personalized learning*. RAND Corporation., DOI: 10.7249/RR1365

Panke, S. (2024). Open Educational Resources and Artificial Intelligence for Future Open Education. *Mousaion: South African Journal of Information Studies*, *42*(1), 23. DOI: 10.25159/2663-659X/15106

Pan, Y. (2016). Heading toward Artificial Intelligence 2.0. *Engineering (Beijing)*, *2*(4), 409–413. DOI: 10.1016/J.ENG.2016.04.018

Papernot, N., McDaniel, P., Goodfellow, I., Jha, S., Celik, Z. B., & Swami, A. (2016). *Practical black-box attacks against machine learning. Proceedings of the 2017 ACM on Asia Conference on Computer and Communications Security*. DOI: 10.1145/3052973.3053009

Pappas, C. (2015). The Successive Approximation Model (SAM): *The Agile eLearning Development Process*. eLearning Industry

Park, S.-M., & Yang, D.-W. (2023). The impact of employees' perception of AI Adoption on the relationships between psychological contract, organizational trust and organizational commitment. *The Korean Academic Association of Business Administration*, *36*(5), 749–775. DOI: 10.18032/kaaba.2023.36.5.749

Parong, J., & Mayer, R. E. (2021). Cognitive and affective processes for learning science in immersive virtual reality. *Journal of Computer Assisted Learning*, *37*(1), 226–241. DOI: 10.1111/jcal.12482

Pasquale, F. (2020). *The black box society: The secret algorithms that control money and information*. Harvard University Press.

Patel, P., Moz-Ruiz, D., Garcia, R., Chatterjee, A., Morreale, P., & Burnett, M. (2024). From Workshops to Classrooms: Faculty Experiences with Implementing Inclusive Design Principles. *SIGCSE 2024 - Proceedings of the 55th ACM Technical Symposium on Computer Science Education, 1*. DOI: 10.1145/3626252.3630861

Paul, R. (2022). Can critical policy studies outsmart AI? Research agenda on Artificial Intelligence technologies and public policy. *Critical Policy Studies*, *16*(4), 497–509. DOI: 10.1080/19460171.2022.2123018

Paul, R. W. (2013). Critical and reflective thinking: A philosophical perspective. In *Dimensions of thinking and cognitive instruction* (pp. 445–494). Routledge.

Paul, R., & Elder, L. (2020). *Critical thinking: Tools for taking charge of your learning and your life* (4th ed.). Pearson.

Pavlov, I. P. (1927). *Conditioned reflexes: An investigation of the physiological activity of the cerebral cortex*. Oxford University Press.

Peck, H.T., Peabody, S.H., & Richardson, C.F. (1897). *The International Encyclopedia, A Compendium of Human Knowledge*. Rev. with large additions. Dodd, Mead and Company.

Pellas, N., Dengel, A., & Müller, W. (2022). Designing personalized VR learning environments. *Education and Information Technologies*, *27*(5), 6509–6530.

Peng, H., Ma, S., & Spector, J. M. (2019). Personalized adaptive learning: An emerging pedagogical approach enabled by a smart learning environment. *Smart Learning Environments*, *6*(1), 9. Advance online publication. DOI: 10.1186/s40561-019-0089-y

Pereira, V., Hadjielias, E., Christofi, M., & Vrontis, D. (2023). A systematic literature review on the impact of Artificial Intelligence on workplace outcomes: A multi-process perspective. *Human Resource Management Review*, *33*(1), 100857. DOI: 10.1016/j.hrmr.2021.100857

Pflanzer, M., Dubljević, V., Bauer, W. A., Orcutt, D., List, G., & Singh, M. P. (2023). Embedding AI in society: Ethics, policy, governance, and impacts. *AI & Society*, *38*(4), 1267–1271. DOI: 10.1007/s00146-023-01704-2

Piaget, J. (1954). *The construction of reality in the child*. Basic Books. DOI: 10.1037/11168-000

Piaget, J. (1972). *Psychology and pedagogy*. Viking Press.

Pirim, A. G. H. (2006). Yapay zeka. *Yaşar Üniversitesi E-Dergisi*, *1*(1), 81–93.

Pizarro Milian, R., & Munro, Y. (2020). Credit transfer, articulation & The future of work: Towards a federal strategy. *Canadian Journal of Higher Education*, *50*(3), 36–48. DOI: 10.47678/cjhe.vi0.188769

Planit Teachers. (n.d.). AI-Enhanced History Teaching. Retrieved from: https://www.planitteachers.ai/subjects/history

Polak, P., & Anshari, M. (2024). Exploring the multifaceted impacts of artificial Intelligence on public organizations, business, and society. *Humanities & Social Sciences Communications*, *11*(1), 10–12. DOI: 10.1057/s41599-024-03913-6

Polat, Z. (2024). Generative artificial ıntelligence in education: Cheating threat or an enhanced learning tool? *Next Frontier for Life Sciences and AI*, *8*(1), 1–5. DOI: 10.62802/gt1b4t58

Popenici, S. A., & Kerr, S. (2017). Exploring the impact of artificial intelligence on teaching and learning in higher education. *Research and Practice in Technology Enhanced Learning*, *12*(1), 22. DOI: 10.1186/s41039-017-0062-8 PMID: 30595727

Poth, R. Dené. (2022). Teaching history/social studies in the era of AI writing tools. https://rdene915.com/2022/12/22/teaching-history-social-studies-in-the-era-of-ai-writing-tools/

Prasanth, A., Vadakkan, D. J., Surendran, P., & Thomas, B. (2023). Role of Artificial Intelligence and business decision making. *International Journal of Advanced Computer Science and Applications*, *14*(6). Advance online publication. DOI: 10.14569/IJACSA.2023.01406103

Prasetyo, M. L., Peranginangin, R. A., Martinovic, N., Ichsan, M., & Wicaksono, H. (2025). Artificial Intelligence in open innovation project management: A systematic literature review on technologies, applications, and integration requirements. *Journal of Open Innovation*, *11*(1), 100445. DOI: 10.1016/j.joitmc.2024.100445

Pressey, S. L. (1950). Development and appraisal of devices providing immediate automatic scoring of objective tests and concomitant self-instruction. *The Journal of Psychology*, *29*(2), 417–447. DOI: 10.1080/00223980.1950.9916043

Przegalinska, A., Triantoro, T., Kovbasiuk, A., Ciechanowski, L., Freeman, R. B., & Sowa, K. (2025). Collaborative AI in the workplace: Enhancing organizational performance through resource-based and task-technology fit perspectives. *International Journal of Information Management, 81*(June 2024), 102853. DOI: 10.1016/j.ijinfomgt.2024.102853

Purdue Libraries. (2025). *Jing Lu*. Purdue University. https://lib.purdue.edu/people/lu59/

Qadhi, S. M., Alduais, A., Chaaban, Y., & Khraisheh, M. (2024, June 2). Generative AI, Research Ethics, and Higher Education Research: Insights from a Scientometric Analysis. *Information (Basel)*, *15*(6), 325. DOI: 10.3390/info15060325

Qian, Y., Siau, K. L., & Nah, F. F. (2024). Societal impacts of artificial intelligence: Ethical, legal, and governance issues. *Societal Impacts*, *3*, 100040. DOI: 10.1016/j.socimp.2024.100040

Qin, F., Li, K., & Yan, J. (2020). Understanding user trust in Artificial Intelligence-based educational systems: Evidence from China. *British Journal of Educational Technology*, *51*(5), 1693–1710. DOI: 10.1111/bjet.12994

Qin, Y., Xu, Z., Wang, X., & Skare, M. (2024). Artificial Intelligence and Economic Development: An Evolutionary Investigation and Systematic Review. *Journal of the Knowledge Economy*, *15*(1), 1736–1770. DOI: 10.1007/s13132-023-01183-2 PMID: 40478928

Quizizz. (n.d.). Quizizz. Retrieved from: https://quizizz.com

Rahiem, M. D. (2021). Storytelling in early childhood education: Time to go digital. *International Journal of Child Care and Education Policy, 15*(1), 1–20. DOI: 10.1186/s40723-021-00081-x

Rahman, M. M., & Watanobe, Y. (2023). ChatGPT for education and research: Opportunities, threats, and strategies. *Applied Sciences (Basel, Switzerland), 13*(9), 5783. DOI: 10.3390/app13095783

Rahwan, I.. (2023). Behavioral AI: Predicting and shaping human behavior in virtual environments. *Nature Communications, 14*(1), 1101–1117. PMID: 36843121

Raji, I. D., & Buolamwini, J. (2020). Actionable auditing: Investigating the impact of publicly naming biased performance of commercial AI products. *Proceedings of the 2019 CHI Conference on Human Factors in Computing Systems.*

Raman, P. (2023). The transformative role of AI in social science research. *Uniathena.* https://uniathena.com/role-of-AI-in-social-science-research

Raman, R., Mandal, S., Das, P., Kaur, T., Sanjanasri, J. P., & Nedungadi, P. (2024). Exploring university students' adoption of ChatGPT using the diffusion of innovation theory and sentiment analysis with gender dimension. *Human Behavior and Emerging Technologies, 2024*(1), 3085910. DOI: 10.1155/2024/3085910

Ramya, R., Priya, S., Thamizhikkavi, P., & Anand, M. (2024). *The pillars of AI ethics.*, DOI: 10.4018/979-8-3693-9173-0.ch004

Rane, N., & Choudhary, S. (2024). Role and challenges of ChatGPT and similar generative artificial intelligence in arts and humanities. *Studies in Humanities and Education, 5*(1), 1–11. Advance online publication. DOI: 10.48185/she.v5i1.999

Rasoolimanesh, S. M. (2022). Discriminant validity assessment in PLS-SEM: A comprehensive composite-based approach. *Data Analysis Perspectives Journal, 3*(2), 1–8.

Rathore, B. (2023). Future of AI & generation alpha: ChatGPT beyond boundaries. Eduzone: International Peer Reviewed/ Refereed Multidisciplinary Journal, 12(1), 63-68. https://www.eduzonejournal.com/index.php/eiprmj/article/view/254

Read, A. W. (Ed.). (1999). *The New International Webster's Comprehensive Dictionary of the English Language-Encyclopedic Edition.* Trident.

Regan, P. M., & Jesse, J. (2019). Ethical challenges of edtech, big data, and personalized learning: Twenty-First Century student sorting and tracking. *Ethics and Information Technology, 21*(3), 167–179. DOI: 10.1007/s10676-018-9492-2

Reigeluth, C. M. (1999). What is instructional design theory, and how is it changing? *Instructional-Design Theories and Models: A New Paradigm of Instructional Theory, 2,* 5-29.

Richardson, R., Schultz, J., & Crawford, K. (2022). Policing, AI, and bias: A critical analysis of predictive policing algorithms. *Columbia Law Review, 122*(5), 1223–1249.

Rink, E., Firemoon, P., Anastario, M., Johnson, O., GrowingThunder, R., Ricker, A., Peterson, M., & Baldwin, J. (2022). Rationale, design, and methods for nen unkumbi/edahiyedo ("We are here now"): A multi-level randomized controlled trial to improve sexual and reproductive health outcomes in a northern plains American Indian Reservation Community. *Frontiers in Public Health, 10*, 823228. Advance online publication. DOI: 10.3389/fpubh.2022.823228 PMID: 35910931

Risso, M., Delbufalo, E., & Di Bernardo, M. (2022). Human-machine interaction and AI for competitive business in the Digital Era. *Symphonya.Emerging Issues in Management, 2*(2), 134–143. DOI: 10.4468/2022.2.12delbufalo.dibernardo.risso

Roberts-Holmes, G., & Bradbury, A. (2016). Governance, accountability and the datafication of early years education in England. *British Educational Research Journal, 42*(4), 600–613. DOI: 10.1002/berj.3221

Robeyns, I., & Fibieger Byskov, M. (2023). *The capability approach.* In E. N. Zalta, U. Nodelman (Eds.). The Stanford Encyclopedia of Philosophy. https://plato.stanford.edu/archives/sum2023/entries/capability-approach/

Robinson, K., & Aronica, L. (2021). *Creative schools: The grassroots revolution that's transforming education*. Penguin Books.

Roblyer, M. D., & Doering, A. H. (2014). *Integrating educational technology into teaching*. Pearson.

Rochi, M., Rauschnabel, P. A., Renner, K., & Ivens, B. S. (2024). Technology paternalism: Development and validation of a measurement scale. *Psychology and Marketing, 41*(5), 1172–1188. DOI: 10.1002/mar.21971

Rodway, P., & Schepman, A. (2023). The impact of adopting AI educational technologies on projected course satisfaction in university students. *Computers and Education: Artificial Intelligence, 5*(April), 100150. DOI: 10.1016/j.caeai.2023.100150

Rogers, C. R. (1969). *Freedom to learn: A view of what education might become*. Merrill.

Rogers, E. M. (1962). *Diffusion of innovations*. Free Press.

Rolnick, D., Donti, P. L., Kaack, L. H., Kochanski, K., Lacoste, A., Sankaran, K., . . . Bengio, Y. (2019). Tackling climate change with machine learning. *arXiv preprint*, arXiv:1906.05433. https://arxiv.org/abs/1906.05433

Rosmayanti, V., Noni, N., & Patak, A. A. (2022). Students' acceptance of technology use in learning English pharmacy. *International Journal of Language Education*, *6*(3), 314–331. DOI: 10.26858/ijole.v6i3.24144

Rotter, J. B. (1954). *Social Learning and Clinical Psychology*. Prentice-Hall. DOI: 10.1037/10788-000

Russell, S. J., & Norvig, P. (2020). *Artificial Intelligence: A Modern Approach* (4th ed.). Pearson.

Saadé, R. G., Zhang, J., Wang, X., Liu, H., & Guan, H. (2023). Challenges and Opportunities in the Internet of Intelligence of Things in Higher Education—Towards Bridging Theory and Practice. *IoT*, *4*(3), 430–465. Advance online publication. DOI: 10.3390/iot4030019

Sabeh, H. N. (2024). What Drives IT Students Toward ChatGPT? Analyzing the Factors Influencing Students' Intention to Use ChatGPT for Educational Purposes. In *2024 21st International Multi-Conference on Systems, Signals & Devices (SSD)* (pp. 533-539). IEEE.

Sætra, E. (2022). An empirical moral philosophy perspective on classroom discussions of controversial issues. *Educational Theory*, *72*(5), 641–662. DOI: 10.1111/edth.12548

Sætra, H. S., & Fosch-Villaronga, E. (2021). Research in AI has implications for society: How do we respond? *Morals & Machines*, *1*(1), 60–73. DOI: 10.5771/2747-5182-2021-1-60

Şahin, O., & Karayel, D. (2024). Generative Artificial Intelligence (GenAI) in business: A systematic review on the threshold of transformation. *Journal of Smart Systems Research*, *5*(2), 156–175. DOI: 10.58769/joinssr.1597110

Saidakhror, G. (2024). The impact of Artificial Intelligence on higher education and the economics of information technology. *Irshad J. Law and Policy*, *2*(3), 1–6. DOI: 10.59022/ijlp.125

Saif, N., Khan, S. U., Shaheen, I., ALotaibi, F. A., Alnfiai, M. M., & Arif, M. (2024). Chat-GPT; validating Technology Acceptance Model (TAM) in education sector via ubiquitous learning mechanism. *Computers in Human Behavior*, *154*, 108097. DOI: 10.1016/j.chb.2023.108097

Sailer, M., & Homner, L. (2020). Educational gamification and immersive learning: A systematic review. *Computers & Education, 147*, 103778. DOI: 10.1016/j.compedu.2019.103778

Salajan, F. D., Barnes, T. L., & Becker, A. (2024). Comparative regionalism cases of artificial intelligence governance in education: The Caribbean Community and the European Union. *The Round Table*, *113*(1), 71–85. Advance online publication. DOI: 10.1080/00358533.2024.2307793

Saleem, R., Torres, M., & Lee, J. (2025). AI-driven adaptive learning systems and student engagement in social science classrooms. *Computers and Education: Artificial Intelligence*, *6*, 100215. DOI: 10.1016/j.caeai.2025.100215

Salgado, N., Meza, J., Vaca-Cardenas, M., & Vaca-Cardenas, L. (2024). Current and emerging trends in the use of AI for community surveillance. *Journal of Infrastructure, Policy, and Development*, *8*(8), 6135. DOI: 10.24294/jipd.v8i8.6135

Sallam, M., Salim, N. A., Al-Tammemi, A. B., Barakat, M., Fayyad, D., Hallit, S., Harapan, H., Hallit, R., & Mahafzah, A. (2023). ChatGPT output regarding compulsory vaccination and COVID-19 vaccine conspiracy: A descriptive study at the outset of a paradigm shift in online search for information. *Cureus*. Advance online publication. DOI: 10.7759/cureus.35029 PMID: 36819954

Samsonovich, A. V., Kitsantas, A., Wahidi, S., & Dolgikh, A. A. (2024). Self-regulated learning (SRL) with AI in problem-based learning. In A. V. Samsonovich & T. Liu (Eds.), *Biologically inspired cognitive architectures 2024. BICA 2024. Studies in Computational Intelligence* (Vol. 477, pp. [345–357]). Springer, Cham. https://doi.org/DOI: 10.1007/978-3-031-76516-2_34

Samuel, Y., Brennan-Tonetta, M., Samuel, J., Kashyap, R., Kumar, V., Kashyap, S. K., Chidipothu, N., Anand, I., & Jain, P. (2023). Cultivation of human-centered Artificial Intelligence: Culturally adaptive thinking in education (CATE) for AI. *Frontiers in Artificial Intelligence*, *6*, 1198180. Advance online publication. DOI: 10.3389/frai.2023.1198180 PMID: 38106981

Sanchez, T. W., Brenman, M., & Ye, X. (2024). The ethical concerns of Artificial Intelligence in urban planning. *Journal of the American Planning Association*, *0*(0), 1–14. DOI: 10.1080/01944363.2024.2355305

Santos, B. de S. (2002). *Toward a new legal common sense: Law, globalization, and emancipation*. Butterworths.

Sanusi, I. T., Oyelere, S. S., Vartiainen, H., Suhonen, J., & Tukiainen, M. (2022). A systematic review of teaching and learning machine learning in K-12 education. *Education and Information Technologies*, *28*(5), 5967–5997. DOI: 10.1007/s10639-022-11416-7

Sapci, A. H., & Sapci, H. (2020). Artificial Intelligence education and tools for medical and health informatics students: Systematic review. *JMIR Medical Education*, *6*(1), e19285. DOI: 10.2196/19285 PMID: 32602844

Saqr, M., Fors, U., & Tedre, M. (2022). How AI is shaping connectivist learning networks. *Computers and Education: Artificial Intelligence*, *3*, 100067. DOI: 10.1016/j.caeai.2022.100067

Sarı, F. (2021). Cahit Arf'in "Makine Düşünebilir mi ve Nasıl Düşünebilir?" Adlı Makalesi Üzerine Bir Çalışma [A study on Cahit Arf's article named "Can machines think and how they think"] [TRT Academy]. *TRT Akademi*, *6*(13), 812–833. DOI: 10.37679/trta.962940

Scheerder, A., Van Deursen, A., & Van Dijk, J. (2017). Determinants of Internet skills, uses, and outcomes. *Telematics and Informatics*, *34*(8), 1604–1616. DOI: 10.1016/j.tele.2017.07.007

Schein, K. E., & Rauschnabel, P. A. (2023). Augmented reality in manufacturing: Exploring workers' perceptions of barriers. *IEEE Transactions on Engineering Management*, *70*(10), 3344–3357. DOI: 10.1109/TEM.2021.3093833

Schiavo, G., Businaro, S., & Zancanaro, M. (2024). Comprehension, apprehension, and acceptance: Understanding the influence of literacy and anxiety on acceptance of Artificial Intelligence. *Technology in Society*, *77*(October 2023), 102537. DOI: 10.1016/j.techsoc.2024.102537

Schleicher, A. (2019). *PISA 2018: Insights and interpretations*. OECD Publishing.

Schleicher, A. (2020). *The impact of COVID-19 on education: Insights from education at a glance 2020*. OECD Publishing.

Schlogl, L., Weiss, E., & Prainsack, B. (2021). Constructing the 'Future of Work': An analysis of the policy discourse. *New Technology, Work and Employment*, *36*(3), 307–326. DOI: 10.1111/ntwe.12202

Schreiber, L. M., & Valle, B. E. (2013). Social constructivist teaching strategies in the small group classroom. *Small Group Research*, *44*(4), 395–411. DOI: 10.1177/1046496413488422

Schüller, K. (2022). Data and AI literacy for everyone. *Statistical Journal of the IAOS, 38*(2), 477–490. DOI: 10.3233/SJI-220941

Schumacker, R. E., & Lomax, R. G. (2010). *A beginner's guide to structural equation modeling* (3rd ed.). Routledge.

Schwab, K. (2016). *The Fourth Industrial Revolution.* World Economic Forum.

Sedrakyan, G., Mannens, E., & Verbert, K. (2019). Guiding the choice of learning dashboard visualizations: Linking dashboard design and data visualization concepts. *Journal of Computer Languages, 50,* 19–38. DOI: 10.1016/j.jvlc.2018.11.002

Selten, F., & Klievink, B. (2024). Organizing public sector AI adoption: Navigating between separation and integration. *Government Information Quarterly, 41*(1), 101885. DOI: 10.1016/j.giq.2023.101885

Selwyn, N. (2016). *Is Technology Good for Education?* Polity Press. http://au.wiley .com/WileyCDA/WileyTitle/productCd-0745696465.html

Selwyn, N. (2014). Data entry: Towards the critical study of digital data and education. *Learning, Media and Technology, 40*(1), 64–82. DOI: 10.1080/17439884.2014.921628

Selwyn, N. (2019). *Should robots replace teachers? AI and the future of education.* John Wiley & Sons.

Selwyn, N. (2022). *Education and technology: Key issues and debates* (3rd ed.). Bloomsbury Academic. DOI: 10.5040/9781350145573

Selwyn, N., Hillman, T., & Eynon, R. (2021). Education and the datafied child: Postdigital childhoods. *Postdigital Science and Education, 3*(1), 8–28. DOI: 10.1007/s42438-020-00168-1

Selwyn, N., Hillman, T., & Eynon, R. (2023). Education and the algorithmic child: Ethics, evidence, and activism. *Postdigital Science and Education, 5*(3), 456–473. DOI: 10.1007/s42438-023-00326-y

Seniutis, M., Gružauskas, V., Lileikienė, A., & Navickas, V. (2024). Conceptual framework for ethical Artificial Intelligence development in social services sector. *Human Technology, 20*(1), 6–24. DOI: 10.14254/1795-6889.2024.20-1.1

Sertalp, E., Moraes, C., & Bütün, E. (2024). Facial reconstruction of a deformed skull from the Roman period of Juliopolis. *Heritage Science, 12*(1), 2. DOI: 10.1186/s40494-023-01124-x

Sevil, Ş., & Saralar-Aras, İ. (2024). *Eğitimde kullanılan yapay zekâ araçları: Öğretmen el kitabı.* Yenilik ve Eğitim Teknolojileri Genel Müdürlüğü.

Seyrek, M., Yıldız, S., Emeksiz, H., Şahin, A., & Türkmen, M. T. (2024). Öğretmenlerin eğitimde yapay zekâ kullanımına yönelik algıları [Teachers' perceptions on the use of artificial intelligence in education] [JSHSR]. *International Journal of Social and Humanities Sciences Research, 11*(106), 845–856. DOI: 10.5281/zenodo.11113077

Shaengchart, Y., Bhumpenpein, N., Kongnakorn, K., Khwannu, P., Tiwtakul, A., & Detmee, S. (2023). Factors influencing the acceptance of ChatGPT usage among higher education students in Bangkok, Thailand. *Advance Knowledge for Executives, 2*(4), 1-14. https://ssrn.com/abstract=4592118

Shafik, W. (2023). *A Comprehensive Cybersecurity Framework for Present and Future Global Information Technology Organizations*. DOI: 10.4018/978-1-6684-9018-1.ch002

Shafik, W. (2024a). An Overview of Artificial Intelligence-Enhanced Teaching Methods. *AI-Enhanced Teaching Methods*, 132–159.

Shafik, W. (2024d). Enhancing AI-Enabled Education Through Mobile Learning and Bring Your Own Device (BYOD) Integration. In *Exploring Youth Studies in the Age of AI* (pp. 140–173). IGI Global.

Shafik, W. (2024e). Generative AI for Social Good and Sustainable Development. In *Generative AI: Current Trends and Applications* (pp. 185–217). Springer. DOI: 10.1007/978-981-97-8460-8_10

Shafik, W. (2024f). Mobile Learning and Bring Your Own Device (BYOD): Enhancing Education in the Digital Age. In *Integrating Cutting-Edge Technology Into the Classroom* (pp. 240–267). IGI Global.

Shafik, W. (2024g). The Role of Generative Artificial Intelligence in E-Commerce Fraud Detection and Prevention. In *Strategies for E-Commerce Data Security: Cloud, Blockchain, AI, and Machine Learning* (pp. 430–469). IGI Global. DOI: 10.4018/979-8-3693-6557-1.ch018

Shafik, W. (2024b). Artificial Intelligence-Enabled Internet of Medical Things for Enhanced Healthcare Systems. In *Smart Healthcare Systems* (pp. 119–134). CRC Press., DOI: 10.1201/9781032698519-9

Shafik, W. (2024c). Deep Learning Impacts in the Field of Artificial Intelligence. In *Deep Learning Concepts in Operations Research* (pp. 9–26). Auerbach Publications., DOI: 10.1201/9781003433309-2

Shafik, W. (2024h). *Towards Trustworthy and Explainable AI Educational Systems*., DOI: 10.1007/978-3-031-72410-7_2

Shafik, W., Kalinaki, K., Fahim, K. E., & Adam, M. (2024). Safeguarding Data Privacy and Security in Federated Learning Systems. In *Federated Deep Learning for Healthcare* (pp. 170–190). CRC Press., DOI: 10.1201/9781032694870-13

Shahid, M. K., Zia, T., Bangfan, L., Iqbal, Z., & Ahmad, F. (2024). Exploring the relationship of psychological factors and adoption readiness in determining university teachers' attitude on AI-based assessment systems. *International Journal of Management Education*, *22*(2), 100967. DOI: 10.1016/j.ijme.2024.100967

Shah, N. H., Milstein, A., & Bagley, S. C. (2022). Making machine learning models clinically useful. *Journal of the American Medical Association*, *322*(14), 1351–1352. DOI: 10.1001/jama.2019.10306 PMID: 31393527

Shahrani, A. S. A., Alhumaidan, N. I., AlHindawi, Z. A., Althobaiti, A., Aloufi, K., Almughamisi, R., & Aldalbahi, A. (2024). Readiness to embrace Artificial Intelligence among medical students in Saudi Arabia: A national survey. *Health Care*, *12*(24), 2504. DOI: 10.3390/healthcare12242504 PMID: 39765931

Sharabati, A.-A. A., Rehman, S. U., Malik, M. H., Sabra, S., Al-Sager, M., & Al-lahham, M. (2024). Is AI biased? Evidence from FinTech-based innovation in supply chain management companies? *International Journal of Data and Network Science*, *8*(3), 1839–1852. DOI: 10.5267/j.ijdns.2024.2.005

Sharma, K., Davidson, B. G. J., George, J. P., & Muttungal, P. V. (2024). Breeding distrust during Artificial Intelligence (AI) Era: How technological advancements, job insecurity, and job stress fuel organizational cynicism? *Evidence-Based HRM: A Global Forum for Empirical Scholarship*. DOI: 10.1108/EBHRM-05-2024-0159

Sharma, P. (2024). Faculty competencies development components: An integrated model for the development of educational leaders in technical education institutes. *International Journal of Educational Management*, *38*(2), 447–468. Advance online publication. DOI: 10.1108/IJEM-07-2023-0363

Shen, C., & Zhang, Y. (2024). Artificial Intelligence for climate resilience: Applications in weather prediction and energy optimization. *Environmental Modelling & Software*, *170*, 105551. DOI: 10.1016/j.envsoft.2023.105551

Sheng, X. (2023). The role of artificial intelligence in history education of Chinese high schools. *Journal of Education Humanities and Social Sciences*, *8*, 238–243. DOI: 10.54097/ehss.v8i.4255

Shen, Y., & Zhang, X. (2024). The impact of artificial Intelligence on employment: The role of virtual agglomeration. *Humanities & Social Sciences Communications*, *11*(1), 1–14. DOI: 10.1057/s41599-024-02647-9

Shermis, M., & Burstein, J. (2013). *Handbook of automated essay evaluation: Current applications and new directions*. Routledge., DOI: 10.4324/9780203122761

Shin, D., & Shin, E. Y. (2023). Human-centered AI: A framework for green and sustainable AI. *Computer*, *56*(6), 16–25. DOI: 10.1109/MC.2023.3241071

Shin, H.. (2023). AI in social science experiments: Applications in psychology and education. *Journal of Experimental Social Psychology*, *61*, 12–26.

Shivley, C. B., Garry, F. B., Kogan, L. R., & Grandin, T. (2016). Survey of animal welfare, animal behavior, and animal ethics courses in the curricula of AVMA Council on Education-accredited veterinary colleges and schools. *Journal of the American Veterinary Medical Association*, *248*(10), 1165–1170. Advance online publication. DOI: 10.2460/javma.248.10.1165 PMID: 27135673

Shneiderman, B. (2020). Human-centered artificial intelligence: Reliable, safe & trustworthy. *International Journal of Human-Computer Interaction*, *36*(6), 495–504. DOI: 10.1080/10447318.2020.1741118

Shukla, A. K., Janmaijaya, M., Abraham, A., & Muhuri, P. K. (2019). Engineering applications of Artificial Intelligence: A bibliometric analysis of 30 years (1988–2018). *Engineering Applications of Artificial Intelligence*, *85*, 517–532. DOI: 10.1016/j.engappai.2019.06.010

Shum, S. B., & Crick, R. D. (2016). Learning analytics for 21st Century competencies. *Journal of Learning Analytics*, *3*(2), 6–21. DOI: 10.18608/jla.2016.32.2

Shute, V. J., Rahimi, S., Smith, G., Ke, F., Almond, R., Dai, C., Kuba, R., Liu, Z., Yang, X., & Sun, C. (2020). Maximizing learning without sacrificing the fun: Stealth assessment, adaptivity and learning supports in educational games. *Journal of Computer Assisted Learning*. Advance online publication. DOI: 10.1111/jcal.12473

Siemens, G., & Long, P. (2011). Penetrating the fog: Analytics in learning and education. *EDUCAUSE Review*, *46*(5), 30–40.

Singapore Smart Nation. (2023). *Singapore National AI Strategy*. https://file.go.gov.sg/nais2023.pdf

Singha, S., & Singha, K. (2024). Revolutionizing content creation and curriculum development through generative AI. In Sharma, R. C., & Bozkurt, A. (Eds.), *Transforming education with generative AI: Prompt engineering and synthetic content creation*. IGI Global., DOI: 10.4018/979-8-3693-1351-0.ch013

Sîrbu, C. L., & Mercioni, M. A. (2024). Fostering trust in AI-driven healthcare: A brief review of ethical and practical considerations. *2024 International Symposium on Electronics and Telecommunications (ISETC)*, 1–4. DOI: 10.1109/ISETC63109.2024.10797264

Skinner, B. F. (1938). *The behavior of organisms: An experimental analysis*. Appleton-Century-Crofts.

Skinner, B. F. (1953). *Science and human behavior*. Free Press.

Small, M. (2022). Combining AI and ethnographic research: A complementary approach. *Field Methods*, *34*(2), 202–216.

Smith, J. (2023). AI in social science research: Opportunities and challenges. *Social Science Review*, *19*(4), 200–215.

Smith, P. L., & Ragan, T. J. (2005). *Instructional design* (3rd ed.). Wiley.

Sobaih, A. E. E., Elshaer, I. A., & Hasanein, A. M. (2024). Examining students' acceptance and use of ChatGPT in Saudi Arabian higher education. *European Journal of Investigation in Health, Psychology and Education*, *14*(3), 709–721. DOI: 10.3390/ejihpe14030047 PMID: 38534908

Social sciences, Columbian Cyclopedia. (1897). (p. 227). Garretson, Cox & Company.

Solak, Y., Dal, H. O., Çınkır, G., & Onu, F. N. (2025). Yapay Zekâ Etiği: Eğitimde kullanımının sınırları ve sorumlulukları [Ethıcs of Artıfıcıal Intellıgence: Limits and responsibilities of its use in education]. *Socrates Journal of Interdisciplinary Social Researches*, *11*(49), 108–116. DOI: 10.5281/zenodo.14762322

Sottilare, R. A., & Holden, H. K. (2013). Motivations for a generalized intelligent framework for tutoring (GIFT) for authoring, instruction, and analysis. In Sottilare, R., Graesser, A., Hu, X., & Holden, H. (Eds.), *Design recommendations for intelligent tutoring systems: Volume 1-learner modeling* (pp. 1–18). Army Research Laboratory.

Sowa, K., Przegalinska, A., & Ciechanowski, L. (2021). Cobots in knowledge work. *Journal of Business Research*, *125*, 135–142. DOI: 10.1016/j.jbusres.2020.11.038

Spreer, P., & Rauschnabel, P. A. (2016). Selling with technology: Understanding the resistance to mobile sales assistant use in retailing. *Journal of Personal Selling & Sales Management*, *36*(3), 240–263. DOI: 10.1080/08853134.2016.1208100

Starkey, L. (2019). A review of research exploring teacher preparation for the digital age. *Cambridge Journal of Education*, *50*(1), 37–56. DOI: 10.1080/0305764X.2019.1625867

Stigall, M., & Choo, K. K. R. (2022). Digital Forensics Education: Challenges and Future Opportunities. *Lecture Notes in Networks and Systems*, *310*, 28–46. Advance online publication. DOI: 10.1007/978-3-030-84614-5_4

Strang, K. D. (2016). Testing young business students for technology acceptance and learning performance. *International Journal of Learning Technology*, *11*(3), 238. DOI: 10.1504/IJLT.2016.079036

Strzelecki, A. (2024). Students' acceptance of ChatGPT in higher education: An extended unified theory of acceptance and use of technology. *Innovative Higher Education*, *49*(2), 223–245. DOI: 10.1007/s10755-023-09686-1

Su, J., & Yang, W. (2023). Unlocking the power of ChatGPT: A framework for applying generative AI in education. *ECNU Review of Education*, *6*(3), 355–366. DOI: 10.1177/20965311231168423

Su, J., & Zhong, Y. (2022). Artificial intelligence (AI) in early childhood education: Curriculum design and future directions. *Computers and Education: Artificial Intelligence*, *3*, 100072. DOI: 10.1016/j.caeai.2022.100072

Sullivan, M., Kelly, A., & Maclaughlan, P. (2023). ChatGPT in higher education: considerations for academic integrity and student learning. ECU. https://ro.ecu.edu.au/cgi/viewcontent.cgi?article=3501&context=ecuworks2022-2026

Sullivan, A., & Bers, M. U. (2019). Investigating the use of robotics to increase girls' interest in engineering during early elementary school. *International Journal of Technology and Design Education*, *29*(5), 1033–1051. DOI: 10.1007/s10798-018-9483-y

Sun, A. Y., & Scanlon, B. R. (2019). How can big data and machine learning benefit environment and water management: A survey of methods, applications, and future directions. *Environmental Research Letters*, *14*(7), 73001. DOI: 10.1088/1748-9326/ab1b7d

Sun, T. Q., & Medaglia, R. (2019). Mapping the challenges of Artificial Intelligence in the public sector: Evidence from public healthcare. *Government Information Quarterly*, *36*(2), 368–383. DOI: 10.1016/j.giq.2018.09.008

Sun, T., Luo, Y., & Tang, K. (2020). AI for emergency services: Predictive modeling of 911 call volumes. *Government Information Quarterly*, *37*(2), 101456. DOI: 10.1016/j.giq.2019.101456

Sureshbhai, S. V., & Nakrani, T. (2024). A literature review : Enhancing sentiment analysis of deep learning techniques using generative AI Model. *International Journal of Scientific Research in Computer Science Engineering and Information Technology*, *10*(3), 530–540. DOI: 10.32628/CSEIT24103204

Sutori. (n.d.). An intuitive timeline maker. Retrieved from: https://www.sutori.com

Taba, H. (1962). *Curriculum development: Theory and practice*. Harcourt, Brace & World.

Taber, K. S. (2018). The use of Cronbach's alpha when developing and reporting research instruments in science education. *Research in Science Education*, *48*(6), 1273–1296. DOI: 10.1007/s11165-016-9602-2

Tafazoli, M. (2024). Generative AI in education: Implications for language learning. *Journal of Educational Technology*, *14*(2), 221–235.

Taheri, M. (2023). Shaping the future together: The inaugural vision for AI and tech in behavioral and social sciences. *Aitechbesosci*, *1*(1), 1–3. DOI: 10.61838/kman.aitech.1.1.1

Tait, I. (2024). Sobbing mathematically: Why conscious, *self-aware AI deserves protection*. DOI: 10.20944/preprints202410.1228.v1

Talan, T. (2021). Artificial intelligence in education: A bibliometric study. *International Journal of Research in Education and Science*, *7*(3), 822–837. DOI: 10.46328/ijres.2409

Tan, C. N.-L., Tee, M., & Koay, K. Y. (2024). Discovering students' continuous intentions to use ChatGPT in higher education: A tale of two theories. *Asian Education and Development Studies*, *13*(4), 356–372. DOI: 10.1108/AEDS-04-2024-0096

The Britannica Dictionary. (2025). Artificial Intelligence. https://www.britannica.com/dictionary/artificial-intelligence

The future of learning: AI is revolutionizing education 4.0. (2024). https://www.weforum.org/stories/2024/04/future-learning-ai-revolutionizing-education-4-0/

Thomas, T. (2024). The role of Artificial Intelligence in Formal and informal education for students. *International Journal for Research in Applied Science and Engineering Technology*, *12*(3), 69–71. DOI: 10.22214/ijraset.2024.58738

Thorndike, E. L. (1911). *Animal intelligence: Experimental studies*. Macmillan.

Thorndike, E. L. (1927). The law of effect. *The American Journal of Psychology*, *39*(1/4), 212–222. DOI: 10.2307/1415413

Tiki-Toki. (n.d.). Online timeline maker. Retrieved from: https://www.tiki-toki.com/

TimeMaps. (n.d.). TimeMaps History Atlas. Retrieved from: https://timemaps.com/history/

Tjebane, M. M., Musonda, I., & Okoro, C. (2022). Organisational factors of Artificial Intelligence adoption in the South African construction industry. *Frontiers in Built Environment*, *8*(March), 1–17. DOI: 10.3389/fbuil.2022.823998

Tlili, A., & Burgos, D. (2024). Unleashing the power of Open Educational Practices (OEP) through Artificial Intelligence (AI): Where to begin? *Interactive Learning Environments*, *32*(10), 6886–6893. DOI: 10.1080/10494820.2022.2101595

Tomašev, N., Cornebise, J., Hutter, F., Mohamed, S., Picciariello, A., Connelly, B., Belgrave, D., Ezer, D., van der Haert, F. C., Mugisha, F., Abila, G., Arai, H., Almiraat, H., Proskurnia, J., Snyder, K., Otake, M., Othman, M., Glasmachers, T., Wever, W. D., & Clopath, C. (2020). AI for social good: Unlocking the opportunity for positive impact. *Nature Communications*, *11*(1), 2468. Advance online publication. DOI: 10.1038/s41467-020-15871-z PMID: 32424119

Tomaževič, N., Murko, E., & Aristovnik, A. (2024). Organisational enablers of Artificial Intelligence adoption in public institutions: A systematic literature review. *Central European Public Administration Review*, *22*(1), 109–138. DOI: 10.17573/cepar.2024.1.05

Topol, E. (2019). *Deep medicine: How artificial Intelligence can make healthcare human again*. Basic Books.

Torrance, E. P. (1972). Can we teach children to think creatively? *The Journal of Creative Behavior*, *6*(2), 114–143. DOI: 10.1002/j.2162-6057.1972.tb00923.x

Touretzky, D., Gardner-McCune, C., Breazeal, C., Martin, F., & Seehorn, D. (2021). A year in K-12 AI education. *AI Magazine*, *40*(4), 88–90. DOI: 10.1609/aimag.v40i4.5289

Touretzky, D., Gardner-McCune, C., Martin, F., & Seehorn, D. (2019). Envisioning AI for K-12: What should every child know about AI? *Proceedings of the AAAI Conference on Artificial Intelligence*, *33*(1), 9795–9799. DOI: 10.1609/aaai.v33i01.33019795

Tovar, E., & Piedra, N. (2023). AI implications in satisfying digital skills training needs through OER. In T. Schlippe, E. C. K. Cheng, T. Wang (Eds.). *Artificial Intelligence in education technologies: New development and innovative practices*. Proceedings of 2023 4th International Conference on Artificial Intelligence in Education Technology. Springer Nature. DOI: 10.1007/978-981-99-7947-9_9

Trabelsi, M. A. (2024). The impact of artificial Intelligence on economic development. *Journal of Electronic Business & Digital Economics, 3*(2), 142–155. DOI: 10.1108/JEBDE-10-2023-0022

Transkribus, A. I. (n.d.). Transkribus. Retrieved from: https://transkribus.ai/

Trunfio, M., Lucia, M. D., Campana, S., & Magnelli, A. (2021). Innovating the cultural heritage museum service model through virtual reality and augmented reality: The effects on the overall visitor experience and satisfaction. *Journal of Heritage Tourism, 17*(1), 1–19. DOI: 10.1080/1743873X.2020.1850742

Tsai, M. J., & Tsai, C. C. (2022). An eye-tracking study of adaptive AR-based biology learning. *Journal of Science Education and Technology, 31*(4), 552–565.

Tsai, Y. S., Poquet, O., Gašević, D., Dawson, S., & Pardo, A. (2019). Complexity leadership in learning analytics: Drivers, challenges, and opportunities. *British Journal of Educational Technology, 50*(6), 2839–2854. DOI: 10.1111/bjet.12846

Tshishonga, N. S. (2023). Student teaching for critical thinking and emancipation at the university: A Freire's liberatory approach. In Makua, M., & Akinlolu, M. (Eds.), *Sustaining higher education through resource allocation, learning design models, and academic development*. IGI Global., DOI: 10.4018/978-1-6684-7059-6.ch007

Tufekci, Z. (2021). *Twitter and tear gas: The power and fragility of networked protest*. Yale University Press.

Tuomi, I. (2018). *The impact of artificial intelligence on learning, teaching, and education*. JRC Science for Policy Report. Luxembourg: European Commission. https://doi:DOI: 10.2760/12297

Turdubaeva, Zh., & Arykbaev, I. (2024). Applications of Artificial Intelligence in education. *Bulletin of Science and Practice, 10*(2), 517–521. DOI: 10.33619/2414-2948/99/56

Turing, A. M. (1950). Computing machinery and intelligence. *Mind: A Quarterly Review of Psychology and Philosophy*, 433–460. https://academic.oup.com/mind/article/LIX/236/433/986238

Turing, A. M. (1950). Computing Machinery and Intelligence. *Mind, 59*(236), 433–460. DOI: 10.1093/mind/LIX.236.433

UNESCO & Microsoft. (2022). *Visual learning and AI: Impact assessment on educational outcomes*. UNESCO Publishing.

UNESCO. (2019). *Artificial intelligence in education: Challenges and opportunities for sustainable development*. UNESCO Publishing. https://unesdoc.unesco.org/ark:/48223/pf0000366994

UNESCO. (2021). *Media and information literate citizens: Think critically, click wisely!* UNESCO Publishing. https://www.unesco.org/mil4teachers/en/curriculum

UNESCO. (2021). *Recommendation on the Ethics of Artificial Intelligence*. https://unesdoc.unesco.org/ark:/48223/pf0000381137

UNESCO. (2023). *Global education monitoring report 2023: Technology in education—A tool on whose terms?* UNESCO Publishing. https://unesdoc.unesco.org/ark:/48223/pf0000385723

UNESCO. (2023). *Guidance for generative AI in education and research*. UNESCO., DOI: 10.54675/EWZM9535

UNESCO. (2024). *Eğitim ve araştırmada üretken yapay zekâ kılavuzu [Guidance for generative artificial intelligence in education and research]*. (Eds. Miao, F., & Holmes, W.). https://unesdoc.unesco.org/ark:/48223/pf0000390842 sayfasından 1.10.2024 tarihinde erişilmiştir.

UNICEF. (2021). *Policy guidance on AI for children*. Author. https://www.unicef.org/globalinsight/media/2356/file/UNICEF-Global-Insight-policy-guidance-AI-children-2.0-2021.pdf

UNICEF. (2023). *The digital divide in education: Global challenges and opportunities*. UNICEF Office of Research.

University of Toronto. (2025). *Cathryn Copper*. University of Toronto, John H. Daniels Faculty of Architecture, Landscape, and Design. https://www.daniels.utoronto.ca/people/staff/cathryn-copper

Urmeneta, A. (2024). *Creative applications of Artificial Intelligence in education* (Urmeneta, A., & Romero, M., Eds.). Springer Nature Switzerland., DOI: 10.1007/978-3-031-55272-4

Uzun, L. (2023a). Are concerns related to Artificial Intelligence development and use really necessary: A philosophical discussion. *Digital Society : Ethics, Socio-Legal and Governance of Digital Technology*, *2*(3), 40. DOI: 10.1007/s44206-023-00070-2

Van Atteveldt, W., Welbers, K., & Jacobi, L. (2021). Analyzing political discourse with AI: Insights from natural language processing. *Political Communication*, *38*(1), 53–75.

VanLehn, K. (2011). The relative effectiveness of human tutoring, intelligent tutoring systems, and other tutoring systems. *Educational Psychologist*, *46*(4), 197–221. https://psycnet.apa.org/doi/10.1080/00461520.2011.611369. DOI: 10.1080/00461520.2011.611369

Varian, H. R. (1992). *Microeconomic analysis* (3rd ed.). W. W. Norton & Company.

Varian, H. R. (2014). Big data: New tricks for econometrics. *The Journal of Economic Perspectives*, *28*(2), 3–28. DOI: 10.1257/jep.28.2.3

Vartiainen, H., Pellas, L., Kahila, J., Valtonen, T., & Tedre, M. (2022). Pre-service teachers' insights on data agency. *New Media & Society*, *26*(4), 1871–1890. DOI: 10.1177/14614448221079626

Veale, M., & Binns, R. (2017). Fairer machine learning in the public sector: Legal and regulatory perspectives. *Computer Law & Security Review*, *33*(3), 361–372.

Veletsianos, G., & Houlden, S. (2021). Learning as agency: AI, tutoring systems, and distributed cognition. *British Journal of Educational Technology*, *52*(1), 242–257. DOI: 10.1111/bjet.13078

Venkatesh, V., Morris, M. G., Davis, G. B., & Davis, F. D. (2003). User acceptance of information technology: Toward a unified view. *Management Information Systems Quarterly*, *27*(3), 425–478. DOI: 10.2307/30036540

Venkatesh, V., Thong, J. Y. L., & Xu, X. (2012). Consumer acceptance and use of information technology: Extending the unified theory of acceptance and use of technology. *Management Information Systems Quarterly*, *36*(1), 157–178. DOI: 10.2307/41410412

Vinuesa, R., Azizpour, H., Leite, I., Balaam, M., Dignum, V., Domisch, S., & Nerini, F. F. (2020). The role of artificial intelligence in achieving the sustainable development goals. *Nature Communications*, *11*(1), 1–10. DOI: 10.1038/s41467-019-14108-y PMID: 31932590

von der Heyde, A. (2022). Digital transformation in higher education: The need for a coordinated approach. *Administrative Sciences*, *14*(3), 48. DOI: 10.3390/admsci14030048

Voogt, J., & McKenney, S. (2017). TPACK in teacher education: Are we preparing teachers to use technology for early literacy? *Technology, Pedagogy and Education*, *26*(1), 69–83. DOI: 10.1080/1475939X.2016.1174730

Vu, P., Tang, J., & Liu, Y. (2022). Personalization trade-offs in AI-based education. *Education and Information Technologies*, *27*(1), 275–295. DOI: 10.1007/s10639-021-10750-2

Vygotsky, L. S. (1978). *Mind in society: The development of higher psychological processes*. Harvard University Press.

Wagner, G., Lukyanenko, R., & Paré, G. (2021). Artificial Intelligence and the conduct of literature reviews. *Journal of Information Technology*, *37*(2), 209–226. DOI: 10.1177/02683962211048201

Wald, N., & Harland, T. (2021). Reconsidering Vygotsky's 'more capable peer' in terms of both personal and knowledge outcomes. *Teaching in Higher Education*, *27*(3), 417–423. DOI: 10.1080/13562517.2021.2007474

Walker, E., Rummel, N., & Koedinger, K. R. (2011). Designing automated adaptive support to improve student-helping behaviors in a peer tutoring activity. *International Journal of Computer-Supported Collaborative Learning*, *6*(2), 279–306. DOI: 10.1007/s11412-011-9111-2

Walter, Y. (2024). Embracing the future of Artificial Intelligence in the classroom: The relevance of AI literacy, prompt engineering, and critical thinking in modern education. *International Journal of Educational Technology in Higher Education*, *2024*(21), 15. DOI: 10.1186/s41239-024-00448-3

Wamba, S. F., Kala Kamdjoug, J. R., & Epie Bawack, R. (2021). Leveraging artificial Intelligence in agriculture for sustainable development. *Technological Forecasting and Social Change*, *169*, 120799. DOI: 10.1016/j.techfore.2021.120799

Wang, F. (2024). AI in vocational training: A qualitative interview study of early-stage practitioners in the real estate brokerage industry in China. *Voprosy Obrazovaniya / Educational Studies Moscow,* *1*(3), 180–200. DOI: 10.17323/vo-2024-17710

Wang'ang'a, A. W. (2024). Consequences of Artificial Intelligence on Teaching and Learning in Higher Education in Kenya: Literature Review. *East African Journal of Education Studies*, *7*(1), 202–215. Advance online publication. DOI: 10.37284/eajes.7.1.1718

Wang, H., & Zhang, W. (2024). ITS-driven simulations in clinical decision-making. *Simulation in Healthcare*, *18*(2), 112–121.

Wang, S., Xiao, Y., & Liang, Z. (2024). Exploring cross-national divide in government adoption of Artificial Intelligence: Insights from explainable Artificial Intelligence techniques. *Telematics and Informatics*, *90*(March), 102134. DOI: 10.1016/j.tele.2024.102134

Wang, W., Lv, Q., Yu, W., Hong, W., Qi, J., Wang, Y., & Tang, J. (2024). Cogvlm: Visual expert for pretrained language models. *Advances in Neural Information Processing Systems*, *37*, 121475–121499.

Wang, W., Wang, Y., Chen, L., Ma, R., & Zhang, M. (2024). Justice at the forefront: Cultivating felt accountability towards Artificial Intelligence among healthcare professionals. *Social Science & Medicine*, *347*(February), 116717. DOI: 10.1016/j.socscimed.2024.116717 PMID: 38518481

Wang, Y., Chen, X., & Zhang, Y. (2024). Integrating the adapted UTAUT model with moral obligation, trust and perceived risk to predict ChatGPT adoption for assessment support: A survey with students. *Computers and Education: Artificial Intelligence*, *6*, 100246. DOI: 10.1016/j.caeai.2024.100246

Ward, M. (2023). ChatGPT: The survey says students love it, but educators, not fans, do not. University Business. https://universitybusiness.com/chatgpt-survey-says-students-love-it-educators-not-fans/#:~:text=Over%2089%25%20of%20students%20have,an%20 outline%20for%20a%20paper

Washburn, J., & McCutchen, J. M. (2024). AI meets AI: ChatGPT as a pedagogical tool to teach American Indian history. *Critical Humanities*, *2*(2). Advance online publication. DOI: 10.33470/2836-3140.1037

Watson, J. B. (1913). Psychology as the behaviorist views it. *Psychological Review*, *20*(2), 158–177. DOI: 10.1037/h0074428

Watters, A. (2015). The algorithmic child: Education and the ethics of big data. In Williamson, B., & Piattoeva, D. (Eds.), *Education Governance and Datafication* (pp. 27–42). Routledge.

Weaver, K. D. (2025). *Kari D. Weaver*. University of Waterloo. https://uwaterloo.ca/scholar/kdweaver

Weaver, K. D., & Muñoz Gómez, A. (2023, February 27). *ChatGPT and Generative Artificial Intelligence (AI)*. University of Waterloo. https://subjectguides.uwaterloo.ca/chatgpt_generative_ai

Weaver, K. D. (2024). The artificial intelligence disclosure (AID) framework: An introduction. *C&RL News*, *85*(10), 407–411. DOI: 10.5860/crln.85.10.407

Wen, C.-H. R., & Chen, Y.-N. K. (2024). Understanding Public perceptions of revolutionary technology: The role of political ideology, knowledge, and news consumption. *JCOM, Journal of Science Communication*, *23*(05). Advance online publication. DOI: 10.22323/2.23050207

Whitburn, B., & Plows, V. (2017). Inclusive Education Making Sense Of Everyday Practice Innovations And Controversies: Interrogating Educational Change. *Sense Publishers, 6.*

Wijayati, D. T., Rahman, Z., Fahrullah, A., Rahman, M. F. W., Arifah, I. D. C., & Kautsar, A. (2022). A study of Artificial Intelligence on employee performance and work engagement: The moderating role of change leadership. *International Journal of Manpower*, *43*(2), 486–512. DOI: 10.1108/IJM-07-2021-0423

Wiley, D. (2023). AI, instructional design, and OER. *Improving learning: Eclectic, Pragmatic, Enthusiastic.*https://opencontent.org/blog/archives/7129

Wiley, D. (2024). The Symmetrical Power of AI in Assessments. *Improving learning: Eclectic, pragmatic, enthusiastic.*https://opencontent.org/blog/archives/7508

Williamson, B. (2017). Big data in education: The digital future of learning, policy and practice. *Sage (Atlanta, Ga.).* Advance online publication. DOI: 10.4135/9781529714920

Williamson, B., & Eynon, R. (2020). Historical perspectives on learning analytics. *Learning, Media and Technology*, *45*(1), 1–14. DOI: 10.1080/17439884.2020.1694942

Williamson, B., & Eynon, R. (2020). Historical threads, missing links, and future directions in AI in education. *Learning, Media and Technology*, *45*(3), 223–235. DOI: 10.1080/17439884.2020.1798995

Williamson, B., Macgilchrist, F., & Potter, J. (2021). Covid-19 controversies and critical research in digital education. *Learning, Media and Technology*, *46*(2), 117–127. DOI: 10.1080/17439884.2021.1922437

Williamson, B., Potter, J., & Eynon, R. (2024). Learning futures: Reclaiming data, equity, and human agency. *Postdigital Science and Education*, *6*(1), 22–45. DOI: 10.1007/s42438-023-00345-9

Willmore, J. (2023). AI education and AI in education | NSF - National Science Foundation. https://www.nsf.gov/science-matters/ai-education-ai-education

Winner, L. (1980). Do artifacts have politics? *Daedalus*, *109*(1), 121–136.

Wirtz, B. W., Weyerer, J. C., & Geyer, C. (2019). Artificial intelligence and the public sector—Applications and challenges. *International Journal of Public Administration*, *42*(7), 596–615. DOI: 10.1080/01900692.2018.1498103

Wood, E., Ange, B. L., & Miller, D. D. (2021). Are we ready to integrate Artificial Intelligence literacy into medical school curriculum: Students and faculty survey. *Journal of Medical Education and Curricular Development*, *8*, 23821205211024078. Advance online publication. DOI: 10.1177/23821205211024078 PMID: 34250242

Woolf, B. P. (2009). *Building intelligent interactive tutors: Student-centered strategies for revolutionizing e-learning*. Morgan Kaufmann.

World Bank. (2020). *Artificial Intelligence in health: Unlocking its potential in low- and middle-income countries*. World Bank Group. https://documents.worldbank.org/en/publication/documents-reports/documentdetail/941981606991679987/artificial-intelligence-in-health-unlocking-its-potential-in-low-and-middle-income-countries

World Economic Forum. (2023a). *Applications of artificial intelligence in education: Promise and challenges*. World Economic Forum Reports.

World Economic Forum. (2023b). *The future of jobs report 2023.* https://www.weforum.org/publications/the-future-of-jobs-report-2023/

Woźniak-Jęchorek, B., Rydzak, W., & Kuźmar, S. (2023). Decoding the interface: Exploring women's perspectives on integrating AI in professional work. *Human Technology*, *19*(3), 325–351. DOI: 10.14254/1795-6889.2023.19-3.2

Wu, Y., Schuster, M., Chen, Z., Le, Q. V., Norouzi, M., Macherey, W., . . . Dean, J. (2016). Google's neural machine translation system: Bridging the gap between human and machine translation. *arXiv preprint arXiv:1609.08144*. https://doi.org//arXiv.1609.08144DOI: 10.48550

Wu, R., & Yu, Z. (2023). Do <scp>AI</Scp> Chatbots improve students' learning outcomes? Evidence from a meta-analysis. *British Journal of Educational Technology*, *55*(1), 10–33. DOI: 10.1111/bjet.13334

Wu, T. T., Lee, H. Y., Li, P. H., Huang, C. N., & Huang, Y. M. (2024). Promoting self-regulation progress and knowledge construction in blended learning via ChatGPT-based learning aid. *Journal of Educational Computing Research*, *61*(8), 3–31. DOI: 10.1177/07356331231191125

Xia, L., & Zhong, B. (2018). A systematic review on teaching and learning robotics content knowledge in K-12. *Computers & Education*, *127*, 267–282. DOI: 10.1016/j.compedu.2018.09.007

Xie, L. (2023). AI and political polarization: A global perspective. *Journal of Political Science and Technology*, *12*(3), 115–130.

Xu, X. (2024). Research on algorithmic ethics in Artificial Intelligence. *2024 6th International Conference on Internet of Things, Automation and Artificial Intelligence (IoTAAI),* 499–503. DOI: 10.1109/IoTAAI62601.2024.10692746

Xu, S., Kee, K. F., Li, W., Yamamoto, M., & Riggs, R. E. (2024). Examining the diffusion of innovations from a dynamic, differential-effects perspective: A longitudinal study on AI Adoption among employees. *Communication Research, 51*(7), 843–866. DOI: 10.1177/00936502231191832

Xu, Z. (2024). AI in education: Enhancing learning experiences and student outcomes. *Applied and Computational Engineering, 51*(1), 104–111. DOI: 10.54254/2755-2721/51/20241187

Yadav, D. S. (2024). Navigating the landscape of AI integration in education: Opportunities, challenges, and ethical considerations for harnessing the potential of Artificial Intelligence (AI) for teaching and learning. *BSSS Journal of Computer, 15*(1), 38–48. DOI: 10.51767/jc1503

Yam, K. C., Tang, P. M., Jackson, J. C., Su, R., & Gray, K. (2023). The rise of robots increases job insecurity and maladaptive workplace behaviors: Multimethod evidence. *The Journal of Applied Psychology, 108*(5), 850–870. DOI: 10.1037/apl0001045 PMID: 36222634

Yang, H., & Boulom, T. (2024). An interactive role-playing game-based learning system for history using artificial ıntelligence and 3D modeling. *12th International Conference of Security, Privacy and Trust Management* (pp.83-90). https://doi.org/ DOI: 10.5121/csit.2024.141107

Yang, S. J., Ogata, H., Matsui, T., & Chen, N. S. (2021). Human-centered artificial intelligence in education: Seeing the invisible through the visible. *Computers and Education: Artificial Intelligence, 2*, 100008. DOI: 10.1016/j.caeai.2021.100008

Yarrow, N., & Bhardwaj, R. (2020). *Indonesia's education technology during COVID-19 and beyond.* East Asia & Pacific on the rise. https://blogs.worldbank.org/eastasiapacific/indonesias-education-technology-during-covid-19-and-beyond

Yaşar, T. (2024). Artificial Intelligence in business operations: Exploring how AI technologies are reshaping processes, enhancing decision-making, and driving efficiency across various industries. *Human-Computer Interaction, 8*(1), 53. DOI: 10.62802/r78f9a37

Yazıcı, C., & Kültür, C. (2020). Medya mı yöntem mi? Bitmeyen tartıma. Kürşat Çağıltay ve Yüksel Göktaş (Ed.), *Öğretim Teknolojilerinin Temelleri* (s. 123-140). Pegem Akademi.

Yıldırım, A., & Şimşek, H., (2016*). Sosyal bilimlerde nitel araştırma yöntemleri [Qualitative research methods in social sciences].* Seçkin Yayınları Vallis, C., Wilson, S., & Casey, A. (2024). *Generative AI: Beyond the binaries with metaphors*. ASCILITE Publications, 590-595.

Yilmaz, H., Maxutov, S., Baitekov, A., & Balta, N. (2023). Student attitudes towards Chat GPT: A technology acceptance model survey. *International Educational Review*, *1*(1), 57–83. DOI: 10.58693/ier.114

Youssef, E., Medhat, M., Abdellatif, S., & Al Malek, M. (2024). Examining the effect of ChatGPT usage on students' academic learning and achievement: A survey-based study in Ajman, UAE. *Computers and Education: Artificial Intelligence*, *7*, 100316. DOI: 10.1016/j.caeai.2024.100316

Yue, C. A., Men, L. R., Mitson, R., Davis, D. Z., & Zhou, A. (2024). Artificial Intelligence for internal communication: Strategies, challenges, and implications. *Public Relations Review*, *50*(5), 102515. DOI: 10.1016/j.pubrev.2024.102515

Yu, H., & Guo, Y. (2023, June). Generative Artificial Intelligence empowers educational reform: Current status, issues, and prospects. [). Frontiers Media SA.]. *Frontiers in Education*, *8*, 1183162. DOI: 10.3389/feduc.2023.1183162

Zahidi, F., Kaluvilla, B. B., & Mulla, T. (2024). Embracing the new era: Artificial Intelligence and its multifaceted impact on the hospitality industry. *Journal of Open Innovation*, *10*(4), 100390. DOI: 10.1016/j.joitmc.2024.100390

Zakharova, G. B., Krivonogov, A. I., Kruglikov, S. V., & Petunin, A. A. (2020). Energy-efficient technologies in the educational programs of the architectural higher education schools. *Acta Polytechnica Hungarica*, *17*(8), 121–136. Advance online publication. DOI: 10.12700/APH.17.8.2020.8.9

Zapata-Ros, M. (2023). Teorías y modelos sobre el aprendizaje en entornos conectados y ubicuos: Bases para un nuevo modelo teórico a partir de una visión crítica del "conectivismo". *Education in the Knowledge Society*, *16*(1), 69–102. DOI: 10.14201/eks201516169102

Zawacki-Richter, O., Marín, V. I., & Bond, M. (2022). The educational metaverse: Hype or hope? *Journal of Computing in Higher Education*, *34*, 457–472. DOI: 10.1007/s12528-022-09318-1

Zawacki-Richter, O., Marín, V. I., Bond, M., & Gouverneur, F. (2019). Systematic review of research on artificial intelligence applications in higher education – where are the educators? *International Journal of Educational Technology in Higher Education*, *16*(1), 1–27. DOI: 10.1186/s41239-019-0171-0

Zeide, E. (2015). Student privacy principles for the age of big data: Moving beyond FERPA and FIPPS. *Drexel L. Rev.*, *8*, 339.

Zhai, X. (2023). ChatGPT and AI: The game changer for education. *Zhai, X.(2023). ChatGPT: Reforming Education on Five Aspects. Shanghai Education*, 16-17. https://ssrn.com/abstract=4389098

Zhai, X. (2024). Transforming teachers' roles and agencies in the era of generative AI: Perceptions, acceptance, knowledge, and practices. *Journal of Science Education and Technology*, •••, 1–11. DOI: 10.1007/s10956-024-10174-0

Zhai, X., Chu, X., Chai, C. S., Jong, M. S. Y., Istenic, A., Spector, M., Liu, J., Yuan, J., & Li, Y. (2021). A review of artificial intelligence (AI) in education from 2010 to 2020. *Complexity*, *2021*(1), 8812542. DOI: 10.1155/2021/8812542

Zhang, H., Lee, I., Ali, S., DiPaola, D., Cheng, Y., & Breazeal, C. (2023). Integrating ethics and career futures with technical learning to promote AI literacy for middle school students: An exploratory study. *International Journal of Artificial Intelligence in Education*, *33*(2), 290–324. DOI: 10.1007/s40593-022-00293-3 PMID: 35573722

Zhang, J., & Zhang, Z. (2024). <scp>AI</Scp> in teacher education: Unlocking new dimensions in teaching support, inclusive learning, and digital literacy. *Journal of Computer Assisted Learning*, *40*(4), 1871–1885. DOI: 10.1111/jcal.12988

Zhang, S.. (2021). Sentiment analysis and public opinion: An AI approach to political science. *Political Analysis*, *29*(3), 319–337.

Zhang, Z. V. (2020). Engaging with automated writing evaluation (AWE) feedback on L2 writing: Student perceptions and revisions. *Assessing Writing*, *43*, 100439. DOI: 10.1016/j.asw.2019.100439

Zhao, J., Li, Q., Chen, Y., & Xu, L. (2023). Societal and economic implications of generative AI. *AI & Society*, *38*(1), 121–135.

Zhou, Q., Chen, K., & Cheng, S. (2024). Bringing employee learning to AI stress research: A moderated mediation model. *Technological Forecasting and Social Change, 209*(January 2023), 123773. DOI: 10.1016/j.techfore.2024.123773

Zimmerman, B. J. (2000). Attaining self-regulation: A social cognitive perspective. In Boekaerts, M., Pintrich, P. R., & Zeidner, M. (Eds.), *Handbook of self-regulation* (pp. 13–39). Academic Press., DOI: 10.1016/B978-012109890-2/50031-7

Zirar, A., Ali, S. I., & Islam, N. (2023). Worker and workplace Artificial Intelligence (AI) coexistence: Emerging themes and research agenda. *Technovation*, *124*, 102747. DOI: 10.1016/j.technovation.2023.102747

Zuboff, S. (2023). *The age of surveillance capitalism: The fight for a human future at the new frontier of power*. PublicAffairs. DOI: 10.4324/9781003320609-27

Zuiderwijk, A., Chen, Y.-C., & Salem, F. (2021). Implications of the use of artificial intelligence in public governance: A systematic literature review and a research agenda. *Government Information Quarterly*, *38*(1), 101577. DOI: 10.1016/j.giq.2021.101577

About the Contributors

Aytekin Demircioğlu (Türkiye) Academic BS (1999): Gazi University, Gazi Education Faculty, Philosophy and Related Sciences Education, Ankara, Turkey. Master's (2009): Gazi University, Gazi Education Faculty, Philosophy and Related Sciences Education, Ankara, Turkey. (Thesis: Knowledge Issue in Ghazali on the Basis of Criticism and Doubt) Ph.D. (2013): Gazi University, Gazi Education Faculty, Philosophy and Related Sciences Education, Ankara, Turkey. (Thesis: Ibn Haldun's Understanding of Human and Civilization) Associate Professorship (2015): Educational Sciences and Teacher Training, Philosophy and Related Sciences Education, Professorship (2021): Philosophy of Education, Philosophy and Related Sciences Education, Turkish-Islamic Philosophy Vice Dean of Faculty of Humanities and Social Sciences Academic Board Member of Kastamonu University Faculty of Humanities and Social Sciences, Head of Department of History of Turkish Islamic Philosophy Chair of the USBED/IJSES International Conferences on Social and Educational Sciences Chief Editor of International Journal of Social and Educational Sciences (USBED) Published Author (8 Books, 5 Chapters, 28 Articles) Stud Fields: Philosophy and Related Sciences Education, Turkish-Islamic Philosophy Professional 1999 – 2002 Teacher at Private Colleges, Ankara, Turkey 2002 – 2010 CEO of Kariyer Dershaneleri (Private Courses), Ankara, Turkey 2010 – 2013 CEO of Batı Kolej (Private College), Ankara, Turkey 2014 - ……. Academic Advisor of many colleges, Turkey 2013 - 2016 Academic member at Sinop University, Turkey 2016 - ……. Academic member at Kastamonu University, Turkey

***

Jacob Adler is the Metadata/Cataloging Librarian of the Lloyd Sealy Library at John Jay College of Criminal Justice. His research interests include generative "artificial intelligence," media studies, science-fiction and fantasy, and tabletop role-playing games.

Gulgun Afacan Adanir is a researcher and learning technologist at Cambridge University Centre for Alternative Finance (CCAF). She holds MSc and PhD degrees in Information Systems with a focus on online learning. Before joining CCAF, she worked at Ankara University, Turkiye, as an academician, teaching ICT courses, developing online course content, and conducting research. Her research interests include artificial intelligence, online learning, social media, and computational thinking.

Aylin (Yavas) Akinlar, Ph.D. is an Assistant Professor in Türkiye. She has worked at Cornell University as a Fulbright Scholar, Yildiz Technical University, and Bandirma Onyedi Eylul University (currently). She holds a Ph.D. in Curriculum and Instruction with a focus on multicultural education, as well as a strong background in curriculum development, equity-minded pedagogy, and instructional design, as well as a passion for improving teaching and learning experiences in higher education gained over 20 years of experience. Her specialized knowledge or areas of interest include curriculum and instruction, multicultural education, international and comparative education, internationalization of higher education, gender equity, teacher careers and development, and qualitative research. Aylin (Yavas) Akinlar, Ph.D. has received many worldwide distinctions, prizes, and awards. She has given international papers and lectures in the United States, Malaysia, the United Kingdom, Norway, Kosovo, Bosnia and Herzegovina, Saudi Arabia, and Turkey, among other places. She is fluent in Turkish and English. She has a basic knowledge of German, Spanish, and Arabic.

Veysel Bilal Arslankara received his Bachelor's and Master's degrees from Necmettin Erbakan University and his PhD degree from Hacettepe University in Computer Education and Instructional Technologies. His research interests include online learning environments, virtual risks, instructional design, material development, digital games, robotic coding, thinking skills and generative artificial intelligence in education.

Ayşegül Nihan Erol Şahin is an Associate Professor in the Division of History Education at Gazi University's Faculty of Education in Ankara, Turkey. From 2012 to 2022, she was a lecturer in the Department of The Principles of Atatürk and The History of The Revolution Research and Implementation at Gazi University. Her research focused on gamification in history education, digital learning, remote teaching implementations, and using AI in history classes. She has participated in numerous national and international projects to advance history education research and practice. Her academic research has received many citations from articles published in academic journals.

Ferah Diba Izgi. After completing her undergraduate education, the author completed her master's degree in psychological counseling and guidance and clinical psychology. She is currently doing her doctorate in psychological counseling and guidance. She worked in the field of pedagogy both in the administrative and professional fields for a long time. She also received advanced training in family counseling, relationship, individual, sexual, psychodynamic, short-term solution-oriented, psychodynamic, transfer-oriented, filial therapy, mindfullnes, self-compassionate awareness. She also received software development engineering tester training from the USA and self-coaching training from the UK. She published two books on values education written in 4 different languages and two books on child education. She is currently continuing her academic studies in Germany.

Vildan Katmer is an Assistant Professor and the Head of the Department of Mathematics and Science Education at Maltepe University, Faculty of Education. She began her academic career by completing her undergraduate degree in Mathematics. She earned a non-thesis master's degree in Mathematics Education in 2009, followed by master's degree in Mathematics Education at Marmara University in 2013, and completed her Ph.D. in Curriculum and Instruction at Yıldız Technical University in 2019. Her research interests include mathematics education, teacher education, curriculum development, the integration of technology into teaching and learning processes, and qualitative research methods. She continues her academic publications in line with her research interests. In addition to her academic work, Dr. Katmer actively participates in various social responsibility projects. She regularly delivers seminars and training sessions for in-service and pre-service teachers as well as students.

Aysha Khalil is an Assistant Professor of Education at Lahore College for Women University (LCWU), Pakistan. Her research focuses on digital education, artificial intelligence in teaching and learning, immersive technologies, and the educational metaverse. She holds a Postdoctoral Certificate in Digital Education and is actively engaged in advancing the intersection of pedagogy and emerging technologies. Dr. Khalil has presented her work at several prestigious international conferences and has published extensively in peer-reviewed, high-impact journals such as the Journal of Positive School Psychology and the Journal of Arts & Social Sciences. Her scholarship emphasizes inclusive, equity-driven educational innovation, with a strong commitment to shaping future-ready teacher education systems. She also contributes to academic peer review and regularly collaborates with scholars across interdisciplinary fields related to educational technology and reform.

Manjit Kour is working as Professor at University Business School at Chandigarh University. She holds a PhD in Business Management from IK Gujral Punjab Technical University, India. She has a good research record with several research papers published in reputed journals. She is an editorial board member and reviewer of many reputed journals including Scopus and ABDC-indexed journals. Her areas of interest include sustainability, green practices, Fintech, online marketing trends and business ethics.

Jaesub Lee's teaching interests include group and organizational communication theory and practice, intercultural/cross-cultural communication, leadership communication, communication theory and research methods courses. His research interests include relationship development and maintenance, leadership, justice, cooperation, bullying, voice and silence, organizational communication, crisis and risk communication, corporate social responsibility, health literacy and patient-care provider relationships. His research has appeared in Management Communication Quarterly, Human Communication Research, Journal of Public Relations Research, Journal of Business Communication, and other publications.

Youmei Liu received her Doctor of Education in Curriculum and Instruction focusing on instructional technology in 2003 from the College of Education at the University of Houston (UH). She has been serving as a Director of Assessment and Accreditation Services since 2011. Before assuming this position, she worked as an educational production specialist and an instructional designer. She is also an adjunct faculty at the Jack J. Valenti School of Communications at UH, and has been teaching Information and Communication Technology course for over 20 years. Dr. Liu functioned as a conference chair for the Society of International Chinese Educational Technology (SICET) and the Chinese American Educational Research and Development Association (CAERDA) in the US. She has rich research experience and has numerous publications in the areas of quality course design, innovative use of educational technology, distance education and mobile learning, cross-cultural communication, and social capital development in e-learning and social media platforms.

Vivit Rosmayanti, S.Pd.I., M.Pd was born in Botta on June 26, 1987. She has over 10 years of experience teaching at the University. She obtained a bachelor's degree in English Education from Alauddin State Islamic University. She completed her master's and doctoral degrees in English Education from Makassar State University. She is currently a lecturer in the Post Graduate Program, Department of English Education at Makassar State University, South Sulawesi, Indonesia. She is also actively writing research articles to be published in nationally and internationally accredited journals. She has written in some chapter books, monographs, and reference books. She is interested in teaching methods for teaching English. Her research interests include language teaching methodology, ICT instruction, and ESP teaching.

Wasswa Shafik (Member, IEEE) received a Bachelor of Science degree in information technology from Ndejje University, Uganda, a Master of Engineering degree in Information Technology (Computer and Communication Networks) from Yazd University, Iran, and a PhD in Computer Science with the School of Digital Science, Universiti Brunei Darussalam, Brunei Darussalam. He is also the Founder and Research Director of the Dig Connectivity Research Laboratory (DCRLab) after serving as a Research Associate at the Network Interconnectivity Research Laboratory at Yazd University. Prior to this, he worked as a Community Data Analyst at Population Services International (PSI-Uganda), a Community Data Officer at the Programme for Accessible Health Communication (PACE-Uganda), a Research Assistant at the Socio-Economic Data Centre (SEDC-Uganda), Uganda, an Assistant Data Officer at TechnoServe, Kampala, Uganda, and Asmaah Charity Organization as Cheif Executive Officer. He has hundreds of publications with renowned publishers. His research interests include Artificial Intelligence, Neural Networks, Computer Vision, Smart Agriculture, Digital Health, and Sustainable Computing.

Marharyta Shyrokova, PhD, Associate Professor of Sociology of Economics at Taras Shevchenko National University of Kyiv. She holds an MA in Economic Cybernetics and a PhD in Sociology of Economics from the NAS of Ukraine, focusing on corporate image and social capital. As a Lane Kirkland Scholar at Wroclaw University, she researched business servitization for regional sustainability. Author of 70+ publications, including monographs on servitization and sustainability, she leads the "Education for Democratic Citizenship" project and contributes to EU-funded initiatives. Recipient of the Lane Kirkland Fellowship and multiple national scholarships, she is fluent in Ukrainian, Russian, English, and Polish.

Tuğçe Şimşek is an academic researcher and lecturer at Gümüşhane University, Department of Human Resources Management. She has demonstrated her commitment to scientific pursuits by completing her doctoral studies in the field of Management and Organization. Her research interests span a wide range of areas, including organizational behavior, human resources management, management and organization studies. Dr. Şimşek has also produced studies covering crisis management and leadership types. With her academic contributions, she has focused intensely on various aspects of management and human resources and shed light on the complexities of these fields. Dr. Şimşek is known for her efforts to combine her knowledge and experiences in various fields by adopting an interdisciplinary approach in her studies. Dr. Şimşek's work reflects her passion for advancing our understanding of management practices and their impact on organizations.

Ibtasam Thakur is an Assistant Professor at Lahore College for Women University, Pakistan, specializing in Special Education. She holds a Ph.D. in Special Education from the University of the Punjab and an M.Sc. in Psychology from Government College University, Lahore. Dr. Thakur is currently on a postdoctoral fellowship in the Department of Education Studies at the University of Warwick, UK. Her research focuses on moral education, inclusive education, and intellectual disabilities. She has authored over twenty-four publications in national and international journals and is a member of the Asia Pacific Network of Moral Education. Dr. Thakur has also served as a visiting scholar at the University of Cambridge.

Index

A

B

C

D

E

F

G

H

I

L

M

N

O

P

Q

R

S

T

V

www.ingramcontent.com/pod-product-compliance
Lightning Source LLC
LaVergne TN
LVHW080614300926
849162LV00005B/1154
9798337326122